SANTA MARIA PUBLIC LIBRARY
809
501 great writers/
c2008
Discarded by
Santa Maria Library
SANTA MARIA PUBLIC LIBRARY
D1165582

501 GREAT WRITERS

GENERAL EDITOR JULIAN PATRICK

First edition for the United States and Canada
published in 2008 by Barron's Educational Series, Inc.

A Quint**essence** Book

Copyright © 2008 Quint**essence**
All rights reserved. No part of this publication may be reproduced,
stored in a retrieval system, or transmitted in any form or by any means,
electronic, mechanical, photocopying, recording, or otherwise,
without the permission of the copyright holder.

ISBN-13: 978-0-7641-6134-6
ISBN-10: 0-7641-6134-2
QSS.FWR

Library of Congress Control Number: 2008931677

All inquiries should be addressed to:
Barron's Educational Series, Inc.
250 Wireless Boulevard
Hauppauge, NY 11788
www.barronseduc.com

This book was designed and produced by
Quint**essence**
226 City Road
London EC1V 2TT

Senior Editor	Jodie Gaudet
Editors	Rebecca Gee, Fiona Plowman
Assistant Editors	Philip Contos, Andrew Smith
Picture Researcher	Sunita Sharma-Gibson
Designer	Rod Teasdale
Editorial Director	Jane Laing
Publisher	Tristan de Lancey

The moral right of the contributors of this Work has been asserted
in accordance with the Copyright, Designs and Patents Act of 1988.

Color reproduction in Singapore by Pica Digital Pte Ltd.
Printed in China by SNP Leefung Printers Ltd.
9 8 7 6 5 4 3 2 1

CONTENTS

FOREWORD

By John Sutherland, writer and literary critic

For no generation before ours has so much literary information, and raw literary text, been available on the Internet. If you want a "fact" or a "great work," a couple of keystrokes will deliver them to your screen. The facts may not, of course, be entirely reliable, and the texts not entirely readable, but you can't have everything. Should you want something pleasurable to handle and trustworthy about good books, my firm belief is that for some (and probably more than "some") years to come you'll need a good book. Like this.

World literature is, for many of us, the finest pleasure of life. But one of its vexations is that unlike other enjoyable consumables—medium-rare hamburgers, for example—it does not, once consumed, vanish. Literature is the most durable of durables. The best of it outlasts its creators and every generation of readers. Literature even outlasts the libraries that contain it. Our copyright and university collections, as "memorious" as Borges's anamnestic Funes, contain pretty well every work of literature ever published. And the mass of literature grows alarmingly. Nor is it just national literature that is growing: Books are also being translated across national borders in ever increasing numbers.

The territory is huge, and getting huger. There was a time (Shakespeare's time, for example) when the work of 501 great writers would pretty well have covered the field. No longer. The field of "books you must read" is growing by more than 501 every week. How to be well-read, when there is so much to read?

The bigger the territory, the more we need maps and aids to discriminating reading. Maps and vade mecums, we can hold physically in our hands. Books that help us with books. This is such a book. It does not tell you what to read, but it opens the way to intelligent reading.

Literature is, as I say, very, very big. And time, in our crazy-hurry, multimedia world is in short supply. We may be living longer than our ancestors (check out the birth and death dates of the authors here), but we are living a lot faster.

What follows is the most reliable of guides from the most reliable guides. Reliable as to the subjects and what is said about those subjects. Every entry is the springboard to follow-up reading, as well as being a repository of essential, impeccably accurate, easily absorbed information, handsomely packaged. A good book about the best writers and their creations.

John Sutherland

London, June 2008

INTRODUCTION

By Julian Patrick, General Editor

"A good preface," as the German writer Friedrich Schlegel once said, "must be at once the square root and the square of its book." It is difficult not to think numerically about the scope and nature of this book, given the rubric. *501 Great Writers* follows on from an earlier series that included *1001 Books You Must Read Before You Die*. The "death sentence" may have been lifted, but the problem of selection is if anything more pressing, as the emphasis shifts from a single work to a body of work, and a name—501 names, to be precise.

Schlegel was interested in the power of the preface to distill the text it introduces. This relationship extends here to the nature of each entry, which aims to introduce a writer—to convey, under extreme compression, a lively sense of why a particular writer may be considered "great" and why he or she may be considered worth reading. This task has been rendered more challenging, and more rewarding, by the range and international inflection of our list. We live in the midst of (and we are ourselves) dispersed peoples. And although inevitably Anglo- and Eurocentric, our list has resulted from a diversified and collaborative effort, involving many contributors and prolonged debate.

Each entry offers a blend of biographical commentary with an indicative selection of works, and aims to be suggestive rather than prescriptive. Like other forms of short writing—the aphorism, the maxim—each entry might operate like those Japanese toys described by Proust that appear to be just tiny pieces of paper, but which, when placed underwater, unfold to reveal a hidden wealth of color and shape. Or if that is too fanciful, you might reflect that we live in the age of "the biobib," by which I mean the life and the list together.

Here then, as with the evocative 1001 (a magical number for all lovers of narrative), the addition of "1" may still indicate the possibility of the additional, thus signaling that a list such as this can never be comprehensive or complete. And needless to say, a list, a collectivity of this kind, can only be gathered together through a dismaying process of subtraction and compromise (a circle, perhaps, that no one could square). We offer not the essence, in essence, but a set of signposts, ways to support your reading habits by making them, we hope, more systematic, serendipitous, and self-starting. Glimpses down roads you may, one day, be traveling.

Toronto, May 2008

HOMER

Born: 8th century B.C.E.

Style and genre: A Greek epic poet whose works celebrated mythical and heroic events, with a focus on aristocracy. He used artificial poetic dialect, repeated phraseology and scenes, and gave prominence to speeches and extended similes.

Just as the English call Shakespeare "the Bard," the ancient Greeks referred to Homer simply as "the Poet." Like Shakespeare, Homer belongs to the very highest echelon of Western literature, and his poetry reveals an understanding of human nature that has rarely been matched and never surpassed. Yet we know virtually nothing about him.

The ancient Greeks themselves had no hard facts concerning the figure whom they revered as the founder not just of epic poetry but of literature *tout court*. Details about Homer's life were collected from supposedly self-referential passages in his poems. The legend of Homer's blindness, for example, derives from his own description of a blind bard named Demodocus. Many scholars, past and present, avoid speaking of any individual poet named Homer and prefer to view Homeric poetry as the product of a long tradition of oral poetry. The linguistic evidence points toward an Ionian origin for Homeric poetry, dating from the late eighth or early seventh centuries B.C.E.

Signature titles

Poetry

Iliad, 8th century B.C.E.

Odyssey, c. 700 B.C.E.

ABOVE: Rembrandt's 1663 depiction of how Homer might have looked.

RIGHT: A third-century C.E. mosaic from Tunisia of Odysseus braving the Sirens.

Later Greeks attributed various early poems to Homer, but only two—the *Iliad* and the *Odyssey*—can truly be described as Homeric. Whether or not the same poet composed both of these poems, they clearly belong to the same tradition of oral poetry and stand apart from other early Greek epic poetry in terms of both quality and length. The *Iliad*, which is set during the tenth and final year of the mythical Trojan War, traces the complicated consequences of a dispute between Achilles and Agamemnon, two Greek commanders at the siege of Troy. The *Odyssey*, which is set after the fall of Troy, tells of the arduous homecoming of another Greek hero, Odysseus, and his struggle to re-establish himself as king of Ithaca. Though there are certain differences in language and religious outlook, both poems are noteworthy for their narrative control, the rhetorical brilliance of their speeches, and their sensitivity to the breadth of human experience. **TP**

ABOVE: *The Sack of Troy* by French artist Jean Maublanc.

Homer: Man or Woman?

There was never any doubt in antiquity that Homer was a man, and for most of the modern period, too, this assumption went unchallenged. On a few rare occasions, however, a dissenting voice has been heard. The British writer Samuel Butler, grandson of the classical scholar of the same name, developed a theory that the author of the *Odyssey* at least was a Sicilian woman, and Robert Graves adopted and developed this theory for his novel *Homer's Daughter*. More recently it has been suggested that the poet who oversaw the writing down of the poems, if not their composition, was a woman.

SAPPHO

Born: *c.* 630 B.C.E. (Lesbos, Greece); died *c.* 580 B.C.E. (place of death unknown, most likely Lesbos).

Style and genre: Sappho was a sixth-century poet from Lesbos called the "tenth muse" by Plato; her songs survive in vivid fragments.

True to her reputation as preeminent poet and lover, Sappho's work intertwines palpable lyrics and erotic charms. Highly regarded throughout antiquity, her poems were collected in nine volumes for the lost library at Alexandria. She even had a meter—Sapphic—named after her verse structure, which contained three long lines and a final short one, like a gasp of desire. Her popularity meant that poem fragments have been found in the prose of many Greek philosophers, as well as—more romantically—on flecks of papyrus found in the desert.

Sappho's life is as much of a puzzle as her complete works, which has not stopped poets, from Ovid through Mary Robinson to lesbian poet Olga Broumas, writing ardently and authoritatively about her. The generally accepted biography, a combination of poetic interpretation and ancient gossip, holds that she was an aristocrat who was part of an artistic and religious community of women on Lesbos, was exiled to Sicily after a coup, and had a daughter, Cleis. According to legend, she committed suicide after rejection by the ferryman Phaon.

The nineteenth century presented a sanitized Sappho, headmistress of a girls' school; twentieth-century classicists argued that her beautifully observed poems mourning the marriage of beloved female friends were just traditional wedding songs. Regardless of these cavils, she remains a figurehead for lesbians, because of her sensual gaze at women, most famously captured in Fragment 31, where the poet imagines herself in a love triangle, looking longingly at a woman flirting with a man. Whatever their basis in biographical fact, and through two and a half centuries of fragmentation and translation, Sappho's poems send a shiver down the spine of any man or woman who has ever loved. **SM**

"Some men say an army of ships is the most beautiful thing. I say it is what you love."—Fragment 16

Signature titles

Poetry

If Not, Winter: Fragments of Sappho, 2002

ABOVE: A fresco that may depict Sappho—her true appearance remains unknown.

AESCHYLUS

Born: *c.* 525 B.C.E. (Eleusis, near Athens, Greece); died *c.* 455 B.C.E. (Gela, Sicily).

Style and genre: With richly descriptive language and complex imagery, Aeschylus made bold innovations in dramatic form and gave prominence to political and religious themes.

Aeschylus's epitaph stated simply that he fought for his native Athens against the Persians at the Battle of Marathon. What it failed to mention was the brilliance of his literary achievement, for Aeschylus's formal innovations played a defining role in the early development of Greek tragedy and his poetry is remarkable for the sustained power and beauty of its imagery.

Born at a time when Athens was still ruled by a tyrant, Aeschylus witnessed the founding of the Athenian democracy and the dawn of the classical age. During a career that spanned nearly half a century, Aeschylus composed some eighty plays, of which just seven survive. Each of these seven plays shows the influence of the transitional age in which they were written, with the political concerns of the fledgling democracy everywhere in evidence. Coupled with this political awareness is a deep-seated religious sensibility that, while acknowledging individual responsibility, regards human activity as inextricably linked with divine will. Human progress is possible, but only through the suffering ordained by the gods (a theme best exemplified in Aeschylus's masterpiece, the trilogy *Oresteia*).

The gravity of the themes tackled by Aeschylus is matched by the majesty of his style. He delights in the piling up of compound adjectives and the mixing of imagery, and values mysterious grandeur more highly than clarity. In addition to being a poet of the first rank, Aeschylus was the most innovative of the ancient tragedians and was responsible for the introduction of the second actor (tragedy having previously involved a single actor and chorus). With this combination of high style and bold innovation, Aeschylus ushered in the golden age of classical drama and set the stage for his successors, Sophocles and Euripides. **TP**

"Zeus has set it down that wisdom comes through suffering . . ."—*Agamemnon*

Signature titles

Plays

Persians, 472 B.C.E.

Seven Against Thebes, 467 B.C.E.

Suppliants, *c.* 463 B.C.E.

Oresteia (Agamemnon; The Libation Bearers; Eumenides), 458 B.C.E.

ABOVE: An undated bust of Aeschylus in Rome's Capitoline Museums.

PINDAR

Born: *c.* 520 B.C.E. (Cynoscephalae, Greece); died *c.* 440 B.C.E. (Argos, Greece).

Style and genre: Widely regarded as the greatest lyric poet of ancient Greece, Pindar wrote poetry that is celebrated for its elaborate and elliptical language, complex metrical patterns, aristocratic outlook, and authorial self-awareness.

The Roman rhetorician Quintilian described Pindar as "by far the greatest" of lyric poets. Some two thousand years later, Quintilian's verdict may still stand, for few exponents of lyric poetry have been able to rival Pindar for nobility of expression, inventiveness of language, and mastery of form.

As with many ancient authors, the details of Pindar's life are obscure. He was born in the town of Cynoscephalae toward the end of the archaic period and was active as a poet throughout the early classical period. Of aristocratic stock, Pindar maintained an unrelentingly aristocratic outlook throughout a career that saw him write under the patronage of some of the leading families of Greece.

Later editors arranged his poetry into seventeen books, of which only four survive. These contain Pindar's victory odes, choral lyric poems written to celebrate the victories of athletes in the Olympian, Pythian, Nemean, and Isthmian athletic contests. The odes provide little in the way of description of the games themselves and instead focus on praising each athlete, along with his family and city. Pindar draws attention to the praiseworthy nature of the athlete's achievements by setting them alongside carefully selected episodes from myth, usually featuring a hero from the athlete's own city. Many of the odes also sound a note of warning, however, and the victorious athlete is advised to avoid attracting the envy of the gods. Pindar's poetry reveals a high level of self-awareness. He constantly compares himself with the athletes whom he is celebrating and reminds them of the reciprocal relationship that they share: athletic victory provides an opportunity for the poet; poetry, in turn, provides a memorial for the athlete. **TP**

"Seek not . . . immortal life; but exhaust the possibilities that are within reach."—*Pythian Odes*

Signature titles

Poetry

Pythian Odes, 498–446 B.C.E.

Olympian Odes, 488–460 B.C.E.

Nemean Odes, 485–444 B.C.E.

Isthmian Odes, 480–454 B.C.E.

ABOVE: A nineteenth-century engraving of Pindar by J. W. Cook.

SOPHOCLES

Born: *c.* 496 B.C.E. (Hippeios Colonus, Greece); died *c.* 406 B.C.E. (Athens, Greece).

Style and genre: Sophocles was a dramatist whose writing is bold, compressed, and understated (compared with that of Aeschylus); he contrasted characters, themes, and moods, and employed irony to great effect.

In his long life, Sophocles of Athens wrote 123 plays and competed with both Aeschylus and Euripides. Seven extant tragedies explore the greatness and suffering of exceptional humans who possessed almost divine abilities and who must choose between certain disaster or a compromise that would betray the heroic nature separating them from mere mortals. Sophoclean dramaturgical skill has been recognized since Aristotle, who praised its masterful sense of timing and unparalleled dramatic tension.

When divinely sent madness causes Ajax to disgrace himself at Troy in *Ajax*, fierce honor and shame permit him (then the mightiest Greek warrior) no other option but suicide. *Oedipus the King* dramatizes how the very intelligence that empowers the monarch drives his excessive and relentless search for truth and eventually leads to his madness, self-blinding, and exile. These tragic dilemmas can be understood in broader political terms as a clash between the values of a past Homeric world that privileged the individual, and those of the contemporary world, the fifth-century Athenian democracy that served the interests of the community and discouraged extreme behavior.

Heroic intransigence leads to a total, dreadful isolation from even the gods in a world governed by a mysterious and cruel fate. *Trachiniae* shows us that Zeus will not even save his son, Heracles, the model of Greek heroism, from an agonizing death that strips him both of his flesh and fabled masculinity. Yet the free and autonomous choice of suffering over the acceptance of human limitations endows Sophocles's heroes with awesomeness and power in a world where the past yields no knowledge, the future no hope, and the present only suffering. **DS**

"Sophocles drew men as they ought to be, Euripides, as they were."—Aristotle, *Poetics*

Signature titles

Plays

Ajax, *c.* 450–440 B.C.E.
Antigone, *c.* 442 B.C.E.
Trachiniae, *c.* 430 B.C.E.
Oedipus the King, *c.* 430–420 B.C.E.
Oedipus at Colonus, 410 B.C.E.
Electra, *c.* 410 B.C.E.
Philoctetes, 409 B.C.E.

ABOVE: An undated depiction of Sophocles drawn from contemporary descriptions.

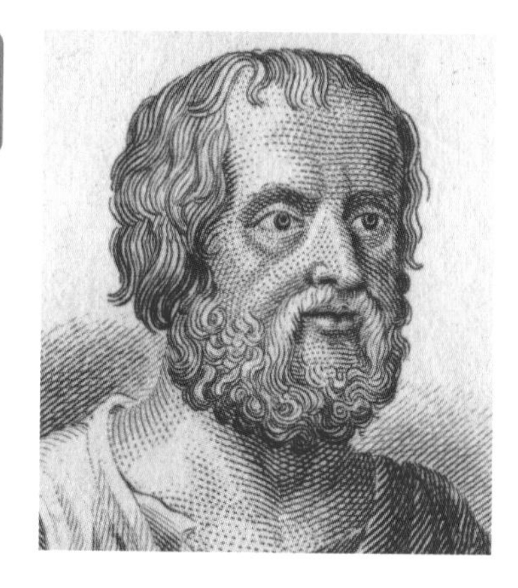

EURIPIDES

Born: 480 B.C.E. (Salamis, Greece); died 406 B.C.E. (Macedonia).

Style and genre: Euripides was the *enfant terrible* of fifth-century B.C.E. Greek tragedy; his war-scarred protagonists exhibit a sophistic and sophisticated skepticism about myths and heroes.

Fascinated by gods and monsters, Euripides could be called the original modern playwright. Although he avoided politics—unlike his older contemporary and competitor Sophocles—Euripides made clear his disillusionment with Athenian culture, clothing his heroes in rags. In *The Trojan Women*, he even openly criticized the city-state's foreign policy by comparing the massacre at Melos to the destruction of Troy—seen, unusually, from the perspective of the Trojans.

To protest against the Vietnam War in 1971, Michael Cacoyannis filmed *The Trojan Women* using the 1937 translation by Edith Hamilton, who saw Euripides as a pacifist in a belligerent age. Certainly, his other plays about Greece's heroic founding myth—*Helen*, *Iphigenia at Aulis*, and *Hecuba*—ask, "War, what is it good for?" Plays such as the *Bacchae*, which satirizes the founding family of Greece, showcase the playwright as iconoclastic contrarian. His gods, like the play's murderously charismatic Bacchus, *are* monsters. More than that, they are politicians.

While Aeschylus's plays suggest a ritual awe at the gods' incomprehensibility, and Sophocles's dramas explore their farsighted logic, Euripides sees gods and humans engaged in a shifty, selfish, profound, and painfully embarrassing dance of power. Although regarded as a less magnificent poet than his predecessors, Euripides is as savagely clever at seeing the underside of words and characters. Several times in *Medea*, the eponymous heroine is credited with *sophrosyne*, the ultimate Greek quality of masculine wisdom. Euripides's point is partially that *sophronsyne* is different for girls, and also that thought, like all gifts of the gods, is a double-edged sword. His plays are still sharp enough to lacerate. **SM**

"[Euripides is,] with all his faults, the most tragic of the poets."—Aristotle

Signature titles

Plays

Medea, 431 B.C.E.
Hippolytus, 428 B.C.E.
Electra, *c.* 420–410 B.C.E.
The Trojan Women, 415 B.C.E.
Iphigenia at Aulis, 410 B.C.E.
Bacchae, 407–406 B.C.E.
Grief Lessons: Four Plays by Euripides, 2006

ABOVE: A nineteenth-century engraving of Euripides by J. W. Cook.

ARISTOPHANES

Born: *c.* 448 B.C.E. (probably Athens, Greece); died *c.* 388–385 B.C.E. (location unknown).

Style and genre: He was the comic dramatist considered by the ancients to be most representative of Greek old comedy for his style that joined obscenity and personal invective with brilliant political satire and subtle parody of contemporary literature.

The earliest picture of Aristophanes occurs in *Symposium* by Plato, in a friendly portrait of a man who enjoyed the pleasures of life and was, like his comedy, both amusing and serious. Most biographical material about Aristophanes, however, is not corroborated and was probably drawn from his plays.

Acharnians, the earliest extant play, embodies the highly topical concerns and fantastic plots characteristic of the "political" plays of old comedy in fifth-century Athens: a sympathetic hero, frustrated with the status quo, employs all his roguish cleverness and ingenuity to overcome his enemies through supernatural means. The poor farmer Dicaeopolis outwits Athens's hawkish demagogues by securing a private peace with the Spartans, thereby acquiring for himself all the pleasures denied by the Peloponnesian war—food, wine, and sex. Coupled with its pervasive obscenity and crude humor, such generic interests of old comedy set its quotidian world of the here-and-now in sharp contrast to the lofty, austere, and removed mythological past of its rival genre: Greek tragedy. *Acharnians* also boasts what is arguably the dirtiest passage in ancient literature, in which the hero bargains for the daughters of a trader through a series of explicit puns about the vagina.

Aristophanes shattered the dramatic illusion preserved at all costs by tragedy with *ad hominem* abuse, a feature adopted from the earlier tradition of iambographic poetry. For laughs, the comic poet abused politicians, private individuals, other poets, and the audience itself with scattered and sustained mockery. *Clouds*'s notorious portrait of Socrates as an eccentric charlatan and representative of the growing sophistic movement was famously blamed as a contributing factor in the philosopher's execution. **DS**

"Demeter . . . may I say much that is funny and much that is serious."—Chorus, *Frogs*

Signature titles

Plays

Acharnians, 425 B.C.E.
Knights, 424 B.C.E.
Clouds, 423 B.C.E.
Wasps, 422 B.C.E.
Peace, 421 B.C.E.
Birds, 414 B.C.E.
Lysistrata, 411 B.C.E.
Thesmophoriazusae, 411 B.C.E.
Frogs, 405 B.C.E.
Ecclesiazusae, c. 393–392 B.C.E.
Wealth, 388 B.C.E.

ABOVE: An undated engraving of the Athenian playwright Aristophanes.

PLATO

Born: *c.* 427 B.C.E. (Athens, Greece); died 347 B.C.E. (Athens, Greece).

Style and genre: Plato was a master teacher-philosopher and founder of the Academy whose own writing took the form of dialogues on subjects as diverse as politics, love, knowledge, and the trial of Socrates.

Plato stands with his teacher Socrates and his pupil Aristotle as one of the three founding figures of the Western philosophical tradition. But whereas Socrates himself wrote nothing, and the surviving works of Aristotle are often little more than lecture notes, we are fortunate to possess more than thirty complete philosophical works by Plato, works that testify to both the flexibility and richness of Plato's thought and his status as one of the great masters of Greek prose style.

Plato, whose real name may have been Aristocles, was descended from distinguished families on both sides. One tradition reports that Plato's father, Ariston, claimed descent from Codrus, a mythical king of Athens. Ariston died while Plato was still a child and his mother, Perictione, married

Signature titles

Dialogues

Euthyphro, c. 380 B.C.E.
Protagoras, c. 380 B.C.E.
Apology, c. 360 B.C.E.
Crito, c. 360 B.C.E.
Phaedo, c. 360 B.C.E.
Republic, c. 360 B.C.E.
Symposium, c. 360 B.C.E.
Laws, c. 360 B.C.E.

ABOVE: A seventeenth-century French School oil painting of Plato.

RIGHT: A mosaic of Plato with his pupils, from the House of T. Siminius in Pompeii.

ABOVE: A sixteenth-century painting of Plato's cave, from the Flemish School.

Pyrilampes, a friend of the great democratic statesman Pericles. Despite his lofty political ties, Plato eschewed a political career and devoted himself to philosophy. The reasons for this choice of career are not clear, but the execution of his friend and master, Socrates, may have been decisive in Plato's rejection not just of Athenian democratic politics but also of democracy itself as a viable system.

"And what, Socrates, is the food of the soul? Surely, I said, knowledge. . . ."—*Apology*

Of Plato's adult life few precise details exist. It is likely that he traveled extensively, possibly to Egypt and certainly to southern Italy and Sicily. Returning to Athens in 387 B.C.E., Plato founded the Academy, a research and teaching institute devoted to philosophy (including mathematics and political theory). Much of the rest of Plato's life was spent teaching and writing, but he did undertake two more voyages to Sicily in 367 B.C.E. (or shortly

Plato the Mythmaker

In a famous passage in the *Republic*, Plato has Socrates declare that most forms of poetry, and especially the myth-based poetry of Homer and the tragedians, should be banned from the ideal city. The reason for this is that mythical poetry is responsible for corrupting character through its depiction of immoral behavior. It is ironic, then, that Plato himself is famous for the use he makes of myth in his own works.

Often Plato is happy to adapt existing myth to fit his philosophical purpose—his *Myth of Er*, for example, is a recasting of Greek myths of the underworld to argue for the rewarding or punishment of the soul after death. Elsewhere, however, Plato simply invents myth.

The best known example of this is the *Myth of Atlantis*, which Plato invented in order to advance certain political ideas. The myth describes the political organization of the island of Atlantis. The *Myth of Atlantis* is a fiction from start to finish, but many people have been seduced by the precision of Plato's description, leading to more than one fruitless search for its location.

RIGHT: Aristotle and Plato in a detail from Raphael's *School of Athens*, 1510–1511.

after) and 361 B.C.E. The purpose of these trips was to educate Dionysius II, the tyrant of Syracuse, and to make of him a true philosopher-king; both were abject failures.

The inspirational form of dialogue

An apocryphal story reported by Diogenes Laertius tells that Plato's first composition was a tragedy, but that he burned it after hearing Socrates talk. Plato's actual works were all written in the form of prose dialogues (the only exception being *Apology*, which purports to be the defense speech from Socrates's trial). The dialogue form represents both a stylistic and philosophical choice. Stylistically, it allows Plato to present philosophical discussion in a vivid and engaging way that gives free reign to his considerable artistic abilities. *Symposium*, to take only one example, is not just a discussion of the nature of love, it is also a dramatic *tour de force*. Philosophically, the dialogue form reinforces Plato's belief that knowledge is only valuable when achieved through individual effort. Each dialogue includes a range of views and aims thereby to rouse the reader to philosophical enquiry.

Plato's contribution to all branches of philosophy is vast, but his most lasting contributions were in epistemology and political theory. His epistemology is built around a dualist cosmology, according to which the everyday world is a pale imitation of a separate world of perfect and unchanging "forms." This world of forms is not open to sensory perception and can only be grasped through philosophical contemplation. Plato's political theory is based on the idea that the structure of the state should reflect the structure of the soul. Justice in the state, as in the individual, exists in the harmonious functioning of its parts: the ruling class, the military class, and the economic class. Such theories are masterfully developed in Plato's *Republic*.

The dialogue form quickly established itself as a philosophical genre and was used by writers from Aristotle to David Hume. Plato's dualist conception of reality was revived in late antiquity by the Neoplatonists and through them profoundly influenced Christian philosophy. **TP**

GAIUS VALERIUS CATULLUS

Born: *c.* 84 B.C.E. (Verona, Italy); died *c.* 54 B.C.E. (Rome, Italy).

Style and genre: A daring, modern writer, Catullus charted the ground between hate and love in personal lyrics of startling intimacy and miniature epics of dazzling freshness.

Gaius Valerius Catullus was the first modern writer. Keen to cultivate a friendship with Julius Caesar, he undertook a hated year of political service in Bithynia, then returned to the bright lights of Rome where—according to his many squibs—he rebelliously devoted himself to sex, drink, and poetry, creating a coterie, the Neoteroi, modeled on fashionable classical Greece.

However, it was Catullus's thinly veiled account of an affair with the consul's wife Clodia Metella, code named "Lesbia," that secured his reputation for social daring. His epyllions, which condensed epic narratives into mere pages, proved his literary daring. In both forms, he invented poetic expression for the passions coursing within his heroes and himself. **SM**

Signature titles

Poetry

Carmina, 1472 (based on thirteenth-century copies of a possible ninth-century manuscript)

Catullus's Carmina, 1949

The Poems of Catullus, 1966

VIRGIL

Born: Publius Vergilius Maro, October 15, 70 B.C.E. (near Mantua, Italy); died 19 B.C.E. (Brindisi, Italy).

Style and genre: To Dante, Virgil is the supreme maestro and creator of "*lo bello stile*." Dryden called the *Georgics* "the best poem of the best poet."

Virgil is generally considered to be one of the most important of the classical Roman poets, and his work has had an enormous influence on European literature. His first work, the *Eclogues*, is set in an idyllic Arcadia, although contemporary political events are discussed by the shepherds and farmers who inhabit this paradise. He included a greater sense of the reality of country life in his subsequent *Georgics*, which described the daily work of a farm. Perhaps his best known work, however, is the *Aeneid*. Virgil traces the journey of Aeneas from the sack of Troy to his founding of Rome, both as an assertion of Rome's heroic origins, and as an attempt to provide Roman culture with a work worthy of comparison with the *Iliad* and *Odyssey*. **PG**

Signature titles

Poetry

Eclogues (also known as *Bucolics*), 42–37 B.C.E.

Georgics, *c.* 36–29 B.C.E.

Aeneid, 19 B.C.E. (published in twelve books but incomplete at Virgil's death)

RIGHT: Charles-Joseph Natoire's depiction of Venus asking Vulcan for weapons for Aeneas, 1734.

HORACE

Born: Quintus Horatius Flaccus, December 8, 65 B.C.E. (Venosa, Italy); died November 27, 8 B.C.E. (Rome, Italy).

Style and genre: Horace was a Roman satirist and critic whose work is full of tolerance, a belief in moderation, and a melancholy recognition of life's brevity.

Signature titles

Poetry

Satires, 35–30 B.C.E.

Epodes, 30 B.C.E.

Odes (Carmina), 23–13 B.C.E.

Criticism

Ars Poetica, or Epistle to the Pisones, 18 B.C.E.

Horace's life—as the coiner of the phrase *carpe diem*—was one filled with opportunities seized. His father, though once a slave, had made enough money as an auctioneer to send his son to school in Rome and subsequently to study at Athens. Horace enrolled in Brutus's republican army and fought at Philippi (42 B.C.E.). With bitter self-irony, he would later say that he threw away his shield and ran from the battlefield. On returning home, he found his property confiscated, but he succeeded in obtaining a secretarial post in the treasury to survive.

The poetry that Horace wrote during the next few years impressed Virgil, who introduced him to the great patron Maecenas. This event marked the beginning of a lifelong friendship. From then on, Horace had no financial worries; he moved freely among the leading poets and statesmen of Rome. Maecenas gave him a farm in the Sabine country, near Rome, which was to be the source of much happiness to Horace and the inspiration of some of the most beautiful passages in his writings. *Epodes and Odes* includes short poems in various lyric meters whose themes involve love and friendship, wine, the joys of the country and the changing seasons, Roman greatness, and the character of the ideal citizen. The urbane and witty poems in *Satires* gently mock the follies and vices of men. Poem II, vi, is the famous satire on town and country life, known as the fable of the town and country mouse.

"It is sweet and fitting to die for one's country."

—*Odes III*

After Virgil's death in 19 B.C.E., Horace became Augustus's Poet Laureate and was commissioned by him to write the hymn, *Carmen Saeculare*. Performed by a chorus of twenty-seven girls and as many boys, it invoked the gods and asked that they assure prosperity for Rome and the rule of Augustus. **PG**

ABOVE: Luca Signorelli's portrait of Horace, c. 1500–1504, San Brizio Chapel, Orvieto.

OVID

Born: Publius Ovidius Naso, March 20, 43 B.C.E. (Sulmona, Italy); died 17 C.E. (Constanta, Romania).

Style and genre: Ovid's poetry is marked by literary self-consciousness; mythological themes; elegant, pithy expression; and a musical flow of verse.

Recognized as the last of the great Augustan poets, Ovid surpassed all of his predecessors in wit, elegance, and charm. Having abandoned a political career for a life of poetry within the fashionable circles and literary haunts of Rome, Ovid found immediate success with his early forays into love elegies. Although he devoted most of his career to the elegiac genre, he is perhaps best known for his grand mythological poem, *Metamorphoses,* his only work in the epic tradition. With the unifying motif of changed bodies, the central theme of love, and embedded narratives that continually reproduce themselves, *Metamorphoses* constitutes the culmination of all of Ovid's learned virtuosity. The poem is at once a catalog of mythology and an erudite examination of literary convention and inheritance.

At the pinnacle of his success, in 8 C.E., Ovid was exiled to Tomis at the farthest reaches of the empire for reasons that are still shrouded in mystery. The suspicion is that behind the formal charge of immorality in his poetry lay the punishment for an adulterous scandal involving the emperor's granddaughter. Expelled from the limelight, Ovid returned to his elegiac roots, bemoaning his separation from the society for which his poetry had been written, and which had applauded his poetic excellence so ardently. His banishment marked an abrupt change in the tone and style of his writing, which became less playful and more brooding and introspective. However, his work written in exile betrayed the same infatuation with his own fame and with the endurance of his poetry that had characterized his writings in Rome. It is indeed befitting that Ovid should remain an influential presence in the Western canon. **MP**

"Here I lie, Naso the poet. I who played amid tender loves was slain by my own talent."—*Sorrows*

Signature titles

Poetry

Loves, c. 25–16 B.C.E.

Letters from Pontus, after 8 B.C.E.

Heroines, c. 5 B.C.E.

Cures for Love, c. 5 B.C.E.

The Art of Love, c. 1 B.C.E.

Metamorphoses, c. 8 C.E.

Sorrows, after 8 C.E.

ABOVE: Luca Signorelli's depiction of Ovid, c. 1500–1504, San Brizio Chapel, Orvieto.

APULEIUS

Born: Lucius Apuleius, *c.* 124 (Madauros, Numidia [near what is now Mdaourouch, Algeria]); died *c.* 170 (Numidia).

Style and genre: Apuleius's prose is an entertaining mixture of magic, farce, religion, and mythology, written in a lively and often picaresque style that is highly polished.

On paper, Apuleius led a privileged life. He was left a substantial amount of money after the death of his father, a provincial magistrate, which he quickly squandered. Matriculating at the university in Carthage and afterward in Athens, he studied Platonic philosophy. After his initiation into the mysteries of Isis, he studied Latin oratory in Rome and began a successful career in the courts. It was this success that allowed him to travel widely in Asia Minor and Egypt, studying philosophy and religion. However, during this time he was accused of using witchcraft and sorcery to gain the affections and fortune of the widow he married. Delivering a speech in his own defense, essentially a discourse on the use of magic, probably secured his acquittal. He reworked and published a version of the speech, which he entitled *Apology*.

Apuleius is primarily well known for the episodic picaresque romance in eleven books known as the *Metamorphoses*, or more popularly as *The Golden Ass*—the only Latin novel to have survived in its entirety. It recounts the boisterous, often bawdy adventures of Lucius, a Greek, who experiments with magic and has the misfortune to be transformed into an ass. In this guise he has many adventures, falls into the hands of robbers, shares their fantastic exploits, and is finally turned back into human shape by the intervention of the goddess Isis. There are multiple digressions: the longest being the well-known fable of the fairy bridegroom, *Cupid and Psyche* (Books IV–VI), which in late antiquity and the Middle Ages was sometimes interpreted as an allegory of the soul (psyche) in relation to love (cupid). *The Golden Ass* was later used by Shakespeare as a source for his popular comedy *A Midsummer Night's Dream*. **PG**

"Familiarity breeds contempt, while rarity wins admiration."—Apuleius

Signature titles

Novel

Metamorphoses (The Golden Ass), date unknown

Speeches

Apology, *c.* 158

ABOVE: Apuleius's *The Golden Ass* is the only Latin novel to have survived in its entirety.

ST. AUGUSTINE

Born: Aurelius Augustinus, November 13, 354 (Souk Ahras, Algeria); died August 28, 430 (Annaba, Algeria).

Style and genre: St. Augustine's analysis of the emotional side of Christian experience in the face of sin remains unsurpassed.

Augustine's father was a pagan, but his mother (St. Monica) was a devout Christian who greatly influenced her son. On reading Cicero's *Hortensius*, Augustine became deeply interested in philosophy. He converted to the Manichean religion, some of whose tenets he continued to hold after he had founded his own school of rhetoric at Rome. During this period he had a son (Adeodatus) by a woman who would be his concubine for more than fifteen years. In Milan he was offered a professorship and came under the influence both of Neoplatonism and of the preaching of St. Ambrose.

After agonizing inward conflict, Augustine renounced all his unorthodox beliefs and devoted himself entirely to serving God and the practices of the priesthood, which included chastity. From his own account, he lived a life of sin until his conversion to Christianity at the age of thirty-two. He gives a moving personal portrayal of his spiritual struggles and search for truth in *The Confessions*, which were written with deep personal introspection for the edification of others.

On his return to North Africa, Augustine converted the family house into a monastic foundation for himself and a group of friends. He now began work on the twenty-two books of *The City of God* that would occupy him for almost fourteen years. It was written to restore the confidence of his fellow Christians, which was badly shaken after the sack of Rome by the Visigoths in 410. In it he sets forth the allegory of two cities: a heavenly city compromising the righteous on earth and the saints in heaven, living in accordance with God's will; and an earthly city, guided by worldly and selfish principles. Augustine died aged seventy-five, as invading Vandals were besieging the city of Hippo. **PG**

"Grant me chastity and continence, but not yet."
—*The Confessions, VII, vii*

Signature titles

Autobiography

The Confessions of Saint Augustine (Confessiones), 397–398

Theological works

The City of God (De Civitate Dei), c. 413–426

ABOVE: Detail from Filippino Lippi's image of *St. Augustine*, c. 1490.

CHRÉTIEN DE TROYES

Born: *c.* 1130s (place unknown); died *c.* 1190 (place unknown).

Style and genre: Chrétien de Troyes was the medieval author of tales of knightly adventure with complex, intertwined plots and mysterious, magical episodes that focused on love and marriage.

As with many medieval authors, little is known of Chrétien's life. His dedication of *The Knight of the Cart* to Marie, Countess of Champagne suggests that he may have been associated with her court at Troyes, France, although it is not clear in what capacity. This mystery notwithstanding, his literary influence extended across Western Europe, throughout the Middle Ages.

Chrétien's career unfolded during a period of significant change in French literature. In the second half of the twelfth century, long verse romances became increasingly popular, at the expense of the traditional epic or *chanson de geste*. Where the *chanson* told of battles and the fate of entire peoples in bold, repetitive stanzas, the romance spoke of the development of one knight or the progress of a pair of lovers. The best medieval romances, with their keen interest in the psychological motivations of their characters, read like distant forebears of the modern novel.

Although Chrétien stands near the beginning of the romance tradition, his work was arguably never surpassed. His five romances (two of which he left unfinished) take place in

Signature titles

Romances

Erec and Enide (Érec et Énide), c. 1170

Cligès, c. 1176

Yvain, The Knight of the Lion (Yvain, le chevalier au lion), c. 1177–1181

Perceval, The Story of the Grail (Le Roman de Perceval ou le conte du graal), c. 1190

Poems

Lancelot, The Knight of the Cart (Lancelot, le chevalier de la charette), c. 1177–1181

ABOVE: ***Sir Perceval and Holy Grail*, 1286.**

BELOW: A thirteenth-century depiction of a scene from the story of Perceval.

ABOVE: ***The Arrival of the Grail*** **(1350), from a French illumination to** ***Le Roman de Perceval.***

the legendary Britain of King Arthur, drawing on a rich tradition of Arthurian lore from England, France, and Wales. Chrétien shifted the focus away from the king himself (who became rather sedentary and even morally ambiguous) and on to his knights and their adventures away from court.

Although the world of his compositions is full of wonders—heroic knights, idealized maidens, magic rings—it is far from a realm of pure fantasy. Human relationships, whether erotic or political, were always Chrétien's central concern. On more than one occasion he gently mocks the elaborate social codes of the courtly aesthetic: *The Knight of the Lion* begins with Arthur unexpectedly leaving the dinner table to go to bed with Guinevere; another romance sees the self-absorbed Lancelot knocked off his horse, unaware, in his lovesick reverie, that he has accepted the challenge of a rival knight.

If the measure of an ideal is the degree to which it provokes thought, the extent to which it can withstand questioning humor, rather than inspire blind devotion, then the ideal of chivalry is very much alive in Chrétien's romances. **CT**

The Holy Grail

Chrétien was the first author to associate the grail with Arthur and his knights. In his unfinished *Story of the Grail* (usually considered his final work), it appears not as the cup of Christ, but as an empty *graal* or fish dish, carried in a mysterious procession before the hero Perceval. Chrétien's romance is more concerned with dynastic rivalry than mysticism: Perceval must choose between his loyalty to Arthur and the demands of his family, hostile to the king. While some characters claim the grail as a holy icon, Chrétien deftly demonstrates its true significance as a symbol of their political cause.

DANTE ALIGHIERI

Born: May 1265 (Florence, Italy); died September 13 or 14, 1321 (Ravenna, Italy).

Style and genre: Known as the father of Italian vernacular poetry, Dante Alighieri lived in exile for political reasons from 1302; in 1308 he began the greatest epic poem of the Middle Ages, *La Divina Commedia*.

Described by Giovanni Boccaccio in his *Treatise in Celebration of Dante* (*c.* 1355), Dante "was our poet of average height, who had reached a mature age and become rather bulky, and it was his solemn and gentle gait, always dressed in the most virtuous clothes, in this dress which, at his age, was most gracious. His face was long, and his nose aquiline, and his eyes big and small at the same time, with a big jaw, and his upper lip protruding. His complexion was dark, and his hair and his beard were thick, black, and frizzy. His face was melancholic and pensive." A fortuitous iconographic tradition confirms the established characteristics of Dante's appearance were his nose, lips, and chin. Boccaccio's descriptors "melancholic and pensive" recall the poet isolated in solitude yet sustained by his unquenchable thirst for knowledge and nourished by a splendid pride that held him from acquiescing to the willful orders of the powerful, even at the cost of compelling him to endure a life spent in exile.

The first piece of literature that can be attributed to Dante with any certainty is *The New Life*. It is composed of a mixture of forty-two prose chapters and thirty-one poems of varying

Signature titles

Poetry

The New Life (La Vita Nuova), 1292–1295

The Banquet (Convivio), 1304–1307

The Divine Comedy (La Divina Commedia: Inferno; Purgatorio; Paradiso), 1308–1321

Essays

On the Eloquence of the Vernacular (De vulgari eloquentia), 1303–1305

ABOVE: Sixteenth-century Italian School portrait of Dante.

RIGHT: Dante's conversation with Justinian in Canto VI of *Paradiso*.

meter, and recounts Dante's love for Beatrice, from their first encounter to her death. In the last chapter, we find the famous lines announcing *The Divine Comedy,* a work Dante claims has been conceived in order to honor his beloved Beatrice: "So that, if it pleases Him by whom all things live, that my life lasts a few years, I hope to write of her what has never been written of any woman."

ABOVE: Dante and Virgil amid the soothsayers and false prophets, whose heads have been reversed in punishment.

Also written in vernacular Italian is *The Banquet,* a collection of four treatises intended as an invitation to the favored table of Knowledge for all those who feel excluded. The book constitutes an academic exercise in medieval philosophy—namely, the attempt to reconcile the doctrine of Christianity with the classical Aristotelian school of thought. In his *Of Vernacular Speech*, a partially completed work written in Latin, the poet discusses the importance of the use of vernacular language, characterizing it as "illustrious," "cardinal," "learned," and "judicial." The three books collected in *On Monarchy (La monarchia,* 1313–1318) are also written in Latin; in these, through the metaphor of two suns, Dante describes his political ideals and advocates for a clear

"Pride, envy, avarice—these sparks have set on fire the hearts of all men."—*Inferno, VI*

Dante's Great Love

Immortalized in Dante's work, Beatrice Portinari has been transformed into one of the great muses in literature—on par with Petrarch's Laura and Shakespeare's Dark Lady.

Dante was only nine and Beatrice eight when they met for the first time. He claims to have fallen in love on first sight, despite never speaking with Beatrice, and, on this somewhat fleeting acquaintance, devoted a considerable amount of his literary output to celebrating her virtues. According to *The New Life*, they met only once more during their lives before Beatrice's death aged twenty-four, although as members of prominent Florentine families, Dante may well be taking a certain amount of poetic license.

Despite marrying Gemma di Manetto Donati, Dante lavished praise on Beatrice in *The New Life*, and she guided him through Heaven in *Paradiso*, taking on a role performed in *Inferno* by no less a figure than Virgil. This lifelong adoration of a woman he claims to have only met twice has led scholars to argue that Beatrice's significance for Dante may have been nothing more than as an emblem of purity. Alternatively, she may have merely provided Dante with an opportunity to display his abilities in the conventions of courtly love. Regardless of the reality, their relationship remains one of literature's great unrequited love stories.

separation between imperial power (politics) and the sphere of papal influence (religion).

The Divine Comedy

The work that makes Dante the ultimate model for Italian writers is undoubtedly *The Divine Comedy* (begun in 1308); the adjective "Divina" was actually a sixteenth-century addition to the title, influenced by Boccaccio's adjudication of the work. It consists of 14,233 verses divided into tercets of linked rhymes. One hundred cantos are divided into three canticles of thirty-three cantos each, plus one initial canto. The eponymous main character in the poem, Dante, describes his journey at the age of thirty-five, "halfway down the road of our lives." The work takes place in 1300 during the Easter triduum, the three days of prayer preceding the feast. In the three subterranean kingdoms of purgatory, hell, and heaven, Dante and his guide Virgil—the foremost poet of classical antiquity and herald of Christianity—encounter personalities of the past and the present. Dante uses these characters as omens; in hell they portend the capital sins that can cause eternal damnation. In purgatory the soul has the ability to ascend to heavenly bliss by purifying the less severe sins it has committed. When he reaches the final zone, earthly paradise, Dante exchanges Virgil's company for Beatrice's, his beloved, and he journeys across the nine skies of paradise with her to reach the supreme experience of gazing at the face of God. *The Divine Comedy* is a fascinating work, veering from criticism of the contemporary political struggles dividing Florence, to abstruse theological debate on the nature of sin and the means of redemption. It blends a variety of mediums and means of communication, from dialectic expressions to neologisms, and from Latinate diction to colloquialisms; as such, it is an Italian equivalent of Geoffrey Chaucer's *The Canterbury Tales* in challenging Latin's preeminence as the language of art and arguing for the literary potential of Italian dialects. These diverse idioms and themes are unified in a sublime text, produced by a genius of poetry. **CC**

RIGHT: ***Scenes from Dante's Divine Comedy*****, 1842–1844, by Carl Vogel von Vogelstein.**

FRANCESCO PETRARCH

Born: July 20, 1304 (Arezzo, Italy); died July 18 or 19, 1374 (Arquà, Italy).

Style and genre: Considered to be the father of European humanism, Petrarch celebrated human potential and justified the pursuit of individual achievement in religious terms, while lamenting the agonies of love in his poetry.

Petrarch is generally considered by scholars to have been instrumental in establishing the humanist movement in Europe. His writings represented a response to earlier Church doctrine, which promoted a passive acceptance of one's lot in life, arguing instead that individuals were capable of choosing their own destiny, and should be allowed to pursue such a choice. Petrarch reconciled this new philosophy with traditional religious belief by suggesting that God would not have bestowed intellect upon humanity without expecting it be used to improve the human condition; these ideas proved fundamental to the creative flowering of the Renaissance.

Petrarch's humanism was informed by western Europe's rediscovery of classical texts; Petrarch himself unearthed a previously unknown collection of Cicero's letters, the *Ad Atticum.* Much of Petrarch's reputation relies on his writings in

Signature titles

Poetry

Song Book (Il Canzoniere), c. 1335–*c.* 1374

My Secret Book (Secretum meum), c. 1342–*c.* 1358

Triumphs (Trionfi), 1351–1374

Letters

Letters on Familiar Matters (Rerum familiarium), c. 1325–1366

Letters on Old Age (Rerum senilium), 1361–1373

ABOVE: A portrait of Petrarch in the museum at Versailles.

RIGHT: A fifteenth-century manuscript of Petrarch's sonnets.

LEFT: Jacopo del Sellaio's *Triumph of Time*, inspired by Petrarch's "Triumph."

Latin, derived from classical exemplars, for example *Letters on Familiar Matters*, *Letters on Old Age*, and *Letter to Posterity* (*Epistula ad posteros, c.* 1372). Also noteworthy is *My Secret Book*, which is a spiritual testament taking the form of a dialogue between the poet and St. Augustine. The work's principal themes are the conflict between striving for purity of soul and the temptations of the flesh; reflections about death; the continuous flow of time; and unspeakable inclinations like sloth—all of which are part of an ongoing spiritual crisis without any solution.

Petrarch's other great achievement was the *Song Book*, inspired by the love of his life, Laura. (There is little information on Laura, but she was married and therefore had little actual contact with him.) Petrarch worked on this text from 1335 until the year of his death and redrafted it several times. At the center of the collection is the story of a restless soul, perennially torn between the beauty of the ideal and the misery of reality, resulting in the poet's continuous soliloquy. On translation into English, the *Song Book* established the Petrarchan form, with its distinctive rhyme scheme and concerns with unattainable love, as one of the main patterns for sonnet composition. **CC**

The Mountaineer

In addition to establishing European humanism, rehabilitating classical works, and developing an influential sonnet form, Petrarch also claimed (inaccurately) to be the first person since Philip V of Macedon to climb mountains for pleasure, after ascending Mont Ventoux in southern France in 1336. His climb has since been interpreted as an allegory of his search for a better life, but in a letter describing the trip to a friend, Petrarch claimed, "My only motive was the wish to see what so great an elevation had to offer."

HAFIZ

Born: Khwajeh Shams al-Din Muhammed Hafez-e Shirazi, *c.* 1310–1325 (Shiraz, Iran); died *c.* 1389 (Shiraz, Iran).

Style and genre: Court poet of spiritual love and Koranic teacher who attained cosmic consciousness, Hafiz embodied the erudite sophistication of medieval Persia.

Signature titles

Poetry

Divan-e-Hafiz, 1410 (compiled by Mohammad Golandaam)

Poems from the Divan of Hafiz, 1897 (translated by Gertrude Bell, reissued 1995)

Like his near-contemporary Petrarch, Hafiz created a crystalline poetry of divine and sexual love. For more than fifty years, Hafiz wrote from divine inspiration, yet many of the 500 *ghazals* sing of the wealth and beauty of Shakh-e Nabat, who stands to his work as Laura stands to Petrarch's. As well as being installed as court poet, first to Abu Ishak and then to Shah Shuja, of Shiraz, Hafiz was a divine Master. His religious scholarship is encoded in his pen name: Hafiz indicates one who has memorized the Koran. Like the Italian poet, he inherited a grand lyric tradition exemplified by Rumi and Nizami—however, Hafiz's tradition, continued by his work, celebrated the interconnections of the erotic and the spiritual. **SM**

GIOVANNI BOCCACCIO

Born: June or July 1313 (possibly Florence, Italy); died December 21, 1375 (Certaldo, near Arezzo, Italy).

Style and genre: Boccaccio is considered to be one of the "three crowns" of Italian literature, together with Dante and Petrarch.

Signature titles

Poetry

Filostrato, 1335–1340

Romances

Decameron, 1349–1353

Biographies

On the Fates of Famous Men (*De Casibus Virorum Illustribus*), 1355–1374

On Famous Women (*De mulieribus claris*), *c.* 1362

Among Boccaccio's many minor works, *Decameron*, a collection of one hundred short stories, stands out for its originality. Written against the backdrop of the plague raging in Florence in 1348, seven children and three youths seek refuge in a house out of town. In the course of ten days, they tell each other ten short stories a day. The work begins with a preface addressed to the "vague women" who have personally experienced love, indicating the symbolic value of this life-bearing feeling compared with the horrors of the plague. In each story, the reader is confronted with the vices and virtues of humankind in a gallery of characters and situations exemplifying heroism, self-denial, foolishness, intelligence, and modesty. **CC**

GEOFFREY CHAUCER

Born: *c.* 1340–1345 (London, England); died October 25, 1400 (London, England).

Style and genre: Chaucer is the most influential medieval English poet, known for his conversational style and earthy sense of humor.

The son of a wine merchant, Geoffrey Chaucer was part of an emerging bourgeois class who were educated and who held high-ranking government positions. Chaucer himself held several important posts, and although his intelligence undoubtedly enhanced his success, being the brother-in-law of John of Gaunt—uncle of King Richard II and a major character in Shakespeare's play—did not hurt.

Chaucer lived through one of the most tumultuous periods of English history. Abroad, the Hundred Years War raged between England and France, and at home signs of unrest were starting to show. Chaucer knew and perhaps sympathized with the popular Lollard heresy and was in London for the Peasant's Revolt of 1381, when revolutionaries executed the Archbishop of Canterbury and ransacked John of Gaunt's palace. This period also saw the first glimmers of the Renaissance on the continent in the writings of Italian poets such as Petrarch and Boccaccio, both of whom Chaucer had read.

Boccaccio's *Decameron* (1349–1353) was a major influence on what is now considered to be Chaucer's greatest work, *The Canterbury Tales*. Chaucer took Boccaccio's scenario of travelers swapping stories on a journey and changed the focus to develop a psychologically nuanced relationship between tale and teller. The result is a lively conversation between a cast of well-rounded characters that has stayed fresh, thought-provoking, and (perhaps most surprisingly) titillating for hundreds of years. Although Chaucer's dream vision poems and his epic tragedy *Troilus and Criseyde* are sophisticated and brilliant in their own right, the meandering and charming *The Canterbury Tales* is the poem that, for many writers, started it all. **SY**

"There's no workman, whatsoever he be, / That may both work well and hastily."

Signature titles

Poetry

The Book of the Duchess, *c.* 1369–1372

The House of Fame, *c.* 1380

Troilus and Criseyde, *c.* 1381–*c.* 1386

Romances

The Canterbury Tales, *c.* 1387–1400

ABOVE: A fifteenth-century manuscript portrait now at the British Museum, London.

FRANÇOIS VILLON

Born: François de Montcorbier, *c.* 1431 (Paris, France); died *c.* 1463 (place unknown).

Style and genre: Villon's life of violence and dissipation—in and out of taverns, brothels, and prisons—proved an irresistible attraction to later generations; he is renowned as the author of *The Legacy* and *The Great Testament.*

Little is known about this celebratedly villainous poet's life, and what is known does not always tally with the life he wrote about, supposedly in the first person, in his poems. Born François de Montcorbier, he was the nephew of a well-to-do clergyman, Guillaume de Villon, who took an interest in him and paid for him to go to university at the Collège de Navarre in Paris. He lived a dissolute life there: In 1455, he stabbed a priest to death during a quarrel and in 1456 he and a group of friends robbed the college. Not surprisingly, he left Paris in a hurry and although pardoned for these crimes it seems he spent much of his life in prison. In 1462 he was condemned to death after another violent brawl in Paris. After an appeal, the sentence was reduced to ten years in exile. Where he went and where he died, still only in his thirties, is uncertain.

Most of Villon's work consists of short poems written in an almost indecipherable underworld argot, or criminals' slang, but he left two longer poems, known as *The Little Testament* and *The Great Testament*, which are admired for their inventiveness and sardonic humour. The first dates from his first time in exile and was supposedly written during a miserable Christmas in 1456 while shivering in a garret and missing a "treacherous and hard" woman with whom he had fallen in love. He goes on to make a will in which he leaves to his friends peculiar objects including inn signs, hair clippings, and his own dubious reputation; he also makes various obscene and vituperative bequests to his enemies. The second, longer poem is another mock will, supposedly dictated in a mood of repentance by the poet to a male secretary and again leaving sardonic bequests while reflecting on death and his own misspent youth. **RC**

Signature titles

Poetry

The Legacy (Le Lais, ou Le Petit testament), *c.* 1456

The Great Testament (Le Grand testament), *c.* 1462

"Mais ou sont les neiges d'antan? (Where are the snows of yesteryear?)" —Ballade, 1461

ABOVE: An 1810 engraving of François Villon by Stich von Rullmann.

NICCOLÒ MACHIAVELLI

Born: May 3, 1469 (Florence, Italy); died June 21, 1527 (Florence, Italy).

Style and genre: The author of a range of works, including poetry, plays, and novellas, Machiavelli has come to be known almost exclusively for his political writings, which reflect on historical examples to illuminate contemporary concerns.

Niccolò Machiavelli's career as a high-ranking Florentine official led to his authorship of one of the most famous political treatises ever written, *The Prince* (*Il Principe*), dedicated to the Duke of Florence, Lorenzo de' Medici. In a letter to a colleague he described the work as a "whim," belying its fierce examination of the problems related to exercising power. Combining erudite quotes, Latin tags, and common sayings, he reviewed some key concepts in politics—virtue, fortune, and occasion—illustrating his arguments with examples from both the classical and modern worlds.

At the center of Machiavelli's reflections, both in *The Prince* and in his other political writings, is the contemporary political crisis in Italy caused by the intense competition between the various rulers. Against this turbulent background, Machiavelli's justification of the occasional need for dubious behavior on the part of rulers to maintain stability becomes easier to understand. While ruthless actions should not be taken if there is an alternative, ultimately, according to Machiavelli, it is better for a ruler to be feared than loved.

The influence of *The Prince* has often overshadowed Machiavelli's other writings, including his comedy in five acts, *The Mandrake* (*La Mandragola*). Nicia, the elderly husband of the beautiful Lucrezia, is profoundly unhappy about not having any heirs. In his foolishness he falls into the trap of the young and robust Callimaco, who is in love with Lucrezia. Nicia is led to believe that Lucrezia will become pregnant if she drinks a concoction of mandrake, but that the mandrake will kill the next man to sleep with her. Callimaco offers to take on the supposedly doomed bedroom task, and Nicia happily gives his consent, losing his wife to his rival. **CC**

"He who is highly esteemed is not easily conspired against."—*The Prince*

Signature titles

Political works

Discourses on the First Ten Books of Titus Livy (Discorsi sopra la prima deca di Tito Livio), 1512–1517

The Prince (Il Principe), 1513, publ. 1532

The Art of War (Dell'arte della guerra), 1519–1520, publ. 1521

Plays

The Mandrake (La Mandragola), 1518, publ. 1524

ABOVE: Santo di Tito's portrait of Machiavelli in the Palazzo Vecchio, Florence.

ERASMUS

Born: Desiderius Erasmus Roterodamus, October 27, 1466 (Rotterdam, Holland); died July 12, 1536 (Basel, Switzerland).

Style and genre: Erasmus is credited with popularizing many phrases still in use, such as "a necessary evil," "cupboard love," "a rare bird," "an iron in the fire."

Signature titles

Theological works

Handbook of a Christian Knight (Enchiridion militis Christiani), 1503

The Praise of Folly (Moriae encomium), 1509

The Gospel Preacher (Ecclesiastes), 1535

Rhetorical works

Adages (Adagia), 1500

Copia: Foundations of the Abundant Style (De ultraque verborum ac rerum copia), 1512

Under pressure from his guardians, Erasmus became an Augustinian monk, but was allowed to travel extensively in Europe. Throughout his life, he focused on producing new Latin and Greek editions of the New Testament with commentaries, which became the starting point for modern biblical exegesis. He declined academic positions, preferring independent literary activity such as writing *The Praise of Folly*, a satire directed against theologians, and *Adages*, a book of proverbs. Although he wrote both on ecclesiastic subjects and those of general human interest, he seems to have regarded the latter as a leisure activity of little consequence. It is, however, on these works that his fame now rests. **PG**

LUDOVICO ARIOSTO

Born: September 8, 1474, (Reggio Emilia, Italy); died July 6, 1533 (Ferrara, Italy).

Style and genre: Thrilling and daring deeds alternate with stately passages of history and prophecy in Ludovico Ariosto's sophisticated and occasionally parodic style of poetry.

Signature titles

Poetry

Orlando Furioso, 1516–1532

Ariosto's fame rests on the mock epic poem *Orlando Furioso*, one of the greatest works of the Italian Renaissance. It combines the chivalric legends of Charlemagne with the Saracen invasion of France in a witty parody of medieval romance. The poem was designed to exalt the house of Este and its legendary ancestor Rogero (Ruggiero), and to continue the story of Orlando's love for Angelica begun by Matteo Maria Boiardo in *Orlando Innamorato* (*c.* 1472–1486). Three principal stories are developed: the love of Orlando for Angelica; the war between the Franks and Saracens; and the love of Ruggiero, a Saracen, for Bradamant, a Christian. The poem was a "model" for Edmund Spenser's *Faerie Queene* (published 1590). **PG**

FRANÇOIS RABELAIS

Born: *c.* 1494 (near Chinon, Indre-et-Loire, France); died April 9, 1553 (Paris, France).

Style and genre: Famous as the author of the comic *Gargantua and Pantagruel* series, Rabelais was known for his humor, bawdy satire, and irreverent depictions of religious life; the author's final bequest was the adjective, "Rabelaisian."

Rabelais made his living as a physician but his lasting reputation comes from his celebrated prose and his talents as a humorist and satirist with an exuberant taste for bawdiness. The son of a prominent lawyer, Rabelais studied medicine at university; a man of contrasts, he also took holy orders, fathered two children by a widow, and then settled in Lyon as a doctor. It was in Lyon that he wrote the first of the books that have remained famous ever since, starting in the 1530s with a series of books that have become known collectively as *Gargantua and Pantagruel*. The books center on the giant Gargantua and his son Pantagruel, whose guiding principle was "eat, drink and be merry"—and the adventures of their roguish friends, who set off on a journey in quest of the Divine Bottle. He published four books in the series and a fifth was published posthumously (although some scholars dispute that the latter was written by Rabelais). A characteristic fictitious creation was the Abbey of Thelema, founded by Gargantua, where the monks lived by the principle of "Do What You Want." They had female servants on hand, and a swimming pool.

Rabelais's humor and sarcastic treatment of Christian institutions did not endear him to the Church. His books were put on the banned list and he was suspected of heresy. Fortunately, he had the support of the powerful du Bellay family and the approval of the French king, François I. Rabelais went to Rome several times with Jean du Bellay, Bishop of Paris, and in the 1540s lived in Turin, but there seem to have been times when he lived in hiding. According to legend, his will consisted of one sentence: "I have nothing, I owe a great deal and I leave the rest to the poor." His last words were "I am off in search of a great perhaps." **RC**

"We always long for the forbidden things. . . ."
—*Gargantua and Pantagruel*

Signature titles

Prose

The Horrible and Terrifying Deeds and Words of the Renowned Pantagruel, King of the Dipsodes (Les horribles et épouvantables faits et prouesses du très renommé Pantagruel, roy des Dipsodes), 1532

The Inestimable Life of the Great Gargantua (La vie inestimable du grand Gargantua), 1534

Third Book of the Heroic Deeds and Words of the Noble Pantagruel (Tiers livre des faits et dits héroiques du noble Pantagruel), 1546

Fourth Book of the Heroic Deeds and Words of the Noble Pantagruel (Quart livre des faits et dits héroïques du noble Pantagruel), 1552

ABOVE: A nineteenth-century lithograph portrait of François Rabelais.

PIERRE DE RONSARD

Born: September 11, 1524 (Couture-sur-Loir, Loir-et-Cher, France); died December 1585 (Saint-Cosme, near Tours, Indre-et-Loire, France).

Style and genre: Hailed in France as "the prince of poets," Ronsard typified the passionate Renaissance enthusiasm for the classical worlds of Greece and Rome.

Signature titles

Poetry

Loves (Les Amours), 1552

Hymns (Les Hymnes), 1555–1556

Remonstrations to the People of France (Remonstrance au peuple de France), 1563

La Franciade, 1572 (unfinished)

The Last Verses (Les Derniers Vers), 1586

Ronsard spent his early life in the highest social circles. The youngest son of a noble family, as a boy he was appointed a royal page and his duties included traveling to Edinburgh with Princess Madeleine, the bride of James V of Scotland. Ronsard seemed headed for a successful career as a diplomat or in the army, but these plans were blighted when it was discovered he was going deaf. As a result, he turned to the world of books, learning Latin and Greek, reading the classics (Homer's *The Iliad* took him a mere three days), founding a literary group called La Pléiade, and starting to pour out a torrent of poetry. His works included odes, sonnets, love poems, nature poems, and memories of the much-loved countryside of his boyhood; poems about death or justice or wine, or poetry celebrating great figures of antiquity. The first collected edition of his work came out in 1560, reportedly published at the behest of Mary, Queen of Scots, who was then also Queen of France.

Ronsard's position has been described as a French equivalent of the poet laureate in England. He was a zealous Roman Catholic and was inevitably embroiled in the religious civil wars which began in the 1560s; as a result his works were fiercely criticized by zealous Protestants. He planned a giant national epic, *La Franciade*, modeled on Virgil's *Aeneid*, but it did not flow smoothly and he eventually gave up on it. He was much admired by Charles IX of France, who employed the poet to write verses in celebration of his marriage to Elizabeth of Austria in 1571. Stricken by an incurable illness, Ronsard spent his last years as an invalid, longing to die, but still compulsively writing. His final poems (*Les Dernier Vers*) were published after his death. **RC**

"When you are very old you will say . . . 'Ronsard sang of me when I was fair.'"—*Sonnets to Hélène*

ABOVE: After going deaf, Ronsard turned to verse, finding favor among the royals.

LUÍS VAZ DE CAMOENS

Born: Luís Vaz de Camoens or Luís Vaz de Camões, *c.* 1524 (possibly in Lisbon, Portugal); died June 10, 1580 (Lisbon, Portugal).

Style and genre: Portugal's great national poet hymned his country's creation of a Roman Catholic world empire.

Information about Camoens's life is scanty, but he seems to have come from an impoverished aristocratic family and his knowledge of classical culture suggests he had a good education. His most famous poem described Vasco da Gama's epoch-making voyage around the Cape of Good Hope to India. Camoens himself spent many years in Africa and India, complaining bitterly in poetry about the difficulty of making a living and the bad luck and injustices he suffered. He served on naval expeditions, apparently reached Macao, and was shipwrecked off the Chinese coast. At another time, a friend found him stranded and penniless in Mozambique and helped pay for his return to Lisbon.

Camoens wrote graceful lyric poems expressing his feelings of profound loneliness and unsatisfied longing, and celebrating desirable women (in later years many more poems were credited to him than he actually wrote). His great epic, *The Lusiads*, was published in Lisbon in 1572. The name Lusiads comes from Lusitania, the old Roman name for Portugal, and the poem recounts the country's entire history to the point when da Gama set sail in 1497. The Olympian gods keep an interested eye on the expedition, with Venus favoring it and Bacchus opposed, and the poem tells how the ships reach India and eventually sail safely home, accompanied by charming nymphs, one of whom predicts future Portuguese achievements. Strongly pro-Catholic (and anti-English), Camoens justified Portuguese imperialism.

"Just like Love is yonder rose, Heavenly fragrance round it throws."—"Rose and Thorn"

The Lusiads was dedicated to King Sebastian of Portugal and Camoens was rewarded with a state pension. He also wrote plays and his work had a powerful influence on later Portuguese and Brazilian literature. **RC**

Signature titles

Poetry

The Lusiads (Os Lusíadas), 1572

The Lyric Poems (Rimas), 1595

ABOVE: A Portuguese oil portrait in the Museu Nacional de Arte Antigua.

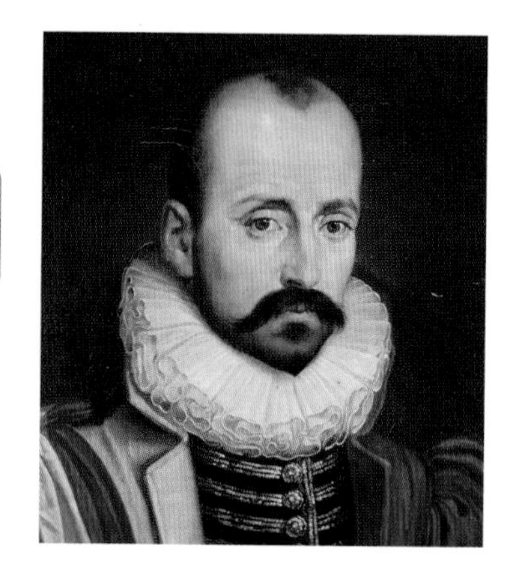

MICHEL DE MONTAIGNE

Born: February 28, 1533 (Château de Montaigne, Dordogne, France); died September 13, 1592 (Château de Montaigne, Dordogne, France).

Style and genre: Skeptic, statesman, and friend of kings, Montaigne was in love with liberty and detested cruelty, corruption, and injustice.

Novelist and essayist Michel de Montaigne was a self-exiled and self-professed skeptic. In his young adulthood he practiced law in Bordeaux, became a councilor in the Bordeaux parliament, and married Françoise de la Chassaigne, another parliament member's daughter. In 1571, he secluded himself in the countryside in order to focus on his writing. There he would publish, expand, revise, and republish his *Essays* (*Essais*), in so doing coining a new term. Indeed, he held his own beliefs on trial as he rigorously assessed himself and the world around him through myriad contemplations. Rich in classical quotation, these compositions on issues ranging from education to drunkenness would be a testament not only to Montaigne's evolving philosophy, but also to his own upbringing—his father insisted he speak nothing but Latin in his early childhood. Ironically, perhaps, he chose to write in colloquial, vernacular French.

A recurring theme throughout Montaigne's work is the damaging power of custom. He believed that people's assessment of the world is limited to their confined surroundings, and that what has become attributed to "nature" is, in fact, a series of small-minded conclusions based on the little bit of information that the mind can conceive. Thus, because so much is impossible for the mind to grasp, individuals should only try to understand themselves within their immediate surroundings. After the public success of his earlier editions, during which time he visited the king of France in 1580 to present to him a copy of his work, Montaigne determined that his desire was to present a written portrait of himself. While narcissistic to some extent—perhaps readers care less than he does that eating radishes

Signature titles

Essays

Essays (Essais), 1588

Journals

Travel Journal, 1580–1581 (first published 1774)

"Everyone runs elsewhere, and to the future, forasmuch as no one is arrived at himself."—*Of Physiognomy*

ABOVE: A nineteenth-century portrait of Montaigne by Jean-Baptiste Mauzaisse.

LEFT: Montaigne's coat of arms, bequeathed to the writer Pierre Charron (1541–1603).

may not agree with him—the theory behind the exercise was that writing one's own existence would still speak to readers in all places, humans being of one fabric. It was during this period between 1580 and 1581 that he also wrote a travel journal, documenting his travels through Europe and recording the differences he found among its peoples.

The impact of Montaigne's writing was not confined to his readers. Indeed literature and philosophy on human consciousness in general owes an enormous debt to the French essayist's works. Although his *Essays* literally became his life work and he consistently revised the writings until he died in 1592, Montaigne's self-deprecating view was that readers may not want to waste their time contemplating "so frivolous and unrewarding a subject." **JS**

Influence of Montaigne

To what extent Shakespeare was directly influenced by Montaigne we shall never know. However, it would appear that the French essayist's imprint rests delightfully on the English bard. Montaigne's determination that the human mind can conceive so little seems remarkably similar to Hamlet's view that there are things outside his philosophy and Bottom's view in *A Midsummer Night's Dream* that "man" is a "patched fool." Echoes of Montaigne are most clearly heard in *The Tempest*. His direct influence is also seen on Pascal, Ralph Waldo Emerson, and Nietzsche, among others.

TORQUATO TASSO

Born: March 11, 1544 (Sorrento, Italy); died April 25, 1595 (Rome, Italy).

Style and genre: Tasso was a poet and scholar who in his *Gerusalemme liberata* attempted to marry the classical Virgilian style of epic poetry with the more modern subject matter of the First Crusade.

Signature titles

Poetry

Rinaldo, 1562

Jerusalem Delivered (Gerusalemme liberata), 1574

Plays

Aminta, 1573

Criticism

Treatise on Epic Poetry (Discorsi del poema eroico), 1594

After a life of wanderings marked by spells in hospitals and prison, Torquato Tasso began to receive attention from the literary world with his poem *Rinaldo*, which consists of twelve cantos. It was published in 1562 and describes the undertakings of the paladin Rinaldo da Montalbano, a topic unequivocally in the tradition of Ludovico Ariosto's writings. A piece of more originality is *Aminta*, a play with a pastoral theme and a setting in classical antiquity. In five acts Tasso describes the shepherd Aminta's unrequited love for the nymph Silvia. In his despair Aminta jumps off a cliff, and when Silvia learns the (false) news of his death she regrets having previously rejected him, thus guaranteeing a happy ending when she finds out that Aminta has survived.

Similar to this composition is the collection of about 2,000 parts called *The Rhymes (Le Rime*), which shows influences of Petrarch. Its poetry contains a complex autobiographical edge informed by anguish and self-doubt.

Tasso's fame is closely linked to *Jerusalem Delivered (Gerusalemme liberata*). The main theme of the work is the First Crusade to liberate the Holy Sepulchre of Jerusalem, a historical event blended with imaginary, idyllic episodes. The magnificent scenery, which makes for a sumptuous framework for the narrative, stands out, as does the meticulous research regarding the arms, the battles, and the costumes. Within this imposing setting, threads are woven that appear to be of little significance, yet they are very well developed, particularly the theme of love in its various guises. The text is informed by Tasso's view that humankind is insignificant compared to nature and that man is ultimately powerless against the mysterious forces that govern the world. **CC**

"None merits the name of Creator but God and the poet."

—*Treatise on Epic Poetry*

ABOVE: A portrait of the Italian Tasso in an undated French illustration.

RIGHT: *Torquato Tasso Reading A Poem to Leonora d'Este,* by Luigi Mussini.

CERVANTES

Born: Miguel de Cervantes Saavedra, September 29, 1547 (Alcalá de Henares, Spain); died April 23, 1616 (Madrid, Spain).

Style and genre: A comic genius with a delightful sense of the absurd, Cervantes made descriptions of travel rich in adventure and mystery.

Spanish poet, playwright, and celebrated author of the first modern novel, *Don Quixote,* (*El ingenioso hidalgo don Quijote de la Mancha*), Cervantes is one of the most important figures in literature. The greatness of *Don Quixote* lies in its everlasting appeal through centuries and cultures, as exemplified by its translation into more than sixty different languages. The book's chief protagonists, Don Quixote and Sancho Panza, are two of the most recognizable and best-loved characters in world literature, and the novel still makes regular appearances in the higher echelons of lists for the greatest works of fiction.

Cervantes's life reads as entertainingly as one of his own novels. He never studied at university. His first published work, concerning the death of Queen Elizabeth of Valois, is attributed to 1569. In the same year, Cervantes traveled to Italy, enlisting as a soldier and seeing active service at the Battle of Lepanto against the Turkish fleet. He endured three separate gun wounds, one of which rendered his left hand permanently

Signature titles

Prose

La Galatea, 1585

Don Quixote Part I (El ingenioso hidalgo don Quijote de la Mancha), 1605

Exemplary Novels (Novelas exemplares), 1613

Don Quixote Part II (Segunda parte del ingenioso hidalgo don Quijote de la Mancha), 1615

The Travails of Persiles and Sigismunda (Los trabajos de Persiles y Segismunda), 1617

Poetry

Journey to Parnassus (Viaje del Parnaso), 1614

Plays

Eight Interludes (Ocho comedias y ocho entremeses nuevos, nunca representados), 1615

ABOVE: A portrait of Cervantes (1600) by Juan de Jauregui y Aguilar (*c.* 1566–1641).

RIGHT: *Don Quixote Setting Out on His Adventures,* by Gustave Doré, 1863.

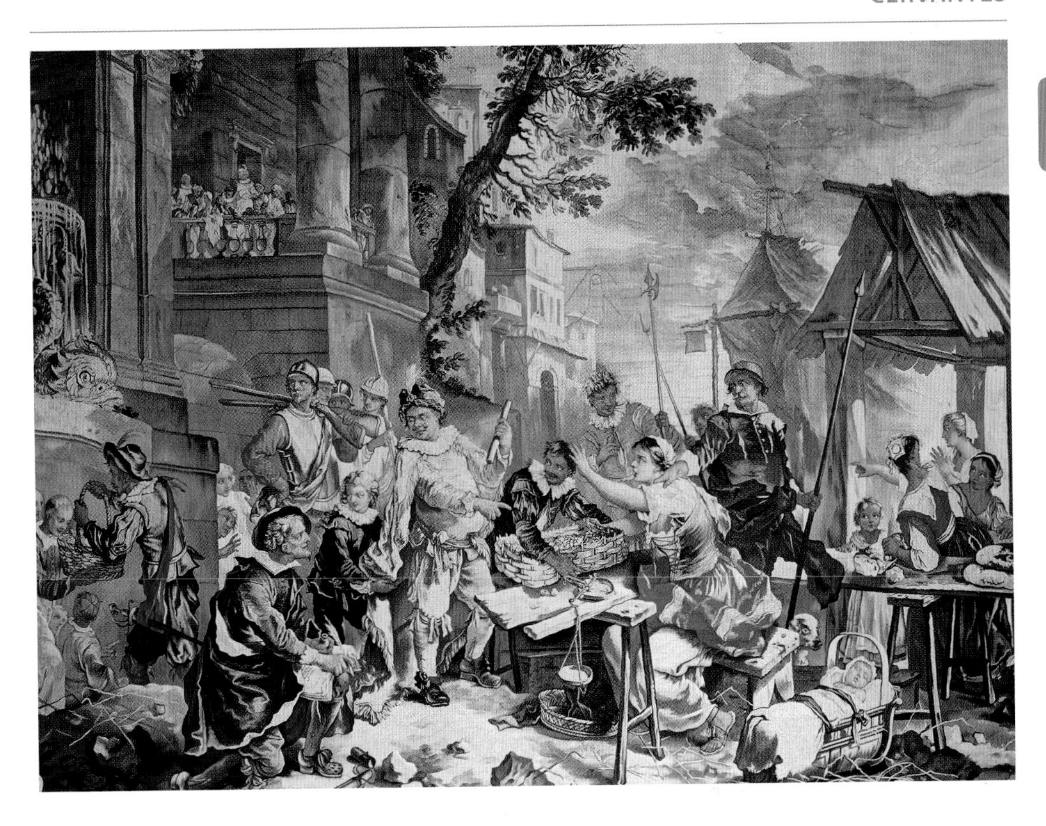

ABOVE: *Sancho Panza and the Nut Seller*, a 1735 tapestry by the Beauvais Workshop, after Charles Joseph Natoire (1700–1777).

maimed. In 1575, he set sail for home, only for his ship to be captured by Barbary corsairs. Along with his brother, Rodrigo, he was sold into slavery in Algiers, remaining in captivity for five years, during which time he made four daring bids for freedom. It was the efforts of his family and Trinitarian monks that delivered his release, ending a period in his life that frequently would be revisited in his literary creations.

"Every man is as heaven made him, and sometimes a great deal worse."—*Don Quixote*

Back in Spain, Cervantes was able to launch a writing career with the publication of his first novel, the pastoral romance *La Galatea*. Using a style popular for its time, the book examined issues of love through the eyes of shepherds and shepherdesses and, despite its modest success,

Living with *Don Quixote*

The enduring popularity of *Don Quixote* has been, in part, increased by its influence over the art world as a whole. Numerous artists have taken the novel as a source of inspiration for their work.

- Painters as diverse as Honore Daumier, Gustav Dore, and Salvador Dalí have used Don Quixote as a muse, but it is Pablo Picasso who drew perhaps the most iconic image of Don Quixote and Sancho Panza. In 1955, he completed a series of illustrations that have been widely reproduced, reinforcing the popular image of the two literary heroes.
- Several film versions based on the novel are in existence. Productions have been made in Spanish, German, French, Russian, Japanese, and English by directors such as Eric Rohmer, Arthur Hiller, Rafael Gil, and Terry Gilliam—evidence of the story's broad appeal.
- The first modern novel was always likely to induce reproduction, but some of the finest authors openly reached within the novel in their own work. Henry Fielding's *Joseph Andrews* brazenly states that it is written in the manner of Cervantes on the title page. Another literary classic, Dostoyevsky's *The Idiot*, explicitly modeled the main character of Prince Myshkin on the noble knight-errant.
- The composer Richard Strauss created the tone poem *Don Quixote*, set to orchestral music and making clear reference to several of the book's outstanding moments, such as the windmill and sheep episodes.

RIGHT: The pen and ink work *Don Quixote*, sketched by Pablo Picasso in 1955.

the novel brought the author to the attention of the literary world. Buoyed by the book's response, Cervantes strove to earn money from writing drama. We only know of two works, the historical tragedy *The Siege of Numantia* (*El Cerco de Numancia*, 1582) and *The Traffic of Algiers* (*El Trato de Argel*, 1580), which survived his time as a contracted playwright.

The rise of Don Quixote

Despite his best efforts, Cervantes was unable to make a living from writing alone and had to find other paid work. While serving as a tax collector in Andalusia, he failed to collect the sum due to the treasury and was imprisoned in Seville. It was while incarcerated that Cervantes began writing *Don Quixote*.

Published in 1605, this monumental work of fiction is a hilarious tale of the fantastical adventures of Don Quixote, a tragic hero obsessed with books of chivalry. Decorated with an old suit of armor, Quixote sets off on his skinny horse, Rosinante, to defend the helpless and destroy the wicked, all for the sake of his true love, a peasant woman whom he renames Dulcinea del Toboso. After an initial failed expedition, Quixote returns and enlists the services of his neighbor, Sancho Panza, as his squire. What follows is an epic journey, incorporating numerous farcical incidents, most memorably encapsulated in Don Quixote's attack on windmills, which his delusional mind views as giants.

Cervantes cemented his reputation as a writer with the publication of *Exemplary Novels (Novelas exemplares)*, *Journey to Parnassus (Viaje del Parnaso)*, and Part II of *Don Quixote*. The second book focused more closely on Sancho Panza, who is tricked into believing he is governor of a fictional fiefdom. Panza "rules" with surprising wisdom but finds the responsibility exhausting and returns to be by his master's side. The novel ends with Don Quixote renouncing chivalry shortly before his death. *Don Quixote* was a landmark achievement, spawning the popular term "quixotic" and influencing a wealth of writers such as Defoe, Dostoevsky, and Joyce. It remains one of the few timeless literary masterpieces. **SG**

10.8.55

EDMUND SPENSER

Born: *c.* 1552 (London, England); died January 13, 1599 (London, England).

Style and genre: Spenser's poetry "is learned wythout hardnes, such indeede as may be perceived of the leaste, understoode of the mooste, but judged onely of the learned." (Introductory epistle to *The Shepheardes Calender.*)

Edmund Spenser was educated in London at the Merchant Taylors' School and in 1569 he matriculated at Pembroke College, Cambridge. Through his college friend, Gabriel Harvey, he obtained a position in the household of the Earl of Leicester and became acquainted with Sir Philip Sidney. In 1579, he published the twelve eclogues of *The Shepheardes Calender* with great success and began the allegorical romantic epic *The Faerie Queene*. He served with the English forces in Ireland as secretary to the Queen's deputy, Lord Grey, and was "granted" Kilcolman Castle in County Cork. Here he settled and occupied himself with literary work, writing his elegy on Sir Philip Sidney and preparing *The Faerie Queene* for the press, the first three books being entrusted to the printer on the poet's visit to London in 1589. He had hoped to secure a place at court through his poetry, but this was never realized.

Spenser reluctantly returned to Kilcolman, which he regarded as a place of exile, and penned the allegorical pastoral *Colin Clout's Come Home Againe* and dedicated it to Sir Walter Raleigh. Although the poem celebrates the glories of Queen Elizabeth and her ladies, it also contains a bitter attack on the envies and intrigues of the court. In 1594, Spenser married Elizabeth Boyle, describing his courtship in the sonnet sequence *Amoretti* and celebrating their marriage in *Epithalamion*. Kilcolman was burned in a sudden insurrection in October 1598, and the family was compelled to flee for refuge to Cork. Spenser's views on the Irish situation were expressed in the controversial prose pamphlet *A View of the Present State of Ireland* (1596). Spenser died in London, aged forty-six. His funeral was attended by most of the poets of the time, who cast their elegies into his grave. **PG**

"It is the mind that maketh good of ill, that maketh wretch or happy, rich or poor."

Signature titles

Poetry

The Shepheardes Calender, 1579

The Faerie Queene, 1590, 1596, 1609

Colin Clout's Come Home Againe, 1595

Astrophel: A Pastoral Elegy Upon the Death of the Most Noble and Valorous Knight, Sir Philip Sidney, 1595

Amoretti, 1595

Epithalamion, 1595

Fowre Hymnes, 1596

Prothalamion, 1596

ABOVE: Color version of an engraving of Spenser made *c.* 1590.

PHILIP SIDNEY

Born: November 30, 1554 (Penshurst, England); died October 17, 1586 (Arnhem, Netherlands).

Style and genre: A poet, courtier, statesman, patron of the arts, and soldier, Sidney was popular during his lifetime and regarded as the quintessential "gentleman."

During his lifetime, Sir Philip Sidney was regarded with great public affection and came to epitomize the essence of the Elizabethan gentleman. He was born into an influential family and was educated at Shrewsbury School, followed by Christ Church, Oxford, which he left before gaining his degree. He became an eminent courtier to Queen Elizabeth I until 1580, when he fell from favor over a misjudged letter to the queen and was forced to retire from court for a period.

Apart from his lively court life, Sidney was also one of the greatest poets of his time and is chiefly remembered for his body of work and the influence it had on the development of English poetry. *Astrophel and Stella* is one of his finest works and was one of the first of the famous English sonnet sequences. The work was inspired by his love for Penelope Devereaux, who was later reluctantly married off to Lord Rich in 1581. Sidney based the poem on the Italian model made famous through Petrarch, but altered the rhyme scheme. Following his dismissal from court, Sidney wrote *The Countess of Pembroke's Arcadia* for his sister, Mary Sidney. A literary romance with intertwined story lines based on a highly idealized depiction of pastoral life, *Arcadia* was of great influence and very popular. William Shakespeare and the dramatists John Day and James Shirley all referred to the work in their writings, and King Charles I is alleged to have quoted from it immediately prior to his execution.

"Each excellent thing, once learned, serves for a measure of all other knowledge."

Sidney's most influential work, however, was *The Defence of Poesy*, which emphasized the importance of the poet in society and their specific artistic role. His use of language and the complex humanist theories laced in the work were borrowed by Percy Bysshe Shelley, William Wordsworth, and Samuel Taylor Coleridge. **TP**

Signature titles

Poetry

The Countess of Pembroke's Arcadia, 1580

Astrophel and Stella, 1581

Essay

The Defence of Poesy, c. 1581

ABOVE: A posthumous portrait of Sidney by John de Critz the Younger, c. 1620.

LOPE DE VEGA

Born: Lope Félix de Vega Carpio, November 25, 1562 (Madrid, Spain); died August 27, 1635 (Madrid, Spain).

Style and genre: The hugely prolific playwright and poet Lope de Vega caught the atmosphere and style of Spain at its apogee as a world imperial power.

Known as "the Spanish phoenix," Vega is believed to have written around 1,800 plays, of which some 400 have survived; he also wrote enough other prose and poetry to fill twenty-one volumes. He was born into a humble family. As a young man, he went to a Jesuit college where he trained to be a priest, but he abandoned the college in pursuit of a married woman, a "remote beauty" who was to have numerous successors in his life. By the time he was in his twenties he was making a living as a playwright in Madrid, while supplementing his earnings in the service of various noblemen, often acting as a pimp. In 1588, Vega joined the forces of the Spanish Armada and fought in their ill-fated sea-battle against England. He later worked for the Duke of Alba and the Duke of Sessa. To make his own name more aristocratic, he changed it to Vega Carpio.

Vega's love-life was varied and controversial. He was imprisoned and then exiled for ferocious written attacks on a beautiful actress, Elena Osorio, after she ended their affair. Later he ran away with a delectable sixteen-year-old from an aristocratic family; he wrote her passionate poems, but did not marry her until he was forced to do so by her family. After his wife's death, he had a twenty-year liaison with another beautiful actress, Micaela de Luján, to whom he wrote more poems, at the same time as a second marriage to a rich butcher's daughter. After the deaths of Micaela and his second wife, he started writing religious works and plays and took holy orders, yet before long was involved in more love tangles. Many of Vega's plays were cloak-and-dagger comedies. With plenty of love interest, master-servant relationships, and witty comment on uppercrust ways, his work gives a vivid impression of life in the Spain of his time. **RC**

"All right, then, I'll say it. Dante makes me sick."

—Lope de Vega's last words

Signature titles

Plays

Collected Plays, published from 1604 onward

Poems

"Dragontea" (on the death of Sir Francis Drake), 1598

"The Tragic Crown" ("La corona tragica"), 1627

"Apollo's Laurel" ("El laurel de Apolo"), 1630

Prose

Arcadia, 1598

Criticism

The Art of Writing Comedies at This Time (Arte nuevo de hacer comedias en este tiempo), 1609

ABOVE: An oil painting (*c.* 1630) of Vega attributed to Eugenio Caxes.

CHRISTOPHER MARLOWE

Born: Baptized February 26, 1564 (Canterbury, England); died May 30, 1593 (Deptford, England).

Style and genre: Marlowe developed blank verse as a powerful vehicle for the stage, using it primarily for stories describing the downfall of the "overreacher."

Christopher Marlowe has attracted notoriety as much for his personal life as for his achievement as one of the Elizabethan Age's leading playwrights. Part of Marlowe's mystique derives from a simple lack of documentation about his life. But there is the intriguing suggestion that he was involved in state espionage. Cambridge University was on the verge of denying him his Masters degree (on suspicion that he had converted to Roman Catholicism and was about to emigrate to the Continent), before the Privy Council intervened and requested he be awarded the degree on account of his unspecified "good service" to the queen. The plot thickens with his untimely death in a brawl over payment of a bill, which some believe may have been connected to his supposed espionage work.

Considering this colorful background, it is perhaps inevitable that he has also been put forward as the true author of at least some of Shakespeare's plays. Whether that claim will ever be proved is highly doubtful, but his authorship of some of the most influential works of the Elizabethan stage is beyond question. *Tamburlaine*, in particular, was one of the first major works in blank verse and was an enormous success when first performed in London. The larger-than-life figure of Tamburlaine conquers a vast empire in *Part I*, but after desecrating a copy of the Koran and claiming to be greater than God in *Part II*, he immediately falls ill and dies. *Doctor Faustus* deals with a similarly arrogant protagonist—a scholar who makes a pact with the Devil for knowledge and power in return for his soul. Faustus's realization of the consequences of his ambition, as the seconds count down to midnight and the Devil approaches to claim his soul, provides one of the most powerful scenes in Elizabethan drama. **AS**

"The stars move still, time runs, . . . / The devil will come and Faustus must be damned."

Signature titles

Plays

Tamburlaine Part I, c. 1586

Tamburlaine Part II, c. 1587

The Jew of Malta, c. 1589

Doctor Faustus, c. 1589

ABOVE: The Corpus Christi portrait of 1585, thought to be of Marlowe.

WILLIAM SHAKESPEARE

Born: Christened April 26, 1564 (Stratford-upon-Avon, Warwickshire, England); died April 23, 1616 (Stratford-upon-Avon, Warwickshire, England).

Style and genre: He was a playwright and poet whose vibrant verse explored the spirit of his age and the human condition with a dazzling, newly accessible lyricism.

It is a well-worn truism that Shakespeare is England's national treasure and the world's all-time greatest writer. Some dispute this, but what seems beyond argument is that Shakespeare had an extraordinary facility with language for his day—or for any day. What he had to say, and how he said it, found enormous popularity when he was alive and has been reinvented in countless ways for new audiences, ever since.

Shakespeare the man—as gleaned from the colorful brew of patchy documentary evidence, traditional tales, and contemporary gossip handed down to us—appears every inch the intriguing superstar. Born into the artistically stimulating era of Elizabethan England, he rose from a provincial background to become the toast of royalty. Along the way he was also an actor and ran with a crowd of his era's leading writers (such as his literary sparring partner, Ben Jonson; 1572–1637). He has been anecdotally implicated as a deer-poacher who fled to London to escape prosecution, and as the illicit lover of his "Dark Lady" (from his sonnets). He has also been

Signature titles

Plays

Romeo and Juliet, 1597
Henry IV, Part One, 1598
Love's Labor's Lost, 1598
Julius Caesar, c. 1599
A Midsummer Night's Dream, 1600
Henry V, 1600
As You Like It, c. 1600
Much Ado About Nothing, 1600
The Merchant of Venice, 1600
Twelfth Night, 1601
Othello, 1602–1604
Hamlet, 1603
Measure for Measure, 1604
King Lear, c. 1604–1608
Macbeth, c. 1606
Antony and Cleopatra, 1606–1607
The Winter's Tale, 1610–1611
The Tempest, 1611

Poetry

Venus and Adonis, 1593
Sonnets, published 1609

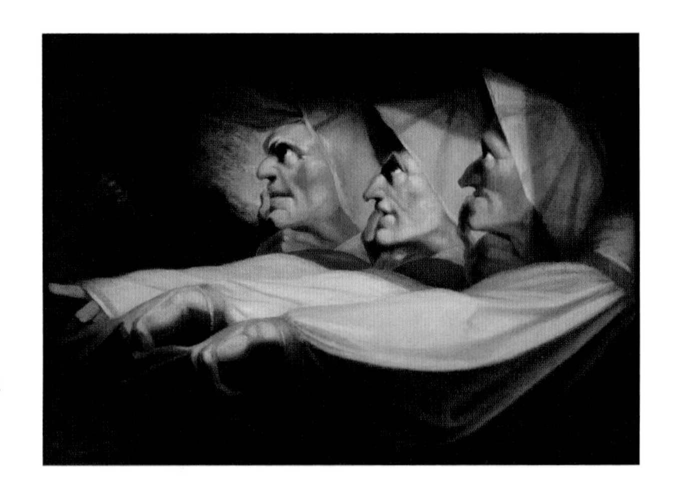

ABOVE: The Chandos Portrait—likely to be of Shakespeare, but impossible to prove.

RIGHT: *The Three Witches*, by Henry Fuseli, c. 1783, based on Shakespeare's *Macbeth*.

ABOVE: **Millais's famous painting of Ophelia (*c.* 1851–1852) inspired by *Hamlet*.**

analyzed for supposedly homoerotic or bisexual leanings, accused of not having written his works, and often reported as dying after a heavy drinking session.

What we can deduce from his work is that Shakespeare had a very human understanding of all kinds of personalities and situations—from power-crazed Scottish kings, to the morally compromised Isabella in *Measure for Measure*; from the ancient-world intrigues of *Antony and Cleopatra* to the broadly comic theatrical troupe in *A Midsummer Night's Dream*. Much material must have been informed by his own life. He grew up in a middle-class family in the country town of Stratford-upon-Avon. His father John was a glover and a local dignitary, who slid into debt. Shakespeare was the third of eight children. Three siblings perished when young and only one would outlive Shakespeare (who died in his early fifties).

"He was not of an age, but for all time."

—Ben Jonson on Shakespeare

His own son Hamnet, one of three children he had with Anne Hathaway (the local girl he married at eighteen, when she was pregnant with their first child), perished during boyhood—connections have been made with grieving passages in many of his works, including *Twelfth Night*.

The mystery of Shakespeare's life

A haze hovers over the chronology of Shakespeare's life and works. He probably caught the theater bug as a child, when Stratford hosted a stimulating succession of traveling theatrical troupes. Shakespeare is likely to have received a solid classical education at Stratford's impressive grammar school. After years about which we know little, he emerges in London during the 1590s as an established actor-dramatist. He probably began writing plays around 1590, with the *Henry VI* trilogy and *Richard III* among his first. Early poetry successes included *Venus and Adonis*. By the early 1600s, he was at the helm of England's leading theater company, the King's Men (named for their patron, King James I). Led by legendary actor, Richard Burbage, the company enjoyed glories both at court and at theaters.

Shakespeare went on to rising success with a rapidly growing canon of plays and his expressive sonnets (1609). Most of his plays were written in iambic pentameter verse form, which he turned into something magical. Reputedly a man of mercurial wit, he could scale heights of poetry, plumb depths of bawdy humor, and turn clever and memorable inversions such as "I wasted time, and now doth time waste me" (*Richard II*). He used language to explore complex personalities, create varied moods, and control twisting plotlines filled with mistaken identities.

Tradition has it that Shakespeare had begun a life of peacefully comfortable retirement in one of his Stratford properties by 1610, but there is no hard evidence for this. He died in Stratford, however, said by one to be from fever brought on by a drunken night out with Ben Jonson and others. The exact cause of death remains yet another unknown in a life of intriguing puzzles. **AK**

Genius or Impostor?

There has been much heated discussion down the centuries—fanned by the lack of firm evidence for his life and work—over whether Shakespeare actually wrote the plays we think as his. One leading suspect was Sir Francis Bacon (1561–1626): towering intellect, accomplished writer, and one-time Lord Chancellor of England. A Victorian scholar had a mental breakdown trying to prove the case. Shakespeare's friend and rival, Ben Jonson, is another suspect. So too are a host of eminent titled gentlemen, including Edward de Vere, Earl of Oxford (a theory supported by Sigmund Freud).

Other cited suspects range from poet and playwright Christopher Marlowe and Sir Walter Raleigh to Queen Elizabeth herself—in other words, the cream of Elizabethan society. The common thread running through many of these theories is, basically, snobbery—the belief that a man of Shakespeare's background could not have been able to write plays that draw on such a broad range of learned allusions. There is, of course, the perennial love of conspiracy theory.

The majority of Shakespeare scholars reject these theories yet acknowledge that some passages (even the occasional entire play) may have been written partly or even wholly by others. Collaboration between writers was a common occurrence in Shakespeare's day.

RIGHT: ***Midsummer Night's Dream*****, by Gustave Doré (undated).**

JOHN DONNE

Born: Between January 24 and June 19, 1572 (London, England); died March 31, 1631 (London, England).

Style and genre: John Donne was one of the great metaphysical poets of his age. His poetry is celebrated for its combination of ingenuity, passion, erudition, and wit.

Signature titles

Poetry

Poems, 1633 (published posthumously)

Sermons

LXXX Sermons, 1640 (published posthumously)

Fifty Sermons, 1649 (published posthumously)

XXVI Sermons, 1660 (published posthumously)

Prose

Pseudo-Martyr, 1610

Ignatius His Conclave, 1611

Devotions Upon Emergent Occasions, 1624

Essays in Divinity, 1651 (published posthumously)

John Donne was born into a prominent Catholic family at a time when it was dangerous to openly worship in the Catholic faith. His father was a prosperous ironmonger and his mother was the daughter of John Heywood, the dramatist. Donne was educated at Oxford and then Cambridge University but was prevented from taking a degree from either institution because of his faith. At the age of twenty, he entered Lincoln's Inn to study law. However, despite his obvious bent for learning, as a younger man he was both a womanizer and an adventurer. In 1596, Donne sailed on the Cadiz expedition and then again with Sir Walter Raleigh in 1597 to hunt for wrecked treasure ships in the Azores. His poems "The Storm" (1597) and "The Calm" (1597) recall these experiences.

In 1601, Donne became the member of parliament for Brackley, but a hugely promising civil career was ruined when he secretly married a teenage girl, Anne More. The union took place against the wishes of More's father, and Donne was briefly imprisoned. As a consequence, the next fourteen years of his life were professionally inauspicious and marked by financial struggle. Donne eventually found favor with James I, who recommended that he pursue a career in the church, which he did very successfully until his death in 1631. Over the course of his profession, the powerful content of his sermons attracted much attention and acclaim. The religious writings also helped him to attain a doctorate from Cambridge University and ultimately the much sought-after deanery of St. Paul's Cathedral. These sermons were published posthumously in three volumes.

"No man is an island, entire of itself . . . any man's death diminishes me . . ."—*Meditation XVII*

Many of Donne's poems are difficult to date. However, it is generally agreed that his love poetry and satires were written

ABOVE: An English School painting of Donne, made *c.* 1595.

LEFT: Donne painted in his funeral shroud only weeks before his death in 1631.

during his younger years and that his more devout poetry, as well as his sermons, emerge from his time as a cleric. Although his writing was circulated widely during his lifetime, the bulk of his work was published after his death.

Donne's early poetry is often frankly sexual and will in part have been inspired by the close physical relationship he shared with a wife who bore him eleven children, although not all survived their childhood. The writer's struggle with the Catholic faith and subsequent conversion to the Anglican Church finds expression in such polemical prose works as *Pseudo-Martyr* (1610) and *Ignatius His Conclave* (1611). **GM**

A Fusion of Blood

In the metaphysic tradition, much of Donne's love poetry melds two disparate ideas to create an elaborate "conceit" (an ingenious extended metaphor) that unifies the emotional with the intellectual. In *The Flea*, a poem that addresses the object of his unreciprocated love, Donne describes how a tiny pest has sucked blood from them both. This slightly unpalatable incident is transformed into the cause for romantic celebration when the fusion of their blood comes to symbolize marriage, sex, and procreation all at once. The poet uses this conceit to argue the case for their actual union.

BEN JONSON

Born: June, 1572 (London, England); died August 6, 1637 (London, England).

Style and genre: An Elizabethan poet and dramatist, and Shakespeare's greatest contemporary rival, Jonson is best known for his wickedly satirical plays in which licentiousness and immorality abound.

Of huge stature, both in terms of his literary reputation and physical presence, Ben Jonson was a colorful and forceful character who grew from relatively humble origins to become Britain's first poet laureate. He started out as a bricklayer, but soon realized the building trade was not for him. Jonson left to join the army, where he saw action in Flanders, killing an enemy in single combat. He then joined a strolling company of actors and soon became an actor-writer. Jonson was at one point imprisoned for his involvement in a seditious play, *The Isle of Dogs,* and again later for killing a fellow actor in a duel. In such circumstances, one imagines he may have wanted to lie low, but he remained a fearlessly outspoken critic of his contemporaries (including Shakespeare) and a shameless promoter of his own talents.

Every Man in His Humour, performed by Lord Chamberlain's company in 1598, turned Jonson into a celebrity. With *Sejanus His Fall*, Jonson's fame became more akin to infamy when he was brought before the Privy Council to answer charges of "popery and treason." He was later imprisoned again for his involvement in *Eastward Ho*, whose anti-Scottish references so offended James I. Jonson's enduring reputation rests with the plays *Volpone* and *The Alchemist*, among others, in which sharp wit combines with ingenious stagecraft to produce masterly satire. It was also as a poet and successful writer of masques that Jonson presided over the literary coterie from which a number of eminent writers emerged. Inevitably Jonson's friendship and contemporaneity with Shakespeare is apt to throw up all kinds of comparisons. These tend to contrast Shakespeare's untutored genius or native wit with Jonson's erudition, classicism, and technical craft. **GM**

"Language most shows a man: Speak, that I may see thee."—*Discoveries*

Signature titles

Plays

Every Man in His Humour, 1598
The Poetaster, 1601
Sejanus His Fall, 1603
Eastward Ho, 1604
Volpone, 1606
The Alchemist, 1610
Bartholomew Fair, 1614

Poetry

The Forest, 1616
Underwoods, 1640

Prose

Timber, or Discoveries, 1640

ABOVE: An undated copy of Gerrit van Honthorst's seventeenth-century portrait.

TIRSO DE MOLINA

Born: Gabriel Téllez, *c.* 1571–1584 (Madrid, Spain); died March 12, 1648 (Soria, Spain).

Style and genre: A Spanish Baroque playwright and poet, Tirso de Molina is known for his depth of characterization, range, and wit. His work comprises tragic, comic, historical, and religious plays.

Tirso de Molina was one of the great playwrights of the Spanish golden age and perhaps only second in prowess to compatriot Lope de Vega. Prolific in his output, De Molina claimed to have written 400 plays, ranging from comedies such as *The Bashful Man at the Palace* to tragedies such as *The Vengeance of Tamar*, but fewer than ninety have survived. The best known is *The Trickster of Seville and the Stone Guest*, in which he created the character of legendary seducer Don Juan Tenorio. This is perhaps ironic, given that De Molina was a priest. He was capable of both wit and pathos and created sympathetic characters and realistic scenarios. This talent got him into trouble in 1625, when some of his works were condemned as obscene. **CK**

Signature titles

Plays

The Bashful Man at the Palace (El vergonzoso en palacio), 1611

Damned for Despair (El condenado por desconfiado), 1624

The Trickster of Seville and the Stone Guest (El burlador de Sevilla y convidado de piedra), 1630

The Vengeance of Tamar (La venganza de Tamar), 1634

JOHN WEBSTER

Born: *c.* 1580 (London, England); died *c.* 1630 (London, England).

Style and genre: An Elizabethan and Jacobean dramatist known for his tragedies, Webster tackled the dark side of human nature with themes of revenge and macabre violence.

Little is known of John Webster's life. He may have trained as a lawyer—a hypothesis backed up by the use of trial scenes in his plays, and their sense of justice, or rather the lack of it. He is first recorded as a writer in 1602, and he wrote and cowrote history plays and tragicomedies with leading playwrights such as Thomas Dekker. Yet the works he is best remembered for are his two tragedies in Italian settings, *The White Devil* and *The Duchess of Malfi*. Renowned for their bloody violence and sense of the macabre, both plays concentrate on the dark side of human nature. The audience feels that evil is never far away in a society that is corrupt to the core. For Webster even a copy of the Bible can be used as a murder weapon. **CK**

Signature titles

Plays

The White Devil, 1612

The Duchess of Malfi, 1623

The Devil's Law Case, 1623

FRANCISCO DE QUEVEDO

Born: September 17, 1580 (Madrid, Spain); died September 8, 1645 (Villanueva de los Infantes, Spain).

Style and genre: Quevedo is famous for his satire and wit, but was also an erudite scholar and writer of love poems, novels, philosophical treatises, and theology.

Quevedo, together with his bitter rival Luis de Góngora, was one of the leading poets of Spain's *Siglo de Oro* (or Golden Century). Quevedo's parents were descended from the Castilian nobility and were very prominent members of the Spanish royal court, but they died when Quevedo was six years old. By all counts their son was an extremely colorful character, who became renowned for his poems, prose, and his work at court. He corresponded with the humanist Justus Lipsius and was acquainted with Miguel de Cervantes.

According to contemporary accounts, Quevedo had an impulsive nature and a mean streak, and he was renowned for making caustic comments about other people's looks. Despite his own disadvantages of having a clubfoot and being near-sighted, he nonetheless attacked other men for their appearance, writing scathing satire or parodying them. He also had a bad temper and on more than one occasion challenged an adversary to a duel over very slight provocation. By far the most prominent of these rivalries was with Luis de Góngora, whose poetry, lifestyle, and physical appearance Quevedo mercilessly satirized. Góngora, of course, reciprocated in kind.

Spanish court life could be tempestuous, dependent on personal friendships and loyalties—all dependent on whomever was currently in power. After a period of exile—caused by having chosen the wrong side in a political quarrel—Quevedo returned to life at court under a new king, Philip IV. On his return Quevedo was even rowdier than before—a drinker, smoker, and visitor of brothels. King Philip IV was equally raucous and held Quevedo in high esteem. In 1632, the king helped Quevedo reach the height of his political ambition, by making the poet his personal secretary. **REM**

"Death, you are wasting time upon my wound, for he who does not live will never die."

Signature titles

Prose

*Paul the Sharper or The Scavenger; The Swindler (El buscón [*Full title: *Historia de la vida del Buscón, llamado Don Pablos, ejemplo de vagamundos y espejo de tacaños]),* 1626

Dreams and Discourses (Sueños y discursos, also known as *Los Sueños),* 1627

Theological works

The Cradle and the Grave (La cuna y la sepultura), 1612

The Providence of God (La providencia de Dios), 1641

Political works

The Politics of the Lord (La political de Dios), 1617–1626

The Life of Marcus Brutus (La vida de Marco Bruto), 1632–1644

ABOVE: A seventeenth-century Spanish School oil on canvas, located in Madrid.

PEDRO CALDERÓN DE LA BARCA

Born: January 17, 1600 (Madrid, Spain); died May 25, 1681 (Madrid, Spain).

Style and genre: Calderón was a leading playwright of the period when Spanish power and influence was at its height. Themes from tragedy, comedy, and religious and secular life are subtly woven together, often inspired by the royal court.

Calderón was born and died in Madrid, spending the majority of his life at the courts of King Philip III and King Philip IV, who gathered a group of favored writers around him. In 1637, King Philip IV made Calderón a Knight of Santiago.

Calderón's parents had moved to Madrid from northern Spain (his mother was purportedly of Flemish descent); they both died young and Calderón was orphaned by the age of fifteen. Initially intended for the priesthood, Calderón entered the Jesuit college in Madrid before changing his mind and choosing to study law at the University of Salamanca. Although sources vary in their opinion, it seems he may have served briefly in the military. He fought on behalf of the king in the Catalan revolt of 1640, and it has been claimed that he also served in campaigns against the Italians and the Dutch.

During his time at university, Calderón began making a name for himself as a writer, and on his return to Madrid, his accessible style and vivid imagination ensured success. He wrote plays for the royal court as well as masques and operas, and his plays were also performed in the public theaters, bringing his name to a much wider audience. His success was so all-encompassing that, after the death of Lope de Vega, Calderón was considered Spain's leading playwright. He never married, although he fathered an illegitimate son. In 1651, he returned to his early vocation and became a priest, later appointed a royal chaplain. He continued to write, on religious themes as well as secular ones, including many scripts for performance at the annual feast of Corpus Christi in Madrid. His comedies have been described as fundamentally serious. "What is life?" he asked in one of them. "A madness. What is life? An illusion, a shadow, a story." **RC**

"He exceeds all modern dramatists with the exception of Shakespeare."—Percy Bysshe Shelley

Signature titles

Plays

The Constant Prince (El príncipe constante), 1629

The Surgeon of His Honor (El médico de su honra), 1635

Life Is a Dream (La vida es sueño), 1635

The Mayor of Zalamea (El alcalde de Zalamea), 1640

The Daughter of the Air (La hija del aire), 1653

ABOVE: Antonio Pereda y Salgado's seventeenth-century portrait of Calderòn.

1600s

PIERRE CORNEILLE

Born: June 6, 1606 (Rouen, France); died October 1, 1684 (Paris, France).

Style and genre: The dramatist credited with inventing French classical tragedy, Corneille is famed for four plays known as his "classical tetralogy." His plays typically hinge on a tricky moral dilemma.

Corneille's celebrated play *Le Cid*, based on tales about the great Spanish hero El Cid, was a watershed production. It is seen as a landmark in French theater for its unique take on classical tragic drama. Although a great hit, the play sparked impassioned artistic controversy among people in high places, leading to official disapproval from the Académie française.

Despite this potential setback and a less-than-easy way with people, Corneille's plays remained very popular. They were much admired by both the public and leading dramatists such as Molière, and Corneille was finally admitted as an Académie member in 1647. By now an established playwright, Corneille had a stream of plays under his belt, which included highly witty comedies such as *Le Menteur* as well as the tragedies for which he is often most praised.

He has become particularly well known for his "classical tetralogy" from the 1630s and 1640s: *Le Cid*, *Horace*, *Cinna*, and *Polyeucte*. Corneille's special gift was a personal reinterpretion of the fashionable theatrical straitjacket of the day—observance of the three supposedly classical "unities" of time, place, and action—in a way that offered expressive psychological insight wedded to a balanced clarity of vision. His plays often pit personal interests against moral issues and offer an uplifting heroism. Perhaps Corneille's unique sense of artistic order came from his birth into a family of lawyers. He himself trained as a lawyer and served as a magistrate and local official during his life. He continued to produce plays into his later years, but was latterly overshadowed by Racine, on whose drama he had a great influence. His work also exerted a profound effect on figures such as the English Restoration playwright John Dryden. **AK**

Signature titles

Plays

Médée, 1635
Le Cid, 1637
Horace, 1640
Cinna, 1641
Polyeucte, 1643
The Liar (Le Menteur), 1643
Andromède, 1650
Nicomède, 1651
Oedipe, 1659

"When there is no peril in the fight, there is no glory in the triumph."—*Le Cid*

ABOVE: A copy of Charles Le Brun's painting of Corneille, located at Versailles, France.

RIGHT: The frontispiece of *Le Cid*, published by Augustin Courbé in 1637.

LE CID

TRAGI-COMEDIE

A PARIS,
Chez AVGVSTIN COVRBE, Imprimeur & Libraire de Monſeigneur frere du Roy, dans la petite Salle du Palais, à la Palme.

M. DC. XXXVII.
AVEC PRIVILEGE DV ROY.

JOHN MILTON

Born: December 9, 1608 (London, England); died November 8, 1674 (Chalfont St. Giles, Buckinghamshire, England).

Style and genre: T. S. Eliot thought Milton "a very great poet indeed," but found the man antipathetic and his poetry characterized by a dominance of sound.

Signature titles

Poetry

Paradise Lost, 1667

Paradise Regained, 1671

Samson Agonistes, 1671

Poems

"On the Morning of Christ's Nativity," 1629

"Lycidas," 1637

Essays

Areopagitica, 1644

The Tenure of Kings and Magistrates, 1649

Second Defence of the English People, 1654

The Readie & Easie Way to Establish a Free Commonwealth, 1659

Play

Comus, performed 1634; published 1637

Milton remains the most powerful poet in the English language, rewarding frequent rereading perhaps more than any other writer. The child who would become a savage controversialist in prose—not least for the strains of misogyny in his work and his unyielding personality—was well-educated by his ambitious parents, first at home with tutors, then at St. Paul's School and Cambridge. He was finally self-educated throughout an extensive period of reading during his twenties, when he put off and finally abandoned a career in the Church.

Despite this apparent belatedness (the theme of "long choosing and beginning late" runs through his work), he had composed, before he was thirty years old, four brilliant poems: "L'Allegro," "Il Penseroso," "Lycidas," and *Comus* (a masque). When he graduated he was already a master of Latin and Greek, could read and write in French and Italian, had enough Hebrew to make a paraphrase, in Greek, of Psalm 114, and was later to defend the execution of Charles I in such robust Latin prose that he became known throughout Europe not only as a successful polemicist but as a great, almost Ciceronian stylist in

ABOVE: A nineteenth-century English School engraving of Milton.

RIGHT: *Satan Tempting Eve*, by John Martin, a scene from Milton's *Paradise Lost*.

ABOVE: ***Satan, Sin & Death*** **(1735–1740) is an unfinished sketch inspired by** ***Paradise Lost*****.**

Latin—he was England's first public intellectual in the international arena.

Milton wrote prose almost exclusively from 1640 to 1656 during the gradual emergence of revolutionary republicanism, which he championed, returning to poetry only when he began *Paradise Lost*. In 1642, Milton married his first wife, Mary Powell, the daughter of a royalist family who owed Milton's father money. They married just two months before civil war broke out in England. Purportedly because of the war, his wife left him for her family home in Oxford, not to return for three whole years. Milton began to write his four tracts on divorce during their separation, arguing that the true basis of marriage is companionship and that incompatibility of temperament is a better reason for divorce than adultery. Mary

"To be blind is not miserable; not to be able to bear blindness, that is miserable."

Superhuman Satan

Milton's Satan is a new kind of character in epic poetry, quite unlike the monstrous Devil represented in medieval and Renaissance literature. Milton's Lucifer is both super- and subhuman:

He trusted to have equalled the most high,
If he opposed; and with ambitious aim
Against the throne and monarchy of God
Raised impious war in heaven and battle proud
With vain attempt. Him the almighty power
Hurled headlong flaming from the ethereal sky
With hideous ruin and combustion down
To bottomless perdition, there to dwell
In adamantine chains and penal fire,
Who durst defy the omnipotent to arms.

Paradise Lost, Book I, 40–49

In his poem *The Marriage of Heaven and Hell*, William Blake made the famous comment, "The reason Milton wrote in fetters when he wrote of Angels and at liberty when of Devils and Hell, is because he was a true poet and of the Devil's party without knowing it." In Blake's view, Satan was a symbol of desire, of energy, and of the vital creative forces that enable humankind to live life to the full. Blake remarks tersely, "In Milton the Father is Destiny, the Son a Ratio of the five senses, and the Holy-Ghost a vacuum."

RIGHT: ***Satan Arousing the Rebel Angels,*** **painted in 1808 by William Blake.**

died in childbirth, leaving him three daughters and a son, who also died shortly after. He married twice more, his third wife outliving him by almost fifty years. He was beset by eye trouble, losing the sight of his left eye in 1648 and becoming completely blind in 1652 (he never saw his second wife, the beloved Katherine Woodcock, and needed to be led, and read to, for the rest of his life).

Paradise Lost and *Samson Agonistes*

Though Milton wrote *Paradise Lost* continuously throughout 1656, at a time when it was becoming clear that Cromwell's Protectorate would soon be replaced by the return of monarchical government, Milton had been planning the epic poem since the late 1630s. No long poem in English has a greater spatial amplitude, and none more intensely realized characters. We read it now as a poem of dramatized, tragic consciousness, our attention focused on Satan, on Eve in the Garden of Eden, and on Milton's self-presentation as a poet "unchanged . . . though fallen on evil days, / On evil days though fallen, and evil tongues, / In darkness, and with dangers compassed round, / And solitude." Satan is glamorous, seductive, and evil, a sublime picture of an actorish hypocrisy so cunning that only a god can see through it, though he is himself straightforward and unillusioned about the personage he has become: "Which way I fly is Hell; myself am Hell; /. . . /All good to me is lost; / Evil be thou my good."

Milton gives Eve an enormously complex character: narcissistic, persuasive in debate with Adam, credulous when she meets Satan as the serpent, and compelling as the fallen mother of humankind when Adam chooses to fall with her. When their paradise is lost, they are promised instead "a paradise within thee happier far."

At the end of *Paradise Lost*, Milton lays emphasis upon inwardness, just as in his redefinition of tragedy in *Samson Agonistes*, he unites the personal with the political and historical to yield an unforgettable image of human solitariness facing the emptiness of the unknown. **JP**

1808

ANDREW MARVELL

Born: March 31, 1621 (Winestead, England); died August 16, 1678 (London, England).

Style and genre: Andrew Marvell was a poet, pamphlet writer, and politician who served under Oliver Cromwell. His writings are suffused with binaries, perhaps representative of his own divided self.

Born in Yorkshire, educated at Trinity College, Cambridge, and well traveled on the continent, Andrew Marvell became tutor to the daughter of Sir Thomas Fairfax in 1648. While there, he is presumed to have written much of his poetry. At some unknown point, Marvell also became acquainted with the great poet John Milton and used his political influence to free Milton from prison.

In 1657, at Milton's recommendation, Marvell was appointed assistant Latin secretary to the Council of State, under Oliver Cromwell's leadership (a surprising turn of events because Marvell had previously been aligned with the Royalists). In 1659, Marvell was elected member of parliament for Hull, a position he held until his death. In the last two decades of his life, he was very politically involved. He wrote numerous scathing political satires and participated in embassies to places as far away as Russia.

Tensions that were evident in Marvell's public existence also permeated his art. He examined, with incredible skill, the rapacious nature of time against pleasure, a thief he was personally well aware of, having experienced the early deaths of both his mother and his father. Marvell also addresses the conflict between the world's pleasures and the soul's moral responsibilities. Perhaps most relevant to his own divided self is his exploration of the individual's role as an aesthete in union with nature, and his or her contrasting and inevitable rational side. For Marvell, in his life experience and his artistic endeavor, two sides would always be in conflict. He died of a tertian ague in 1678 and is remembered as a loyal patriot. His poetry was not published until 1681. **JS**

"Society is all but rude,
To this delicious Solitude."
—"The Garden"

Signature titles

Poems

"An Horatian Ode," 1650

"The Coronet," *c.* 1650–1652

"A Dialogue Between the Soul and the Body," *c.* 1650–1652

"To His Coy Mistress," *c.* 1650–1652

"The Mower Against the Gardens," *c.* 1650–1652

"The Garden," *c.* 1650–1652

"Upon Appleton House, to my Lord Fairfax," 1651

Prose

The Rehearsal Transpos'd; or, Animadversions Upon a Late Book, Intituled, A Preface, Shewing What Grounds There Are of Fears and Jealousies of Popery, 1672

The Growth of Popery and Arbitrary Government, 1677

ABOVE: A *c.* 1880 engraving from *Old England's Worthies* by Lord Brougham.

JEAN DE LA FONTAINE

Born: July 8, 1621 (Château-Thierry, France); died April 13, 1695, (Paris, France).

Style and genre: La Fontaine was a French writer who made the moral fable his own. His verses about animals and ancient heroes borrowed from Aesop and other sources were full of vibrant humor and rich language.

Every French-speaking school child has heard of La Fontaine's *Fables*. These elegant little moral tales have been recited by children for the last 300 years. But on closer examination, the morals drawn in La Fontaine's famous *Fables* are not homey wisdom, but satirical comments on contemporary society.

La Fontaine was born in Château-Thierry to the east of Paris, the son of a government official. He studied theology, law, and perhaps even medicine, but he was something of a dilettante and never put these studies to practical use. He did not begin writing until the age of thirty-three, but once he had started, he dedicated himself to the art. To finance his writing, he held several government posts, which brought him an income but required little attention. He also had a series of aristocratic patrons to support him. The first, Nicolas Fouquet, Louis XIV's superintendent of finances, was to give him problems in later years. When Fouquet was disgraced, La Fontaine continued to support him, earning himself such royal suspicion that the king personally blocked his admission to the Académie Française for a year.

La Fontaine's first writing success came with his *Tales and Novels in Verse*, a collection of scurrilous tales of lecherous priests, wanton women, and cuckolds. When he turned to religion in old age, La Fontaine regretted the licentious tone of the *Tales* and renounced them. He dabbled in all the fashionable forms of writing, from long romance to elegy, but it was his 240 *Fables* that earned him a place in the canon of French literature. In an age when most writers used formal, constrained language, these tales of animals and ancient heroes, written in fabulously rich language and full of archaic words and colloquialisms, buzz with life and wit. **CW**

"Every flatterer lives at the expense of him who listens to him."—*The Fox and the Crow*

Signature titles

Prose

Tales and Novels in Verse (Contes et nouvelles en vers), 1664–1674

Selected Fables in Verse (Fables choisies, mises en vers), 1668–1694

The Love of Psyche and Cupid (Les Amours de Psyché et de Cupidon), 1669

ABOVE: Portrait of La Fontaine from the studio of Hyacinthe Rigaud (1659–1743).

MOLIÈRE

Born: Jean Baptiste Poquelin, January 15, 1622 (Paris, France); died February 17, 1675 (Paris, France).

Style and genre: Seventeenth-century French dramatist, widely recognized as one of the greatest comic playwrights of all time.

The influential comic playwright Molière was born Jean Baptiste Poquelin, the son of a well-to-do upholsterer to the French court. Even at a young age, Molière found it more pleasing to make fun of the aristocracy than be classed among them. Using his share of his mother's estate, he set up a theater group called L'Illustre Théâtre, which toured the provinces and allowed Molière to start honing his craft. By the time he returned to Paris, he had picked up the name Molière.

In 1658, Molière gained an audience before King Louis XIV, but he and his court were unimpressed with the company's chosen play, a tragedy. At its conclusion, Molière approached the king and asked his permission to perform "one of the little pieces with which he had been used to regale the provinces." The king acceded and Molière's own farce, called *The Lovesick Doctor*, proved so popular that the actors were granted the use of the Hôtel du Petit Bourbon theater. It was here that he staged his first Parisian success, *The Affected Young Ladies*, a play that infuriated members of the French court who believed it was about them and tried to get it shut down. Despite this,

Signature titles

Plays

The Jealous Husband (La Jalousie de Barbouillé), c. 1645
The Flying Doctor (Le Médecin volant), c. 1648
The Affected Young Ladies (Les Précieuses ridicules), 1659
The School for Husbands (L'École des maris), 1661
The School for Wives (L'École des femmes), 1662
The Forced Marriage (Le Mariage forcé), 1664
Tartuffe, 1664 (rewritten 1667 and 1669)
Don Juan, 1665
The Misanthrope, 1666
The Doctor In Spite of Himself (Le Médecin malgré lui), 1666
The Miser (L'Avare), 1668
Amphitryon, 1668
George Dandin, 1668
The Bourgeois Gentleman (Le Bourgeois gentilhomme), 1670
Scapin, 1671
The Learned Ladies (Les Femmes savantes), 1672

ABOVE: Detail from a portrait by Jean-Baptiste Mauzaisse located at Versailles.

RIGHT: *Crispin and Scapin, or Scapin and Sylvester, c.* 1863–1865, by Honoré Daumier.

the king granted Molière the use of the Palais Royale, where he would stay for the rest of his life and where his theater company was later appointed "the King's Troupe."

Over the next thirteen years, Molière wrote comic creations that continued to ruffle the feathers of the aristocracy, medical professionals, and the clergy, including one of his best known and most controversial plays, *Tartuffe*. His clashes with his young wife seem to have inspired his writings, too, including another comic masterpiece, *The Misanthrope*.

Having churned out plays that were to be envied by dramatists for centuries, Molière died after playing a lead role on stage, ironically in *The Imaginary Invalid*. His troupe begged him not to go on, but he replied, "There are fifty poor workers who have only their daily wage to live on. What will become of them if the performance does not take place?" It is said he was so good the audience was completely unaware he was ill. **JM**

ABOVE: ***Molière Dining with Louis XIV*** **(1857), by Jean Auguste Dominique Ingres.**

Molière and Religion

Molière spent much of his life surrounded by controversy because of his habit of poking fun at the controlling classes, particularly the Roman Catholic clergy. When Molière wrote *Tartuffe* in 1664, a mocking look at the hypocrisy rife within the church, the archbishop of Paris issued a decree threatening to excommunicate anyone performing, attending, or even reading the play. Even with Molière's sway with the king, it took five years and at least two rewrites before the play was finally granted an official public performance. It became a great success, but made Molière numerous enemies.

MADAME DE SÉVIGNÉ

Born: Marie de Rabutin-Chantal, Marquise de Sévigné, February 5, 1626 (Paris, France); died April 17, 1696 (Grignan, Drôme, France).

Style and genre: Madame de Sévigné's flow of correspondence from her base in Parisian high society made her one of the most famous letter-writers of all time.

Signature titles

Collected letters

The Letters of Madame de Sévigné to Her Daughter and Friends, 1869

Selected Letters of Madame de Sévigné, 1947

Letters from Madame de Sévigné, 1955

A highly educated Burgundian aristocrat, Marie de Rabutin-Chantal lived in fashionable Paris, of which she gave shrewd, highly enjoyable accounts in her correspondence. She had married a nobleman, who spent most of her money before being killed in a duel over another woman in 1651. Her life and the lives of those around her are recorded in the hundreds of gossipy letters, to friends and to her daughter, Madame de Grignan. She wrote of the latest events and people in Paris, "everything from birth-control to hair-dos." Until Madame de Sévigné, correspondence was expected to conform to formal rules; she ignored them and her liveliness and literary skill gave letter-writing a serious place in French tradition. **RC**

JOHN BUNYAN

Born: Baptized November 30, 1628 (Harrowden, England); died August 31, 1688 (London, England).

Style and genre: Bunyan is most famous for the heavy allegory in *The Pilgrim's Progress*—the action enacts the spiritual progression of a Christian toward salvation.

Signature titles

Allegories

The Pilgrim's Progress, 1678

The Holy War, 1682

Autobiography

Grace Abounding to the Chief of Sinners, 1666

John Bunyan was imprisoned on two occasions for preaching without a license, and it was during his first incarceration that he began *The Pilgrim's Progress*. First published in 1678, his allegorical tale of Christian's search for spiritual salvation has become one of the most influential works in English literature. Bunyan was certainly not the first to allegorize Christianity in such a way, but his simple language, vivid descriptions, and his stylistic echoes of the magisterial King James Bible made such an allegory far more accessible to a general readership. Indeed, Dr. Johnson believed the strength of the book was that "the most cultivated man cannot find anything to praise more highly, and the child knows nothing more amusing." **AS**

JOHN DRYDEN

Born: August 19, 1631 (Aldwinkle, Northamptonshire, England); died May 12, 1700 (London, England).

Style and genre: Dryden established the heroic couplet as a major verse component, using it for grandiose effect, as well as for satiric, mock-heroic verse.

Few figures had a greater impact on literature in Restoration England than John Dryden. Writing during times of extreme tension between the monarchy and parliament, Dryden found it prudent to celebrate both sides of the political divide. He composed *Heroic Stanzas* (1658) on the death of Oliver Cromwell, which praised the life of the man responsible for the execution of Charles I, and went on to celebrate the restoration of Charles II with *Astraea Redux* (1660).

In 1671, Dryden was appointed poet laureate, but in 1688 he was removed from the position, in a break from the tradition that laureates serve for life, when he refused to take the oath of allegiance to the new government after the Glorious Revolution that deposed James II. In a cruel twist of fate, the position was then awarded to Thomas Shadwell, the playwright who had been the target of one of Dryden's most vicious satirical poems, *MacFlecknoe*. Dryden's achievements extended far beyond poetry, with a reputation as a leading playwright, literary critic, and translator, but his poetic influence proved extremely long-lived thanks to his popularization of one of the period's most common poetic devices, the heroic couplet—a rhyming pair of lines in iambic pentameter. Appropriately, one of the most famous of these couplets comes from Dryden's *Absalom and Achitophel*: "Great wits are sure to madness near allied,/And thin partitions do their bounds divide." As its name suggests, the form was the basis for epic, heroic poetry but it also came to be used for the mock-heroic form, in which a large part of the satire derives from the sense that the subject is unworthy of such adulation. *MacFlecknoe* is the best example of Dryden's use of this form, and his satirical influence can be clearly seen in Alexander Pope's *The Dunciad* (1728). **AS**

"All things are subject to decay; when fate summons, monarchs must obey."—*MacFlecknoe*

Signature titles

Poetry

Absalom and Achitophel, 1681

Religio Laici, 1682

MacFlecknoe, 1682

A Song for St. Cecilia's Day, 1687, 1687

Translation

Juvenal: The Sixth Satire, 1693

ABOVE: A portrait of Dryden engraved by William Falthorne (1616–1691).

SAMUEL PEPYS

Born: February 23, 1633 (London, England); died May 26, 1703 (London, England).

Style and genre: Pepys is most famous for his diaries; begun in 1660, they provide a detailed and personal account of contemporary life, as well as important accounts of historical events.

Signature titles

Diaries

The Diaries of Samuel Pepys, 1825

There is perhaps no other account of seventeenth-century life in England that is so captivating and historically enlightening than that depicted in Samuel Pepys's diaries. The influential member of parliament and naval administrator, who led a colorful life and was imprisoned on several occasions and charged with treason (though he was acquitted), first began his diaries on January 1, 1660. He continued for the next nine years, until May 31, 1669, when he made his last entry, blaming his failing eyesight for his decision to stop writing.

The diaries were a personal account of Pepys's life, including the trivia of his domestic forum and the fraught relations with his wife, as well as forthright accounts of his various liaisons with different women. These include a particularly vivid description of an incident on October 25, 1668, when his wife caught him embracing Deborah Willet, who ironically had been hired to keep Pepys's wife company. Alongside these highly personal entries, which have done much to rekindle the character of the man for the modern reader, are fascinating accounts of the social and political atmosphere of the time, and major historical events. The diaries provide a firsthand account of the Great Plague in 1665 and the Fire of London the following year in 1666, for example, written with tremendous compassion and perspicacity, as well as a vivid description of Charles II's coronation and various accounts of events during the Second Anglo–Dutch War (1665–1667). The diaries were written in a form of shorthand that was standard for the time and were clearly devised as a personal record rather than for publication. However Pepys had the volumes bound to preserve them, indicating that he was aware that one day the books would be read by others. **TP**

"As happy a man as any in the world, for the whole world seems to smile upon me!"

ABOVE: Godfrey Kneller's portrait of Pepys at the Royal Society of Arts, London.

MADAME DE LA FAYETTE

Born: Marie-Madeleine Pioche de La Vergne, baptized March 18, 1634 (Paris, France); died May 25, 1693 (Paris, France).

Style and genre: La Fayette has been hailed as the founder of the French tradition of the serious historical novel, using the past to illuminate the present.

1600s

Madame de La Fayette was a sprig of the lesser French nobility, who married into a grander family in 1655; her husband was the Comte de La Fayette. They lived at first on his country estate and she bore him two sons, but after a few years she moved to Paris, leaving him behind, and made herself one of Parisian society's most redoubtable hostesses. She was a close friend of Madame de Sévigné and many celebrated literary figures gathered at Madame de La Fayette's glittering salons; they included the poet Jean de Segrais, who collaborated with her on her *Zayde* (set in Moorish Spain), the flirtatious Gilles Ménage, who was supposedly her and Madame de Sévigné's tutor, and most notably of all, the Duke de La Rochefoucauld, who has been famed ever since for his marvelously disillusioned maxims.

Madame de La Fayette's husband remained living on his country estate, although he often visited her in Paris. The tragedy of a loveless marriage is the theme of several of her novels, including the most famous one, *The Princess of Clèves*, which for its psychological insight has been called the first modern novel. It contains a portrait of La Rochefoucauld, who was closely involved with its creation. The heroine is a rivetingly desirable ornament of the French court in the sixteenth century, married off to a man she does not love. Finding herself threatened with entanglement in court intrigues and seductions, she eventually keeps her virtue intact by leaving the court and spends her last years alone. Readers thought the story implied that marriage and true love are incompatible and many of them wrote letters to the *Mercure galant* magazine implying that they considered the heroine as a real person of their own time. **RC**

"Shame is the most violent of the passions."

—The Princess of Clèves

Signature titles

Novel

The Princess of Clèves (La Princesse de Clèves), 1678

Romance

Zayde, 1670

ABOVE: A colored engraving by Amedée Felix Geille after Friedrich Bouterwek.

JEAN RACINE

Born: December 1639 (La Ferté-Milon, France); died April 21, 1699 (Paris, France).

Style and genre: A leading French dramatist of his time (and a rival of Molière and Corneille), Racine worked in a classical tradition, creating compelling characters in his works. He was also a historian.

Signature titles

Plays

The Thébaïde or The Enemy Brothers (La Thébaïde ou les frères ennemis), 1664
Alexander the Great (Alexandre le grand), 1665
Andromaque, 1667
Bérénice, 1670
Phèdre, 1676
Esther, 1689
Athalie, 1691

ABOVE: **Jean Baptiste Santerre's *Portrait of Jean Racine*, c. 1700.**

Jean Racine can be considered one of the leading French dramatists of the seventeenth century. During his lifetime he achieved great success with his dramas and was financially and critically acclaimed, becoming one of the first French literary figures to support himself through his writing. His style was notably different to that of his main rivals, Molière (1622–1673) and Pierre Corneille (1606–1684), and was characterized by a more rigidly classical tone. Racine's direct and frill-free approach appealed to the public and lent him an edge with the critics. He was also friends with one of the leading critics, Nicolas Boileau-Despréaux (1636–1711), which certainly helped his general reception.

Racine was brought up by his grandmother, Marie des Moulins, and educated at the convent of Port-Royal, run by members of the controversial Jansenist movement. Here he was given broad instruction in classic Greek and Roman literature and language—and especially mythology—which would shape his later literary career. His teachers encouraged him to study law, but Racine turned instead toward the artistic and literary circles of Paris. He began writing poetry, which came to the attention of Boileau-Despréaux. The critic encouraged the young writer to continue on a literary path. Racine next wrote his first play *Amasie*, which was never produced, and shortly afterward met Molière.

In 1664, Molière produced Racine's second play, the tragedy *The Thébaïde*, and the following year Molière's theater company staged Racine's next play, *Alexander the Great*, which received an enormously enthusiastic response from the public. Racine then decided to approach a rival theater company with a better reputation for staging tragedies. *Alexander the Great* was canceled from Molière's stage and given a second opening night by the Hôtel de Bourgogne troupe less than two weeks

after it first opened. In a further act of betrayal, Racine stole Molière's leading lady, Thérèse du Parc, transferring her to the Bourgogne company. Understandably, Molière cut all ties with Racine and the two were never reconciled.

Racine continued to produce dramatic plays (and one comedy) to increasing public acclaim and mostly based on classical stories, including *Bérénice* and *Phèdre*. By this time, Racine had also made a number of prominent enemies and, partly due to this, he stopped writing and took a post as historian to Louis XIV. For the next twelve years, he worked at the court, married, and raised a family, before being persuaded back to writing by Madame de Maintenon (1635–1719), Louis XIV's consort, who requested that he write two plays for the children at the school of Saint-Cyr. *Esther* and *Athalie* were well received, but they were the last works he wrote before he died some years later in 1699. **TP**

ABOVE: ***Racine Reads "Athelie" to Louis XIV,*** **1819, by Julie Philipault.**

Leading Ladies

According to some, Racine led something of a scandalous private life, which was given as part of the reason he stopped writing in 1677. One scandal erupted when he stole leading lady Thérèse du Parc from Molière's acting troupe and embarked on a turbulent affair with her. The actress, who was married, died in suspicious circumstances, and Racine was at first suspected of poisoning her. He was later acquitted, with one possible cause of death cited as an ill-fated abortion. Racine was later alleged to have had an affair with another actress, La Champmeslé, the leading lady in his play *Bérénice*.

APHRA BEHN

Born: Aphra Johnson, July, 1640 (Harbledown, England); died April 16, 1689 (London, England).

Style and genre: Behn was the first English professional female writer. Her life (as a spy and lesbian) and work were highly unconventional and ahead of her time.

Signature titles

Plays

Abdelazer, 1677

The Rover, 1677–1681

The Lucky Chance, 1686

Novels

Oroonoko, or the History of the Royal Slave, 1688

Like Christopher Marlowe, Aphra Behn is cloaked in the mystery befitting a spy. However, unlike Marlowe, she wrote an extensive body of work between 1670 and 1689, consisting of eighteen plays, two novels, and several poems celebrated now for their witty exploration of lesbian desire. Although her plays were successful at the time, not least because they embodied the buoyant mood of the Restoration, her contemporary reputation rests largely on *Oroonoko, or the History of the Royal Slave*. The earliest written narrative to explore African slavery, *Oroonoko* is framed, like Daniel Defoe's novels, as reportage. Oroonoko is a character both of and before his time, just as Behn—canny and determined—was a woman of and before hers. **SM**

CARLOS DE SIGÜENZA Y GONGÓRA

Born: August, 1645 (Mexico City, Mexico); died August 22, 1700 (Mexico City, Mexico).

Style and genre: A true Renaissance man, Sigüenza wrote poetry, belonged to the Society of Jesus, and acted as historian, royal cartographer, and geologist—he was the foremost intellectual figure of colonial Mexico.

Signature titles

Scientific works

The Book of Astronomy (Libra astronómica y philosóphica), 1691

Philosophical works

A Philosophical Treatise Against Comets (Manifiesto philosóphico contra los cometas), 1681

Western Paradise, the Plants and Gardens of the Magnificent Royal Convent of Jesus Maria of Mexico (Parayso Occidental, plantado y cultivado en su magnífico Real Convento de Jesüs María de México), 1684

Poetry

The Glories of Queretaro (Las Glorias de Queretaro), 1668

Novels

The Misadventures of Alonso Ramírez (Infortunios de Alonso Ramírez), 1690

Sigüenza's father, tutor to the Spanish royal family, taught his son mathematics and astronomy. The young Sigüenza took vows as a Jesuit in 1662, although he was expelled from the college for not observing the correct discipline. Despite this, he later became a hospital chaplain. A scholarly man revered for his learning, he published an almanac in 1671, and produced *El Mercurio Volante*, the first newspaper in New Spain, in 1693. As royal geographer, Sigüenza was the first person born in the colony to prepare a map of New Spain and, during the 1680s, he began his acclaimed histories of Mexico. His works encompass poetry, philosophy, and astronomy and he was a huge influence on later Latin American novelists. **REM**

JOHN WILMOT

Born: April 1, 1647 (Ditchley, England); died July 26, 1680 (Woodstock, England).

Style and genre: John Wilmot, the Second Earl of Rochester, was an early English Restoration courtier and wit who famously satirized the decadent life of late seventeenth-century England.

If John Wilmot, the Second Earl of Rochester, burned bright, he also cast dark shadows. He was immersed in the politics (often petty and sexual) of the court of Charles II. At an early age, Rochester became a favorite of the king, serving as a courtier and "Gentleman of the Bedchamber." The young earl quickly fell into the company of court wits who embraced the moral and sexual license of the Restoration. In his early twenties, Rochester contracted syphilis, which, combined with his copious drinking, killed him at the young age of thirty-three. Despite his ill health, he continued to frequent brothels and acquire numerous mistresses. Rochester spent much of his life scraping around for money and he rarely paid his debts.

Rochester was famous for his wit, which was often expressed in biting satirical poetry about the people of the court, including the king and the king's mistresses. His satire about courtly ladies, *Signior Dildo*, aroused the king's interest, but Rochester mistakenly handed him a copy of his *Satyr on Charles II*. Rochester had to flee the court into temporary exile: it was not the first or last time he would anger the king.

Rochester's disillusionment grew as his health declined, and his poetry reflects his regrets and dependence on alcohol. His poetry was not published in his lifetime; it was instead passed around in manuscript and often copied into the personal books of his friends and acquaintances. Even some of his extemporaneous poetry has been preserved by his friends, who transcribed it as best they remembered. On his deathbed he repented his sins and his atheism. His family burned many of his papers, particularly anything licentious, so much of his writing unfortunately has been lost. **IJ**

"Man differs more from Man, than Man from Beast."

—*A Satyr Against Reason and Mankind*

Signature titles

Poetry

A Ramble in St. James's Park, 1672

Signior Dildo, 1673

A Satyr Against Reason and Mankind, 1675

To the Postboy, 1676

Satyr on Charles II, 1679

The Imperfect Enjoyment, 1685

Upon His Drinking Bowl, 1685

Plays

Valentinian, 1685

The Farce of Sodom, or the Quintessence of Debauchery, 1685

ABOVE: ***Portrait of John Wilmot*** **by Sir Peter Lely (1618–1680).**

DANIEL DEFOE

Born: Daniel Foe, 1660 (London, England); died April 26, 1731 (London, England).

Style and genre: Defoe was the inventor of the adventure novel; his capable and practical-minded protagonists came to typify the Protestant work ethic, if not always Protestant morality.

Signature titles

Novels

Robinson Crusoe, 1719
Captain Singleton, 1720
Colonel Jack, 1722
Moll Flanders, 1722
A Journal of the Plague Year, 1722
A New Voyage Around the World, 1724
Roxana, 1724

Daniel Defoe was prolific in every sense of the word. As a pamphleteer, essayist, and writer of books, he was easily one of the most widely read men of his era: conservative estimates of his canon ascribe over 300 works to his name. His publication *The Review*, which he produced almost single-handedly, revolutionized English journalism. He worked as a propagandist and spy, both in London and Scotland, with such success that he has been called a "one-man secret service." He had eight children, six of whom survived to adulthood. As an economist, he played an early role in drafting the blueprints for the British Empire of the following century. And his first novel, *Robinson Crusoe*, published at the age of fifty-nine, has not only inspired scores of imitators but it has never been out of print.

Despite the wide variety of genres that Defoe tackled, his work is characterized by a singular clarity of focus: trade, fairly practiced according to peaceful, rational principles, provides the best means by which the human condition can be improved. This is not to say that Defoe wrote purely as a dismal scientist, though an obsessive cataloguing of material possessions is a notable feature of his technique. His best work is characterized by astute psychological profiles and a sensitivity to the fact that the problems of economic circumstances will not be easily resolved. The protagonists of his novels, male and female, tend to be mercenaries thrust into their roles by situations beyond their control. Though they do not attempt to justify their actions, nor are we given reason to judge them harshly. In his writing, Defoe accomplished the difficult double task of giving a voice to both an emergent capitalist society, and to the people it had callously thrust aside. **SY**

"The first English author to write without imitating or adapting former works."—James Joyce

ABOVE: Daniel Defoe, engraved by Michael Van der Gucht (1660–1725).

RIGHT: The front cover of the 1881 edition of Defoe's *Robinson Crusoe*.

ROBINSON
CRUSOE

JONATHAN SWIFT

Born: November 30, 1667 (Dublin, Ireland); died October 19, 1745 (Dublin, Ireland).

Style and genre: Jonathan Swift was an unwilling and combative clergyman who ruthlessly satirized the religious and political landscapes of Ireland in publications that provoked both laughter and outrage.

Signature titles

Novel

Gulliver's Travels, 1726

Prose

A Tale of a Tub, 1704

The Battle of the Books, 1704

An Argument Against Abolishing Christianity, 1711

Drapier's Letters, 1724

A Modest Proposal, 1729

Poetry

Cadenus and Vanessa, 1713

To Stella, Who Collected and Transcribed His Poems, 1720

The Grand Question Debated, 1729

A Beautiful Young Nymph, Going to Bed, 1731

Verses on the Death of Dr. Swift, 1731

Swift's was a life of frustrated expectations. Fatherless from the moment he was born, he was shunted from place to place as a child, eventually graduating from Trinity College, Dublin, and becoming secretary to Sir William Temple in southern England. It was here that he began to write poetry, although it was in prose that he would make his most significant marks. Unhappy at having been educated in Ireland, which he described as a "vile country," Swift found himself back there after Temple's death in 1699 as chaplain to the Lord Justice. He published his first satirical works in 1704, in which he railed against pedantry and religious fanaticism.

As his literary reputation grew, so did the animosity he inspired in the establishment, with satirical publications such as *An Argument Against Abolishing Christianity* proving too much to stomach for those who might have given him preferment. A regular visitor to England, where he became friends with some of the leading literary figures of the day, he only really settled in Ireland when he became the Dean of St. Patrick's Cathedral, Dublin, in 1713. It was from this position that he wrote the works that have come to define him. The extraordinary *Gulliver's Travels*, a satire on humanity's irrationality (and now a children's favorite read) provided fuel to those who felt Swift was merely a misanthrope. The later pamphlet *A Modest Proposal*, in which he ironically advocated the rearing of poor children in Ireland for food to resolve the nation's high birth rates and famine at the same time, reinforced such views. A brain tumor meant that for the last years of his life he suffered from dementia, a tragic yet perversely appropriate end for this most precise and infuriating of thinkers. **PS**

"I never wonder to see men wicked, but I often wonder to see them not ashamed."

ABOVE: Charles Jervas's eighteenth-century *Study Portrait of Jonathan Swift*.

RIGHT: *Gulliver in Lilliput* from a drawing by Frédéric Théodore Lix.

ALEXANDER POPE

Born: May 22, 1688 (London, England); died May 30, 1744 (Twickenham, England).

Style and genre: The signature characteristics of Pope's work are intelligent satire, witty sarcasm, bawdy sexual themes, and keen observation of human nature and weaknesses.

Alexander Pope was used to mockery from his literary rivals, being an unhealthy, hunchbacked adult of well under 5 feet (1.5 m) in height, and a Roman Catholic in the midst of an Anglican majority. He learned to deflect the abuse with a well-honed sense of humor and a sharp, sarcastic tongue. Furthermore, as the son of a self-made man—a tradesman turned wealthy merchant—he created for himself an illustrious background, with aristocratic ancestors and valiant histories. Pope inherited a large fortune on his father's death, which seemed to add credence to his claims of noble birth.

Unable to play sports as a child, he loved books and began writing at a young age, claiming to have written his first proper work, an "Ode on Solitude," before the age of twelve. Influenced by the Earl of Rochester, he wrote poems on a sexual theme, disguising them as witty comedy of social manners. His most famous poem, *The Rape of the Lock*, is the jocular story of a stolen lock of hair—the traditional gift from one lover to another. Based on a true story, which turned into a feud between two families, it is written in a high-blown style, its prosaic subject matter deliberately built up into a drama. Full of symbolism, the poem can be read on two levels, either as a light comedy or as a bitingly subversive view of Pope's contemporary society.

"Know then thyself, presume not God to scan; / The proper study of mankind is man."

His other works, including his "moral essays," poked fun at the hierarchical class system and the rigid social rules. Many of his letters were also intended for publication and written accordingly. In 1717 he was a celebrated poet and a favorite of many society women. He bought a villa in Twickenham—then a village outside London—that became a highly fashionable place to visit. He died there at the age of fifty-six. **LH**

Signature titles

Poetry

An Essay on Criticism, 1711

The Rape of the Lock, 1712–1714

Windsor Forest, 1713

Eloisa to Abelard, 1717

Elegy to the Memory of an Unfortunate Lady, 1717

The Dunciad, 1728

An Essay on Man, 1733–1734

Translations

Homer's Iliad, 1715–1720

Homer's Odyssey, 1726

ABOVE: A detail from *Alexander Pope and His Dog, Bounce*, c. 1718, by J. Richardson.

SAMUEL RICHARDSON

Born: August 19, 1689 (Mackworth, Derbyshire, England); died July 4, 1761 (London, England).

Style and genre: Often called the "father of the novel," Richardson explored contemporary moral issues through an innovative use of the epistolary form.

It is hard to imagine the popularity of Samuel Richardson's work in the eighteenth century, when the trials, dilemmas, and misfortunes of the characters of his novels were as much a topic of conversation as that of characters in today's TV soap operas. Yet his ability to create psychologically convincing characters has stood the test of time, and his romantic stories written in epistolary form prove to be rewarding reading.

Richardson is famous for his novels *Pamela: or, Virtue Rewarded*, *Clarissa: or, the History of a Young Lady*, and *Sir Charles Grandison*, yet he was a printer by trade and did not start writing novels until he was in his fifties. The novel as a literary genre was in nascent form when Richardson made his debut with *Pamela*. It set out to appeal to a literate middle class both as an entertainment, but also as a means of moral instruction. The moral tone of this and his later novels may jar with modern readers, but is also fascinating as an insight into eighteenth-century English life. Yet even then the story of Richardson's protagonist, the housemaid Pamela, and her attempts to protect her "virtue," against the advances of her master were satirized, most notoriously by Henry Fielding in his novels *Shamela* (1741) and *Joseph Andrews* (1742).

Richardson's greatest work is *Clarissa*, which consists of letters written by several of its characters rather than just one as in *Pamela*, achieving a wider perspective on events and greater insight into the characters' feelings and motivations than in Richardson's other works. Richardson's ability to create realistic characters, both in speech and action, and plausible scenarios still makes for compelling reading and marks one of the first forays of the novel into quality romantic fiction. **CK**

"The more you read him, the more pleasure you take in him."—Denis Diderot on Richardson

Signature titles

Novels

Pamela: or, Virtue Rewarded, 1740

Clarissa: or, the History of a Young Lady, 1747–1748

Sir Charles Grandison, 1753–1754

ABOVE: ***Samuel Richardson*, a portrait by Joseph Highmore painted in 1747.**

VOLTAIRE

Born: François-Marie Arouet, November 21, 1694 (Paris, France); died May 30, 1778 (Paris, France).

Style and genre: Author of historical works and tragic dramas, Voltaire was a satirical polemicist who infused his critical works with biting wit.

The embodiment of the Age of Enlightenment, Voltaire's writings brim with wit in their deconstruction of moral and social issues. His work encompassed poetry, plays, essays, and philosophy, expounding his belief in civil liberties, freedom of religion, and the need for social progress. Although much of his work no longer reaches a wide audience, his reputation as an opponent of tyranny and bigotry remains undiminished.

Voltaire was educated at the Jesuit college of Louis-le-Grand, where the first sense of his disillusionment with religion surfaced. Despite graduating in law, he chose to become a writer. Early on in his career, in what was to be a regular occurrence, Voltaire angered the authorities by daring to mock the Duc d'Orléans, resulting in banishment from Paris and eventual imprisonment in the Bastille. During this time he wrote the tragedy *Oedipe*, a triumphant success when performed after his release, and he assumed the pen name Voltaire. He worked on an epic poem about the life of the

Signature titles

Prose

Zadig, 1747

Micromégas, 1752

Candide, 1759

The Ingenue (L'Ingénu), 1767

Poetry

Henriade, 1723

Plays

Oedipe, 1718

Alzire, 1736

Mahomet, 1741

The Princess of Navarre (La princesse de Navarre), 1745

Nonfiction

Letters on the English (Lettres philosophiques sur les Anglais), 1733

Elements of Newton's Philosophy (Elements de la philosophie de Newton), 1738

The Age of Louis XIV (Le siècle de Louis XIV), 1751

Treaty on Tolerance (Traité sur la tolerance), 1763

Philosophical Dictionary (Dictionnaire philosophique), 1764

ABOVE: Nicholas de Largilliere's *Portrait of Voltaire*, painted after 1718.

RIGHT: An illustration from *Candide*, after Jean Michel Moreau the Younger.

ABOVE: *Voltaire Conversing with the Peasants in Ferney*, by Jean Huber (1721–1786).

popular French king Henry IV, which initially failed to find authorization for publication, due to its vigorous espousal of religious tolerance. *Henriade* delighted the freethinkers of Parisian high society and earned Voltaire a career as court poet. Established in the company of some of France's finest thinkers of the day, Voltaire's intellectual development blossomed until his pen once again landed him in trouble when he insulted a member of a leading French family, the Chevalier de Rohan. After a visit to prison, Voltaire accepted enforced exile and headed for London in May 1726.

"Men are equal; it is not birth but virtue that makes the difference."

He spent two years in England mastering the language and digesting the philosophy of John Locke and scientific thought of Sir Isaac Newton. His high regard for the liberalism of England's institutions and religious tolerance inspired Voltaire to write *Letters on the English* upon return to his homeland. The thinly veiled attack on the French establishment created more

Voltaire and His Enemies

For Voltaire, falling out with people was a way of life. Throughout his twenties and thirties, he spent time in and out of the Bastille for various attacks on the French aristocracy and monarchy. He appeared to have finally made his peace with the cream of French society when he made an ill-advised quip about the integrity of certain persons during a card game. Fearing the usual response to one of his witticisms, he made a hasty retreat to the country mansion of Duchess du Maine.

After succumbing to the repeated invitations of Frederick II to join him in Berlin, Voltaire took little time in upsetting the king by ridiculing Maupertuis, the president of Frederick's academy of science, in the pamphlet *Diatribe du Docteur Akakia*. So enraged was the king that he had Voltaire placed under house arrest at Frankfurt on his way back to France. He never reached his homeland, as word circulated that Louis XV would not allow him back to Paris as punishment for previous indiscretions.

Voltaire did not reserve his spleen solely for attacks on the upper classes; he clashed frequently with the other great thinker of the day, Rousseau, on philosophical matters. To gain revenge for Rousseau's criticism of his work, Voltaire anonymously published a pamphlet informing the public that Rousseau had abandoned his children.

Even in death Voltaire aroused strong feelings. In 1814, a group of religious zealots stole his remains and dumped them in a pit.

RIGHT: A French School engraving on the title page of *Elements of Newton's Philosophy.*

outrage, forcing him to leave Paris and take refuge in the château of Madame du Chatelet at Cirey in Champagne. He wrote many dramas during this time, including *Alzire*, a play that embraced notions of moral superiority in those who preach tolerance over repression, as well as exposing a new audience to natural sciences with his *Elements of Newton's Philosophy*. Further indiscretions brought more run-ins with the French royal court amid the success of his stage plays *Merope* and *The Princess of Navarre*. The constant fleeing to preserve himself exhausted Voltaire and acted as a source of inspiration for the novel *Zadig*. The story of the Babylonian philosopher Zadig, who suffers persecution and ill fortune, eventually casting doubt over man's ability to affect his own outcome in favor of destiny, bears more than a passing resemblance to the author's own experiences.

In July 1750, Voltaire arrived in Berlin at the invitation of Frederick II. During his time in the royal palace he completed the historical work *The Age of Louis XIV*, an exhaustive study of the reign of Louis XIV using the accounts of those who lived through the period. An inevitable disagreement with Frederick forced Voltaire to leave Prussia, eventually relocating to Ferney in Switzerland, where he wrote the satirical masterpiece *Candide*. The novel follows the young man Candide on an odyssey around the world, with his teacher, Dr. Pangloss, a disciple of the philosophical optimism of Gottfried Liebniz. The extraordinary human atrocities witnessed and the hardships endured on the odyssey force Candide to dismiss his master's belief that "all is for the best in the best of all possible worlds." The endless misery is dampened by the wit and satire that accompanies each tragedy, conveniently masking pointed criticism of the State and the Church.

Voltaire dedicated much of his later life to the continuing struggle for the establishment of religious tolerance and the abolition of torture, something that prompted him to intervene on behalf of victims of fanaticism. Considered a hero of the French Revolution, Voltaire's body was finally laid to rest in the Panthéon in 1791. **SG**

ELÉMENS
DE LA
PHILOSOPHIE
DE NEUTON,

Mis à la portée de tout le monde.

Par Mr. DE VOLTAIRE.

A AMSTERDAM,

Chez JACQUES DESBORDES.

M. DCC. XXXVIII.

HENRY FIELDING

Born: April 22, 1707 (Sharpham Park, Somerset, England); died October 8, 1754 (Lisbon, Portugal).

Style and genre: English novelist, dramatist, and magistrate, Fielding is famous for his satirical plays, humor, and his capacious, picaresque novels.

Signature titles

Novels

Shamela, 1741
Joseph Andrews, 1742
Tom Jones, 1749
Amelia, 1751

In spite of his remarkable late success as a novelist, Fielding's first career was as a dramatist. His plays—from the comic *Tom Thumb* to the political satires *Pasquin* and *The Historical Register*—dominated the London stage in the 1730s. His career as a playwright was, however, thwarted when censorship, introduced by the Theater Licensing Act, effectively pushed him into political journalism, translation, and the law.

In 1741, Fielding's literary career took off in new directions with the publication of *Shamela*, a searing parody of Samuel Richardson's *Pamela, or Virtue Rewarded*. Fielding carried forward this richly burlesque mode, with comic gender inversions, into his second novel, *Joseph Andrews*, which he memorably referred to as "a comic Epic-Poem in Prose."

As a writer, Fielding is probably best known for *Tom Jones*, a novel that combines his interest in human nature (beyond the hypocrisy of what passes for "virtue") with an elaborate plot that Samuel Taylor Coleridge referred to as one of the most perfect ever planned. The novel, with its intrusive narrator, large cast of characters, and panoramic depiction of English life in the 1740s, follows the fortunes of its hero from his mysterious and humble origins to the revelation of his identity at the end—whereupon, needless to say, he gets the girl. In 1748, Fielding, still involved actively in political journalism and writing pamphlets on important legal issues, was made Justice of the Peace for Westminster. From this position he founded London's first effective police force, for which he is still honored today at New Scotland Yard. A fitting end, perhaps, for someone who had been, in the spirit of *Tom Jones*, bound over to keep the peace at the age of eighteen for attempting to abduct an heiress. **ST**

"Make money your God and it will plague you like the devil."

ABOVE: A 1762 etching of Henry Fielding based on a William Hogarth engraving.

SAMUEL JOHNSON

Born: September 18, 1709 (Lichfield, Staffordshire, England); died December 13, 1784 (London, England).

Style and genre: Known for the serious, moral tone of his essays; the lighter, satirical tone of his novellas; and the witty, grumpy, old man style of his epigrams.

Samuel Johnson has come to be regarded as one of the presiding figures of eighteenth-century English literature, as much for his personality as for his work. He came from an impoverished background, and was forced to leave Oxford University after only a year because he was unable to afford the fees; his title, "Dr. Johnson," derives from the honorary degrees conferred on him later in life by both Oxford and Trinity College, Dublin.

Best known for his groundbreaking *A Dictionary of the English Language*, and his novella *The History of Rasselas, the Prince of Abissinia*, Johnson established himself on London's literary scene through his moral and philosophical essays in *The Rambler*, which he later followed with his satires in *The Idler*, poking fun at everything from politics to marriage, to the English obsession with the weather. The *Dictionary*, however, was his most exacting commission, taking him nine years to compile. There was nothing new in the idea of producing a collection of all the words in the English language, but Johnson's work was unparalleled in the depth of its research, its comprehensiveness, and its use of quotation from other authors to illustrate meaning. Despite the need for objectivity, Johnson still managed to inject some of his own character into the work: "patron" was defined as "Commonly a wretch who supports with insolence, and is paid with flattery," and a "lexicographer" was "a writer of dictionaries; a harmless drudge."

"The reciprocal civility of authors is one of the most risible scenes in . . . life."

Yet a significant part of Johnson's reputation is because of the work of his biographer, James Boswell. His colorful *Life of Johnson* (1791) related what have become some of the most well-known stories about Johnson, and virtually established the modern genre of biography. **AS**

Signature titles

Essays

The Rambler, 1750–1752

The Idler, 1758–1760

Taxation No Tyranny, 1775

Novellas

The History of Rasselas, the Prince of Abissinia, 1759

Poetry

London, 1738

Prologue at the Opening of the Theatre in Drury Lane, 1747

The Vanity of Human Wishes, 1749

Nonfiction

A Dictionary of the English Language, 1755

ABOVE: An oil painting of Dr. Samuel Johnson (1775), by Sir Joshua Reynolds.

JEAN-JACQUES ROUSSEAU

Born: June 28, 1712 (Geneva, Switzerland); died July 2, 1778 (Ermenonville, France).

Style and genre: Rousseau was a Swiss philosopher and novelist who was famous for his uncompromising views on society and the nature of man.

Rousseau's profound influence, as a political philosopher and novelist, extended well beyond the Enlightenment with which he was, in any case, frequently in conflict. He first rose to prominence as a social theorist with his *Discourse on the Sciences and the Arts*, written in 1750 for an essay competition—which he won. *Discourse*, and the works that followed, announced a radically fresh line of thought. His religious views, his championing of an authentic inner life lived in preference to outward social conformity, his argument that man in a state of nature is inherently virtuous and moral because political and even cultural institutions are inherently corrupting, his emphasis on individual freedom and equality, his openness to sensation—all this drew him to the attention of philosophers such as Diderot and Voltaire, and ultimately made Rousseau an important figure in the ideological struggles leading up to the French Revolution.

Signature titles

Essays

Discourse on the Sciences and the Arts (Discours sur les sciences et les arts), 1750

Novel

Julie, or the New Eloisa (Julie, ou la Nouvelle Héloïse), 1761

Political works

The Social Contract (Du Contrat social), 1762

Philosophical works

Emile, or On Education (Émile, ou de l'éducation), 1762

Autobiographies

Reveries of the Solitary Walker (Rêveries du promeneur solitaire), 1782

Confessions Part I, 1782

Confessions Part II, 1789

ABOVE: *Portrait of Jean-Jacques Rousseau*, by Maurice Quentin de la Tour (1704–1788).

RIGHT: A page from one of Rousseau's collections of preserved plant specimens.

ABOVE: Eighteenth-century illustrations from Rousseau's *Émile*, by the French School.

"Man is born free, and everywhere he is in chains." Thus begins *The Social Contract*, one of Rousseau's best known works, in which he argued for the close connection between freedom and justice, and for the sovereignty of the collective will. His novel *Émile*, a narrative treatise on education, dramatized Rousseau's philosophical views regarding the individual, nature, and society. Both *The Social Contract* and *Émile* were received as an affront to the religious and political establishment and were burned in Geneva and banned in Paris. Rousseau arguably never recovered from the vehemence of these attacks, which led to periodic homelessness and paranoia.

Rousseau's last book, *Reveries*, engages in self-exploration and self-defense. Structured around ten walks, Rousseau variously argues with those who misunderstood him, celebrates the virtues of solitude, copies music, and studies botany. Unfinished at his death, it nevertheless offers a moving final portrait. **ST**

Baring All

Rousseau regarded his life and writings as interrelated, and is often credited with inventing modern autobiography. In his *Confessions* particularly, he casts the self as irreducibly unique, and yet subject to transformation. With extraordinary sensitivity, he explores not only the events of his life, but his feelings: not only outward circumstances, but their formative effect on his development in childhood, as well as on his adult beliefs and sexual proclivities. With searching honesty, he analyzes and defends his conflicts and liaisons. Rousseau presents his text as the "history of his soul," and in it he bares all.

LAURENCE STERNE

Born: November 24, 1713 (Clonmel, Ireland); died March 18, 1768 (London, England).

Style and genre: Sterne was an English novelist and clergyman, famous for his eccentric, humorous novels, in particular *Tristram Shandy*.

Signature titles

Novels

The Life and Opinions of Tristram Shandy, Gentleman, 1759–1767 (serialized over nine volumes)

A Sentimental Journey through France and Italy, 1768

Raised in Ireland and Yorkshire, and educated at Cambridge for a career in the church, Sterne spent much of his adult life devoted to his rural parish—and, in his last decade, writing witty, eccentric novels. His first published work was a pamphlet, *A Political Romance*, but it was the novel *The Life and Opinions of Tristram Shandy* that made him a celebrity. *Tristram Shandy* received some criticism for its bawdy qualities—certainly, it played fast and loose with narrative conventions—but was overall considered a literary triumph. Despite its biographical pretensions, it had little to say about the "life and opinions" of its titular hero (though much to say about class, sexuality, and family foibles in the eighteenth century), and very little to do with plot and character, those mainstays of narrative fiction. Sterne's self-conscious playfulness—which included inserting two black pages to commemorate the passing of "poor Yorick"—inspired such monumental experimental fictions of the twentieth century as James Joyce's *Ulysses*.

Sterne died in the year *A Sentimental Journey* was published. Intriguingly, its central character and narrator, Parson Yorick, had not only appeared (and died) in *Tristram Shandy*, but also figured as an alter ego for Sterne himself, who had signed letters and published sermons under that name. Sterne's final novel came from a seven-month trip through France and Italy. In spite of the recognizable narrative rubric of a journey, however, the novel is not just digressive but disordered and virtually plotless, offering an ironic and at times ludicrously funny portrayal of the excesses of the cult of sensibility. As Virginia Woolf remarked, his "road" is "often through his own mind, and his chief adventures [are] . . . with the emotions of his own heart." **ST**

"In contrast [to Sterne] all others seem stiff, square, intolerant, and boorishly direct."—Nietzsche

ABOVE: ***Portrait of Laurence Sterne*** **(nineteenth century), by the English School.**

DENIS DIDEROT

Born: October 5, 1713 (Langres, Haute-Marne, Champagne-Ardenne, France); died July 31, 1784 (Paris, France).

Style and genre: Editor and contributor to the *Encyclopédie*, Diderot was a philosopher, writer, freethinker, and a leading figure of the French Enlightenment.

Denis Diderot was one of the great freethinkers of the French Enlightenment whose radical ideas and groundbreaking writing challenged conventional thought across the board. His contribution to Enlightened thought, and to the foundations of modern liberalism was virtually unequaled, but his complexity and vigorous beliefs were also misunderstood or simply rejected during his time. The scope of his writing ranged from plays to novels, and translations and essays covering many topics, but most significantly religion and politics.

He worked as an editor and contributor on the monumental *Encyclopédie, ou dictionnaire raisonné des sciences, des arts et des métiers*, for twenty-five years. **TP**

Signature titles

Nonfiction

Letter About the Blind For the Use of Those Who Are Able to See (Lettre sur les aveugles à l'usage de ceux qui voient), 1749

Encyclopedia, or A Systematic Dictionary of the Sciences, Arts, and Crafts (Encyclopédie, ou dictionnaire raisonné des sciences, des arts et des métiers), 1751–1772

Plays

The Natural Son (Le Fils naturel), 1757

The Father of the Family (Le Père de famille), 1758

Novels

The Indiscreet Jewels (Les Bijoux indiscrets), 1748

Jacques the Fatalist and His Master (Jacques le fataliste et son maître), 1796

The Nun (La Religieuse), 1796

TOBIAS SMOLLETT

Born: Tobias George Smollett, March 19, 1721 (Dalquhurn, West Dumbartonshire, Scotland); died September 17, 1771 (Livorno, Tuscany, Italy).

Style and genre: His novels epitomize the spirit of the Scottish Enlightenment, fluctuating between surreal or grotesque representation and realistic resolution.

Tobias Smollett wrote drama, criticism, satirical vignettes, and travel literature, but he is primarily known for his picaresque novels, *The Adventures of Roderick Random* and *The Adventures of Peregrine Pickle*. Born in Scotland, to a landowning family, Smollett intended on a medical profession, but in 1739 moved to London to embark on a literary career.

Smollett is credited as a progenitor of the modernist novel, many of which feature characters with distinctive dialects that anticipate modern literary characters such as James Joyce's Molly Bloom. His novels also celebrate individualized perspective in a manner that looks forward to Virginia Woolf's experimentation with stream-of-consciousness narration. **SD**

Signature titles

Nonfiction

Travels through France and Italy, 1766

Novels

The Adventures of Roderick Random, 1748

The Adventures of Peregrine Pickle, 1751

The Adventures of Ferdinand Count Fathom, 1753

The Life and Adventures of Sir Launcelot Greaves, 1760

The History and Adventures of an Atom, 1769

The Expedition of Humphry Clinker, 1771

Translations

Don Quixote, 1755

GIACOMO CASANOVA

Born: April 2, 1725 (Venice, Italy); died June 4, 1798 (Dux, Bohemia; now Duchov, Czech Republic).

Style and genre: Writer, diplomat, and essayist, Casanova recounted the mundane and the lascivious with equal aplomb in his salacious, erotic autobiographical writing.

It is much too easy to associate the name of Casanova solely with the stereotype of a man who turned the pursuit of sexual satisfaction into an art form. Known to his contemporaries as "healthy and robust," Casanova's autobiography, *The Story of My Life* (written in French in the hopes of reaching a wider audience), portrays him as a bohemian in search of adventures. His travels satisfied this need but also exposed him to the connected risks of the time. Hence, the initially unknown and impecunious writer ended up spending his nights in guesthouses of ill repute, turning toward theft and violence. Added to this was his sexual desire: so unrestrained, it puts any kind of contemporary erotic literature in the shade. The range of his amorous encounters was eclectic. Once Casanova entered the circle of Venetian aristocracy, using his acquaintance with a local nobleman, his life underwent major changes that brought him, on the whole, brief anguish and eternal fame.

One of the most famous incidents of his reckless life is his arrest by the Venetian authorities. Casanova managed to escape from the famous Piombi di Venezia prison in scarcely believable fashion, relived in the extraordinary scenes of his autobiography with a sense of rhythm and plotting reminiscent of cinematography. In fact, he fits in some mundane endeavors with the more accomplished undertakings of his life, which he turned into what became his most successful book during his lifetime, *I Piombi: The Story of My Escape from the Prisons of the Republic of Venice Called the Leads*. The fact remains that, despite having been exiled from his beloved Venice, his reputation preceded him at every court in Europe, where the writer displayed his wit regarding sexuality, finance, and even medicine. **FF**

"You can learn a lot from inexperienced women."
—*Story of My Life*

Signature titles

Autobiographies

I Piombi: The Story of My Escape from the Prisons of the Republic of Venice Called the Leads (Histoire de ma fuite des prisons de la République de Venise qu'on appelle les Plombs), 1787

The Story of My Life (Histoire de ma vie), published posthumously in 1960

ABOVE: A portrait of Casanova by Anton Raphael Mengs (1728–1779).

GOTTHOLD LESSING

Born: January 22, 1729 (Kamenz, Germany); died February 15, 1781 (Brunswick, Gemany).

Style and genre: His Germany was still a patchwork of independent states, but Lessing was a major figure in the creation of a distinctive German literature.

Considered the first important German playwright, Lessing was the son of a Lutheran pastor. A bright, bookish boy who learned Greek, Latin, and Hebrew at school, he went on to study theology at university in Leipzig, but he was much more interested in literature, the arts, and philosophy. To his family's dismay, he started writing plays, which were produced in Leipzig. In one of them, *Die Juden*, he struck a blow against anti-semitism.

Lessing later lived in several German cities, including Berlin, where he gained a reputation as a brilliant book reviewer and literary critic. A great admirer of Shakespeare, he has been called "the father of German criticism." He also worked as a translator and was employed for a time by Voltaire, until they fell out. Lessing's plays have been described as "bourgeois drama," significantly taking middle-class life and characters seriously instead of focusing on the aristocracy, as was the previous norm. His 1767 play *Minna von Barnhelm* was the first German comedy set in the contemporary German world.

As well as his plays, Lessing wrote about painting and produced philosophical works. He defended the Christian's right to think for himself and, in the Enlightenment spirit of the time, believed in a Christianity of reason rather than clerical dogma. He also believed in tolerance for the world's other principal religions. He earned very little, but in 1770 he was given the post of court librarian to the Duke of Brunswick. It gave him a regular income and meant that he could at last afford to marry. He married a widow named Eva König but, tragically, she and their baby son died within two years. His last years were unhappy and impoverished, and he was buried in a pauper's grave. **RC**

"One can drink too much, but one never drinks enough."

—Preface to *Lieder*

Signature titles

Plays

The Jews (Die Juden), 1749

Minna von Barnhelm, 1767

Emilia Galotti, 1772

Nathan the Wise (Nathan der Weise), 1779

Essay

Laocoon: An Essay on the Limits of Painting and Poetry (Laokoon oder Über die Grenzen der Malerei und Poesie), 1766

Philosophical works

The Education of the Human Race (Die Erziehung des Menschengeschlechts), 1780

ABOVE: A portrait of German writer Gotthold Lessing (c. 1769).

BEAUMARCHAIS

Born: Pierre-Augustin Caron, January 24, 1732 (Paris, France); died May 18, 1799 (Paris, France).

Style and genre: The creator of Figaro was many things besides a playwright—music teacher, inventor, financial dealer, arms supplier, and publisher.

The crafty, scheming, infinitely resourceful manservant who persistently outwits his employer is an archetype who goes far back to the Roman stage, but the supreme example of the genre is Figaro, created in two popular plays by Beaumarchais, on which Rossini and Mozart were to base operas—*The Barber of Seville* and *The Marriage of Figaro*—that have delighted audiences ever since. The plays mocked the upper classes and showed a distinct fellow-feeling for the lower orders.

Pierre-Augustin Caron was the son of a Parisian watchmaker. As a young man, he invented a new escapement mechanism and in 1756 he married the first of his three wives, a rich widow who was one of his father's customers, Madeleine Francquet. She owned the estate of Beaumarchais, which provided her husband with a new and much grander surname. She died not long after they were married. Beaumarchais was a skilled musician and by this time he had gained an appointment as music teacher to Louis XV's daughters.

Through the court, Beaumarchais attracted the attention of a rich financier, who employed him in various dealings connected with the slave trade. Beaumarchais made plenty of money and in the 1770s supplied arms to the Americans to fight for their independence from Britain. He was also sent to England and Austria on secret missions by Louis XV and Louis XVI, and in the 1780s he published the first complete edition of Voltaire's works, in seventy volumes, which cost him a fortune. An object of suspicion during the French Revolution because of his court links, he tried to sell Dutch muskets to the revolutionary armies, but spent time in prison until released through the intervention of a former mistress, and he died comparatively poor. **RC**

"Of all serious things, marriage is the most farcical."

—*The Marriage of Figaro*

Signature titles

Plays

The Barber of Seville (Le Barbier de Séville), 1775

A Day's Follies or the Marriage of Figaro (La Folle journée ou le mariage de Figaro), 1785

ABOVE: A portrait of Beaumarchais by Paul Soyer after Jean-Baptiste Greuze.

RESTIF DE LA BRETONNE

Born: Nicolas-Edme Rétif, October 23, 1734 (Sacy, Yonne, France); died February 2, 1806 (Paris, France).

Style and genre: Restif's themes include peasant life and the underworld in his sexually explicit, often autobiographical novels, as well as in his essays.

His unusual blend of eroticism with high-minded social reforming zeal earned Rétif the nicknames of "the Rousseau of the gutter" and "the chambermaid's Voltaire." He started life with the surname Rétif, born on a farm in the village of Sacy in Burgundy, the eighth of fourteen children and the oldest by his father's second wife. He later added to his name the name of the farm, La Bretonne, to celebrate his peasant roots. Later still he altered the spelling of his surname to Restif so as to imply that stability was the key element of his character. He was someone *"qui est porté à rester, à ne pas avancer"* ("who is inclined to stay, not to move forward").

Restif did not care for the rapidly changing world in which he found himself after he moved to Paris, where he worked as a printer and where, so he said, he had as many women as his tally of books. A compulsive writer with a huge output, he poured out some 250 volumes of stories, plays, improving essays, and utopian fantasies. In *Pornography*, he advocated sexual freedom and state-run brothels. His other works include a huge and explicit sixteen-volume autobiography, *Monsieur Nicolas*. Much of his other work was also based on his own life and often focuses on his nostalgia for the innocence and security of his childhood years in the country with his adored and delightful mother and his loving, if stern father, who was celebrated in *My Father's Life*. His novels took a rosy view of peasant life as a pastoral idyll, contrasted with the restlessness of city life and the corrupting, crime-prone city streets. He also published a large number of essays calling for social reform. Set as they were among the peasant classes and Parisian underworld, Restif's novels did not find favor with highbrow literary critics and readers. **RC**

"I shall dissect ordinary man, as Jean-Jacques Rousseau dissected greatness."

Signature titles

Novels

The Corrupted Peasant (Le Paysan perverti), 1775

My Father's Life (La Vie de mon père), 1779

The Corrupted Peasant Girl (La Paysanne pervertie), 1784

The Parisians (Les Parisennes), 1787

Autobiography

Monsieur Nicolas, 1794–1797

Nonfiction

Pornography, or The Reorganized Prostitution (Le Pornographe ou La prostitution réformée), 1769

ABOVE: A detail from an eighteenth-century French School portrait of Restif.

MARQUIS DE SADE

Born: Donatien Alphonse François de Sade, June 2, 1740 (Paris, France); died December 2, 1814 (Charenton, France).

Style and genre: Sade was a controversial French author of sexual and philosophical works exploring the darkest side of human nature.

The Marquis de Sade was born into an aristocratic family, and his rank and wealth assured him of a privileged future, but he was destined to spend a third of his life in prison. He was imprisoned at the request of his mother-in-law after embarrassing her family with public scandal. Under a *lettre de cachet* (a royal order of arrest and imprisonment) Sade was imprisoned without trial, and without knowing if, or when, he would be released. As such the marquis is, for some, a symbol of the oppression of the *ancien régime* (old regime), who lived an adventurous life dedicated to the pursuit of pleasure.

In prison Sade channeled his energies into writing; in the Bastille he wrote *The 120 Days of Sodom* on 4-inch (10 cm) slips of paper that were pasted together forming a roll that could be easily concealed. When the storming of the Bastille took place in 1789, the incomplete manuscript was lost, but resurfaced a century later. During the French Revolution he was free, and he published *The Crimes of Love* under his own name and *Justine* anonymously. The short stories of *The Crimes of Love* deal with

Signature titles

Short stories

The Crimes of Love (Les Crimes de l'amour), 1800

Plays

Philosophy in the Bedroom (La Philosophie dans le boudoir), 1795

Oxtiern, The Misfortunes of Libertinage (Le Comte Oxtiern ou les effects du liberinage), 1800

Dialogue Between a Priest and a Dying Man (Dialogue entre un prêtre et un moribond), 1926

Novels

Justine, or The Misfortunes of Virtue (Justine ou les infortunes de la vertu), 1791

Juliette, or Vice Amply Rewarded (Histoire de Juliette ou les prospérités du vice), 1797

The 120 Days of Sodom, or the School of Licentiousness (Les 120 journées de Sodome ou l'école du libertinage), 1905

Nonfiction

A Citizen of Paris Addressing the King of France (Adresse d'un citoyen de Paris au roi des Français), 1791

ABOVE: A detail from a colored etching of the Marquis de Sade (*c.* 1830).

RIGHT: *Thérèse* (1748) was one of Sade's favorite erotic books.

LEFT: An engraving by Eustache l'Orsay depicting Sade in a characteristic pose.

the same themes as his novels—vice, atheism, and crime—but have moralistic endings. Nonetheless, the collection represents some of Sade's finest work.

He was arrested on spurious charges in 1793 during the Reign of Terror, and sentenced to death. Yet when the day of his execution arrived, he could not be found, perhaps because of a bureaucratic error or a bribe. The next day Maximilien Robespierre was executed, and the Reign of Terror was over. Sade was freed, but also destitute. He published an expanded version of *Justine* with an accompanying novel about her libertine sister, *Juliette*, which is the fullest account of Sade's libertine philosophy.

In 1801 Sade was betrayed by his publisher, and arrested as the author of obscene works. He was sent to an asylum on the grounds that he was suffering from libertine dementia, where he spent the rest of his life. **IJ**

Charenton Asylum

The asylum at Charenton was a progressive medical institution, where Sade enjoyed relative freedom. His mistress and longtime companion Marie-Constance Quesnet lived with him, pretending to be his daughter. In 1805, under Sade's direction, the asylum opened a theater as part of its therapeutic program. Sade had a lifelong passion for theater; he was a failed playwright whose plays lacked the fire of his novels. The asylum theater was in vogue with Paris intellectuals, with whom Sade mingled and dined. Yet objections to the theater and Sade's involvement grew, and its productions were shut down in 1813.

1700s

PIERRE CHODERLOS DE LACLOS

Born: Pierre-Ambroise-François Choderlos de Laclos, October 18, 1741 (Amiens, France); died September 5, 1803 (Taranto, Puglia, Italy).

Style and genre: Laclos was the author of one of the first psychological novels—one of the most celebrated, banned, and perfect epistolary novels ever written.

At the age of forty, Pierre Choderlos de Laclos was a soldier in the French army, posted to a tedious military outpost in the Bay of Biscay. To pass the time, he set himself to writing a novel set in the heart of Paris society. The novel he produced, *Dangerous Liaisons*, was to become a literary sensation.

In the book, a pair of aristocrats, Vicomte de Valmont and Marquise de Merteuil, searching for a fresh diversion to stimulate their idle, frivolous lives, challenge each other to seduce some innocents newly arrived in Paris society. Written in the form of letters between the main characters, *Dangerous Liaisons* lays open the psychological workings of each character with startling effectiveness, demonstrating the malicious intent of Valmont and Merteuil and the moral turmoil of their victims. The fictional editor who "gathered" the letters claims a didactic, moral purpose to the book, but virtue does not triumph in the end, and indeed one is led rather to admire the cold intelligence of the characters. From its first publication, *Dangerous Liaisons* was considered scandalous, and in 1824 the novel was banned in France for immorality.

Laclos did produce other writings, but nothing to match this gem, the perfect example of an epistolary novel. His *Letter to the Gentlemen of the Académie Française about the Praise for Marshall Vauban* was an outspoken condemnation of the army, and lost him his army commission. He moved into politics in the 1780s, a dangerous move in those turbulent times, and survived the French Revolution by the skin of his teeth. Under Napoleon Bonaparte, he rejoined the army, and rose to the rank of general, seeing action in several campaigns. He died of dysentery and malaria on the way to a posting in Naples in Italy. **CW**

"What you call happiness is nothing but a tumult in the mind. . . ."—*Dangerous Liaisons*

Signature titles

Nonfiction

Letter to the Gentlemen at the Académie Française about the Praise for Marshall Vauban (Lettre à MM. de l'Académie Française sur l'éloge de M. le Maréchal de Vauban), 1786

Essay

Of Women's Education (De l'éducation des femmes), 1783

Novel

Dangerous Liaisons (Les Liaisons dangereuses), 1782

Opera

Ernestine, 1776

ABOVE: A detail from an eighteenth-century pastel portrait of Laclos in uniform.

RIGHT: *Couple Hugging*, by Georges Barbier from *Dangerous Liaisons*.

GEORGE BARBIER
MXMXXX

JOHANN WOLFGANG VON GOETHE

Born: August 28, 1749 (Frankfurt am Main, Germany); died March 22, 1832 (Weimar, Germany).

Style and genre: Goethe's exposition of traditional Germanic language and voice intricately blends intellectual thought with a dramatic story line.

Few writers embody a nation's literary culture as fully as Goethe does for his native Germany. A true polymath who excelled in the fields of poetry, drama, literature, science, philosophy, painting, and politics, his standing as the preeminent writer in the German language is uncontested. A leading figure in the cultural movements *Sturm und Drang* (Storm and Stress) and Weimar classicism that sought to imitate Greek classicism, Goethe's influence spread throughout Europe as the emblematic representative of Romanticism.

Goethe was born into relative privilege, enjoying private tutelage before following his father's wishes to study law in Leipzig. At university, he preferred to attend poetry lessons rather than reciting ancient laws, perfecting his writing style and burning numerous works as unacceptable before beginning the mature comedy *Partners in Guilt*. Ill health precipitated a return to Frankfurt without a degree, and after a lengthy period of convalescence, Goethe relocated to Strasbourg to conclude his studies. It was here that he

Signature titles

Novels

The Sorrows of Young Werther (Die Leiden des jungen Werthers), 1774

Wilhelm Meister's Apprenticeship (Wilhelm Meisters Lehrjahre), 1795–1796

Elective Affinities (Die Wahlverwandtschaften), 1809

Poetry

Roman Elegies (Römische Elegien), 1790

Hermann and Dorothea (Hermann und Dorothea), 1798

Plays

Götz von Berlichingen, 1773

Clavigo, 1774

Partners in Guilt (Die Mitschuldigen), 1787

Egmont, 1788

The Lover's Caprice (Die Laune des Verliebten), 1806

Faust: Part One, 1808

Faust: Part Two, 1832

Nonfiction

Italian Journey (Italienische Reise), 1816–1817

ABOVE: A detail of J. H. W. Tischbein's *Goethe on His Italian Journey* (1788).

RIGHT: *Dorothea's Farewell* by Heinrich Maria von Hess, from *Hermann and Dorothea*.

ABOVE: *The Meeting of Faust and Marguerite* (1860), by French painter James Tissot.

experienced an intellectual awakening after meeting with the literary critic and philosopher Johann Gottfried Herder. He encouraged Goethe to look at language and literature in a scientific manner, exploring notions of national identity, folk songs, and the genius of individuals such as Martin Luther in comparison to those beyond the German borders such as William Shakespeare. Goethe journeyed through Alsace familiarizing himself with the oral tradition of German-speaking villages and the popular roots of his native tongue, deepening his desire to write a Germanic play that would meet Herder's approval. This arrived with his play *Götz von Berlichingen*, the story of a sixteenth-century imperial knight. Its publication was significant in literary history, triggering a resurgence across Europe for drama based on the

"The decline of literature indicates the decline of a nation."

The Omnipresence of Faust in Popular Culture

Few literary works can have inspired or been a constant point of reference for so many creative minds as that of Goethe's *Faust*. Since its publication it has acted as the basis for countless literary, cinematic, artistic, and musical works, and the book's influence still pervades today.

Music

- Radiohead's 2007 album *In Rainbows* contains underlying themes from the Faust legend. In particular, the song "Faust Arp," and closing track "Videotape," which contains the lines: "When Mephistopheles is just beneath / And he's reaching up to grab me."
- During U2's Zooropa tour of the early 1990s, reputedly performed before an audience of more than five million people, lead singer and world statesman Bono introduced the stage persona Mr. MacPhisto—a loose play on words for the character Mephistopheles.

Film

- In the Coen Brothers' 2000 production *O Brother, Where Art Thou?* the character Tommy Johnson makes a brief appearance, insisting he has sold his soul to the devil in exchange for being able to play guitar. Besides *Faust* comparisons, this also mirrors the tale of the pact between the legendary Delta blues singer Robert Johnson when he sold his soul to the devil in order to play.
- *Ghost Rider* is a 2007 film based on the Marvel Comics superhero of the same name. The character Johnny Blaze (Nicolas Cage) inadvertently signs a contract with Mephistopheles (Peter Fonda) to cure his father's cancer and in turn forsakes his soul.

RIGHT: Poster by Jules Massenet for a Paris production of *Werther* in 1893.

history of individual nations as reflected in the works of Sir Walter Scott, Victor Hugo, and Alexandre Dumas.

For Goethe it brought immediate fame, although this was taken to new heights with the release of *The Sorrows of Young Werther*, a novel that captured the imagination of a generation, and intimately associated the author with the Storm and Stress movement. Werther was a young man at odds with the world, unable to express himself and find happiness. His obsessive love for the engaged Lotte, and his failure to overcome the pain of rejection contribute to his violent suicide. Goethe created in Werther the ultimate tortured soul; a creature too sensitive for the harsh environment in which he exists, and destined to be misunderstood. A cult emerged from the novel as hundreds of young people who identified with Werther dressed in the blue coat and yellow trousers of their hero, and in some extreme cases, tragically carried out copycat suicides.

With his star in the ascendancy, Goethe accepted the post of court official and privy councilor to Charles Augustus, the young Duke of Saxe-Weimar-Eisenach in 1776. For ten years he served diligently as the duke's adviser, gaining ennoblement, but the creative gene had been stymied by state duties. It was his friendship with the poet and dramatist Friedrich Schiller that signaled a fresh period of productivity. For Goethe this incorporated *Wilhelm Meister's Apprenticeship*, a novel of self-realization, and the successful *Hermann and Dorothea*, a tale of ordinary Germans, and the effects of the French Revolution.

Goethe's unparalleled masterpiece *Faust*, a tragic play that he had been working on for most of his adult life, finally surfaced in his later years. The first part follows Faust, who in his quest for happiness makes a pact with the Devil in the form of Mephistopheles. This brings him to the brink of moral degradation after a love affair with Margarete results in infanticide and execution. *Faust: Part Two*, cloaked in classical allusion, politics, history, and psychology, witnesses the redemption of Faust through the divine love of Margarete. It is a work of staggering complexity and literary daring, and arguably the pinnacle of German literature. **SG**

THEÂTRE NATIONAL DE L'OPERA COMIQUE
Drame lyrique
d'après
GOETHE
par M.M
Edouard Blau
Paul Milliet
et Georges Hartmann
WERTHER
Musique
de
J. MASSENET
En vente au MENESTREL 2bis Rue Vivienne
HEUGEL & Cie Editeurs pour tous Pays. PARIS
Sté DES IMPies LEMERCIER PARIS

RICHARD BRINSLEY SHERIDAN

Born: October 30, 1751 (Dublin, Ireland); died July 7, 1816 (London, England).

Style and genre: Sheridan was an Irish playwright and radical Whig politician who was famous for popular comedies that feature witty dialogue and caricatured characters.

Richard Brinsley Sheridan was buried in Poets' Corner in Westminster Abbey, London, but it was not as a literary man that he wanted to be remembered. His playwriting career lasted until he was only thirty years old; politics was his first vocation and he was a member of parliament until his death.

Born into a literary family—his father, an actor and theater manager of the Smock Alley Theater, and his mother a novelist and playwright—he learned little of his art from his parents. He spent most of his youth with a nurse. His parents, constantly leaving the country to escape creditors, enrolled him in an English school with the idea that he should learn to "shift for himself." There he met Elizabeth Ann Linely, a singer. He married her against the wishes of his father, who disowned him.

Shifting for himself, Sheridan began playwriting to support his new family. His first play, *The Rivals*, was poorly received, but after he rewrote it, and cast a famous actor in the lead, it was both a commercial and artistic success. Sheridan cemented his reputation with *The Duenna* (about tyrannical fathers and secret marriages), *The School for Scandal* (mocking superficial sentimentality), and *The Critic* (a satire on journalism). Having secured himself financially, Sheridan entered politics as a radical Whig, friends with James Charles Fox and Edmund Burke. Sheridan was as celebrated a speaker as he was a writer, a truly great eighteenth-century orator. Like his speeches—championing radical and revolutionary politics—his plays mock and expose political and social problems through witty dialogue and unique characters. Most famous of all is Miss Malaprop from whom the English language receives the word "malapropism," the unintentional and therefore comedic misuse of words. **SD**

"Certainly nothing is unnatural that is not physically impossible."—*The Critic*

Signature titles

Plays

The Rivals, 1775

The School for Scandal, 1777

The Camp, 1778

The Critic, 1779

Pizarro, 1799

Libretto

The Duenna, 1775

ABOVE: A 1788 pastel portrait of Sheridan by John Russell (1745–1806).

FANNY BURNEY

Born: Frances Burney, later Madame d'Arblay, June 13, 1752 (King's Lynn, England); died January 6, 1840 (London, England).

Style and genre: Burney was an English novelist famous for her perceptive and often comic narratives of women and society in the eighteenth-century.

Over the course of her long and eventful life, Fanny Burney wrote four major novels, eight plays, a biography, and many volumes of journals and letters. Her father, Dr. Charles Burney, was a well-known musician, teacher, and scholar, of whom her final work was a reverential memoir. Although her family found her an unremarkable child, Fanny turned out to be a prolific, if closeted, writer. She wrote her first manuscript novel by the age of ten, then burned it, along with numerous poems and stories, in a futile effort to curb "this writing passion," as she called it in her memoirs.

Since Burney's first writings were composed secretly, it is perhaps not surprising that she published her first novel, the epistolary *Evelina, or The History of a Young Lady's Entrance into the World*, anonymously, and only revealed the truth to her father once the novel had been publicly approved. And well received it was, with some prominent figures (such as Edmund Burke and Joshua Reynolds) claiming to have read it in a night, and reviewers describing it as "one of the most sprightly, entertaining, and agreeable productions of this kind. . . ." Her reputation was thus established, and confirmed by the success of her later works.

Burney's letters and journals, which recount her time as "Second Keeper of the Robes" in Queen Charlotte's court, her marriage to an émigré French aristocrat, and her time living in France, have been of lasting interest to historians. As a novelist, however, Burney was credited more for her influence on such writers as Austen and Edgeworth than for her own achievements. Now, though, her writing is recognized as more subtle and complex than the phrase "cheerful Georgian satirist" might otherwise suggest. **ST**

"It's writ by somebody that knows the highest and lowest of Mankind."—Hester Thrale on *Evelina*

Signature titles

Novels

Evelina, or The History of a Young Lady's Entrance into the World, 1778

Cecilia, or Memoirs of an Heiress, 1782

Camilla, or A Picture of Youth, 1796

The Wanderer, or Female Difficulties, 1814

ABOVE: A detail from an engraving by Evert A. Duyckinck after a painting by E. Burney.

WILLIAM BLAKE

Born: November 28, 1757 (London, England); died August 12, 1827 (London, England).

Style and genre: Poet, writer, and artist whose work is considered visionary, creative, and enlightened, Blake's poems are imbued with mystical, religious, philosophical, and political themes.

Today William Blake is widely recognized as one of the most creative and visionary artistic talents of his time. He was intensely interested in mysticism and Christianity, although was opposed to formalized religion, and brought his penetrating insight and deep beliefs to both his art and his writing. His fascination with the spiritual began in childhood, when at the age of ten he allegedly experienced his first vision, seeing a tree in Peckham Rye, London, filled with angels. Blake claimed that he experienced visions like this throughout his life, and that they inspired the profound spirituality inherent in his written and illustrated works.

He trained for seven years under the engraver James Basire in London as well as studying at the Royal Academy. In 1782 Blake married Catherine Boucher, who went on to assist him with the printing of many of his engravings, and became a stalwart emotional and spiritual support to the artist and writer. The year after his marriage he published his first collection of poems, *Poetical Sketches*, and in 1784 opened a printing shop with his brother Robert. He continued to work on illustrations, and evolved a new type of etching called relief

Signature titles

Poetry

Poetical Sketches, 1783
Songs of Innocence, 1789
The Book of Thel, 1789
The Marriage of Heaven and Hell, 1790–1793
Visions of the Daughters of Albion, 1793
America, a Prophecy, 1793
Europe, a Prophecy, 1794
Songs of Experience, 1794
The First Book of Urizen, 1794
The Book of Los, 1795
The Book of Ahania, 1795
Milton, a Poem, c. 1804–1811
Jerusalem, The Emanation of the Giant Albion, 1804–1820

Poems

"Tiriel," 1789
Poems from the Pickering Manuscript (*c*. 1802–1804)
"The Mental Traveller"
"The Crystal Cabinet"
"Auguries of Innocence"

ABOVE: A detail from an 1807 oil portrait of poet and artist William Blake.

RIGHT: Blake's watercolor, *Newton* (1795), reveals his suspicion of science.

etching that he used for illustrating the majority of his written works including *Songs of Innocence* and *Songs of Experience*. After completion of the latter, Blake published both works together to form a contrasting body of poetry. *Songs of Innocence* celebrates the natural world with a childlike enthusiasm. *Songs of Experience*, written toward the end of the French Revolution, is much darker in tone, and addresses the loss of innocence as an inevitable consequence of adult comprehension and life.

From 1800 Blake worked on *Milton, a Poem*, and part of its preface was turned into the moving hymn *Jerusalem*, and the long and visionary prophetic book *Jerusalem, The Emanation of the Giant Albion*.

Throughout his life Blake was deeply immersed in spirituality and believed strongly in racial and sexual equality, and an encompassing humanity. He utterly rejected formalized religion, some of his comments causing outrage during his day, and instead focused on the power of the imagination; the creative boundaries of his mind were limitless. His work and his perception of the world has been of enormous influence on a succession of writers, artists, and singers. **TP**

ABOVE LEFT: Blake often illustrated his own work, as here, with *Pity* (1795).

ABOVE: Plate 7: *The Lamb*, from *Songs of Innocence and of Experience* (1794).

Blake on Trial

In 1803 Blake had to physically remove a drunken soldier, John Schofield, from his garden in Felpham, West Sussex. Schofield was reportedly causing a disturbance and urinating. Later Schofield alleged that Blake had uttered the words, "Damn the King. The soldiers are all slaves," and brought charges of assault and high treason against the writer. Blake was put on trial at Chichester, but was acquitted due to the lack of substantiated evidence. After his trial he moved back to London, and later included a drawing of Schofield wearing "mind forged manacles" to illustrate a passage in his masterpiece, the prophetic book *Jerusalem*.

MARY WOLLSTONECRAFT

Born: April 27, 1759 (London, England); died September 10, 1797 (London, England).

Style and genre: Mary Wollstonecraft was an English writer and educationalist famous for her outspoken stance on contemporary politics; she is hailed as the first major feminist writer.

The second of seven children in a downwardly mobile farming family, Wollstonecraft grew up resenting the preference automatically extended to her older brother. Clever and vivacious, she began early to study and articulate the inherent injustices of patriarchal society; largely self-taught, she worked as a governess, founded her own school, and published a treatise on the education of girls in 1787. She lived in Paris during the French Revolution, traveled in Scandinavia, and had an ill-fated affair with an American adventurer in Paris, Gilbert Imlay, with whom she had a child. In London, Wollstonecraft moved in a circle connected to the radical publisher Joseph Johnson, including William Blake, the Swiss painter Henry Fuseli, Tom Paine, and William Godwin—whom she would marry in 1797. This alliance was tragically short-lived: Wollstonecraft gave birth to a second daughter, the future Mary Shelley, and died shortly after from complications.

Wollstonecraft's writings have not been entirely overshadowed by her extraordinary life. Both *A Vindication of the Rights of Man* and *A Vindication of the Rights of Woman* brought her widespread fame. The central argument of the latter was dramatized in *Maria*, a novel that explored the fate of one woman "Bastilled" for life by marriage, and another trapped by class and poverty. Wollstonecraft's polemical linking of politics and private life also attracted hostility. In the conservative climate of the later 1790s, she was regarded as scandalously unconventional, a "hyena in a petticoat," a sentiment inadvertently fueled by Godwin's memoir with its unflinching account of her life (including two suicide attempts) and writings. Now, however, she enjoys a secure and well-deserved place in history. **ST**

"Was not the world a vast prison, and women born slaves?"—*Maria*

Signature titles

Philosophical works

A Vindication of the Rights of Man, 1790

A Vindication of the Rights of Woman, 1792

Travel writing

Letters Written During a Short Residence in Sweden, Norway, and Denmark, 1796

Novel

The Wrongs of Woman, or, Maria, 1798

ABOVE: Detail from a c. 1793 portrait of Mary Wollstonecraft by John Keenan.

RIGHT: *Women March on Versailles, 5/6 October 1789*, a French School engraving.

FRIEDRICH SCHILLER

Born: Johann Christoph Friedrich Schiller, November 10, 1759 (Marbach, Germany); died May 9, 1805 (Weimar, Germany).

Style and genre: Schiller was a Romantic dramatist, poet, and philosopher whose writings on aesthetics revived the classicism movement in Germany and abroad.

Friedrich Schiller was the only son among ten daughters. Although his parents wanted him to become a pastor, Schiller chose to study medicine. In addition his love for the works of Rousseau and Goethe inspired him to write his first play, *The Robbers*. It is a dramatic feast, exploring the conflict between two aristocratic brothers, one a rebellious student leader, the other a schemer who contrives to inherit his father's estate. Dealing with physical freedom, political oppression, and the tyranny of social convention, the play was an immediate sensation when it was first performed in 1782 at the National Theatre of Mannheim, but its proto-revolutionary sentiments proved too much for Karl Eugen, the Duke of Württemberg. The play was banned in Stuttgart and Schiller was temporarily arrested and forbidden from writing further plays.

Schiller fled Stuttgart, but not his political vision. His next drama, *Don Carlos*, concerned the relationship between King Phillip II of Spain and his son. Significant for German theater, the play was in blank verse, a medium that thereafter became a signature of German drama. Arriving in Weimar in 1789, Schiller met Goethe and took up a position as professor of history and philosophy in Jena. From 1793 to 1801, after reading the philosophy of Immanuel Kant, he wrote a series of essays in an attempt to define aesthetic activity and its relation to ethical experience. His essays remain influential on modern philosophy and literary criticism. Although his later writings are less overtly concerned with political conditions, Schiller maintained a lifelong interest in the ideals of human freedom in art, philosophy, and history. In 1802, three years before his death, Schiller's name was ennobled; hence, the addition of "von" to his full name. **SD**

"Lose not yourself in a far off time, seize the moment that is thine . . ."

Signature titles

Plays

The Robbers (Die Räuber), 1781

Don Carlos, 1787

The Wallenstein Trilogy (Wallenstein), 1796–1799

Mary Stuart (Maria Stuart), 1800

William Tell (Wilhelm Tell), 1804

Philosophical works

On the Aesthetic Education of Man (Über die ästhetische Erziehung des Menschen), 1795

ABOVE: A detail from a nineteenth-century German School portrait of Friedrich Schiller.

MADAME DE STAËL

Born: Anne Louise Germaine Necker, April 22, 1766 (Paris, France); died July 14, 1817 (Paris, France).

Style and genre: Novelist and intellectual, de Staël was famous for her political commentary, social satire, and minute observations of contemporary life.

1700s

Germaine de Staël, daughter of Louis XVI's famous finance minister, Jacques Necker, and product of the Paris salons of the late eighteenth century, was by all accounts a force to reckon with. An intellectual, political commentator, conversationalist and novelist, she was—alongside Byron, Goethe, and Walter Scott—one of the best-known writers of her own period and exercised remarkable political influence. Indeed, de Staël's novels were a vehicle for her canny political observations and for much of her adult life she lived in exile from Paris, having repeatedly aroused the ire of Napoleon for her critical views.

The publication of *Delphine* in 1802, which she dedicated to "silent France," brought on her first ten years of exile, but the experience of living in different European capitals marked her work with a distinctly internationalist perspective, and she was credited with having developed a new "science of nations." Initially de Staël fled to Germany, where she met leading political and intellectual figures such as Goethe, Schiller, and the Schlegels (August W. Schlegel would become the tutor of her children). *De L'Allemagne*, a work Napoleon had pulped because it was "not at all French," drew from this experience.

De Staël's most influential work, however, lent wit and distinction to another, she claimed, out-of-fashion European nation: Italy. *Corinne* combines guidebook with romance. It sets the story of an ill-fated love affair between Corinne (a semi-autobiographical portrait of a woman of genius with a talent for improvisation) and a traveling Scottish peer against a warm appreciation of the cultural and historical landscapes of Italy. De Staël's exposure of national prejudice extended to a damning portrait of patriarchal privilege, for which *Corinne* has become a feminist classic. **ST**

"Her works are my delight, and so is she herself . . . she ought to have been a man."—Lord Byron

Signature titles

Nonfiction

About Literature (De la littérature), 1800

On Germany (De L'Allemagne), 1810

Novels

Delphine, 1802

Corinne, or Italy (Corinne, ou l'Italie), 1807

ABOVE: A detail from a portrait of de Staël by Anne-Louis Girodet de Roucy-Trioson.

FRANÇOIS CHATEAUBRIAND

Born: François-Auguste-René, Vicomte de Chateaubriand, September 4, 1768 (St.-Malo, France) ; died July 4, 1848 (Paris, France).

Style and genre: Novelist, Christian apologist, and diplomat, Chateaubriand had a powerful influence on French literature from the early 1800s.

Chateaubriand came from a run-down Breton noble family and spent much of his childhood at their country estate with his sister Lucille. He later wrote a novella (*René*) about a brother and sister's incestuous feelings for one another which has been called a thinly veiled piece of autobiography.

The "father of French Romanticism" started the nineteenth-century fashion for tales of star-crossed love and melancholy heroes despondently tortured by vague unsatisfied longings. Away from his writing, he was actively involved in current affairs. He fought on the royalist side in the French Revolution and in the 1790s spent time in the United States and England. Back in Paris under a false name from 1800, he scored a popular success with his novel, *Atala*, about a Christian girl who is sworn to virginity, but falls in love with an American Indian in Louisiana and kills herself in despair.

Chateaubriand also wrote in defence of Christianity, as a reaction against the Enlightenment's attacks on his religion. *The Genius of Christianity* came out at the right moment to attract the approval of Napoleon Bonaparte, who was restoring Roman Catholicism as the French state religion; as a result Chateaubriand was briefly the first secretary at the French embassy in Rome. After the return of the Bourbons in 1814 he was created a viscount and he also began a long affair with a fashionable hostess, Madame Récamier. In the 1820s he was ambassador to Berlin and then to London, minister for foreign affairs and ambassador to Rome. His most lasting work, the autobiography *Mémoires d'outre-tombe*, written for publication after his death, gives an account of French history in his lifetime, his love of women, the beauties of nature, and his tendency to melancolia. **RC**

"The original writer is . . . he who can be imitated by none."

—*The Genius of Christianity*

Signature titles

Novel

Atala, 1801

Novella

René, 1802

Nonfiction

The Genius of Christianity (Le Génie du Christianisme), 1802

Autobiography

Memories from Beyond the Grave (Mémoires d'outre-tombe), 1848–1850

ABOVE: A detail of an 1811 portrait by Anne-Louis Girodet de Roucy-Trioson.

FRIEDRICH HÖLDERLIN

Born: Johann Christian Friedrich Hölderlin, March 20, 1770 (Lauffen am Neckar, Germany); died June 7, 1843 (Tübingen, Germany).

Style and genre: Hölderlin's poetry hauntingly resuscitates the lyrical spirit of ancient Greece—and gives a fascinating example of madness writ large.

Hölderlin's upbringing was marked by the early death of his father. His mother, who was the daughter of a pastor, expected her son to become a pastor as well. Hölderlin studied philosophy and theology as a scholarship student in Tübingen, where he entered into spiritual communion with Hegel and Schelling, who became philosophers of epochal significance. In 1794, Hölderlin went to Jena and met the legendary Goethe. Like many German writers of his day who wanted to avoid a religious career, Hölderlin then embarked on a ten-year stint of insecure jobs, working as a private tutor in the households of well-to-do families.

Most scholars believe that, whatever his mental state had previously been, as of 1806 Hölderlin was completely mad. He was forcibly removed to Tübingen, where he was institutionalized, spending the next thirty-six years in a tower (today endearingly called the Hölderlin Tower) overlooking the River Neckar, until his death in 1843. There he continued to write, choosing to sign his poems as "Scardanelli" instead of his own name. The post-1806 poetry that survived, some of which is now viewed as Hölderlin's most fascinating work, was largely dismissed as insane until the twentieth century.

Prior to Hölderlin's residence in the tower, he published some seventy poems in various journals, as well as a volume of Sophocles translations and the epistolary novel *Hyperion*, a powerful disclosure of the role played by ancient Greece in the construction of the modern German imagination. In the twentieth century, luminaries as diverse as the philosopher Martin Heidegger and the poet John Ashbery cited Hölderlin as a powerful and perplexing influence, securing his singular place in the history of modern poetry. **JK**

"If you have brains and a heart, show only one at a time."

—from "Good Advice" (1797)

Signature titles

Novel

Hyperion, or The Hermit in Greece (Hyperion, oder Der Eremit in Griechenland), 1797–1799

Poetry

Poems of Friedrich Hölderlin (Gedichte von Friedrich Hölderlin), 1826

Translation

Tragedies of Sophocles (Trauerspiele des Sophokles), 1804

ABOVE: A detail from a 1792 pastel portrait of Hölderlin by Franz Karl Hiemer.

WILLIAM WORDSWORTH

Born: April 7, 1770 (Cockermouth, England); died April 23, 1850 (Rydal Mount, England).

Style and genre: Wordsworth was a Romantic poet whose poems of landscape, memory, and the imagination are closely identified with the English Lake District.

Signature titles

Poetry

Lyrical Ballads, 1798, 1800

Poems, in Two Volumes, 1807

The Excursion, 1814

Yarrow Revisited, 1835

The Poems of William Wordsworth, 1849

The Prelude, 1850

Essays

Essays upon Epitaphs, 1810

A Description of the Scenery of the Lakes in the North of England, 1810, 1822

Autobiography

Home at Grasmere, 1960

Wordsworth's early years were happy ones, despite the deaths of his parents and long separations from much loved siblings, particularly his sister Dorothy. His childhood in the Lake District of England left a profound impression, which he analyzed at length in his epic poem on the growth of his mind, "The Prelude." Begun during a long German winter in 1799, and expanded in 1805 to thirteen books (and revised again in 1850 and published within months of his death), this extraordinary poem follows the course of his life up to 1798, covering his time at Cambridge, his walking tour through France and the Alps in 1790, his time spent in London, and a long stay in France in 1791–1792 that stimulated his enthusiastic support for the French Revolution ("Bliss was it in that dawn to be alive, / But to be young was very heaven!")—but neglecting to mention his affair with Annette Vallon at Orleans, which resulted in the birth of a daughter, Caroline. The title was not chosen by Wordsworth, but the poem does offer a fitting "prelude" to the poetic homecoming that marked his return to the Lake District with Dorothy at the end of 1799, and to all

ABOVE: A detail from an 1840 portrait of Wordsworth by Henry William Pickersgill.

RIGHT: *Portrait of William and Mary Wordsworth* (1839), by Margaret Gillies.

that followed: his residence at Dove cottage in Grasmere (now a museum), his marriage to Mary Hutchinson, settled family life, and the "restoration" of his imaginative powers after periods of pain and loss of direction.

ABOVE: *North View of Tintern Abbey* from *Picturesque Illustrations of the River Wye* (1818), by Anthony Fielding.

Early books of "The Prelude" recount his experiences "running wild among the Mountains" and tell of boyish antics—from stealing boats to raiding birds' nests—which, by exposing him to the forms and forces of nature, laid the foundations of his mind, and nourished his developing imagination. Nature left its "impressions," some of which would lie dormant "Until maturer seasons called them forth / To impregnate and to elevate the mind." By the late 1790s, Wordsworth had found what would be his characteristic themes (the "still, sad music of humanity"), and his poetic voice.

"One impulse from a vernal wood / May teach you more of man . . . Than all the sages can."

Coleridge Collaboration

Lyrical Ballads, which belongs to one of the most fertile periods of Wordsworth's life, was in its inception a collaborative project, undertaken with Coleridge to raise funds for their trip to Germany in 1798. The first edition, published anonymously, had Coleridge's "Rime of the Ancient Mariner" as its leading poem, and Wordsworth's "Tintern Abbey" at its close—both poems for which each poet is justly famous.

A second edition in 1800 added a volume of poems principally by Wordsworth (and named him as its author), and included an extended preface—a critical manifesto that defended the project's experimental status, and that became an influential document in the history of literary theory and criticism. The stated aim of the poets was first to "choose incidents and situations from common life, and to relate or describe them … in a selection of language really used by men, and, at the same time, to throw over them a certain coloring of imagination." The preface had much to say about what defined "good" poetry, and included two of Wordsworth's most famous proclamations: that poetry is "the spontaneous overflow of powerful feelings" and that its origin is "emotion recollected in tranquillity."

RIGHT: The printer's copy of "Daffodils," handwritten by Wordsworth's wife, Mary.

In the famous preface to *Lyrical Ballads*, Wordsworth defended his interest in the lives and language of rural communities, arguing that they are instructive of the link between "the essential passions of the heart" and "the beautiful and permanent forms of nature." Wordsworth is thus typically thought of as a nature poet, but his interest in the natural world is far more complex than that suggests. The topographic details of a place are, for him, less important than visionary apprehension, than seeing with the heart and mind so that, in the words of his "Lines Composed a Few Miles Above Tintern Abbey," "... with an eye made quiet by the power / Of harmony, and the deep power of joy, / We see into the life of things." Wordsworth's relaxed and meditative style, developed out of the creative meeting with Samuel Coleridge, has greatly influenced much later English poetry.

Later life and achievements

Wordsworth lived long enough to revise his poetic works, which went through several expanding editions during his lifetime, to temper his early radicalism, and to become poet laureate. Although it was subject to increasing strain from the early 1800s, Wordsworth would maintain that his friendship with Coleridge was one of the most important of his life. At the height of their creative collaboration in the 1790s, Coleridge's assessment of Wordsworth as a potentially great poet, capable of writing "the First Genuine Philosophic Poem," did much to consolidate his sense of poetic vocation. Wordsworth never did write the great philosophical poem Coleridge had in mind: "The Recluse," which had been conceived as a comprehensive poem on man, nature, and society was, Wordsworth finally admitted, beyond his powers to complete. On the other hand, "The Prelude," which Wordsworth referred to as the "poem to Coleridge," and which was to function as a preface or preparation for that great work, is a fitting substitute: a lasting monument to their friendship, and to Wordsworth's achievement as one of the great poets of the English language. **ST**

To the Printer

80

(after the Poem (in the set under the title of "Moods of my own mind") beginning "The Cock is crowing" please to insert the two following properly number'd & number the succeeding accordingly)

~~I wandered like a cloud~~

I wandered lonely as a Cloud
That floats on high o'er Vales and Hills,
When all at once I saw a crowd
A host of dancing Daffodils;
Along the Lake beneath the trees,
Ten thousand dancing in the breeze.

The Waves beside them danced, but they
Outdid the sparkling Waves in glee —
A Poet could not but be gay
In such a laughing company:
I gaz'd — and gaz'd — but little thought
What wealth the shew to me had brought.

For oft when on my couch I lie
In vacant or in pensive mood,
They flash upon that inward eye
Which is the bliss of solitude
And then my heart with pleasure fills,
And dances with the Daffodils.

Who fancied what a pretty sight
This Rock would be if edged around
With living Snowdrops? circlet bright!

WALTER SCOTT

Born: August 15, 1771 (Edinburgh, Scotland); died September 21, 1832 (Abbotsford, Roxburgh, Scotland).

Style and genre: Scott was a Romantic novelist and poet who had a fascination with Scottish history and legend, upon which he based many of his stories.

Signature titles

Poetry

The Lay of the Last Minstrel, 1805

The Lady of the Lake, 1810

Novels

Waverley, 1814

Guy Mannering, 1815

Rob Roy, 1817

Ivanhoe, 1819

A Legend of Montrose, 1819

Kenilworth, 1821

Peveril of the Peak, 1822

Woodstock, 1826

Anne of Geierstein, 1829

Sir Walter Scott was the consummate writer of dashing romantic stories, epitomized by the popular *Ivanhoe* and tales like *Waverley*, based around Scottish history. His dramatic and descriptive works reawakened an interest in the Scottish Highlands among the general public in England and abroad, as well as popularizing the genre of the historical novel.

Scott produced a large number of novels, as well as poetry, and literary criticism, with his prose fiction being particularly popular during his lifetime. For a period following the end of World War I, his work came under attack and was cited as fickle, poorly put together, and lacking in humor, although he has since been lauded as a master of the historical novel. **TamP**

NOVALIS

Born: Friedrich Leopold von Hardenberg, May 2, 1772 (Oberwiederstedt, Germany); died March 25, 1801 (Weißenfels, Germany).

Style and genre: A founder of German Romanticism, Novalis was a multitalented poet, philospher, and mystic, who pioneered freer forms of literary expression.

Signature titles

Poetry

Hymns to the Night (Hymnen an die Nacht), 1800

Nonfiction

Christendom or Europe (Die Christenheit oder Europa), 1799

Fragments

Pollen (Blüthenstaub), 1798

Faith and Love (Glauben und Liebe, oder Der König und die Königin), 1798

Novalis was a protégé of the dramatist and poet Friedrich von Schiller, whom he met while studying at the University of Leipzig. He became one of the most important figures of the early German Romantic movement and his poetry and prose express a mystical sense of the symbolic meaning of life. In 1795, Novalis became engaged to thirteen-year old Sophie von Kühn. Her death two years later from tuberculosis affected him deeply and as a result he produced his most famous work, *Hymns to the Night*, a series of poems in which he longs for death so he can be reunited with his beloved. He continued to write but much of his work was left unfinished when he died, also from tuberculosis, at the age of twenty-eight. **HJ**

SAMUEL TAYLOR COLERIDGE

Born: October 21, 1772 (Ottery St. Mary, Devon, England); died July 25, 1834 (London, England).

Style and genre: Coleridge was an English Romantic poet best known for his supernatural masterpiece "The Rime of the Ancient Mariner."

Coleridge was a brilliant and precocious figure, whose imagination was caught early by the revolutionary spirit of his times. In 1795, in a bid to raise funds for the establishment of a "pantisocratic" commune in Pennsylvania, he could be found lecturing in Bristol on contemporary issues—the slave trade, the war against France—and gaining notoriety as an impassioned public speaker and political radical; it was an image that he spent much of his later life disavowing.

It was during this period that Coleridge met Wordsworth, and though the friendship would later founder, it gave rise to the poems for which Coleridge is best known: "The Rime of the Ancient Mariner" and the richly symbolic "Kubla Khan," allegedly composed during an opium-induced reverie at a remote farmhouse. Coleridge's most lasting innovation, however, was his "conversation" poems, such as "Frost at Midnight" and "This Lime-Tree Bower My Prison." The style of these meditative poems, which follow the spontaneous movements of imaginative thought, was a profound influence on Wordsworth and on much later English poetry.

So various were Coleridge's gifts and pursuits (not just as a poet, literary critic, and religious thinker, but as a journalist, playwright, and philosopher) that his achievements are difficult to summarize. In the long term, it is perhaps ironic that his impact has been greatest in the very area he increasingly abandoned to others, his poetry. The promise of Coleridge's early brilliance was undermined by illness and mounting disappointment—and both were compounded by increasing dependence on opium—but he was always, as his friend Charles Lamb described him in his later life, "an archangel a little damaged." **ST**

"The only man I ever met who corresponded to the idea of a man of genius."—William Hazlitt

Signature titles

Poems

"The Rime of the Ancient Mariner," 1798

"Kubla Khan, or A Vision in a Dream," 1816

"Frost at Midnight," 1798

Autobiography

Biographia Literaria, 1817

Nonfiction

Notebooks, 1794–1834

ABOVE: A detail from an 1804 portrait of Coleridge by James Northcote.

JANE AUSTEN

Born: December 16, 1775 (Steventon, Hampshire, England); died July 18, 1817 (Winchester, England).

Style and genre: Austen is an enduringly popular English novelist whose novels abound with sharp social observations and ironic commentary.

Signature titles

Novels

Sense and Sensibility, 1811
Pride and Prejudice, 1813
Mansfield Park, 1814
Emma, 1815
Persuasion, 1818 (published posthumously)
Northanger Abbey, 1818 (published posthumously)

What little we actually know of Jane Austen's life has had a disproportionate effect on how we read her novels, with their spirited, attractive, and usually impoverished heroines rewarded by happy and successful marriages against the odds. Born into the large family of a clergyman, and raised on the margins of the rural gentry in Hampshire, Austen herself never married and died at a relatively young age. Arguably, the film *Becoming Jane* is just one of the more recent manifestations of a perennial desire to write Austen into her own novels—but it is also a testament to those novels' enduring power.

Offering advice to a budding novelist, Austen suggested that "3 or 4 Families in a Country Village is the very thing to work on." This formula is at the heart of all her novels, which are carefully attuned to the social politics of a small circle, and particularly to the lot of women in an era when patriarchal inheritance practices made marrying well a form of survival. Structured, perhaps inevitably, by the conventions of the courtship plot, Austen's novels nevertheless reveal her extraordinary gift for satire and sharp social commentary.

ABOVE: A portrait of Jane Austen (*c.* 1810) by her sister Cassandra.

RIGHT: An 1894 engraving of the Bingley sisters from *Pride and Prejudice*.

Ostensibly about morals and manners, they also display a winning tendency toward the comic and the irreverent. Austen described her technique self-deprecatingly to her nephew as "the little bit (two inches wide) of ivory, on which I work with so fine a brush, as produces little effect after much labour."

Certainly this meticulous attention to the everyday, which was her great strength, also meant that her novels were narrow in scope, which put her out of step with cultural trends in her own lifetime, and indeed later in the nineteenth century. What Margaret Oliphant referred to as her "fine vein of feminine cynicism" was not what Twain had in mind when he commented, "Every time I read *Pride and Prejudice* I want to dig her up and beat her over the skull with her own shin-bone." In the twentieth century, however, Austen came to the cultural prominence she now enjoys and she has become a formidable English icon. **ST**

ABOVE: An 1806 painting of *The Pump Room in Bath*, by John Claude Nattes.

Kipling's *The Janeites*

In 1924, Rudyard Kipling published his short story *The Janeites*, a tribute to the works and influence of Jane Austen. It appeared in the magazine *The Storyteller*.

It tells the story of British soldiers in World War I, living in their trenches and seeking to escape from the horrors of the war by reading Jane Austen.

Almost all the soldiers are killed in the war—as Kipling's own son had been. The one soldier who survives to tell their story comments, "There's no one to touch Jane where you're in a tight place."

E. T. A. HOFFMANN

Born: Ernst Theodor Wilhelm (changed to Amadeus in 1813) Hoffmann, January 24, 1776 (Kaliningrad, Russia); died June 25, 1822 (Berlin, Germany).

Style and genre: The author of fantastic and grotesque tales, Hoffmann was one of the most important representatives of the German Romantic movement.

1700s

"Councilor of the Court of Justice, excellent in his office, as a poet, as a musician, as a painter, dedicated by his friends." The epitaph to E. T. A. Hoffmann sums up the astonishing life story of this Romantic genius. Today, Hoffmann is best remembered for his fantastic tales, such as *The Sandman*, which became bestsellers in his native Prussia as well as all over Europe.

Hoffmann's first career, in jurisprudence, was interrupted in 1806 when Warsaw, where he was a law officer, was occupied after Napoleon's victory over Prussia. Hoffmann refused to swear allegiance to the new government, deciding instead to follow his artistic vocation. Working first as a music director and later as a dramatist in Bamberg, he also wrote music criticism for a paper in Leipzig, which had already published his novella *Ritter Gluck*.

By the time Napoleon was defeated and Hoffmann reinstated as judiciary official in Berlin, publication of his short story collection *Fantasiestücke* (1814) had already brought him literary fame. *Nachtstücke*, published in 1817 and equally successful, included *The Sandman*, a horror story in which a mentally troubled youth falls in love with an automaton that eventually drives him to suicide. *The Life and Opinions of Tomcat Murr* (1816) is an unflattering parody of Prussian aristocracy and Berlin bourgeoisie. Hoffmann's satires infuriated his superiors on more than one occasion, and only his death in 1822 saved him from disciplinary proceedings over mocking a police commissioner in *Master Flea* (1822), his last novel. Hoffmann's novellas inspired Jacques Offenbachs's opera *The Tales of Hoffmann*. His own opera, *Undine*, successfully premiered in 1814 in Berlin and is considered the first German Romantic opera. **FHG**

"How prone Humanity is to build an artificial roof to prevent it looking up to the sky."

Signature titles

Novels

The Devil's Elixirs (Die Elixiere des Teufels), 1815
Nutcracker and the Mouse King (Nußknacker und Mausekönig), 1816
The Life and Opinions of Tomcat Murr (Lebensansichten des Katers Murr), 1819–1821
Master Flea (Meister Floh), 1822

Short stories

The Chevalier Gluck (Ritter Gluck), 1809
The Golden Pot (Der goldne Topf), 1814
The Sandman (Der Sandmann), 1817
The Entail (Das Majorat), 1817
Doge and Dogaressa (Doge und Dogaressa), 1819
Mademoiselle de Scudéry (Das Fräulein von Scuderi), 1819
Princess Brambilla (Prinzessin Brambilla), 1820

ABOVE: An 1821 engraving of Hoffmann by Johann Passini (1798–1874).

HEINRICH VON KLEIST

Born: Bernd Heinrich Wilhelm von Kleist, October 18, 1777 (Frankfurt an der Oder, Germany); died November 21, 1811 (Berlin-Wannsee, Germany).

Style and genre: Kleist's dramas and novellas crash through love, violence, and illusion with an intensity matched only by his short and peaceless life.

Born into a noble Prussian family, at the age of fifteen Bernd Heinrich von Kleist was already a member of the king's elite guard. A thirst for knowledge and distaste for subordination soon made a military career untenable. A restless traveler and problematic disciple of the Enlightenment, Kleist found broken dreams at every turn. A Rousseauian fantasy of becoming a farmer in Switzerland, in which his wife refused to join, ended his brief marriage. An attempt to walk from Königsberg to Dresden landed him in a Napoleonic jail as a suspected spy. His plays saw little success during his lifetime and the great Goethe simply refused to understand him. Kleist's life concluded in double suicide with his soul mate, Henriette Vogel. **JK**

Signature titles

Plays

The Family Schroffenstein (Die Familie Schroffenstein), 1803

Penthesilea, 1808

Novellas

The Earthquake in Chile (Das Erdbeben in Chili), 1807

The Marquise von O . . . (Die Marquise von O . . .), 1808

Michael Kohlhaas, 1808

The Betrothal in Santo Domingo (Die Verlobung in St. Domingo), 1811

The Duel (Der Zweikampf), 1811

Essay

On the Marionette Theater (Über das Marionettentheater), 1810

STENDHAL

Born: Marie-Henri Beyle, January 23, 1783 (Grenoble, France); died March 23, 1842 (Paris, France).

Style and genre: His bold ideas and ironic hedonism often hide great complexity; he uses a mix of literary devices to probe big questions about life and society.

At the heart of Stendhal's *Le rouge et le noir* is a young man whose philosophical battles reflect the author's own conflicted preoccupations. Stendhal's life mixed politics (an army career) with writing and alternated spells in Italy with time in Paris as a darling of the salons and freethinking wit. Deeply affected by his mother's death when he was seven, the quest for love and happiness became his recurrent literary theme, played out for real in a string of affairs and one major doomed love. His works were admired by his contemporaries and continue to be so. His novels' themes and preoccupations are expressed in a style that throws lyricism, satire, cynicism, hope, and psychological insight into a compelling brew. **AK**

Signature titles

Novels

Armance, 1827

The Scarlet and the Black (Le rouge et le noir), 1830

The Charterhouse of Parma (La Chartreuse de Parme), 1839

Lucien Leuwen (unfinished), 1894

Autobiographies

The Life of Henri Brulard (La vie de Henri Brulard, unfinished*),* 1890

Memoirs of an Egotist (Souvenirs d'egotisme, unfinished*),* 1892

Nonfiction

On Love (De l'amour), 1822

Life of Rossini (La vie de Rossini), 1823

Walks in Rome (Promenades dans Rome), 1829

THOMAS DE QUINCEY

Born: August 15, 1785 (Manchester, England); died December 8, 1859 (Edinburgh, Scotland).

Style and genre: Celebrated author, essayist, and critic, de Quincey is most famous for his description of opium hallucinations in *Confessions of an English Opium Eater.*

Thomas de Quincey's brilliance was apparent from an early age. He was particularly gifted at the classics, speaking and writing Greek fluently by the age of fifteen, and appeared destined for a superb academic career. In 1800, he entered Manchester Grammar School to prepare for a scholarship to Oxford University, but eighteen months later he ran away, and spent the following months destitute. He was reunited with his family, and took up a place at Oxford, where he stayed until around 1807, leaving before earning his degree.

It was during his Oxford years that he first began using opium, initially to combat neuralgia pains, though he would gradually increase the quantities he took throughout his life. He met and was befriended by Samuel Taylor Coleridge in 1807, and through him was introduced to Robert Southey and William Wordsworth. De Quincey moved to the Lake District in 1809, living in Wordsworth's old house Dove Cottage, and stayed there for around ten years. Having depleted his money, he turned to journalism, writing articles and reviews for various periodicals over the next thirty years. In 1822, he published *Confessions of an English Opium Eater,* an autobiographical collection of stories detailing the effects of his addiction. It was an instant success and his most famous work. Following this he continued to write articles, publishing several hundred on a wide range of topics, and from 1853 to his death worked on his collected writings, published together as *Selections Grave and Gay, from the Writings, Published and Unpublished by Thomas de Quincey*.

His writing had a large influence on his contemporaries such as Edgar Allan Poe and Charles Baudelaire, and continues to find a large readership today. **TamP**

"I have struggled against this fascinating enthrallment with a religious zeal. . ."—*Confessions*

Signature titles

Autobiographies

Confessions of an English Opium Eater, 1822

Recollections of the Lake Poets, 1830–1840

Suspiria de Profundis, 1845

Essays

On the Knocking at the Gate in Macbeth, 1823

On Murder Considered as One of the Fine Arts, 1827

Anthologies

Collected Writings, 1889

Uncollected Writings, 1890

ABOVE: A twentieth-century English School lithograph of Thomas de Quincey.

LORD BYRON

Born: George Gordon Byron, January 22, 1788 (London, England); died April 19, 1824 (Messolonghi, Greece).

Style and genre: Legendary Romantic poet and satirist, Byron is almost as famous for his exotic and dramatic lifestyle as for his writing.

Lord Byron composed some of the most famous and influential Romantic works of the nineteenth century. His character and lifestyle matched the literature he produced, his private life comprising a turbulent catalog of affairs, and various allegations ranging from incest to pederasty. Despite, or perhaps because of these scandals, he remains the quintessential embodiment of the Romantic hero and writer.

Byron arrived in Cambridge in 1805 and soon published his first major collection of poems, *Hours of Idleness*. The book was poorly received and he published the satire, *English Bards and Scotch Reviewers*, as revenge against his critics. He embarked on his Grand Tour, traveling through the Mediterranean, and began work on *Childe Harold's Pilgrimage*. The first two cantos were published in 1812 and were an instant success. They were followed by *The Corsair*, which sold approximately 10,000 copies on the first day of publication. During the same period, Byron embarked on a tumultuous affair with Lady Caroline Lamb, then married Anne Isabella Milbanke, who bore his daughter Ada the same year, although the couple separated shortly afterward. By then, details of Byron's private life had tarnished his reputation in polite society. Rumors of a relationship with his half sister and allegations of debt haunted him, and in 1816 he left England, never to return.

He settled in Geneva with Percy Bysshe Shelley, Mary Wollstonecraft Shelley, and Claire Clairmont and wrote *The Prisoner of Chillon* before traveling to Italy where he started work on his epic *Don Juan*. He settled in Genoa until 1823, when he sailed to Greece to help in the fight against the Turks. He died from a fever in 1824 in Messolonghi before seeing any serious military action. **TamP**

"Mad, bad, and dangerous to know."
—Lady Caroline Lamb on Lord Byron

Signature titles

Poetry

English Bards and Scotch Reviewers, 1809
Childe Harold's Pilgrimage, 1812–1818
The Corsair, 1814
Hebrew Melodies, 1815
The Prisoner of Chillon, 1816
Beppo, 1818
Don Juan, 1819–1824 (incomplete)

Play

Manfred, 1817

ABOVE: An 1813 portrait of Byron in Albanian dress, by Thomas Phillips.

JAMES FENIMORE COOPER

Born: September 15, 1789 (Burlington, New Jersey, U.S.); died September 14, 1851 (Cooperstown, New York, U.S.).

Style and genre: Writer of historic romance, sea adventures, and frontier life; Cooper's works were often critical of contemporary social and political trends.

James Fenimore Cooper was one of the first major American novelists, and he enjoyed international success during his lifetime, enjoying praise on both sides of the Atlantic. His richly sweeping historical romances, and in particular his depictions of frontier life and contemporary America, led to him being heralded as America's "national novelist"; and, although fictional, his books still provide an important account of this period in America's history.

Despite his enormously prolific output, today Cooper's fame rests chiefly on one book, *The Last of the Mohicans*, which has

Signature titles

Novels

Precaution, 1820
The Spy, 1821
The Pioneers, 1823
The Last of the Mohicans, 1826
The Prairie, 1827
The Pathfinder, 1840
The Deerslayer, 1841

ABOVE: A detail from an engraving of Cooper by Julien Léopold Boilly.

RIGHT: An 1826 illustration of Cooper's *The Last of the Mohicans*.

gained popularity with successive generations thanks to several big-screen adaptations. *The Last of the Mohicans* was one of five books that formed the Longstocking Series, which featured a pioneering frontiersman character called Natty Bumppo. With his rugged individualism and bravery, Bumppo epitomized the adventurous spirit of the times and quickly became a hero to the public. Through these books, Cooper cleverly created a romanticized, historically inaccurate picture of relations between the Native American tribes and the white settlers, which was nevertheless very popular and palatable to his audience, both in America and overseas.

For all his literary success, Cooper came upon a career in writing by chance. Allegedly when he was reading a book out loud to his wife, he threw it to one side announcing that, "I could write you a better book than that myself," whereupon his wife urged him to do so. His first novel, *Precaution*, was well received and clearly reflected the influence of the historical romances of Sir Walter Scott, Amelia Opie, and Jane Austen. His second work, *The Spy*, based on the American Revolution, was an instant success. It was quickly followed by *The Pioneers*, the first of his Longstocking Series. Cooper continued to write prolifically, frequently placing his stories within the context of American history and addressing themes such as the various challenges of frontier life and conflict over lands, the displacement of the Native Americans by white settlers, and the experiences of British Loyalists during the American Revolution.

During the 1820s, and at the height of his fame, Cooper traveled to Europe with his family, staying there for seven years. During this period he wrote *Notions of the Americans* (1829) and worked on four travel books. He returned to America in 1833 and the following year published *A Letter to His Countrymen*, in which he criticized American provincialism. These works, compounded by a number of lawsuits he successfully brought against journalists, affected Cooper's popularity, but despite this, his work was widely appreciated and he remains one of America's great authors. **TamP**

ABOVE: A 1925 Scribner's edition of *The Deerslayer*, illustrated by N. C. Wyeth.

Unpopular American

Despite the popularity of his books, Cooper's work was not immune to criticism, with his critics led by Mark Twain, who wrote the scathing essay *Fenimore Cooper's Literary Offenses*, in 1895. Cooper's over-romanticizing, lack of credible and rounded female characters, and didacticism over his personal, social, and political views were the main target for his detractors. Certainly, over the years Cooper's acerbic comments regarding American politics and the perceived crisis in American democracy, detailed in his final social and political critique, *The American Democrat* (1838), made him unpopular in some circles. However, his position as America's first true literary giant was never usurped, and his popularity continued unabated despite the attacks from his critics.

FRANZ GRILLPARZER

Born: January 15, 1791 (Vienna, Austria); died January 21, 1872 (Vienna, Austria).

Style and genre: Regarded as Austria's finest playwright, Grillparzer also wrote lyrical poetry and prose. His themes include the classical world, medieval history, and a deeply held belief in individualism.

Franz Grillparzer is one of Austria's finest writers. Although best known as a playwright, he also wrote lyrical poetry, prose, and a novella. He used a variety of settings for his drama, including Greek antiquity and the medieval period, but he always related them to the age in which he lived.

Grillparzer wrote his first play while still a student but it was *The Ancestress*, a fate-tragedy first performed in 1817, that brought him fame. His next drama, *Sappho*, inspired by ancient Greece, further enhanced his reputation and was translated into a number of different languages. Grillparzer used more stories from ancient Greece in his 1822 trilogy *The Golden Fleece*, which comprises *The Guest-Friend*, *The Argonauts*, and *Medea*, and is based on the stories of Jason and Medea.

Turning to a different period from history for inspiration, Grillparzer produced a series of historic tragedies, including *King Ottokar, His Rise and Fall,* which was completed in 1823 but due to censorship problems was not able to be performed (or published) until 1825. The problems the Austrian court's censorship created caused him to fall into a depression, further compounded by the failure of his relationship with his fiancée Katharine Fröhlich. Despite Grillparzer's state of mind, he went on to produce his two finest works: *The Waves of Love and the Sea* and *A Dream is Life*. Continuing with his theme of tragedy, *The Waves of Love and the Sea* retells the love story of Hero and Leander; it is regarded as the finest German-language love tragedy ever written.

Subsequently Grillparzer turned his hand to comedy and wrote *Woe to Him Who Lies*; its poor reception caused him never to publish another play, although three finished plays were found among his papers after his death. **HJ**

Signature titles

Plays

The Ancestress (Die Ahnfrau), 1817
Sappho, 1818
The Golden Fleece Trilogy (Das Goldene Vlies), 1821
The Guest-Friend (Der Gastfreund)
The Argonauts (Die Argonauten)
Medea
King Ottokar, His Rise and Fall (König Ottokars Glück und Ende), 1825
The Waves of Love and the Sea (Des Meeres und der Liebe Wellen), 1831
A Dream is Life (Der Traum ein Leben), 1834
Woe to Him Who Lies (Weh dem, der lügt), 1838

"When . . . a mob pours inside . . . it is the poet's task to turn it into an audience."—"Audience" from *Poems*

ABOVE: A detail from an 1820 portrait print of Franz Grillparzer.

PERCY BYSSHE SHELLEY

Born: August 4, 1792 (Horsham, West Sussex, England); died July 8, 1822 (at sea near Livorno, Italy).

Style and genre: Shelley was the *enfant terrible* of the British Romantic movement. He lived a turbulent life but produced lyrically brilliant, intellectually rigorous poetry.

Percy Shelley was born into the English establishment but spent his short life rebelling against it. After he was expelled from Oxford in 1811 for publishing an atheist pamphlet, he eloped with the sixteen-year-old Harriet Westbrook and turned his back on his inheritance. His domestic arrangements were always improvised and never stable—in 1814, he abandoned Harriet for Mary Godwin, who would later become his second wife. Shelley was briefly active in radical politics and remained committed to it throughout his life.

In 1818, Shelley ran away from both his creditors and a hostile intellectual climate when he moved to Italy. He had met Byron in 1816, and they now became the most influential figures in the nomadic coterie of exiles who had fled Britain and chosen Italy as their home; Shelley's *Julian and Maddalo* details their complex relationship. Both Percy and Mary Shelley suffered from extended periods of depression, exacerbated by the deaths of their son and daughter. Nonetheless, Shelley's artistic production during these years was intense, and he wrote a series of great poetical works that balance his philosophical and political idealism with his personal despondency.

Shelley has been justly celebrated for gem-like lyrics such as "To a Skylark" and "Ode to the West Wind." His posthumously published poetic manifesto, *A Defence of Poetry*, declares his belief that poets are "the unacknowledged legislators of the world"; much of his own verse could not find an audience during his lifetime, but it strongly advocates the power of song to bring felicitous order to the world. His own life was tempestuous and disordered; how apt it was that when he drowned, it was in the boat he had renamed *Ariel* after the mischievous sprite in Shakespeare's *The Tempest*. **TM**

"Poets are the unacknowledged legislators of the world."

—*A Defence of Poetry*

Signature titles

Poems

"Queen Mab," 1813
"Mont Blanc," 1816
"Ozymandias," 1818
"The Revolt of Islam," 1818
"To a Skylark," 1820
"Ode to the West Wind," 1820
"Adonais," 1821
"Epipsychidion," 1821
"Julian and Maddalo," 1824
"The Triumph of Life," 1824
"The Mask of Anarchy," 1832

Play

Prometheus Unbound, 1820

Essay

A Defence of Poetry, 1840

ABOVE: A detail from *Portrait of Percy Bysshe Shelley* (1819), by Amelia Curran.

1700s

JOHN CLARE

Born: July 13, 1793 (Helpstone, Northamptonshire, England); died May 20, 1864 (Northampton, England).

Style and genre: Clare was a rural English poet whose humble origins and descent into madness overshadowed his artistic achievement.

The most authentic of the "peasant poets" who became popular in the 1820s, John Clare came from genuinely humble beginnings. Born in rural Northamptonshire, the son of an agricultural laborer, Clare had little formal schooling and was helping with his father's work from the age of seven. He was a voracious and indiscriminate reader and began writing poems at the age of thirteen, attempting to publish a volume while working as a gardener in 1817.

Although he failed to gain any subscriptions, Clare attracted the attention of Keats's publishers, who produced *Poems Descriptive of Rural Life and Scenery* in 1820. It was extremely successful, enabling Clare to marry. He then published *The Village Minstrel and Other Poems*; this was much less successful and forced him to return to laboring in order to support his increasingly large family. The difficulty of his circumstances is evident in the time it took to prepare his next collection. The *Shepherd's Calendar* was a commercial and critical disaster, principally because of Clare's vain attempts to write what he thought his publishers and public wanted rather than what he wished to write. Clare had long trod a fine psychological line, and the stress of this failure took its toll; in 1837, Clare was committed to an Essex asylum, two years after his final publication, *The Rural Muse*. Although seemingly happy in the asylum, Clare absconded and was recommitted five months later, this time to an institution in Northampton. He spent the rest of his life there, occasionally writing, but more often suffering delusions. His poems, largely ignored in his life, underwent a critical reevaluation in the twentieth century, and are now seen as some of the finest evocations of landscape and rural life ever written. **PS**

Signature titles

Poetry

Poems Descriptive of Rural Life and Scenery, 1820

The Village Minstrel and Other Poems, 1821

The Shepherds Calendar with Village Stories and Other Poems, 1827

The Rural Muse, 1835

Letters

The Letters of John Clare, 1951

"I long for scenes where man has never trod . . . where woman never smiled or wept."

ABOVE: A detail from an engraving of English poet John Clare.

RIGHT: John Constable's *The Lock* depicts rural life in paint the way Clare did in verse.

JOHN KEATS

Born: October 31, 1795 (London, England); died February 23, 1821 (Rome, Italy).

Style and genre: Keats was an English Romantic poet whose rich verse sought to capture "the truth of the imagination"; a contemporary of Lord Byron and Percy Bysshe Shelley, Keats wrote with passion and fervor of beauty and nature.

Keats's short life was dominated by financial insecurity, but in spite of this he abandoned a promising career in medicine, after several years of training, to dedicate himself to poetry. Keats's life was also dominated by family tragedy: his father died when the young Keats was only eight and tuberculosis killed his mother, his brother, and finally Keats himself (at the age of twenty-five), just when his star was rising.

In the last months of his life, Keats traveled to Italy in a last-ditch effort to relieve his tubercular symptoms, leaving behind his fiancée Fanny Brawne, and knowing he would not return. The brevity and intensity of his literary career has no doubt contributed to the popular view of Keats as the quintessential Romantic poet, who yearned for a life of sensation and imaginative transcendence.

From his early sonnets to his unfinished "Hyperion" poems, Keats's work was always more intellectually rigorous than that characterization suggests. In the nineteenth century, Keats's poetry, especially "La Belle Dame sans Merci" and "Isabella, or

Signature titles

Poetry

Poems, 1817

Endymion, 1818

Lamia, Isabella, The Eve of St. Agnes, and other Poems, 1820

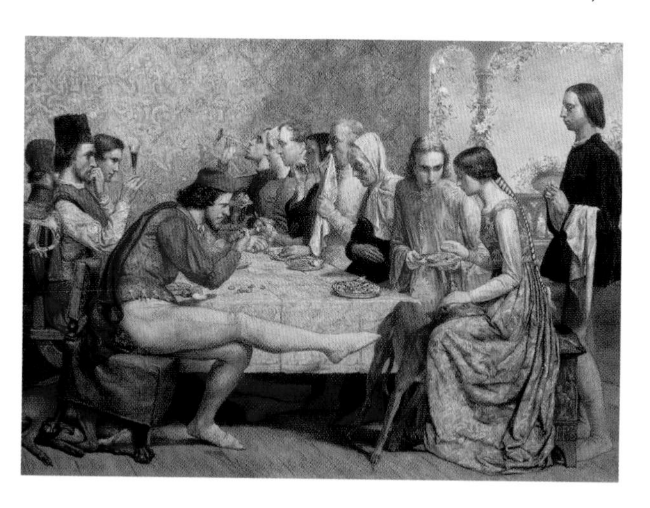

ABOVE: A miniature of Keats painted by his friend Joseph Severn in 1819.

RIGHT: John Everett Millais's *Isabella* (1848–1849), based on Keats's 1818 poem.

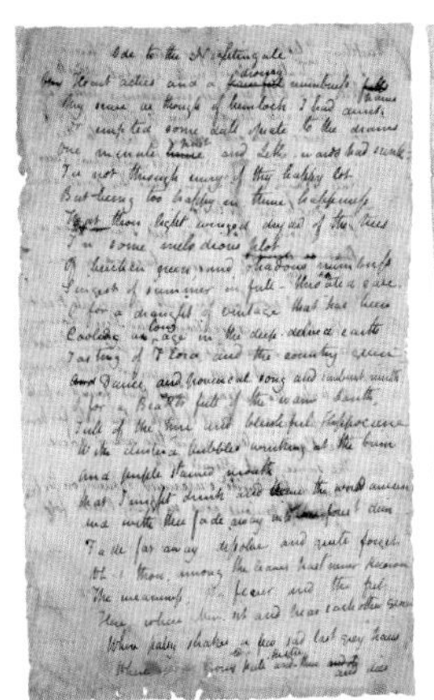
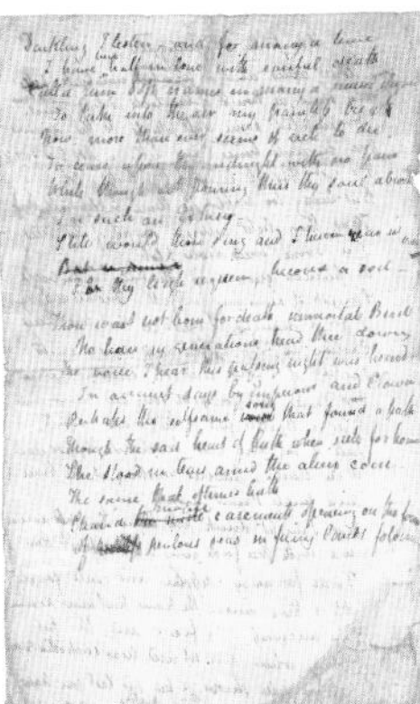
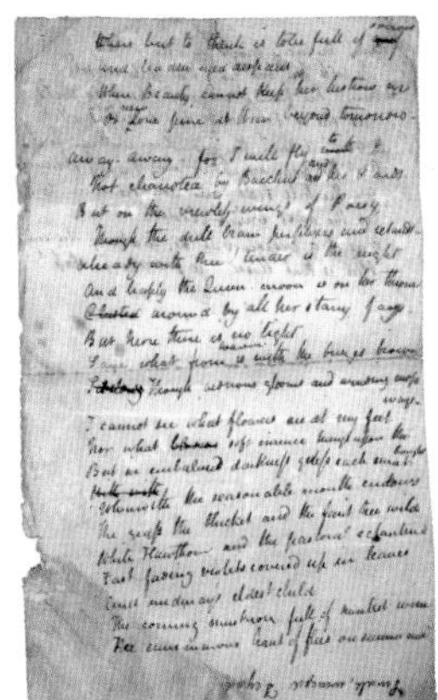
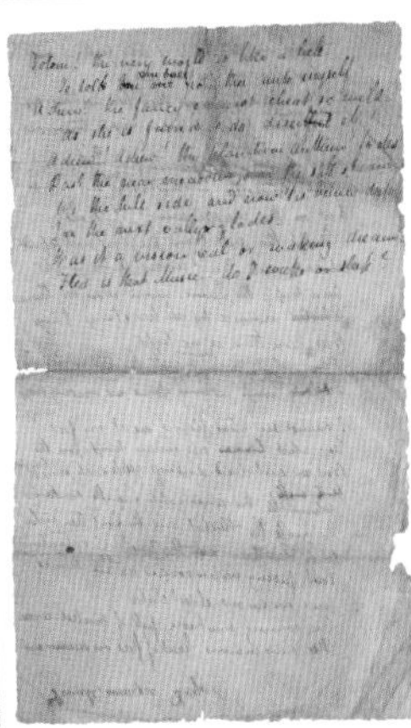

the Pot of Basil," greatly influenced several groups of artists, including the Pre-Raphaelite Brotherhood and the Symbolists. In the twentieth century, Keats's odes remained a huge influence on writers and critics. The enigmatic closing lines of his "Ode on a Grecian Urn": "Beauty is truth, truth beauty,—that is all / Ye know on earth, and all ye need to know" are some of the most discussed—and argued over—in English poetry.

Keats was a lively, intelligent, and deeply sympathetic figure who forged connections easily with other writers and influential cultural figures, such as Leigh Hunt. He met Hazlitt, Wordsworth, and Shelley. He was remembered by his friend John Hamilton Reynolds as having "the greatest power of poetry in him, of anyone since Shakespeare."

In spite of growing recognition of his talent, his first published volumes of poetry, *Poems* and *Endymion*, attracted derision, much of it directed at his humble origins, his "Upstart" pretensions, and his "Cockney rhymes." Shelley made much of this crushing attack in his elegiac poem to Keats, "Adonais," noting that "where cankerworms abound," it was no wonder if the "young flower" of Keats's genius was "blighted in the bud." But Keats himself managed to dismiss it as "the mere matter of the moment—I think I shall be among the English poets after my death." How right he was. **ST**

ABOVE: A manuscript of Keats's "Ode to a Nightingale" (1819).

Man of Letters

Keats's letters are, as much as his poems, fine expressions of his unique critical intelligence. They contain a wealth of information about his views on poetry, including his famous definition of "negative capability," that quality possessed by "men of achievement," and a number of suggestive axioms: "I think Poetry should surprise by a fine excess and not by Singularity—it should strike the Reader as a wording of his own highest thoughts, and appear almost a remembrance. . . ." Indeed, he concludes, "if poetry comes not as naturally as the Leaves to a tree it had better not come at all."

1700s

MARY WOLLSTONECRAFT SHELLEY

Born: Mary Wollstonecraft Godwin, August 30, 1797 (London, England); died February 1, 1851 (London, England).

Style and genre: Daughter of literary lions Mary Wollstonecraft and William Godwin, Percy Bysshe Shelley's wife virtually invented science fiction with *Frankenstein*.

Mary Shelley outlived her better-known husband, the poet Percy Bysshe Shelley, by nearly thirty years, during which time she preserved his legacy and raised his son, despite opposition from his family, by writing silver-spoon novels. Although her literary output between 1822 and 1851 was considerable, she remains known largely for *Frankenstein, or The Modern Prometheus*, which numbers among the rare literary works whose characters have passed into popular culture.

While Hammer horror films perpetuated the fame of Dr. Frankenstein, his monster, and the monster's extra-literary bride, attention has turned to Shelley's other work. She has been reinstated within her literary milieux: not just the famous storytelling session at the Villa Diodati on Lake Geneva that also produced John Polidori's novel *The Vampyre*, but also the radical household of her parents, the social reformers and writers Mary Wollstonecraft and William Godwin.

Wollstonecraft died in childbirth, but her feminist legacy can be seen in her daughter's novels, which focus on the thorny question of what constitutes humanity within the Gothic style of the time. Shelley miscarried several times, and a number of her children died in infancy. Her experiences as a mother come through in *Maurice, or The Fisher's Cot*, an unpublished novella that, like *Frankenstein*, considers the dangers of reproduction.

Godwin's legacy can be felt in the monster's desire for education, and in the political debates of Shelley's apocalyptic novel *The Last Man*, in which a thinly disguised Lord Byron rules an epidemic-swept Britain. The novel is framed by a visit to the Sibyl's Cave, where the story is found on blowing leaves. Shelley's work is similarly prophetic and similarly neglected. **SM**

Signature titles

Novels

Frankenstein, or The Modern Prometheus, 1818

The Last Man, 1826

Children's story

Maurice, or The Fisher's Cot, 1998

Nonfiction

Mary Shelley's Journal, 1947

"I present the public with my latest discoveries in the slight Sibylline pages."—*The Last Man*

ABOVE: A detail from an 1818 portrait of Gothic novelist Mary Shelley.

RIGHT: An illustration from Shelley's *Frankenstein* by Theodor M. von Holst.

HEINRICH HEINE

Born: Christian Johann Heinrich Heine, December 13, 1797 (Düsseldorf, Germany); died February 17, 1856 (Paris, France).

Style and genre: Heine was a Jewish-German Romantic poet and political journalist who combined a devastating wit with unmatched lyrical versatility.

No German writer has endured the tension between art and politics with the same searing wit and tragic lightheartedness as Heinrich Heine. Born "Harry" into a Jewish-German family in 1797, the young poet was heir to an aesthetic and nostalgic Romanticism he found to be politically vapid. Heine's appropriation of Romanticism restored political currency to the movement by turning it inside out, while pushing it to cartoonish limits from which it never recovered. His lyric poems, many of which were set to music by Robert Schumann and others, inspired Friedrich Nietzsche to call him the first artist of the German language.

After achieving little success in commerce, Heine earned a law degree in 1825. He converted to Lutheranism in an attempt to circumvent the institutional exclusion of Jews in Germany, but his outsider status continued to crucially inform his literary innovations. As a poet, he desanctified literary German by infusing it with everyday language, and as a journalist he turned the feuilleton—scorned by the literary establishment of his day—into a politically charged form of art. Under the pressure of increasingly harsh German press laws, Heine went into exile in Paris following the July Revolution in 1831. Four years later, his works, along with those of other members of the Young Germany movement, were banned outright in Prussia and Austria, but the authorities' frantic attempts at suppression did little to keep Heine's voice from reaching revolutionary activists across Restoration Europe. As his Hungarian admirer, Karl-Maria Kertbeny, wrote to him in 1849, "You yourself will perish with Europe, but the noble, healthy youth will carry you with it to the new world, where you are to stand in the niche of the house-gods." **JK**

"Whether my poems are praised or criticized is of little concern to me."

Signature titles

Poetry

Book of Songs (Buch der Lieder), 1827

Germany: A Winter's Tale (Deutschland: Ein Wintermärchen), 1844

New Poems (Neue Gedichte), 1844

Atta Troll: A Summer Night's Dream (Atta Troll. Ein Sommernachtstraum), 1847

Nonfiction

The Harz Journey (Die Harzreise), 1826

Travel Images (Reisebilder), 1826–1831

French Conditions (Französische Zustände), 1832

The Romantic School (Die romantische Schule), 1836

Shakespeare's Girls and Women (Shakespeares Mädchen und Frauen), 1838

ABOVE: *Portrait of Heinrich Heine* (1831), by Moritz Daniel Oppenheim (1800–1882).

ALEKSANDR PUSHKIN

Born: June 6, 1799 (Moscow, Russia); died February 10, 1837 (St. Petersburg, Russia).

Style and genre: Pushkin's writing is beautifully lyrical with detailed (and often romantic) plots and politically astute themes, enlivened with much dramatic tension.

Aleksandr Pushkin's life was one of contrasts. Almost as soon as he published his first poem, he was lionized as a literary genius, yet he would always be despised by some for his skin color—his great-grandfather was an African slave who had become the favorite of Peter the Great and raised to the aristocracy.

Pushkin was always controversial. His "Ode to Liberty," written when he was twenty, so alarmed Tsar Alexander I that Pushkin found himself in enforced exile—although it was shrouded in the guise of an administrative post—far from Moscow. His political writings were so powerful that in the Decembrist Uprising of 1825, the rebels carried copies of his work. Pushkin was not part of the movement and panicked afterward, destroying his papers for fear he would be accused.

The poet's love life was filled with scandal, with rumors of affairs with married women. In 1831, he married the beautiful and flirtatious Natalia Goncharova, with whom he had four children. They always lived beyond their means, trying to keep up the facade of a wealthy lifestyle, while earning very little. In 1834, they met the soldier George d'Anthès who was envious of Pushkin and adoring of Natalia. He goaded Pushkin, claiming publicly that he had slept with Natalia (for which there was no proof). After two years of provocation, the poet challenged the soldier to a duel in which Pushkin was killed, at the age of thirty-seven. Ironically, the plot of his most acclaimed work, *Eugene Onegin*, hinges on a duel between rival lovers. After his death, the Russian people went into mourning and the authorities panicked, wanting to suppress the outpouring of emotion and the possible resurgence of rebellion. Pushkin was not honored publicly as a great literary figure for another three decades. **LH**

"Make plans to live. Look, all is dust, and we shall die."

—"Tis Time, My Friend"

Signature titles

Poetry

Ruslan and Ludmilla, 1820

Ode to Liberty, 1820

The Gypsies, 1824

Eugene Onegin, 1825–1832

The Bronze Horseman, 1833

Plays

Boris Godunov, 1831

Mozart and Salieri, 1830

Novel

The Moor of Peter the Great (unfinished), 1827

ABOVE: A detail of A. P. Yelagina's copy of V. A. Tropinin's original portrait of Pushkin.

HONORÉ DE BALZAC

Born: May 20, 1799 (Tours, Loire Valley, France); died August 18, 1850 (Paris, France).

Style and genre: One of the founders of realism in literature, Balzac was a leading novelist and playwright of the nineteenth century; an observer of humanity without idealism.

Honoré de Balzac was one of the founding fathers of realism in literature. He wrote prolifically throughout his life publishing some works under pseudonyms, such as the outrageous *The Vicar of the Ardennes* (under the name Horace de Saint-Aubin), which featured a married priest and alluded to incest, and other works anonymously. However the main body of his work, *The Human Comedy* (*La Comédie humaine)*, was published under his own name, and represents one of the most complicated and astonishing feats of realist writing. *The Human Comedy* comprises almost one hundred novels that paint in vivid, gritty detail urban and provincial French life following the fall of Napoleon Bonaparte. The works broach universal themes such as love, politics, and social conventions, with the same characters reappearing in many of the books.

Following a troubled early life Balzac entered the law offices of a family friend for three years before becoming disillusioned and deciding to be a writer. His first, though uncompleted, work was the comic opera *Le Corsaire* followed in 1820 by the tragedy *Cromwell*. It was not until 1832, and after writing several novels, that the author conceived the idea for *The Human Comedy*, and the following year published *Eugénie Grandet*, which became his first best-selling novel, and then the successful *Old Goriot* (or *Father Goriot*) in 1835.

Balzac worked voraciously until his death, with his tone evolving through his oeuvre from bleak despondency toward greater positivity, although his observation of humanity remained firmly rooted in realism. His work was of profound influence on the development of literature, affecting writers such as Gustave Flaubert, Marcel Proust, Emile Zola, Charles Dickens, and Henry James. **TamP**

"He will shine . . . among the brightest stars of his native land."

—Victor Hugo on Balzac

Signature titles

Novels

The Vicar of the Ardennes/The Vicar's Passion (Le Vicaire des Ardennes), 1822

The Human Comedy (La Comédie humaine)

The Wild Ass's Skin (La peau de chagrin), 1831

Eugénie Grandet, 1833

Old Goriot (Le Père Goriot), 1835

The Splendors and Miseries of Courtesans (Splendeurs et Misères des courtisanes), 1838–1847

ABOVE: *Honoré de Balzac in His Monk's Habit*, an 1829 painting by Louis Boulanger.

ALEXANDRE DUMAS

Born: Dumas Davy de la Pailleterie, July 24, 1802 (Villers-Cotterêts, Aisne, France); died December 5, 1870 (Puys, Dieppe, Seine-Maritime, France).

Style and genre: Dumas was a writer whose serial novels reinvigorated the French historical romance with their gripping tales of chivalry and derring-do.

Alexandre Dumas remains one of the most popular French authors, with many of his historical novels turned into blockbuster movies. He was one of the first authors to exploit the serial novel, although he was helped by the lifting of press censorship in the 1830s that saw a sudden increase in the circulation of periodicals, and a public demand for exciting adventure stories. Dumas virtually single-handedly revitalized the French historical novel, blending fact and fiction in works that appealed to a wide audience.

One of his first successful works was the play *Henry III and His Court*, and Dumas went on to write a number of plays in addition to his prolific output of novels and articles. In 1838 he rewrote one of his plays to create his first serial novel, *Captain Paul*, and based on its success, he established a production company with a large staff who produced many stories under his supervision. He continued to use collaborators when working on his novels, most famously Auguste Maquet, who, although uncredited on the title pages, outlined the serials and worked on the plots of *The Three Musketeers* and *The Count of Monte Cristo* while Dumas provided the detailing and dialogue.

Dumas managed to spend his fortune several times over because of his lavish, indulgent lifestyle, and multiple affairs. Because of his credit problems and unpopularity with Napoleon III, he fled to Brussels in 1851, then traveled to Russia, and finally Italy. Seeking adventure, he joined the fight for a united Italy and set up the *Indipendente* newspaper. He later spent four years in Naples as keeper of the museums, and only returned to France in 1864 where he continued to work and spend more than he earned. **TamP**

"All human wisdom is summed up in . . . two words, 'Wait' and 'Hope.'"—*The Count of Monte Cristo*

ABOVE: A portrait of Dumas (*c.* 1825–1830) attributed to Eugène Delacroix.

Signature titles

Novels

Captain Paul (Le Capitaine Paul), 1838

The Three Musketeers (Les Trois mousquetaires), 1844

The Count of Monte Cristo (Le Comte de Monte-Cristo), 1845–1846

The Vicomte de Bragelonne (Le Vicomte de Bragelonne, ou Dix ans plus tard), 1847

The Black Tulip (La Tulipe noire), 1850

Plays

Henry III and His Court (Henri III et sa cour), 1829

Antony, 1831

Nonfiction

Celebrated Crimes (Les Crimes célèbres), 1839–1840

VICTOR HUGO

Born: Victor-Marie Hugo, February 26, 1802 (Besançon, France); died May 22, 1885 (Paris, France).

Style and genre: Hugo's acute social conscience and progressive interpretation of traditional literary values was a reflection of the political climate in which he wrote.

Revered in France as a poet, but remembered abroad for his novels—chiefly *The Hunchback of Notre-Dame (Notre-Dame de Paris)* and *Les Misérables*—Hugo was the leading figure of French romanticism. A law graduate, he was influenced by the work of François-René de Chateaubriand whom he sought to emulate. At twenty-one he published his first novel, *Hans of Iceland*, attracting the attention of the journalist Charles Nodier who introduced him to a close literary circle of romantics. He produced a series of important poems and plays including the never-staged verse drama *Cromwell* that contained a long, provocative preface urging artists to abandon the formal rules of classic tragedy, fiercely dividing opinion among the intelligentsia. As a statement on the principles of romanticism it has remained more important than the play.

The success of his next play *Hernani* set a fresh course for French literature, and wider fame arrived for Hugo with his *The Hunchback of Notre-Dame*. It tells the story of the corrupt archdeacon Claude Frollo, who is thwarted in his attempts to kidnap the gypsy girl La Esmerelda by the hunchback bell ringer Quasimodo, who in turn transforms from her captor to

Signature titles

Novels

Hans of Iceland (Han d'Islande), 1823

The Hunchback of Notre-Dame (Notre-Dame de Paris), 1831

Les Misérables, 1862

Toilers of the Sea (Les Travailleurs de la mer), 1866

Ninety-Three (Quatre-vingt-treize), 1874

Plays

Cromwell, 1827

Hernani, 1830

Ruy Blas, 1838

Poetry

The Punishments (Les Châtiments), 1853

The Legend of Centuries (La Légende des siècles), 1859–1883

ABOVE: A detail from a portrait of Victor Hugo by Léon Bonnat (1833–1922).

RIGHT: A poster advertising the publication of *Les Misérables* in 1886 by Jules Chéret.

savior. Dominated by the gothic architecture of Paris's cathedral, the novel was an international success, and sparked a national campaign to preserve much fine architecture.

An intensely creative period followed as Hugo used his plays to espouse political and social ideas. By 1848 he was an elected member of the French Assembly, but criticism of Napoleon III forced him into exile. During this time he achieved extraordinary success with *Les Misérables*, an epic tale of social injustice, and a study of the nature of good and evil. The novel centers on the reformed criminal Jean Valjean, who despite paying back his debt to society, is remorselessly hounded by the detective Javert, who refuses to let Valjean forget his past. Set against a backdrop of the Parisian underworld and revolutionary France, it is a story that still captivates audiences today. Afforded a state funeral upon his death, Hugo's body rests in the Panthéon in Paris. **SG**

ABOVE: Lon Chaney stars as Quasimodo in *The Hunchback of Notre-Dame* (1923).

The Battle of *Hernani*

Battle lines were drawn between the romantics and the classicists at the premiere of *Hernani* in Paris in February 1830. Anticipating a hostile attack from the traditionalists, Hugo positioned his supporters at strategic points throughout the Théâtre Français, enabling them to counteract any dissident voices. As much as defenders of the old school hissed, the soldiers of the new applauded. Fights broke out as panic engulfed the theater, yet the play continued unabated. Finally, despite inferior numbers, the romantic army ensured the cheers drowned out the jeers, handing victory to Hugo.

RALPH WALDO EMERSON

Born: May 25, 1803 (Boston, Massachusetts, U.S.); died April 27, 1882 (Concord, Massachusetts, U.S.).

Style and genre: Emerson's themes include a belief in the divinity of the individual, an emphasis on originality, and nature as a source of ethical instruction.

Signature titles

Poetry

Concord Hymn, 1837
The Rhodora, 1847
Poems, 1847
May-Day and Other Pieces, 1867

Essays

Nature, 1836
The American Scholar, 1837
Divinity School Address, 1838
Self-Reliance, 1841
Essays, First Series, 1841
Essays, Second Series, 1844
Representative Men, 1850
The Conduct of Life, 1860

In his own lifetime, Ralph Waldo Emerson became his country's most important intellectual, and he remains the most influential American thinker. His call for a new national literature, attentive to the new form that society had taken in the United States, inspired many great writers, including Herman Melville, Walt Whitman, and Emily Dickinson. *Self-Reliance*, his most widely read essay, exhorts his audience to pay attention to their own "inner laws" ahead of societal expectation or religious belief. It is the individual, rather than the institution, which is truly sacred.

Born into an old Puritan family, Emerson seemed destined to become a preacher. Following the death of his father, a Unitarian minister, he was raised by his deeply religious mother, and his eccentric, intellectual aunt. Emerson's growth as a philosopher can be measured by a series of breaks with religious orthodoxy. In 1832 he resigned as pastor of the Second Church of Boston because he could not administer the Eucharist in good conscience. Six years later he scandalized the Harvard Divinity School with an address that attacked Christ's divinity, and insisted that God was made incarnate in every man and woman. Rather than remaining in Boston, Emerson settled in nearby Concord, pursuing a career as an essayist, poet, and lecturer.

"Whoso would be a man must be a nonconformist."
—*Self-Reliance*

Although he stressed the importance of living close to nature, Emerson was very much a man of the world. As a speaker he achieved considerable public fame, embarking on many lecture tours across both the United States and Europe. While chiefly interested in the ethical and religious, he was outspoken on a number of political issues: His fierce opposition to slavery was testament to his deep commitment to personal freedom. **CT**

ABOVE: A detail from a nineteenth-century American School portrait of Emerson.

NATHANIEL HAWTHORNE

Born: Nathaniel Hathorne, July 4, 1804 (Salem, Massachusetts, U.S.); died May 19, 1864 (Plymouth, New Hampshire, U.S.).

Style and genre: Hawthorne was a novelist whose rich portraits of the United States were among the first to gain widespread recognition on a global stage.

If the mandate to write "the Great American Novel" continues to stand before all U.S. novelists as a challenge of their abilities, then Nathaniel Hawthorne is one of the writers who issued it. When Hawthorne's first novel, *The Scarlet Letter*, was published, U.S. bookshelves were still crammed only with what had managed to make it across the Atlantic; the novel sold out within days, and became a best seller. But perhaps part of the reason for his success is that his fiction has less to say about what Europeans had discovered in the New World than it does about what they brought with them.

The story of adultery in the Massachusetts colonies, *The Scarlet Letter*, is resolutely American in its themes, as the author makes clear when he begins by noting that the first task of any utopian society is to designate one spot for a cemetery, and another for a prison. Ideologically allied with the transcendentalism of contemporaries Ralph Waldo Emerson and Walt Whitman, Hawthorne's novel evokes the beauty of the pristine Massachusetts setting, and his sympathetic portrait of the outcast Hester Prynne has been praised as an early antecedent of the feminist movement.

As a struggling young writer, Hawthorne worked in a customs house that later formed the setting for the autobiographical preface of *The Scarlet Letter*. He also spent a brief stint in the utopian community Brook Farm, an experience he fictionalized in his third novel, *The Blithedale Romance*. The novel is like all of Hawthorne's fiction, in that it borders on allegory, but is too focused on the inexpressible beyond his paradigms for any clear argument to emerge. Hawthorne may have helped invent the American novel, but already he was gesturing beyond it. **SY**

"The style of Hawthorne is purity itself."

—Edgar Allan Poe

Signature titles

Novels

The Scarlet Letter, 1850

The House of the Seven Gables, 1851

The Blithedale Romance, 1852

The Marble Faun, 1860

The Dolliver Romance, 1863

Short stories

Twice-Told Tales, 1837

Mosses from an Old Manse, 1846

The Snow-Image, and Other Twice-Told Tales, 1852

Tanglewood Tales, 1853

ABOVE: An 1840 portrait of American writer Nathaniel Hawthorne by Charles Osgood.

GEORGE SAND

Born: Amantine Aurore Lucile Dupin, July 1, 1804 (Paris, France); died June 8, 1876 (Nohant, Indre, France).

Style and genre: Sand was a freethinking female writer of fiction with pastoral themes, unconventional characters, and realistic dialogue.

A renowned freethinking female novelist, George Sand became as famous for her lifestyle as for her writing. She chose a man's name as her pseudonym, often dressed in men's clothing, and asked people to address her as "*mon frère*" ("my brother"). She was also unusual for her time because her work was admired and read by men as well as women. Her contemporary, Elizabeth Barrett Browning, wrote a poem entitled *To George Sand: A Desire* (1844) that describes the Frenchwoman as a "large-brained woman and large-hearted man."

George Sand was raised largely by her grandmother, whose forceful personality informed Sand's own, and that of many of her characters. They lived in the family estate at Nohant, south of Paris, an area that features prominently in Sand's works. Sand also spent two years living in a convent at her grandmother's request. Her grandmother died in 1821, and in 1822 at the age of eighteen, Sand married a baron, several years her senior, with whom she had two children. The marriage was deeply unhappy, and she left him and her children nine years later, to live in Paris.

Sand began her career writing articles for publications including *Le Figaro*. Her first novel, *Rose et Blanche*, was published under the name Jules Sand—it was cowritten with her then lover Jules Sandeau. Sand became as famous for her love affairs as her writing; she had turned against the institution of marriage, and believed in free love. Her most famous affair was with the composer Frédéric Chopin; her book *A Winter in Majorca* (*Un Hiver à Majorque*) is about the months they spent living together on the island. Her works and the way she lived her life were instrumental in bringing forward the emancipation of women in France. **LH**

Signature titles

Novels

Rose et Blanche, 1831
Indiana, 1832
Lélia, 1834
Spiridion, 1839
Horace, 1842
Consuelo, 1842–1843
The Devil's Pool (La Mare au diable), 1846
Little Fadette (La Petite Fadette), 1849
The Bagpipers (Les Maîtres sonneurs), 1853

Autobiographies

A Winter in Majorca (Un Hiver à Majorque), 1842
Story of My Life (Histoire de ma vie), 1854–1855

"There is only one happiness in life, to love and be loved."
—Letter to Lina Calamatta, 1862

ABOVE: *Portrait of George Sand* (detail), by Auguste Charpentier (1813–1880).

ELIZABETH BARRETT BROWNING

Born: Elizabeth Barrett Moulton-Barrett, March 6, 1806 (Coxhoe Hall, County Durham, England); died June 29, 1861 (Florence, Italy).

Style and genre: Browning was a Victorian poet whose fertile imagination was an antidote to the social constraints of the period—and to her own poor health.

Elizabeth Barrett was unlucky enough to be born into a privileged Victorian family; even as she approached the age of forty, her father continued to guard her so closely that she was forced to marry Robert Browning in secret, before returning to the family home to spend her wedding night alone. She was already a celebrated poet, and her husband's fame only eclipsed hers long after her death. Their correspondence is unique and compelling because it offers a glimpse into the evolution of a remarkable creative partnership.

Browning encouraged his wife to publish the sonnets she had written to him during their courtship. They became *Sonnets from the Portuguese*, probably the greatest sequence produced in a period when sonneteering was all the rage. The Brownings eloped to Italy, where "E. B. B." (as she chose to call herself) flourished in the idealistic intellectual climate of the group of British and American exiles who had chosen Florence as their home. Her Republican sympathies are most evident in *Casa Guidi Windows*, where she promotes the cause of Italian nationalism in a revolutionary era. It was in Florence that she developed her interest in spiritualism, a pursuit that angered Browning, and left a small crease in their otherwise smooth and happy marriage.

E. B. B.'s greatest poetical achievement is her verse novel, *Aurora Leigh*. It is partially autobiographical, because it narrates the bold artistic development of a female poet who is hampered by the strictures of Victorian society. E. B. B. had overcome much to speak out herself—let alone find an audience for her passionate voice. Her health remained poor in Italy but although her happiness was brief, it was genuine; she died in her husband's arms in 1861. **TM**

"How do I love thee?
Let me count the ways."
—*Sonnets from the Portuguese*

Signature titles

Poetry

An Essay on Mind and Other Poems, 1826
Poems, 1844
Sonnets from the Portuguese, 1850
Casa Guidi Windows, 1851
Aurora Leigh, 1856
Poems Before Congress, 1860
Last Poems, 1862

Nonfiction

The Letters of Robert Browning and Elizabeth Barrett, 1845–1846

ABOVE: A detail from an 1853 portrait of Browning by Thomas Buchanan Read.

HENRY WADSWORTH LONGFELLOW

Born: February 27, 1807 (Portland, Maine, U.S.); died March 24, 1882 (Cambridge, Massachusetts, U.S.).

Style and genre: Longfellow wrote melodious poetry with memorable rhymes and patriot themes; he had a joyous love of language, history, and mythology.

1800–19

Signature titles

Poetry

Voices of the Night, 1839
The Skeleton in Armor, 1840
Ballads and Other Poems, 1842
The Wreck of the Hesperus, 1842
Poems on Slavery, 1842
Evangeline, A Tale of Acadie, 1847
The Seaside and the Fireside, 1850
The Song of Hiawatha, 1855
Paul Revere's Ride, 1861
Tales of a Wayside Inn, 1863
The Masque of Pandora and Other Poems, 1875
Ultima Thule, 1880
In the Harbor, 1882

One of the first recognized poets from the United States, Henry Wadsworth Longfellow continues to affect the English language; many of the phrases he first coined have passed into common usage—such as the expressions "ships that pass in the night," and "into each life some rain must fall." He went to school with Nathaniel Hawthorne, who became a close friend, and in adult life he moved in literary circles, befriending, among others, Charles Dickens and Alfred, Lord Tennyson.

Longfellow was born into a wealthy family, the son of a lawyer. He wrote his first poem at the age of thirteen, and saw it published in his local newspaper. After school he traveled in Europe learning languages. He was a brilliant linguist, and on his return to the United States began teaching at universities, including Harvard. He married in 1831, but his wife died four years later. He married again in 1843, a happy marriage that produced five children, but in 1861 his second wife also died tragically, killed when her dress caught fire.

The poetry Longfellow created was inspired by the rich history of North America. He was a passionate supporter of Native American rights, and of the abolition of slavery; he wrote his epic poem *The Song of Hiawatha* as a tribute to a culture that was being so terribly eroded. Longfellow also translated classic works of literature, including Homer's *Odyssey* and Dante Alighieri's *The Divine Comedy* (*La Divina Commedia*). He was so celebrated in his own lifetime that his seventieth birthday was made a day of national celebration. He was also honored with a monument in Poets' Corner in London's Westminster Abbey —an honor usually reserved for British writers. **LH**

"All your strength is in your union,
All your danger is in discord. . . ."
—*The Song of Hiawatha*

ABOVE: A detail from a painting of American poet Henry Wadsworth Longfellow.

GÉRARD DE NERVAL

Born: Gérard Labrunie, May 22, 1808 (Paris, France); died January 26, 1855 (Paris, France).

Style and genre: French romantic poet, translator, and short-story writer, Nerval's literary experiments made him a precursor to the symbolists.

An archetype of the *poète maudit* (accursed poet), Gérard de Nerval began life as Gérard Labrunie, taking his pseudonym based on his belief that he was a descendent of the Roman Emperor Nerva. The son of a doctor in Napoleon I's army, his mother died when he was two-years-old, and he was brought up by a great uncle in the French countryside. When his father returned from the Peninsular War in 1814, they went to Paris. There he acquired a bohemian set of friends, including Charles Baudelaire, Théophile Gautier, and Alexandre Dumas, all of whom were members of the Club des Haschichins (Hashish Club) that sought to experiment with drugs.

Nerval first made his mark in the 1820s with a brilliant translation of Johann Wolfgang von Goethe's *Faust* (1808) with which Goethe himself was pleased, and which composer Hector Berlioz used in his libretto *The Damnation of Faust* (*La Damnation de Faust*, 1846). However, Nerval lost all his money in a business venture, and fell in love with singer and actress, Marguerite "Jenny" Colon, who did not return his feelings. From 1841 he became mentally unstable, and it was even claimed he took a pet lobster for walks. He had a nervous breakdown, and was put into a mental institution; he was interred again between 1853 to 1854, and wrote about his experience of madness in *Aurélia*.

The symbolism of his poetry, such as the sonnets, *The Chimeras*, and his fascination with dreams, which he regarded as journeys into another life in an invisible world, influenced generations of writers including Marcel Proust, Antonin Artaud, Louis Aragon, André Breton, and T. S. Eliot. He died by hanging himself from a bar in a sewer grate. **RC**

"This life is a hovel and a place of ill repute. I'm ashamed that God should see me here."

Signature titles

Short stories

Girls of Fire (Les Filles du feu), 1854

Poetry

The Chimeras (Les Chimères), 1854

Nonfiction

Voyage to the Orient (Voyage en Orient), 1851

Aurélia, 1855

ABOVE: A photograph of French writer Nerval in Paris (1852).

EDGAR ALLAN POE

Born: Edgar Poe, January 19, 1809 (Boston, Massachusetts, U.S.); died October 7, 1849 (Baltimore, Maryland, U.S.).

Style and genre: Poe was a poet, short-story writer, and essayist whose tales of mystery and the macabre redefined the "American Gothic."

Although William Carlos Williams would call him the first truly American writer, Edgar Allan Poe was not a celebrated author in his own country until decades after his reputation had been established in France. His talent as a storyteller had been acknowledged even by his contemporaries, yet his writing has, as Robert Louis Stevenson described it: "A certain jarring note, a taint of something that we do not care to dwell upon or find a name for." Part of what gives this uncanny quality its power is the difficulty in identifying whether it is a deliberately cultivated effect on the author's part, or caused by a mental illness. In an age of reason that had just begun to doubt its own sanity, this was exactly the quality that made Poe's work so resonant.

Poe tried his hand at a large number of genres, and arguably invented several—science fiction, detective fiction, and horror,

Signature titles

Short stories

The Masque of the Red Death, 1838
The Fall of the House of Usher, 1839
The Murders in the Rue Morgue, 1841
The Pit and the Pendulum, 1842
The Tell-Tale Heart, 1843
The Purloined Letter, 1845
The Cask of Amontillado, 1846

Poetry

Tamerlane and Other Poems, 1827
Poems, 1831
The Raven, 1845
Annabel Lee, 1849

ABOVE: A detail from a portrait photograph of Edgar Allan Poe (*c.* 1848).

RIGHT: Arthur Rackham's *Fortunado and Montresor* from *The Cask of Amontillado*.

to name a few. Yet the complete, unabridged works of Poe can fit into a single fat volume. That such a volume would contain some of the most influential literature of the past two centuries is testimony to his mastery of structure and understatement. When the protagonist of *The Tell-Tale Heart* decides to murder someone because he does not like their eyes, it is barely commented on; but this brief story nonetheless paints a portrait of insanity all the more vivid and terrifying for its matter-of-fact narration. This is all the stronger in his poetry, most famously *The Raven* and *Annabel Lee*, whose simple diction and almost sing-song rhyme schemes frame narratives of deep psychological complexity. Poe's best stories—among them *The Fall of the House of Usher*, and *The Pit and the Pendulum*—all have this quality. They suggest there is more to the story than what happens on the surface; but leave readers with a sense that they would rather not find out what it is. **SY**

ABOVE: Gustav Doré's illustration for "The Raven" (nineteenth-century).

An Early Sleuth

Poe's stories about his recurring character C. Auguste Dupin constitute one of the earliest examples of the genre that came to be called "detective fiction." The four Dupin stories, most famously *The Purloined Letter* and *The Murders in the Rue Morgue*, describe how Dupin uses the powers of observation and logic to help the Paris police deduce the improbable solutions to impossible problems. But where his successors like Sherlock Holmes use reason to demystify the unknown, Poe's Dupin often leaves the reader with answers that are more disquieting than the questions were in the first place.

NIKOLAY GOGOL

Born: Nikolay (or Nikolai) Vasilievich Gogol, March 31, 1809 (Sorochyntsy, Poltava Oblast, Ukraine); died March 4, 1852 (Moscow, Russia).

Style and genre: Gogol is known for satirical humor, minute observances, surrealism, political satire, farcical situations, and larger-than-life characters.

Signature titles

Novels

Taras Bulba, 1835

Dead Souls, 1842

Short stories

Evenings on a Farm near Dikanka, 1831–1832

Mirgorod, 1835

Diary of a Madman, 1835

The Nose, 1836

The Overcoat, 1842

Plays

The Government Inspector, 1836

Marriage, 1842

The Gamblers, 1843

Nonfiction

Letters of Nikolai Gogol, 1967

An experimental writer, Nikolay Gogol is best known today for the superbly original *Diary of a Madman.* Influenced by Russian masters and by Sir Walter Scott, his writing would go on to influence Leo Tolstoy, Fyodor Dostoevsky, Vladimir Nabokov, and Franz Kafka. His works were surrealist decades before the movement began—*The Nose*, for instance, relates the adventures of a nose severed from its face, and its attempts to live an independent life.

Gogol was born into a wealthy family, and grew up on an estate which was deeply divided by the vast gulf between rich and poor. Determined to become a poet, Gogol moved to St. Petersburg, where he also toyed with becoming an actor. He worked for the government in minor administrative jobs until 1831, when he became a history teacher. In the same year, Gogol met one of his idols, the poet Aleksandr Pushkin. They became good friends, with Pushkin influencing Gogol's literary taste, and convincing him to persevere with his first published book, the collection of short stories *Evenings on a Farm near Dikanka*. Pushkin also published Gogol in his magazine. Three years later, Gogol became a full-time writer.

ABOVE: A portrait of Nikolay Gogol by Otto Moeller from 1845.

RIGHT: An illustration for *The Nose* (1904), by Russian painter Léon Bakst.

Gogol's early years in St. Petersburg inspired his brilliant *The Government Inspector*. A play that works as a basic ludicrous farce, as well as on a subversive level, it is a biting satire about bureaucracy. The first performance was attended by the tsar, whose sharp comments caused Gogol to fear for his safety. He left Russia for twelve years, traveling through Europe and the Middle East, and settling in Rome, where he penned *Dead Souls*. It proved successful and he returned to Russia as a celebrated author. At the end of his life, Gogol turned to fanatical religion, deeply influenced by Father Konstantinovskii, a priest who persuaded Gogol his writing was blasphemous, leading the author to burn some of his manuscripts. By the time he died, Gogol was considered insane, a cruel irony for the author of the iconic *Diary of a Madman*. His final years were so strange that rumors abounded, including one that he was not actually dead when put into his grave. **LH**

ABOVE: A stage design for composer Rodion Shchedrin's opera of *Dead Souls* (1976).

Dead Souls

Allegedly, it was Pushkin who suggested the idea of *Dead Souls* to his friend. Gogol began the book in 1835, the year he gave up teaching to become a full-time writer, but it was not completed until his self-enforced exile in Rome. The idea Pushkin suggested was that of a man who travels through Russia buying the ownership of serfs, who had already died—the "souls" of the title. Although a comedy, the book is an indictment of the rigidly hierarchical class system, and the corruption it engendered—a corruption Gogol experienced in Russia and in Rome, where the pope held absolute power.

ALFRED, LORD TENNYSON

Born: August 6, 1809 (Somersby, Lincolnshire, England); died October 6, 1892 (Aldworth House, Surrey, England).

Style and genre: Tennyson's lyrically flowing poetry involved high-blown dramatic themes, medieval subject matter, and intense emotions.

Signature titles

Poetry

Poems Chiefly Lyrical, 1830
The Lady of Shalott, 1832
Poems, 1832
The Lotos-Eaters, 1833
Poems, 1842
In Memoriam A. H. H., 1850
Ode on the Death of the Duke of Wellington, 1852
The Charge of the Light Brigade, 1854
Maud; A Monodrama, 1855
The Idylls of the King, 1859–1885

Play

The Foresters, Robin Hood and Maid Marion, 1892

Alfred, Lord Tennyson, the most popular of all Victorian poets, was one of twelve children born to a parson and his wife. Money was scarce, and although Alfred went to Cambridge, where he won a gold medal for poetry, when his father died he left university to support his mother financially. Tennyson did not inherit his title; it was awarded to him by Queen Victoria in 1884. He had been a friend of Prince Albert, and dedicated his Arthurian collection, *The Idylls of the King*, to Albert's memory.

Tennyson became famous for *In Memoriam A. H. H.*, a mourning poem to his friend Arthur Henry Hallam, who died in the same year that Tennyson's brother Edward was admitted to an asylum. The exquisite poetry that miserable year produced has become the pinnacle of Tennyson's work; *In Memoriam A. H. H.* was absolutely of its time, in keeping with the fashion of deep mourning so associated with Victoria's reign. *In Memoriam A. H. H.* led to Tennyson being chosen to succeed William Wordsworth as poet laureate in 1850.

In the same year Tennyson married his childhood sweetheart, Emily Sellwood; they had two sons, Hallam and Lionel. The family lived in London and at Freshwater on the Isle of Wight. Tennyson's presence, and that of his friends including Julia Margaret Cameron, the Prinseps, and G. F. Watts, made Freshwater a fashionable destination. Virginia Woolf later wrote a play entitled *Freshwater: A Comedy* (1923), whose characters include Tennyson and his set.

"Tis better to have loved and lost / Than never to have loved at all."—*In Memoriam A. H. H.*

Tennyson's poems remain well known, including such masterpieces as *The Lady of Shalott* and *The Lotos-Eaters*. As poet laureate he was also responsible for producing poems at times of national importance, such as his *Ode on the Death of the Duke of Wellington*. **LH**

ABOVE: *Portrait of Alfred, Lord Tennyson*, a nineteenth-century engraving by C. Laurie.

ELIZABETH GASKELL

Born: Elizabeth Stevenson, September 29, 1810 (London, England); died November 12, 1865 (Holybourne, Hampshire, England).

Style and genre: Gaskell was a chronicler of her era who provided fascinating descriptions, minute observations of human nature, and social commentary.

Elizabeth Gaskell, wife of William Gaskell a Unitarian minister, lived the majority of her life in the north of England, where she wrote, and helped her husband in his ministry to the struggling poor. It was this landscape with its industry, and the gaping void between the wealthy and the poor that she depicted through her novels. She addressed the rights of women, or lack thereof, and championed the working classes—famously her characters speak in local dialect—subtly commenting on the different social levels of Victorian England.

Her first novel, *Mary Barton: A Tale of Manchester Life*, drew a hostile reaction from some critics because of its sympathy for the working classes Yet undeterred, later she returned to its themes of the relationship between employers and workers in *North and South*. Her third novel, *Ruth*, also caused scandal among contemporary society thanks to its explorations of the fate of a seduced, and thereby "fallen" woman, and her subsequent experience of being ostracized by society. Gaskell's keen eye for observation of small-town communities and moral convention makes her work valuable to social historians, as well as possessing literary merit. Her last novel, *Wives and Daughters: An Every-Day Story*, is considered her best, and was written when her powers of depicting relationships were at their peak.

She was widely respected by John Ruskin, William and Mary Howitt, and Charles Dickens. The latter published a series of gothic-style ghost stories by Gaskell in his magazine *Household Words* that were stylistically quite different from her novels.

Gaskell was friendly with Charlotte Brontë, and wrote the first biography of her. It is still considered the definitive biography of the author. **TamP**

"... the most powerful and finished female novelist of an epoch. . . ."—*The Athenaeum*, 1865

Signature titles

Novels

Mary Barton: A Tale of Manchester Life, 1848
Cranford, 1851–1853
Ruth, 1853
North and South, 1854–1855
Sylvia's Lovers, 1863
Cousin Phyllis, 1864
Wives and Daughters: An Everyday Story, 1864–1866

Short stories

The Poor Clare, 1856
The Grey Woman, 1861

Nonfiction

The Life of Charlotte Brontë, 1857

ABOVE: A detail from a lithograph (after George Richmond) of Elizabeth Gaskell.

HARRIET BEECHER STOWE

Born: Harriet Elizabeth Beecher, June 14, 1811 (Litchfield, Connecticut, U.S.); died July 1, 1896 (Hartford, Connecticut, U.S.).

Style and genre: Stowe wrote controversial works—particularly against slavery—in a realistic, insightful style, often with strongly Christian themes.

The importance of Harriet Beecher Stowe's work toward the abolition of slavery was paramount, and today she is remembered chiefly for her novels about this subject. So great was her influence on the public, urging them to support the anti-slavery movement, that according to her daughter, Hattie, when Harriet finally met President Abraham Lincoln in 1862, he greeted her with the words: "So you're the little woman who wrote the book that started this great war!"

Stowe wrote a number of books, some of which addressed strongly Christian themes, but her work championing the anti-slavery movement is considered her finest. Her early, and most significant, work was *Uncle Tom's Cabin; or, Life Among the Lowly*. Initially it was serialized in the anti-slavery periodical *The National Era* in 1851. Its appreciative reception, led her to publish it in book form the following year, and it proved an instant success. Although controversial, it reached a wide audience, selling thousands of copies within the first week. Sales were particularly good in Britain, and the book went on to be translated into many different languages. In 1853 Stowe traveled to England, where she was enthusiastically received, and lectured on the abolition of slavery. She also garnered great support from the Northern states of the United States, but in the Southern states her novel caused public outcry, and was banned in many areas. Here, she was accused of fabrication and inaccuracy; in retaliation, Stowe published *A Key to Uncle Tom's Cabin* that charted her research in an irrefutable manner. Stowe's books have left a lasting and poignant account of this passage in U.S. history, and apart from her anti-slavery themes, also depict with gritty realism the people, culture, and fabric of her times. **TamP**

Signature titles

Novels

Uncle Tom's Cabin; or, Life Among the Lowly, 1852
Dred: A Tale of the Great Dismal Swamp, 1856
The Minister's Wooing, 1859
Little Foxes, 1866
Old Town Folks, 1869
Pink and White Tyranny: A Society Novel, 1871

Short stories

Queer Little Folks, 1897

Nonfiction

A Key to Uncle Tom's Cabin, 1853
Sunny Memories of Foreign Lands, 1854

"I did not write it. God wrote it. I merely did his dictation."
—Introduction, *Uncle Tom's Cabin*

ABOVE: A nineteenth-century English School engraving of Harriet Beecher Stowe.

WILLIAM MAKEPEACE THACKERAY

Born: July 18, 1811 (Calcutta, India); died December 24, 1863 (London, England).

Style and genre: Thackeray's writing is marked by bitingly witty satire, intelligently thought-out and complex plots, superb and detailed characterization, and a thorough understanding of human nature.

Although born in India—where his father worked for the East India Company—William Makepiece Thackeray was sent to school in England and settled there. He was studying for a law degree when he took to writing, entering a poetry competition (in which he was beaten by the young Alfred, Lord Tennyson). Thackeray then began working as a journalist. He became one of the nineteenth century's most popular novelists, and an integral part of London's literary scene.

At the age of twenty-five, Thackeray married Isabella Shawe. They had three daughters: Jane, who died in infancy; Minny, who died in childbirth at the age of thirty-five; and Anny, the eldest, a successful novelist. Isabella suffered from mental illness following the birth of her youngest child, and spent the rest of her life living with a nurse-carer. With his wife's expenses and two daughters to support, Thackeray worked feverishly, writing for magazines. He garnered fame in *Punch* for his "Snob Papers," and it is claimed it was he who brought the word "snob" into regular usage. His novels, published in monthly chapters, proved hugely popular, most notably *Vanity Fair: A Novel without a Hero* and *The Newcomes*, and he made an unusually large income from his writing. In 1859, Thackeray set up *Cornhill Magazine* with George Smith; its first issue sold more than 100,000 copies. After a bout of poor health, Thackeray died suddenly at his home on Christmas Eve 1863, aged fifty-two. The public went into mourning over the demise of this giant of literature: a kind, loyal friend, and an adoring father. More than 2,000 mourners went to his funeral—the painter John Everett Millais later recorded his outrage about the large number of gaudily dressed prostitutes who had attended. **LH**

"Next to the young, I suppose the very old are the most selfish."—*The Virginians*

ABOVE: A detail from a portrait of Thackeray by William Drummond (*c.* 1800–1850).

Signature titles

Novels

Catherine: A Story, 1839–1840
The Luck of Barry Lyndon, 1844
Vanity Fair: A Novel without a Hero, 1847–1848
Pendennis, 1848–1850
Rebecca and Rowena, 1850
Men's Wives, 1852
The History of Henry Esmond, 1852
The Newcomes, 1853–1855
The Rose and the Ring, 1855
The Virginians, 1857–1859
The Adventures of Philip on His Way Through the World, 1860–1862

Nonfiction

The Book of Snobs, 1848

CHARLES DICKENS

Born: Charles John Huffam Dickens, February 7, 1812 (Portsmouth, England); died June 9, 1870 (Gad's Hill Place, Kent, England).

Style and genre: Grotesquely comic characterization, intricate plots, evocatively atmospheric description, and a social conscience runs through Dickens's fiction.

Very few writers attain the status of being used as an adjective, their name employed to describe the era in which they lived and about which they wrote; Charles Dickens is one of those select few. The word "Dickensian" has made its way into everyday usage: it is used to describe something grotesque, witty, ludicrous, socially deprived, or even to encompass the nineteenth century as a whole.

A hugely prolific writer, Dickens wrote novels, short stories, journalistic articles, and plays—not to mention numerous letters that have been collected and edited. He also cowrote with Wilkie Collins and Elizabeth Gaskell, and edited the magazines *Household Words* and *All The Year Round*. Dickens's career began as a legal reporter in London, leading to his lampooning of the legal profession in a number of novels. His first fictional works were a series of sketches of London life, published in magazines under the pseudonym "Boz" from 1833. They became the talk of London, an unwitting publicity stunt as readers longed to know the identity of Boz. In *The Pickwick Papers*, Dickens revealed his identity, and his next

Signature titles

Novels

The Pickwick Papers, 1836–1837
The Adventures of Oliver Twist, 1837–1839
The Life and Adventures of Nicholas Nickleby, 1838–1839
The Old Curiosity Shop, 1840–1841
Barnaby Rudge: A Tale of the Riots of 'Eighty, 1841
A Christmas Carol, 1843
The Life and Adventures of Martin Chuzzlewit, 1843–1844
Dombey and Son, 1846–1848
David Copperfield, 1849–1850
Bleak House, 1852–1853
Hard Times for These Times, 1854
Little Dorrit, 1855–1857
A Tale of Two Cities, 1859
Great Expectations, 1860–1861
Our Mutual Friend, 1865
The Mystery of Edwin Drood, 1870

Short stories

Sketches by Boz, 1836

Nonfiction

The Uncommercial Traveller, 1860–1869

ABOVE: A photograph of Charles Dickens in 1868, two years before his death.

RIGHT: A Hablot K. Browne ("Phiz") illustration from *Nicholas Nickleby*.

novel, *The Adventures of Oliver Twist*, made him a household name. His novels were written in monthly installments, each chapter being published as it was written.

ABOVE: George Cattermole's *The Grave of Little Nell*, inspired by *The Old Curiosity Shop*.

One of the most important aspects of Dickens's work is the social conscience with which it is infused. His books highlighted vitally important social issues of the day: child abuse, poverty, domestic violence, prostitution, the conditions of the workhouses, the lack of work and paucity of education for the working classes, to name just a few of the causes he espoused. Dickens's journalistic talent meant his fictional works had a direct influence and genuinely brought about change. A fervent campaigner, he worked with a number of fellow philanthropists on projects such as sanitary reform, education reform, rescuing "fallen women," and helping

"The children of the very poor are not brought up but dragged up."—*Bleak House*

Haunted by Childhood

Much of Dickens's work was directly affected by his childhood. His father (a clerk for the navy, ironically in the payroll office) was not good with money, and often was unable to support his family. The author's childhood was haunted by creditors and bailiffs. When he was twelve-years-old, his father was arrested for debt and the whole family, except Charles and his oldest sister, Fanny (who was away at boarding school), were taken into the Marshalsea debtors' prison. The young Charles had to leave school, and work in a factory to earn money for his family. He worked and lived alone in lodgings for just three months, but they were months that would haunt him for the rest of his life. As an adult, he told just two people about the experience: his wife, Catherine, and his friend and biographer, John Forster.

The episode was highly influential on his books. The factory made shoe blacking, and Dickens's job was to paste labels onto the bottles. In all of his novels, a blacking bottle is mentioned; usually it is merely a passing reference, but the blacking bottle and what it represented to Dickens is always present. The people Dickens met, and the poverty he witnessed daily as he walked through London between work, the Marshalsea and his lodging house, led to his fervent social-reform work. It also led to empathetic creations of characters, such as the prostitute Nancy in *Oliver Twist* and the neglected child, Jo the crossing sweeper, in *Bleak House*.

RIGHT: Arthur Rackham's illustration of Bob Cratchit from *A Christmas Carol*.

establish the Great Ormond Street Hospital for Children. In *The Life and Adventures of Nicholas Nickleby*, he exposed what he had learned about Yorkshire Schools—abusive establishments to which unwanted children were sent and forgotten. As he intended, the novel led investigative journalists to Yorkshire to discover if such places actually existed. The discovery that they did caused a public and political outcry, and within a few years of the novel's publication, all Yorkshire Schools had been closed down.

The breakdown of family life

Dickens married young and had ten children with his wife, Catherine (née Hogarth). A writer whose works espoused the glories of family life, the idyll was shattered when Dickens separated from his wife very publicly in 1858, although he maintained her until she died. At the age of forty-six, he had fallen in love with an eighteen-year-old actress, Ellen Ternan. Such was his popularity that the newspapers refrained from writing about his affair, knowing that a publication that sneered at Dickens would lose its own readership. Instead, vicious rumors appeared about Catherine, claiming she was an alcoholic and a bad mother; all entirely untrue.

Dickens was the first celebrity author. His popularity was international, spanning from the poorest to the queen of England. When he published *A Christmas Carol*, written in less than six weeks, he said he was striking a blow in favor of "the poor man's child." The initial print run of 6,000 copies sold out in five days. At the age of thirty-one, Dickens had become the most successful English writer since William Shakespeare.

Despite his immense body of work, Dickens was just fifty-eight when he died, leaving *The Mystery of Edwin Drood* unfinished. His daughter, Katey, claimed he had worked himself to death. His death provoked international mourning and outpourings of public grief. He had become such an extraordinarily famous, almost mythical, figure that it was reported a small child, hearing of Dickens's death, asked if that meant Father Christmas would die too. **LH**

ROBERT BROWNING

Born: May 7, 1812 (London, England); died December 12, 1889 (Venice, Italy).

Style and genre: Robert Browning was a Victorian poet of challenging but playful dramatic monologues; having married Elizabeth Barrett, he was one half of the greatest celebrity couple of the mid-nineteenth century.

Robert Browning served his poetic apprenticeship in his father's large and colorful library. His adolescent enthusiasm for Lord Byron and his lasting admiration of Percy Bysshe Shelley informed not only his writing, but also a dandyish appearance that seemed misplaced in the 1830s. His early poetry was learned and precocious, and led many critics to charge the young poet with wilful obscurity; such accusations were to dog Browning throughout his career.

In 1845, Browning began to correspond with Elizabeth Barrett, who was six years his senior and already a highly respected poet. Although Elizabeth was confined by poor health and by her draconian father, the poets allowed their love to flourish in a celebrated exchange of heartfelt letters. They married in secret in 1846 and eloped to Italy, where they became part of the large expatriate community in Florence. It was here that Browning developed his remarkable talent for poetic ventriloquism, composing the dramatic monologues that make up the collection *Men and Women*. They include *Fra Lippo Lippi*, *Bishop Blougram's Apology*, and *Andrea del Sarto*, poems that brilliantly interweave the unique idioms of their speakers with the distinctive texture of Browning's blank verse.

Browning was inwardly devastated by his wife's death in 1861, but reacted with a stoicism that surprised many of his friends. He left Florence immediately and returned to London, where he published the highly acclaimed *Dramatis Personae* in 1864. Writing became a way of curbing his grief, and he spent the second half of the decade immersed in the creation of his masterpiece, *The Ring and the Book*. It is a marvelous cacophony of competing voices and opinions—as if a great Victorian novel had been rendered in verse. **TM**

"I count life just a stuff / To try the soul's strength on."
—"In a Balcony"

Signature titles

Poetry

Paracelsus, 1835
Sordello, 1840
Christmas-Eve and Easter-Day, 1850
Men and Women, 1855
Dramatis Personae, 1864
The Ring and the Book, 1868–1869
Asolando, 1889

Poems

"In a Balcony," 1855
"Fra Lippo Lippi," 1855
"Bishop Blougram's Apology," 1855
"Andrea del Sarto," 1855

Nonfiction

The Letters of Robert Browning and Elizabeth Barrett, 1845–1846

ABOVE: A photograph of Robert Browning, master of the dramatic monologue.

GEORG BÜCHNER

Born: Karl Georg Büchner, October 17, 1813 (Goddelau, Germany); died February 19, 1837 (Zurich, Switzerland).

Style and genre: A playwright, poet, and novelist, Büchner wrote works that explore the revolutionary spirit and the struggles of the working class.

Georg Büchner is often called "the father of modern theater," somewhat strangely in that none of his plays were performed in his short life, and his dramatic oeuvre is small. He wrote a romantic comedy, *Leonce and Lena* (*Leonce und Lena*), and two historic tragedies, *Danton's Death* (*Dantons Tod*) and *Woyzeck*. The latter was sadly incomplete when Büchner died of typhus aged only twenty-three; it was later famously adapted into an opera by composer Allan Berg, and first performed in 1925.

It was almost sixty years after Büchner's death when one of his plays, *Leonce and Lena*, was performed in his native Germany. The delay may have been partly because of Büchner's early demise, but it is also an indication of how much he was ahead of his time. He depicted working-class characters, and his works are notable for their revolutionary spirit: *Danton's Death* portrays the disillusionment of activist George Danton with the French Revolution, and *Woyzeck* deals with the lot of a persecuted Slavic soldier.

Büchner's works reflect his own political leanings. Born to a middle-class family, he studied zoology and comparative anatomy in Strasburg. He also became a radical, going on to found the revolutionary group, the Society of Human Rights. In 1834 he wrote and distributed an illegal political pamphlet, for which he was soon denounced to the authorities—although he denied being the author. Frightened, he soon fled to France, and then on to Switzerland. He spent the rest of his life in exile and never engaged in political activities again, but he continued to write fiction, using it as an outlet for his critique of social convention. The innovative style and content of his works saw him being hailed as a forerunner of naturalism and expressionism. **CK**

"Individuals are so much surf on a wave, greatness the sheerest accident."

ABOVE: A steel engraving of Georg Büchner by A. Limbach.

Signature titles

Novella

Lenz, 1836 (published posthumously, 1839)

Plays

Danton's Death (Dantons Tod), 1835, first performed in 1902

Leonce and Lena (Leonce und Lena), 1836 (published posthumously, 1895)

Woyzeck, 1836–1837 (published posthumously, 1879)

MIKHAIL LERMONTOV

Born: Mikhail Yuryevich Lermontov, October 15, 1814 (Moscow, Russia); died July 27, 1841 (Pyatigorsk, Russia).

Style and genre: A Russian romantic poet, Lermontov was one of the first writers of Russian prose whose work took an anti-authoritarian stance against the tsar.

Mikhail Lermontov was brought up by his rich grandmother after his mother's death when he was three years old. His father, a poor army officer, was kept at arm's length and, not surprisingly, the author was an angry and difficult boy. While attending university in Moscow, Lermontov began to write. His play *A Strange Man* denounced the tyranny of the tsarist regime and the plight of the serfs. He took Lord Byron as the model for his personality and his early poetry. After university he attended cadet school, and took a commission in the cavalry.

Lermontov first made his name after Aleksandr Pushkin was killed in a duel in 1837. He penned a poem that praised the dead poet's love of liberty, and attacked the court aristocrats who supported the tsarist tyranny as "the hangmen who kill liberty, genius, and glory." He was promptly exiled to the Caucasus, where he was fascinated by the local folklore and the work of contemporary Georgian poets. This was Lermontov's first banishment for his libertarian opinions, and inspired what was to prove an extremely influential novel known for its beautiful descriptions of the Caucasus, *A Hero of Our Time*, in which he surveyed the Russia of his day, and which he described as a portrait of "all our generation's vices in full bloom." Its Byronic anti-hero is intelligent and highly educated, but his lack of freedom channels his energy into self-destructive courses. Admirers took the character as an all too typical figure in the Russia of the tsars, and Lermontov, who described his poetry as "iron verse steeped in bitterness and hatred," began to be hailed in liberal circles as Pushkin's successor. Banished back to military action in the Caucasus, he fought bravely in battles before a quarrel with another officer led to a duel in which he was killed. **RC**

"Passions are merely ideas in their initial stage."

—*A Hero of Our Time*

Signature titles

Novel

A Hero of Our Time, 1840

Poetry

Borodino, 1837

Death of the Poet, 1837

The Song of the Merchant Kalashnikov, 1837

The Tambov Treasurer's Wife, 1837–1838

Clouds, 1840

The Demon, 1841

The Dream, 1841

Prophet, 1841

Sashka, 1862

Plays

A Strange Man, 1831

Masquerade, 1834–1836

ABOVE: A detail from *Painting of Lermontov* (1837), by Piotr Yefimovich Sabolotsky.

ANTHONY TROLLOPE

Born: April 24, 1815 (London, England); died December 6, 1882 (London, England).

Style and genre: Trollope's style includes plots led by the characters, social hierarchies and injustices, a deep understanding of human nature, the theme of love, and strong and emancipated female characters.

The author of forty-seven novels, Anthony Trollope spent his adult life working for the General Post Office (GPO), rising at 5:30 A.M. to write solidly for three hours before work. He was friends with a number of artists and writers, including William Thackeray, who published Trollope's work in *Cornhill Magazine*. Trollope became one of the most highly respected of London's literary figures, yet he did not give up his job.

Trollope used his novels to air his political opinions and pillory what he saw as the hypocritical views of contemporary society. Although his first novels were comparatively unsuccessful, by the time he was in his thirties he was famous.

A tempestuous childhood had caused the young Trollope to suffer severe depression. His father—an erratic, difficult man—had little money, but insisted on his sons going to the most expensive schools. The disparity between his expected circumstances and his actual home life led to severe bullying, and Trollope later admitted he had felt suicidal. The family's finances were saved by Trollope's mother, Frances, who became a successful writer, influencing her son's future. His career with the GPO, which had begun as a lowly position, led to a highly important post that took him all over the world. He traveled to Africa, the Middle East, Australia, New Zealand, the Caribbean, the U.S. and throughout Europe—to places most of his contemporaries were unaware existed. Yet despite the wide variety of places in which he wrote, Trollope is firmly identified with England, and is best known for his "Barsetshire'" chronicles, about a fictitious English county.

"There is no road to wealth so easy and respectable as that of matrimony."—*Doctor Thorne*

In addition to changing the face of English literature, Trollope also changed the British landscape—it was he who introduced the now iconic postbox to Britain. **LH**

ABOVE: A nineteenth-century English School photograph of Anthony Trollope.

Signature titles

Novels

The Warden, 1855
Barchester Towers, 1857
Doctor Thorne, 1858
Framley Parsonage, 1861
The Small House at Allington, 1864
Can You Forgive Her?, 1864
The Last Chronicle of Barset, 1867
Phineas Finn, 1869
He Knew He Was Right, 1869
The Eustace Diamonds, 1873
Phineas Redux, 1874
The Way We Live Now, 1875
The Prime Minister, 1876
The Duke's Children, 1880

CHARLOTTE BRONTË

Born: April 21, 1816, (Thornton, Yorkshire, England); died March 31, 1855 (Haworth, Yorkshire, England).

Style and genre: Brontë was a Victorian novelist who helped create a new type of female figure in literature—the unconventional, independent, and strong woman.

Signature titles

Novels

Jane Eyre, 1847

Shirley, 1849

Villette, 1853

The Professor, 1857

Poetry

Poems by Currer, Ellis, and Acton Bell, 1846

Charlotte Brontë remains most famous for *Jane Eyre,* a novel that combines gothic imagery and sweeping romanticism with a keenly wrought social commentary. It introduced a new female role: An unconventional, independent, intelligent woman who rises above adversity. *Jane Eyre* and *Shirley* were published under the pseudonym "Currer Bell" because Brontë felt a male name would give the works a better chance of being taken seriously. Brontë later revealed her true identity but, although she published several other works, none matched the great success of *Jane Eyre*. Brontë's life ended tragically early in 1855, while she was pregnant with her first child, and following the deaths of both her sisters Emily and Anne. **TamP**

HENRY DAVID THOREAU

Born: David Henry Thoreau, July 12, 1817 (Concord, Massachusetts, U.S.); died May 6, 1862 (Concord, Massachusetts, U.S.).

Style and genre: Thoreau's robust, complex prose style complemented his philosophical inspiration in nature and strong opposition to slavery and injustice.

Signature titles

Nonfiction

A Week on the Concord and Merrimack Rivers, 1849

Civil Disobedience, 1849

Slavery in Massachusetts, 1854

Walden; or, Life in the Woods, 1854

A Plea for Captain John Brown, 1859

Walking, 1862

Life Without Principle, 1863

The Maine Woods, 1864

A Yankee in Canada, with Anti-Slavery and Reform Papers, 1866

Student, teacher, handyman, hermit, naturalist, protestor, and man of letters: Henry David Thoreau lived a life of many parts. He possessed a strong practical sense and a commitment to philosophy. In 1845 he built a cabin by the side of Walden pond, in Concord. He lived there alone for two years, and later crafted his experiences into *Walden; or, Life in the Woods*, now an acknowledged American classic. Although he prized solitude, and at Walden sought to live entirely by his own means, Thoreau was fiercely political. His life in the backwoods was no retreat from society but an attempt to find a more just way of living, part of his campaign of civil disobedience against corrupt and selfish government. **CT**

EMILY BRONTË

Born: Emily Jane Brontë, July 30, 1818 (Thornton, Yorkshire, England); died December 19, 1848 (Haworth, Yorkshire, England).

Style and genre: Brontë was a Romantic novelist who chronicled the wild places of the soul, as well as the Yorkshire Moors where she lived and wrote.

Few novels have topped the music charts, but in 1978 *Wuthering Heights* did just that, in the form of Kate Bush's debut single in the voice of Emily Brontë's heroine, Catherine Earnshaw. Bush became the first female artist to top the charts with a self-penned song—an appropriate tribute to Brontë, whose much-loved tale of a headstrong heroine first appeared under the male *nom de plume* of "Ellis Bell."

It was Emily's older sister Charlotte who determined that she, Emily, and middle sister Anne (the three surviving daughters of a Yorkshire clergyman) should take male pen names to counter Victorian sexism, having decided to publish an anthology of the sisters' poetry. Aside from *Wuthering Heights*, the poems collected in *Poems by Currer, Ellis, and Acton Bell* are Emily Brontë's only published work.

Emily Brontë's verses show a restlessly inquisitive mind exploring the bleak frontiers of the human relationship with nature and divinity. Yet she is generally regarded primarily as a romantic novelist, and *Wuthering Heights* regularly tops polls for the most romantic book of all time. This is something of an anomaly given that Brontë's excoriating investigation of class and gender oppression, told in the narrative of a gothic ghost story, suggests there can be no happily ever after. Perhaps the most remarkable character in the novel is not one of the romantic leads, but the geographic heights whose gothic weather informs the title. These moors were her imaginative and literal world, informing not only the setting but the drama of the novel. From an isolated parsonage at Haworth, Yorkshire, she created a novel that has assumed the status of modern myth, perhaps consolation for the work left undone by her death at the age of thirty. **SM**

"Whatever our souls are made of, his and mine are the same."—*Wuthering Heights*

Signature titles

Novel

Wuthering Heights, 1847

Poetry

Poems by Currer, Ellis, and Acton Bell, 1846

ABOVE: Emily Brontë, from a painting of the family group by Branwell Brontë.

IVAN TURGENEV

Born: Ivan Sergeyevich Turgenev, November 9, 1818 (Oryol, Oryol Oblast, Russia); died September 3, 1883 (Paris, France).

Style and genre: A controversial Russian realist writer, Turgenev's detailed, descriptive works depict everyday life and the plight of the peasantry.

Ivan Turgenev is generally rated along with Fyodor Dostoevsky and Leo Tolstoy as one of the three greatest of all Russian novelists, although his personal relationships with the other two were difficult, and for seventeen years he and Tolstoy refused to speak to each other. From a well-to-do landed family, Turgenev was brought up harshly by a mother who often beat him. A timid young man, he went to university in Moscow, St. Petersburg, and then Berlin. He returned to Russia in 1841 to become, at his mother's insistence, a civil servant.

He first made his reputation with a collection of short stories, *A Sportsman's Sketches*, published in 1852. They were based on his experiences while hunting at his mother's estate at Spasskoye where he observed the abuse of the peasants, and the injustices of the Russian system: The need to improve their condition was one of his abiding preoccupations, and heralded a new age. Allegedly the book influenced Tsar Alexander II's decision to emancipate the serfs, although at the time the author's liberal opinions made him a suspect to the regime, and he underwent house arrest for eighteen months.

Turgenev went on to write a succession of novels, short stories, and plays that earned the plaudits of the Russian literary world, and often reflected his own frustration in love because he had a long relationship with the married French opera singer, Pauline García-Viardot, with whom he was infatuated. His most famous works are the play *A Month in the Country*, and the novel *Fathers and Sons* that made his reputation outside Russia. Adverse reaction to *Fathers and Sons* in Russia saw Turgenev leave his homeland, and move to Germany, then London, and finally Paris. García-Viardot was at his bedside when he died of cancer, aged sixty-four. **RC**

Signature titles

Novels

Rudin, 1856
Home of the Gentry, 1859
First Love, 1860
On the Eve, 1860
Fathers and Sons, 1862
Smoke, 1867
Virgin Soil, 1877

Short stories

A Sportsman's Sketches, 1852
"Torrents of Spring," 1872

Plays

A Rash Thing to Do, 1843
A Month in the Country, 1850
Fortune's Fool, 1848

"A nihilist is a man who does not bow to any authorities . . ."
—*Fathers and Sons*

ABOVE: *Portrait of Ivan S. Turgenev* (1879), by Ilya Efimovich Repin (1844–1930).

GEORGE ELIOT

Born: Mary Ann Evans, November 22, 1819 (South Farm, Arbury, Warwickshire, England); died December 22, 1880 (London, England).

Style and genre: Eliot was a leading nineteenth-century writer of insightful and philosophical novels that depict humanity in all its forms and character.

Mary Ann Evans became one of the greatest Victorian authors, under the pen name of "George Eliot." She adopted a male pseudonym for two reasons: She wished to distance her scandalous private life from her work, and she felt her work would be more seriously considered if she were believed to be a man. Eventually her true identity was revealed, and her reputation as an author did not suffer unduly.

Mary Ann grew up in a conventional, conformist, and religious family. After her mother died, she took over running the family home and in 1841 moved to a house near Coventry with her father. Here she became acquainted with Charles Bray and his wife, and started attending gatherings of open-minded intellectuals at their home. Her evolving religious skepticism caused problems within her family, although she attended church until her father's death in 1849. After he died, she visited Switzerland with the Brays before moving to London, where she worked as assistant editor of the *Westminster Review*, organizing and contributing articles for three years.

In 1851 she met George Henry Lewes, an unhappily married critic and editor. The two shocked society by moving in together in 1854. Around this time, Eliot decided to become a writer, and Lewes arranged for the publication of a collection of short stories, *Scenes of Clerical Life*. Her characters play out their lives against a backdrop of historical and social change with penetrating psychological observations, a style that was to mark the rest of her oeuvre. She published her first novel, *Adam Bede,* in 1859 to instant success. She wrote for the next fifteen years, books of realism and piercing insight, such as *The Mill on the Floss*, *Silas Marner,* and *Middlemarch*. **TamP**

"But what we call our despair is often only the painful eagerness of unfed hope."—*Middlemarch*

ABOVE: A portrait of Mary Ann Evans (1864), who wrote as George Eliot.

Signature titles

Novels

Adam Bede, 1859
The Mill on the Floss, 1860
Silas Marner, 1861
Romola, 1863
Felix Holt, the Radical, 1866
Middlemarch, 1871–1872
Daniel Deronda, 1876

Short stories

Scenes of Clerical Life, 1858

Poetry

The Spanish Gypsy, 1868
A Minor Prophet, 1874
A College Breakfast Party, 1879
The Death of Moses, 1879

WALT WHITMAN

Born: Walter Whitman, May 31, 1819 (West Hills, Huntington, Long Island, New York, U.S.); died March 26, 1892 (Camden, New Jersey, U.S.).

Style and genre: A visionary American poet, Whitman helped shape the identity of the modern United States through his use of free verse and themes of democracy.

Signature titles

Poetry

Leaves of Grass, 1855, 1856, 1860, 1867, 1870, 1876, 1881, 1891

Poems

"Song of Myself," 1855
"I Sing the Body Electric," 1855
"Crossing Brooklyn Ferry," 1856
"Mannahatta," 1860
"O Captain! My Captain!," 1867
"I Hear America Singing," 1867
"A noiseless patient spider," 1871

Nonfiction

Democratic Vistas, 1871
Memoranda During the War, 1875
Specimen Days and Collect, 1882

The child of a Quaker mother and a radical father, Walt Whitman was raised in Brooklyn, had little formal education and was largely self-taught. Years as a printer, wandering schoolteacher and magazine contributor occupied his teens and twenties, while his own writing began to reflect the unorthodoxy of his thinking—editorships at the New York *Aurora* and the Brooklyn *Eagle* were curtailed because Whitman's vociferous radicalism proved unpopular. A journey across the United States to New Orleans in 1848 was central to the development of his poetic project, and he returned profoundly altered, with a new awareness of the implications of the fledgling American nation and the responsibilities of its chroniclers. This was expressed in Whitman's appearance, his beard and rough clothes expressing his democratic idealism, coupled with a fierce individualism that found its greatest outlet in *Leaves of Grass*, Whitman's self-published 1855 poetry collection.

Although the collection was largely ignored, praise from Ralph Waldo Emerson spurred Whitman on, and by its third edition, the collection had swelled to 156 poems. During the American Civil War, Whitman sent dispatches to the *New York Times*, and nursed wounded soldiers from both sides, including his brother George. These experiences proved transformative, and the poems of *Drum Taps*, incorporated into the 1865 edition of *Leaves of Grass*, are among his finest on any subject. Although not especially popular with his American peers, many of whom felt his focus on the male body and its sensual and sexual potential inappropriate, he exerted great influence on later poets. After a stroke in 1873 he remained in Camden, New Jersey, where, as his reputation finally began to grow, his health began to wane. **PS**

"I hear and behold god in every object, yet understand god not in the least."—"Song of Myself"

ABOVE: ***Portrait of Walt Whitman*** **(1887), by Thomas Cowperthwait Eakins (1844–1916).**

RIGHT: A full-length portrait photograph of poet Walt Whitman taken in 1879.

Signature titles

Novels

Typee, or a Peep at Polynesian Life, 1846
Omoo: Adventures in the South Seas, 1847
Mardi, and a Voyage Thither, 1849
Redburn: His First Voyage, 1849
White-Jacket; or The World in a Man-of War, 1850
Moby-Dick, or, The Whale, 1851
Pierre, or, The Ambiguities, 1852
Israel Potter: His Fifty Years of Exile, 1855
The Confidence-Man: His Masquerade, 1857
Billy Budd, Sailor: (An Inside Narrative), 1924

Short stories

The Piazza Tales, 1856
Bartleby, the Scrivener, 1856

Poetry

Battle-Pieces and Aspects of the War, 1866
Clarel: A Poem and Pilgrimage in the Holy Land, 1876
John Marr and Other Sailors, 1888
Timoleon, 1891
Weeds and Wildings, and a Rose or Two, 1924

ABOVE: A detail from a portrait of American novelist Herman Melville.

HERMAN MELVILLE

Born: August 1, 1819 (New York, New York, U.S.); died September 28, 1891 (New York, New York, U.S.).

Style and genre: Melville wrote of sailors and the sea with a blend of narrative realism and a fixation on religious faith tempered by acute skepticism and humor.

By the year of his death, Herman Melville was a stranger to the American literary scene. He had published his last novel, *The Confidence-Man: His Masquerade*, in 1857, subsequently pursuing an ill-fated career as a lecturer. In 1866 he withdrew from public life, taking up a post in the New York Custom House, where he worked until his retirement in 1885. His writing seemed destined to be forgotten; his passing scarcely noticed outside his family. There was little to suggest Melville would secure a central position in the canon of American literature, yet ever since the "Melville Revival" of the 1920s, his reputation has retained the grandeur and proportion of Moby-Dick, his most famous creation.

The genteel New York-Dutch family into which Melville was born fell into financial difficulties in his late childhood. His first ten years were spent in comfortable Manhattan town houses, but in 1830 the family moved to a more humble abode in Albany, following the collapse of his father's business. Escalating misfortune forced Melville into the adult world: after his father's death from a fever in 1832, he took a position as a clerk in a bank, aged twelve. He found a refuge in his father's library until he was able to return to school a few years later.

Melville's real education for life began with his first sea voyage in 1839. He had always been a restless spirit, and his family misguidedly hoped the short journey to Liverpool, England, would cure him of his wanderlust. Instead, exhilarated by his newfound freedom, he made a number of long trips over the next five years, working on ships that sailed to Tahiti, Hawaii, Lima, and Rio de Janeiro. His experiences on deck formed the inspiration for most of his fiction: *Typee, or a Peep at Polynesian Life* and *Omoo: Adventures in the South Seas*, his first two novels, provide a fictionalized account of the month he spent among the people of Taipi Valley in the Marquesas

ABOVE: ***The Whaler "Acushnet" (. . .)*** **by Louis Dodd depicts the whaler Melville served on.**

Islands, after he had jumped the whaling ship on which he had been sailing. The success of *Typee* turned Melville into a minor celebrity. Readers were fascinated by his racy account of island life, which they took for a factual travelog.

Commercially, Melville never hit the high points of *Typee* and *Omoo* again, but while his sales declined, his ambition grew. His third novel, *Mardi, and a Voyage Thither* added philosophical and allegorical dimensions to his trademark jump-ship story line. The two books that followed were dashed off quickly for financial gain, although, their fresh realism spoke of the expansion of his literary horizons.

"Let the ambiguous procession of events reveal their own ambiguousness."—*Pierre*

August 1850 laid the foundations for Melville's greatest achievements, when he met Nathaniel Hawthorne at a picnic atop Monument Mountain, Massachusetts. Melville formed a

Moby-Dick

As they finish Melville's epic novel, most readers feel that they too have wrestled with a whale; *Moby-Dick* is worth the effort. An ambitious amalgam of encyclopedia, drama, and romance, it sets the story of Ishmael, a restless wanderer, against that of Ahab, a man almost psychotically fixed to a single purpose.

Ahab is the captain of the whaler *Pequod*, on which Ishmael and his Polynesian companion, the harpooner Queequeg, set sail. Some time after the ship leaves harbor, Ahab reveals that he is abandoning the commercial purpose of the voyage in favor of his own personal quest: The pursuit and destruction of the great white whale that has taken his leg. Ishmael, as narrator, offers the reader a comprehensive course in cetology, the study of whales. He celebrates the whaling trade as a symbol of cooperation between the nations, of civilization itself. As the book reaches its climax, however, Ishmael's perspective is gradually subordinated to the tale of Ahab and his monomaniacal obsession—a story that draws on the high-flown rhetoric and deep gravitas of Shakespearian tragedy. Seen by some readers as a selfish tyrant, and others as a brave political and religious radical, the captain is the quintessential overreacher. In his eyes, the whale is an emblem of every philosophical issue that has ever eluded human understanding: the inscrutable otherness of God, the problem of radical evil, and the impossibility of attaining truth. Despite his realization that the whale may actually be nothing more than a blank vessel, that he has constructed its meaning himself, Ahab leads his crew into a disastrous confrontation with the beast, from which only Ishmael escapes alive.

lasting admiration for his fellow author, who shared his fascination with the problem of evil and the darker side of human character. A few weeks later he moved to a small estate outside Pittsfield, where he continued work on what was to become his masterpiece, *Moby-Dick, or, The Whale*. Hawthorne continued to inspire Melville, whose next novel, *Pierre: or, The Ambiguities*, was a gothic romance that, like *The Scarlet Letter* (1850), probed the connections between faith and sexuality. Dismissed by contemporary reviewers, *Pierre* is among the most important American novels. It saw its author in blackly humorous mood, recasting his family history and the struggles of his career into a cautionary tale about the dangers of idealism. As his fame dwindled he produced much of his finest writing, including *Billy Budd, Sailor: (An Inside Narrative)*. **CT**

RIGHT: A *c*. 1851 illustration of the white whale by A. Burnham Shute for *Moby-Dick*.

THEODOR FONTANE

Born: December 30, 1819 (Neuruppin, Brandenburg, Germany); died September 20, 1898 (Berlin, Germany).

Style and genre: Fontane was a realist novelist who portrayed the lives of the upper classes in nineteenth-century Prussia with humor, compassion, and sensitivity.

Theodor Fontane followed in his father's footsteps and trained as an apothecary, but at the age of twenty he began writing poetry and stories to relieve the boredom of his job. His first novella, *Sibling Love* (*Geschwisterliebe*) was serialized in Berlin's *Figaro* newspaper in 1839, although it did not shows signs of his future greatness.

He joined the Prussian Army in 1844, and after finishing military service in 1849 he became a full-time journalist and writer. He spent several years in London as a foreign correspondent, and visited Paris as a war correspondent where he was mistakenly arrested as a spy. In addition to his journalism, he wrote poetry, theater reviews, and travelogues. He published his first novel *Before the Storm* (*Vor dem Sturm*) at the age of fifty-eight. He then wrote another sixteen novels that were to establish his reputation as Germany's greatest realist novelist: Fontane was able to write with equal skill about the Berlin bourgeoisie as well as life in parochial nineteenth-century Germany.

He believed that "women's stories are generally far more interesting," and depicted their lives with great sensitivity. His novel *The Woman Taken in Adultery* (*L'Adultera*) was considered so shocking that it took two years to find a publisher, but it is *Effi Briest*, the story of a woman who refuses to bow to convention that is perhaps his best-loved work. Set in Chancellor Otto von Bismarck's Germany, it relates the tale of seventeen-year-old Effi Briest, and her marriage to a dull baron who is twice her age, but whom her family deem is a socially suitable match. Fontane depicts with great sensitivity how the narrow-minded strictures of social convention can lead to personal tragedy. **HJ**

"[*Effi Briest* is] one of the six most significant novels ever written."—Thomas Mann

Signature titles

Novels

Before the Storm (Vor dem Sturm), 1878

The Woman Taken in Adultery (L'Adultera), 1882

Trials and Tribulations (Irrungen, Wirrungen), 1888

Beyond Recall (Unwiederbringlich), 1891

Jenny Treibel (Frau Jenny Treibel), 1893

Effi Briest, 1895

Novella

Sibling Love (Geschwisterliebe), 1839

ABOVE: A detail from a photograph of Theodor Fontane taken c. 1880–1890.

CHARLES BAUDELAIRE

Born: April 9, 1821 (Paris, France); died August 31, 1867 (Paris, France).

Style and genre: French critic, poet and translator and a founding figure of the symbolist movement, Baudelaire's poetry was highly controversial for its description of sacred and profane love, morality and death, and eroticism.

Signature titles

Poetry

The Flowers of Evil (Les Fleurs du mal), 1857

The Flowers of Evil (Les Fleurs du mal), 1861 (second edition, with additional poems)

Short Prose Poems / The Spleens of Paris (Petits poèmes en prose / Paris Spleen), 1869

Novel

La Fanfarlo, 1847

Translations

Les Paradis artificiels, 1860

Criticism

Curiosités Esthétiques, 1868 (published posthumously)

L'Art romantique, 1868 (published posthumously)

Charles Baudelaire played a significant role in the development of modern English and French literature, not only as the infamous author of an incendiary collection of poems but as a critic whose then-controversial theories of literature are now widely accepted. His early years were marked by a dissolute lifestyle (which he called a "*vie libre*") and it is during this period that he contracted the venereal disease that may have left him impotent for the remainder of his life.

Baudelaire's father, a priest, died when he was a young boy and his mother remarried an army officer who was to rise to the rank of General. It was this disciplinarian figure who sent the young Charles off to board at the Collège Royal, Lyons, and thereafter to the Collège Louis-le-Grand, in Paris, from which he was expelled for indiscipline in 1839. The next two years were spent living a decadent existence in Paris, during which time Baudelaire dissipated a large part of his paternal

ABOVE: A portrait photograph of Charles Baudelaire by the Goupil Studio.

RIGHT: One of Charles Maurin's 1891 illustrations from *Les Fleurs du mal*.

inheritance and built up debts. Consequently his family insisted his money be transferred into the hands of a trustee who reduced his spending to more temperate levels.

It was during these bohemian years that Baudelaire became a part of the literary-artistic milieu and wrote a number of the poems that were to make up part of the collection *Les Fleurs du mal* (*The Flowers of Evil*), which would attract much attention when it was published in 1857. By this time he had established a reputation for his critical reviews of the salons of 1845 and 1846, for his only completed novel, *La Fanfarlo* (1847), and for his translations of, and critical essays on, Poe and de Quincey. During the early 1860s, Baudelaire focused much of his energy on writing prose poetry. It was also around this time that he fell into a state of very poor physical and mental health, in large part due to a recurrence of the syphilis that had afflicted him as a young man. After an unsuccessful two years in Belgium, a serious fall left him unable to read and write, and he spent the last year of his life in a Parisian nursing home. **GM**

ABOVE: Baudelaire (in profile with hat) in Manet's *Music in the Tuileries Gardens* (1862).

Indecent Poems

Baudelaire's poetry collection *Les Fleurs du mal* is, for many, synonymous with scandal. His audacious treatment of sex and death quickly arrested the attention of the authorities and the publication was withdrawn and Baudelaire fined, after a court found six of the poems to be indecent. In it, he uses the lyrical mode to explore his taste for vice and sin, an exasperated sense of existential ennui, the profligacy of Parisian life, as well as his romantic and carnal cravings. In his poetic graspings for the ideal, in his seer-like attempts to attain the transcendent, Baudelaire anticipated much of what was to follow in the symbolist movement.

GUSTAVE FLAUBERT

Born: December 12, 1821 (Rouen, France); died May 8, 1880 (Croisset, France).

Style and genre: A member of the class he held so much in contempt, Flaubert never had to work for a living and was able to write and travel as he liked, allowing him to choose his words with impeccable care and publish at his own pace.

In his novel *Flaubert's Parrot*, Julian Barnes lists some of the titles applied to the French author, all of them apt: "The hermit of Croisset. The first modern novelist. The father of Realism. The butcher of Romanticism. . . . The bourgeois bourgeoisophobe." Flaubert is a legend, one of the great innovators of the realist novel, but also something of a contradiction. The son of a wealthy surgeon, the young Flaubert rebelled against his comfortable life—he was expelled from school for rowdiness at eighteen—and maintained a continued contempt for the bourgeoisie. After his father and sister died, and an epileptic attack forced Flaubert to quit law school, he moved to Croisset, where he lived with his mother until he was fifty; he traveled and wrote, but otherwise never worked, enjoying the spoils of a moneyed existence. Perhaps this maxim of his explains it best: "Be regular and orderly in your life like a bourgeois, so that you may be violent and original in your work."

The scandal that resulted from the publication of his first novel, *Madame Bovary*, catapulted Flaubert to fame. The

Signature titles

Novels

Madame Bovary, 1857

Salammbô, 1862

Sentimental Education (L'Éducation sentimentale), 1869

The Temptation of Saint Anthony (La Tentation de saint Antoine), 1874

Short stories

Three Tales (Trois contes), 1877

Nonfiction

Dictionary of Received Ideas (Dictionnaire des idées reçues), 1911 (published posthumously)

ABOVE: ***Portrait of Gustave Flaubert*** **(1881), by Eugène Giraud (1806–1881).**

RIGHT: ***The Death Bed of Madame Bovary*** **(before 1889) by Albert-Auguste Fourie.**

LEFT: A nineteenth-century engraving of Emma Bovary.

painstakingly realistic story of Emma Bovary's adultery and suicide was a critique of the type of romantic novels that instilled in Emma herself the desire for a love life of thunderbolts and fury, with a man vastly unlike the devoted but dull provincial doctor she married. *Madame Bovary* was also a critique on the level of form: the narrator never intrudes to tell the reader to pity Emma, or to judge her, but leaves that decision up to us—in fact, this may be what outraged its detractors most.

Flaubert only published every five or six years—indicative of his famous phrase: "le seul mot juste," or, "the one precise word." Flaubert believed that every thought deserved its most perfect expression, and that "the more beautiful an idea, the more sonorous the sentence." Although his work was hugely successful, his extravagant lifestyle left him penniless. **CQ**

Madame Bovary

Madame Bovary was first published in serial form in the *Revue de Paris*, edited by Flaubert's friend, Maxime du Camp, who cut the most explicit scenes. Despite this, the novel was accused of having "outraged public morals and religion." Flaubert and the magazine managed to escape conviction, though he would have willingly gone to jail rather than censor his own work. Besides his oft-quoted line, "Madame Bovary, c'est moi," the most Flaubert would say on the scandal was that, "I would not like to die before having emptied a few more buckets of shit on the heads of my fellow men."

FYODOR DOSTOEVSKY

Born: Fyodor Mikhailovich Dostoevsky, November 11, 1821 (Moscow, Russia); died February 9, 1881 (St. Petersburg, Russia).

Style and genre: Russian novelist whose powerful dramas of moral confusion mark the beginning of modern psychological fiction.

If an eventful life makes for better literary output, then circumstance gave Fyodor Dostoevsky all the material he could need. In the 1840s, he became caught up in the optimistic liberalism of the Russian intelligentsia and joined a society called the Petrashevsky Circle. He was arrested for his involvement, sentenced to death, and was on the verge of execution before being given a last-minute reprieve and sent to Siberia for four years of hard labor. He fictionalized these experiences in his novel *The House of the Dead*. By the time Dostoevsky returned to St. Petersburg in 1859, he was deeply ambivalent about the cultural movement he had left behind, and turned with increasing fascination back to Russian orthodoxy and traditionalism; the influence of this belief system on his fiction becoming stronger as he grew older.

What makes Dostoevsky's writing so compelling is that he asks the big questions, but never finally decides between faith and politics; thus what comes across in his work is less a coherent system of beliefs than an urgent desire to believe. This is why the philosophical arguments and allegorical

Signature titles

Novels

Poor Folk, 1846
The Double: A Petersburg Poem, 1846
Netochka Nezvanova, 1849
The Insulted and the Injured, 1861
The House of the Dead, 1862
Notes from Underground, 1864
Crime and Punishment, 1866
The Gambler, 1867
The Idiot, 1868
The Possessed, 1872
The Brothers Karamazov, 1880

ABOVE: An portrait photograph of Russian novelist Fyodor Dostoevsky.

RIGHT: Marian Marsh and Peter Lorre in the 1935 film of *Crime and Punishment*.

ABOVE: **Boris Grigoryev's illustration (1916–1932) based on** ***The Brothers Karamazov.***

elements that characterize his novels, which would be heavy-handed in less capable hands, have remained fresh and compelling for over a century.

This aspect of Dostoevsky's fiction is perhaps clearest in *Crime and Punishment*, which follows the aftermath of a murder poorly conceived and poorly executed. In its sympathetic approach to a sensational subject, the novel helped to reinvent crime fiction from the ground up; the entire literary genre of the hard-boiled thriller (and with it the cinematic genre film noir) occupies the same uneasy moral haze that this novel dramatizes so successfully. As with Dostoevsky's other masterpiece, *The Brothers Karamazov*, the narrative is both relentlessly gripping and excruciatingly slow, racheting up the tension without ever collapsing under

"Seething whirlpools, waterspouts that hiss and boil and suck us in."

—Virginia Woolf on Dostoevsky's novels

Existentialism and *Notes from Underground*

In the title of his popular reader *Existentialism from Dostoevsky to Sartre*, Walter Kaufman identifies Dostoevsky with "existentialism"—a modern philosophical approach that focuses on the personal and ethical over the universal and metaphysical, in contrast to "essentialist" philosophy, which works the other way around. Kaufman says the first expression of existentialism can be found in the writing of Dostoevsky. In particular, his early novel *Notes from Underground* represents, in Kaufman's words, an "altogether new voice," which had a direct influence on Nietzsche, Sartre, and most of the major philosophers of the twentieth century.

In two parts, the novel is a response to the "rational egoism" of Dostoevsky's contemporary, Chernychevsky, which takes as a starting premise that human beings always act out of their perception of their own self-interest. The unnamed narrator responds that he does not act out of his own interest, and in fact consciously chooses to do the opposite of what he knows to be good for him. Part one is a statement of these principles, and part two is a story in which the narrator appears so revolting that many readers read it as ironically undercutting the first. But the whole point is that it does not matter what we think of the underground man; he has chosen to be the person he is, whether we like it or not.

RIGHT: *Portrait of Fyodor Dostoevsky* (1872), by Vasili Grigorevich Perov (1833–1882).

the weight of its own ambivalence. Dostoevsky is able to accomplish this by keeping things in constant motion, even at the level of the sentence, and his novels propel their readers forward in a surge of inevitability while they draw them backward with an undertow of dread. Unlike the protagonists of a classical tragedy, his characters are wholly responsible for their own suffering, and conscious of their culpability; unfortunately for them, this knowledge only draws the noose all the tighter.

A character type that Dostoevsky seemed fascinated by is the amoralist, or someone with a worldview that modern psychologists would diagnose as sociopathic. In contrast to the merely immoral person, who chooses selfishly to pursue their own short-term gain, Dostoevsky's amoral characters—such as Svidrigailov in *Crime and Punishment* and Smerdyakov in *The Brothers Karamazov*—are bound by no such consistent motivations. They seem to have only the dimmest conception of the ethical implications of their behavior, and the best explanation for their actions seems to be simply that they want to hurt the people around them, just to see what it is like.

In *The Possessed*, Dostoevsky creates perhaps his most purely amoral character in Stavrogin, the indifferent figurehead of a radical organization not unlike the Petrashevsky Circle. The difference is that the radicals in *The Possessed* are significantly less innocent; the novel is set in the 1860s, after the intelligentsia had shed many of the utopian ideals that characterized the intellectual climate of Dostoevsky's youth, in exchange for a nihilistic practical materialism. Many readers have suggested that the cynical propagandists and ruthless economists who populate this novel are proof that Dostoevsky already saw the dangers that would culminate in the rise of the Bolsheviks, half a century later. If true, this would not be the only time Dostoevsky anticipated the future; in fact, it is safe to say that there are not many writers of the nineteenth century who belong so completely to the intellectual climate of the twentieth. But if Dostoevsky was able to see the future, it was because of his unwavering fixation on the dilemmas right in front of him, in his unstable, uncertain present. **SY**

WILKIE COLLINS

Born: William Wilkie Collins, January 8, 1824 (London, England); died September 23, 1889 (London, England).

Style and genre: Collins's work is known for its dramatic themes interspersed with humor, melodramatic plots, and an air of sometimes sinister mystery.

Widely read and admired in his lifetime, Wilkie Collins is most famous today for *The Moonstone* and *The Woman in White*. His works are filled with vivid imagery, like that of a drug-induced dream, inspired by his own addiction to the opiate, laudanum, which he took for gout-induced pain. He lived a bohemian existence with two women: Caroline Graves, a widow with a daughter, and Martha Rudd, with whom he had three children. He didn't marry either but openly lived with them both, in separate houses. His works reflect this refusal to conform, dealing as they do with subjects such as illegitimacy, divorce, and even vivisection. He had a vast circle of literary friends, most notably Charles Dickens. **LH**

Signature titles

Novels

Mr. Wray's Cash-Box, 1852
The Woman in White, 1860
No Name, 1862
Armadale, 1866
The Moonstone, 1868
The Haunted Hotel, 1878
Heart and Science, 1883

Plays

The Lighthouse, 1855
The Frozen Deep, 1857 (cowritten with Charles Dickens)

JULES VERNE

Born: Jules Gabriel Verne, February 8, 1828 (Nantes, France); died March 24, 1905 (Amines, France).

Style and genre: A popular French author of adventure stories based on scientific fact, Jules Verne has a claim to the title "the father of true science fiction."

Jules Verne trained as a lawyer before turning to writing accounts of realistic adventures whose plots hinged on as yet uninvented technologies. His books predicted submarines (*20,000 Leagues Under the Sea*), space travel (*From the Earth to the Moon*), helicopters (*Robur the Conqueror*), and skyscrapers (*In the Year 2889*). However, as Verne himself pointed out, these were not his inventions, merely extrapolations of contemporary scientific developments. Nevertheless, some of his ideas ring impressively true: his moon-rocket was the same dimensions and launched from the same vicinity (Florida) as that of the U.S.'s Apollo space missions. Verne's thrilling plots have made him one of the most translated authors of all time. **JM**

Signature titles

Novels

Five Weeks in a Balloon (Cinq semaines en ballon), 1863
Journey to the Center of the Earth (Voyage au centre de la terre), 1864
From the Earth to the Moon (De la terre à la lune), 1865
Round the Moon (Autour de la lune), 1870
20,000 Leagues Under the Sea (Vingt mille lieues sous les mers), 1870
A Floating City (Une ville flottante), 1871
Around the World in Eighty Days (Le Tour du monde en quatre-vingts jours), 1873
Kéraban the Inflexible (Kéraban-le-têtu), 1883
Paris in the 20th Century (Paris au XX siècle), 1994 (published posthumously)

RIGHT: The cover of Verne's *Kéraban the Inflexible*, published by Hetzel in 1883.

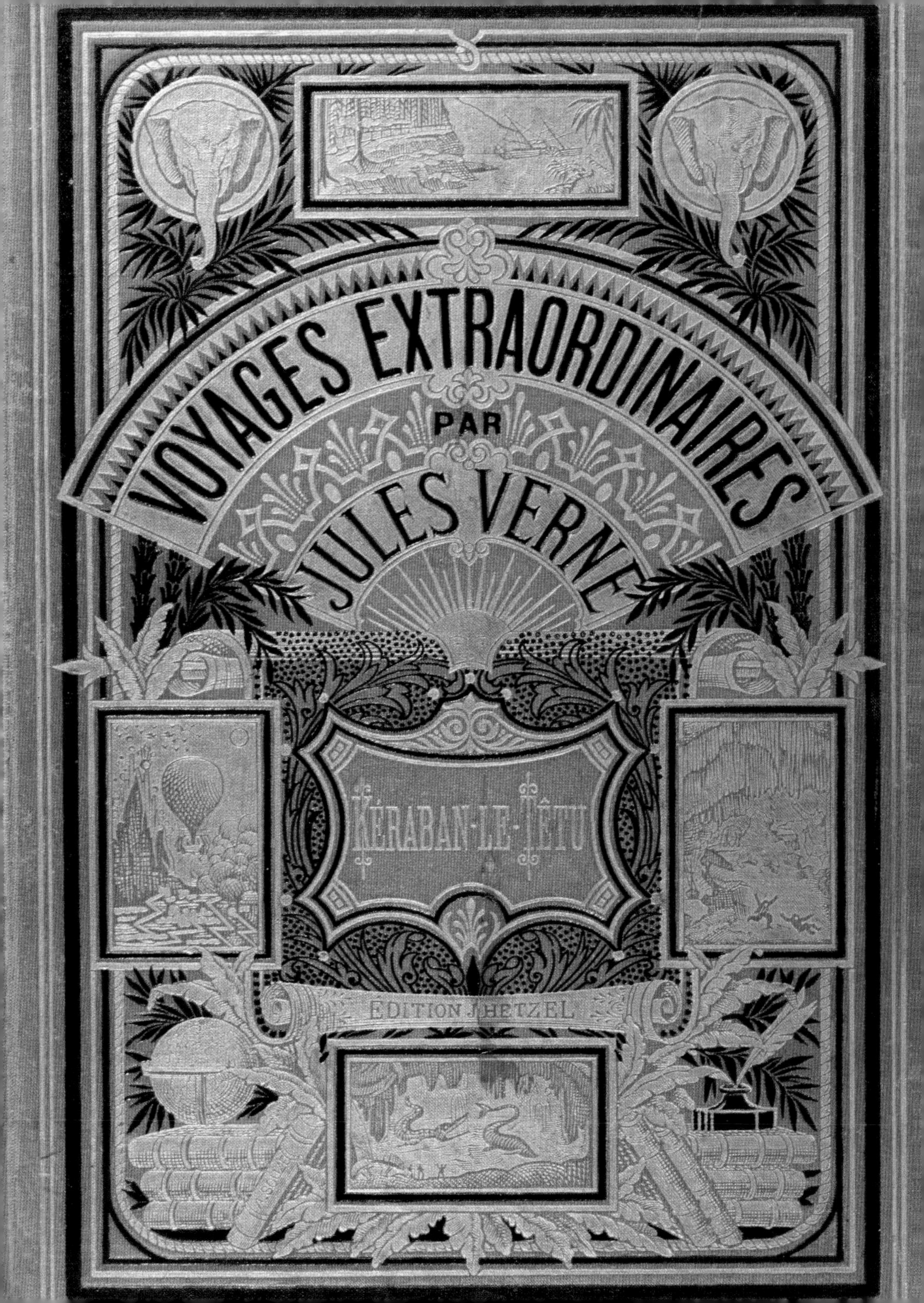
VOYAGES EXTRAORDINAIRES
PAR
JULES VERNE
KÉRABAN-LE-TÊTU
ÉDITION J. HETZEL

HENRIK IBSEN

Born: March 20, 1828 (Skien, Norway); died May 23, 1906 (Oslo, Norway).

Style and genre: Ibsen's unflinching dialogue reassesses the moral values of his day. The plays contain portraits of middle-class life, often with tragic themes evolved through male hypocrisy and the futility of idealism.

Signature titles

Plays

Brand, 1866
Peer Gynt, 1867
Emperor and Galilean 1873
The Pillars of Society, 1877
A Doll's House, 1879
Ghosts, 1881
An Enemy of the People, 1882
Hedda Gabler, 1890
The Master Builder, 1892

A major playwright of the late nineteenth century, Ibsen was responsible for the introduction of modern realistic drama to the stage. His love for the theater took him firstly to Bergen and later Christiana (present day Oslo) working as a stage manager writing and directing plays. Despite gaining valuable practical experience Ibsen failed to connect intellectually with an audience he thought to be petty and small-minded. A self-imposed, twenty-seven-year period of exile ensued, taking him to Rome, Dresden, and Munich. Seemingly released from the constraints of his homeland, Ibsen wrote the bulk of his dramas abroad beginning with *Brand*, a play concentrated on a priest who puts his own religious and moral principles before the well-being of his family. The "all or nothing" philosophy of Brand, which ultimately leaves him broken and alone, proved hugely popular, as did follow-up *Peer Gynt*, an egotistical, aimless character, very much the antithesis of Brand.

It was *A Doll's House* that elevated him to international attention with its controversial denouement and scandalous (to Victorian audiences) lack of a happy ending. The ordinary household setting witnesses the heroine Nora become gradually disillusioned with her husband, whom she comes to view as a stranger, leaving him and her children behind. He courted yet more damnation in *Ghosts* with its subject matter of venereal disease and central belief that to ignore ugly truths is only to create dire consequences at a later point. Later works shifted focus from societal pressures on women to the psychological interpersonal conflicts of control and domination as explored in *Hedda Gabler* and *The Master Builder*. Ibsen rewrote the rules of drama remaining challenging and provocative to the end. **SG**

"The strongest man in the world is he who stands most alone." —*An Enemy of the People*

ABOVE: A photograph of the hirsute Ibsen *c.* 1900, just a few years before his death.

RIGHT: Arthur Rackham's *Peer Gynt* Act II Scene vi, Peer Before the King of the Trolls.

Rackham

LEO TOLSTOY

Born: Lev Nikolayevich Tolstoy, September 9, 1828 (Yasnaya Polyana, Russia); died November 20, 1910 (Astapovo, Russia).

Style and genre: Russian author, essayist, playwright, and philosopher, Tolstoy is celebrated as one of the greatest novelists of all time.

Count Leo Tolstoy was born into a noble Russian family. After being orphaned at the age of nine, he was brought up by his aunts and private tutors. He left university early without a degree, but was a great believer in education, and when he returned to his parents' estate in Yasnaya Polyana, he made unfruitful attempts to educate his workers. He often traveled to Moscow and St. Petersburg with his brother, following the self-indulgent lifestyle expected of a young Russian nobleman, but he grew weary of this debauched way of life, and was prone to bouts of self-hating introspection. In 1851, he joined the army, and the next year published *Childhood*, the first of an autobiographical trilogy followed by *Boyhood* and *Youth*. During the Crimean War he fought at Sevastopol; his ensuing forthright articles made him well known in the literary circles of St. Petersburg and gained the attention of the tsar.

Signature titles

Novels

The Cossacks, 1863

War and Peace, 1865–1869

Anna Karenina,1873–1877

The Death of Ivan Ilyich, 1886

The Kreutzer Sonata, 1889

What Is Art?, 1897–1898

Resurrection, 1899

Hadji Murad, 1912 (published posthumously)

Nonfiction

A Short Exposition of the Gospels, 1881

What I Believe In, 1882

Confession, 1882

What Then Must We Do?, 1886

What Is Art?, 1897–1898

The Law of Love and the Law of Violence, 1908

Plays

The Power of Darkness, 1886

The Living Corpse, 1911 (published posthumously)

Autobiographies

Childhood, 1852

Boyhood, 1854

Youth, 1857

ABOVE: A portrait of Leo Tolstoy, created in approximately 1887.

RIGHT: Chekov and Tolstoy at the estate of Countess Paniva near Yalta, 1901.

ABOVE: An illustration of the revered Tolstoy with Russian children.

Although Tolstoy is remembered mostly for being a novelist, he actually only wrote three full-length novels: *War and Peace*; *Anna Karenina*, which Vladimir Nabokov described as "one of the greatest love stories in world literature"; and *Resurrection*. In his day, Tolstoy was known more as a moral philosopher and his political writings won him a great following in Russia. He believed in a simple existence of toiling for what was needed in life, with no material possessions. He wrote long tracts on his anti-capitalist viewpoints, the path of non-violent protest (later adopted by Gandhi) and religious reform. In 1901, he was excommunicated from the Orthodox Church for his quest to try to create a new, simpler version of Christianity, but this only made him more popular with his followers.

In the last years of his life, Tolstoy lived by his creed, doing away with his titles and possessions, much to the chagrin of his wife and family. He died a hermit. **JM**

War and Peace

- Voted by *Time* magazine as the greatest novel of all time, *War and Peace* is an epic historical saga following the lives of four aristocratic families against the backdrop of the invasion of Russia by Napoleon.
- It began as a magazine serialization but became a truly staggering work, taking seven years to complete and featuring 580 characters (some based on real-life people, others fictional).
- Its overarching theme explores the value of the family and how victory in life and war is based on nothing more than chance and circumstance.

EMILY DICKINSON

Born: December 10, 1830 (Amherst, Massachusetts, U.S.); died May 15, 1886 (Amherst, Massachusetts, U.S.).

Style and genre: Dickinson used everyday language in poetic form, accentuated by rapid—often broken—phrases, unusual punctuation, and soul-searching lyrics.

Signature titles

Poetry

Selected Works, 1924

Bolts of Melody, 1945

The Collected Poems of Emily Dickinson, 1998

Letters

Emily Dickinson's Correspondences, 2005

A poet who lived in as eccentric a manner as possible for a nineteenth-century woman—without being confined to an asylum—Emily Dickinson was little known during her life but became celebrated after her death. The stories of her eccentricities, affectations, and insanity have kept the Dickinson legend alive, ensuring new generations will keep wanting to rediscover her. Dickinson wrote more than 1,700 poems, as well as a large number of letters, although barely any of her poems were published in her lifetime. Much of her poetry can appear unfathomable, seemingly a series of riddles allowing varied interpretations; the poems' meanings have kept academics and scholars debating for well over a century.

The Dickinsons were a wealthy and well-respected family. Emily's father, a lawyer and strict Christian, ruled over his children sternly, probably resulting in his daughter's fragile emotional state. According to family history, Mr. Dickinson

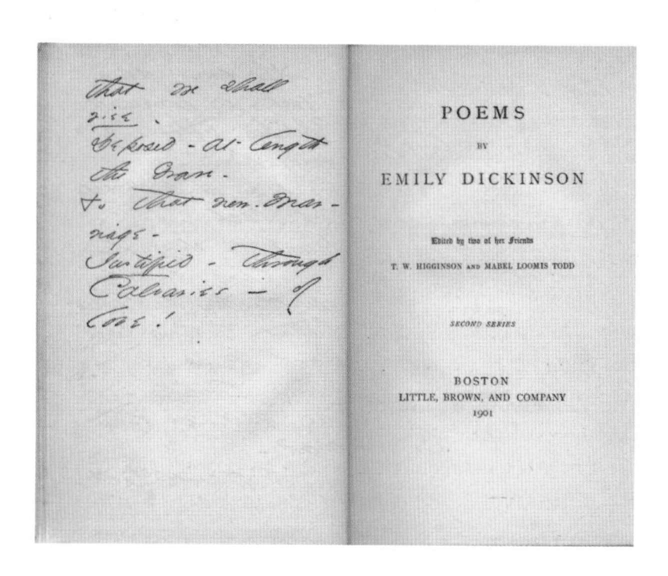

that we shall
rise.
Deposed - at - length
the Grave -
to that new - Mar-
riage -
Justified - through
Calvaries - of
Love!

POEMS

BY

EMILY DICKINSON

Edited by two of her Friends

T. W. HIGGINSON AND MABEL LOOMIS TODD

SECOND SERIES

BOSTON
LITTLE, BROWN, AND COMPANY
1901

ABOVE: A portrait of the young, reclusive Emily Dickinson *c.* 1850.

RIGHT: The end of "Renunciation," from the first volume of Dickinson's poems.

would not even allow his daughters to choose the books they wanted to read or who they would be friends with; he made all such decisions for them. Emily Dickinson remained childlike even as an adult, reluctant to grow up. In her twenties, she made the decision to wear no colors, insisting every item of her clothing be white; by the time she was in her thirties, she had become almost entirely reclusive, refusing to leave home even to attend her father's funeral. Her poetry records Dickinson's frustration with the world and with her own inability to live in it, recorded in such lines as "I felt a cleaving in my mind / as if my brain had split." Her many periods of depression can also be witnessed through the poems she left behind, a poignant glimpse into the world of mental illness.

After Emily's early death, from Bright's Disease, her younger sister, Lavinia, discovered the wealth of poetry she left behind. Emily had asked for the poems to be destroyed but Lavinia could not bring herself to do so. She published the first volume (of three) of her sister's poems in 1891. Since that time, Emily Dickinson, nicknamed "the nun of Amherst," has become a cult figure. The place of her birth has become a shrine for poetry lovers from around the world. **LH**

ABOVE: The Dickinson family home in Amherst, Massachusetts, now the Emily Dickinson Museum.

Intimate Friendships

Despite writing such passionate and sexual poetry, the poet appears to have had no genuine love affairs—although scholars have attempted to prove her correspondents could have been her lovers. Despite her reclusive life, she cultivated a number of intimate friends and correspondents, men and women, including her beloved sister-in-law, Susan (wife of Austin Dickinson). Among her regular correspondents were writer, abolitionist, and social reformer Thomas Wentworth Higginson (1823–1911) and writer Helen Hunt Jackson (née Fiske; 1830–1885), who campaigned fervently for equal rights for Native Americans.

CHRISTINA ROSSETTI

Born: December 5, 1830 (London, England); died December 29, 1894 (London, England).

Style and genre: An unworldly poet of the Pre-Raphaelite circle, whose Tractarian religious devotion was at odds with her most famous works' pagan imagination.

Few female poets of the nineteenth century have survived into the twentieth-century canon. Most have been consigned to the back shelves, while Christina Rossetti and Elizabeth Barrett Browning are widely anthologized. It is largely Elizabeth Barrett's romantic elopement with poet Robert Browning that continues to capture the imagination, but with Christina Rossetti it is her work—1,100 poems—that has passed into popular knowledge. In particular, her wintry lyric, "In the Deep Midwinter," and her feverish vision and novella-length-poem *Goblin Market* (which was first published with illustrations by her brother, poet and painter Dante Gabriel Rossetti).

Christina was the youngest of the four remarkable Rossetti siblings. She socialized with many of her brothers' friends, who comprised the artistic elite of 1860s England, including Whistler, Charles Dodgson (Lewis Carroll) and the poet W. H. Swinburne. *Goblin Market* is an exploration of Victorian female adolescence on the cusp of sexual awareness; like Swinburne's poetry, it is ornately medieval in its language and references.

Although Rossetti's creative impetus apparently stemmed from her strict Christianity, her works include many poems that are suffused with the same female erotic as *Goblin Market*, including melancholy poems to, or in the voice of, Sappho. Like her brother, Christina Rossetti revived the sonnet form, with a similarly strong gift for visual imagery. Echoing the sonnet structure, her poems often explore a deep dichotomy—in her case, between the spiritual and sensual, both of which are symbolized by striking use of the natural world. Although she never married and was only briefly engaged, Christina Rossetti used the sonnet form to sound feelings of (metaphysical) love. **SM**

"Better . . . you should forget and smile than . . . remember and be sad."—"Remember"

Signature titles

Poetry

Goblin Market and Other Poems, 1862

The Poetical Works of Christina Georgina Rossetti. With Memoir and Notes, & c., by William Michael Rossetti, 1904

Complete Poems of Christina Rossetti: A Variorum Edition, 1986

ABOVE: A lithograph of Christina Rossetti after a drawing by Dante Gabriel Rossetti.

LEWIS CARROLL

Born: Charles Lutwidge Dodgson, January 27, 1832 (Daresbury, Cheshire, England); died January 14, 1898 (Guildford, Surrey, England).

Style and genre: Author of two of the world's most popular children's books, Carroll also wrote poetry, pamphlets, and articles.

Lewis Carroll, the pen name adopted by Charles Dodgson, is synonymous with some of the most imaginative writing of the nineteenth century. Today he has become a cult figure, with societies and clubs around the world dedicated to keeping his work alive. Ironically, Lewis Carroll has assumed an identity almost completely separate from the real Charles Dodgson, and there are numerous and unsubstantiated myths attached to the "persona." The name Lewis Carroll has also been subjected to a number of (unproven) accusations of pedophilia, based on Dodgson's affection for young girls and photographs, including nude studies, that he took of children.

In 1851 Dodgson entered Christ Church College, Oxford, the beginning of a lifelong association with the university which culminated in him becoming a Professor of mathematics. He did not greatly enjoy his job, yet even after literary and financial success, he remained in his teaching position.

In 1856 Henry Liddell, the new dean of Christ Church, arrived in Oxford with his wife and three young daughters, Lorina, Edith, and Alice. Dodgson became good friends with the family, and frequently took the girls out on picnics. It was during one such trip that he began to tell them a story about a little girl and her adventures. Alice Liddell persuaded him to write the story down and Dodgson showed it to his friend, the author George MacDonald. In 1863 Dodgson submitted the manuscript to the publisher Macmillan, and in 1865 *Alice's Adventures in Wonderland* was published. It met with immediate success and was followed by *Through the Looking Glass and What Alice Found There* (1872), and *The Hunting of the Snark* in 1876. None of his works reached the same level of popularity as the original story of Alice. **TP**

"Everything has got a moral, if you can only find it."
—Lewis Carroll

Signature titles

Children's fiction

Alice's Adventures in Wonderland, 1865

Through the Looking Glass and What Alice Found There, 1871

Sylvie and Bruno, 1889; volume 2 1893

Nonsense verse

The Hunting of the Snark, 1876

ABOVE: A portrait photograph of Lewis Carroll taken by Oscar Gustav Rejlander.

Signature titles

Novels

The Gilded Age, 1873 (with C. D. Warner)

The Adventures of Tom Sawyer, 1876

The Prince and the Pauper, 1882

Adventures of Huckleberry Finn, 1884

A Connecticut Yankee in King Arthur's Court, 1889

The Tragedy of Pudd'nhead Wilson, 1894

Nonfiction

The Innocents Abroad, 1869

Roughing It, 1872

Life on the Mississippi, 1883

Is Shakespeare Dead?, 1909

Mark Twain's Autobiography, 1924

Short stories

The Celebrated Jumping Frog of Calaveras County and Other Sketches, 1867

The Man that Corrupted Hadleyburg, 1899

Extracts from Adam's Diary, 1904

Captain Stormfield's Visit to Heaven, 1909

ABOVE: A studio portrait photograph of Twain taken at the height of his fame.

RIGHT: An illustration from *The Adventures of Tom Sawyer*.

MARK TWAIN

Born: Samuel Langhorne Clemens, November 30, 1835 (Florida, Missouri, U.S.); died April 21, 1910 (Redding, Connecticut, U.S.).

Style and genre: Twain's writing features a folksy, mischievous authorial persona; skepticism toward religion; roguish, innocent heroes; and sharp social satire.

White suit, mustache, cigar: Mark Twain's sartorial trademarks are as well-known as his best-loved characters, Tom Sawyer and Huckleberry Finn. As the most prominent man of letters in America's first great commercial age, Twain understood that how he presented himself in public was as important to his audience as the quality of his writing. A hugely prolific writer, he published more than thirty books as well as numerous essays and hundreds of short stories. An icon in his own

lifetime, Mark Twain still stands at the center of the American literary tradition—his social satires, compassion and biting wit remaining an inspiration for writers today.

Twain was born Samuel Clemens in Florida, Missouri, although his formative years were spent in the town of Hannibal, on the banks of the Mississippi. Although he moved away in 1853, a few months shy of his eighteenth birthday, the frontier spirit of the Midwest and the life of the river would always infuse his work. He adopted his famous pseudonym ten years later, while working as a journalist amid the silver mines of Virginia City, Nevada. Although he didn't strike it rich in Nevada, Twain amassed a considerable fortune through the course of the literary career that began there. His first two books, *The Innocents Abroad* and *Roughing It*, were tremendous commercial successes, the first describing his travels in Europe, the second his time on the Nevada frontier.

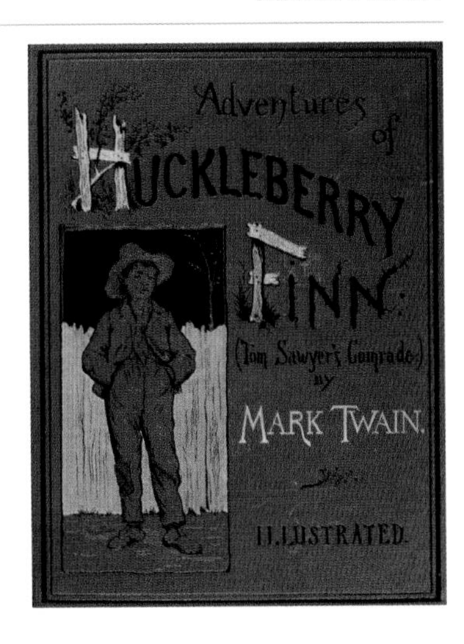

ABOVE: The cover of the first American edition of *Adventures of Huckleberry Finn*.

Creating Tom Sawyer and Huckleberry Finn

While Twain's fame as a humorist and journalist spread ever wider, reaching even the shores of Europe, his career as a novelist would begin with a return to the Hannibal of his youth. Although intended as a book for boys, *The Adventures of Tom Sawyer* proved to have a much broader appeal. Along with its sequel, *Adventures of Huckleberry Finn*, it proved to be his most popular and critically acclaimed work. Although both books are brimming with nostalgia, they showcase Twain's sharp, skeptical tongue as much as his keen eye for provincial color and detail.

If he retained the manner of a bluff Missourian on the make, Twain's political values sat more comfortably with the liberal New England where he spent much of his later life. His works showcase his own political views, thinly veiled in fiction, as well as his observations about contemporary society. His views on the racial problems that faced America were particularly progressive. Twain was no naive idealist, however; despite his egalitarian beliefs, his best work is shot through with a healthy contempt for the gross stupidity and venality of humanity. **CT**

Huckleberry Finn

Famously described by Hemingway as the book "all modern American literature comes from," *Adventures of Huckleberry Finn* is still the quintessential American coming-of-age story. The moment when Huck realizes that he would rather go to hell for breaking the law than shop his friend Jim, the fugitive slave, to the authorities retains all of its startling power. Twain uses Huck's innocent perspective on his misadventures to expose the hypocrisies and petty vanities of Southern society. The raft on the Mississippi proves to be the only place where white and black can approach each other as equals.

MACHADO DE ASSIS

Born: Joaquim Maria Machado de Assis, June 21, 1839 (Rio de Janeiro, Brazil); died September 29, 1908 (Rio de Janeiro, Brazil).

Style and genre: Brazilian writer who reflected many contemporary European trends, used irony in his social criticism, and satirized bourgeois manners and ideals.

Signature titles

Poetry

Chrysalids (Crisálidas), 1864

Americanas, 1875

Novels

Mistress Garcia (Iaiá Garcia), 1878

The Posthumous Memoirs of Brás Cubas, or Epitaph for a Small Winner (Memórias Póstumas de Brás Cubas), 1881

Philosopher or Dog? (Quincas Borba), 1891

Sir Dour (Dom Casmurro), 1900

Short stories

Stories of Midnight (Histórias da Meia Noite), 1873

Machado de Assis, one of Brazil's greatest novelists, also wrote plays, poetry, and critical essays. The son of an impoverished housepainter, he managed to become one of the literary elite, although he had received little education. Machado taught himself French and English, and in 1897 he founded and became president of the Brazilian Academy of Letters. His first novels, poetry, and plays were written in the romantic style, but with his novel, *The Posthumous Memoirs of Brás Cubas*, Machado entered into a new phase of writing, breaking many literary conventions of his day. Influenced by Laurence Sterne and Xavier de Maistre, his novels, in their psychological depth, have been compared to the work of Henry James. **REM**

THOMAS HARDY

Born: June 2, 1840 (Higher Bockhampton, Dorset, England); died January 11, 1928 (Dorchester, England).

Style and genre: Poet and novelist, Hardy created sympathetic and vivid descriptions of rural life and a fatalistic world full of injustice.

Signature titles

Novels

Far From the Madding Crowd, 1874

The Return of the Native, 1878

The Mayor of Casterbridge, 1886

The Woodlanders, 1887

Tess of the d'Urbervilles, 1891

Jude the Obscure, 1895

Poetry

Wessex Poems, 1898

Poems of the Past and Present, 1902

Satires of Circumstance, 1914

Hardy set his novels predominantly in the semifictional county of Wessex, describing in exacting detail life in rural southwest England. The countryside witnesses the dramatic, romantic, and tragic events that dominate the author's work. Many of Hardy's characters are victims of their own passions and emotions, resulting in catastrophic consequences. His final novels, *Tess of the d'Urbervilles* and *Jude the Obscure*, are his finest and most controversial. They challenged Victorian morality and society's sexual mores with a sympathetic treatment toward issues such as illegitimacy. Widely criticized for his seemingly inherent pessimism, Hardy retired from writing novels in 1898 to concentrate on poetry. **SG**

ÉMILE ZOLA

Born: Émile-Édouard-Charles-Antoine Zola, April 2, 1840 (Paris, France); died September 28, 1902 (Paris, France).

Style and genre: Zola was a novelist and journalist; he is considered the founder of naturalist fiction and famed for his involvement in the notorious Dreyfus case.

On the day of Émile Zola's funeral, the streets were lined with people paying their respects; but the road to such a successful place at the heart of progressive Paris life had not been easy. Zola's boyhood in Aix-en-Provence was marked by poverty, as was his time as a young man in Paris. In 1865, he celebrated the publication of his first novel, *Claude's Confession* (*La Confession de Claude*), but also received his first taste of controversy. The book's graphic realism led to police interest and Zola's expulsion from a job at Hachette publishers.

A writing career, in both journalism and fiction, was soon underway. This was dominated by a twenty-volume novel series of stunning ambition and breadth, charting a time of great change in France. The *Rougon-Macquart* series told of two families during France's Second Empire (1852–1870). Using a heady mixture of Romantic lyricism and sordid realism, the series swept across every aspect of contemporary French life, from the lot of rural peasants to the rise of the impressionists. Zola's aim was to study how heredity and environment fashioned behavior. Along the way, he incurred wrath from several quarters, including those offended by the grimmer side of modern life; his boyhood friend Cézanne, who believed himself to be unflatteringly portrayed in *L'oeuvre*; and opponents of Zola's criticisms of the French government in *La Débâcle*.

Political controversy returned in 1898 when Zola defended army officer Alfred Dreyfus in a high-profile treason case. His famous defense, published in *L'Aurore* newspaper, began "J'accuse . . . " and led to Zola's prosecution and flight to England. He and Dreyfus were ultimately exonerated, but some still believe that Zola's death from asphyxiation was engineered by anti-Dreyfus plotters. **AK**

"Modern life in all its aspects, that's the subject!"
—*L'oeuvre*, 1886

Signature titles

Novels

Claude's Confession (La Confession de Claude), 1865
Thérèse Raquin, 1867
The Rougon-Macquart series, (1871–1893), including:
- *The Club or The Drunkard (L'assommoir)*, 1877
- *Nana*, 1880
- *Germinal*, 1885
- *The Masterpiece (L'oeuvre)*, 1886
- *The Human Animal (La Bête humaine)*, 1890
- *The Downfall (La Débâcle)*, 1892

Journalism

J'accuse . . . !, 1898

ABOVE: A portrait of Émile Zola taken in c. 1875.

STÉPHANE MALLARMÉ

Born: March 18, 1842 (Paris, France); died September 9, 1898 (Paris, France).

Style and genre: Mallarmé was a leading symbolist poet whose work was particularly influential on modern French, German, and American poetry. He was host to group of intellectuals, philosophers, and artists known as *Les Mardistes*.

Stéphane Mallarmé was a leader in the development of modern poetry, adopting a then radical approach to his works which placed the phonetics, symbolic qualities, and visual shape of his words over and above their literal meaning. His poems thus evolved to become virtual works of art, combining visual and auditory stimuli in such a way that the lines between literature and art were blurred. He dispensed with conventional syntax, creating works that are enigmatic and at times complicated to digest.

Mallarmé wrote poetry from a young age, studying the works of Charles Baudelaire, who was a major influence on his early style. He learned English, and absorbed the works of Edgar Allan Poe, which also profoundly affected him. Working as an English teacher in French schools, and writing his poetry in his free time, Mallarmé produced relatively few finished works. He was a great perfectionist, deliberating over his poetry at length to achieve the exact and unequaled marriage

Signature titles

Poetry

Poems (Poésies), 1887

Divagations, 1897

Poems

"The Afternoon of a Faun" ("L'après-midi d'un faune"), 1876

"The English Words" ("Les Mots anglais"), 1878

"The Ancient Gods" ("Les Dieux antiques"), 1879

"Hérodiade," 1896

"A Throw of the Dice Will Never Abolish Chance" ("Un Coup de dés jamais n'abolira le hazard"), 1897

Essays

The Impressionists and Edouard Manet, 1876

Music and Letters (La Musique et les lettres), 1891

Anthologies

Selected Poetry and Prose, 1982

Selected Letters, 1988

Mallarmé in Prose, 2001

ABOVE: A silver bromide print of Mallarmé from *c.* 1895.

RIGHT: A detail of Edouard Manet's *Portrait of Stéphane Mallarmé* (1876).

ABOVE: Edouard Manet's 1876 illustration for "L'après midi d'un faune."

of style, content, and sound. He began two of his most famous works in the early 1860s, "Hérodiade" and "The Afternoon of a Faun" ("L'après-midi d'un faune"), but neither was published until many years later. Both works were of considerable influence on his contemporaries: "The Afternoon of a Faun" in particular inspired several pieces of music, includingthe orchestral *Prélude à l'après-midi d'un faune* (1894) by Claude Debussy. Mallarmé became a leading figure in the French avant-garde, hosting meetings attended by a wide circle of intellectuals, philosophers, artists, and writers including W. B. Yeats and Paul Valéry—the group later became known as Les Mardistes. He became friendly with Edouard Manet and, through him, the circle of impressionist and post-impressionist painters striving for recognition in Paris. In 1876 he published *The Impressionists and Edouard Manet*, an important and favorable critique of their style.

The year before his death Mallarmé published his most complicated poem, "A Throw of the Dice Will Never Abolish Chance," which was later illustrated by Odilon Redon, and became one of Mallarmé's most influential poems. **TamP**

Loss of Mother

Mallarmé's mother died when he was just five years old, and he later recounted how he was so mortified at not feeling more emotion that he threw himself down to the floor, tearing at his hair, in an effort to convince those around him of his grief. He explained that his lack of emotion was due to the fact that he had been raised by a wet-nurse and had not grown to know his mother. He had experienced the wrench of leaving the wet-nurse, as well as the complex layers of feelings associated with his mother, with whom he had not bonded; even at such a young age, he clearly felt that he should have.

HENRY JAMES

Born: April 15, 1843, (New York, New York, U.S.); died February 28, 1916 (London, England).

Style and genre: James was an American novelist who wrote psychologically complex novels that contrasted American values with their European heritage.

In his 1893 short story "The Private Life," Henry James described an author with the uncanny ability to be in two places at once. He can be grafting away at his writing desk even while he is entertaining company downstairs with his literary anecdotes and opinions. James himself was a consummate socialite who nonetheless produced a prolific body of writing during his long career. He was a solitary man and a committed bachelor, yet never said no to a dinner invitation.

James became a Europhile at an early age after reading voraciously from the European canon and spending three years of his youth in Europe under the auspices of his father's educational experiments. He abandoned his studies at Harvard Law School after a year to become a full-time writer, and after early success as a critic he began to concentrate on fiction. He relocated to Europe in 1875 and settled in London, though he traveled for extended periods on the continent, notably in Italy. It was this pattern of emigration and exploration that informed the adventures of his great heroines, such as Isabel Archer in *The Portrait of a Lady* and Milly Theale in *The Wings of the Dove*.

James was a versatile writer, celebrated both for the perceptive social satire of the novels that he wrote from the 1880s onward, and the linguistic and psychological obscurity of his great late works. He wrote a number of plays and was a master of shorter fiction, from the beguiling literary mystery *The Aspern Papers* to the claustrophobic ghost story *The Turn of the Screw*. In 1915, as a gesture of loyalty to his adopted country, James renounced his American citizenship and became a British citizen, with the prime minister among his sponsors; he died the following year, having firmly established himself as a European. **TM**

Signature titles

Novels

Roderick Hudson, 1875
The Europeans, 1878
Washington Square, 1881
The Portrait of a Lady, 1881
The Bostonians, 1886
The Tragic Muse, 1890
The Spoils of Poynton, 1897
What Maisie Knew, 1897
The Wings of the Dove, 1902
The Ambassadors, 1903
The Golden Bowl, 1904

Novellas/Short fiction

Daisy Miller, 1879
The Aspern Papers, 1888
The Turn of the Screw, 1897

"Summer afternoon: the two most beautiful words in the English language."—*The Portrait of a Lady*

ABOVE: A portrait of the young Henry James taken when he was twenty years old.

RIGHT: Henry James relaxing in his garden in Rye, East Sussex, England.

BENITO PÉREZ GALDÓS

Born: May 10, 1843 (Las Palmas, Canary Islands, Spain); died January 4, 1920 (Madrid, Spain).

Style and genre: The prolific Pérez Galdós wrote unique historical fiction; his short narratives chronicled the history of Spain and individuals within Spanish society.

Pérez Galdós is considered the Tolstoy of Spain and has been compared to Dickens and Balzac. He grew up in the Canary Islands until the age of nineteen, when he moved to Madrid to study law; he soon abandoned this to take up journalism. His first novel, *The Fountain of Gold*, published in 1870, earned him fame and led to the beginning of a series of novels chronicling Spain's history from the Napoleonic Wars (1805) to the Bourbon restoration in Spain in 1874. These forty-six novels, known as *National Episodes* (*Episodios nacionales*, 1873–1912), mix historical fact with fictional characters, and are the result of meticulous documentary research using memoirs, newspaper articles, and eyewitness accounts.

Beginning in the 1880s, and concurrently with *Episodios nacionales*, Pérez Galdós began another enormous series of novels, the *Contemporary Spanish Novels* (*Novelas españolas contemporáneas*). Written at the height of his literary development, his masterpiece, *Fortunata and Jacinta*, is a four-volume novel almost as long as *War and Peace;* it provides a view of Madrid's social spectrum through the lives of an affluent but weak young man, his wife, Jacinta, his lower-class mistress, Fortunata, who is also the mother of his son, and Fortunata's husband. The story varies depending on the narrator and focuses particularly on the working classes in Madrid. The Spanish idea of *quedar bien*, the need to portray oneself as financially or mentally secure (even when the opposite is true), appears often in his works, especially in his female characters.

Pérez Galdós also wrote approximately twenty controversial and often successful plays. In 1912, he went blind, but continued to dictate narratives for the rest of his life. The quality and output of his final works showed, however, a decline in mental power, which was sadly compounded by his blindness. **REM**

Signature titles

Novels

The Fountain of Gold (La Fontana de oro), 1870
Doña Perfecta, 1876
Marianela, 1878
The Disinherited Lady (La Desheredada), 1881
Miau, 1888
Fortunata and Jacinta (Fortunata y Jacinta), 1886–1887
Ángel Guerra, 1891
Tristana, 1892
Nazarín, 1895
Compassion (Misericordia), 1897

ABOVE: A photo of the wildly prolific Pérez Galdós taken in the early 1900s.

RIGHT: A tiled memorial to Pérez Galdós adorns a wall in Spain.

Benito Perez Galdos

GERARD MANLEY HOPKINS

Born: July 28, 1844 (London, England); died June 8, 1889 (Dublin, Ireland).

Style and genre: Hopkins was a priest and poet who was unpublished during his lifetime but whose complex, experimental verse was later championed by the modernist movement.

Signature titles

Poems (published posthumously)

"The Wreck of the Deutschland," 1918

"God's Grandeur," 1918

"The Windhover," 1918

"Pied Beauty," 1918

"Spelt from Sibyl's Leaves," 1918

"Carrion Comfort," 1918

"To seem the stranger lies my lot, my life," 1918

"That Nature is a Heraclitean Fire and of the comfort of the Resurrection," 1918

Prose

The Journals and Papers of Gerard Manley Hopkins, 1959

Gerard Manley Hopkins was an observant man in more than one sense; a devout Catholic who dedicated his life to the church, he was also one of the greatest chroniclers of the natural world that English poetry has ever known. Hopkins converted to Catholicism while an undergraduate at Oxford in the 1860s, at a time when the university was embroiled in religious controversy. He entered the Jesuit order and spent most of his lonely, brief life teaching and preaching in unfulfilling pastoral postings across the country before taking up a position at University College, Dublin, in 1884. Hopkins worked in Dublin for five years before his premature death; it was a miserable period in which he produced his most soul-searching poetry, including the so-called "terrible" sonnets.

Hopkins wrote verse to explore both himself and the minutiae of his personal faith. He was embarrassed by his poetry and once burned everything he had written. His sporadic attempts at publication were unsuccessful; when he submitted his masterpiece, "The Wreck of the Deutschland," to a Jesuit journal, it was rejected for its religious and stylistic idiosyncrasies. After his death, his manuscripts were safeguarded by his close friend Robert Bridges, and no edition of the poetry appeared until 1918. It is an extraordinary achievement, however—as linguistically and rhythmically energetic as the natural phenomena it so frequently describes. In both verse and prose, Hopkins developed a theory of what he called the "inscape" and "instress" of all things—God-given qualities that gave order to the apparent chaos of the natural world. They also offer a useful way of thinking about the felicitous surprises, echoes, and imaginative leaps of Hopkins's intricately structured verse. **TM**

"Brute beauty and valor and act, oh, air, pride, plume, here / Buckle!"—"The Windhover"

ABOVE: An 1863 portrait of Gerard Manley Hopkins when he was just nineteen.

PAUL-MARIE VERLAINE

Born: March 30, 1844 (Metz, France); died January 8, 1896 (Paris, France).

Style and genre: Verlaine was a decadent lyrical poet and writer whose themes include eroticism, sexuality, addiction, and religion. He is associated with fellow Decadents Stéphane Mallarmé and Charles Baudelaire.

One of Paul Verlaine's most admired works was his study of *Accursed Poets*—and he himself was one of the breed. A thrilling lyrical poet with a taste for the erotic, both heterosexual and homosexual, he grew up in comfortable middle-class circumstances, worked for an insurance company, and then moved into fashionable literary circles in Paris and began writing poetry. He had a gift for using ordinary French language to communicate delicate nuances and his first major success came in 1869 with his second book of verse, *Brave Parties*; the title refers to eighteenth-century aristocratic country gatherings and references the paintings of artists such as Watteau. Unstable, unpredictable, and sometimes violent, he fell in love with a sixteen-year-old and married her, yet became infatuated with a younger poet, Arthur Rimbaud, and in 1872 abandoned his wife and their baby to go traveling with Rimbaud. In 1873, they were in Brussels when they quarreled and Verlaine, in drunken misery, shot Rimbaud in the wrist.

After two years in prison in Belgium, where he wrote *Songs Without Words*, he returned to the Roman Catholic faith in which he had been brought up and retreated briefly to a Trappist monastery. Returning to France in 1877, he attempted farming unsuccessfully and, now a celebrated figure in Paris, wrote poetry, short stories, and studies of contemporary writers, while living an increasingly sad life of drunkenness and decay with aging prostitutes. In 1885, he was in prison again for attacking his mother. In addition, absinthe addiction, syphilis, and other illnesses put him in and out of the hospital. Admirers in France and England helped him financially and from 1895 he was awarded a state pension, but he still died in poverty at fifty-one. **RC**

"Take elegance and wring its neck!"

—*Yesteryear and Yesterday*

Signature titles

Poetry

Brave Parties (Fêtes galantes), 1869

Songs Without Words (Romances sans paroles), 1873–1874

Wisdom (Sagesse), 1880–1881

Accursed Poets (Les Poètes maudits), 1884

Yesteryear and Yesterday (Jadis et Naguère), 1885

Love (Amour), 1888

ABOVE: A *c*. 1890 colored image of Verlaine, from an original sepia photograph.

1840–59

ANATOLE FRANCE

Born: Jacques-Anatole-François Thibault, April 16, 1844 (Paris, France); died October 12, 1924 (St.-Cyr-sur-Loire, France).

Style and genre: Considered the model French literary man, France wrote with ironic intelligence; his themes include contemporary events, history, and religion.

A bookseller's son who decided to devote himself to literature, Anatole France worked as a reviewer before turning briefly to poetry and then to novels and short stories, written in a skeptical, worldly, mockingly ironic vein, with little time for bourgeois values. In 1877 he married, but in 1888 he met the love of his life, Arman de Caillavet, and their affair inspired his novel *Thaïs*, about an Egyptian courtesan who became a Christian saint, as well as a love story set in Florence, *The Red Lily*. His later work revealed his increasing disillusionment with French society and politics, and in the 1890s he was a supporter of the army officer Alfred Dreyfus, a victim of anti-Semitism. In 1921, he was awarded the Nobel Prize in Literature. **RC**

Signature titles

Novels

Thaïs, 1890

The Red Lily (Le Lys rouge), 1894

Mr. Bergerat in Paris (Monsieur Bergerat à Paris), 1901

The Gods are Thirsty (Les Dieux ont soif), 1912

The Rebellion of the Angels (La Rèvolte des anges), 1914

JOSÉ MARIA EÇA DE QUEIROS

Born: November 25, 1845 (Póvoa de Varzim, Portugal); died August 16, 1900 (Paris, France).

Style and genre: Eca de Queiros was a controversial intellectual who satirized and criticized the Portuguese elite and religious hypocrisy.

Eça de Queiros was the illegitimate son of a lower aristocratic mother and a judge who did not marry until Eça de Queiros was four years old, and did not acknowledge him as their son until he was in his forties. This early abandonment is felt in all his work—parents are rarely portrayed. Eça de Queiros studied law at the University of Coimbra, where he lobbied for artistic and social change and became known as the "Portuguese Zola." He was in the influential literary and thinkers' group called, ironically, *Os vencidos da vida* ("Those defeated by life"). Because of his work's controversial subject matter, his conservatively Catholic, relatively uneducated wife blocked some of his writing from publication after his death. **REM**

Signature titles

Novels

The Sin of Father Amaro (O Crime do Padre Amaro), 1876

Cousin Bazilio: A Domestic Episode (O Primo Basilio), 1878

The Relic (A Relíquia), 1887

The Maias (Os Maias), 1888

The Illustrious House of Ramires (A Ilustre casa de Ramires), 1900

The City & the Mountains (A Cidade e as serras), 1901

The Last Pages (Últimas páginas), 1912

Short stories

The Mandarin and Other Stories (O Mandarim), 1880

HENRYK SIENKIEWICZ

Born: May 5, 1846 (Wola Okrzejska, Russian-ruled Poland); died November 15, 1916 (Vevey, Switzerland).

Style and genre: Sienkiewicz was known for his novels of sweeping historical scope and his reproduction of natural speech, use of bathos, and absurdist humor.

Henryk Sienkiewicz was the person who really created the modern Polish novel, writing fiction of sweeping historical scope that fulfilled an important social role for a people who were struggling under foreign rule.

Born into a family of Polish nobility, Sienkiewicz began his career working for newspapers and writing short stories. He went to university to study law and medicine but transferred to study history. He was a vocal advocate for the rights of the peasant classes and a benefactor who set up a trust fund for artists and a school for children, as well as being a stylish "dandy" renowned for his many love affairs. While living in Switzerland during World War I, Sienkiewicz founded the organization that would become the Polish Provisional Government at the close of the war (two years after his death).

Sienkiewicz's novels give a human face to political events by depicting mass movements of humanity on an individual, personal scale. *Teutonic Knights* and *The Trilogy* describe the uprisings, invasions, and expulsions that characterized Polish history in the fourteenth and seventeenth centuries. For these, he would become enormously popular within his native country. After touring America for three years and with the publication of *Quo Vadis?*, his popularity became international. In 1905, he was awarded the Nobel Prize. *Quo Vadis?* dramatizes the legendary cruelty of the Emperor Nero, who sets fire to Rome and blames the event on Early Christians. The novel's uncritical portrayal of the latter seems biased and unconvincing to a modern reader; however, his absurdist humor and vibrant recreation of everyday life amid the decadence of Rome—which at times reaches a nail-bitingly gruesome pitch—make for an enjoyable read. **ER**

"Eros called the world out of chaos. Whether he did well is another question."—*Quo Vadis?*

Signature titles

Novels

Quo Vadis?, 1895

The Trilogy, 1884–1888

Teutonic Knights, 1900

ABOVE: A photograph of the popular Polish novelist Henryk Sienkiewicz, *c.* 1870.

BRAM STOKER

Born: November 8, 1847 (Dublin, Ireland); died April 20, 1912 (London, England).

Style and genre: Stoker was the author of horror stories suffused with elements of romance, nightmares, curses, and the supernatural, with the inclusion of folklore tales and superstitions.

Now globally famous for his Gothic horror novel *Dracula*, Bram Stoker turned to writing fiction late in life. As a child he was unable to walk until the age of seven, yet he overcame this disability to become an outstanding athlete at Trinity College, Dublin. Despite harboring dreams of becoming a writer, Stoker acquiesced to his father's wishes and followed him into the civil service, where he remained for ten years. He also worked as a theater critic for the *Dublin Mail*, making the acquaintance of the English actor Sir Henry Irving. In 1878, Irving requested that Stoker act as his manager, a task Stoker undertook for twenty-seven years, writing as many as fifty letters a day for his boss and accompanying him on tours of America.

Amid this heavy workload Stoker managed to write the novel *The Snake's Pass*—a brooding tale of a troubled romance, set in western Ireland—and his eternal masterpiece, *Dracula*. The story of the vampire Count Dracula is told through the diary entries, letters, and journals of the principal characters: Jonathan Harker, his wife Mina, Dr. Seward, and Lucy Westenra, as well as occasional newspaper clippings that lend the story an air of realism. The Transylvanian vampire—who exhibits supernatural powers, requires human blood to preserve his existence, and is killed with a Bowie knife to the heart, thereby lifting his spell—has become one of the most enduring characters of both literature and film. Further horror novels followed, in which Stoker adopted the familiar thread of seemingly inexplicable occurrences—as in *The Jewel of Seven Stars,* in which an archeologist attempts to revive an ancient Egyptian mummy. None, however, was able to capture the public's imagination to the extent that *Dracula* did. In fact, few novels by any writer have. **SG**

"How blessed are some people, whose lives have no fears, no dreads."—*Dracula*

Signature titles

Novels

The Primrose Path, 1875
The Snake's Pass, 1891
The Shoulder of Shasta, 1895
Dracula, 1897
Miss Betty, 1898
The Mystery of the Sea, 1902
The Jewel of Seven Stars, 1904
Lady Athlyne, 1908
The Lady of the Shroud, 1909
The Lair of the White Worm, 1911

Short stories

Under the Sunset, 1881
Snowbound: The Record of a Theatrical Touring Party, 1908

ABOVE: A photograph of Bram Stoker from the 1890s.

RIGHT: An early engraving of Vlad the Impaler, known as Count Dracula.

Van deme quaden thyrāne Dracole wyda·

JORIS-KARL HUYSMANS

Born: Charles-Marie-Georges Huysmans, February 5, 1848 (Paris, France); died May 12, 1907 (Paris, France).

Style and genre: Huysmans's works display a refined aestheticism enlivened by sardonic humor, verbal inventiveness, intellectual curiosity, and surreal fantasy.

Signature titles

Novels

Marthe, 1876
The Vatard Sisters (Les Soeurs Vatard), 1879
Parisian Sketches (Croquis Parisiens), 1880
Married Life (En ménage), 1881
Downstream/With the Flow (À vau-l'eau), 1882
Against Nature/Against the Grain (À rebours), 1884
Becalmed/A Haven (En rade), 1887
Down There/The Damned (Là-bas), 1891
En route, 1895
The Cathedral (La Cathédrale), 1898
The Oblate (L'oblat), 1903
The Crowds of Lourdes (Les Foules de Lourdes), 1906

Born in Paris of a Dutch father, Huysmans was a Parisian intellectual and aesthete, convinced of the supreme value of art and corrosively cynical about everything else. Supporting himself through a sinecure in the civil service—a post that he held without visible effort for thirty years—he embarked on a literary career. At first under the influence of Zola's version of realism, he discovered his own voice in the 1880s to become one of the founders of the fin-de-siècle Decadent movement.

In Des Esseintes, antihero of the novel *Against Nature (À rebours)*, Huysmans created the iconic figure of the decadent aesthete, a self-obsessed sensualist bent on the pursuit of refined sensation and the indulgence of perverse tastes, without regard for morality or social convention. As well as his subject—the hypersensitive, exquisitely cultivated individual at odds with a vulgar materialistic society—Huysmans found his style, remarkable for its bravura set pieces, torrents of verbal fantasy or comic crescendos of serial frustration, enriched by a recondite vocabulary and obscure learning. His novels won notoriety and reasonable sales, no doubt boosted by sometimes lurid material. *Down There (Là-bas)*, his most popular work, includes no-holds-barred descriptions of satanic rites and homicidal pedophilia. But Huysmans is equally good at generating comedy from observation of the minutiae of everyday life—for example, detailing the sordid indignities of bachelorhood. Huysmans finally found a resting place for his angst in Catholicism. The story of his progression from a cynical interest in satanism and the occult to a reluctant commitment to faith runs through his later novels, where they are enacted by his alter ego, Durtal. Huysmans died of cancer, which he had endured with laudable stoicism. **RG**

"It is impossible not to feel that Huysmans's life was a sad moral fable."—Colin Wilson

ABOVE: A c. 1905 photograph of Huysmans, a leader of the Decadent movement.

AUGUST STRINDBERG

Born: Johan August Strindberg, January 22, 1849 (Stockholm, Sweden); died May 14, 1912 (Stockholm, Sweden).

Style and genre: Strindberg is considered the father of modern Swedish theater; his themes include conflict between the sexes and classes, and erosion of tradition.

Writer, painter, experimental photographer, and alchemist, August Strindberg was an innovator, and one of the leading Scandinavian playwrights of the nineteenth century. His style shifted from early naturalism to symbolism, and then to expressionism, taking the theater into the modern age.

His works focus on the tensions between the classes, and the battle between the sexes—leading some to suggest that Strindberg was a misogynist. Perhaps he was more a creature of his time and his own personal history. The son of a shipping merchant and his former maidservant, Strindberg was often moody and depressive. He was married three times and led a peripatetic existence, living in Sweden, Denmark, Germany, and France. Contemporary Sweden, like much of Europe, was undergoing a metamorphosis from an agricultural nation to an industrial one, with ensuing social and political changes leading to the rise of socialism, the transformation of town and country, new class structures, and eventually female suffrage.

Strindberg wrote sixty plays, as well as novels, short stories, and essays. He first came to public attention with his novel *The Red Room*. He is most famous for his plays, especially the oft-performed tragedy *Miss Julie*, which tells the story of a Midsummer's Eve liaison between a young upper-class woman and her father's valet, and its deadly consequences, in the claustrophobic society of the time.

"Superstition and prejudice taught in childhood can't be uprooted in a moment."—*Miss Julie*

Strindberg depicts a society in which the old order is crumbling, where everything is in limbo in a post-Nietzschean world where God is dead, and characters are motivated by the enduring sentiments of love or lust, leaving them on the verge of hysteria as they too fail to prove rewarding pursuits—the preoccupations of the modern European mind. **CK**

Signature titles

Novel

The Red Room, 1879

Short stories

From Fjerdingen and Svartbäcken, 1877

Life of an Island Lad, 1888

Plays

The Outlaw, 1871

Master Olof, 1872

The Father, 1887

Miss Julie, 1888

To Damascus (trilogy), 1898–1902

Gustav Vasa, 1899

The Dance of Death, 1900

A Dream Play, 1902

The Ghost Sonata, 1907

ABOVE: An 1881 portrait of the eccentric Swedish writer August Strindberg.

GUY DE MAUPASSANT

Born: Henri René Albert Guy de Maupassant, August 5, 1850 (Château de Miromesnil, Normandy, France); died July 6, 1893 (Paris, France).

Style and genre: Maupassant was a French nineteenth-century short-story writer known for his economy of style and gift of societal observation.

Guy de Maupassant is often credited with having invented the French short story. Guided by Gustave Flaubert, Maupassant developed his own economically descriptive method of telling a story, often creating a social portrait of his central character and placing it alongside contrasting social figures and pressures. Hypocrisy, in particular, was an attribute he identified and despised in the multi-class France of his time.

In 1870, Maupassant fought in the Franco-Prussian war, which later became the setting for "Boule de Suif," a short story published in 1880 to resounding success. The story tracks the wartime journey of a group of Normans from vastly differing backgrounds. Boule de Suif is one of the party, an exceedingly rotund but desirable courtesan of good nature, who is used and then cast out by her hypocritical traveling companions. Throughout the tale, Maupassant remains critical, questioning the religious, moral, and class-related beliefs of the passengers in the carriage, and ultimately exposing their ungenerous and self-serving behavior. Strengthened by the unanimous praise of this short but astute work, Maupassant went on to write copiously and make a healthy living, producing many volumes of his succinct, popular stories. The first was the lauded *The House of Madame Tellier*, followed by further collections and a handful of well-received novels, notably *Pierre et Jean*. Maupassant harbored a fear of sickness and dying, and developed an intense desire to remain alone and undisturbed by the society he excoriated. Having contracted syphilis as a young man, his physical and mental health deteriorated in his forties. Ironically, in view of his intense interest in psychiatry, Maupassant was declared insane in 1891; it was the end of a prolific period of writing. **LK**

"Patriotism is a kind of religion; it is the egg from which wars are hatched."

Signature titles

Novels

A Life/A Woman's Life (Une vie), 1883

Bel Ami, or The History of a Scoundrel (Bel-ami), 1885

Pierre et Jean, 1888

Short stories

"Boule de Suif," 1880

Evenings at Médan (Les Soirées de Médan), 1880

The House of Madame Tellier and Other Stories (La Maison Tellier), 1881

Mademoiselle Fifi and Other Stories (Mademoiselle Fifi), 1882

Poetry

Des Vers, 1880

ABOVE: An oil portrait of Maupassant by François N. A. Feyen-Perrin, from 1876.

ROBERT LOUIS STEVENSON

Born: Robert Lewis Balfour Stevenson, November 13, 1850 (Edinburgh, Scotland); died December 3, 1894 (Vailima, Samoa).

Style and genre: Stevenson was a Scottish novelist and poet who also wrote children's fiction, essays, short stories, and factual works.

Robert Louis Stevenson was an adventurer and a traveler with a keen sense of the romantic, and it is these qualities that are invested in his adult and children's novels. It was also these themes that led to his fall from literary grace in the years following World War I, when his novels came to be considered too frivolous. It is only relatively recently that the author has been reevaluated and the true worth of his broadly eclectic and imaginative writing acknowledged.

Stevenson studied engineering at Edinburgh University before studying law but, although he passed his exams, he never practiced. He began to travel frequently, in part seeking a more temperate climate to suit his weak lungs, but also fueled by his adventurous spirit. He visited France often and was welcomed into artistic and literary circles there. His first published works were travel writings, such as *An Inland Voyage*, detailing his trip by canoe from Antwerp to northern France.

In 1876, Stevenson met Fanny Vandegrift Osbourne, a married American woman. He followed her to America, she divorced her husband, and, in 1880, she and Stevenson married. Between 1880 and 1887 the couple, with Fanny's children, moved around England, during which period Stevenson wrote perhaps his most famous work, *Treasure Island*, and *The Strange Case of Dr. Jekyll and Mr. Hyde*. After the death of Stevenson's father in 1887 they moved back to America and the following year set sail for the South Pacific. Finally, in 1890, the writer bought a large tract of land on Upolu, one of the Samoan Islands, and began building a house there. He became popular among the local people, whose rights he fought for, and on his death in 1894 he was buried near Mount Vaea, overlooking the sea. **TP**

"There is no duty we so much underrate as the duty of being happy."

Signature titles

Novels

Treasure Island, 1883

The Strange Case of Dr. Jekyll and Mr. Hyde, 1886

Kidnapped, 1886

The Master of Ballantrae, 1889

Catriona, 1893

Weir of Hermiston, 1896 (unfinished)

Poetry

A Child's Garden of Verses, 1885

Travel writing

An Inland Voyage, 1878

Travels with a Donkey in the Cévennes, 1879

The Silverado Squatters, 1883

ABOVE: A sepia photograph of Stevenson from the 1880s.

LEOPOLDO ALAS

Born: Leopoldo Alas y Ureña, April 25, 1852 (Zamora, Spain); died June 13, 1901 (Orviedo, Spain).

Style and genre: Alas wrote sensitive novels about psychological and physical isolation and the search for deeper meaning in life in a biting, belligerent style.

Though he studied law and held the position of professor of law and political economy at the University of Orviedo until his death, Leopoldo Alas is best known for his journalism and literary criticism. Often using the pseudonym Clarín, he published thousands of articles on fiction, poetry, and drama in national newspapers and magazines, and was much respected and feared for his sharp tongue. Alas's advocacy of literary naturalism, anticlericalism, and liberalism in these *paliques* ("chitchat") gained him many enemies.

In addition to these articles, which were eventually collected into thirty volumes, *Solos de Clarín*, Alas wrote several novels. The two most important, among the greatest Spanish novels of the nineteenth century, are *The Regent's Wife* and *His Only Son*. *The Regent's Wife* depicts a woman caught in the net of her husband's negligent love and victimized and shunned as an outsider by the narrow-minded, misogynistic Restoration society. Often called "the Spanish Madame Bovary," Ana Ozores's psychological and physical decline mirrors what Alas thought of as the country's own ailments and degeneration. In *His Only Son*, Alas sensitively explores the dissatisfaction the main character feels with his marriage and his life, the title ironically referring to his doubts as to whether his only son is his, or his wife's by another man. These novels utilize techniques such as internal monologue or free indirect style, and are often, perhaps wrongly, called naturalistic works. They place more emphasis on the inner turmoil and psychological search rather than the physical or behavioral aspects of the characters. Sometimes inscrutably, his works of fiction seem to simultaneously encourage the search for God as well as the search for humanism. **REM**

"He who would prove all life, leaves it empty."
—*Socrates' Rooster*

Signature titles

Novels

The Regent's Wife (La Regenta), 1884–1885
His Only Son (Su único hijo), 1890
Doña Berta, 1892
Goodbye Cordera! (¡Adiós, Cordera!), 1892
God and the Rest Is Fairy Tales (El Señor y lo demás son cuentos), 1893
Moral Stories (Cuentos morales), 1896
Socrates' Rooster (El Gallo de Sócrates), 1900

Essays

Solos de Clarín, 1881
La literatura en 1881, 1882
Sermón perdido, 1885
Nueva campaña, 1887
Ensayos y revistas, 1892

ABOVE: A portrait of the young Alas, whose strong opinions gained him many enemies.

ARTHUR RIMBAUD

Born: Jean Nicholas Arthur Rimbaud, October 20, 1854 (Charleville, France); died November 10, 1891 (Marseille, France).

Style and genre: A dissident and vagabond French poet, Rimbaud's wild lifestyle and subversive poetry earned him a reputation as one of the first true *enfants terribles*.

Rimbaud's eventful life is obscured by a thick haze of rumor, speculation, and controversy, and his considerable reputation rests on only the slim body of work he produced between the ages of sixteen and nineteen. A brilliant student, he soon grew restless with his mother's conventionalism and his provincial, bourgeois roots, and ran away from home on a number of occasions. On one of these excursions he may have briefly joined the Paris Commune of 1871. More famously, he became the lover of the older poet Paul Verlaine, with whom he had a violent and tempestuous affair that ended when Verlaine shot him in the hand with a pistol.

Rimbaud's shabby appearance, outrageous behavior, and iconoclasm often scandalized those with whom he came into contact on his European travels, but following his break-up with Verlaine he ventured even further, first into the Middle East and then to Abyssinia. By this time, he had long since given up his literary endeavors and was instead focused on making money as a trader and arms dealer. He returned to France only when he fell ill with cancer and died, aged thirty-seven, in 1891, six months after having a leg removed.

Although little known during his lifetime, Rimbaud's writing has had a major impact on the writing of succeeding generations and is seen by many as anticipating the surrealism of the 1920s and 1930s. His poetry rejects the classical mode and is dissonant in its use of disparate language levels, tones, and registers, its subversive treatment of classical themes and its use of base language. In "Vénus Anadyomène," for example, the goddess Venus is transmuted into a fat, ugly woman, whose unceremonious exit from a dirty bath affords us a glimpse of the ulcer on her anus. **GM**

"Idle youth, enslaved . . . by being too sensitive I have wasted my life."

Signature titles

Poetry

"Vénus Anadyomène," 1870

"The Drunken Boat" ("Le bateau ivre"), 1871

A Season in Hell, (Une saison en enfer), 1873

Illuminations, 1886

Letters

Lettres, 1899

ABOVE: An image of the seventeen-year-old Arthur Rimbaud.

OSCAR WILDE

Born: Oscar Fingal O'Flahertie Wills Wilde, October 16, 1854 (Dublin, Ireland); died November 30, 1900 (Paris, France).

Style and genre: Playwright, novelist, poet, aesthete, campaigner, and writer of short stories, Wilde was famed for his unparalleled wit and decadence.

Although at times Oscar Wilde's private life seems to overshadow his work, what is in no doubt is his vast literary talent and unparalleled wit. Until he was famously imprisoned in 1895 for "gross indecency," Irish-born Wilde was one of Britain's leading literary lights, famed for his plays, his decadent dress, hedonism, and aesthetic philosophy. After two years in prison, he was bankrupt and ostracized from society. He spent the rest of his life abroad, eventually living in the Hotel d'Alsace in Paris under the pseudonym "Sebastian Melmoth." Prison life and his sentence of "hard labor" took its toll on Wilde's health, and he died aged forty-six, just three years after his release.

Wilde came from an upper-class Anglo-Irish family, and studied classics at Trinity College, Dublin, and Magdalen College, Oxford, where he became involved in the aesthetic movement. In 1879, he moved to London, and was in demand as a lecturer on aesthetics at home and abroad.

Wilde's poetry was first published in 1881, beginning a decade of prolific output that saw him write short stories akin to fairy tales, such as *The Happy Prince*; popular plays satirizing the customs and hypocrisy of Victorian society, such as *Lady Windermere's Fan*; and his only novel, *The Picture of Dorian Gray*, which proved controversial for its homoerotic themes.

Although he was married, with two sons, he had a number of homosexual affairs, most notoriously with Lord Alfred Douglas, whose father (the ninth Marquess of Queensberry) had Wilde arrested. The series of trials (where Wilde defended same-sex love) led to his imprisonment.

Wilde's last published work, *De Profundis*, is based on a letter written to Alfred Douglas while in jail. Its title refers to the biblical Psalm 130, and means "From the Depths." In it Wilde talks of his life, humiliation at his prosecution, suffering in prison, and religious beliefs. **CK**

Signature titles

Novel

The Picture of Dorian Gray, 1890

Short stories

The Canterville Ghost, 1887

The Happy Prince and Other Tales, 1888

Lord Arthur Savile's Crimes and Other Stories, 1891

Plays

Lady Windermere's Fan: A Play About a Good Woman, 1892

Salomé, 1893 and 1894

A Woman of No Importance, 1893

An Ideal Husband, 1895

The Importance of Being Earnest, 1895

Poetry

Poems, 1881

The Sphinx, 1894

The Ballad of Reading Gaol, 1898

Essays

The Soul of Man under Socialism, 1891

De Profundis, 1905

ABOVE: A portrait of Wilde taken in 1882 during the poet's tour of America.

RIGHT: "The Climax," an illustration by Aubrey Beardsley for Wilde's play *Salomé*.

GEORGE BERNARD SHAW

Born: July 26, 1856 (Dublin, Ireland); died November 2, 1950 (Ayot St. Lawrence, Hertfordshire, England).

Style and genre: Shaw was an Irish playwright known for his dry humor, political overtones, well-rounded female characters, and unhappy endings.

The son of an alcoholic father and a professional singer mother, the young George Bernard Shaw grew up with a stammer and little self-confidence. When he was sixteen, his mother left and moved to London; he followed later and lived with her until he was forty-two. Many of his plots center on dysfunctional relationships, often between parents and children.

Shaw began as a theater and arts critic before becoming one of the world's foremost playwrights and the inspiration for the expression "Shavian wit." A committed vegetarian, teetotaller, and Socialist, he was often perceived by his contemporaries as self-righteous and preachy. Yet he had a wide-ranging and fascinating circle of friends, including IRA leader Michael Collins, the actresses Ellen Terry and Mrs. Patrick Campbell, Lord Alfred Douglas (Oscar Wilde's lover), and Charles Dickens's daughter Kate Perugini—who once called him "Shernard Bore." A regular orator at London's Speaker's Corner, he was fervently in support of female emancipation and Irish Home Rule and campaigned for equal pay for men and women—themes that occur frequently in his writings.

Shaw's plays include *Mrs. Warren's Profession*, a sympathetic view of prostitution, and *Pygmalion*, best known as the inspiration for *My Fair Lady* (which provides the happy ending that Shaw had denied it). In 1884, together with Beatrice Potter and Sidney Webb, he founded the Fabian Society. In 1925, Shaw was awarded the Nobel Prize in Literature and, in 1938, an Oscar for the film of *Pygmalion*. In 1898, Shaw married a wealthy Irish woman, Charlotte Payne-Townsend. The indomitable playwright died at their home at the age of ninety-four, after falling off a ladder when pruning a tree. He was halfway through a new play at the time. **LH**

"A government that robs Peter to pay Paul can always depend on the support of Paul."

Signature titles

Plays

Mrs. Warren's Profession, 1893
Arms and the Man, 1894
Candida, 1894
The Man of Destiny, 1895
Caesar and Cleopatra, 1898
Man and Superman, 1903
Major Barbara, 1905
Pygmalion, 1913
Saint Joan, 1923

Nonfiction

Fabian Essays in Socialism, 1889
The Intelligent Woman's Guide to Socialism and Capitalism, 1912
Everybody's Political What's What, 1944

ABOVE: *Portrait of George Bernard Shaw as a Young Man*, a pastel by Louise Jopling.

RIGHT: Shaw speaking at a protest meeting against the visit of the tsar of Russia, 1909.

JOSEPH CONRAD

Born: Józef Teodor Konrad Korzeniowski, December 3, 1857 (Berdichev, Russian-occupied Polish Ukraine); died August 3, 1924, (Canterbury, England).

Style and genre: Conrad was a novelist poised on a knife edge between the moral certainties of the nineteenth century and the existential despair of the twentieth.

Signature titles

Novella

Heart of Darkness, 1902

Novels

Lord Jim, 1900

Nostromo, 1904

The Secret Agent, 1907

Under Western Eyes, 1911

What often astounds people about Conrad is that he did not learn English until he was twenty-one. Writing, too, came late in life: he spent sixteen years as a mariner, on and off, before publishing his first book, *Almayer's Folly*, in 1895.

Conrad's experiences at sea formed the basis for much of his fiction, most notably the novella *Heart of Darkness*, which drew on his own disastrous journey up the Congo river. The book—given new life in 1979 by Francis Ford Coppola's loose film adaptation, *Apocalypse Now*—still stands as an astonishingly powerful and prescient exploration of the evils of colonialism, the hypocrisy of humankind, and the elusive nature of any single, objective, communicable truth. All these themes would surface throughout Conrad's writing, with which he persevered despite ill health and a lack of commercial success. Yet he managed to impress many of his literary peers, such as H. G. Wells, Henry James, and Ford Madox Ford, with whom he collaborated.

They may have recognized that Conrad was an author ahead of his time. His best works—*Lord Jim*, *The Secret Agent*,

ABOVE: An undated photograph of Joseph Conrad in England.

RIGHT: A still from *Apocalypse Now* (1979), a film loosely based on *Heart of Darkness*.

The Secret Sharer—deal with men who, in a moment of crisis, must make a moral decision that has life-or-death consequences. In the early, seafaring novels, such choices often go against the unwritten code of the sea. But Conrad also suggests that the code is unworkable—even nonsensical—in an age where capitalism, anarchy, and moral relativism were taking hold. This pessimistic approach is even more marked in the later, political novels, *Nostromo* and *Under Western Eyes*. Both deal with revolutions and revolutionaries, yet are remarkably devoid of idealism—or happy endings.

All this obfuscation is reflected in Conrad's feverish narrative style, which anticipates the experiments of modernism, such as multiple narrators and confusing time frames. Commenting on this, E. M. Forster disparagingly remarked that Conrad's writing was "misty in the middle as well as at the edges," but it is this very quality—the revelation that there is no final, central, graspable meaning or truth—that keeps readers coming back to Conrad more than one hundred years on. **COG**

ABOVE LEFT: A photograph of Conrad and his wife at home with their son John.

ABOVE: A 1904 sketch of Henry James and Joseph Conrad by Max Beerbohm.

Shades of Black

In 1977, Chinua Achebe wrote an essay calling Conrad a racist and describing *Heart of Darkness* as "offensive and deplorable" toward black Africans. This started a debate that continues, fueled by advances in post-colonial theory. Certainly, the modern reader will find much distasteful, but it is clear that Conrad had an even worse opinion of the white colonizers. In his first novel, he contrasted the "savage sincerity" of the Malays with the "sleek hypocrisy" of the Europeans. This is not so much racism as all-pervasive skepticism: in other words, we are all as bad as each other.

SELMA LAGERLÖF

Born: November 20, 1858 (Mårbacka, Sweden); died March 16, 1940 (Mårbacka, Sweden).

Style and genre: Lagerlöf was the first woman to win the Nobel Prize in Literature, which was awarded for her vivid imagination and spiritual perception.

Selma Lagerlöf's work is steeped in Nordic myth and legend and the landscape of northern Sweden. Her first novel, *Gösta Berling's Saga*, is a masterpiece of Swedish romanticism. Lagerlöf began writing it while working as a schoolteacher, submitted its early chapters to a literary competition, and was awarded a publishing contract. The novel went unnoticed in Sweden until a later Danish translation was well received by critics. *Gösta Berling's Saga* then became hugely successful in Sweden and remains her most popular work.

Like most of Lagerlöf's novels, *Gösta Berling's Saga* is a lyrical depiction of life in nineteenth-century Sweden and features a wide array of characters. She draws on myth and legend to tell the tale of Gösta Berling, a priest disgraced by drunkenness, who falls in with a band of twelve cavaliers. Berling eventually falls in love with a woman called Elizabeth and is thus redeemed.

The success of *Gösta Berling's Saga*, together with financial support from the Swedish Academy and the Swedish royal family, allowed Lagerlöf to give up teaching and devote herself

Signature titles

Novels

Gösta Berling's Saga, 1891
The Outlaws, 1894
The Miracles of Antichrist, 1897
Jerusalem, 1901–1902
The Wonderful Adventures of Nils, 1906
The Ring of the Löwenskölds, 1925
Charlotte Löwensköld, 1925
Anna Svärd, 1928

ABOVE: A photograph of Lagerlöf from 1909, the year she won the Nobel Prize.

RIGHT: A scene from *Herr Arnes Pengar*, 1919, based on Selma Lagerlöf's novel.

to writing. In 1897, she traveled to Italy where she wrote *The Miracles of Antichrist*, a story of life in Sicily. Following a journey to Egypt and Palestine in 1900, she published *Jerusalem*, which was inspired by a true story about a group of Swedish peasants who emigrate to the Holy Land. In 1906, Lagerlöf wrote the work for which she became best known internationally—the children's book *The Wonderful Adventures of Nils*.

In 1909, Lagerlöf was the first Swede and the first woman to be awarded the Nobel Prize in Literature. She continued writing and in the 1920s published the Varmland trilogy, comprising *The Ring of the Löwenskölds*, *Charlotte Löwensköld*, and *Anna Svärd*. With the approach of World War II, Lagerlöf helped a number of German writers to escape the Nazis by organizing Swedish visas, and donated her Nobel medal to Finland to help its people during a blockade by the Soviet Union. She died of a stroke in 1940. **HJ**

ABOVE: Sweden's most famous female author, Selma Lagerlöf at work in her study.

Magical Mystery Tour

Selma Lagerlöf's best-loved work is *The Wonderful Adventures of Nils*. Written originally as a geography book for Swedish schools, it tells the story of Nils Holgersson, a mischievous boy who shrinks to the size of an elf and flies on the back of a goose across Sweden. It explores the geography, nature, and climate of the country, and through a series of perilous and exhilarating adventures, Nils learns about the nature of friendship and goodness, before returning home to his parents. It is so well loved that Nils Holgersson features on Swedish 20 Kronor bills.

ARTHUR CONAN DOYLE

Born: Arthur Ignatius Conan Doyle, May 22, 1859 (Edinburgh, Scotland); died July 7, 1930 (Windlesham, Sussex, England).

Style and genre: Conan Doyle is revered for his vivid imagination, Gothic imagery inspired by Edgar Allan Poe, atmospheric descriptions, and daring adventure tales.

Sir Arthur Conan Doyle, the creator of Sherlock Holmes, is less famous than the character he invented. Yet his violin-playing, cocaine-taking detective is a globally recognizable "brand"—an irony that would not be lost on Conan Doyle, who wanted to be taken seriously as a man of literature. He also wrote nonfiction, essays, novels, and another series featuring two characters he hoped would become as famous Holmes, but none was as well received as his crime novels. Even when he was knighted for his medical work during the Boer War, rumors claimed it was because the king was a Sherlock Holmes fan.

Conan Doyle attributed his imagination to his mother's "vivid stories," an escape from life with his alcoholic father. It was while training as a doctor that Conan Doyle began writing short stories. He traveled to the Arctic, Africa, and Europe before opening a doctor's practice in London, writing all the while. In 1888, *A Study in Scarlet* introduced Sherlock Holmes, who was inspired by Conan Doyle's former tutor, Dr. Joseph Bell. Holmes's sidekick, Dr. Watson, was the author's alter ego—on occasion he would sign his autograph as "Dr. John Watson."

In 1906, Doyle's wife, Louisa, died from tuberculosis, and in 1907 he married a woman with whom he had been in love for many years, but Louisa's death still led to depression and an interest in spirituality and seances. He became a member of and spokesperson for the Society for Psychical Research. Turned down for active service in World War I, Conan Doyle dreamed up inventions to help those serving overseas. The war killed many in his family, including his only son. He retreated into a world of spiritualism and a belief in fairies, antagonizing the Catholic Church and the media who derided and mocked his beliefs very publicly. **LH**

"As a rule . . . the more bizarre a thing is the less mysterious it proves to be."

Signature titles

Novels

Sherlock Holmes

- *A Study in Scarlet,* 1887
- *The Sign of Four,* 1890
- *Adventures of Sherlock Holmes,* 1892
- *The Hound of the Baskervilles,* 1902
- *The Valley of Fear,* 1915

The Surgeon of Gaster Fell, 1885

The Mystery of Cloomber, 1889

The Lost World, 1912

Plays

The Exploits of Brigadier Gerard, 1910

The House of Temperley, 1912

Nonfiction

The Great Boer War, 1900

The Roman Catholic Church. A Rejoinder, 1929

ABOVE: A photograph of the Scottish writer Arthur Conan Doyle from 1925.

KNUT HAMSUN

Born: Knut Pedersen, August 4, 1859 (Vågå, Gudbrandsal, Norway); died February 19, 1952 (Nørholm, Norway).

Style and genre: Nobel Prize–winning Norwegian writer Knut Hamsun alienated many with his support for German National Socialism in World War II.

Born in central Norway, Hamsun's independence of mind was evident from an early age. He rarely went to school, preferring instead the company of the landscape and air surrounding the northern farm to which his family had moved. The farm's name was Hamsund, and the debt that Hamsun felt to it is clear in his change of name. He left home at a young age, and at seventeen was apprenticed to a rope maker. At the age of twenty, he wrote a novella, *Frida*, but failed to get it published. Short of money and friends, Hamsun descended into a period of near-starvation, an experience that would inform his greatest work, the 1890 novel *Hunger*.

When he was twenty-three, Knut Hamsun traveled to America, where he worked in a variety of jobs, including in a lumber yard and as an auctioneer. He was diagnosed with terminal tuberculosis and returned to Norway—but not before curing himself of the disease (as he claimed) by hanging his head out of a train window.

Despite Hamsun's improved health, literary success remained conspicuously absent and two more years of extreme poverty followed. It took another trip to America and a further one to Copenhagen before *Hunger* was finally published. It was a great and instant success, signaling an upturn in Hamsun's fortunes that culminated in *Growth of the Soil* in 1917 and the Nobel Prize in 1920. At the time, it was a popular award, but Hamsun's gift of the Nobel medal to Nazi propaganda minister Josef Goebbels in 1943 led to widespread condemnation. He carried on writing into his dotage, and died, aged ninety-three, in Norway, a political pariah, whose prodigious literary achievement had ultimately failed to conceal his personal shortcomings. **PS**

"When good befalls a man he calls it Providence, when evil, fate."

Signature titles

Novels

Hunger, 1890
Mysteries, 1892
Shallow Soil, 1893
At the Gate of the Kingdom Dreamers, 1895
A Wanderer Plays on Muted Strings, 1909
Children of the Age, 1913
Growth of the Soil, 1917
The Women at the Pump, 1920
The Last Chapter, 1923
Wayfarers, 1927
August, 1930
The Road Leads On, 1933
The Ring Is Closed, 1936
On Overgrown Paths, 1949

ABOVE: A 1914 portrait of Knut Hamsun at the height of his fame.

ANTON CHEKHOV

Born: Anton Pavlovich Chekhov, January 29, 1860 (Taganrog, Russia); died July 15, 1904 (Badenweiler, Germany).

Style and genre: Chekhov wrote tragic and tragicomic plays and stories portraying domestic dramas of provincial life with a focus on the emotions of the characters.

Signature titles

Short stories

At Dusk, 1887

My Life, 1896

A Visit to Friends, 1898

The Lady with the Little Dog, 1899

In the Ravine, 1900

Plays

Ivanov, 1888

The Seagull, 1896

Uncle Vanya, 1899

Three Sisters, 1900

The Cherry Orchard, 1904

Anton Chekhov was one of the nineteenth-century playwrights who moved the theater into modernity. Spurning melodrama and action, he produced works that focused on the emotional lives of the protagonists in domestic settings, and which went on to influence twentieth-century dramatists such as Tennessee Williams and Eugene O'Neill.

He was born when Russia was still under the rule of the tsar, but serfdom had been abolished, and the October Revolution was in the air. Chekhov was the son of a former serf turned grocery-store man, who later became bankrupt. Part of an emerging middle class, Chekhov trained and worked as a physician, writing sketches for newspapers to subsidize his studies. His job brought him into contact with both the peasants and the nobility, under the great leveler of disease, and his insight into human nature and philanthropic attitude informed his work.

Chekhov was a prolific writer of short stories, yet he is most famed for his plays, notably *The Seagull*, *Uncle Vanya*, *Three Sisters*, and *The Cherry Orchard*. They focus on the boredom of life in the provinces, and the declining fortunes of the bourgeoisie wracked by frustration and frequently unrequited love. He began writing plays after a prize for his short story *At Dusk* led to him being commissioned to write the hit play *Ivanov*. His now acclaimed *The Seagull* did not encounter success on opening night. It was booed by the audience and panned by critics, and Chekhov vowed never to put on a play again. Just a year later, influential director Constantin Stanislavski put on the play; it was a triumphant performance. He also directed Chekhov's later plays, overseeing the theatrical shift to ensemble pieces. **CK**

"Medicine is my lawful wife and literature my mistress."

—Letter to A. S. Suvorin, 1888

ABOVE: A detail of an 1898 oil painting of Chekhov by Osip E. Braz.

RABINDRANATH TAGORE

Born: May 7, 1861 (Calcutta, India); died August 7, 1941 (Calcutta, India).

Style and genre: Tagore had multifarious interests—he was a playwright, poet, novelist, composer, and painter whose innovative use of Bengali colloquial language created lyrical works.

Winner of the Nobel Prize in Literature in 1913, Rabindranath Tagore is a rare example of an Indian writer who was widely read and greatly admired in the West. He came from a rich and prominent family in Calcutta, and in his boyhood learned Sanskrit and English as well as his native Bengali. He started writing poetry as a boy, studied briefly in England, and in 1890 published *The Ideal One* (*Manasi*), a collection of his poetry that made a considerable impression. From 1891 he spent ten years managing his family's estate in what was then East Bengal, and learned much about the local peasantry and their lives, joys and sorrows that influenced his poetry and short stories (some of which have been adapted for films by Satyajit Ray). He also set his own songs to music; wrote plays, novels, and essays; and late in life took up painting.

Tagore broke with classical Bengali tradition by using everyday colloquial language and abandoning traditional Sanskrit models. His English translations of his work gained him many admirers in the West, W. B. Yeats and André Gide among them. His wife and two of their children died in the early 1900s, events that imbued much of his later work with deep sadness. He believed that the best in Indian and Western cultural traditions could be harmonized together in the cause of world unity, and in 1901 he founded a school and later a university, called "the Abode of Peace," in West Bengal to advance this ideal. He lived at the school until 1921, but spent much of his time in Europe and the Americas reading his poetry, lecturing, and eloquently advocating independence for India. The British knighted him in 1915, but he renounced it four years later in protest at the Amritsar Massacre of Indians by British troops.

"We do not raise our hands to the void for things beyond hope."—"The Gardener"

Signature titles

Novels

The Broken Nest (Nastanirh), 1901

The Home and the World (Ghôre Baire), 1916

Short stories

The Beggar Woman (Bhikharini), 1877

The Runaway (Atithi), 1895

Plays

Valmiki (The Genius of Valmiki), 1881

Sacrifice (Visajan), 1890

Poetry

The Ideal One (Manasi), 1890

The Golden Boat, (Sonar Tari), 1894

Song Offerings (Gitanjali), 1912

The Gardener, 1913

Fruit-Gathering, 1916

ABOVE: A photograph of Tagore from 1930, when he was sixty-nine years old.

ITALO SVEVO

Born: Aron Ettore Schmitz, December 19, 1861 (Trieste, Italy); died September 13, 1928 (Motta di Livenza, Treviso, Italy).

Style and genre: Italy's first modernist novelist, Svevo was also a playwright and short-story writer known for his witty prose and narcissistic, introspective characters.

Signature titles

Novels

A Life (Una vita), 1892

As a Man Grows Older (Senilità), 1898

Confessions of Zeno (La Coscienza di Zeno), 1923

The Hoax (Una burla riuscita), 1928

Short stories

The Nice Old Man and the Pretty Girl, and Other Stories (La Novella del buon vecchio e della bella fanciulla, ed altri scritti), 1929

Of the great subjects of nineteenth-century literature, that of ineptitude was the most developed in Italo Svevo's novels: ineptitude in the sense of being totally unable to respond to people's ruthlessness in business affairs and to deal with guile in general, whether in emotional, sexual, or other matters. Svevo's characters are absentminded, fascinated by the little things in life. All of his protagonists excel at making fools of themselves, but this is by no means a criticism—Svevo's rejection of efficiency and the notion of well-defined, self-assured personalities as an ideal allows for protagonists who are forever caught in indecision but who, precisely because of this, are able to savor life on a deep and authentic level. **FF**

RIGHT: A photograph, taken in 1892, of Italo Svevo holding the pages of *A Life*.

ARTHUR SCHNITZLER

Born: May 15, 1862 (Vienna, Austria); died October 21, 1931 (Vienna, Austria).

Style and genre: Schnitzler was a master of sexual frankness, who concentrated on the themes of love and death in hedonistic fin-de-siècle Vienna; he was also known for his stance against anti-Semitism.

Signature titles

Novels

The Road to the Open (Der Weg ins Freie), 1908

Rhapsody: A Dream Novel (Traumnovelle), 1925

Short story

Lieutenant Gustl, 1900

Plays

Anatol, 1893

Playing with Love (Leibelei), 1895

The Dance of Love/La Ronde (Der Reigen), 1900

Professor Bernhardi, 1912

Born to middle-class Jewish parents, Arthur Schnitzler abandoned his medical studies to become a writer. He portrayed the decadence of fin-de-siècle Vienna, in works such as *The Dance of Love/La Ronde* (*Der Reigen*) that are famous for a sexual frankness derived from his own private life. Yet Schnitzler's oeuvre is about much more than pleasure seeking. He was interested in the theories of Sigmund Freud, and was one of the first writers to use the stream-of-consciousness technique, in *Lieutenant Gustl*. His stance against anti-Semitism frequently gained him censure at a time when anti-Semitic feeling was on the rise, and his works were banned when the Nazi Party came to power. **CK**

EDITH WHARTON

Born: Edith Newbold Jones, January 24, 1862 (New York, New York, U.S.); died August 11, 1937 (Saint-Brice-sous-Forêt, Val-d'Oise, France).

Style and genre: Wharton was an author known for her interest in the manners and mores of upper-crust American society and her keen sense of dramatic irony.

Signature titles

Novels

The Valley of Decision, 1902
The House of Mirth, 1905
The Fruit of the Tree, 1907
Ethan Frome, 1911
The Custom of the Country, 1913
Summer, 1917
The Age of Innocence, 1920
The Glimpses of the Moon, 1922
Twilight Sleep, 1927
The Children, 1928

Nonfiction

A Backward Glance, 1934
Life and I, 1990

There was little in the upbringing of Edith Newbold Jones to suggest the astonishing heights she would attain. Born to leisure-class parents—her family supposedly inspired the phrase "keeping up with the Joneses"—Edith's childhood was characterized by the unique privileges and limitations of her Old New York lineage. Her profound ambivalence toward this, combined with an unhappy, sexless marriage to Teddy Wharton in 1885 (whom she divorced in 1913) provided the author with her defining subject matter and thematic preoccupations.

Wharton's greatest characters are strangled by the very social codes and decorums that constitute their privileged caste. In *The House of Mirth*, Lily Bart has become addicted to the trappings of wealth, but as she refuses numerous lucrative marriage proposals, she is gradually ostracized from the leisure class. She ends up in a cheap boardinghouse, effectively murdered by the culture that rejected her. Wharton examines the same tension in a radically different milieu in *Ethan Frome*, a claustrophobic novel set in a derelict New England township. Ethan longs to elope with Mattie Silver, the antithesis of his shrewish and ailing wife, Zeena, yet he cannot bring himself to do so, largely for fear of what the neighbors might think.

"The only way not to think about money is to have a great deal of it."—*The House of Mirth*

Wharton wrote more than forty books—fiction and nonfiction—and was the first woman to win the Pulitzer Prize for Fiction. She moved in literary circles, being close friends with Henry James and others. She traveled widely, and after her divorce and a passionate affair, she chose to leave the United States and move to France. During World War I, Wharton undertook serious war work including visiting the front line and working with refugees that in turn inspired her writing. She died in France at the age of seventy-five. **IW**

ABOVE: Wharton, known for her portrayals of upper-class New York society, in the 1930s.

GABRIELE D'ANNUNZIO

Born: March 12, 1863 (Pescara, Abruzzo, Italy); died March 1, 1938 (Gardone Riviera, Brescia, Lombardy, Italy).

Style and genre: D'Annunzio was an Italian symbolist poet, playwright, and novelist who caused controversy with his decadent, violent, and sensuous works.

The greatest proof of the complex personality of "*Il Vate*," or "The Bard," as Gabriele d'Annunzio called himself, is the house where he spent the last years of his life, the Vittoriale degli Italiani (Shrine of Italian Victories). The poet, a major representative of European symbolism, turned his house into a temple of excess. D'Annunzio was known as a modern-day Casanova, and he justified such legendary status with books such as *The Child of Pleasure* and *The Flame of Life: A Novel.* Scandalous at the time of its publication, *The Flame of Life* was strongly influenced by Friedrich Nietzsche's concept of the *Übermensch*, or Superman, and is also a perfect description of open, all-encompassing eroticism. **FF**

Signature titles

Novels

The Child of Pleasure (Il piacere), 1889

The Intruder (L'innocente), 1892

The Triumph of Death (Il trionfo della morte), 1894

The Book of the Virgins (Le vergini delle rocce), 1895

The Flame of Life: A Novel (Il fuoco), 1900

Play

The Dead City: A Tragedy (La città morta), 1899

Poetry

Primo Vere, 1879

Heavenly Poem (Poema paradisico), 1893

CONSTANTINE P. CAVAFY

Born: Constantine Petrou Photiades Cavafy, April 17, 1863 (Alexandria, Egypt); died April 29, 1933 (Alexandria, Egypt).

Style and genre: The youngest poet of the Hellenistic tradition, Cavafy's works shaped Greek and European literature with themes of homosexuality and nostalgia.

In Constantine P. Cavafy's elegiac and angry poems, such as the famous *Waiting for the Barbarians*, he prefigured the eradication of the Greek community in Alexandria that World War II would bring. Few of Cavafy's poems made it beyond his Greek coterie there, the exception being the publication of *Ithaka* in T. S. Eliot's influential *Criterion* magazine in 1911. Refusing to enter the literary marketplace, Cavafy resonated with the classicism of Eliot and Ezra Pound. It was writers such as Thom Gunn, however, who would follow the course marked out by his deft marriage of the personal and political in his colloquial yet classical poems of homosexual desire. Few writers have matched Cavafy's skill in making the classical world contemporary. **SM**

Signature titles

Poetry

Waiting for the Barbarians, 1904

Ithaka, 1911

Poems of C. P. Cavafy (Poiimata), 1935 (published posthumously)

MIGUEL DE UNAMUNO

Born: Miguel de Unamuno y Jugo, September 29, 1864 (Bilbao, Spain); died December 31, 1936 (Salamanca, Castile-Leon, Spain).

Style and genre: Unamuno was an essayist, novelist, poet, and philosopher who explored the vigorous and agonizing tension between reason and faith.

A political and philosophical writer of beautiful verse and profound prose, Miguel de Unamuno spent his intellectual life searching for the balance between Christian faith and reason, and the links between existence and immortality. He was born in Bilbao to Basque parents, the third of six children, and went on to have ten children with his wife and childhood sweetheart.

After attaining a doctorate in philosophy from the University of Madrid, Unamuno taught Greek language and literature at the University of Salamanca, where he was later elected rector. In 1914, he had to leave this post because of his support of the Allied cause in World War I. Although he returned to the post in 1924, when he opposed the military dictatorship of General Primo de Rivera, Unamuno was exiled without his family to Fuerteventura in the Canary Islands. He escaped to Paris, where he wrote *From Fuerteventura to Paris*. While in Paris he completed *Ballads of Exile* (*Romancero del destierro*), which would be the last book of poetry published in his lifetime. His friends and these works helped to bring public attention to his exile, and when King Alfonso of Spain removed the dictator in 1930, Unamuno returned to Spain. A legend at

Signature titles

Novels

Love and Pedagogy (Amor y pedagogía), 1902

Mist (Nebla), 1914

Abel Sánchez (Abel Sánchez: una historia de pasión), 1917

Saint Manuel the Good, Martyr (San Manuel Bueno, mártir), 1933

Poetry

Rhymes from Within (Rimas de dentro), 1923

From Fuerteventura to Paris (De Fuerteventura a París), 1925

Ballads of Exile (Romancero del destierro), 1928

Songbook (Cancionero), 1953

Nonfiction

The Tragic Sense of Life in Men and People (Sentimiento trágico de la vida en los hombres y en los pueblos), 1913

The Agony of Christianity (La Agonía del cristianismo), 1925

ABOVE: Spanish writer Miguel de Unamuno photographed in 1920.

RIGHT: Unamuno leaving the university after an argument with General Astray, 1936.

LEFT: A portrait of Unamuno by Joaquin Sorolla y Bastida, *c.* 1920.

Salamanca claims that the day he returned, Unamuno began his lecture with: "As we were saying yesterday . . ." as if he had never been gone.

Unamuno is considered a predecessor of existentialist philosophy. A religious crisis from 1896 to 1897 made him realize he could not find a rational explanation of God and meaning in life. He turned from universal, academic philosophies to examining the individual's struggles with questions of death or immortality. He concluded that rationalism would never provide what faith could offer. "Faith which does not doubt is dead faith," he said. Works such as *The Tragic Sense of Life in Men and People* deal with these and other questions. Unamuno's thoughts influenced Juan Ramón Jiménez and Graham Greene, among others. **REM**

The Death of Unamuno

Unamuno became increasingly scared that Spain's identity would be crushed by outside influence and initially welcomed General Francisco Franco's revolt. Soon the harshness of the regime caused Unamuno to oppose it, however, and in 1936 Unamuno and the fascist General José Millán-Astray had a brief public quarrel at the University of Salamanca. Millán-Astray forced Unamuno out of the university at gunpoint. Although Franco allegedly gave permission to shoot him, Unamuno was placed under house arrest to avoid an international outcry. He died from a heart attack two months later.

W. B. YEATS

Born: William Butler Yeats, June 13, 1865 (Sandymount, County Dublin, Ireland); died January 28, 1939 (Menton, Provence-Alpes-Côte d'Azur, France).

Style and genre: Irish poet, dramatist, and a leading figure in the late-nineteenth-century "Irish Literary Revival," Yeats used Celtic, political, and mystical themes.

W. B. Yeats lived in London until his middle teens, making return trips to Ireland to visit his mother's family in County Sligo. The west of Ireland provides the inspiration for many of his best early poems, including "The Lake Isle of Innisfree." From 1880 he was based in Dublin, enrolling as a student at the Metropolitan School of Art, developing his interests in poetry, and exploring the attractions of mysticism and the occult. From 1887 he worked in London and Dublin, energetically committing himself to the ideal of a distinctive Irish literary movement. His meeting with the poet and Fenian leader John O'Leary in 1885 was instrumental in turning his attention to an existing Irish tradition of poetry, songs, and stories, and in giving a strongly nationalist dimension to his work. Yeats's involvement in nationalist politics was intensified through his meeting with the revolutionary Maud Gonne in 1889, to whom he unsuccessfully proposed marriage on numerous occasions. Yeats saw theater as having a powerful role to play in the emergence of a

Signature titles

Plays

The Countess Cathleen, 1892

Purgatory, 1938

Poetry

The Lake Isle of Innisfree, 1893

The Rose, 1893

The Wanderings of Oisin and Other Poems, 1889

The Wind Among the Reeds, 1899

Responsibilities, 1914

Easter 1916, 1916

The Wild Swans at Coole, 1919

In Memory of Major Robert Gregory, 1919

The Tower, 1928

The Winding Stair and Other Poems, 1933

New Poems, 1938

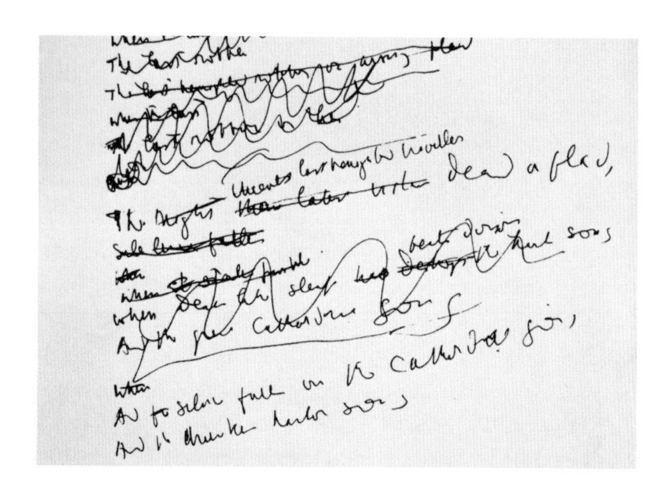

ABOVE: A portrait of William Butler Yeats taken on July 15, 1911.

RIGHT: The lower half of page two of Yeats's handwritten manuscript of "Byzantium."

unified culture, and in 1889 cofounded the Irish Literary Theatre, out of which Dublin's Abbey Theatre was born.

His later books of poems included *The Wind Among the Reeds*, and *The Wild Swans at Coole*. In these, Yeats established himself both as an Irish nationalist poet, and as a symbolist writer with visionary, transcendental impulses. Yeats's reputation rests partly on his powerful adaptation in English of Irish myths and legends, but also on his unflinching grasp of events in Irish political history. *Easter 1916* remains one of the greatest political elegies, and *In Memory of Major Robert Gregory* reveals an intensely personal side to Yeats's poetry of loss and mourning.

In 1917 he married George (Georgie) Hyde-Lees. He purchased a Norman tower near Coole Park, County Galway, which became their home. After the establishment of the Irish Free State in 1922, Yeats became a senator, and he won the Nobel Prize in Literature in 1923. **SR**

ABOVE: French soldiers carry Yeats's coffin for its reburial in Ireland.

The Symbolic Tower

The old ruined tower known as Thoor Ballylee that Yeats acquired in 1917 was a Norman keep. It took on immense symbolic importance in Yeats's imagination and provided the setting for the poems in his collection, *The Tower*. It was a potent reminder of centuries of English colonial domination over Ireland, but it also had powerful literary associations in Yeats's mind. A romantic emblem of the poet's solitary vocation, with links back to poems by Percy Bysshe Shelley and Lord Byron. Throughout the violent political tumult of the 1920s, it provided a refuge and a watching place.

RUDYARD KIPLING

Born: Joseph Rudyard Kipling, December 30, 1865 (Bombay, India); died January 18, 1936 (London, England).

Style and genre: He wrote rich, colorful tales that evoke the senses, characterized by gentle humor and a love of unusual words, alliteration, and onomatopoeia.

Rudyard Kipling's birth and his early years in India informed the style of all his literary works, no matter where they were written. He wrote for adults and children, producing stories infused with the color and vibrancy of his formative years that had been spent in the care of an Indian nanny. At the age of five, he was sent to school in England, an experience he found so miserable that he sought solace by escaping into the imagination that would later create his works of fiction. As soon as he was able, he left England to return to India, where he worked as a journalist. His *Just So Stories for Little Children* and his most famous work, *The Jungle Book*, were directly inspired by his love of the Indian landscape and its animals.

Kipling's father was a professor of architecture, and his mother came from a remarkable family of sisters whose marriages meant Rudyard was related to the artists Edward Burne-Jones and Edward Poynter, and the Prime Minister Stanley Baldwin. His family home was filled with fascinating, unusual people, whose lives and works influenced his own.

Kipling has become renowned as the voice of an era, his words, thoughts, and literary images defining the worlds in which he lived—both prewar and during the World War I. Despite his privileged background his life turned into a tragedy. His daughter Josephine, for whom he wrote the *Just So Stories*, died at the age of six, and his son John was killed in World War I at the age of eighteen. Kipling's grief led to some of his most poignant writings, and it was he who first coined the phrase used on most war memorials in Britain: "Their Name Liveth For Evermore." In 1907 Kipling was awarded the Nobel Prize in Literature. His grave is in Poets' Corner in Westminster Abbey, London. **LH**

"Come you back, you British soldier; come you back to Mandalay!"—"Mandalay"

Signature titles

Novel

Kim, 1901

Short stories

Plain Tales from the Hills, 1888

The Phantom Rickshaw and Other Eerie Tales, 1888

The Jungle Book, 1894

Just So Stories for Little Children, 1902

Puck of Pook's Hill, 1906

Poetry

Departmental Ditties, 1886

Mandalay, 1890

If—, 1910

Nonfiction

Something of Myself, 1937

ABOVE: A portrait of Rudyard Kipling taken by E. O. Hoppé *c.* 1912.

H. G. WELLS

Born: Herbert George Wells, September 21, 1866 (Bromley, Kent, England); died August 13, 1946 (London, England).

Style and genre: Known as the father of science fiction, Wells was also a novelist, journalist, sociologist, and historian.

The son of a shopkeeper, a onetime draper's assistant then teacher, a biology graduate, a Labour Party parliamentary candidate, and a member of the Fabian Society—H. G. Wells drew on all his experiences in his writing. A prolific author of short stories, essays, histories, and novels, he is best known for his science-fiction novels, notably *The Time Machine*, *The Island of Doctor Moreau*, *The Invisible Man*, *The War of the Worlds*, and *The First Men in the Moon*. They led to him being described as "the father of science fiction," along with Jules Verne.

What set Wells apart was his ability to foresee technological advances and societal changes with uncanny accuracy, predicting events such as the development of tanks, atomic bombs, genetic engineering, space travel, sexual liberation, the European Union, and the rise of fascism. Such was his foresight that during World War II Sir Winston Churchill gave Wells access to army technicians to build one of his creations, a "teleferic" (the weapon was introduced in insufficient numbers late in the war and made little difference). It is not just Wells's prophetic powers that make his work interesting, he is a masterful storyteller, and his belief in a utopia and new world order paints a future that ultimately spells hope for humanity in its inventiveness, and ability to learn lessons from history. Nor was Wells without humor, satirical novels such as *Kipps the Story of a Simple Soul* and *The History of Mr. Polly* see him examine class and marital disillusionment, and draw on his early life. Wells inevitably ruffled feathers; he was as profligate in his love life as he was extravagant in the wide range of topics he explored in his writing. Yet he remains a great and influential thinker, whose work is both entertaining and fascinating. **CK**

"There is no intelligence where there is no change and no need of change."—*The Time Machine*

Signature titles

Novels

The Time Machine, 1895
The Island of Doctor Moreau, 1896
The Invisible Man, 1897
The War of the Worlds, 1898
The First Men in the Moon, 1901
Kipps the Story of a Simple Soul, 1905
The War In The Air, 1908
Ann Veronica, 1909
Tono-Bungay, 1909
The History of Mr. Polly, 1910

Nonfiction

A Short History of the World, 1922
World Brain, 1938

ABOVE: A *c.* 1925 photograph of H. G. Wells, the father of science fiction.

RAMÓN DEL VALLE-INCLÁN

Born: Ramón María del Valle-Inclán y de la Peña, October 28, 1866 (Villenueva de Arosa, Pontevedra, Spain); died January 5, 1936 (Santiago de Compostela, Spain).

Style and genre: Spanish modernist playwright, poet, novelist, and member of the Generation of '98, he wrote subversive works satirizing the Spanish establishment.

Ramón del Valle-Inclán deliberately perpetuated a mysterious demeanor, growing his hair and beard long, wearing a dark hat and long, black, bell-shaped cloak, and moving about with an elegant and aristocratic manner that belied his Galician birth. Influenced by French symbolism and modernist techniques, his first well-known works were a collection of four novellas called *The Pleasant Memoirs of the Marquis de Bradomin* (*Sonatas*). Beautifully aesthetic, they chronicle the seasons of nature in the life of a character called Don Juan Manuel de Montenegro, a Galician womanizer, and part-autobiographical figure. De Montenegro and his six wild sons are captured in lyrical and evocative prose; humor and delicate parody, nostalgia for a decadent and aristocratic past, and intertextual allusions all combine to make these grand stories come alive.

Valle-Inclán's second literary phase moves away from this modernista tradition and its quest for beauty, with a violent trilogy about the nineteenth-century Carlist Wars. His third transition was marked by his invention of the *esperpento* style of grotesque caricature that he used to satirize and criticize certain Spanish ideals of the nineteenth century. In particular, he attacked attitudes to the royalty and the Roman Catholic Church, militarism and the concept of masculine honor. He satirized bourgeois viewpoints and those of the ruling classes, by a systematic and deliberate distortion of heroic figures and values. His writing is intentionally absurd and expressionistic, and the best plays of this period are *Bohemian Lights* (*Luces de bohemia*) and *Don Friolera's Horns* (*Los cuernos de Don Friolera Esperpento*). *The Iberian Circle* (*El ruedo ibérico*) is an unfinished set of nine novels dealing with the social ruin and political corruption in Spain. **REM**

"The most beautiful images are absurd in a concave mirror."

—*Bohemian Lights*

Signature titles

Novella

The Pleasant Memoirs of the Marquis de Bradomin (Sonatas), 1902–1905

Novels

Los cruzados de la causa, 1908

Tyrant Banderas: A Novel of Warm Lands (Tirano Banderas: Novela de Tierra caliente), 1926

The Court of Miracles (La Corte de los milagros), 1927

The Iberian Circle (El ruedo ibérico), 1927–1936

Plays

Bohemian Lights (Luces de bohemia), 1920

Don Friolera's Horns (Los cuernos de Don Friolera Esperpento), 1921

Poetry

Claves líricas, 1930

ABOVE: A late portrait of Valle-Inclán, a master of grotesque satire.

LUIGI PIRANDELLO

Born: June 28, 1867 (Agrigento, Sicily, Italy); died December 10, 1936 (Rome, Italy).

Style and genre: Pirandello was a famed Italian playwright and novelist who challenged theatrical traditions and believed that personal identity was no more than a performance.

Sicilian Luigi Pirandello was born in a suburb of Agrigento called Caos; it often suited him to think that he had been born into chaos. He was a prolific writer, but his anxious life was peppered with ill luck. He was financially ruined when his father's sulfur mine flooded in 1903, and he spent long periods of his life caring for his mentally ill wife before being forced to commit her to an asylum.

Prior to World War I, Pirandello concentrated on prose writing, producing a number of important critical essays and novels, including *The Late Mattia Pascal*, a comic masterpiece in which the hero abandons his identity after reading reports of his own death, and subsequently drifts from exhilaration to despondency. The intense emotions stirred by the war urged Pirandello to turn to the more public arena of theater; he wrote forty-four plays and in the 1920s became internationally renowned as a playwright.

When Pirandello's greatest play premiered in Rome, he was booed out of the theater, and forced to escape by running out of a side exit. *Six Characters in Search of an Author* disrupted traditional assumptions about theatrical space. Now considered a groundbreaking play about a group of actors rehearsing a play, it insinuates that life mirrors art as no more than a series of performances in different masks; a theme that Pirandello was to develop in his comic study of madness, *Henry IV*. Many critics cite these works as important influences on the "Theater of the Absurd." Pirandello has been criticized for his canny relationship with the Italian fascists, but he of all people recognized that he would need to don a mask to continue his work in the theater. He was awarded the Nobel Prize in Literature in 1934. **TM**

"... a character can laugh even at death. He cannot die."
—*Six Characters in Search of an Author*

Signature titles

Novels

The Late Mattia Pascal (Il fu Mattia Pascal), 1904

One, No One, and One Hundred Thousand (Uno, nessuno, e centomila), 1926

Plays

Right You Are (If You Think So) (Così è [se vi pare]), 1917

Six Characters in Search of an Author (Sei personaggi in cerca d'autore), 1921

Henry IV (Enrico IV), 1922

Each in His Own Way (Ciascuno a suo modo), 1924

Tonight We Improvise (Questa sera si recita a soggetto) 1930

Nonfiction

On Humor (L'umorismo), 1908

ABOVE: The Nobel Prize–winning Pirandello in the 1930s.

MAXIM GORKY

Born: Aleksey Maksimovich Peshkov, March 16, 1868 (Nizhny Novgorod, Nizhny Novgorod Oblast, Russia); died June 18, 1936 (Moscow, Russia).

Style and genre: Gorky was a writer who championed the poor and working classes as a revolutionary, Marxist, and a founder of social realism in literature.

Signature titles

Novels

The Mother, 1906

The Artamov Business, 1925

Short story

Twenty-Six Men and a Girl, 1899

Plays

The Lower Depths, 1902

Summerfolk, 1903

Children of the Sun, 1905

Poetry

The Song of the Stormy Petrel, 1901

Nonfiction

My Childhood, 1913

In the World, 1916

My Universities, 1922

RIGHT: Achille Beltram's depiction of Gorky at a meeting of Russian revolutionaries, 1907.

Aleksey Maksimovich Peshkov adopted the pseudonym "Maxim Gorky" ("Bitter One") in 1892, encapsulating his views. He grew up impoverished, and championed the cause of the poor for the rest of his life. A founding figure in literary social realism, his works describe the brutalities of poverty, and the courage and pride of those affected. His political views landed him in prison on many occasions. He wrote highly charged political novels and plays, such as *The Lower Depths* and *Children of the Sun*, written while he was imprisoned. Gorky lived for a while in Italy, but returned to Russia in 1932. He died under suspicious circumstances, and Genrikh Yagoda, police chief to Joseph Stalin, was implicated in his death. **TamP**

ANDRÉ GIDE

Born: André Paul Guillaume Gide, November 22, 1869 (Paris, France); died February 19, 1951 (Paris, France).

Style and genre: Gide's work explored the search for one's self and displayed an openness about sex and sexual practices that was considered shocking at the time.

Signature titles

Novels

The Immoralist (L'immoraliste), 1902

The Pastoral Symphony (La Symphonie pastorale), 1919

The Counterfeiters (Les Faux-monnayeurs), 1925

Short story

The Return of the Prodigal (Le Retour de l'enfant prodigue), 1907

Play

Saul, 1903

Nonfiction

Corydon, 1924

If It Die... (Si le grain ne meurt), 1924

Return from the U.S.S.R. (Retouches â mon retour de l'U.R.S.S.) 1936

André Gide's works and life are inseparable. He traveled widely, imbuing his writings with his experiences. He wrote fiction and autobiography, and was a symbolist, an aesthete, a political activist (proudly left wing, although disillusioned after visiting the Soviet Union in the 1930s), a campaigner against fascism, and a sexual experimentalist whose beliefs often shocked. A complex and strong personality, his life was filled with paradoxes. In 1895, in Algiers, he met Oscar Wilde and felt free to acknowledge his homosexuality—although he would later marry and have a daughter. Gide spent much of his life, and his works, focusing on the individual's rights. He won the Nobel Prize in Literature in 1947. **LH**

JOHN MILLINGTON SYNGE

Born: April 16, 1871 (Rathfarnham, Ireland); died March 24, 1909 (Dublin, Ireland).

Style and genre: Although his writing career lasted just six years, J. M. Synge's spare, lyrical prose and realistic portrayals of Irish peasant life established his reputation as one of Ireland's greatest playwrights.

J. M. Synge originally intended to become a musician and studied music in Germany, but his shyness and his own doubts about his abilities meant that he abandoned music for a literary career. After traveling in France and Italy, Synge was encouraged by the writer W. B. Yeats to visit the Aran Islands off the west coast of Ireland. He wrote about the people he met and cast off the stereotypical romanticized ideas of Irish peasant life. His writing was published in the *New Ireland Review* in 1898 and later in book form as *The Aran Islands* in 1907.

His first play, *In the Shadow of the Glen*, a one-act black comedy, was performed in 1903. It was based on an Irish folktale about an elderly husband in a loveless marriage who fakes his own death to test his younger wife's fidelity. The play was attacked by Irish nationalists as a slur on Irish womanhood but was the first play to run at Dublin's groundbreaking Abbey Theatre, in 1904.

In the Shadow of the Glen was followed by *Riders to the Sea,* which is generally regarded as one of the great short tragedies in modern drama. It is set on the Aran Islands and is the story of Maurya, a mother who has lost five sons to the sea and fears she will lose her sixth as he leaves the island for a horse fair in Galway. Synge's play *The Tinker's Wedding*, a comedy that features a priest being tied up in a sack, was considered too inflammatory to be performed during his lifetime. But it was *The Playboy of the Western World*—a comic satire that tells of a young stranger who claims to have killed his father—that is now considered his masterpiece. It was his most controversial play and caused riots when it was first performed in 1907.

Synge continued writing, but his health failed and in 1909 he died of Hodgkin's disease. His writing influenced the Irish playwright Samuel Beckett and his plays were a mainstay of the repertoire of the Abbey Theatre until the 1950s. **HJ**

Signature titles

Plays

In the Shadow of the Glen, 1903
Riders to the Sea, 1904
The Well of the Saints, 1905
The Playboy of the Western World, 1907
The Tinker's Wedding, 1908

Nonfiction

The Aran Islands, 1907
Poems and Translations, 1909

ABOVE: A portrait of John Millington Synge by John Butler Yeats, from 1905.

RIGHT: Detail of Harry Clarke's illustration for J. M. Synge's poem "Queens."

MARCEL PROUST

Born: Valentin Louis Georges Eugène Marcel Proust, July 10, 1871 (Auteuil, Paris, France); died November 18, 1922 (Paris, France).

Style and genre: Proust was a French novelist, essayist, and critic who wrote fiction that blended confessional writing into the genre of the novel.

In 1909, Marcel Proust dipped a madeleine into a cup of linden tea and changed the course of world literature. The aroma of lime flowers mingled with the sweetness of cake powerfully summoned long-forgotten childhood memories. Inspired by the idea that memory could be triggered by sensory experience—what has come to be widely known as involuntary, or "Proustian," memory—Proust began writing *In Search of Lost Time* (*À la recherche du temps perdu*), a seven-volume semi-autobiographical masterpiece that immortalized him as an inventor of the modern novel.

Born an asthmatic child into a middle-class family, Proust spent much of his childhood in his bedroom, sealed away from the dusty streets and blooming trees of Paris. Despite his poor health, in 1882 he was able to attend and graduate from the Lycée Condorcet, an elite secondary school offering rigorous training in Greek, Latin, French, and philosophy. In 1889, he enlisted for a year of military service in Orléans. Proust complained of his experience in letters home to his mother, to whom he was closely attached, although he would idealize a similar service in the third volume of *In Search of Lost Time.*

Returning to Paris, Proust studied law and politics at the prestigious École Libre des Sciences Politiques, where, in addition to taking courses in diplomacy, he became a frequenter of aristocratic and artistic salons meeting, among others, the Irish writer Oscar Wilde.

His first book of short stories, *Pleasures and Days* (*Les plaisirs et les jours*), was written with unwieldy sentences and packaged with a luxurious floral design. It drew slight sales and tepid reviews. From 1900 to 1906, Proust left off his own writing to become completely absorbed with translating English writer and art critic John Ruskin. It was from reading and reworking Ruskin's prose that Proust honed his characteristic writing

Signature titles

Novels

In Search of Lost Time (À la recherche du temps perdu), 1913–1927

Jean Santeuil, 1954

Short stories

Pleasure and Days (Les Plaisirs et les jours), 1896

Nonfiction

On Reading Ruskin, 1987

By Way of Sainte-Beuve (Contre Sainte-Beuve), 1954

ABOVE: A photograph of Proust taken in Illiers-Combray, France, *c.* 1895.

LEFT: *Art nouveau interior 1900* by Georges de Feure (1868–1943), an illustration for Proust's *In Search of Lost Time*.

style: labyrinthine sentences and contorted syntax unfurling minutiae of the natural and social world. It was also from Ruskin that Proust developed a sense of the importance of reading. In a prefatory essay to one of his translations of Ruskin—his first serious piece of writing—Proust argued for the importance of reading in awakening a child's imagination, an idea that would infiltrate his magnum opus, *In Search of Lost Time*. His mother's death in 1905 also greatly affected his writing; the fact of her death, coupled with the fortune it left him, made Proust aware of his own mortality. He had believed that death, like writing, might be put off, but he now felt an intense yearning to write and had the money to do so.

To precipitate his newfound determination, Proust moved out of his parents' apartment. In an effort to make his new

Social Being

As much as Proust's asthma drew him into long periods of solitude, as a young adult he was also a well-known dandy and social climber.

Proust's parents grew concerned that he was becoming too much of a dilettante and erring from his middle-class status. He conceded to their wishes and accepted a position at the Bibliothèque Mazarine in 1896. However, when he was not ill, all of his energy and ambition was devoted to socializing. After a prolonged period of absence, claimed to be on account of a nervous breakdown, Proust abandoned his position at the library entirely. He would live with his parents for the remainder of their lives.

Involuntary Memory

In addition to the digressive style and philosophical scope of *In Search of Lost Time*, the work is renowned for presenting and coining the idea of involuntary memory. It differs from ordinary memory in that it cannot be recalled by an act of will; instead recollections of the past are triggered by sensory experience.

The most famous example of this type of memory occurs at the start of the novel, when the taste and smell of lime blossom mixed with madeleine spontaneously recall the narrator's childhood at Combray with startling clarity. This is arguably the most significant moment in the novel, as the memories uncovered by this experience allow the narrator to begin to tell his story. Beyond its function in the novel, Proust's idea of involuntary memory also became an important concept for modern psychology.

environment conducive to his failing health and efforts at writing, he sealed the walls of his bedroom with cork. It was in this room that he wrote most of *In Search of Lost Time*. The first volume of the novel, *Swann's Way* (*Du côté de chez Swann*) was published in 1913, and received mixed reviews. But subsequent volumes gathered critical acclaim. Proust died in 1922, before the final opus could be published. While most of his worldwide acclaim was garnered after his death—with writers such as Virginia Woolf, Graham Greene, and Vladimir Nabokov extolling his influence—Proust at lived long enough to be revered in his native country: In 1919 he received the Prix Goncourt, the most prestigious literary prize in France. **SD**

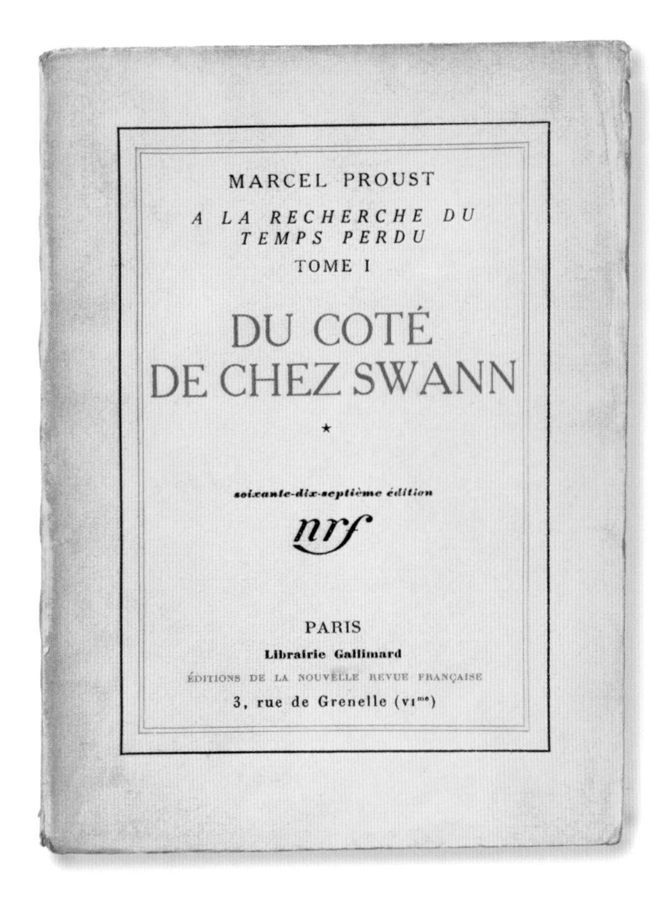

RIGHT: "Swann's Way," volume 1 of *In Search of Lost Time,* by Marcel Proust.

THEODORE DREISER

Born: Theodore Herman Albert Dreiser, August 27, 1871 (Terre Haute, Indiana, U.S.); died December 28, 1945 (Hollywood, California, U.S.).

Style and genre: Dreiser's work combined dense textual detail, journalistic documentation, interest in the conflict of innate drives, and civilization's strictures.

The first major U.S. author of the twentieth century, Theodore Dreiser was also the first professional American writer of non-British descent—his father was a German immigrant. Dreiser's class affiliations were humble; he taught his own mother how to read when he reached the age of twelve. When Henry James was not writing, he could pose as a "man of leisure"; when Dreiser was not writing, he was simply out of work. As a literary figure, Dreiser not only confronted Victorian sexual timidities, he also challenged assumptions about who could be an author.

Critical approval was not always forthcoming. A polarizing figure, Dreiser often attracted critical reproach: F. R. Leavis said that he wrote as though he did not have a native language; Lionel Trilling used him to exemplify U.S. anti-intellectualism; John Berryman said that he "wrote like a hippopotamus." Dreiser periodically achieved sentences of toe-curling embarrassment, yet despite this his finest novels successfully reimagined established cultural paradigms while capturing the definitive pictures of the urban United States.

Sister Carrie is the "fallen woman" story purged of its moralistic conclusions, written against a social canvas capacious enough to include the opulent hotels and department stores, as well as the squalid factories and flophouses of New York and Chicago. *An American Tragedy* begins in similarly well-worn grooves—a poor boy falls in love with a rich man's daughter—but ends with an execution rather than marriage, therefore establishing a pattern for the true-crime documentary that led to Truman Capote's *In Cold Blood*, (1966) and Norman Mailer's *The Executioner's Song* (1979). **IW**

"... words are but the vague shadows of the volumes we mean."—*Sister Carrie*

Signature titles

Novels

Sister Carrie, 1900
Jennie Gerhardt, 1911
The Financier, 1912
The Titan, 1914
The Genius, 1915
An American Tragedy, 1925
The Bulwark, 1946
The Stoic, 1947

Short stories

Free and Other Stories, 1918

Nonfiction

A Book About Myself, 1922
Dawn, 1931

ABOVE: A portrait of American author Theodore Dreiser *c.* 1915.

PAUL VALÉRY

Born: Ambroise-Paul-Touissaint-Jules Valéry, October 30, 1871 (Sète, Hérault, France); died July 20, 1945 (Paris, France).

Style and genre: Valéry was a leading French poet, essayist, critic, philosopher, and public speaker whose poetry reflected symbolist thinking.

Paul Valéry was one of the towering intellectual figures of nineteenth-century France, best remembered for his poetry and public speaking. A member of poet and critic Stéphane Mallarmé's circle, attending his famous literary "Tuesday evening" meetings, he is widely considered one of the last great symbolist poets. Valéry published his first poem in 1889, and described seeing his name in print as inducing: "an impression similar to that experienced in dreams where you are deeply mortified to discover yourself stark naked in an elegant drawing-room." He traveled to Paris in 1892, befriending Mallarmé and artist Berthe Morisot among others.

In 1896 Valéry spent time in London and published *An Evening with Monsieur Teste*, which he tried to dedicate to artist Edgar Degas, who refused the offer. In 1900 Valéry went to work for Édouard Lebey, director of the advertising group Agence Havas; he remained there for the next twenty years, ceasing writing his poetry but continuing to write his *Notebooks* (*Cahiers*). He began these invaluable diaries in 1894, and they contain his many mathematical and scientific investigations, as well as drafts of passages that appeared in his works. Valéry began writing poetry again in 1917, producing *The Young Fate* (*La Jeune parque*). The complex poem—a soliloquy of a young woman reflecting on the forces of life, love, and death—is written along classical alexandrine lines, and is considered a masterpiece. His poetry was greatly influenced by the works of Mallarmé, Edgar Allan Poe, and Robert Louis Stevenson. In 1927 Valéry was elected to the Académie française, and became a dedicated public speaker, lecturing on France's social and cultural issues. **TamP**

"Literature is thronged with people who don't really know what to say. . . ."—*Tel Quel*

Signature titles

Novel

An Evening with Monsieur Teste (La Soirée avec monsieur Teste), 1896

Poetry

The Young Fate (La Jeune parque), 1917

Album of Ancient Verses (Album des vers anciens), 1920

Charms (Charmes), 1922

Nonfiction

Notebooks (Cahiers), 1957–1960

Tel Quel, 1941–1943

ABOVE: A *c.* **1935 portrait photograph of Valéry, one of France's greatest poets.**

PÍO BAROJA

Born: Pío Baroja y Nessi, December 28, 1872 (San Sebastián, Gipuzkoa, Spain); died October 30, 1956 (Madrid, Spain).

Style and genre: Baroja was a Spanish author who wrote with directness and simplicity, using colloquial language to explore the difficulties of city life for the poor.

Pío Baroja was a key member of the "Generation of '98," the group of young writers who were preoccupied with Spain's social and political degeneration at the turn of the nineteenth century. A prolific author, Baroja often grouped his works into volumes or trilogies (the largest of which is twenty-two volumes), many of which address contemporary social problems. His semiautobiographical masterpiece of 1911, *The Tree of Knowledge* (*El árbol de la ciencia*), is a coming-of-age story, full of pessimism and misunderstanding of life, whose protagonist eventually commits suicide. Often using colloquial language, Baroja's austere and sparse style was a great influence on American author Ernest Hemingway. **REM**

Signature titles

Novels

The House of the Aizgorri (La casa de Aizgorri), 1900

The Lord of Labraz (El mayorazgo de Labraz), 1903

Zalacain the Adventurer (Zalacaín el aventurero), 1909

Caesar or Nothing (César o nada), 1910

The Tree of Knowledge (El árbol de la ciencia), 1911

Memoirs of a Man of Action (Memorias de un hombre de acción), 1913–1931

The Struggle for Life (La Lucha por la Vida), 1922–1924

ALFRED JARRY

Born: September 8, 1873 (Laval, Mayenne, France); died November 1, 1907 (Paris, France).

Style and genre: Jarry was a playwright whose surreal plays of savage humor and grotesque characters are regarded as the forerunners of absurdist theater.

Alfred Jarry wrote his first work at the age of fifteen. It was a satirical piece about his physics teacher, and it formed the basis for *King Ubu* (*Ubu roi ou les Polonais*) published in 1896. This parody of William Shakespeare's *Macbeth* (*c.*1603–1606) used scatological humor to present Jarry's view of the world. It was unlike anything that had been seen on the French stage, and there was uproar at its first performance. The play was not performed again until 1907, but it established his reputation. Jarry wrote more plays featuring the same character, as well as poetry, essays, and novels. Jarry's behavior became erratic: He drank heavily, carried a loaded pistol, and when his inheritance ran out, lived in poverty before dying of tuberculosis. **HJ**

Signature titles

Novels

Days and Nights (Les Jours et les Nuits), 1897

Exploits and Opinions of Dr. Faustroll, Pataphysician (Gestes et opinions du docteur Faustroll, pataphysicien), 1898–1911

The Supermale (Le Surmâle), 1902

Plays

Caesar Antichrist (César Antéchrist), 1895

King Ubu (Ubu Roi ou les Polonais), 1896

Ubu Cuckolded (Ubu cocu), 1899

Ubu Chained (Ubu enchaîné), 1900

COLETTE

Born: Sidonie-Gabrielle Colette, January 28, 1873 (Saint-Sauveur-en-Puisaye, Yonne, Bourgogne, France); died August 3, 1954 (Paris, France).

Style and genre: Colette's erotic fiction celebrates sensuality with characterizations that expose superficiality and provide a dose of witty satire.

That Colette was known simply by one name is a true measure of her status as an author and celebrity. Her 1954 obituary in the *New York Times* noted that she was only the second woman ever admitted as a grand officer of the Légion d'honneur (Legion of Honor). Although Colette's success transcended gender, with Paul Claudel calling her "the greatest living writer in France," much of her writing is concerned with the construction of femininity. Her best-known novel, *Gigi* (adapted for Broadway by Anita Loos, with a starring role for the then-unknown Audrey Hepburn) deals with the socialization of a young woman. Under the light-hearted glamor that made it a success, *Gigi* is a telling account of the ways in which women learn to be objects in a male-dominated world.

Colette's name in adulthood, Sidonie-Gabrielle Claudine

Signature titles

Novels

Claudine at School (Claudine à l'école), 1900
Claudine in Paris (Claudine à Paris), 1901
Claudine Married (Claudine en ménage), 1902
The Innocent Wife (Claudine s'en va), 1903
The Vagabond (La Vagabonde), 1910
Mitsou, 1919
Chéri, 1920
My Mother's House (La Maison de Claudine), 1922
The Ripening Seed (Le Blé en herbe), 1923
The Last of Chérie (La Fin de Chéri), 1926
The Cat (La Chatte), 1933
Gigi, 1944

ABOVE: A 1900 photographic portrait of the French author Colette.

RIGHT: A lithograph by Alexandre Rzewuski for Colette's "Procession of Precious Stones."

Colette Gauthier-Villars de Jouvanel Goudeket, gives some sense of her many-storied life that she took as subject for much of her work. She was married three times, first and most significantly to Henri Gauthier-Villars, a populist writer under the pseudonym "Willy," who persuaded her to turn her private accounts of schoolgirl life into the *Claudine* novels (published under his name). Their direct charm and erotic undertones made them best sellers—and Willy rich. *Claudine* was one of the first franchises, inspiring uniforms, soaps, and perfumes.

Divorcing Willy in 1906 after thirteen years of marriage and forced writing, Colette became a music-hall dancer (an experience that provided background for many subsequent novels), and then a journalist covering a wide beat from politics to cinema. In the 1920s, she took to the stage to play the central character in *Chéri*, her adaptation of her most successful novel. A daring tale of love, sex, and class, its blend of melancholy and desire is representative of Colette's oeuvre. Spoiled young Chéri is subject to the gaze of aging courtesan Léa—a role that Colette made her own as she continued to take lovers both male and female into her seventies. **SM**

ABOVE: Colette posing for the camera on a lion-skin rug.

A Riotous Career

Few writers have had careers as varied as Colette's, moving from page to stage and screen. Beyond her literary diversity, Colette was also a well-known performer in the Parisian music-hall scene in the early years of the twentieth century, and many of her fictional characters derive from the bohemian environment. An advocate of sexual liberation, Colette courted scandal: She was known for baring her breasts on stage, and once simulated sex in a sketch at the Moulin Rouge, almost causing a riot. Even so, she was accorded the honor of a state funeral, attended by thousands of mourners.

WILLA CATHER

Born: Wilella Sibert Cather, December 7, 1873 (Back Creek Valley, Virginia, U.S.); died April 24, 1947 (New York, New York, U.S.).

Style and genre: Cather was an American modernist author, poet, and essayist who wrote about frontier life in Nebraska with a spare but elegiac precision.

Signature titles

Novels

Alexander's Bridge, 1912
O Pioneers!, 1913
The Song of the Lark, 1915
My Ántonia, 1918
One of Ours, 1922
A Lost Lady, 1923
The Professor's House, 1925
My Mortal Enemy, 1926
Death Comes for the Archbishop, 1927
Shadows on the Rock, 1931
Lucy Gayheart, 1935
Sapphira and the Slave Girl, 1940

Poetry

April Twilights, 1903

American modernist writer Willa Cather wrote with equanimity about the passion and violence of frontier life, and with understated elegy about the beauty of the landscape that shaped both the people and the stories they tell. Like the flat, rolling landscape of the prairies, her stories spread out as an evenly paced series of arresting tableaux.

Cather grew up in Nebraska, and it was there she met and gathered information from the pioneers and immigrants the likes of whom were to populate her later work, as she said: "Of course Nebraska is a storehouse of literary material. Everywhere is a storehouse of literary material. If a true artist was born in a pigpen and raised in a sty, he would still find plenty of inspiration for his work. The only need is the eye to see."

When Cather traveled to Paris as a student, she was struck by French painter Pierre Puvis de Chavannes's frescoes of the life of St. Genevieve, in which all the events in the saint's life are depicted with the same distance, from the same perspective. It is as if, Cather wrote: "all human experiences, measured against one supreme spiritual experience, were of about the same importance." She achieves the same effect with her fiction: Cather writes about preparing a meal in the kitchen of a sod hut with the same spare precision as she treats suicide, murder, or a love affair.

"Nothing is far and nothing is near, if one desires."
—*The Song of the Lark*

Cather was overlooked as a major American writer but is today receiving her share of attention. Some are interested in her as a lesbian writer, although little can be said about this, because she stipulated in her will that no one be allowed to quote from her personal writings. That said, her quietly innovative fiction is important in its own right. As writer A. S. Byatt said: "She was a modernist when Dos Passos, Hemingway, and Fitzgerald were boys." **CQ**

ABOVE: A *c.* 1930 photograph of American modernist author Willa Cather.

FORD MADOX FORD

Born: Ford Hermann Hueffer, December 17, 1873 (Merton, Surrey, England); died June 26, 1939 (Deauville, Normandy, France).

Style and genre: Ford was a novelist, poet, and critic whose flowing style of storytelling is marked by introspective, pensive prose exploring patriotic themes.

An unhappy, troubled man whose works reflect his inward-thinking nature, Ford Madox Ford was never quite sure what or who he should be. His father was German, a music critic for *The Times*; his mother was English, the daughter of Pre-Raphaelite painter Ford Madox Brown. As anti-German feeling grew in Britain, the writer changed his surname from Hueffer to Ford, giving himself a palindromic quality of a thoroughly English man, seemingly negating his father's influence.

Ford's private life was erratic, symptomatic of the depressive nature that lurks behind his writing. He married Elsie Martindale, after an exciting elopement—only to discover incompatibility. Elsie would not divorce him, but he left her so he could live with a prominent literary hostess and fellow writer, the temperamental and passionate Violet Hunt. In 1915, he gladly left both women behind when he enlisted to fight for his country; the same year his most famous book, *The Good Soldier*, was published. The traumatic fighting at the Somme left him suffering from shell shock.

After World War I, he moved to France, having fallen in love with painter Stella Bowen. He left her for a U.S. artist, Janice Biala, and began spending much of his time in the United States. A difficult man, his reputation has often been damaged by contemporaries who disliked him; yet he was also a kind man who took pains to help younger writers further their careers. As editor of the well-respected *The English Review*, he had influence. He worked closely with Joseph Conrad with whom he collaborated. When Conrad later turned against him, Ford was deeply wounded—it seems to have been a sad and regular feature of Ford's life that those who had once loved him ended up disliking him. **LH**

"It is a queer and fantastic world. Why can't people have what they want?"—*The Good Soldier*

Signature titles

Novels

The Good Soldier, 1915

Parade's End, 1924–1928

It Was the Nightingale, 1933

Ladies Whose Bright Eyes, 1935

Vive le Roy, 1936

Poetry

Collected Poems, 1936

Nonfiction

Ford Madox Brown: A Record of His Life and Work, 1896

Rossetti: A Critical Essay on His Art, 1902

The English Novel, 1929

ABOVE: English novelist Ford Madox Ford photographed by E. O. Hoppé.

HUGO VON HOFMANNSTHAL

Born: February 1, 1874 (Vienna, Austria); died July 15, 1929 (Vienna, Austria).

Style and genre: Hofmannsthal was a novelist, playwright, poet, and translator who is best known for the heartbreaking and comedic librettos he wrote for operas by composer Richard Strauss.

Born into a cultivated Roman Catholic family distantly of Jewish descent, Hugo von Hofmannsthal began publishing poetry in his teens and after university moved in an avant-garde literary circle known as "*Junges Wien,*" or "Young Vienna" that included the dramatist Arthur Schnitzler.

In the 1890s he began writing plays, initially in verse. His *Elektra*, which he called "a new version" of the classical Greek drama by Sophocles, attracted the attention of the composer Richard Strauss, who saw the Berlin production directed by Max Reinhardt, and made an opera out of it. Their next joint project, suggested by Hofmannsthal in 1909 and set in the Vienna of the eighteenth century, was to prove the most popular of all Strauss's operas: the delightful *The Cavalier of the Rose* (*Der Rosenkavalier*). The duo worked together for more than twenty years until Hofmannsthal's death. Few authors of such distinction have spent so much time and effort on the librettos for operas, or written words of such quality in their own right.

In the theater Hofmannsthal scored a great success with *Everyman* (*Jedermann*), his adaptation of the English medieval morality play. He admired England and its solid national identity and cohesion that he believed provided the ideal background for writers as contrasted with fragmented German culture. He regarded World War I and its aftermath, with the end of the Austro-Hungarian Empire, as a disaster not only for Austria but for the whole cultural future of Europe, and after the war he joined Strauss and Reinhardt in founding the prestigious Salzburg Festival.

"[Hofmannsthal] would prove to be one of the finest librettists opera has seen. . . ."—Jan Swafford

Hofmannsthal was working on the libretto of *Arabella* in 1929 when his eldest son committed suicide. He himself died of a stroke two days later while dressing for the funeral. **RC**

Signature titles

Plays

Elektra, 1903

Everyman (Jedermann), 1912

The Difficult Man (Der Schwierige), 1921

Librettos

Elektra, 1909

The Cavalier of the Rose (Der Rosenkavalier), 1911

Ariadne on Naxos (Ariadne auf Naxos), 1912

The Woman without a Shadow (Die Frau ohne Schatten), 1919

The Egyptian Helen (Die ägyptische Helena), 1928

Arabella, 1933

ABOVE: A photograph of Hofmannsthal in the early twentieth century.

GERTRUDE STEIN

Born: February 3, 1874 (Allegheny, Pennsylvania, U.S.); died July 27, 1946 (Paris, France).

Style and genre: Stein's style includes modernist reinventions of poetic language and polymathic ventures into opera, history, and food writing.

Poet William Carlos Williams noted that Gertrude Stein's "theme is writing," connecting her complex, often frustrating oeuvre to the investigation of language—a reflection of his own grappling with setting down the material world in textual form. While Williams practiced a deceptive simplicity, Stein, an American in Europe, explored the complexities of vision with the eye of an outsider. Her cubist style is best exemplified by the funny, intimate *Tender Buttons: Objects, Food, Rooms*. An elliptical prose-poetry journal of her life with lover and lifelong companion Alice B. Toklas, it gives the reader a sense of a world of things busy becoming and doing. It is a cue to the enjoyably active apprehension that her work requires.

Poet and critic Juliana Spahr places Stein front and center in her account of teaching "difficult" poetry, as well as claiming her as a central influence in postmodern poetry. Meanwhile, biographers such as Janet Malcolm see Stein not least as a Jew living in Nazi France, but as key to understanding the vivid community of writers and artists gathered in the Left Bank of Paris between the wars. Stein, who grew up in 1880s suburban California, which she described pithily as "there is no 'there' there," then studied psychology with William James and emigrated to Paris in 1904 with her brother Leo. An avid collector, Leo was Gertrude's link to modernist artists, including Pablo Picasso, whose ambitious remaking of the world reflected and informed her own.

Stein's writing explained France to Americans in *Paris France*, Americans to themselves in her monumental *The Making of Americans*, herself to the world in *Everybody's Autobiography*—and most significantly through her unparalleled rethinking of poetic language, explained the world to the world. **SM**

"I like a view but I like to sit with my back turned to it."
—*The Autobiography of Alice B. Toklas*

Signature titles

Novels

Three Lives, 1909

The Making of Americans; Being a History of a Family's Progress, 1934

Poetry

Tender Buttons: Objects, Food, Rooms, 1914

Nonfiction

The Autobiography of Alice B. Toklas, 1933

Everybody's Autobiography, 1937

Paris France, 1940

Wars I Have Seen, 1945

ABOVE: A portrait of the eccentric modernist Gertrude Stein in 1942.

ROBERT FROST

Born: Robert Lee Frost, March 26, 1874 (San Francisco, California, U.S.); died January 29, 1963 (Boston, Massachusetts, U.S.).

Style and genre: Frost's poetry plays off the stresses of the spoken voice against poetic meter and explores themes of rural New England.

Although Robert Frost is generally regarded as a poet of rural New England, his earliest poems include some troubled meditations on the urban, industrial United States. A Californian by birth, Frost briefly attended Dartmouth College in New Hampshire in 1892, and studied at Harvard University from 1897 to 1899. His first book of poems, *A Boy's Will*, was published in Britain during a three-year visit, and was favorably reviewed by Ezra Pound. The celebrated early volume *North of Boston* appears to ground Frost's work in a precise location and a known community. However, many of the poems were composed in England in Buckinghamshire and Gloucestershire shortly before the outbreak of World War I, and they reveal an acute awareness of both British and U.S. literary traditions and ideals. During those early years, Frost and the poet Edward Thomas strived to establish "the sound of sense" in their poetry, playing off the stresses of the spoken voice against those of poetic meter. Frost also proposed the idea of poetry as an existential "stay against confusion," and a momentary illumination of darkness.

Later volumes, including *Mountain Interval*, *New Hampshire*, and *West-Running Brook*, established Frost's identity as a New England poet. Many of his best-known poems, including *Stopping by Woods on a Snowy Evening* and *The Road Not Taken*, appear to be simple moral fables, but embody a profound and troubling ambivalence. If Frost excels in the writing of dramatic and narrative verse, he is also a supreme lyricist and sonneteer, as poems such as *Nothing Gold Can Stay* and *The Silken Tent* attest. He famously recited *The Gift Outright* at the inauguration of President John F. Kennedy in 1961. **SR**

"In the capriciousness of summer air / Is of the slightest bondage made aware."—*The Silken Tent*

Signature titles

Poetry

A Boy's Will, 1913
North of Boston, 1914
Mountain Interval, 1916
The Road Not Taken, 1916
Stopping by Woods on a Snowy Evening, 1922
New Hampshire, 1923
Nothing Gold Can Stay, 1923
West-Running Brook, 1928
The Gift Outright, 1941
The Silken Tent, 1942

Anthology

Robert Frost: Collected Poems, Prose & Plays, 1995

ABOVE: A portrait photograph of the New England pastoral poet Robert Frost.

ANTONIO MACHADO

Born: Antonio Cipriano José María y Francisco de Santa Ana Machado y Ruiz, July 26, 1875 (Seville, Spain); died February 22, 1939 (Collioure, France).

Style and genre: Poet, playwright, and member of the Generation of '98, Machado used early dreamlike, nostalgic, romantic, and later existentialist themes.

Antonio Machado was born in Seville, but his family moved to Madrid when he was eight years old. After graduating from the University of Madrid, he traveled to Paris, where he studied at the Sorbonne. On his return to Spain Machado became a French teacher at a secondary school in Soria, and in 1903 published his first volume of poetry *Solitudes* (*Soledades*) that established his ties with the romantic poets of Europe. The poems describe his connection with natural phenomena, especially the sunset, and evoke images of memories and dreams by which the poet captures his subject matter.

During his years in Soria, Machado met the young Leonor Izquierdo, whom he married in 1909 when she was fifteen years old and he was thirty-four. Tragically, she died three years later of tuberculosis, just after the publication of *Castilian Plains* (*Campos de Castilla*), a collection of poems capturing the stark landscape of the Castilian countryside and spirit in spare, somber style. Machado used geographical realities to discuss the larger and deeper questions of the psyche of Spain's common people, which became a precedent for social-realist poets. Machado grappled with the social and political problems of Spain. He coined the phrase "the two Spains" to describe the one that dies, and the one that yawns, referring to the political divisions that led to the Spanish Civil War. As such he was typical of the "Generation of '98," a group of novelists, poets, and philosophers who declared a cultural and ethical rebirth for Spain after its defeat in the Spanish-American War in 1898. Loyal to the Spanish Republic, Machado was forced across the French border into Collioure when the Republic collapsed in 1939, where he died from an illness caught on the journey. **REM**

"... wanderer, there is no road, / the road is made by walking."

—*Castilian Plains*

Signature titles

Poetry

Solitudes (Soledades), 1903

Solitudes, Galleries and other poems (Soledades, Galerías y Otros poemas), 1907

Castilian Plains (Campos de Castilla), 1912

New Songs (Nuevas canciones), 1924

Complete Poems (Poesías completas), 1928

Nonfiction

Juan de Mairena, 1936

ABOVE: A portrait of Antonio Machado in the early twentieth century.

THOMAS MANN

Born: Paul Thomas Mann, June 6, 1875 (Lubeck, Schleswig-Holstein, Germany); died August 12, 1955 (Zurich, Switzerland).

Style and genre: Mann was a writer whose works examine the nature of Germany and the need to balance art with the demands of everyday life.

Thomas Mann was born into a wealthy merchant family. After his father died in 1891, the family moved to Munich where Mann started writing short stories. They were well received, so his publisher encouraged him to try a longer work. The result was the best-selling *Buddenbrooks*. Hailed a masterpiece, the novel follows the rise and subsequent fall from social grace of a family during four generations.

In *Buddenbrooks* Mann began to explore a recurring theme: the need to balance the pursuit of art and the demands of practical life. It is also found in *Death in Venice* (*Der Tod in Venedig*), the story of an artist who falls in love with a young boy and slowly spirals into self indulgence, and in *The Magic Mountain* (*Der Zauberberg*), which examines bourgeois society via the discussions of the inhabitants of a health sanitarium.

Although Mann began life as a staunch conservative, his ideology became increasingly liberal, leading him to publicly oppose the policies of Adolph Hitler in 1930. Mann left Germany when the Nazis gained power in 1933 and spent years in self-imposed exile, mostly in Switzerland, before settling in the United States in 1939. Increasingly politically vocal, he made anti-Nazi radio broadcasts to Germany during World War II. In 1947 he published *Doctor Faustus* (*Doktor Faustus*), the story of a musician who sells his soul to the devil in return for a mastery of music, and is an allegory of Germany's slow destruction by Nazism. In 1952 Mann moved his family back to Switzerland, where he remained until his death. His last work, *Confessions of Felix Krull, Confidence Man: The Early Years*, remains unfinished.

As well as being an outstanding German novelist , through his essays Mann became a leading spokesperson for German values and literature, helping to keep their recognition alive in some of the darkest periods for German culture. **JM**

Signature titles

Novels

Buddenbrooks, 1901
Tristan, 1903
Royal Highness (Königliche Hoheit), 1909
Death in Venice (Der Tod in Venedig), 1912
Disorder and Early Sorrow (Unordnung und frühes Leid), 1925
The Magic Mountain (Der Zauberberg), 1924
Mario and the Magician (Mario und der Zauberer), 1930
Joseph and His Brothers (Joseph und seine Brüder, 1933–1943
Doctor Faustus (Doktor Faustus), 1947
Confessions of Felix Krull, Confidence Man: The Early Years (Bekenntnisse des Hochstaplers Felix Krull. Der Memoiren erster Teil), 1955

ABOVE: Thomas Mann photographed by Eric Schaal in May 1938.

RIGHT: The first-edition cover of *Buddenbrooks* designed by Wilhelm Schulz.

Thomas Mann

Buddenbrooks

Berlin
S. Fischer, Verlag.

RAINER MARIA RILKE

Born: René Karl Wilhelm Johann Josef Maria Rilke, December 4, 1875 (Prague, Czechoslovakia); died December 29, 1926 (Montreux, Switzerland).

Style and genre: Rilke was a poet, novelist, and essayist poised between melancholy romanticism and modernism who explored spiritual and mystic themes.

Modernist before his time, and romantic long after it was fashionable, Rainer Maria Rilke bridged the chasm in German literature between lyric poet Heinrich Heine and the "–isms" of the 1920s. Rilke's work can be read as a product of his own divided identity: His mother called him Sophia until he was five years old, dressing him in the feminine clothes belonging to his dead sister. She also encouraged his love of poetry, introducing him to the works of Friedrich Schiller.

Throughout his life, Rilke would be surrounded by influential and intriguing women, none more so than novelist and psychoanalyst Lou-Andreas Salomé, who introduced him to the artists' colony at Worpswede where pioneering expressionist painter Paula Modersohn-Becker lived. There Rilke met his future wife, artist Clara Westhoff, who introduced him to her teacher, the sculptor Auguste Rodin, for whom Rilke worked as amanuensis from 1902 onward.

Inspired by Rodin, Rilke developed a new type of poetry, deliberately modeled on Rodin's sculptures, these were his "*Dinggedichten*" ("Thing poems") that condensed objective observation into powerful lyrics. Between 1912 and 1922, dislocated by World War I, Rilke worked on his masterpiece, the *Duino Elegies* (*Duineser Elegien*). In a frenzied two-month creative period in 1922, he completed the elegies, and then wrote the beautiful *Sonnets to Orpheus* (*Die Sonette an Orpheus*), in which the poet can be heard speaking of his approaching death. After these major sequences, Rilke's health failed, and he spent the next five years moving between a sanatorium at Territet in Switzerland and Paris. Despite his diagnosis of leukemia, he produced a body of poems in French meditating on the rose that he believed would kill him. **SM**

"And the point is, to live everything. Live the questions now."—*Letters to a Young Poet*

Signature titles

Novel

The Notebooks of Malte Laurids Brigge (Die Aufzeichnungen des Malte Laurids Brigge), 1910

Poetry

Life and Songs (Leben und Lieder), 1894

New Poems (Neue Gedichte), 1907

Another Part of the New Poems (Der neuen Gedichte anderer Teil), 1908

Duino Elegies (Duineser Elegien), 1912–1922

Sonnets to Orpheus (Die Sonette an Orpheus), 1922

Nonfiction

Letters to a Young Poet, 1934

Anthology

Tender Taxes, 2002

ABOVE: A portrait of Rainer Maria Rilke, one of the great German lyric poets.

JACK LONDON

Born: John Griffith Chaney, January 12, 1876 (San Francisco, California, U.S.); died December 22, 1916 (Glen Ellen, California, U.S.).

Style and genre: London was a socialist novelist, short-story writer, and journalist, acclaimed for masterful, realistic adventure stories often based on his own exploits.

The U.S. novelist Jack London had a short but adventure-filled life not unlike an exciting work of fiction. It provided him with a wealth of material from which he drew inspiration for his best-selling novels. He grew up in poverty, making ends meet in a variety of professions including sailor, factory worker, oyster pirate, and prospector in the Klondike Gold Rush. During this time, he often used alcohol to escape from the misery of menial labor; it became a lifelong addiction.

London's big break was with a realistic short adventure story called *An Odyssey of the North* drawn from notes made when gold prospecting in Alaska. He had hit on a winning formula of writing gripping fiction based on firsthand experiences. Using this graphic yet compelling style, he went on to write more Alaskan-based adventures: *The Son of the Wolf*, *The Call of the Wild*, and *White Fang*, all of which became immensely popular. A lot of his own life ended up in his work, particularly his memoirs *John Barleycorn*, in which he tells of his battle with alcoholism, and the acclaimed novel, *The Sea-Wolf*, based on his experiences at sea.

A true adventurer and eloquent public speaker, who often fought for improved conditions for the poor, London cut a controversial, dashing, and romantic figure. A prolific writer, between 1900 and 1916, he wrote more than fifty books, hundreds of short stories, and numerous articles, not to mention hundreds of thousands of letters to admiring fans. He became one of the United States's highest-paid authors, although he was terrible with money and often in debt. Sadly, London died of alcohol-induced kidney failure when he was forty, depriving the United States of one of its most prolific, vivid, and naturalistic writers. **JM**

"I shall not waste my days in trying to prolong them, I shall use my time."

Signature titles

Novels

The Call of the Wild, 1903

The Sea-Wolf, 1904

White Fang, 1906

The Iron Heel, 1908

Burning Daylight, 1910

The Valley of the Moon, 1913

The Little Lady of the Big House, 1915

Short stories

The Son of the Wolf, 1900

An Odyssey of the North, 1900

Nonfiction

The People of the Abyss, 1903

Autobiography

John Barleycorn, 1913

ABOVE: Jack London in the photo studio of A. J. Mills in San Jose, California, c. 1905.

HERMANN HESSE

Born: July 2, 1877 (Calw, Württemberg, Germany); died: August 9, 1962 (Montagnola, Collina d'Oro, Ticino, Switzerland).

Style and genre: Hesse was a novelist, poet, essayist, and painter whose works analyze the search for self-enlightenment within the constraints of society.

Hermann Hesse was born into a staunchly Christian family. His father was a Pietist missionary and Hesse went to a monastic school, expected to become a theologian. Hesse rebelled and ran away, later he said: ". . . from my thirteenth year on, it was clear to me that I wanted to be a poet or nothing at all."

Hesse left the education system depressed, resentful, and defiant. He first became an apprentice mechanic, and then a bookseller, where he withdrew into a world of books, studying and appreciating writers such as Johann Wolfgang von Goethe and Friedrich Nietzsche. In 1899, he managed to publish a collection of his poetry. He had also had some success with a few articles, and a publisher who liked his work approached him to write a book. Hesse produced a masterpiece, *Peter*

Signature titles

Novels

Peter Camenzind, 1904
Beneath the Wheel (Unterm Rad), 1906
Gertrude (Gertrud), 1910
Rosshalde, 1914
Demian: The Story of Emil Sinclair's Youth (Die Geschichte von Emil Sinclairs Jugend), 1919
Siddhartha, 1922
Steppenwolf (Der Steppenwolf), 1928
Narcissus and Goldmund (Narziss und Goldmund), 1930
The Journey to the East (Die Morgenlandfahrt), 1932
The Glass Bead Game/Magister Ludi (Das Glasperlenspiel), 1943

Short stories

An Hour Behind Midnight (Eine Stunde hinter Mitternacht), 1899

Poetry

On the Road (Unterwegs), 1911
Poems (Die Gedichte), 1942

Nonfiction

Reminiscences (Gedenkblätter), 1937
War and Peace (Krieg und Frieden), 1946

ABOVE: Hermann Hesse photographed in 1958 for *Der Spiegel* magazine.

RIGHT: A page of Hesse's fairy tale *Piktor's Metamorphosis* with his own illustration.

LEFT: Hesse in his library in Montagnola, Switzerland, photographed in 1937.

Camenzind, the story of a failed writer finding a new life by retreating from a faceless society and returning to nature. The book brought Hesse fame and enough money to write full time. This first novel already contained the first glimpse of the philosophy Hesse would spend his life extolling: the need to balance one's own spiritual individuality against the expected mundane, intellectual routines that society enforces.

Hesse traveled extensively, including a visit to India and Sri Lanka in 1911, and immigrated to Switzerland in 1912. When World War I broke out, Hesse appealed to the German public for peace; as a result the German press labeled him a traitor, and German journals stopped printing his articles. Hesse worked tirelessly in Switzerland helping prisoners of war, and this, combined with a failing marriage, a very ill son, and his father's death, brought him close to a nervous breakdown. He was psychoanalyzed by J. B. Lang, a

"Knowledge can be communicated, but not wisdom."—*Siddhartha*

Eastern Philosophy

Hesse was fascinated by the mysticism of India, his mother's birthplace. As a child he was surrounded by exotic Indian mementoes that helped to fire his imagination regarding the continent.

Siddhartha took three years to complete and Hesse described it as the fruit of "nearly twenty years of familiarity with the thought of India and China." The English translation had a major effect on popularizing Hinduism and Buddhism in the United States. In the 1960s *Siddhartha* was adopted by Jack Kerouac and other "Beat Generation" poets. They identified with the character's struggle for enlightenment. Hesse became a cult figure, representing pacifism and humanitarianism during turbulent times.

Although celebrated as one of Eastern philosophy's major proponents in the West, when Hesse traveled to India he did not find the enlightenment for which he was searching. He realized that the Indian and Chinese philosophy he was imagining was more a representation of a state of mind than something that could be found in a particular location.

RIGHT: Hesse in 1952 with his wife, Ninon, in Montagnola, Switzerland.

student of Karl Jung, and later used these experiences to create the widely acclaimed novel *Demian: The Story of Emil Sinclair's Youth* (*Die Geschichte von Emil Sinclairs Jugend*). It made Hesse popular throughout Europe, but because of his increasing unpopularity in Germany, it was first published under the pen name "Emil Sinclair," who is the protagonist in the novel. Ironically, it was awarded the Fontane Preis for first novels, and Hesse had to admit to writing the book and return the award. He described the book as a story of "individuation," but many people see *Demian* as a thinly disguised autobiography.

Hesse and dualities

In 1922, Hesse published one of his most famous works, *Siddhartha*, following an Indian youth's philosophical search for himself, combining Eastern and Western philosophy in its exploration of self-enlightenment. This was followed by the more surreal *Steppenwolf* (*Der Steppenwolf*), a nightmarish exploration of the dual nature of humanity, and *Narcissus and Goldmund* (*Narziss und Goldmund*), which explores the conflict between reason and creativity.

The pinnacle of Hesse's creative work was *The Glass Bead Game/Magister Ludi* (*Das Glasperlenspiel*) written between 1931 and 1942. It describes a utopian future where the ideals of the spirit are actively preserved. He also published a collection of almost all his published poetry written over the previous fifty years, some 600 poems, in 1942. During this time Hesse wrote book reviews and articles on poetry as well. His work in recognizing new talent helped to critique and to define the literature of his time.

When Hesse died he left behind a legacy of more than fifty novels, hundreds of poems, and countless articles and letters. His literary genius seemed to stem from his uneasiness with the world, and his constant examination of the human struggle to maintain ideals within the confines of society. It is this search for the self that struck such a chord with a worldwide audience, earning him numerous plaudits, including the Nobel Prize in Literature in 1946. **JM**

EINO LEINO

Born: Armas Einar Leopold Lönnbohm, July 6, 1878 (Paltamo, Oulu, Kainuu, Finland); died January 10, 1926 (Tuusula, Uusimaa, Finland).

Style and genre: Leino was a poet, novelist, journalist, translator, and critic best known for his songlike poetic forms inspired by Finnish nature, culture, and folklore.

Eino Leino is regarded as one of Finland's greatest poets. His first published work was a poem, *The Castle of Kajaani* that appeared in a Finnish newspaper when he was just twelve years old. His first collection of poems, *The Songs of March*, was published six years later. Leino was influenced by the *Kalevala* (1849), an epic poem compiled from Finnish and Karelian folklore. Perhaps his greatest work is *Whitsuntide Songs I–II,* which uses the traditional meter of Finnish folk poetry and portrays the past in a heroic light. Leino was a prolific writer (thirty-two books of poetry, twenty-five plays, and twenty-five novels) and has translated Racine, Runeberg, Schiller, Goethe, Dante, and Rabindranath Tagore into Finnish. **HJ**

Signature titles

Novels

Slave of Work, 1911
Slave of Money, 1912
Slave of Woman, 1913
Slave of Fortune, 1913

Poetry

The Castle of Kajaani, 1890
The Songs of March, 1896
Whitsuntide Songs I–II, 1903–1916
Winter Night, 1905
Frost, 1908

ALFRED DÖBLIN

Born: August 10, 1878 (Stettin, West Pomeranian Voivodeship, Poland); died June 26, 1957 (Emmendingen, Baden-Württemberg, Germany).

Style and genre: Döblin was a member of the German "New Objectivity" movement whose novels examine how society shapes the individual.

Alfred Döblin studied medicine at the University of Berlin and then worked as a psychiatrist. His work focuses on the suffering of humanity, and his first novel, *The Three Leaps of Wang-lun*, describes the crushing of a rebellion in eighteenth-century China by the state. However, it was his novel *Alexanderplatz, Berlin: The Story of Franz Biberkopf*—the story of a petty criminal released from prison, stylistically reminiscent of James Joyce and told from multiple points of view—which established his reputation. A Jew and a socialist, Döblin fled Germany in 1933. He moved first to the United States where he worked as a scriptwriter, and then to Paris after World War II. His works influenced Günter Grass and Bertolt Brecht. **HJ**

Signature titles

Novels

The Three Leaps of Wang-lun (Die drei Sprünge des Wang-Lun), 1915
Mountains, Seas, and Giants (Berge Meere und Giganten), 1924
Alexanderplatz, Berlin: The Story of Franz Biberkopf (Berlin Alexanderplatz: die Geschichte vom Franz Biberkopf), 1929
Men Without Mercy (Pardon wird nicht gegeben), 1935
The Land without Death (Das Land ohne Tod), 1937
November 1918: A German Revolution (November 1918. Eine deutsche Revolution), 1949–1950

E. M. FORSTER

Born: Edward Morgan Forster, January 1, 1879 (London, England); died June 7, 1970 (Coventry, Warwickshire, England).

Style and genre: Forster was a modernist whose irony, symbolism, and wit evoked the interior lives and longings of his characters, as well as a sense of the eternal.

"Only connect the prose and the passion, and both will be exalted, and human love will be seen at its height." This famous quotation from *Howards End* encapsulates E. M. Forster's personal and artistic goals: to infuse the everyday with fervor, a commitment to personal relationships, and an appreciation for natural beauty.

After graduating from King's College, Cambridge, Forster traveled to Italy and Greece, and found their cultures more vital, dynamic, and authentic than rigid Edwardian England—crystallizing his sense that there was more to life than upright suburban mores. Italy also provides the setting for two of his novels, *Where Angels Fear to Tread* and *A Room with a View*, both of which deal with the intoxicating emotions that Italy evokes in repressed English visitors, and in the choices such a climate and culture seduces his characters to make. More travel, this time the experience of living in India, inspired Forster's last novel, and what many consider to be his strongest work, *A Passage to India*.

Despite this credo, Forster was lonely much of his life. He did not admit to himself that he was attracted to men until he was in his twenties, and he lived a largely solitary life. His novel *Maurice*, written in his thirties, is one of a very few works about homosexual love written before gay liberation; however, it was not published until after his death. Forster stopped writing novels at the age of forty-five, but remained prominent as an essayist and broadcaster who stood for secular humanist values. Most of his novels have been successfully made into films, yet Forster refused permission to adapt them while he was alive, fearing the medium would render his stories nostalgic and sentimental. **CQ**

"Life is easy to chronicle, but bewildering to practice."

—*A Room with a View*

Signature titles

Novels

Where Angels Fear to Tread, 1905
The Longest Journey, 1907
A Room with a View, 1908
Howards End, 1910
A Passage to India, 1924
Maurice, 1971 (published posthumously)

Short stories

The Celestial Omnibus (and Other Stories), 1911
The Eternal Moment and Other Stories, 1928
The Life to Come and Other Stories, 1972 (published posthumously)

Nonfiction

Aspects of the Novel, 1927
Two Cheers for Democracy, 1951
The Hill of Devi, 1953

ABOVE: The British modernist E. M. Forster photographed in 1949.

WALLACE STEVENS

Born: October 2, 1879 (Reading, Pennsylvania, U.S.); died August 2, 1955 (Hartford, Connecticut, U.S.).

Style and genre: Stevens was a modernist poet famed for his lush and elaborate late-romantic diction and imagery, and his view of poetry as the supreme fiction.

Wallace Stevens is a figure of contrasts. Much of his best poetry is full of rococo colorings, extravagantly flamboyant diction, and the sensuously imagined landscape of Florida, the South Seas, or the "green and actual Guatemala." Yet he spent almost his entire professional life adjudicating bond claims for the Hartford Accident and Indemnity Company, quietly amassing wealth, and rising to be vice president in 1934. Stevens was known for his reticence. As his daughter recalled: "We held off from each other . . . one might say that my father lived alone." Fellow poet William Carlos Williams wrote: "He was always the well-dressed one, diffident about letting down his hair, precise when we were sloppy." In fact, Stevens lived such a private life that many of his long-term colleagues were unaware "Wally" was one of the most highly esteemed poets of his generation.

Stevens's blend of elegance, cool wit, and enigmatic, playful gestures made his work stand out. His poems show a love of goofy Francophone puns, such as *Le Monocle de Mon Oncle*, and of playful musicality. The poem *A High-Toned Old Christian Woman* revels in the "tink and tank and tunk-a-tunk-tunk" of poetry's "jovial hullabaloo," and delights in poets' ability to ignore polite sensibilities and "wink most when widows wince." It is characteristic of Stevens that this high-spirited eccentricity is the vehicle for a careful and detailed argument about the functions of poetry and religion. His work embodies a serious engagement with the nature of aesthetics. *A High-Toned Old Christian Woman* begins: "Poetry is the supreme fiction," and this phrase was taken up in Stevens's late, long poem *Notes Toward a Supreme Fiction*. As he sums up: "After one has abandoned a belief in god, poetry is that essence which takes its place as life's redemption." **MS**

"Verses wild with motion, full of din, Loudened by cries, by clashes."—*Le Monocle de Mon Oncle*

Signature titles

Poetry

Sunday Morning, 1915
Thirteen Ways of Looking at a Blackbird, 1917
Le Monocle de Mon Oncle, 1918
Anecdote of the Jar, 1919
The Snow Man, 1921
The Emperor of Ice-Cream, 1922
The Comedian as the Letter C, 1922
A High-Toned Old Christian Woman, 1923
Harmonium, 1923
Sea Surface Full of Clouds, 1924
Ideas of Order, 1935
The Man with the Blue Guitar, 1937
Notes Toward a Supreme Fiction, 1942
Collected Poems, 1954

ABOVE: A detail from a July 1950 photograph of Wallace Stevens.

GUILLAUME APOLLINAIRE

Born: Wilhelm Apollinaris de Kostrowitzki, August 26, 1880 (possibly Rome, Italy); died November 9, 1918 (Paris, France).

Style and genre: The "herald of surrealism," Apollinaire was closely involved in new developments in French literature and art in the early twentieth century.

Apollinaire's unconventional life and career began with his birth as the illegitimate child of a Polish immigrant woman in Italy. His father seems to have been a Swiss-Italian nobleman who refused to recognize him. Apollinaire spent his childhood in France with his mother and her succession of lovers and pretended to be a mysterious Russian prince. At the age of twenty, he went to Paris, plunged into bohemian circles in Montparnasse, became close to avant-garde writers, painters, and musicians, including Pablo Picasso, Gertrude Stein, Jean Cocteau, Erik Satie, Marc Chagall, and Raoul Dufy, and had a tempestuous affair with the painter Marie Laurencin. Apollinaire wrote anonymous pornography as well as short stories. A notable early work is *L'Enchanteur pourrissant* about the great magician Merlin, the enchantress Viviane, and other figures of the Arthurian legends. In 1911, as a foreigner and subversive, he was arrested as a suspect in the theft of the *Mona Lisa* (Picasso was another) and published his first collection of poems, illustrated with woodcuts by Dufy.

Apollinaire wrote a book on cubist painting, with which Picasso disagreed. His principal published collections of poetry were *Alcools* and *Calligrammes*. In the latter, some of the poems were written in the shape of objects. Much of his work was experimental and enigmatic, and it was apparently he who coined the term "surrealist," in the program notes for the 1917 ballet *Parade* by Cocteau and Satie. Apollinaire joined the French army during World War I, in 1915, much enjoyed military life, and has been described as the only French poet to deal with the experience of the war. A head wound suffered in the trenches contributed, along with the influenza epidemic, to his early death. **RC**

"Without poets, without artists, men would soon weary of nature's monotony."

Signature titles

Poetry

The Rotting Magician (L'Enchanteur pourrissant), 1909

The Bestiary or the Cortege of Orpheus (Le Bestiaire, ou Cortège d'Orphée), 1911 (illustrated by Dufy)

Alcools, 1913

Calligrammes: Poems of Peace and War, 1918

Essay

The Cubist Painters (Les Peintres Cubistes), 1913

Play

The Breasts of Tiresias (Les Mammelles de Tirésias), 1917

1880–99

ABOVE: Apollinaire in Picasso's studio at the Bateau-Lavoir in Paris in the early 1900s.

ROBERT MUSIL

Born: November 6, 1880 (Klagenfurt, Austria); died April 15, 1942 (Geneva, Switzerland).

Style and genre: Musil is regarded as one of the most important modernist novelists and his work is characterized by subtle psychological analysis.

Signature titles

Novels

The Confusions of Young Törless (Die Verwirrungen des Zöglings Törleß), 1906

The Man Without Qualities (Der Mann ohne Eigenschaften), 1930, 1932, 1942 (unfinished)

Short stories

Unions (Vereinigungen), 1911

Three Women (Drei Frauen), 1924

After his death in exile, Robert Musil was all but forgotten until interest in his long, unfinished novel *The Man Without Qualities* revived in the 1950s and the first English translation appeared. The novel, which has been compared with the works of Proust, is a sweeping and often comic exploration of the decline of the Austro-Hungarian Empire seen through the eyes of Musil's antihero Ulrich. Musil published his first novel, *The Confusions of Young Törless*, to critical acclaim in 1906. It was based on his own experiences at a military boarding school. Collections of short stories followed, but it was the publication of the first two volumes of *The Man Without Qualities* in 1930 and 1932 that cemented his reputation. **HJ**

RIGHT A color lithograph of the title page for *The Confusions of Young Törless* (1906).

STEFAN ZWEIG

Born: November 28, 1881 (Vienna, Austria); died February 23, 1942 (Petropolis, Brazil).

Style and genre: Famous principally as a biographer, Zweig helped to introduce great figures of European literature and culture to a wider audience.

Signature titles

Novel

Beware of Pity (Ungeduld des Herzens), 1938

Libretto

The Silent Woman (*Die Schweigsame Frau*), 1935

Nonfiction

Three Masters: Balzac, Dickens, Dostoevsky (*Drei Meister*), 1920

The Master Builders (*Der Kampf mit dem Dämon*), 1925

The World of Yesterday (*Die Welt von Gestern*), 1941

Zweig was influenced by the avant-garde "Young Vienna" literary group and by Sigmund Freud. From a wealthy Jewish family, he went to university in Berlin and Vienna, traveled widely, and wrote studies of Tolstoy and Dostoyevsky as well as Stendhal, Dickens, Nietzsche, Balzac, Marie Antoinette, and others. He also wrote plays and short stories and translated Baudelaire and Verlaine. After the death of Hugo von Hofmannsthal in 1929, Zweig wrote the libretto for one of Richard Strauss's operas, but because he was Jewish, the Nazis forced the composer to drop him. Zweig lived in Salzburg, Austria, from 1913 until he was driven out by the Nazis in the 1930s. He ended up in Brazil, where he and his second wife committed suicide. **RC**

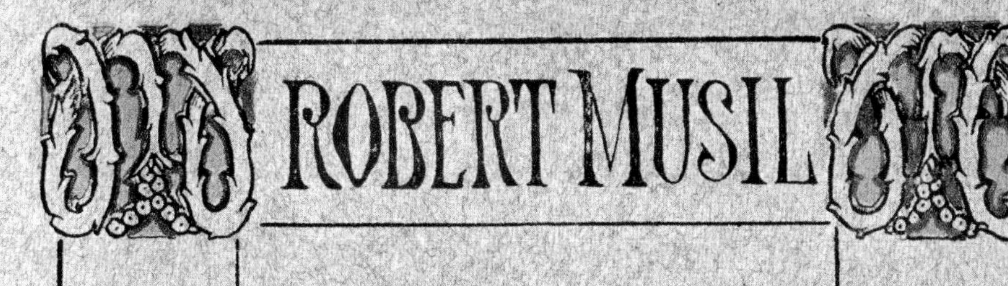

Die Verwirrungen des Zöglings Törless

Plessner

WIENER VERLAG
WIEN u. LEIPZIG.

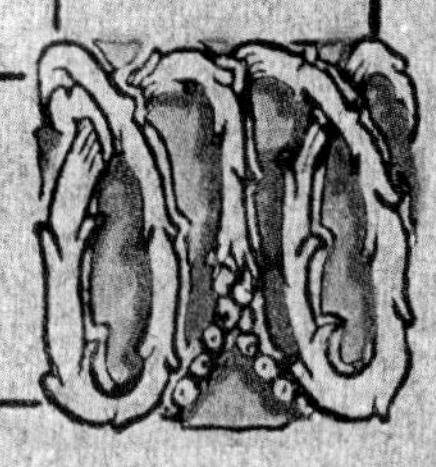

JUAN RAMÓN JIMÉNEZ

Born: December 24, 1881 (Moguer, Andalusia, Spain); died May 29, 1958 (Santurce, Puerto Rico).

Style and genre: One of the great Spanish poets, Jiménez's work is romantic, visual, and often associated with the colors green, yellow, and later, white.

Winner of the Nobel Prize in Literature in 1956, Juan Ramón Jiménez grew up in a Spanish literary climate that emerged after the loss of Spain's colonies to the United States in 1898. These poets and novelists called themselves *modernistas*, and the leader of this movement, poet Rubén Dario, invited Jiménez to Madrid. There he encouraged the poet and supported the publication of his first volume of poetry in 1900. In this same year, however, Jiménez's father died, and he fell into a deep depression that developed into a bout of mental illness. He went to a sanatorium in France to recover, but his preoccupation with death lasted for the rest of his life.

Throughout his life, Jiménez was an incredibly prolific poet, producing sometimes a book of poetry a year, in addition to establishing two literary reviews and acting as critic and editor of various Spanish literary journals. In 1912, he moved to Madrid, where he worked with the poet, writer, and translator Zenobia Camprubí Aymar to translate the work of Hindu poet Rabindranath Tagore and they fell in love. Their love enabled Jiménez to cope with his depression and four years later, he followed her by boat to New York. This transatlantic voyage led him to contemplate the emptiness of the ocean surrounding the boat that mirrored one of his principal themes: how poetry and the experience of beauty are a means of struggling against the feeling of nothingness he experienced when depressed. He married Camprubí Aymar in 1916 and in the 1920s became the recognized leader of a new generation of Spanish poets.

Jiménez's later poetry exhibited a religious ideology and symbolic references to color and music permeated his work. His early work was romantic and associated with the colors green and yellow, whereas his later poetry was more ascetic, and dominated by references to the color white. He left Spain

Signature titles

Poetry

Souls of Violet (*Almas de violeta*), 1900
Pure Elegies (*Elejías puras*), 1908
Sonorous Solitude (*La Soledad Sonora*), 1911
Magic Poems of Sorrow (*Poemas mágicos y dolientes*), 1911
Platero and I (*Platero y yo*), 1914
Diary of a Newly-Wed Poet (*Diario de un poeta recién casado*), 1917
Eternities (*Eternidades*), 1918
Stone and Sky (*Piedra y cielo*), 1919
Poetry (*Poesía*), 1923
Beauty (*Belleza*), 1923
Spaniards of Three Worlds (*Españoles de tres mundos*), 1942
Voices of My Song (*Voces de mi copla*), 1945
Animal of Depth (*Animal de fondo*), 1949

ABOVE: A photograph of Jiménez in 1956, the year he won the Nobel Prize.

ABOVE: Jiménez addressing a class at the University of Puerto Rico, October 1956.

for Cuba and the United States as a result of the Spanish Civil War that broke out in 1936, and in 1951 he moved permanently to Puerto Rico.

Zenobia died three days after he received the Nobel Prize in 1956, and when the Nobel Laureate was unable to attend the Nobel Banquet in Stockholm (in his own words, he was "besieged by sorrow and sickness"), his acceptance speech was read by Jaime Benitez, rector of the University of Puerto Rico. He said on Jiménez's behalf, "My wife Zenobia is the true winner of this prize. Her companionship, her help, her inspiration made, for forty years, my work possible. Today, without her, I am desolate and helpless." Unable to cope with his loss, Jiménez died two years later in the same clinic where she had died. **REM**

"Your voice of white fire / in the universe of water, the ship, the sky . . ."—"Full Consciousness"

VIRGINIA WOOLF

Born: Adeline Virginia Stephen, January 25, 1882 (London, England); died March 28, 1941 (Rodmell, East Sussex, England).

Style and genre: Woolf is known for deploying a range of narrative techniques, the most influential of which was stream-of-consciousness representation of character.

The third of four children, Virginia Woolf was born into an upper-middle-class family in Kensington, London. Her beginnings, from a literary point of view, were auspicious. Her father, Sir Leslie Stephen, descended from the intellectual aristocracy of Victorian England and was himself a critic and first editor of the *Dictionary of National Biography*, as well as the widower of novelist William Makepeace Thackeray's eldest daughter. Thus, while she received no formal education, Woolf grew up surrounded by books and intellectuals. Numbered among the visitors to her first home were Henry James, George Eliot, and George Henry Lewes; so it is unsurprising that she resolved to become a writer from the earliest age.

The recurring breakdowns to which Woolf was subject over the course of her lifetime have been attributed to the losses she experienced in later childhood, and much speculation has been made regarding the extent to which the sexual abuse she suffered at the hands of her half-brothers impacted on her mental stability. When she was thirteen years old, her mother died suddenly, a tragedy that was followed only two years later

Signature titles

Novels

The Voyage Out, 1915
Night and Day, 1919
Jacob's Room, 1922
Mrs. Dalloway, 1925
To the Lighthouse, 1927
Orlando: A Biography, 1928
The Waves, 1931
The Years, 1937
Between the Acts, 1941

Short stories

The Complete Shorter Fiction, 1985

Nonfiction

Modern Fiction, 1919
The Common Reader, 1925
A Room of One's Own, 1929
On Being Ill, 1930
The London Scene, 1931
The Common Reader: Second Series, 1932
Three Guineas, 1938
The Death of the Moth and Other Essays, 1942

ABOVE: The English novelist and essayist Virginia Woolf at the age of twenty.

RIGHT: Virginia Woolf photographed with her father, Sir Leslie Stephen.

ABOVE: The original Bloomsbury Group, picnicking. Woolf is center-right with hat.

by the death of her half-sister. An even more serious collapse followed her father's death in 1904. A retrospective diagnosis would seem to indicate bipolar disorder, a condition that caused Woolf to drown herself near her Sussex home when she was only fifty-nine years old and depressed by World War II.

As a young woman, her home in Gordon Square became the convening point for members of the Bloomsbury Group, a collection of freethinking artists and intellectuals. Key members included John Maynard Keynes, Lytton Strachey, E. M. Forster, Clive Bell, and Leonard Woolf, whom she married in 1912. Together the couple formed the Hogarth Press, a company that was committed to publishing new and experimental work by writers such as T. S. Eliot, Katherine Mansfield, and Woolf herself.

"A woman must have money and a room of her own if she is to write fiction."

Filmic Qualities

Woolf's trailblazing literary style, feminist credentials, ebullient personality, and precarious mental state have made her the object of Hollywood fascination. Her character and work has been the subject of a number of films, including *Orlando* (1992), *Mrs. Dalloway* (1997), and the Academy Award–nominated *The Hours* (2002). The latter is based on the Pulitzer Prize–winning novel of the same name, by Michael Cunningham. In it he adopts many of Woolf's stylistic devices to produce a text that is rich with Woolfian allusion. Many critics have noted the filmic quality of Woolf's narrative, including close-up effects, the subjective viewpoint, flashbacks, swift scene and character cuts, as well as an obsessive concern for the visual.

Woolf wrote for the *Times Literary Supplement* almost until her death and produced a number of novels, of which four stand out as being particularly significant. What unifies much of her fictional writing is a concern with the feminine consciousness as explored through the now widely exploited stream-of-consciousness (or interior monologue) device. Other characteristics combined the temporal rearrangement of events to match the protagonist's internal experience of time and the juxtaposition of multiple points of view. This produced a subjective style of narration that was different from the conventional, omniscient narrative voice of nineteenth-century realist literature.

The surface action of *Mrs. Dalloway* occurs over only one day and tracks the eponymous hostess's thoughts as she prepares for a high-society party. Setting forth to purchase some flowers, the sights and sounds of central London interweave with flashes of memory that span a lifetime. The novel culminates at the party, where characters from the past crash into the present. *To the Lighthouse* draws inspiration from the author's happy childhood memories of holidays spent at St. Ives in Cornwall, as well as from her parents, on whom the central figures, Mr. and Mrs. Ramsay, are to some extent based. *The Waves* traces the lives of a group of friends over a number of years. The very formal structure of the novel is made up of a rotating series of thoughts in which the characters reflect on themselves and each other.

Orlando stands out as being a more playful novel and adopts the form of a mock biography, taking as its source the writer Vita Sackville-West, with whom Woolf formed a very close, and possibly sexual, relationship. In this fictional incarnation, she lives for more than three centuries, alternately as both man and woman.

Characteristically, Woolf's novels explore the response of characterful women to their social, familial, or domestic environment that alongside her classic critical essay, *A Room of One's Own* (among others), has served to make her a prominent feminist icon. **GM**

RIGHT: The dust jacket for *Mrs. Dalloway* (1925), designed by Vanessa Bell.

MRS
DALLOWAY
VIRGINIA WOOLF

JAMES JOYCE

Born: James Augustine Aloysius Joyce, February 2, 1882, (Dublin, Ireland); died January 13, 1941 (Zürich, Switzerland).

Style and genre: Joyce was an Irish novelist and master prose stylist whose portraits of turn-of-the-twentieth-century Dublin are strikingly innovative.

To say that James Joyce towers over the literary landscape of the twentieth century is, if anything, an understatement. In 1999, Joyce's novel *Ulysses* was not only selected as the best English language novel of the twentieth century (by critics on both sides of the Atlantic), it won the votes handily because it was the obvious choice.

The novel chronicles a single day in the life of the son of a Hungarian Jew named Leopold Bloom in Dublin, in a narrative based on Homer's epic poem the *Odyssey* (*c.* 700 B.C.E.). Along the way, Joyce makes use of every device in his well-stocked tool cabinet, from stream of consciousness to pastiche, and parodies everything from dime-store romances to Irish heroic poetry. The novel has even been criticized for displaying too much virtuosity—such as when the chapter set in a newspaper office employs every classical rhetorical technique, or the Sirens episode that is composed in four interlaying parts as a kind of poetic fugue. But when a work's imitations include literature as significant in its own right as Virginia Woolf's

Signature titles

Novels

Stephen Hero, written 1904–1906, published 1944

A Portrait of the Artist as a Young Man, 1916

Ulysses, 1922

Finnegans Wake, 1939

Short stories

*Dubliners,*1914

Play

Exiles, 1918

Poetry

Giacomo Joyce, written 1907, published 1968

Chamber Music, 1907

Pomes Penyeach, 1927

ABOVE: A photograph of James Joyce in Paris *c.* 1938.

RIGHT: The lost Eumaeus draft from *Ulysses,* fragment of leaf twenty-three, verso.

ABOVE: Ford Madox Ford, James Joyce, Ezra Pound, and John Quinn in Paris (1923).

Mrs. Dalloway (1925) and T. S. Eliot's *The Waste Land* (1922), for example, such criticisms are, in a sense, academic. Even the novel's detractors must acknowledge that there are few works in English literature outside those of William Shakespeare whose influence has been more significant and ongoing.

Joyce was the oldest of ten children, who grew up in Dublin in dire poverty. His first published fiction was a collection of short stories, *Dubliners*, which set the tone for his later work in two ways. First, the work is set entirely in the Dublin of Joyce's childhood and anatomizes the Irish people, demonstrating on the one hand Joyce's intimate knowledge of and sympathy with his countrymen, and on the other his ambivalence about Irish nationalism and the strictures of Roman Catholicism. Second, the book inspired strong negative

"A man of genius makes no mistakes."

—Stephen Dedalus, *Ulysses*

Lucia Joyce

Although Bloomsday (June 16, the date on which *Ulysses* is set) is perhaps the best-known Joyce-related holiday, the Irish also have Lucia Day on July 26, the birthday of Joyce's daughter, Lucia. The holiday was declared in order to promote awareness of schizophrenia; Lucia was first institutionalized at twenty-five years old and was still in psychiatric care when she died at the age of seventy-five.

Joyce wrote of his daughter: "Whatever spark or gift I possess has been transmitted to Lucia and it has kindled a fire in her brain." An avant-garde dancer who studied under Raymond Duncan (brother of Isadora), Lucia was in a brief relationship with her father's friend, writer Samuel Beckett, but it ended in her rejection. She was first institutionalized when, in a fight with her family, she threw a chair at her mother; she would be shuffled between institutions in France and Switzerland for the rest of her life, and at one time was psychoanalyzed by Carl Jung himself. Jung described the father and daughter as, "two people going to the bottom of a river, one falling and the other diving."

RIGHT: A pavement plaque commemorating *Ulysses* on Dawson Street, Dublin.

reactions. In this case, one reader in Dublin purchased the entire run of the first edition and had it burned, an event perhaps not unrelated to Joyce's voluntary exile from his homeland. He left in 1904 and lived in Europe for the rest of his life, primarily in Trieste and Paris.

Joyce's next work and first novel was ultimately printed under the name *Portrait of the Artist as a Young Man*. The story is a thinly veiled autobiography about the childhood of Joyce's alter ego Stephen Dedalus. The character's first name is after the first Christian martyr and his surname after the mythological builder of labyrinths and maker of wings for Icarus. The novel is particularly vivid in its evocation of Joyce's Jesuit education and his protagonist's desire to fly away and escape from the religious and political conventions that stifle his artistic creativity.

Ulysses is a sequel to *Portrait of the Artist*, as an older Dedalus plays the son Telemachus to Bloom's fatherly Odysseus—Joyce essentially creating through fiction his own spiritual father. The novel is, at its core, a meditation on the filial bond—and, in a larger sense, love itself. It is set on the date of Joyce's first rendezvous with his life partner and eventual wife, Nora Barnacle. This is what keeps his verbal pyrotechnics from dissolving into mere intellectual exercises. If Joyce goes to such extremes to tell this story, it is in part because all of literature cannot contain the beauty of one genuine encounter between two human beings. If this novel deserves to be considered the best of the twentieth century, it is as much for its humanity as it is for its virtuosity.

Joyce's talent for inciting controversy did not end with *Dubliners*; *Ulysses* was banned as an obscene book in the United States and Britain, until a landmark decision in 1933 by Judge John Woolsey of the U.S. District Court for the Southern District of New York found it not pornographic, and hence it could not be obscene. By the time U.S. and British readers could freely get a copy of the book, Joyce was already ten years into his final novel, *Finnegans Wake*. His health and eyesight declined as he wrote, and he died only two years after its publication. **SY**

ULYSSES
—You're in Dawson street, Mr Bloom said. Molesworth street is opposite. Do you want to cross? There's nothing in the way.
P. 148
C&C
proudly sponsored by
Cantrell & Cochrane (Dublin) Limited

WYNDHAM LEWIS

Born: Percy Wyndham Lewis, November 18, 1882 (Amehurst, Nova Scotia, Canada); died March 7, 1957 (London, England).

Style and genre: Lewis examined brutalism and the exaltation of violence and the machine age; he had a vivid dislike of sentimentality and Victorianism.

Signature titles

Novels

Tarr, 1918
The Apes of God, 1930
The Revenge for Love, 1937
Self-Condemned, 1954
The Human Age, 1955

Poetry

One-Way Song, 1933

Nonfiction

Hitler, 1931
Blasting and Bombadiering, 1937
The Hitler Cult and How it Will End, 1939
The Jews, Are They Human?, 1939
America and Cosmic Man, 1948

Known primarily as an artist and one of the founders of the artistic movement vorticism, Wyndham Lewis was also a published novelist, poet, and editor. As a young man, he spent several years traveling through Europe and studying art; it was on his return to England in 1912 that he founded vorticism. Two years later he began *Blast*, a ground-breaking vorticist magazine in which he parodied the sentimentalism of the Victorian era and called for the world to embrace the machine age. Ironically, this coincided with the start of World War I. Wyndham Lewis spent the final two years of the war fighting on the Western Front. Two decades later, he published his experiences in *Blasting and Bombadiering*.

After the war, Wyndham Lewis became increasingly right wing. He considered the contemporary art and literary worlds degenerate and launched stinging attacks on those who inhabited them, such as Roger Fry and the Bloomsbury Group. His reputation has unsurprisingly been etched by those same contemporaries, so it is hard to know what is truth and what spite. According to reports, he was a misogynist lover, an uninterested father, and a selfish friend. His writing and art became informed by his politics, most prominently his dislike of the new avant-garde (of which, ironically, he had once been at the forefront), and his allegiance to fascism. He supported Sir Oswald Mosley in Britain and Adolph Hitler in Germany, publishing *The Hitler Cult and How it Will End*. In the same year, he traveled to the United States, where he lived during World War II, returning to London in 1945. He gave up art, although he continued to write and became a notable art critic. In the final years of his life, he went blind as a result of a cancerous tumor. **LH**

"If the world would only build temples to machinery . . . then everything would be perfect."

ABOVE: English novelist, painter, and critic Wyndham Lewis smoking a cigarette in 1914.

JAROSLAV HAŠEK

Born: April 30, 1883 (Prague, Czechoslovakia); died January, 1923 (Lipnice, Czechoslovakia).

Style and genre: A master of political satire, social realism, anecdotes, and comic relief, Hašek was an antimilitarist and a regular contributor to the *Anarchist Press*.

A master of political satire, Jaroslav Hašek has been labeled the Mark Twain of Czech letters. Vitriolic critique of the monarchy and humorous accounts of the Czechs living under the Austro-Hungarian Empire pervade his sketches and stories. His narratives are acute studies of human character, targeting the so-called heroism of the Austro-Hungarian dignitaries, mocking their nationalism and imposed conventions. A passionate critic of social injustice, Hašek became one of the major contributors to the *Anarchist Press*, writing libelous articles against the empire for the Progressive Youth. Stories such as "The Gypsy's Funeral" or "Three Sketches from the Hungarian Plain" spoke for the various nations and nationalities living under the yoke of the Habsburg Empire. Hašek also mocked the excesses of the Catholic Church, which he saw as the primary legislator of imperial rule.

Although Hašek wrote more than 1,000 stories, he is primarily known for his novel *The Good Soldier Švejk*, a collage of sketches and stories about Švejk (who first appeared in a short story in 1912), the common-folk jester and people's philosopher, whose big heart and overzealous desire to serve during World War I wreak havoc with established conventions. While he is viewed as the regiment's idiot, Švejk's double talk parodies the contradictory attitudes of military officers. Through his endless stories and anecdotes, he not only diverts their attention from the grand business of the war but also inevitably exposes the shortcomings of the empire he humbly serves. With the exception of Lieutenant Lukáš, who patiently tolerates Švejk's humorous and at times dangerous excesses, the military officers serve as mere vehicles of Hašek's astute criticism of the imperial rule. **PR**

"Great times call for great men."

—*The Good Soldier Švejk*

Signature titles

Short stories

The Good Soldier Švejk and Other Stories, 1912

The Tourists' Guide and Other Satires from Travels Abroad and At Home, 1913

Two Dozen Stories, 1920

Novels

The Good Soldier Švejk, 1920–1923 (4 volumes)

ABOVE: The Czech writer Jaroslav Hašek photographed in 1910.

FRANZ KAFKA

Born: July 3, 1883 (Prague, Czechoslovakia); died June 3, 1924 (Kierling, Austria).

Style and genre: Kafka is best known for his influential, lucid, concise prose describing incomprehensible scenarios and for his naturalistic landscapes in which individuals are overwhelmed by the state.

A German-language fiction writer of immeasurable influence, Franz Kafka's outstanding originality of thought broods with a nightmarish vision of an oppressive state machine suffocating the individual through bureaucratic complexities. He published only a handful of works during his lifetime and left instructions to his friend and literary executor, Max Brod, to destroy all unpublished manuscripts; a request never honored.

Kafka's works flicker from normalized situations to the point of the ridiculous. Despite regular employment as an insurance official, Kafka published his first collection of short stories, *Meditation*, in 1913. His breakthrough came with *The Judgment*, a tale of a son committing suicide at the behest of his father, and *The Metamorphosis*, the surreal story of a traveling salesman, Gregor Samsa, who awakes one morning to find himself transformed into a giant insect. There is frustratingly little explanation for this change, and Samsa at first behaves as though nothing is drastically amiss. His family, however, are ashamed by his condition and leave him to die alone. Critical interpretation of the symbolic nature of the story implies a condemnation of society's treatment of those who appear different and the isolation that this generates.

The central figure of *The Trial*, Josef K., is arrested without clear reason and spends the duration of the book consumed in search of an explanation for his situation that drags him into a labyrinth of bureaucratic offices, nameless officials, and bewildering procedures. Kafka expertly creates a terrifying, claustrophobic tension in the novel, pertinently describing a state system that prefigured the totalitarian regimes that would shortly devour Europe. Further wrangling with petty officials and authority ensues in *The Castle*. Dark, maddening, and equally compelling, the novel exhibits perfectly Kafka's representation of the anxiety and alienation of twentieth-century life. **SG**

Signature titles

Novels

The Metamorphosis (*Die Verwandlung*), 1915
The Trial (*Der Prozess*), 1925
The Castle (*Das Schloss*), 1926
Amerika, 1927

Short stories

Meditation (*Betrachtung*), 1913
The Judgment (*Das Urteil*), 1913
In the Penal Colony (*In der Strafkolonie*), 1914
A Message from the Emperor (*Eine kaiserliche Botschaft*), 1919
The Refusal (*Die Abweisung*), 1920
Investigations of a Dog (*Forschungen eines Hundes*), 1922
A Hunger Artist (*Ein Hungerkünstler*), 1924

ABOVE: Franz Kafka's passport photograph from 1915.

RIGHT: The cover of Penguin's 2006 edition of Kafka's *Metamorphosis*.

FRANZ KAFKA

METAMORPHOSIS

AND OTHER STORIES

NIKOS KAZANTZAKIS

Born: February 18, 1883 (Heraklion, Crete); died October 26, 1957 (Freisburg-im-Breisgau, Germany).

Style and genre: Kazantzakis is the most highly regarded modern Greek author; he lost the Nobel Prize by only one vote in 1957 (it went to Albert Camus).

Signature titles

Poetry
The Odyssey: A Modern Sequel, 1938
Novels
Zorba the Greek, 1946
Freedom or Death, 1950
The Last Temptation of Christ, 1951
Essay
Report to Greco, 1961

Crete had a special place in Kazantzakis's life and work. It was the Ithaca from which this latter-day Odysseus set out on his wanderings, and he insisted that after his death he should be buried there, at his birthplace. During his childhood in Crete, he witnessed repeated rebellions against Ottoman Turkish rule. He grew up to study law at university in Athens and philosophy under Henri Bergson in Paris before returning to Greece before World War I.

Kazantzakis wrote in modern Greek, which meant that he had little readership outside Greece until his work began to be translated. To earn a living, he had to produce a great quantity and range of work: poetry, novels, plays, children's stories, travel books, and translations into Greek—including Goethe's *Faust* (1808) and Dante's *Divine Comedy* (1308–1321). In 1924, he began years of writing and rewriting a massive sequel to Homer's *Odyssey* (*c.* 700 B.C.E.), which eventually ran to 33,333 lines and which he considered his most important work. Meanwhile, Kazantzakis traveled restlessly in Europe and to Egypt and Palestine. Also involved in politics, he was briefly a minister without portfolio in the Greek government in 1945, worked for UNESCO in Paris in 1947 to 1948, and then settled in France, at Antibes. The two books that brought him the greatest attention outside Greece were novels, which were both made into celebrated films: *Zorba the Greek* and *The Last Temptation of Christ*, whose unorthodox treatment of Christ was condemned by both the Roman Catholic and the Greek Orthodox churches. Returning from China and Japan in 1957, Kazantzakis was taken fatally ill. He was buried in Heraklion city wall because the Orthodox Church would not allow his interment in a cemetery. **RC**

"I hope for nothing. I fear nothing. I am free."
—Epitaph on Kazantzakis's tomb in Crete

ABOVE: A photograph of the Greek writer Nikos Kazantzakis.

WILLIAM CARLOS WILLIAMS

Born: September 17, 1883 (Rutherford, New Jersey, U.S.); died March 4, 1963 (Rutherford, New Jersey, U.S.).

Style and genre: Williams is known for his remarkably vivid, spare, imagistic work, and belief in socialism; his poems have a jazzlike rhythm and themes of everyday life.

Although he made ends meet as the physician of Rutherford, New Jersey, William Carlos Williams moonlighted as one of the most important American poets of the twentieth century.

Williams studied in Geneva, Paris, and New York before attending medical school at the University of Pennsylvania. His early foreign schooling gave him an appetite for travel, and he frequently spent weekends in New York and went to Europe throughout his life, mixing with avant-garde artists and writers such as Marcel Duchamp, Francis Picabia, James Joyce, and Marianne Moore.

He was also a personal friend of fellow poets Ezra Pound and H. D. (Hilda Doolittle) from his medical school days. Williams shared Pound's emphasis on simplicity, but where Pound's verse is tense and gnomic, Williams is just precise, and his best poems have a clarity that is startlingly suggestive. Although he describes plums as simply "so sweet/ and so cold," one can nonetheless almost taste them. He is regarded as a poet who attempted to write about the everyday existence of ordinary people in everyday language, deliberately spurning classical allusion in favor of creating an idiom that reflected a contemporary American lifestyle.

The height of Williams's influence was in the 1950s on writers of the Beat Generation, the Black Mountain school, and the New York school; Jack Kerouac's Dean Moriarty in *On the Road* (1957) starts out from Paterson, New Jersey, in homage to Williams's epic poem. Yet Williams was more than an influence, he was also a mentor to young writers, notably to Allen Ginsberg. Two months after his death in 1963, Williams was posthumously awarded the Pulitzer Prize for *Pictures from Brueghel and Other Poems*. **SY**

"[Williams uses] plain American which cats and dogs can read."—Marianne Moore

Signature titles

Poetry

Poems, 1909

Al Que Quiere, 1917

Sour Grapes, 1921

Spring and All, 1923

An Early Martyr and Other Poems, 1935

Paterson, Books I to IV, 1946–1958

The Desert Music and Other Poems, 1954

Journey to Love, 1955

Pictures from Brueghel and Other Poems, 1962

Prose

The Great American Novel, 1923

ABOVE: William Carlos Williams photographed *c.* 1950.

D. H. LAWRENCE

Born: David Herbert Richards Lawrence, September 11, 1885 (Eastwood, Nottinghamshire, England); died March 2, 1930 (Vence, Alpes Maritimes, France).

Style and genre: A writer of poetry, short stories, and novels, Lawrence employed strict realism in the exploration of relationships between men and women.

Signature titles

Novels
The White Peacock, 1911
The Trespasser, 1912
Sons and Lovers, 1913
The Rainbow, 1915
Women in Love, 1920
The Lost Girl, 1920
Kangaroo, 1923
The Plumed Serpent, 1926
Lady Chatterley's Lover, 1928
Short stories
The Prussian Officer and Other Stories, 1914
England, My England and Other Stories, 1922
Nonfiction
Twilight in Italy and Other Essays, 1916
Sea and Sardinia, 1921
Mornings in Mexico, 1927

An influential and controversial author, D. H. Lawrence's writing explored human emotions, the psyche, and sexuality in a frank and honest manner, breaking down moral conventions. The ill-matched union of his father, an illiterate, alcoholic miner, and his schoolteacher mother created tension at home, and alongside the unspoiled Nottinghamshire countryside his upbringing provided raw material for his early work. This was most evident in his novel *Sons and Lovers*. The book borders on the autobiographical with its vivid descriptions of life in a working-class mining community. The central character, Paul Morel, is unable to release himself from the overbearing influence of his mother, affecting his relationships with other women. The book reads like a psychoanalytical study of the author, a theme that underpins much of his work.

His next novels created uproar on their eventual release because of their sexual subject matter. *The Rainbow* follows three generations of the Brangwen family, allowing Lawrence to weave emotional and social change into the story while

ABOVE: British modernist author D. H. Lawrence photographed in 1930.

RIGHT: Lawrence with writer Aldous Huxley at Bandol, France, in 1929.

LEFT: The Lawrentian phoenix, a powerful symbol Lawrence often used on his covers.

skillfully examining sexual desires and relationships. The follow-up, *Women in Love*, revolves around two modern and educated sisters and their aspirations in life and love.

Blighted by his reputation as a subversive writer, Lawrence left England, yet fell foul of the censors once again after the completion of his most famous novel, *Lady Chatterley's Lover*. The tender treatment of an affair between the upper-class Lady Chatterley and her gamekeeper Oliver Mellors contained graphic descriptions of sexual acts and the use of a certain four-letter word. The book remained banned until 1960. Despite his lowly reputation during his lifetime and criticism from feminists at his representation of women, Lawrence is now regarded as a significant modernist writer who moved fiction away from Victorian social and moral norms. **SG**

The Savage Pilgrimage

Accused of spying and confined to a cottage in Cornwall, it was little wonder Lawrence took a self-imposed exile after World War I. He termed this the "savage pilgrimage" and with his wife Frieda they traveled the world, inspiring Lawrence to produce some of the first recognized English language travel books. The couple journeyed through Italy as recounted in *Sea and Sardinia* before visiting Sri Lanka and Australia, an experience covered in his novel *Kangaroo*. Yet his best travel writing derived from his time in the United States and Mexico as he described the New World in *Mornings in Mexico*.

SINCLAIR LEWIS

Born: Harry Sinclair Lewis, February 7, 1885 (Sauk Center, Minnesota, U.S.); died January 10, 1951 (Rome, Italy).

Style and genre: Lewis's works include themes on women's rights and race issues and are written in an insightful and direct manner with a satirical wit.

Sinclair Lewis was possibly one of the most successful American writers of the first half of the twentieth century, with his dry, satirical wit and brilliantly descriptive style appealing to the American public at large. His novels are characterized by their criticism of American society and consumerism, but this acerbic tone is perfectly balanced by his droll humor, creating insightful yet subtle works.

Lewis began writing at a young age, first poetry, and then short stories, contributing to the Yale University publication the *Yale Literary Magazine*, of which he was editor. After graduating from Yale in 1908, he worked as a freelance writer and for various publishing houses for some years before publishing his first novel, *Hike and the Aeroplane,* in 1912 under the pseudonym Tom Graham. This was the first of several potboilers he wrote, but two years later he published his first serious novel *Our Mr. Wrenn: The Romantic Adventures of a Gentle Man*, which was relatively well received.

It was not until 1920 and the publication of *Main Street*, an instant best seller that Lewis achieved the success and fame for which he is now known. *Main Street* was the result of extensive research and critiqued the narrow mindset of "small-town America," with its protagonist being Carol Kennicott, a strong and emancipated woman. He followed it with *Babbitt*, an equally pithy and insightful work, and later *Arrowsmith* for which he was awarded a Pulitzer Prize that he refused. Lewis was awarded the Nobel Prize in Literature in 1930, the first American to win it. In later years, Lewis never quite recaptured his piercing insight, and although he published nine more novels, only *It Can't Happen Here* comes close in depth and perspicacity to his earlier work. **TamP**

"Our American professors like their literature clear and cold and pure and very dead."

Signature titles

Novels

Hike and the Aeroplane, 1912

Our Mr. Wrenn: The Romantic Adventures of a Gentle Man, 1914

Main Street, 1920

Babbitt, 1922

Arrowsmith, 1925

Elmer Gantry, 1927

Dodsworth, 1929

It Can't Happen Here, 1935

ABOVE: American author Sinclair Lewis photographed in 1940.

ISAK DINESEN

Born: Baroness Karen von Blixen-Finecke, April 17, 1885 (Rungsted, Denmark); died September 7, 1962 (Rungsted, Denmark).

Style and genre: Isak Dinesen is acclaimed for her fantastical fiction, but it is *Out of Africa*, the story of her time spent in Kenya, for which she is best remembered.

Isak Dinesen was born into a bourgeois family in Denmark and studied art in Copenhagen, Paris, and Rome. In 1914, she married a distant cousin, Baron Bror von Blixen-Finecke and moved to Kenya to run a coffee plantation. However, her husband was unfaithful and she developed syphilis. At around this time, she met the big game hunter Denys Finch Hatton and they began a relationship. After he died in an air crash in 1931 and the coffee plantation failed, Dinesen returned to Denmark.

Her first work, *Seven Gothic Tales,* was published in 1934 and was well received by critics in Denmark, the United Kingdom, and the United States. Set in eighteenth- and nineteenth-century Europe, these tales combine elements of traditional gothic fantasy with modern psychological insight. Dinesen wrote *Seven Gothic Tales* and all her subsequent work in English and then translated them into Danish. After her initial success, Dinesen turned to her life in Africa for inspiration and wrote her novel *Out of Africa*, which was published in 1937. During World War II, she wrote *Winter's Tale*—stories based on folk tales—which was smuggled out of Denmark via Sweden. In the United States, it was given to American soldiers fighting abroad. Dinesen also wrote her only full-length novel, *The Angelic Avengers*, as an allegory of Nazism.

After the war, Dinesen turned again to short tales. *Anecdotes of Destiny* was published in 1958 and contains five stories, including *Babette's Feast*, one of her best-loved works, which tells the tale of an elderly cook who finally shows off her real talent.

"Difficult times have helped me understand how infinitely rich and beautiful life is. . . ."

Dinesen was short-listed twice for the Nobel Prize in 1954 and 1957, but she lost out to Ernest Hemingway and Albert Camus. During the 1950s, Dinesen suffered from increasingly poor health and was unable to write. She died in 1962. **HJ**

ABOVE: Baroness Karen von Blixen, who wrote as Isak Dinesen, in January 1959.

Signature titles

Novels

Out of Africa, 1937

The Angelic Avengers, 1946

Short stories

Seven Gothic Tales, 1934

Winter's Tale, 1942

Last Tales, 1957

Anecdotes of Destiny, 1958

Shadows on the Grass, 1960

Carnival, 1977

FRANÇOIS MAURIAC

Born: October 11, 1885 (Bordeaux, France); died September 1, 1970 (Paris, France).

Style and genre: Mauriac was a novelist, essayist, poet, playwright, and journalist whose major novels hinge on the struggle between sin and salvation in the modern world.

Born into a wealthy, bourgeois, Roman Catholic family in Bordeaux, François Mauriac studied literature in Bordeaux and Paris, before his family wealth allowed him to devote himself to writing. His first real success came in the 1920s, with the publication of his novel *A Kiss for the Leper*.

Mauriac's early novels portray the provincial bourgeois world of his childhood. The atmosphere is suffocating and morally bereft, but his religious intentions are not immediately apparent. Struck by a crisis of faith between 1928 and 1931, Mauriac battled with what he saw as the dilemma of every Christian writer: how to portray human evil without placing temptation before the reader.

The dramatic change in his subsequent work is evident in the contrast between Mauriac's two most widely read works. In *Thérèse*, the heroine tries to murder her husband to escape her suffocating life. Although the psychological portrait of Thérèse is sympathetic, it is clear that her actions will only entrap her. However, in his most successful novel, *The Knot of Vipers*, the central character's ill will toward his family and greed is redeemed through his spiritual awakening. In addition to fiction and poetry, Mauriac was a distinguished journalist, writing hard-hitting political articles for several newspapers. During World War II, he was at the forefront of the writers of the French Resistance, and afterward a prominent supporter of Charles de Gaulle. He also communicated widely about writing itself, seeking to justify himself to his critics, and outline his moral intentions. In 1952, Mauriac was awarded the Nobel Prize in Literature, for "deep spiritual insight and the artistic intensity with which he has in his novels penetrated the drama of human life." **CW**

"... sin is the writer's element; the passions of the heart are the bread and wine he savors daily."

Signature titles

Novels

A Kiss for the Leper (*Le Baiser au lépreux*), 1922

The Desert of Love (*Le Désert de l'amour*), 1925

Thérèse (*Thérèse Desqueyroux*), 1927

The Knot of Vipers (*Le Noeud de vipères*), 1932

The End of the Night (*La Fin de la nuit*), 1935

A Woman of the Pharisees (*La Pharisienne*), 1941

Plays

Asmodée, or The Intruder, 1938

The Poorly Loved (*Les Mal-Aimés*), 1945

Poetry

Clasped Hands (*Les Mains jointes*), 1909

Nonfiction

De Gaulle, 1964

ABOVE: François Mauriac photographed on November 14, 1946.

EZRA POUND

Born: Ezra Weston Loomis Pound, October 30, 1885 (Hailey, Idaho, U.S.); died November 1, 1972 (Venice, Italy).

Style and genre: A flamboyant, innovative poet, critic, and polemicist who defined literary modernism, Pound was imprisoned for his pro-fascist broadcasts.

In 1945, after four decades as a tireless controversialist, never attaining the public influence he desired, Ezra Pound found his life overtaken by public controversy. When the Italian war effort collapsed, Pound was locked in an outdoor cage in a U.S. military camp outside Pisa and charged with treason for the pro-fascist, anti-Semitic radio broadcasts he had made in Rome openly attacking the American war effort. Tried in Washington, D.C., Pound escaped the death penalty only by entering a plea of insanity, and was held for the next twelve years in the city's St. Elizabeth's Hospital for the criminally insane. Yet against the odds, Pound managed to compose some of his greatest poetry during this period, and when *The Pisan Cantos* were published in 1948, they were heralded by many as his strongest work yet and awarded the prestigious Bollingen Prize, despite public outcry against the selection.

Pound had been dedicated to his work on *The Cantos*, his modernist epic, since at least 1917 and was to continue the endeavor for the rest of his life. He defined the epic work as a "poem including history," and *The Cantos* shows Pound making an attempt to reorder human history according to his own gallery of exemplary heroes and his economic theories.

The poem includes, among much else, portraits of Odysseus, Confucius, U.S. President John Adams, and Italian mercenary Sigismondo Malatesta, along with condemnations of usury and consignments of the politically wicked to a Dantescan hell. After 800 pages, this effort runs into the ground of its own vast ambition: "I am not a demigod, / I cannot make it cohere," Pound admits. But what remains has the grandeur of a ruined palace, with luminous details among the darkness. **MS**

"But to have done instead of not doing . . . This is not vanity."—*The Pisan Cantos*

Signature titles

Poetry

A Lume Spento, 1908
Des Imagistes, 1914
Cathay, 1915
Lustra, 1916
Quia Pauper Amavi, 1919
Homage to Sextus Propertius, 1919
Hugh Selwyn Mauberley, 1920
The Cantos, 1930–1969
The Pisan Cantos, 1948

Nonfiction

ABC of Economics, 1933
ABC of Reading, 1934
Jefferson and/or Mussolini, 1935

ABOVE: Ezra Pound photographed by E. O. Hoppé in 1918.

SIEGFRIED SASSOON

Born: September 8, 1886 (Matfield, Kent, England); died September 1, 1967 (Heytesbury, Wiltshire, England).

Style and genre: Sassoon's work adopts themes of ironic antiwar commentary with pacifistic overtones and an idealized vision of the English countryside.

Siegfried Sassoon was a leading antiwar poet and writer of fictionalized autobiographies depicting English country life. He volunteered for the British army at the outbreak of World War I, yet by its climax he had become a vociferous pacifist. Sassoon recorded the horrors he witnessed in a satirical and acerbic fashion in poems such as *The General* and *Glory of Women*, which aired familiar grievances against the military staff and those left at home. His public protests at the war resulted in him being admitted to a war hospital where he met fellow war poet Wilfred Owen. He went on to publish the *Complete Memoirs of George Sherston*, a semifictional account of his own life in the English countryside before the onset of war. **SG**

Signature titles

Poetry

The Old Huntsman, 1917

Glory of Women, 1917

The General, 1917

Counter-Attack, 1918

The Path to Peace, 1960

Autobiographies

Memoirs of a Fox-Hunting Man, 1928

Complete Memoirs of George Sherston, 1937

Siegfried's Journey, 1945

RIGHT: Siegfried Sassoon in uniform in camp during World War I.

FERNANDO PESSOA

Born: Fernando António Nogueira Pessoa, June 13, 1888 (Lisbon, Portugal); died November 30, 1935 (Lisbon, Portugal).

Style and genre: Underappreciated (in fact, mostly unknown in his lifetime), Pessoa's contribution to modernism put Portuguese literature on the map.

Fernando Pessoa's first volume of English poetry, *Antinous*, appeared in 1918. One year before his death, his first book of poems in Portuguese, *Mensagem*, was published but largely ignored. Pessoa's extraordinary abilities shone through in his use of seventy-two heteronyms, characters through which he produced a rich dream world of poetry and fiction. Some of his most famous heteronyms include Alberto Caeiro, Álvaro de Campos, and Ricardo Reis. Pessoa imbued these writers with personalities that influenced how they wrote. Bernardo Soares, the heteronym closest to Pessoa's own personality, authored a sweeping, two-decade-long project, a diarylike work of fragments known as *Livro do dessassogego* (Book of Disquiet). **REM**

Signature titles

Poetry

English Poems (Poemas Ingleses), 1921

Message (Mensagem), 1934

Poems of Fernando Pessoa (Poesias de Fernando Pessoa), 1942

The Collected Poems of Alberto Caeiro (Poemas de Alberto Caeiro), 1946

Prose

Book of Disquiet (Livro do dessassogego por Bernardo Soares), 1982

Always Astonished: Selected Prose, 1988

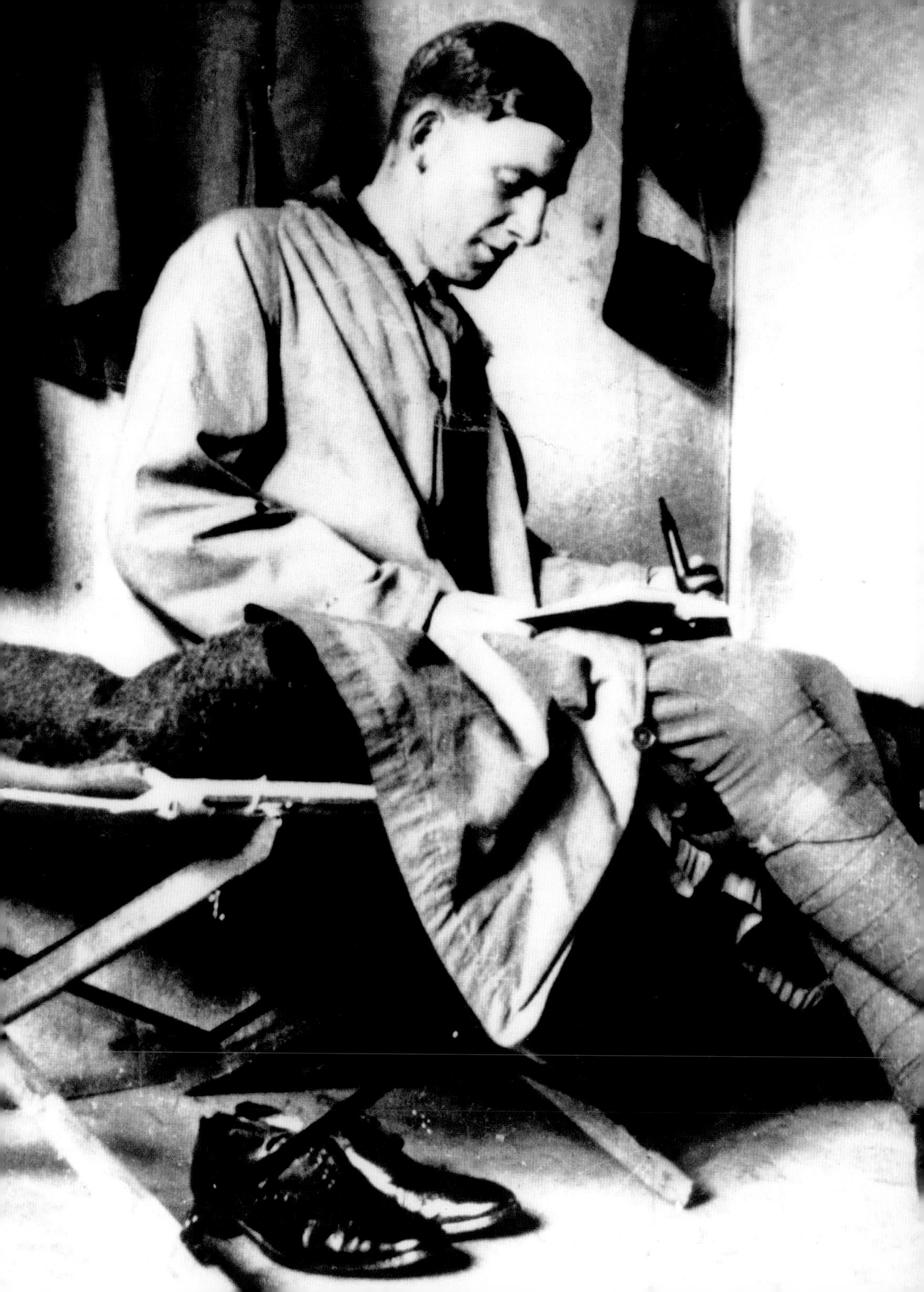

KATHERINE MANSFIELD

Born: Kathleen Mansfield Beauchamp, October 14, 1888 (Wellington, New Zealand); died January 9, 1923 (Fontainebleau, France).

Style and genre: A master of light prose that masks deeper undercurrents, Mansfield's work features marginalized characters and depictions of class struggle.

Katherine Mansfield is acclaimed as one of English literature's finest short-story writers and is rivaled only by novelist Janet Frame as New Zealand's greatest writer. She was brought up in a well-to-do, middle-class family in Wellington, and after four years of schooling in England, beginning at the age of fourteen, she returned to New Zealand, where she began to write.

Colonial New Zealand could not compete with the attractions of London, however, and she returned to London in 1908, where she quickly fell in with the Bloomsbury Group. After an abortive marriage that lasted three weeks from the first meeting to divorce, and the miscarriage of a baby conceived with a family friend, Mansfield came to live with, and eventually marry, the influential editor and critic John Middleton Murry. Her health became a major concern; apart from the miscarriage, she contracted gonorrhea in 1911, suffered from depression, and became infected with tuberculosis in 1917, before succumbing to the disease in France in January 1923.

Mansfield left behind a body of work that draws both on her travel experiences, such as her first collection, *In a German Pension*, but which increasingly looks back to her childhood in New Zealand. Although she never returned to New Zealand after leaving in 1908, *At the Bay*, *The Doll's House*, and *The Garden Party* are all set in the colony and are some of the finest stories she ever wrote. Each of them is a delicate portrait of privileged life in the "young country," underpinned with some vague sense of unpleasantness—often rooted in class conflicts between the working class and the bourgeoisie, or social hypocrisy—that prevents Mansfield from ever lapsing into meaningless nostalgia. **AS**

"I was jealous of her writing. The only writing I have ever been jealous of."—Virginia Woolf

Signature titles

Short stories

In a German Pension, 1911
The Woman at the Store, 1912
Miss Brill, 1920
Marriage à la Mode, 1921
Her First Ball, 1921
The Daughters of the Late Colonel, 1921
At the Bay, 1922
The Doll's House, 1922
The Garden Party, 1922
A Married Man's Story, 1923
The Canary, 1923

ABOVE: A photographic portrait of Katherine Mansfield.

GEORGES BERNANOS

Born: February 20, 1888 (Paris, France); died July 5, 1948 (Neuilly-sur-Seine, France).

Style and genre: French writer Georges Bernanos was a staunch Catholic. His personal spiritual struggle and his deeply felt religious beliefs resonate throughout his novels, especially *Diary of a Country Priest*.

Georges Bernanos, a veteran of World War I, was a devout Catholic and a loyal monarchist. He was deeply critical of modern society as a whole and was violently opposed to defeatism in France in World War II. Throughout his life, he advocated a moral order based on the teaching of the Catholic Church, and a common thread in his writing is his belief in the existence of evil.

After World War I, during which he served on the Somme and at Verdun and was wounded on a number of occasions, Bernanos worked in the insurance industry before writing his first novel *Under the Sun of Satan* in 1926. The book tells the haunting and powerful story of a young, naive Catholic priest who tragically becomes involved with a woman who has committed murder.

Almost all of Bernanos's major works were written in a highly productive period between 1926 and 1937. These include *The Imposter,* which appeared in 1927 and details the spiritual crisis of a priest, and its sequel *Joy,* published in 1929. His masterpiece, *Diary of a Country Priest*, was written in 1936 and recounts the life of a young priest, his spiritual struggle as he attempts to improve the lives of his parishioners, and how he deals with his own approaching death from cancer. It was later made into a film by the French director Robert Bresson.

"To be able to find joy in another's joy, that is the secret of happiness."

After its publication, Bernanos became preoccupied with the coming war and in 1938 he emigrated to Brazil, from where he denounced the spiritual exhaustion of France and strongly supported General de Gaulle's Free French forces. He returned to France and in 1948, shortly before he died, completed a film script, *Dialogues des Carmelites*, about nuns who were martyred during the French Revolution. **HJ**

Signature titles

Novels

Under the Sun of Satan (Sous le soleil de Satan), 1926

The Impostor (L'Imposture), 1927

Joy (La Joie), 1929

Diary of a Country Priest (Journal d'un curé de campagne), 1936

Essay

A Diary of my Times (Les Grandes cimetières sous la lune), 1938

1880–99

ABOVE: Bernanos during the Geneva Peace Conference of Thought, 1946.

EUGENE O'NEILL

Born: Eugene Gladstone O'Neill, October 16, 1888 (New York, New York, U.S.); died November 27, 1953 (Boston, Massachusetts, U.S.).

Style and genre: A dramatist whose work was defined by gritty realism, O'Neill dealt with religion and tragedy and frequently depicted the working classes.

Eugene O'Neill was one of the most influential American playwrights of the early twentieth century and single-handedly changed the nature of American theater through his plays. His work was unconventional and introduced gritty drama, the individual tragedies of human life, uncomfortable subject matter, and expressionistic performance to the American stage.

O'Neill's early life and upbringing had a profound effect on his later life and work, with one of his best plays, *Long Day's Journey into Night*, being a searingly poignant autobiographical account. His father was a well-respected actor whose job entailed constant traveling. The family was dysfunctional: his mother was a drug addict and his brother an alcoholic who died young. Eugene's own family life would prove similarly shadowed by tragedy.

As a young man, O'Neill left home and lived as an itinerant working in various jobs, becoming an alcoholic, and finally attempting suicide. At the end of 1912, he became seriously ill and was hospitalized for six months. It was a turning point for O'Neill, who began to write short, one-act plays during his recuperation, drawing inspiration from his family and life on the perimeter of society. In 1916, O'Neill met a group of young, experimental actors, the Provincetown Players, who began to stage his early plays. The relationship was symbiotic, and between 1916 and 1920, they produced all his short plays. O'Neill's first full-length play, *Beyond the Horizon*, appeared on Broadway in 1920 to positive reviews, winning him the first of four Pulitzer Prizes. Over the next twenty years, he wrote twenty full-length plays and numerous short ones. It was a period of tremendous creativity and saw him win the Nobel Prize in Literature in 1936. **TamP**

"None of us can help the things life has done to us."

—*Long Day's Journey into Night*

Signature titles

Plays

Beyond the Horizon, 1920
Anna Christie, 1922
All God's Chillun Got Wings, 1924
Desire Under the Elms, 1925
Strange Interlude, 1928
Dynamo, 1929
Mourning Becomes Electra, 1931
Ah, Wilderness!, 1933
The Iceman Cometh, 1939 (produced 1946)
Long Day's Journey into Night, 1941 (produced 1956)

ABOVE: A portrait of the American playwright Eugene O'Neill.

RAYMOND CHANDLER

Born: July 23, 1888 (Chicago, Illinois, U.S.); died March 26, 1959 (La Jolla, California, U.S.).

Style and genre: Hard-boiled with a soft center, Chandler's tough-talking, hard-drinking, dame-ogling detectives see the funny and sad side of murder.

Until 1933, Raymond Chandler drew a regular paycheck as vice-president of an oil company. The job did not agree with his creative side and he took up writing instead—to the eternal benefit of pulp-fiction readers everywhere. Even in his earliest stories, written for cheap magazines such as *Dime Detective*, Chandler took the hard-boiled detective story to new levels. He introduced not only a physical realism—where the detective is not always in the right place at the right time—but also an emotional realism, confronting the harsh truths of poverty, jealousy, greed, and crime.

That is not to say, however, that his books do not feature a fair few saps getting thumped by thugs and heavies. Philip Marlowe, his main hero, spends nearly as much time unconscious as he does drinking bourbon and making jokes. It is Marlowe's voice, complete with period slang and unlikely similes ("The walls here are as thin as a hoofer's wallet"), that carries the books along, rather than the plots, which can be Byzantine in their twists and double-crosses. By the time Marlowe gets around to wrapping up the tale, explaining the who, how, and why of the murder—usually murders—the reader is often as flummoxed as the witless cops who gave up trying to solve the case 200 pages ago.

Chandler's books are oddly timeless, with little sense of progression between them. Highlights include *Farewell, My Lovely*, which introduced the world to Moose Molloy, famously not more than 6 feet 5 inches (2 m) tall and no wider than a beer truck, and *The Long Goodbye*, in which Marlowe grapples with the betrayal of his friend, Terry Lennox. This last book, written while Chandler's wife was dying, is considered by some to be his finest work. **CO**

"The private detective of fiction is a . . . creation who acts and speaks like a real man."

Signature titles

Novels

The Big Sleep, 1939

Farewell, My Lovely, 1940

The High Window, 1942

The Lady in the Lake, 1943

The Little Sister, 1949

The Long Goodbye, 1954

Playback, 1958

Short stories

Smart-Aleck Kill, 1934

The Man Who Liked Dogs, 1936

Screenplays

Double Indemnity, 1944

Strangers on a Train, 1951

ABOVE: A casual portrait of Raymond Chandler taken on November 30, 1943.

T. S. ELIOT

Born: Thomas Stearns Eliot, September 26, 1888 (St. Louis, Missouri, U.S.); died January 4, 1965 (London, England).

Style and genre: Eliot was a modernist whose haunting, disjointed lyricism has led to some of the most memorable evocations of unfulfillable longing in literature.

As a poet, essayist, critic, playwright, editor, and even as a children's book author (his *Old Possum's Book of Practical Cats* was the basis for Andrew Lloyd Webber's *Cats*, one of the most successful musicals of all time), T. S. Eliot's influence on the cultural landscape of the twentieth century is such that any description of his writing is also a description of his era. Eliot was an assistant editor at Ezra Pound's *The Egoist* and edited his own quarterly *The Criterion* until 1939; he also worked as a literary editor at the press Faber and Faber until his death. He wrote a series of essays and reviews in the late 1910s—published together under the title *The Sacred Wood*—that continue to influence both poetic and critical conceptions of what, on its most basic level, literature is supposed to do. Although he is most famous as a poet, Eliot would have a claim to being one of the most influential writers and thinkers of his generation, even if none of his poems had been published.

Eliot was born in St. Louis into a wealthy, patrician family with strong New England roots. Among Eliot's relatives are three U.S. presidents and an original settler at the Massachusetts

Signature titles

Plays

The Rock, 1934
Murder in the Cathedral, 1935
The Family Reunion, 1939
The Cocktail Party, 1950
The Confidential Clerk, 1954
The Elder Statesmen, 1959

Poetry

Preludes, 1917
The Love Song of J. Alfred Prufrock, 1917
The Waste Land, 1922
The Hollow Men, 1925
The Journey of the Magi, 1927
Ash Wednesday, 1930
Old Possum's Book of Practical Cats, 1939
Four Quartets, 1942

Nonfiction

The Sacred Wood: Essays on Poetry and Criticism, 1920
The Use of Poetry and the Use of Criticism, 1933
Notes Towards the Definition of Culture, 1948

ABOVE: A portrait of Eliot, winner of the Nobel Prize in Literature in 1948.

RIGHT: Eliot with his mother and sister Marian in England, 1921.

ABOVE: T. S. Eliot inspecting manuscripts at his desk.

Bay Colony. Eliot attended Harvard and had begun to study a doctorate in philosophy when he was catapulted on to the modern poetry scene with *The Love Song of J. Alfred Prufrock*. He never got around to finishing the degree. Although, in substance, the poem is an ironically titled monologue by one of world literature's most pathetic and repressed wallflowers, the poem's lyricism and rich sound play invest Prufrock with an intense pathos that may not redeem his humdrum existence, but certainly makes it compelling reading.

"A great sorcerer of words . . . the very key keeper of the language."—Igor Stravinsky

It was several years before Eliot wrote his next and perhaps greatest poem, *The Waste Land*. The poem is a fractured, disjointed journey through a landscape exhausted both ecologically and culturally, inhabited by fragmented, almost ghostly voices that are connected only by their yearning

The Waste Land

T. S. Eliot's obituary in *Life* magazine was only slightly exaggerating when it said, "Our age beyond any doubt has been, and will continue to be, the Age of Eliot." *The Waste Land* specifically has become to the literary branch of the twentieth-century aesthetic movement called "modernism" what William Wordsworth's *Lyrical Ballads* (1798) is to ninteenth-century romanticism. These texts are both manifesto and example, harbingers of things to come and proof that they were already here.

It is not hard to imagine that a poem so revolutionary in form and content as *The Waste Land* would be subjected to criticism when it was published in 1922. What is more surprising is that it would be criticized for its lack of originality. But it was soon pointed out that, like James Joyce's *Ulysses* (1922), *The Waste Land* borrowed its underlying structure from an ancient myth—in Eliot's case, the legend of the Fisher King. Eliot responded to these criticisms by saying that Joyce's innovation had "the importance of a scientific discovery." As in science, the innovation is only as important as it is useful to one's colleagues, looking to apply it to their own experiments.

It has also been noted that Pound's contributions in editing *The Waste Land* are extensive enough to make him its second author. However, this very collaborative method is arguably one of Eliot's most influential contributions to the movement he personifies. As the author himself wrote, "Immature poets imitate; mature poets steal."

RIGHT: A caricature of T. S. Eliot with three cats.

for rebirth. *The Waste Land* tapped into the zeitgeist of the "Lost Generation" after World War I, who were beginning to question the faith in science and progress that had characterized the preceding century.

Eliot himself later denied any intent to let the work's pessimism speak for this generation, calling the poem "the relief of a personal and wholly insignificant grouse against life." His change of heart can perhaps be ascribed to a larger shift in his perspective, culminating in 1927, in both his naturalization as a British citizen and his baptism into the Anglican Church. The juxtaposition of these two events is not accidental. In an essay on the metaphysical poets, Eliot wrote about a shift in English literature he called the "dissociation of sensibility," which he located in the seventeenth century. Before this shift, he argued, poets could "feel their thought as immediately as the odor of a rose."

Underlying all of Eliot's work is a nostalgia for this more genuine intellectual and aesthetic experience, allegedly erased in the wake of John Dryden and John Milton at roughly the same time that Eliot's own ancestors settled in the United States. It is particularly a feature of Eliot's later work that his desire for rebirth and renewal should be phrased so explicitly in terms of a wish to turn back the clock. Among his strongest statements in this vein is his poetic play *Murder in the Cathedral*, about the death of the medieval saint Thomas à Becket. The play uses its subject—one of the most dramatic encounters between ecclesiastical and secular authority before the Reformation—to comment on the politics of the 1930s and the rising tide of fascism in Europe.

Eliot's final poetic achievement is his *Four Quartets*. These four lyrical poems, considered by Eliot himself to be his best, put into practice his idea of a classicizing, Christian poetic with a modern sensibility, and are in this sense the closest he came to producing his ideal poetry. As Eliot himself wrote in the final quartet, *Little Gidding*, "We shall not cease from exploration/ And the end of all our exploring/ Will be to arrive where we started/ And know the place for the first time." **SY**

JOHN MINNION

JEAN COCTEAU

Born: Jean Maurice Eugène Clément Cocteau, July 5, 1889 (Maisons-Laffitte, Île-de-France, France); died October 11, 1963 (Milly La Forêt, Essonne, France).

Style and genre: A precociously prolific polymath who saw himself as the Orpheus of modernist Paris, Cocteau enlivened every art form that he attempted.

Jean Cocteau may not have coined the phrase *"enfant terrible"* that formed the title of his 1929 novel, but he certainly embodied it. After his father committed suicide, wealthy ten-year-old orphan Jean was enrolled in a private school. Five years later, in 1904, he was expelled and ran away to Marseille, the French port notorious for its homosexual red-light district. Although the police returned him to his uncle's care, Jean did not return to middle-class provinciality. From 1908, when he met the leading tragedian Édouard de Max, Cocteau reveled in the Parisian limelight, when Paris itself enjoyed an international cultural limelight.

In an era of possibility, Cocteau was aware of his own potential and the potential of the new aesthetic practices. Having worked with Igor Stravinsky on the notorious *Rite of Spring* (1913), he reinvented ballet with Serge Diaghilev, Léonide Massine, Erik Satie, and Pablo Picasso with *Parade* (1917). Cocteau soon fell out of favor with the powerhouses of Parisian art, including Picasso and André Breton, some argue due to his homosexuality, yet he continued to generate art, including his classic dramatic rewriting of the Oedipus narrative, *The Infernal Machine*. Cocteau's stage play *Orpheus* dramatizes the plight of the avant-garde artist, whose work is so far ahead of its time that it draws the attention of Death—echoing Cocteau's tragic loss of his young and brilliant lover, novelist Raymond Radiguet, in 1923. *Orpheus* was later made into a film, starring Cocteau's muse and alleged lover, Jean Marais. Much of Cocteau's art was inspired by a combination of classical models and himself, riffing on them to bring the jazz age into drama, poetry, fiction, drawing, and film. **SM**

"History is facts which become lies in the end; legends are lies which become history. . . ."

Signature titles

Novel

The Holy Terrors, 1929

Plays

Orpheus, 1926

The Human Voice, 1930

The Infernal Machine, 1934

The Eagle Has Two Heads, 1946

The Storm Within, 1948

Screenplay

Beauty and the Beast, 1946

ABOVE: A portrait photograph of polymath Jean Cocteau in 1925.

PIERRE REVERDY

Born: September 13, 1889 (Narbonne, France); died June 17, 1960 (Solesmes, France).

Style and genre: An enigmatic French cubist-surrealist poet, Reverdy's syntactical experiments created new realities and pushed the limits of language.

Little is known about Reverdy the man. He shunned giving biographical details and his experimental poetry is not easily accessible and is difficult to translate meaningfully from the French. However, his abandonment of conventional forms, thought shockingly strange in the earlier 1900s, continues to speak to new audiences.

Reverdy used a very personal syntax to construct an internally logical world inspired by cubist and surrealist techniques. Having settled in Paris circa 1910, he lived through a thrilling artistic era when ways of representing "reality" were turned inside out. Part of a group of French cubist poets that included Guillaume Apollinaire and Jean Cocteau, Reverdy was a particular admirer of the cubist painter Juan Gris.

In 1917, Reverdy started the influential, although short-lived journal, *Nord-Sud* (*North-South*) to further the cubist aesthetic—both visual and literary. His sympathies became more surrealist during the 1920s, but later returned to cubism. This fruitful decade also saw the publication of works such as *Shipwrecks from Heaven*. Reverdy's affinity with visual cubism parallels the way in which he, like Picasso, takes apart what appears to be real and rebuilds new forms. His poems try to reveal a more authentic state where unconditioned emotional and sensory responses are possible. Despite a certain transcendence, Reverdy's work is carefully controlled and does not altogether shun "normal" reality. He tries to make sense of life and ask the big questions, but has no concrete answers. To find some answers, the reclusive Reverdy retreated to the Benedictine Abbey of Solesmes around 1930. Here he lived the rest of his life in an isolated existence, punctured by occasional forays back into Paris. **AK**

"So many of the poems are simple gestures laying bare the heart."—Kenneth Rexroth

Signature titles

Poetry

Painted Stars (*Étoiles peintes*), 1921

Shipwrecks from Heaven (*Les Épaves du ciel*), 1924

Glass Puddles (*Flaques de verre*), 1929

The Horsehair Glove (*Le Gant de crin*), 1927

The Book Beside Me (*Le Livre de mon bord*), 1948

ABOVE: A 1940 portrait of Pierre Reverdy smoking a cigarette.

H. P. LOVECRAFT

Born: Howard Phillips Lovecraft, August 20, 1890 (Providence, Rhode Island, U.S.); died March 15, 1937 (Providence, Rhode Island, U.S.).

Style and genre: Author of science fiction, fantasy, and horror novels, Lovecraft was a compulsive letter writer, as well as a poet, essayist, and columnist.

Signature titles

Novels

The Call of Cthulhu, 1926

At the Mountains of Madness, 1931

Novella

The Case of Charles Dexter Ward, 1941

Short stories

"The Lurking Fear," 1923

"The Rats in the Walls," 1924

"The Outsider," 1926

"The Color Out of Space," 1927

"The Shadow Out of Time," 1936

"The Thing on the Doorstep," 1937

H. P. Lovecraft is one of the most important horror, fantasy, and science fiction writers of the twentieth century. The last decade of Lovecraft's life was his most prolific, when he wrote classics *The Call of Cthulhu* and *The Shadow Out of Time*. Lovecraft and his contemporaries (the Lovecraft Circle) shared ideas, characters, and themes, with Lovecraft as the chief influence. He based many of his ideas on his own nightmares, often painting a pessimistic view of the future and incorporating alternative realities populated by monstrous entities. Lovecraft has had a profound influence on subsequent writers such as Stephen King and Clive Barker, as well as on popular culture, film, music, and television. **TamP**

KAREL ČAPEK

Born: January 9, 1890 (Malé Svatonovice, Northeastern Bohemia); died December 25, 1938 (Prague, Czechoslovakia).

Style and genre: A Nobel Prize nominee and biographer of the first Czech president, Čapek is associated with futurism, science fiction, and humanitarianism.

Signature titles

Novels

Wayside Crosses, 1917

The Absolute at Large, 1922

Three Novels: Hordubal, Meteor, An Ordinary Life, 1934

The War with the Newts, 1936

Travelogues

Letters from Italy, 1923

Letters from England, 1924

Travels in the North, 1936

Plays

R.U.R., 1920

Insect Play, 1922

The White Plague, 1937

Karel Čapek's philosophical prose questioning the limits of human intelligence contributed greatly to the science fiction genre. While celebrating technological progress, Čapek's work cautions against narrow-minded thinking, corruption, and greed. In his trilogy, *Hordubal, Meteor,* and *An Ordinary Life*, he debunks the idea of universal truth by calling for tolerance and diversity. His interest in exploring alternative human life forms and the impact of modern science on human civilization shapes his writing (see *The War with the Newts, R.U.R.*, and *Insect Play*). *R.U.R.* garnered much attention for its critique of social exploitation and racism and for first using the word *robot*, derived from the Czech term *robota* meaning "work." **PR**

RIGHT: Talking robot Asimo lays a bunch of flowers at the bust of Karel Čapek in tribute.

HONDA

VICTOR SERGE

Born: Victor Lvovich Khibalchich, December 30, 1890 (Brussels, Belgium); died November 17, 1947 (Mexico City, Mexico).

Style and genre: Victor Serge's life was so extraordinary that it often overshadows his masterful, lyrical novels about the Russian Revolution and Stalin's purges.

Victor Serge was born in Brussels, Belgium, of a Russian émigré family. In 1919, he moved to Russia in support of the revolution and quickly rose through the ranks of the Comintern. However, he became increasingly disturbed by the rise of Stalinism and was expelled from the Communist Party in 1928. He turned his attention to writing and produced a work of history, *Year One of the Russian Revolution*, and two novels *Men in Prison* and *Birth of Our Power*. All three were banned in Russia but were published in France and Spain. In 1933, Serge was imprisoned and then exiled to France three years later. When France was occupied by the Nazis, he left Europe and moved to Mexico City.

These are the historic events that provide the backdrop to his novels. *The Case of Comrade Tulayev*, published in 1948, is one of the great Russian novels of the twentieth century. It focuses on the murder of a government official and the search for his killer. The state draws in more and more suspects, elicits false confessions, and sends innocent people to the gulags, reflecting the purges that took place during Stalinist Russia. Serge's other great novel, *Unforgiving Years,* is a sweeping, deeply humane, epic adventure with a hallucinatory quality, in four sections. It follows a lifelong revolutionary known as "D" fleeing Paris and his past, a fellow revolutionary trapped in Leningrad under the German siege, the experiences of a woman called Daria during the fall of Germany, and finally the reuniting of "D" and Daria in Mexico after the war. Plagued by ill health brought on by his periods in prison, Serge died in Mexico in 1948 and *The Case of Comrade Tulayev* and *Unforgiving Years* were published posthumously. **HJ**

Signature titles

Nonfiction

Year One of the Russian Revolution, 1930

Novels

Men in Prison, 1930

Birth of Our Power, 1931

The Case of Comrade Tulayev, 1948

Unforgiving Years, 1948

"Why write, why read, if not to offer, to find, a larger image of life?"—*Unforgiving Years*

ABOVE: A photograph of the revolutionary Victor Serge in 1912.

BORIS PASTERNAK

Born: February 10, 1890 (Moscow, Russia); died May 30, 1960 (Peredelkino, near Moscow, Russia).

Style and genre: Pasternak was much admired abroad, but in constant trouble in his own country for not toeing the Soviet line.

Boris Pasternak is best known for his romantic novel *Doctor Zhivago*, which was smuggled out of Russia in the 1950s. It had been translated into eighteen languages by 1958, the year in which he won the Nobel Prize in Literature, and was later made into a famous film directed by David Lean.

Pasternak had begun life in a highly civilized Jewish family in Moscow and originally planned to be a musician. He switched to study philosophy before publishing his first volumes of poetry between 1913 and 1922. His poetry was avant-garde, yet highly regarded, but in the 1930s he was unable to publish because his work did not fit the pattern of socialist realism established for literature and the arts by Soviet communism. There is a story that Stalin called him a "holy fool" and only spared his life because he had translated Georgian poetry from the dictator's homeland. Translating was the only way Pasternak could earn a living and he produced Russian versions of Shakespeare, Shelley, Swinburne, Goethe, Verlaine, and Rilke, among others.

In 1956, he sent the manuscript of *Doctor Zhivago* to a Moscow magazine, which rejected it for libeling the Bolshevik Revolution and the Soviet system. It reached the West through an Italian publishing firm and there it created a sensation. It was only available in secret in Pasternak's own country until the 1980s. The awarding of the Nobel Prize to Pasternak aroused a storm of abuse, and there were demands for him to be deported. He felt forced to decline the prize and issue an apology and told Nikita Khruschev, the Soviet prime minister, that "leaving the motherland will equal death for me." He lived his last months suffering from lung cancer and heart disease at his home outside Moscow. **RC**

"Immensely thankful, touched, proud, astonished, abashed."

—On winning the Nobel Prize

Signature titles

Poetry

Above the Barriers, 1917

My Sister Life, 1922

Safe Conduct, 1931

Novel

Doctor Zhivago, 1956

ABOVE: A portrait of the Russian writer Boris Pasternak *c.* 1935.

1880–99

AGATHA CHRISTIE

Born: Agatha Mary Clarissa Miller, September 15, 1890 (Torquay, Devon, England); died January 12, 1976 (Cholsey, Oxfordshire, England).

Style and genre: Cleverly created plots, coincidences, red herrings, and minute observances of human weakness can all be found in Christie's works.

Dame Agatha Christie is a global phenomenon. All her works remain in print, and regular film, television, and stage adaptations continue to draw large audiences. In addition to her seventy-eight detective novels, she wrote romantic fiction (under the name Mary Westmacott), plays, a children's book, short stories (often starring her most famous detectives, Hercule Poirot and Miss Jane Marple), and nonfiction. It is estimated that four billion of her novels have been sold worldwide.

Agatha Miller married Colonel Archibald Christie in 1914, thus assuming the name she made famous. During World War I, she worked in a hospital dispensary, and the knowledge she amassed—in particular about poisons—was used in her fiction to great acclaim. She also befriended a number of Belgian refugees, which inspired her to create a Belgian detective. The fastidious and charming Hercule Poirot first appeared on the literary scene in 1920 in *The Mysterious Affair at Styles*.

By the time of this first success, her marriage was already in trouble. In 1928, after the couple divorced, Agatha traveled to the Middle East alone by train. In Mesopotamia (modern-day Iraq) she met her second husband, archeologist Sir Max Mallowan, who was fourteen years her junior. She spent many contented years traveling with him, learning about archeology, and being inspired to write novels, including *Death on the Nile*, *Murder in Mesopotamia*, *Murder on the Orient Express*, and the thrilling *Appointment with Death*. She also wrote the nonfiction work *Come, Tell Me How You Live* about their life on archeological digs.

Her other famous detective, Miss Marple, is the epitome of an elderly English lady, whose knowledge of human nature Christie based on herself, despite being the detective's junior by many years. Miss Marple exhibits a confidence that Christie was seldom able to display in real life. Despite her great fame

Signature titles

Novels

The Mysterious Affair at Styles, 1920
The Secret of Chimneys, 1925
The Murder of Roger Ackroyd, 1926
The Murder at the Vicarage, 1930
Murder on the Orient Express, 1934
Three Act Tragedy, 1935
Death in the Clouds, 1935
Murder in Mesopotamia, 1936
Dumb Witness, 1937
Death on the Nile, 1937
Appointment with Death, 1938
Sparkling Cyanide, 1945
Taken at the Flood, 1948
A Murder is Announced, 1950
The Pale Horse, 1961
Curtain: Poirot's Last Case, 1975
Sleeping Murder, 1976

Play

The Mousetrap, 1952

Nonfiction

Come, Tell Me How You Live, 1946

ABOVE: The doyenne of British detective fiction photographed in the mid-1930s.

LEFT: Hercule Poirot on the front cover of a magazine featuring a Christie story in 1936.

and wealth, Agatha Christie always lacked confidence and, even in old age, felt uncomfortable in many social situations. Always happiest in the fictional world she had created, she spent hours every day with her characters, often publishing several books a year.

Although occasionally derided by writers of serious fiction as being too formulaic, Christie's popularity has never waned throughout the years. Her style of writing, her carefully planned plots, and her lovable characters continue to spellbind generations of readers. Her eventful life itself has also inspired several biographers. **LH**

Mystery Disappearance

In 1926, when Agatha Christie had been married for twelve years, she discovered her husband was having an affair. In one of the greatest publicity stunts ever staged, Christie disappeared. Her crashed car was found, containing suitcases and bloodstains, but there was no sign of her. The newspapers offered a reward to anyone who found her. Archibald Christie was believed to have murdered his wife. After an eleven-day search, she was found in a hotel in Harrogate, in North Yorkshire, England, registered under the surname of her husband's mistress, claiming to have lost her memory.

JEAN RHYS

Born: Ella Gwendolen Rees Williams, August 24, 1890 (Roseau, Dominica); died May 14, 1979 (Exeter, Devon, England).

Style and genre: Known for her minimalist prose, Rhys explored Caribbean and British culture, feminine sensibility, and themes of loneliness, dislocation, and exile.

Jean Rhys, a West Indian modernist writer, came to England in 1907 to study acting in Cambridge. When her dreams of becoming an actor failed, Rhys worked as a model, chorus girl, and ghost writer. Encouraged by Ford Madox Ford, Rhys began writing short stories, using displaced, socially marginalized characters to probe into the expatriate ethos of modernity. She explores the theme of exile and displacement, the clash between West Indian and English cultures, feminine sensibility, and cultural dispossession. *Wide Sargasso Sea*, Rhys's masterful re-visioning of *Jane Eyre*, explores the female exilic plight in the face of cultural, racial, and gender discrimination, through the lens of a white Creole's toxic marriage and double exile. **PR**

Signature titles

Novels

Postures, 1928 (published as *Quartet* in the U.S.)

After Leaving Mr. Mackenzie, 1930

Voyage in the Dark, 1934

Good Morning, Midnight, 1939

Wide Sargasso Sea, 1966

Short stories

The Left Bank and Other Stories, 1927

Tigers Are Better Looking, 1968

Sleep It Off Lady, 1976

Autobiography

Smile Please: An Unfinished Autobiography, 1979

PÄR LAGERKVIST

Born: May 23, 1891 (Växjö, Sweden); died July 11, 1974 (Stockholm, Sweden).

Style and genre: One of Sweden's leading radical figures, Lagerkvist was a poet, playwright, and novelist whose themes of socialism, religion, and the battle between good and evil won him the 1951 Nobel Prize in Literature.

Novelist, poet, and dramatist, Lagerkvist was the son of a railroad official and had a conventional upbringing in a small town in southern Sweden. He was brought up a Lutheran, but later distanced himself from the faith. After university at Uppsala he lived in Denmark, France, and Italy before returning to Sweden in 1930. A socialist and fierce opponent of fascism, he described himself as "a religious atheist" and was concerned with the perplexing mixture of good and evil in human nature, as in his novels *The Hangman* and *The Dwarf*. The latter, a best seller, made him a major figure in Sweden, and *Barabbas* made his name abroad. His modernizing influence on Swedish poetry has been compared to that of T. S. Eliot in England. **RC**

Signature titles

Novels

Guest of Reality, 1925

The Dwarf, 1944

Barabbas, 1950

Novella

The Hangman, 1933 (dramatized 1934)

Essay

The Triumph over Life, 1927

MIKHAIL BULGAKOV

Born: Mikhail Afanasievich Bulgakov, May 15, 1891 (Kiev, Ukraine); died March 10, 1940 (Moscow, Russia).

Style and genre: Bulgakov was an intelligent and thought-provoking writer of grotesque, anti-authoritarian subject matter, with wittily unsettling, theatrical plots.

In the early 1920s, the work of Mikhail Bulgakov was lauded, but after falling out of favor with Joseph Stalin, his writings were banned. Before he became a writer, Bulgakov trained as a doctor, working for the anti-Bolshevik White Army during the Russian Civil War. Afterward he moved to Moscow, giving up medicine to become a journalist, novelist, and playwright.

Bulgakov's strong beliefs and the joy he took in poking fun at authority earned him censure under the new Soviet leadership and in 1929, his plays were banned. Bulgakov had no choice but to appeal to Stalin, who appointed him to the Moscow Art Theater, where he could be monitored. Trapped by red tape, Bulgakov began secretly writing his masterpiece, *The Master and Margarita,* a brilliantly subversive, witty, and unsettling novel that speaks volumes about the pressure that its author was under and his need to break free of Stalin.

After adapting other authors' plays for Russian audiences, Bulgakov dared to produce his own play, *Molière, A Cabal of Hypocrites*, about Molière's persecution by the authorities. It was performed only seven times before being stopped. His next play, about Alexander Pushkin, was also shut down. Despite writing a play especially for Stalin that glorified the dictator's early days as a revolutionary, Bulgakov remained ostracized, and the play was never performed. He died a broken man. Bulgakov married three times and it was the tenacity of his third wife, Elena, that saw Bulgakov's works published after his death. In 1930, Bulgakov destroyed the first manuscript of *The Master and Margarita*, terrified that the authorities would raid his home and seize it. He began rewriting it the following year and Elena finished it after his death. **LH**

"... where would your good be if there were no evil?"

—*The Master and Margarita*

Signature titles

Novels

The White Guard, 1925

The Heart of a Dog, 1925

The Fatal Eggs, 1925

Black Snow: A Theatrical Novel, 1936

The Master and Margarita, 1966–1967

Plays

The Days of the Turbins, 1926

Molière, A Cabal of Hypocrites, 1934

Batum, 1939

Pushkin, The Last Days, 1943

Short stories

Notes on the Cuff and Other Stories, 1922–1923

Nonfiction

A Country Doctor's Notebook, 1963

ABOVE: A portrait photograph of the Russian writer taken in *c.* 1930.

HENRY MILLER

Born: Henry Valentine Miller, December 26, 1891 (New York, New York, U.S.); died June 7, 1980 (Los Angeles, California, U.S.).

Style and genre: Novelist, travel writer, essayist, critic, and philosopher, Miller wrote on semi-autobiographical and sexual themes using stream-of-consciousness.

Signature titles

Novels

Tropic of Cancer, 1934

Black Spring, 1936

Tropic of Capricorn, 1939

Remember to Remember, 1947

The Rosy Crucifixion

Sexus, 1949

Plexus, 1953

Nexus, 1960

Play

Just Wild About Harry, 1963

Travel writing

The Colossus of Maroussi, 1941

The Air-Conditioned Nightmare, 1945

Big Sur and the Oranges of Hieronymus Bosch, 1957

Henry Miller is perhaps best remembered for his novel *Tropic of Cancer*, which is widely considered to be a masterpiece of twentieth-century literature. It was written while Miller was living in Paris, having moved there in 1930 and lived in straitened circumstances. During this period, he met the author Anaïs Nin, who became his lover and benefactor, and the author Alfred Perlès. *Tropic of Cancer* was based on Miller's life and loves in Paris, with sexual encounters graphically described, using a complex narrative style combining stream-of-consciousness passages with those of realism. The book was published in Paris, and earned him recognition as an influential, although controversial modern writer, and turned him into an underground hero. It was banned in the United States, and remained unpublished until 1961, when it became the subject of an obscenity trial. George Orwell heralded it as "the most important book of the mid-1930s," and it has since been named one of the fifty top books of the twentieth century.

Miller followed this with the loosely autobiographical *Tropic of Capricorn*, which parallels his life in New York when he was working for the Western Union Telegraph Company in the 1920s. Shortly after publication, Miller left Paris and traveled to Greece, where he spent six months with his friend, novelist Lawrence Durrell. Miller later wrote the important *The Colossus of Maroussi*, a searching account of Greece and its past in which he amalgamated a travel book with something infinitely more poignant.

"I hate inspiration. It takes you over completely. I could never wait until it passed. . . ."

Miller returned to the United States in 1940 and continued to write prolifically, producing works such as the travel volume *The Air-Conditioned Nightmare* and the eloquent *Big Sur and the Oranges of Hieronymus Bosch*. **TamP**

ABOVE: An undated photograph of Miller taken during his later life.

RIGHT: Miller with his wife Eve McClure on a Spanish beach in 1953, the year they married.

MARINA TSVETAEVA

Born: Marina Ivanovna Tsvetaeva, October 9, 1892 (Moscow, Russia); died August 31, 1941 (Yelabuga, Tatarstan, Russia).

Style and genre: An outstanding Russian poet of the twentieth century, Tsvetaeva's work covers a range of themes, including Russian history and the role of women.

Marina Tsvetaeva was born into a wealthy intellectual family in Moscow; her mother, Maria Mein, was a talented concert pianist, and her father, the classical philologist Ivan Tsvetaev, founded the Pushkin Museum of Fine Arts. After attending schools in Germany, Switzerland, and Paris, she returned to Russia and published her first collection of poetry, *Evening Album*, at the age of eighteen. In 1912 she married Sergei Efron, and the couple went on to have two daughters and a son. But throughout her marriage she had a number of affairs that inspired a series of poems. These included *Girlfriend*, about her relationship with the opera librettist Sophia Parnok, and *Poem of the Mountain* and *Poem of the End*, recounting the ending of an affair with Konstantin Borisovich Rodzevich, a former Red Army officer.

Tsvetaeva's poetry is marked by its cadence and rhythm and has a musical quality. Much of her work reflects the great suffering she endured throughout her life and the historical events in which she was caught up—one of her daughters died of starvation in the Russian Revolution. During the subsequent Russian Civil War, Tsvetaeva was separated from her husband, and wrote a long cycle of poems, *The Desmesne of the Swans*, about the White Army in which her husband served, and their struggle against the communists. Although written in 1921, it was not published until 1957.

Tsvetaeva and her family went into exile in 1922, and moved between Berlin, Prague, and Paris, living in increasing poverty. She published essays, plays, five collections of verse, and narrative poetry, some of which evoked Russian folklore and Russian Orthodox prayers. *The Ratcatcher* is a narrative poem based on the legend of the Pied Piper of Hamelin, in which the rats represent revolutionaries. Tsvetaeva's family scraped a living on her writing but were ostracized by the exiled literary

Signature titles

Plays

Theseus-Ariadne, 1927

Phaedra, 1928

Poetry

Evening Album, 1910

The Magic Lantern, 1912

Girlfriend, 1914

Mileposts, 1921

Separation, 1922

Psyche, 1923

Craft, 1923

Poem of the End, 1924

Poem of the Mountain, 1924

The Ratcatcher, 1925–1926

After Russia, 1928

The Demesne of the Swans, 1957

ABOVE: Much of Tsvetaeva's work reflects the suffering of her troubled life.

LEFT: One of the few known images of Tsvetaeva, taken in 1914.

community in Paris when her husband began to work for the Soviet secret police, the People's Commissariat for Internal Affairs, or the NKVD.

Tsvetaeva returned to live in Russia with her family in 1938. But in 1941 tragedy struck: Her husband was executed for espionage, her daughter was sent to a labor camp, and under Joseph Stalin's regime the author could no longer get her work published. After the German invasion in 1941, Tsvetaeva was evacuated from Moscow to the small town of Yelabuga. Unable to get work and facing starvation, she hanged herself, although there have been claims that NKVD agents visited her home and forced her to commit suicide. Interest in her poetry began to grow in the 1960s, and her work was translated into a number of languages, especially English. **HJ**

The Inspiration for Lara

Tsvetaeva had a long and fruitful relationship, conducted purely by letter, with the Russian writer and poet Boris Pasternak. Weeks after Tsvetaeva went into exile in 1922, Pasternak discovered her poetry and was swept away by its lyricism. He wrote to his sister: "it's as though my heart has ripped open my shirt. I've gone crazy, splinters are flying: something akin to me exists in the world, and what kin!" He began writing to Tsvetaeva, and their correspondence lasted for more than a decade. Tsvetaeva formed the basis of the heroine Lara in his masterpiece *Doctor Zhivago* (1957).

J. R. R. TOLKIEN

Born: John Ronald Reuel Tolkien, January 3, 1892 (Bloemfontein, South Africa); died September 2, 1973 (Bournemouth, England).

Style and genre: J. R. R. Tolkien was a scholar and fabulist whose dense world-building transformed the fantasy genre.

Signature titles

Novels

The Hobbit, or There and Back Again, 1937
The Fellowship of the Ring, 1954
The Two Towers, 1954
The Return of the King, 1955
The Silmarillion, 1977 (published posthumously)

Nonfiction

The Monsters and the Critics, 1983 (published posthumously)

1880–99

In a famous lecture J. R. R. Tolkien delivered to the British Academy, as a part of his day job as chair of Anglo-Saxon language and literature at the University of Oxford, he made an analogy: an English farmer finds an ancient ruin on his property, and uses the stones to build a tower. Although his sons are angry with him for destroying the ruin, Tolkien says that if they had climbed to the top of the tower, they would have realized that from the new vantage point, the farmer was able to see the sea.

Tolkien uses this image to make a point about the layers of Christianity and paganism in the Old English poem *Beowulf* (*c.* 700–1000). But the analogy also works to characterize Tolkien's own use of existing mythology in the creation of his beloved series of novels, *The Hobbit, or There and Back Again* and its sequel trilogy *The Lord of the Rings*. Like many students of the oldest surviving British literature, Tolkien lamented that only mere traces of the early Anglo-Saxon and Celtic traditions were left after centuries of conquest and Roman Catholicism; but rather than content himself with the ruins, he set out to build a tower instead. The world of Tolkien's novels starts small, and his hobbits are a gentle satire of the quiet, humdrum routines of small-town England. But it is not long into their adventures that a broad, epic mode takes over, and very quickly his readers find themselves referring to the detailed maps at the beginning of each volume. The novels are nostalgic for an earlier era, but with a mature sadness lacking in the hordes of imitators that practically constitute a genre to themselves. Tolkien may have built a tower, but he did not forget the loss that allowed him to do so. **SY**

"Tolkien's themes are timeless in the genuine sense of being timeless. . . ."—Peter Jackson

ABOVE: Tolkien, photographed toward the end of his life, in the early 1970s.

IVO ANDRIĆ

Born: October 9, 1892 (Travnik, Bosnia); died March 13, 1975 (Belgrade, Serbia).

Style and genre: Ivo Andrić's work focuses on Bosnia, its history, culture, folklore, and the ties that bind the people of the region; he was the winner of the Nobel Prize in Literature in 1961.

Ivo Andrić's writing career spanned six decades. In 1919, he published his first work *Anxieties*—a book of lyrical prose that focused on his experiences in prison during World War I. Andrić then became a diplomat and traveled extensively while continuing to write short stories, but it was while under house arrest during the Nazi occupation of Belgrade that he began to write novels. In 1945 he published his Bosnian trilogy: *The Bridge on the Drina*, *Bosnian Chronicle,* and *The Woman from Sarajevo*. Considered his masterpiece, *The Bridge on the Drina* is a series of elegantly simple vignettes in which we see the lives of a range of characters—Muslim, Christians, and Jews—who have lived in the shadow of the bridge for generations. **HJ**

Signature titles

Novels

The Bridge on the Drina, 1945

Bosnian Chronicle, 1945

The Woman from Sarajevo, 1945

Lyrical prose

Anxieties, 1919

DJUNA BARNES

Born: June 12, 1892 (Cornwall-on-Hudson, New York, U.S.); died June 18, 1982 (New York, New York, U.S.).

Style and genre: Barnes is known for her acerbic wit, stylistic versatility, melancholy vision of women's condition, and grotesque parody of sexuality.

Djuna Barnes, a modernist writer and playwright, started her career as a journalist. In the 1920s, she left New York for Paris where she belonged to the modernist expatriate bohemia. She was famous for her tongue-in-cheek style and cynicism, often highlighted with Beardsley-inspired drawings and caricatures. Her first novel, *Ryder*, parodies patriarchal conventions through the misogyny of Wendell Ryder, the father who dreams of a Ryder race. *Nightwood*, her most celebrated novel, features Dr. O'Connor, a Socratic transsexual amid decadent, fin-de-siècle angst. It is a literary masterpiece and a cult novel; its characters' individual histories challenge normative ideologies of gender, sexuality, and identity—and showcase Europe in crisis. **PR**

Signature titles

Novels

Ryder, 1928

Ladies Almanack, 1928

Nightwood, 1936

Short stories

A Book, 1923 (reprinted as *A Night among the Horses* in 1929, and as *Spillway* in 1962)

Plays

At the Roots of the Stars, 1995

The Antiphon, 1958

Poetry

The Book of Repulsive Women, 1915

The Creatures in the Alphabet, 1982

REBECCA WEST

Born: Cicily Isabel Fairfield, December 21, 1892 (London, England); died March 15, 1983 (London, England).

Style and genre: Strong feminist themes, minutely observed details, fervent political views, and a brusquely witty sense of humor permeate West's work.

Harboring dreams of becoming an actress, Cicily Isabel Fairfield went to the Royal Academy of Dramatic Art in London, where she chose the stage name "Rebecca West"; a name she took from the heroine of a Henrik Ibsen play, and one she would make famous. West began her writing career before World War I with articles for the suffragist publication *The Freewoman*. Her political opinions and strong feelings would inform all her writing, no matter what genre. One of her most famous feminist essays was *The Sterner Sex* published in 1913.

While in her teens, she had become interested in the fight for the emancipation of women, and became a fervent and politically active suffragette who believed in free love. In 1913 she met the married H. G. Wells with whom she had a decade-long affair—and a son. She is rumored to have had numerous lovers, including Charlie Chaplin, before marrying financier Henry Maxwell Andrews in her late thirties.

West became famous for her fiction and travel writing, as well as for her hard-hitting journalism that she produced for a number of left-wing publications. During World War II she worked for the BBC in London, and from 1945 to 1946 she covered the Nuremberg Trials for the *New Yorker*, an experience that caused her much anguish although it gained her international acclaim. Her most famous piece of travel writing is the excellent *Black Lamb and Grey Falcon*, about her travels through what was then Yugoslavia. A committed socialist and social reformer who hated the brutalities of both fascism and communism, her book *The Birds Fall Down* was about the Russian Revolution; it was her last novel. By the end of her life, West was renowned as one of Britain's foremost literary figures. **LH**

Signature titles

Novels

The Return of the Soldier, 1918
The Judge, 1922
Harriet Hume, 1929
The Thinking Reed, 1936
The Fountain Overflows, 1957
The Birds Fall Down, 1966

Nonfiction

The Sterner Sex, 1913
Henry James, 1916
The Strange Necessity: Essays and Reviews, 1928
D. H. Lawrence, 1930
Black Lamb and Grey Falcon, 1941
The Phoenix: Meaning of Treason, 1949
A Train of Powder, 1955

"Motherhood is the strangest thing, it can be like being one's own Trojan horse."

ABOVE: The writer and journalist Rebecca West photographed in 1930.

WILFRED OWEN

Born: Wilfred Edward Salter Owen, March 18, 1893 (Oswestry, Shropshire, England); died November 4, 1918 (Sambre-Oise Canal, France).

Style and genre: Owen's innovative, shocking, and realistic poetry describes in great detail the horrors of the World War I trenches and gas warfare.

Wilfred Owen was the outstanding English poet of World War I. Once he enlisted in the British Army in 1915 he remarked that the subject of his poetry was: "war, and the pity of war." While recuperating from shell shock at Craiglockhart War Hospital he met fellow poet Siegfried Sassoon, who encouraged him to write of his own experiences. His use of realism, allied to technical experiments with assonance, can best be appreciated in *Dulce et Decorum Est* where brutal descriptions of the cruelty of trench warfare and gas attacks denounce romantic notions of war. In *Anthem for Doomed Youth* the anger and resentment at the fate that awaits young soldiers is expertly exposed. Tragically, Owen was killed a week before Armistice Day. **SG**

Signature titles

Poetry

Anthem for Doomed Youth, 1917
Dulce et Decorum Est, 1917
Greater Love, 1917
Disabled, 1918
Exposure, 1918
Futility, 1918
Insensibility, 1918
Spring Offensive, 1918
Strange Meeting, 1918
The Send-Off, 1918
Collected Poems, 1920
Collected Poems of Wilfred Owen, 1965

VLADIMIR MAYAKOVSKY

Born: July 19, 1893 (Bagdati, Georgia); died April 14, 1930 (Moscow, Russia).

Style and genre: One of the leading poets of the Russian Revolution and part of the Russian Futurism movement, Mayakovsky was fascinated with the dynamism of modern life.

After attending the Moscow Institute of Painting, Sculpture and Architecture, Vladimir Mayakovsky moved to St. Petersburg where he helped create a Russian Futurist manifesto, *A Slap in the Face of Public Taste*, obviously courting controversy. His own first great poem, "A Cloud in Trousers," was about unrequited love. The start of the Russian Revolution then inspired him to write poems supporting the Bolsheviks and he also wrote plays including *Mystery-Bouffe*—a religious mystery play that mocked religion. A recurring theme in Mayakovsky's work is death and suicide. In 1930, denied a visa to travel abroad, in love with the wife of his publisher, and savaged by literary critics, he shot himself. **HJ**

Signature titles

Essay

A Slap in the Face of Public Taste, 1912

Poetry

"A Cloud in Trousers," 1915
"The Backbone Flute," 1916

Plays

Mystery-Bouffe, 1918
The Bedbug, 1928
The Bathhouse, 1930

JOSEPH ROTH

Born: Moses Joseph Roth, September 2, 1894 (Brody, Lviv Oblast, Ukraine); died May 27, 1939 (Paris, France).

Style and genre: Roth's journalism and fiction long for a more humane world he could imagine with nostalgic clarity existing only in Austria's imperial past.

ABOVE: Portrait of the Austrian writer Joseph Roth in an undated photograph.

When Joseph Roth was born, Brody, Ukraine, had itself become an outsider. As an important node in the Austro-Russian trade circuit, the town had risen to affluence by the nineteenth century, but by 1894, his birthplace still had neither a train station nor modern industries. Yet it was a center of learning, a *shtetl* (small town) that was home to Enlightened as well as Orthodox Jews, settled bourgeois German-speakers, and poor immigrants arriving from points farther east.

In many ways, Roth never left Brody. He took it with him to school in Lemberg, then to university in Vienna, and from there into the Austrian army press corps during World War I, where he published his first articles. His childhood, he said, was marred by poverty. Some biographers point out photographs that show him well dressed and mention his violin lessons, but as his late novella *The Legend of the Holy Drinker* shows, the empathy that was Roth's great strength was also his most profound weakness.

Without money to finish his studies after the war, Roth went to Berlin, and there too he found Brody: in the unsettled, the working poor, and the unemployed. In his literary nonfiction, Berlin's golden 1920s continuously choke on cocktails of hardship and addiction. Roth's marriage was troubled by financial worries, constant travel, and his wife's schizophrenia. In January 1933, on the day of Adolph Hitler's appointment as chancellor, Roth left Germany for Paris. While his books were being burned in Germany, Roth continued to drink, write, and travel as much as he ever had, but his health and financial situation worsened. He died poor in Paris in the spring of 1935 from pneumonia exacerbated by alcohol withdrawal. **JK**

"My most unforgettable experience was the war and the end of my fatherland. . . ."

Signature titles

Novels

The Spider's Web (Das Spinnennetz), 1923

Hotel Savoy, 1924

The Blind Mirror (Der Blinde Spiegel), 1925

The Flight without End (Die Flucht ohne Ende), 1927

Job (Hiob), 1930

Radetzky March (Radetzkymarsch), 1932

The Emperor's Tomb (Die Kapuzinergruft), 1938

The Legend of the Holy Drinker (Die Legende vom heiligen Trinker), 1939

The Leviathan (Der Leviathan), 1940

Short story

"The Bust of the Emperor" ("Die Büste des Kaisers"), 1935

LOUIS-FERDINAND CÉLINE

Born: Louis-Ferdinand Destouches, May 27, 1894 (Courbevoie, Haute-Seine, France); died July 1, 1961 (Paris, France).

Style and genre: Céline created a vivid prose style based on the rhythms of everyday speech to express his rage at the modern human condition.

Louis-Ferdinand Céline poses, in acute form, the question of the relation between an author's political views and the value of his work. Revered as an innovative master of literary modernism, he has simultaneously been reviled for his rabid anti-Semitism and his association with pro-Nazi collaborators.

The irrational violence of war was Céline's bedrock experience. Severely wounded on the Western Front in 1914, he survived the slaughter of World War I to view the postwar world with a savagely disillusioned eye. He wrote his debut novel, *Journey to the End of the Night*, while working as a doctor in a municipal clinic in the seedy Clichy district of Paris. Chiming with the mood of the Depression era, the book was an instant critical and popular success. The lacerating black humor of its enraged colloquial monologue carries the reader on a nightmare tour of the modern world, from the wartime trenches to the African colonies and the factories of Detroit.

Céline followed up with *Death on the Installment Plan*, a scabrous and anarchic coming-of-age story that introduced a new stylistic trademark, the use of ellipses (. . .). In these two episodic masterpieces, the bleak vision is offset by a superb gift for storytelling, over-the-top comedy, and a streak of tenderness. In the late 1930s, Céline published anti-Semitic pamphlets, and the last year of World War II found him on the run from the Allies, though he did not actively collaborate with the Nazis. His wanderings through the collapsing Third Reich provided most of the material for his bitter, rambling, postwar novels. Imprisoned for a year in Denmark and condemned in France in absentia, he was allowed to return home in 1951. The reputation of his novels has survived their author's disgrace. **RG**

> "To evoke one's posterity is to make a speech to maggots."
> —*Journey to the End of the Night*

Signature titles

Novels

Journey to the End of the Night (Voyage au bout de la nuit), 1932

Death on the Installment Plan (Mort à crédit), 1936

Guignol's Band, 1943

Fable for Another Time (Féerie pour une autre fois), 1952

Castle to Castle (D'un château à l'autre), 1957

North (Nord), 1960

London Bridge (Le pont de Londres), 1964

Rigodon, 1969

ABOVE: Louis-Ferdinand Céline photographed in France in 1955.

DASHIELL HAMMETT

Born: Samuel Dashiell Hammett, May 27, 1894 (St. Mary's County, Maryland, U.S.); died January 10, 1961 (New York, New York, U.S.).

Style and genre: Hammett wrote detective stories brimming with sex and violence amid sordid urban backgrounds with fast-paced, slang-filled dialogue.

Signature titles

Novels

Red Harvest, 1929
The Dain Curse, 1929
The Maltese Falcon, 1930
The Glass Key, 1931
The Thin Man, 1932

Short stories

The Adventures of Sam Spade, 1944
The Continental Op, 1945
The Return of the Continental Op, 1945
Hammett Homicides, 1946
Nightmare Town, 1948
The Creeping Siamese, 1950
Woman in the Dark, 1951
A Man Named Thin, 1962

Dashiell Hammett is the father of the hard-boiled detective novel, and creator of one of fiction's most famous sleuths. He worked for seven years as a detective for the Pinkerton National Detective Agency, which provided a bountiful supply of material for his writing. Pulp magazines were the first outlet for Hammett's work before he released two novels, *Red Harvest* and *The Dain Curse* in 1929. His following novel, *The Maltese Falcon*, featured Sam Spade, a wisecracking loner detective with a rigid code of personal honor. Hammett's last novel, *The Thin Man*, features the detective couple of Nick and Nora Charles, who spend much time inebriated. After 1934 he devoted himself to the defense of civil liberties. **SG**

E. E. CUMMINGS

Born: Edward Estlin Cummings, October 14, 1894 (Cambridge, Massachusetts, U.S.); died September 3, 1962 (North Conway, New Hampshire, U.S.).

Style and genre: Unconventional and idiosyncratic experimentation with language forms and punctuation permeate Cumming's poetry.

Signature titles

Poetry

Tulips and Chimneys, 1923
is 5, 1926
ViVa, 1931
95 Poems, 1958
Complete Poems, 1981 (two volumes, published posthumously)

Nonfiction

The Enormous Room, 1922
Eimi, 1933

Play

him, 1927

Ballet

Tom, 1935 (based on *Uncle Tom's Cabin*)

RIGHT: Cummings's *Self-portrait with a Sketchpad*, painted *c.* 1939.

Harvard-educated Cummings is popularly celebrated as a poet, but he also wrote prose and drama, and was an artist. While an ambulance driver in France during World War I, Cummings was imprisoned for allegedly criticizing the war effort. A sign of his modernist, anti-establishment ethos, the experience is recorded with outspoken wit in *The Enormous Room*. With influences ranging from English Romanticism to Ezra Pound, Cummings's anarchically styled seesawing between lyricism, naivety, and frank street talk brought immense public (but less critical) acclaim. The folkloric view that he officially restyled his name as e. e. cummings is incorrect; he also used the upper-case form. **AK**

ALDOUS HUXLEY

Born: July 26, 1894 (Godalming, Surrey, England); died November 22, 1963 (Los Angeles, California, U.S.).

Style and genre: Huxley's work explores the impact of science and technology with intellectual theorizing delivered in a witty and pessimistically satirical fashion.

A novelist and essayist born into a family of intellectuals, Aldous Huxley was educated at Eton College, and Balliol College, Oxford. Despite suffering from partial blindness, he established himself as a novelist of extreme wit and insight with his first two published novels *Crome Yellow* and *Antic Hay*.

Signature titles

Novels

Crome Yellow, 1921
Antic Hay, 1923
Those Barren Leaves, 1925
Point Counter Point, 1928
Brave New World, 1932
Eyeless in Gaza, 1936
After Many a Summer Dies the Swan, 1939
Ape and Essence, 1948
The Genius and the Goddess, 1955
Island, 1962

Nonfiction

The Devils of Loudon, 1952
The Doors of Perception, 1954
Heaven and Hell, 1956

ABOVE: Aldous Huxley photographed with a cigarette in 1946.

RIGHT: The dust jacket of the first edition of *Brave New World*.

Few writers have captured so perfectly the mood of disenchantment that existed within the youth of 1920s Britain. These early works were scintillating satires on the upper classes and intelligentsia, in which the characters discuss morals, behavior, and culture in country houses, and ultimately detach themselves from the seriousness of their conversations in favor of triviality and sexual topics.

By the time of his fourth novel, *Point Counter Point*, which expresses concern at the unrestricted progress of science and technology, Huxley was synonymous with thought-provoking fiction that spewed forth opinion and arresting ideas.

His next work, *Brave New World*, would come to define the author. In part inspired by a trip to the United States (he moved there in 1937, and remained there for the rest of his life), which he feared was accelerating toward world domination, Huxley offered a nightmarish vision of the future where genetic science has brought about a perfect human race subdivided by caste at the expense of family, culture, religion, and philosophy. *Brave New World* defies literary categorization and is regarded as one of the principal anti-utopian novels of the twentieth century—a catchphrase wheeled out by the media in relation to any development considered overtly modern or a threat to human liberty.

Huxley continued to paint a bleak image of a violent and aimless society in *Eyeless in Gaza*, although he suggested viable alternatives with his own conversion to pacifism that offered a counterpoint to his previous biting cynicism. Of his later works, *The Doors of Perception* is the most keenly remembered as the author detailed his experiences of taking the hallucinogenic drug mescaline in an attempt to understand how the mind works. Not surprisingly the book became a must-read for the emerging hippy and psychedelic culture of the 1960s, perhaps more so because Huxley famously took LSD on his deathbed.

A writer of huge intellect, Huxley's humor and caustic satire combined with his visionary exploration of the impacts of science and technology made him one of the twentieth century's foremost writers. **SG**

ABOVE: A drawing of Huxley by Sir David Low for *The New Statesman*, 1926.

The Devils of Loudon

Huxley's rare foray into nonfiction produced one of his most compelling works, *The Devils of Loudon*. This historical account set in seventeenth-century France expertly reveals the events that led to a promiscuous priest, Urbain Grandier, being burned at the stake after being convicted of witchcraft. Grandier was charged with being in league with the devil and seducing an entire convent of nuns, a charge to which he maintained his innocence until the grisly end. Demonic possession, superstition, religious fanaticism, and sexual hysteria are all covered in detail offering a unique insight into the age. The overriding themes of human persecution, bigotry, envy, and greed dovetail perfectly with much of Huxley's fictional oeuvre.

ROBERT GRAVES

Signature titles

Poetry

Over the Brazier, 1916

Goliath and David, 1917

Fairies and Fusiliers, 1917

Collected Poems, 1975

Novels

I, Claudius, 1934

Claudius the God and His Wife Messalina, 1935

The Golden Fleece, 1944

Nonfiction

Lawrence and the Arabs, 1927

A Survey of Modernist Poetry, 1927

Good-Bye to All That, 1929

The White Goddess, 1948

The Greek Myths, 1955

Born: July 24, 1895 (London, England); died December 7, 1985 (Deià, Majorca, Spain).

Style and genre: Graves's poetry centers on his early recollections of trench warfare; he later wrote historical novels dealing with ancient Mediterranean civilizations and infused his works with studies of mythology.

Robert Graves was an English poet, novelist, and scholar, who rose to prominence with his poems written while serving in World War I. These graphic collections of the conditions of war include *Over the Brazier*, and *Fairies and Fusiliers*, although his autobiographical novel *Good-Bye to All That* became the definitive account of the horrors of the war. The book's success allowed Graves to move to Majorca, where he completed the historical novels *I, Claudius* and *Claudius the God and His Wife Messalina*. A fascination with Greek myths inspired *The White Goddess*, a controversial study of the language of poetic myth. In his later years, Graves wrote numerous love poems, admired as some of the finest poetry written in the last century. **SG**

PAUL ÉLUARD

Signature titles

Poetry

The Duty and the Anxiety (Le Devoir et l'Inquiétude), 1917

Poems for Peace (Poèmes pour la paix), 1918

Capital of Pain (Capitale de la douleur), 1924

Love Poetry (L'amour la poésie), 1929

Poetry and Truth (Poésie et vérité), 1942

Uninterrupted Poetry (Poésie ininterrompue), 1946

The Hard Wish to Endure (Le dur désir de durer), 1946

Political poems (Poèmes politiques), 1948

The Phoenix (Le Phénix), 1951

Born: Eugène-Émile-Paul Grindel, December 14, 1895 (Saint-Denis, France); died November 18, 1952 (Charenton-le-Pont, France).

Style and genre: One of the founding figures of surrealism, Éluard wrote poetry noted for its lyricism; it often reflects social and political events of the time.

Paul Éluard is remembered as one of the founding members of surrealism in poetry (although he later rejected this), along with his two friends André Breton (with whom he collaborated) and Louis Aragon. Éluard's poetry is notable for its direct and striking language that evokes passages of time, place, and action through economic use of words. His work reflects his personal triumphs and loves as well as losses, and the greater world at large, especially social and political events. Éluard was a strongly political figure, and a member of the French Communist Party. He saw his poetry as a way of inspiring emotion and action in his readers, to showcase the leftist struggle for social and political power. **TamP**

RIGHT: Photo of Éluard with André Breton and Robert Desnos in an amusement park.

F. SCOTT FITZGERALD

Born: Francis Scott Key Fitzgerald, September 24, 1896 (St. Paul, Minnesota, U.S.); died December 21, 1940 (Hollywood, California, U.S.).

Style and genre: Fitzgerald provided a sense of elegance in the Jazz-Age decay; his characters teem with pronounced fatal flaws and veneers of insouciance.

With what seems like prescience of how short his life would be, F. Scott Fitzgerald lived at a fast pace. A love of writing shaped his character from an early age, and his first stories were published in his school magazine. During World War I, he joined the army, yet continued to write articles for magazines and lyrics for songs, as well as unsuccessfully submitting his first novel, *The Romantic Egoist* (1917) to publishers. After the war, Fitzgerald worked in advertising, an experience that honed the often jaded, cynical outlook he would convey in his novels.

Fitzgerald was the Jazz Age personified—and he made the jazz age itself into an integral character presiding over all his works. His characters, so charming and full of life, often doom themselves to unavoidable failure or misery, as excess takes its toll, and often leads to tragedy; a depressing indictment on the life Fitzgerald himself lived. He created the "flapper," a modern, independent-minded, and often controversial woman. He also married one: the dialogue spoken by his female characters is often direct quotations from his wife, Zelda Sayre.

His first success, *This Side of Paradise*, provided the Fitzgeralds with the income to travel widely and to live a privileged, glamorous life. They lived in an almost continual state of tension and hedonism, and Fitzgerald wrote intensely about it, entwining his experiences into works of fiction, such as the meaningfully titled *The Beautiful and the Damned*, and his most famous work, *The Great Gatsby*. His wife's schizophrenia and his attempts to deal with it are lovingly but tragically portrayed in *Tender Is the Night*. He died before finishing his last novel, *The Last Tycoon*. The works, style, and life of Fitzgerald led to the subversive, underground writing that was exemplified by Jack Kerouac in the 1960s. Fitzgerald not only gave the United States the Jazz Age in words, but also the freedom to expose the less palatable elements of life. **LH**

Signature titles

Novels

This Side of Paradise, 1920
The Beautiful and the Damned, 1922
The Great Gatsby, 1925
Tender Is the Night, 1934
The Last Tycoon, 1941

Short stories

Flappers and Philosophers, 1920
Tales of the Jazz Age, 1922
All the Sad Young Men, 1926
The Pat Hobby Stories, 1962
The Collected Short Stories of F. Scott Fitzgerald, 2000

Nonfiction

The Crack-Up, 1945

ABOVE: A portrait photograph of F. Scott Fitzgerald taken *c.* 1946.

RIGHT: A girl's face floats over Coney Island on the 1925 cover of *The Great Gatsby*.

The GREAT GATSBY

F·SCOTT·FITZGERALD

ANTONIN ARTAUD

Born: Antoine Marie Joseph Artaud, September 4, 1896 (Marseille, France); died March 4, 1948 (Ivry-sur-Seine, France).

Style and genre: Poet, essayist, playwright, actor, and director, Artaud influentially redefined theater with his advocacy of a sensual rather than literary experience.

Signature titles

Plays

Jet of Blood (Jet de Sang), 1925

The Cenci (Les Cenci), 1935

Nonfiction

The Theater and its Double (Le Théâtre et son double), 1938

Heliogabalus: Or, the Crowned Anarchist (Héliogabale ou l'anarchiste couronné), 1934

Voyage to the Land of the Tarahumaras (D'un voyage au pays des Tarahumaras), 1945

Screenplay

The Seashell and the Clergyman (La Coquille et le clergyman), 1928

In 1931 Antonin Artaud saw a Balinese theater performance at the Colonial Exposition in Marseille. It was a defining moment, and he was influenced by the dramatic and mystic approach of the Balinese to the stage. He went on to write *The Theater and its Double*, a selection of essays contributing to his two manifestos of the "Theater of Cruelty." He attacked the conventionality of French theater, advocating the need for more drama, and that theater should be a holistic experience, with the audience and actors forming part of a whole. His concept of "cruelty" was based on creating drama through extreme experience: violence, lighting, sound, and language designed to shatter the complacency of reality. **TamP**

GIUSEPPE TOMASI DI LAMPEDUSA

Born: December 23, 1896 (Palermo, Sicily, Italy); died July 23, 1957 (Rome, Italy).

Style and genre: Lampedusa was a Sicilian writer, duke of Palma, and prince of Lampedusa whose posthumously published novel about the unification of Italy became an international best seller.

Signature titles

Novel

The Leopard (Il gattopardo), 1958

Short stories

Stories (I racconti), 1961

Nonfiction

Lessons on Stendahl (Le lezioni su Stendhal), 1959

Introduction to Sixteenth-Century French Literature (Invito alle lettere francesi del Cinquecento), 1970

Giuseppe Tomasi di Lampedusa started writing seriously two years before his death. His life had been a preparatory exercise for the composition of *The Leopard*, as he had spent years watching the gradual disintegration of his aristocratic status, and the traditional way of life that it entailed. Disillusioned first with corrupt liberals, and then with violent fascists in the interwar years, he became introverted and began to meditate on the melancholy disappointments of historical progress. Set during the Italian Risorgimento, *The Leopard* charts the political paralysis of the Sicilian aristocracy. Poignantly told, it is a deeply thought exploration of the conflicting human urges to resist and submit to change. **TM**

ANDRÉ BRETON

Born: February 18, 1896 (Tinchebray, Orne, France); died September 28, 1966 (Paris, France).

Style and genre: Black humor, left-wing political themes, surrealism, symbolism, and a fascination with psychology and insanity all meld in Breton's works.

André Breton, a founder of the surrealist movement, remains most famous for his manifestos, the first of which was published in 1924, announcing the birth of surrealism to the world. A poet and psychiatrist, Breton used his medical studies to inform his poetry and his belief system. Initially a dadaist, he grew disillusioned not only with dadaist art but with the world in general, after living through the horrors of World War I. During the war, he worked in a hospital, treating physically as well as mentally damaged soldiers. From this time, his search for what he saw as the simplicity of life before the war encouraged his imagination and his works.

Breton's writings often focus on the harsh realities of life and the darkest recesses of the human mind. He saw life through the eyes of the insane he treated and won acclaim for his *Mad Love (L'Amour fou)*, a collection of poems that defend the crazy actions lovers commit. He wrote books and essays as well as poetry. His novel *Nadja* was more favorably received in his lifetime than his poetry, but since his death his poetry has been rediscovered. Breton also edited collections of other poets and writers, choosing those whose works had influenced him such as Edgar Allen Poe, Lewis Carroll, and Franz Kafka.

World War II affected Breton as deeply as the previous world war. Before combat he had become a communist; he left France, traveling to countries untainted by war, writing poetry that dwelled on issues of exile. In 1946, he returned to France, continuing his work as a surrealist with a new generation of followers. He famously said, "The mind which plunges into surrealism, relives with burning excitement the best part of childhood"—a poignant comment on the simplicity and innocence to which he longed to return. **LH**

"It is living and ceasing to live that are imaginary solutions. Existence is elsewhere."

Signature titles

Novel

Nadja, 1928

Poetry

Mad Love (L'Amour fou), 1937

Earthlight (Clair de terre), 1937

Arcane 17, 1945

Poems 1919–48 (Poèmes 1919–48), 1948

Nonfiction

Manifesto of Surrealism (Manifeste du surréalisme), 1924

Second Manifesto of Surrealism (Second manifeste du surréalisme), 1930

The Communicating Vessels (Les Vases communicants), 1932

What Is Surrealism? (Qu'est-ce le que le surréalisme?), 1934

ABOVE: A photograph of Breton taken in the mid-1930s, at the height of his fame.

JOHN DOS PASSOS

Born: John Roderigo Dos Passos, January 14, 1896 (Chicago, Illinois, U.S.); died September 28, 1970 (Baltimore, Maryland, U.S.).

Style and genre: Dos Passos's novels combine fiction with biography to create sweeping and critical studies of life in the United States.

The son, or ostensibly the son, of a well-to-do American lawyer of Portuguese descent, Dos Passos spent his early years traveling with his mother as what he called a "hotel child."

After graduating from Harvard University in 1916, he went to Europe and served in World War I as a volunteer ambulance driver. The experience inspired his fiercely antiwar novel *Three Soldiers*. He also came to see his own country as not one nation, but as two: the rich and powerful, and the poor and powerless. It was his novel about New York City, *Manhattan Transfer*, that made his reputation.

In his 1930s trilogy of novels, *U.S.A*, he skillfully blended fiction with biographies of real Americans, including J. P. Morgan, Woodrow Wilson, Rudolph Valentino, and Henry Ford. He used real newspaper headlines, advertisements, and popular songs of the period, along with simulated "newsreels" and extracts from political speeches to produce a chronicle of American history and society since 1900, which attacked what he saw as a system powered by greed and exploitation.

He supported left-wing causes, approved of communism and visited Russia. Backing the Republican side in the Spanish Civil War, he went to Spain with Ernest Hemingway, but the two men fell out and Dos Passos increasingly disliked what he saw of communism in action. He was moving steadily to the right politically. In another trilogy of novels, *District of Columbia*, he expressed his mounting disillusionment with American politics and President Roosevelt's New Deal, as well as with radical politicians and labor unions. He also wrote plays, poetry, travel books, and essays, but by the time of his death his conservatism had robbed him of influence with liberal intellectuals. **RC**

"Marxism has not only failed to promote human freedom. It has failed to produce food."

Signature titles

Novels

Three Soldiers, 1921
Manhattan Transfer, 1925
The U.S.A Trilogy
The 42nd Parallel, 1930
1919, 1932
The Big Money, 1936
The District of Columbia Trilogy
Adventures of a Young Man, 1939
Number One, 1943
The Grand Design, 1949

Autobiography

The Best of Times: An Informal Memoir, 1966

ABOVE: A later portrait (*c.* 1955) of Dos Passos with his ever-present cigar.

EUGENIO MONTALE

Born: October 12, 1896 (Genoa, Italy); died September 12, 1981 (Milan, Italy).

Style and genre: Montale was an Italian poet, journalist, and essayist whose poems are rife with existential themes that vindicate the value of humankind tempered by subtle humor.

Eugenio Montale's first collection of poems, *Cuttlefish Bones*, established a fresh, experimental idiom in Italian poetry while at the same time capturing the Mediterranean landscape with imagistic sharpness and precision. In 1938 he was dismissed as director of the Gabinetto Vieusseux Library in Florence for antifascist sentiments. *The Occasions* maintained a stoical vision and a resilient voice in a time of political oppression. It was followed by *The Storm and Other Things*, a harrowing distillation of wartime and postwar experience. In 1948 Montale became literary critic for the newspaper *Corriere della Sera*. He carried on writing poetry and essays on modern literature, and won the Nobel Prize in Literature in 1975. **SR**

Signature titles

Poetry

Cuttlefish Bones (Ossi di sepia), 1920–1927

The Coastguard's House and other verses (La Casa dei doganieri e altri versi), 1932

The Occasions (Le occasioni), 1939

The Storm and Other Things (La bufera e altro), 1956

Satura, 1971

Selected Poems, 1966

Nonfiction

Selected Essays ,1978

The Second Life of Art: Selected Essays of Eugenio Montale, 1982

GEORGES BATAILLE

Born: September 10, 1897 (Billom, Auvergne, France); died July 9, 1962 (Paris, France).

Style and genre: An essayist, philosophical theorist, and novelist, Bataille wrote on themes ranging from surrealism, transgression, and eroticism to death, degradation, and obscenity.

Georges Bataille's work influenced French twentieth-century theorists such as Jacques Lacan and Michel Foucault. Himself influenced by Friedrich Nietzsche and the Marquis de Sade, his essays and cult novels such as *The Story of the Eye* pushed the boundaries of sexual taboos as he explored the concept of the sacred within Dionysian excess and the erotic. Sometimes he wrote under pseudonyms, and on occasion his work was deemed pornographic and banned. Writing at a time when Europe stumbled from one war to another, and fascism hit its peak, he sought, like many, to find meaning when the existing social order had collapsed and the tenets of bourgeois society were called into question. **CK**

Signature titles

Novels

The Story of the Eye (Histoire de l'oeil), 1928

Blue of Noon (Le Bleu du ciel), 1945

Nonfiction

The Inner Experience (L'Expérience intérieure), 1943

The Guilty (Le Coupable), 1944

On Nietzsche (Sur Nietzsche), 1945

WILLIAM FAULKNER

Born: September 25, 1897 (New Albany, Mississippi, U.S.); died July 6, 1962 (Byhalia, Mississippi, U.S.).

Style and genre: Faulkner was a modernist writer whose poetic language and mythologizing portraits of the postbellum American South are legendary.

Signature titles

Novels

The Sound and the Fury, 1929
As I Lay Dying, 1930
Sanctuary, 1931
Light in August, 1932
Absalom, Absalom!, 1936
If I Forget Thee, Jerusalem, 1939
The Hamlet, 1940
The Town, 1957
The Mansion, 1959
The Reivers, 1962

Short stories

These 13, 1932

Poetry

The Marble Faun, 1924

William Faulkner once famously observed that part of the reason for human misery is that the only thing people are capable of doing for eight continuous hours a day is work. That the Nobel Prize winner could work longer than that is demonstrated by his output: besides his early poetry and his stint as a Hollywood screenwriter, Faulkner wrote twenty novels and eighty-five short stories, many of which are among the most important literature produced by any U.S. writer. Most of his works are set in the fictional "Yoknapatawpha County" of northern Mississippi, and the overlapping strands of shared history give them a richly evoked sense of place.

Faulkner's first great novel is *The Sound and the Fury*. It has all of the hallmarks of his best fiction: innovative, stream-of-consciousness narrative techniques are used to frame an almost classical tragedy, with characters both well developed and symbolic, toeing the line between exemplifying and allegorizing the violent nostalgia of the Depression-era South. He revisited these themes with the more complex structure of *As I Lay Dying* within a year. He also wrote *Sanctuary*—a gripping and horrific novel set during the Prohibition era that he described as "cheap," despite it being the biggest commercial success of his early career. Faulkner's other celebrated works include *Light in August*, his most explicit treatment of race relations; *Absalom, Absalom!*, the story of a young man's obsession with a local family; and the Snopes trilogy—*The Hamlet*, *The Town*, and *The Mansion*—about a family who personify the opportunistic greed underlying the emergence of the New South. Working eight hours a day may not have made Faulkner happy, but readers are lucky that he decided to do it anyway. **SY**

"I'm trying to say it all in one sentence, between one Cap and one period."

ABOVE: Faulkner photographed on February 5, 1954.

THORNTON WILDER

Born: April 17, 1897 (Madison, Wisconsin, U.S.); died December 7, 1975 (Hampden, Connecticut, U.S.).

Style and genre: An iconic American playwright and novelist, Wilder addresses universal philosophical themes within a modern context.

Thornton Wilder's first work, his novel *The Cabala*, was published in 1926, and from then on the writer's fame was destined. He primarily wrote plays, but also novels, although he considered himself to be first and foremost a teacher. This self-effacement was characteristic of the man who won two Pulitzer Prizes, as well as numerous other awards, for his writing, and whose work often broached deeply philosophical themes and examined the human condition.

Wilder was born into an illustrious family, his father a diplomat, and his siblings all highly talented. He grew up in an environment that fostered intellectual thought, and started to write plays while still at school. His first, *The Russian Princess* (1913), was written while he attended the Thatcher School at Ojai in California, where he was allegedly unhappy, and spent most of his time in the library. Wilder's first major success, and first Pulitzer Prize, came in 1927 with the novel *The Bridge of San Luis Rey*, which relates the intertwined stories of several people who die during the collapse of the bridge, and the events that placed them there. It explored the philosophical reasons behind random tragedy and death of the innocent, and set a precedent for future epic disaster stories; it is a model that has been consistently readdressed in literature and filmography since Wilder's time. After the early triumph of *The Bridge of San Luis Rey*, Wilder continued to publish a number of successful works, including the plays *The Skin of Our Teeth* and *Our Town*, which won him his second Pulitzer Prize.

Wilder's work is characterized by the poignant and insightful manner in which he addresses humanity and the complexities of human behavior, as well as examining deep philosophical themes that are inherent in all parts of life. **TamP**

Signature titles

Novels

The Cabala, 1926
The Bridge of San Luis Rey, 1927
The Woman of Andros, 1930
Heaven's My Destination, 1935
Ides of March, 1948
The Eighth Day, 1967
Theophilus North, 1973

Plays

The Trumpet Shall Sound, 1926
Our Town, 1938
The Skin of Our Teeth, 1942
The Matchmaker, 1955
Childhood, 1960
Infancy, 1960

"I am interested in those things that repeat and . . . repeat in the lives of the millions."

ABOVE: A c. 1950 portrait of Thornton Wilder.

LOUIS ARAGON

Born: October 3, 1897 (Paris, France); died December 24, 1982 (Paris, France).

Style and genre: Aragon was a leading French poet, novelist, and surrealist whose work was heavily influenced by his political activity and broke traditional literary conventions.

In 1924 Louis Aragon became a founding member of the surrealist movement with André Breton and Philippe Soupault. Along with Breton, Aragon produced a periodical called *Littérature* that set out their theories of surrealism. Their aim was to free the imagination by using the unconscious as a source of inspiration. By using automatic writing—writing without any form of conscious control—they believed the mind could be freed of all inhibitions. They also believed that poetry should take risks and emancipate language by disrupting and breaking literary conventions.

In 1924 Aragon wrote *The Libertine* (*Le Libertinage*), a collection of short fragmentary stories. In scenes of everyday life, Aragon explores the subconscious mind and the result blends a series of impressions with fantasy. Two years later, Aragon produced *Paris Peasant* (*Le paysan de Paris*), one of the central works of surrealism. Aragon said that it was neither a story nor a character study but "a novel that would break all the traditional rules governing the writing of fiction . . . a novel that the critics would be obliged to approach empty-handed."

As well as his surrealist writing, Aragon, who had joined the French Communist Party, worked as a journalist and publisher. During World War II, he was a member of the French Resistance, and built up a network of writers who wrote for underground journals and used literature to undermine the occupation. Many of the poems he wrote during this period were set to music.

After the war, Aragon increasingly drew on his own experiences as the basis for the fiction of his last novels, often peppering them with news articles, speeches, journal essays, and his theories on art. **HJ**

Signature titles

Novels

Paris Peasant (Le paysan de Paris), 1926

The Communists (Les Communistes), 1949–1951

Holy Week (La Semaine sainte), 1958

The Kill (Le mise à mort), 1965

Blanche or Forgetting (Blanche; ou L'oubli), 1967

Théâtre/Roman, 1974

Short stories

The Libertine (Le Libertinage), 1924

Poetry

Bonfire (Feu de joie), 1920

Perpetual Movement (Le Mouvement perpétuel), 1926

The Red Front (Le Front rouge),1930

"We know that the nature of genius is to provide idiots with ideas twenty years later."

ABOVE: A 1936 photograph of surrealist writer Louis Aragon.

FEDERICO GARCÍA LORCA

Born: June 5, 1898 (Fuente Vaqueros, Spain); died August 19, 1936 (Víznar, Spain).

Style and genre: Personal, collective, mythological, avant-gardist, and cosmic—Lorca's poetic, dramatic works fuse the elemental in nature with the spirit worlds of childhood and folklore.

Federico García Lorca's upbringing was animated by folklore and nursery rhymes, the natural world, and music, painting, and puppetry. He took a degree in law, but immediately plunged into the world of the arts, where he soon distinguished himself as a personality of force: producing plays, composing at the piano, transcribing folk songs, and in particular, reciting his poems in performances that contemporary accounts describe as electrifying.

His first plays and poems dramatizing a conflicted transition from child to adult established his reputation, and confirmed his conviction that the ideal medium for verse was popular, oral, and dramatic. *Gypsy Ballads* evokes the rhythms and passions of a violent, sensual world, and many of his poems in *Songs* reflect a child's point of view, so expressing the duality of his character.

Facing a crisis about his homosexuality, Lorca visited New York from 1929 to 1930 and encountered an alien world. The experience gave rise to Lorca's most surreal works, including *A Poet in New York*, in which experiences of fear and isolation are laced with a condemnation of the city. In 1931, Lorca took directorship of La Barraca theater company, charged with presenting the Spanish classics to rural audiences. For the next five years, Lorca toured extensively and wrote his most highly regarded works, such as the rural dramatic trilogy of *Blood Wedding*, *Yerma*, and *The House of Bernardo Alma*.

Lorca's public profile as a producer of popular theater, as well as his sexuality, made him a target; he was assassinated by fascist partisans in the first days of the Spanish Civil War. His body was buried in an unmarked grave and has never been found. **CH**

"A dead man in Spain is more alive than a dead man anywhere. . . ."—*A Poet in New York*

Signature titles

Poetry

Poem of the Deep Song (Poema del cante jondo), 1921

Songs (Canción de jinete), 1927

Gypsy Ballads (Primer romancero gitano), 1928

Lament for Ignacio Sánchez Mejías (Llanto por Ignacio Sánchez Mejías), 1936

Sonnets of Dark Love (Sonetos del amor oscuro), 1936

A Poet in New York (Poeta en Nueva York), 1940

The Diván of Tamarit (Diván del Tamarit), 1941

Plays

Blood Wedding (Bodas de sangre), 1932

Yerma, 1934

The House of Bernardo Alma (La casa de Bernarda Alba), 1936

ABOVE: Federico García Lorca posing in a library in 1930.

BERTOLT BRECHT

Born: Eugen Berthold Friedrich Brecht, February 10, 1898 (Augsburg, Bavaria, Germany); died August 14, 1956 (Berlin, Germany).

Style and genre: A Marxist playwright, poet, and theater director, Brecht's didactic dramas are famed for their lack of illusionistic artifice and use of song.

Marxist playwright and theater director Bertolt Brecht changed drama to such an extent that the term "Brechtian" is now in existence to describe his and others' exposition of plays and films. Brecht's political beliefs saw him use theater as a form of didactic experience to educate the proletariat, and he frequently adapted historical events into plays ensuring they had a relevance to contemporary times and its social problems, as in *Life of Galileo.*

However, perhaps it is the form his plays took when staged that has had most impact. Brecht spurned illusionism, and sought to make his audiences aware they were watching a fiction, leading him to austere sets, incorporating songs, and employing projections to reiterate a point in what is possibly the first use of multimedia in theater.

Brecht's strong Marxist commitment also saw him espouse the concept of the collective. This brought about successful collaborations with scenographers, actors, and composers, most notably with composer Kurt Weill, when the duo cowrote *The Threepenny Opera*, pitting the criminal underworld of Mack the Knife against the Victorian upper classes.

Signature titles

Plays

Baal, 1918

St. Joan of the Stockyards (Die heilige Johanna der Schlachthöfe), 1929–1931

Life of Galileo (Leben des Galilei), 1937–1939

Mother Courage and Her Children (Mutter Courage und ihre Kinder), 1938–1939

The Good Person of Szechwan (Der gute Mensch von Sezuan), 1939–1942

The Resistible Rise of Arturo Ui (Der aufhaltsame Aufstieg des Arturo Ui), 1941

The Caucasian Chalk Circle (Der kaukasische Kreidekreis), 1943–1945

Musical

The Threepenny Opera (Die Dreigroschenoper), 1928

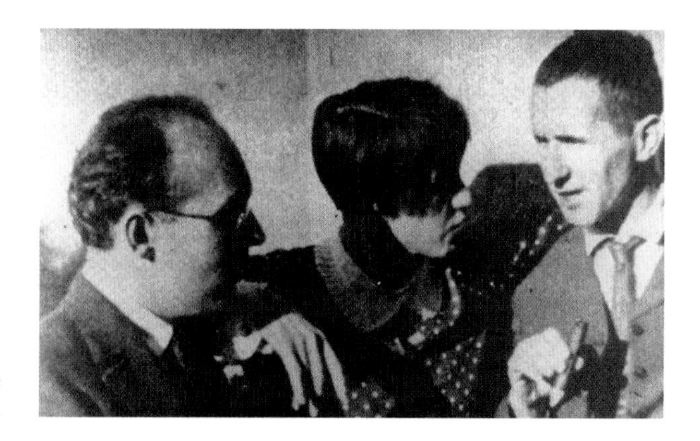

ABOVE: A portrait of dramatist Bertolt Brecht taken during the 1930s.

RIGHT: Brecht with Kurt Weill (left) and Lotte Lenya during rehearsals of *Threepenny Opera*.

Brecht studied drama at Munich University and worked as a theater reviewer. He wrote his first play, *Baal*, in 1918, but it was in the 1920s that he became the darling of the Weimar Republic's theater world as a playwright, director, and notable theorist. The Nazi era saw Brecht fall out of favor with the authorities because of his opposition to fascism displayed in works such as *Mother Courage and Her Children*, and he emigrated to the United States in 1941. There he worked as a Hollywood screenwriter, but his belief in art as propaganda did not endear him to many.

After World War II, Brecht fell foul of the House Un-American Activities Committee, and was called to testify in 1947. He denied being a member of the Communist Party—despite being a Marxist he had never joined. He left the United States, and headed for Switzerland before being invited by the then East German communist government to return to Germany. **CK**

ABOVE: A set design sketch for the musical *Happy End* (1929), written with Kurt Weill.

The Threepenny Opera

Written with composer Weill, Brecht's musical is based on the English opera *The Beggar's Opera* (1728) written by John Gay. When it opened in Berlin in 1928 it soon became the most successful show of the then Weimar Republic. There were forty-six productions of the musical across Europe within a year of its premiere, and film director G. W. Pabst made the first cinematic version in 1931. The musical reached the height of its glory after World War II when an off-Broadway production ran from 1954 through 1961, making it the longest-running musical ever at the time.

ERNEST HEMINGWAY

Born: Ernest Miller Hemingway, July 21, 1899 (Oak Park, Illinois, U.S.); died July 2, 1961 (Ketchum, Idaho, U.S.).

Style and genre: A writer of the "Lost Generation," Hemingway is known for his spare, terse prose that established the style of the age.

By the fall of 1950, Ernest Hemingway was all but finished. He had just released *Across the River and Into the Trees*, his first novel since *For Whom The Bells Tolls*, to perhaps the worst reviews of his life. It follows a fifty-year-old U.S. colonel, who returns to a site near Venice where he had fought in World War I in order to spend his final days duck hunting, eating, drinking, and making love to an eighteen-year-old countess. Because Hemingway had recently taken a less than wholesome interest in a young *amorosa* of his own, critics read the novel as an embarrassing display of male menopause. It had been more than a decade since his last successful novel, and Hemingway was veering toward self-parody. The prodigy of U.S. modernism, who had been called "Papa" since his twenties, seemed to have skipped middle age entirely: He was already an old man in a sea of drink, sickness, and depression. At fifty-one years old—an age at which a typical major author has barely finished clearing his throat—Hemingway's career was considered over.

Unbelievably, however, his greatest successes—and torments—were still ahead of him. In 1952 he regained his

Signature titles

Novels

The Torrents of Spring, 1926
The Sun Also Rises, 1926
In Another Country, 1927
A Farewell to Arms, 1929
To Have and Have Not, 1937
For Whom the Bell Tolls, 1940
Across the River and Into the Trees, 1950
The Old Man and the Sea, 1952
Islands in the Stream, 1970
The Garden of Eden, 1986

Short stories

In Our Time, 1925
Men without Women, 1927
Winner Take Nothing, 1933
The Snows of Kilimanjaro, 1936

Nonfiction

Death in the Afternoon, 1932
The Green Hills of Africa, 1935
A Moveable Feast, 1964

ABOVE: Hemingway in Malaga, Spain, photographed a year before his death.

RIGHT: Hemingway and friend Taylor "Beartracks" Williams hunting antelope.

ABOVE: The writer in conversation with Cuban leader Fidel Castro in late 1959.

reputation with his novel *The Old Man and the Sea*, which won both the Pulitzer Prize and Nobel Prize in Literature. In subsequent years he continued to produce a great deal of valuable fiction, which was published posthumously. But these years also brought mental and physical anguish for Hemingway. Had he foreseen the serious internal injuries and burns from two successive plane crashes, his worsening hypertension and cirrhosis, as well as his deepening depression, paranoia, and the electroshock therapy sessions that left his memory permanently damaged, it is reasonable to suspect that Hemingway would have reached his final conclusion, and committed suicide rather sooner than he did.

"Writing and travel broaden your ass if not your mind and I like to write standing up."

Nevertheless, few U.S. authors have achieved the iconic status enjoyed by Hemingway. The beard, the sweater, the

A Love of Bullfighting

Hemingway witnessed his first bullfight in 1923 in Spain, at the recommendation of Gertrude Stein. The experience had a profound effect on the young author. He became a lifelong *aficionado* of the ritual, and wrote about it in *The Sun Also Rises*, as well as in the nonfiction *Death in the Afternoon*. He first traveled to Pamplona in Navarre in July 1923 for the great fiesta of San Fermín, a Christian holiday that dates to 1126. The most popular event associated with the festival is the daily "running of the bulls" down a stretch of streets. To this day, misguided Hemingway enthusiasts travel to the Spanish town in order to run with the bulls—the author himself, however, did no such thing.

Tauromaquia, or bullfighting, is not just about stabbing an animal to death—it is a complex, balletic ritual, and during Hemingway's thirty-year relationship with the sport he appreciated the theatrical and spiritual aspects of the ceremony. Hemingway admired the dignity and honesty of bullfighting, the "art and valor" of the struggle, and responded imaginatively to the "grace under pressure" demonstrated by the matador.

As the author put it: "Bullfighting is the only art in which the artist is in danger of death and in which the degree of brilliance in the performance is left to the fighter's honor."

RIGHT: The cover of the first U.K. edition of his 1952 novel published by Jonathan Cape.

intense stare—the image of Hemingway, and what he stands for, overwhelms any one of his novels. And while he certainly participated in the production of his own legend, he also lived an impossibly full life.

At eighteen years old, Hemingway became a volunteer ambulance driver on the Italian front in World War I, where an Austrian trench mortar shell left more than 200 shrapnel fragments in his legs. Recuperating in Milan, he fell hopelessly in love with his nurse Agnes von Kurowsky, who, more than six years his senior, finally broke off their engagement because she felt he was too young. (Two years later Hemingway married Hadley Richardson, who was a year older than Kurowsky.) By his twenty-fifth birthday he was residing in Paris, and had formed friendships with Gertrude Stein, Ezra Pound, and James Joyce. Aged twenty-seven, he solidified his literary reputation with *The Sun Also Rises*. Aged thirty, Hemingway had buried his father—a suicide—married his second wife, and written his second major novel, *A Farewell to Arms*. The author then delved into politics with *To Have and Have Not*, but it was considered an artistic failure. He responded by publishing what is perhaps his finest novel, *For Whom the Bell Tolls*, not long after wedding bells announced the author's third marriage.

Hemingway was at home in war. Indeed, he sought it out. In 1942, with the blessing of the U.S. government, he outfitted his fishing boat to hunt German U-boats off the coast of Cuba. He reported on the Greco-Turkish War in 1922, and the Spanish Civil War from 1937 to 1939. In 1944 he documented the Allied assault on Omaha Beach, Normandy, on D-Day from a landing craft. Later that same year, Hemingway covered the fighting on the German-Belgian border, and killed an advancing Nazi soldier. He eventually observed the Liberation of Paris, where he met his fourth wife.

It is frequently insisted that a writer's life is the single greatest determinant of the nature of his or her literary expression. In the case of Hemingway the opposite is true: his life came to approximate the romance, adventurousness, despair, and epic scale of his fiction. **IW**

HEMINGWAY

THE OLD MAN
AND
THE SEA

ELIZABETH BOWEN

Born: Elizabeth Dorothea Cole Bowen, June 7, 1899 (Dublin, Ireland); died February 22, 1973 (Hythe, Kent, England).

Style and genre: A modernist with an outsider's eye for passionate interiority, Bowen populated her novels with semi-autobiographical awkward orphans falling in love.

Elizabeth Bowen published her first short stories—already marked by her flawless command of language and tone—at the age of twenty-four. Bowen hovered at the edge of the Bloomsbury Group, and her novels resonate with the experiments into interiority that define the fiction of Virginia Woolf and James Joyce.

Unlike her better known contemporaries, Bowen was a best seller in her day, writing for fashionable magazines such as *Tatler* and *Harper's Magazine*. Her work was neglected after her death from cancer in 1973, but has seen a recent revival on the back of Deborah Warner's film adaptation of *The Last September*. (1999). This was Bowen's second novel, and her most autobiographical in its account of the fading culture of the Anglo-Irish Protestant ascendancy.

The Last September's central consciousness is that of Lois Farquar, the niece of ascendancy grandees clinging to their country house and way of life. By contrast, the young girl is inchoate with conflicting desires: to stay in Ireland and to study art in London; and to get engaged to her English soldier and to be kissed by an Irish rebel. Sharply observant within this cloud of amorphous thoughts, Farquar prefigures Portia Quayne, the willful, passionate antiheroine of Bowen's most critically acclaimed novel, *The Death of the Heart*. Bowen's caustic observations from the margins of good society were rooted in a peripatetic period similar to her female protagonists, staying with relatives and in boardinghouses while her father recovered from a nervous breakdown. Her novels are often structured through a displaced adolescent consciousness, whose misperceptions of mysterious adult ways leads to a tragic denouement. **SM**

Signature titles

Novels

The Hotel, 1926
The Last September, 1929
Friends and Relations, 1931
To the North, 1932
The House in Paris, 1935
The Death of the Heart, 1938
The Heat of the Day, 1949
A World of Love, 1955
Eva Trout, 1968

Short stories

Encounters, 1923
Joining Charles and Other Stories, 1929
The Cat Jumps and Other Stories, 1934
The Demon Lover, and Other Stories, 1945

"I don't mind feeling small myself, but I dread finding the world is."—*The House in Paris*

ABOVE: Elizabeth Bowen photographed outside her home.

NOËL COWARD

Born: December 16, 1899 (Teddington, Middlesex, England); died March 26, 1973 (Port Maria, Jamaica).

Style and genre: Coward found fame with his bitingly witty song lyrics and plays that border on farce, but which are saved by intelligent plots.

Sir Noël Coward was a playwright, lyricist, novelist, musician, actor, film director, and television star—not to mention a world-class celebrity and icon. From the jazz age to the swinging sixties, he remained at the forefront of the literary world, and his works still attract large audiences today. Several of his plays have been turned into films, most notably *This Happy Breed* (1944) and *Blithe Spirit* (1945).

Coward first appeared on stage at the age of eleven and remained in the spotlight until the end of his life. A gay man in an age when homosexuality was still illegal in most countries, he lived a surprisingly open lifestyle, although the public seemed blind to his homosexuality abetted by the media that constantly hinted at relationships with women, in particular actress Gertrude Lawrence. His longest relationship was with actor Graham Payn and it lasted for almost thirty years, ending only with Coward's death.

Coward's erratic romantic life, and the farcical lengths the media would go to in order to present him as a heterosexual man, added poignancy to his comedies, in which he coyly alludes to same-sex relationships, yet keeping most of his characters firmly heterosexual. His cynicism about love per se is apparent in most of his works, with usually at least one couple unable to live with, or without, each other—most notably Elyot and Amanda in *Private Lives*. This duality of personality was a prominent feature in almost every area of Coward's life. In recent years it has emerged that in World War II when he traveled regularly ostensibly as an entertainer of the troops, he was working as an undercover agent for the British government. Coward was so well known and well liked that he was nicknamed "The Master." **LH**

"I like long walks, especially when they are taken by people who annoy me."

ABOVE: A press shot of Noël Coward taken in the late 1950s.

Signature titles

Plays

The Vortex, 1923
Fallen Angels, 1923
Hay Fever, 1924
Easy Virtue, 1924
Semi-Monde, 1926
This Was a Man, 1926
Private Lives, 1929
Cavalcade, 1931
Design for Living, 1932
Present Laughter, 1939
This Happy Breed, 1939
Blithe Spirit, 1941
Star Quality, 1967

VLADIMIR NABOKOV

Born: Vladimir Vladimirovich Nabokov, April 23, 1899 (St. Petersburg, Russia); died July 2, 1977 (Montreux, Switzerland).

Style and genre: Novelist and short-story writer known for his flamboyant, inventive, erudite, and elaborate prose, and his bold treatment of the taboo.

Vladimir Nabokov was a master prose stylist, whose most famous novel is undoubtedly *Lolita*, a work that explores, in witty and elegant terms, the story of a middle-aged academic's obsession for a young teenage girl. Despite his brilliant mastery of the English language, Nabokov spent the first twenty years of his life in Russia. His facility for language may, in part, have grown from the trilingual household in which he grew up, and his later transition from Russian to English-language-based writing would have been a reversion to the language he had mastered as a child. His family was wealthy, and his father a member of the Russian Constituent Assembly.

In 1919, the family fled the country to escape the Bolshevik Revolution, fully expecting to return after the troubles were over. They did not. Soon afterward, Nabokov arrived in England to study modern languages at the University of Cambridge, and after graduating moved to Berlin, where he wrote, in Russian, nine novels, more than three hundred poems, and approximately fifty short stories. On the basis of this output, he slowly acquired a reputation among the Russian émigrés, although not enough of one to derive a full-time income. After

Signature titles

Novels

Bend Sinister, 1947
Lolita, 1955
Pnin, 1957
Pale Fire, 1962
Ada or Ardor: A Family Chronicle, 1969
Transparent Things, 1972
Look at the Harlequins!, 1974

Short stories

Nine Stories, 1947
Nabokov's Dozen: A Collection of Thirteen Stories, 1958

Poetry

Poems, 1916
The Cluster, 1922

Nonfiction

Notes on Prosody, 1963
Speak, Memory: An Autobiography Revisited, 1967

ABOVE: Nabokov searching for butterflies in Switzerland, *c.* 1975.

RIGHT: A poster for Stanley Kubrick's 1962 film starring Sue Lyon as Lolita.

three years in Paris, he fled again, this time from the advancing Nazi troops to the United States. Here he made a living lecturing in comparative literature at Wellesley College. His lectures were unique, entertaining, and witty, and his courses popular. At the same time, he worked at Harvard's Museum of Comparative Zoology as a research fellow in entomology, a discipline in which he also rose to some eminence.

His next appointment was at Cornell University, where he was professor of Russian literature from 1948 to 1959. In 1957 he published *Pnin*, a novel in which the protagonist, a U.S.-based academic with a Russian émigré past, shares many obvious similarities with Nabokov.

After the financial success of the U.S. publication of *Lolita* in 1958—three years after the less hesitant Olympian Press publication in France—Nabokov was able to retire to Montreux, in Switzerland, where he devoted himself to writing. **GM**

ABOVE: Nabokov photographed writing in his car in September 1958.

Erotic Infatuation

In just four years, *Lolita* went from being regarded as a dangerously obscene underground publication to being hailed as a sophisticated and masterly prose work that explored, and subverted, the genre of courtly love. It is narrated by Humbert Humbert, a scholar who has a self-confessed attraction to nymphets. The novel traces his erotic infatuation with Lolita, the twelve-year-old daughter of his reviled landlady, whom he eventually seduces into a sexual relationship. It was briefly banned in France and Britain, although in the United States it was an instant hit.

JORGE LUIS BORGES

Born: Jorge Francisco Isidoro Luis Borges, August 24, 1899 (Buenos Aires, Argentina); died June 14, 1986 (Geneva, Switzerland).

Style and genre: Borges was a fabulist, poet, short-story writer, essayist, and self-described mythographer who wrote laconic but dazzling and inimitable prose.

Born into a bilingual Anglophile household, Jorge Luis Borges first learned to read not in Spanish but in English, under the tutelage of his paternal grandmother. A precocious youngster, at the age of six, he declared his intent to be a writer; aged seven, he wrote, in English, a survey of Greek mythology; aged eight, he penned his first story; and aged nine, he published his first work, a translation into Spanish of Oscar Wilde's *The Happy Prince* (1888). Since he shared the same name as his father, a professor of English and minor writer, the translation was widely assumed to be the work of the elder Borges.

Borges was educated at home, largely in his father's extensive library. Two results of this upbringing were to become leitmotifs of Borges's aesthetic: an encyclopedic knowledge of "literature"—for Borges an undifferentiated category including fiction, poetry, metaphysics, and mythology—and an Anglophile sensibility. He once remarked that it was not until late in his childhood that he realized Spanish and English were different languages.

Signature titles

Short stories

A Universal History of Infamy (Historia Universal de la Infamia), 1935

Pierre Menard, Author of the Quixote (Pierre Menard, autor del Quijote), 1939

The Library of Babel (La biblioteca de Babel), 1941

Funes the Memorious (Funes el memorioso), 1942

Ficciones (Fictions), 1944

The Aleph (El Aleph), 1949

Nonfiction

Other Inquisitions 1937–1952 (Otras Inquisiciones 1937–1952), 1952

Seven Nights (Siete noches), 1977

Anthologies

Dreamtigers (El Hacedor), 1960

A Personal Anthology (Antología Personal), 1961

Labyrinths: Selected Stories and Other Writings, 1962

ABOVE: Borges at his National Library office in Buenos Aires in 1973.

RIGHT: A photograph taken in 1968 of Borges with his first wife Elsa.

LEFT: A copy of the Argentine edition of Borges's *Poems (1922–1943)*.

Under the influence of the Spanish ultraist avant-garde poets, Borges established himself in the 1920s as a poet and essayist who combined international avant-garde sensibilities with the local color of the bustling, melting-pot culture of Buenos Aires, and popular mythology of the tango, gangsters, and street slang. During the 1930s Borges began to experiment with short prose pieces, or "fictions," and in doing so began to become the Borges of renown. His 1935 *A Universal History of Infamy* (*Historia Universal de la Infamia*) masqueraded as the work of an editor and bibliophile who merely recounted a series of outré biographical anecdotes lifted from forgotten

"Every novel is an ideal plane inserted into the realm of reality."—*Labyrinths*

books. In 1937 Borges took a job as a municipal librarian, resigning in response to Juan Perón's rise to power in 1946. With the fall of Perón in 1955, he was named the director of the National Library of the Argentine Republic, a post he held until 1973. The theme of the library, cataloguing, and the infinite worlds created by words pervade a number of Borges's subsequent works.

In 1938 Borges suffered a wound to the head that became infected, and left him hovering on the verge of death for several weeks, hallucinating. As a result, Borges's eyesight began to fail, eventually leading to blindness in the late 1950s. During his recovery, Borges composed his first truly Borgesian fiction, *Pierre Menard, Author of the Quixote* (*Pierre Menard, autor del Quijote*). The story is an obituary of a little-known man of letters who had set himself the heroic, absurd, and infinite task of writing—word for word—*Don Quixote* (*Don Quijote*, 1605). The story was revolutionary in its suggestion that fiction could be composed out of the raw material of other fictions.

Over the next two decades, Borges pursued the "infinite," fantastic, and labyrinthine theme of fiction in a series of stories and parables of mythic resonance, and gemlike precision. Fantastic literature, as Borges came to define it, is not an evasion of reality, but a more lucid, rigorous, and authentic vision of it. Other permutations of the Borgesian universe consider the vanity of identity and originality; the folly of erudition; the impossibility of an absolute delimitation between good and evil, original sin and grace; the symmetry of absolute chaos and absolute order, pure certainty and pure futility. The bleakness of his vision is tempered by the self-effacing humility, sly humor, and irony of his narrators.

From the late 1950s until his death, Borges lectured widely, and because his blindness made composing prose narratives difficult, he returned to writing poetry. International recognition came in the form of the 1961 International Publishers' Formentor Prize, and in the 1960s "boom" of Latin-American magic realists, for many of whom Borges was an acknowledged precursor. **CH**

Helpful Hallucinations

Many of Borges's stories are animated by what he called "the immanence of a revelation which does not occur," the feeling of a quasi-narcotic, lucidly controlled delirium. Ironically, this may have stemmed from Borges's 1938 life-threatening illness and its accompanying hallucinations. During his recovery, Borges experienced a crisis of fear that his mental and poetic faculties had been damaged permanently, and that he would never write poetry again. To put his powers to a "safe" test, Borges conceived the idea of attempting a short story (*Pierre Menard*) that, should it fail, could be attributed to his inexperience in fiction. The infinite dilation of time and space characteristic of delirium, as well as its attendant terrors and astonishments, would receive masterful exposition in *The Library in Babel* (*La biblioteca de Babel*) and *Funes the Memorious* (*Funes el memorioso*).

ANTOINE DE SAINT-EXUPÉRY

Born: June 29, 1900 (Lyon, France); died July 31, 1944 (at sea near southern France).

Style and genre: Saint-Exupéry is known for his dreamlike narrative, weaving travel writing into his fiction and nonfiction works, with the theme of flying ever present; he tentatively experimented with magical realism.

Antoine de Saint-Exupéry is best known for his magical, thought-provoking children's novel *The Little Prince*, a classic of French literature. He also wrote nonfiction and novels that read like travel writing, inspired by his life as a pilot and the countries he lived in and visited.

Saint-Exupéry's early career was spent in North Africa, which inspired him to write about the landscape, the people, and the desert he adored. His writing is imbued with the otherworldliness of a life spent flying above the clouds and the ethereal thoughts he conjured up while living in the desert. In 1929, he moved to Argentina, where he learned to fly the intensely difficult air routes through the Andes. In 1931, he married the widowed Consuelo Gomez Carillo—but theirs was a turbulent marriage and he was frequently unfaithful. Most at home in the skies and something of a nomad, Saint-Exupéry seemed to possess a charmed life when he survived what was believed to have been a fatal air crash in the North African desert in 1935, about which he wrote in *Wind, Sand, and Stars*. He also survived a crash in Guatemala in 1937. At the start of World War II, he confidently joined the French air force but became increasingly depressed at the continuing helplessness of France against the occupying Germans.

In 1944, Saint-Exupéry's P-38 Lightning plane disappeared over the Mediterranean. It was unknown whether he was shot down, suffered an accident, or had committed suicide. His body and the plane were never recovered and for decades the story remained a tantalizing mystery. In 1998, it seemed the mystery was over when a French fisherman discovered an engraved bracelet believed to have belonged to the author. More recent claims, however, suggest the bracelet was a forgery. **LH**

"I know but one freedom, and that is the freedom of the mind."

Signature titles

Nonfiction

The Aviator (L'Aviateur), 1926
Southern Mail (Courier Sud), 1929
Wind, Sand, and Stars (Terre des Hommes), 1939
Flight to Arras (Pilote de Guerre), 1942
Wisdom of the Sands (La Citadelle), 1948 (published posthumously)

Children's fiction

The Little Prince (Le Petit Prince), 1943

ABOVE: An undated photo of the author and pilot who disappeared during World War II.

1900–19

THOMAS WOLFE

Born: October 3, 1900 (Ashville, California, U.S.); died September 15, 1938 (Baltimore, Maryland, U.S.).

Style and genre: A highly influential novelist, Wolfe's works are defined by his use of richly emotive language and were greatly respected by Beat Generation writers.

Despite his tragically short life, Thomas Wolfe left an important legacy in his work. Aside from the works published during his lifetime, three further novels—*The Web and the Rock* (1939), *You Can't Go Home Again* (1940), and *The Hills Beyond* (1941)—were extricated from his remaining manuscripts.

Wolfe was writing at a critical time in the United States's history, as the Great Depression was sweeping across the country with devastating effects. Inevitably perhaps, this change in mood forms the background for much of his work, which is also frequently autobiographical. Wolfe's use of descriptive and expressionistic language brings to life the United States of the 1930s.

After graduating from Harvard University, Wolfe traveled to Europe. It was on his return journey, in 1925, that he met the wealthy Mrs. Berstein, with whom he began an affair. Berstein supported Wolfe financially, allowing him to write his first work, *Look Homeward, Angel*, which he then dedicated to her. Their turbulent affair ended and Wolfe went back to Europe, funded by the Peggy Guggenheim Fellowship.

He finished his second novel, *Of Time and the River,* in New York, where it was edited by the famous editor Maxwell Perkins of Scribners, who also worked with F. Scott Fitzgerald and Ernest Hemingway. Wolfe's works were extremely lengthy, and the editing process was therefore a complicated one. This eventually led to problems between the writer and Perkins, and Wolfe switched to the publishers Harpers. He then remained with Harpers and was still working until the time of his death from tuberculosis of the brain. While on his deathbed, he wrote a heartfelt letter to Perkins about the times the two had spent together. **TamP**

"... loneliness ... is the central and inevitable fact of human existence."

Signature titles

Novels

Look Homeward, Angel, 1929
Of Time and the River, 1935
From Death to Morning, 1935
The Story of a Novel, 1936

ABOVE: An undated portrait photograph of Thomas Wolfe.

1900–19

JACQUES PRÉVERT

Born: February 4, 1900 (Neuilly-sur-Seine, France); died April 11, 1977 (Omonville-la-Petite, France).

Style and genre: Jacques Prévert was one of the most popular twentieth-century French writers. He wrote poetry, ballads, and a number of important screenplays.

Jacques Prévert's poetry ranges from the wildly satirical to the melancholic and often ridicules the establishment. He was, and remains, one of France's most popular poets and a great deal of his work focuses on Parisian life. Many of his poems such as "Autumn Leaves" ("Les Feuilles mortes") were put to music and sung by vocalists including Edith Piaf, Yves Montand, and Juliette Greco.

In the 1920s Prévert worked for an advertising agency and began writing poetry in his spare time. He became associated with the surrealist movement along with André Breton and Louis Aragon until he was thrown out by Breton for his "irreverence." In 1932 he joined the agitprop "Groupe Octobre," a left-wing acting ensemble whose members took part in the surrealist film *L'Affaire Est Dans le Sac* (1932), which Prévert cowrote. He became a prominent screenwriter throughout the 1930s and wrote the script for Jean Renoir's *Le Crime de Monsieur Lange* (1936). Together with the film director Marcel Carné, Prévert developed a cinema movement called poetic realism, which formed the basis for American film noir.

After World War II, Prévert published a number of books of poetry including *Paroles*, *Spectacle*, *Rain and Good Weather*, and *Things and Others*. Prévert was notable for his disregard of convention and the liberties he took with language, traits he retained from his time with the surrealists. In his poems, he breaks rules on rhyme and punctuation and draws attention to the arbitrary nature of language by punning, creating new words and phrases, and playing on the literal meaning of words and their sounds. Prévert was France's biggest selling poet and his work is still widely taught in French schools. **HJ**

"Even if happiness forgets you a little bit, never forget about it."

Signature titles

Poetry

Paroles, 1946

Spectacle, 1951

Rain and Good Weather, 1955

Things and Others, 1973

ABOVE: Prévert caught on camera at an exhibition of his collages in 1966.

1900–19

NATHALIE SARRAUTE

Born: July 18, 1900 (Ivanovo, Russia); died October 19, 1999 (Paris, France).

Style and genre: Russian-born French novelist and essayist Nathalie Sarraute was one of the pioneers of the *nouveau roman* movement that radically departed from conventional ideas about plot, dialogue, characterization, and narrative.

Signature titles

Novels

Tropisms (Tropismes), 1939

Portrait of a Man Unknown (Portrait d'un inconnu), 1949

Martereau, 1953

The Age of Suspicion (L'ère du soupcon), 1956

The Golden Fruits (Les Fruits d'ór), 1963

Childhood (L'Enfance), 1983

Here (Ici), 1997

Nathalie Sarraute was born in Russia but grew up in Paris. She practiced as a lawyer until the war and then became a writer, but as a Jew was forced into hiding during the Nazi occupation. Her first work *Tropisms* was published in 1939. It focuses on "tropisms"—the involuntary, inner movements of the mind that guide our behavior. In the 1950s and 1960s Sarraute developed her ideas in *Portrait of a Man Unknown*, which Sartre described as an anti-novel. It explores the relationship between a father and daughter but the narrator's observations change constantly and are unreliable. Sarraute was awarded the *Prix international de litterature* in 1963 for her novel *The Golden Fruits,* which brought her wider public attention. **HJ**

RIGHT: Sarraute photographed in a thoughtful mood in 1986.

ANDRÉ MALRAUX

Born: November 3, 1901 (Paris, France); died November 23, 1976 (Paris, France).

Style and genre: Novelist, art critic, and pro-Gaullist politician, Malraux's life and work illustrated his two core passions: taking bold political action and exploring aesthetic ideas.

Signature titles

Novels

The Conquerors (*Les Conquérants*), 1928

The Royal Way (*La Voie Royale*), 1930

Man's Fate (*La Condition Humaine*), 1933

Days of Hope (*L'Espoir*), 1937

The Walnut Trees of Altenburg (*Les Noyers d'Altenburg*), 1943

Nonfiction

The Voices of Silence (*Les Voix du silence*), 1951

The Imaginary Museum of World Sculpture (*La Musée imaginaire de la sculpture mondiale*), 1952–1954 (three volumes; translated later as *Museum Without Walls*, 1967)

Autobiography

Anti-memoirs (*Antimémoires*), 1967

A charismatic man of extraordinary intellect and energy, Malraux cemented his place at the forefront of French literary life with his prize-winning novel, *Man's Fate*. To Malraux, the human condition was essentially a somewhat wretched and lonely affair, but he believed that salvation came through joining with others in direct political involvement and also through creativity. Action-filled but questioning novels such as the earlier *The Conquerors* and the later *Days of Hope* directly reflect Malraux's hands-on participation in revolutionary activities in the Far East and Spain during the 1920s and 1930s. From the 1940s, Malraux turned increasingly to writings on art, producing his masterpiece *The Voices of Silence*. **AK**

JOHN STEINBECK

Born: February 27, 1902 (Salinas, California, U.S.); died December 20, 1968 (Sag Harbor, New York, U.S.).

Style and genre: Steinbeck's naturalistic novels often focused on agricultural laborers, the Great Depression, and themes from myths and the Old Testament.

One of the great U.S. writers and winner of the Nobel Prize for Literature, Steinbeck's social novels perfectly captured the hardships endured by workers during the Great Depression. He studied at Stanford University but left for New York before graduating, trying to establish himself as a freelance writer. He returned to California, writing short stories and working as a manual laborer, witnessing firsthand those people who would later become the subject of his most successful works. Such experiences lent authenticity to Steinbeck's documentary intensity and his depiction of agricultural laborers who would later brave starvation and unemployment.

In 1929 he had his first novel, *Cup of Gold*, published, but it was not until the release of *Tortilla Flat* in 1935 that Steinbeck received critical and commercial success. The novel dealt sympathetically with illegal Mexican immigrants in California with an earthy humor interwoven with the story of the knights of King Arthur from British myth. The mood in the trio of works that followed became markedly darker. With *In Dubious Battle, Of Mice and Men*, and *The Grapes of Wrath*, Steinbeck tackled

Signature Titles

Novels

The Pastures of Heaven, 1932
Tortilla Flat, 1935
In Dubious Battle, 1936
Of Mice and Men, 1937
The Grapes of Wrath, 1939
The Sea of Cortez, 1941
The Moon is Down, 1942
Cannery Row, 1945
The Wayward Bus, 1947
The Pearl, 1947
East of Eden, 1952
The Short Reign of Pippin IV, 1957
The Winter of Our Discontent, 1961

ABOVE: John Steinbeck photographed in the 1960s, toward the end of his life.

RIGHT: A photograph of the novelist with a companion in Venice, Italy, in 1952.

the issues of displaced workers searching in vain for a slice of the "American Dream" while battling the unjust working conditions to which they were subjected. *The Grapes of Wrath*, arguably Steinbeck's greatest literary feat, tells the story of Oklahoma tenant farmers unable to make a living in the dust bowl, who are forced to migrate to California, and their subsequent exploitation at the hands of the plantation owners and harassment from the police. The aggressive mixture of proletarian characters and political radicalism caused uproar upon its release as conservative observers criticized the socialist theorizing and anti-capitalist messages that emanated from the novel. Despite the banning of the book in several parts of the country it became a best seller and later a celebrated Hollywood film.

Steinbeck withdrew from writing to explore his fascination with marine life before serving as a war correspondent for the *New York Herald Tribune* in World War II. His postwar works became less harsh in their social criticism, but in *East of Eden* he delivered a novel of staggering ambition that draws many parallels with the biblical story of Cain and Abel. His books continue to be key texts in U.S. schools. **SG**

ABOVE LEFT: The cast of the acclaimed movie *The Grapes of Wrath* (1940).

ABOVE: The dust jacket for the 1947 edition of the best-selling novel *Of Mice and Men*.

Steinbeck on Screen

Steinbeck's work received numerous Hollywood treatments:

- *The Grapes of Wrath*—Directed by the legendary John Ford, for which he won an Academy Award for Directing, and starring a young Henry Fonda, John Carradine, and Jane Darwell, who won Best Supporting Actress.
- *Of Mice and Men*—The 1939 adaptation starring Lon Chaney Jr. and Burgess Meredith received four Oscar nominations.
- *East of Eden*—Directed by Elia Kazan and forever immortalized as one of the few screen appearances by James Dean.
- *O. Henry's Full House*—Five separate screenplays all narrated by Steinbeck, who made a rare appearance in front of the camera to introduce each film.

CARLO LEVI

Born: November 29, 1902 (Turin, Italy); died January 4, 1975 (Rome, Italy).

Style and genre: A writer, painter, essayist, and political activist, Levi wrote sympathetically of society's disenfranchised and forgotten in a style that put him at the forefront of Italian neorealism.

Signature titles

Novels

Christ Stopped at Eboli—The Story of a Year (*Cristo si è fermato a Eboli*), 1945

The Watch: A Novel (*L'orologio*), 1950

Nonfiction

Fear of Freedom (*Paura della libertà*), 1946

Words are Stones: Impressions of Sicily (*Le parole sono pietre*), 1955

Carlo Levi was an intellectual engaged on several fronts, making it difficult to tell which one was his main focus. Above all, though, he was a writer whose book *Christ Stopped at Eboli* garnered international praise. The story is set in southern Italy, during the days of Levi's confinement at the hands of the ruling fascist party. In fact, he adopted a firm stance against Mussolini's regime, continually fighting for society's and individual freedom. This "expressionist" inclination for protest also revealed itself in his forays into the visual arts. He painted haunted figures suffering abuse, strongly influenced by an existentialist philosophy whose proponents challenge a more materialistic and hollow way of life. **FF**

LANGSTON HUGHES

Born: James Mercer Langston Hughes, February 1, 1902 (Joplin, Missouri, U.S.); died May 22, 1967 (New York, New York, U.S.).

Style and genre: Hughes's work was influenced by and reflected the emergence of jazz, and depicted the life of African-Americans in rich, evocative language.

Signature titles

Novel

Not Without Laughter, 1930

Poetry

The Weary Blues, 1926

Shakespeare in Harlem, 1942

Montage of a Dream Deferred, 1951

Play

Black Nativity, 1961

Langston Hughes was one of the leading poets writing during the Harlem Renaissance in New York, whose work captured the turbulence of the times within black culture and life. Jazz music, in particular, profoundly affected his work, especially seen in *Montage of a Dream Deferred*, a volume of poetry that is now considered among his best. Hughes's work expressed the social trials and triumphs of black Americans living through changing times, concentrating on the working classes. In 1926, he published the important essay "The Negro Artist and the Racial Mountain" in *The Nation*, a political and cultural journal. Powerfully worded and expressively put, this essay came to be seen as a manifesto for Hughes and his contemporaries. **TamP**

ISAAC BASHEVIS SINGER

Born: November 21, 1902 (exact date debated; in Russian Poland); died July 24, 1991 (Miami, Florida, U.S.).

Style and genre: Written in Yiddish, Singer's novels and short stories preserved the memory of pre-Holocaust Jewry in Eastern Europe.

Both the place and the date of Singer's birth are disputed, but he grew up mainly in Warsaw and apparently dated his birth to July 14, 1904 to make himself younger and avoid conscription. His father was a rabbi, his mother a rabbi's daughter, and his brother and eldest sister were also writers. Singer decided not to follow in his father's footsteps and in 1935, after starting his writing career in Warsaw after World War I, he emigrated to the United States and settled in New York as a writer for a Yiddish-language newspaper. He began to pour out a stream of novels and short stories, which quickly gained attention and were particularly admired. His work was almost entirely in Yiddish, but he oversaw the English translations, which made his reputation and won him the Nobel Prize for Literature in 1978.

Imbued with humanity and humor, Singer's output was inspired by his memories of his youth and by traditional Jewish piety, legends, and folkore. Novels such as *The Family Moskat*, *The Manor,* and *The Estate* told the stories of Jewish families over several generations and the changes that destroyed the Jewish world of the late nineteenth century. In an interview in 1979 he said he thought that something of that vanished world, "call it spirit or whatever," was "still somewhere in the universe." He also drew on his own personal experience to write about the world of immigrants coming to America. One of his recurring themes was the link between the tyranny of human passions and their creative power. In addition, *Schlemiel Went to Warsaw* is an especially delightful collection of stories for children and *A Day of Pleasure* is an autobiographical account of his Warsaw childhood. **RC**

"God is a writer and we are both the heroes and the readers."

Signature titles

Novels

The Family Moskat, 1950

The Manor, 1967

The Estate, 1969

The Golem, 1983

Short stories

Schlemiel Went to Warsaw and Other Stories, 1968

The Image and Other Stories, 1985

The Death of Methuselah and Other Stories, 1988

Autobiography

A Day of Pleasure: Stories of a Boy Growing Up in Warsaw, 1969

Lost in America, 1981

1900–19

ABOVE: Singer photographed in New York, five years before his death.

GEORGE ORWELL

Born: Eric Arthur Blair, June 25, 1903 (Motihari, Bihar, India); died January 21, 1950 (London, England).

Style and genre: A leftist intellectual and prolific writer of allegory, political memoir, and eyewitness journalism, Orwell joined literary craft to political purpose.

George Orwell was born into a family he described as "lower-upper-middle English class." He reacted to the inequities of social immobility in his youth by becoming a vocal advocate for the breakdown of class barriers. He graduated from Eton without the funds to go to university and joined the Indian Imperial Police in Burma, acquiring an extreme dislike of imperialism. On returning to England, he chose to live in poverty among the working class and the homeless, whom he wrote about. In *Down and Out in Paris and London*, Orwell documents toiling for poor wages in the kitchens of Paris hotels, before running aground on the shoals of another kind of despair, jobless among the "tramps" in London. It was likely during these years that Orwell contracted the tuberculosis that would eventually kill him.

Homage to Catalonia documents Orwell's experience as a volunteer in the Spanish Civil War. It exposes the deep economic and ideological divisions among soldiers on the left. Orwell was sensitive to the problematic impact of "soldier-intellectuals" such as W. H. Auden, whom he accused of romanticizing the war. His form of dissident socialism has caused him to be used as a political cudgel by both left-wing and right-wing groups. In 1997, a *Guardian* article revealed that Orwell had provided a list of names of Stalinist sympathizers to an intelligence officer in the year before his death. Eyewitness journalism attracted Orwell as a counterweight to propaganda. His trust in visuality over the written word carries over to his anti-Soviet allegory, *Animal Farm*. Longing for the future is a powerful weapon of resistance for the animals because it resides in mental images and thus falls outside of language and political rhetoric.

In *Nineteen Eighty-Four*, human decency has disappeared alongside memory, and the emotions that bind people to one another have been channeled into fear. Orwell's foreboding and most powerful novel describes the extreme consequences

Signature titles

Novels

Burmese Days, 1934

Animal Farm, 1945

Nineteen Eighty-Four, 1949

Nonfiction

Down and Out in Paris and London, 1933

The Road to Wigan Pier, 1937

Homage to Catalonia, 1938

Collected Essays, Letters and Journalism, 1968

ABOVE: The novelist and journalist photographed in the early 1940s.

87.

... from his arm. NP.

On the one hand she took it for granted that nearly everyone, at any rate nearly everyone who was not in a privileged position, secretly hated the Party & would break the rules if it were safe to do so: on the other hand she refused to believe in the existence of any widespread, organised opposition. The talk on the telescreens about Goldstein & his conspiracy, she said, was simply a lot of rubbish that you had to pretend to believe in. In reality, there was no such conspiracy. Times beyond number, at Party rallies & spontaneous demonstrations, she had signed petitions & helped to pass unanimous resolutions demanding sterner measures against the thought-criminals & saboteurs. She had shouted at the top of her voice for the execution of people whose names she had never heard & in whose supposed crimes she had not the faintest belief. When public trials were happening, she had taken her place in the detachments from the Youth League who ~~stood all day~~ surrounded the courts from morning to night, chanting at intervals "Death to the traitors!" During the Two Minutes Hate she always excelled all others in shouting insults at Goldstein. Yet she had only a dim idea of who Goldstein was & what doctrine he was supposed to represent. Having grown up since the Revolution, she was not able to think in terms of political movements or concerted insurrections. She started out with the assumption that the Party would always exist & would always be the same. Your job was to get your own back on it in your own individual way. Rebellion either meant breaking the rules successfully, or it meant committing isolated acts of violence, such as killing somebody or blowing something up. //

(cont. p. 153)

ABOVE: Orwell's experience in the Indian Imperial police inspired his 1934 novel.

LEFT: An excerpt from the uncorrected manuscript of *Nineteen Eighty-Four*.

of curtailing freedoms of the press and speech: language and literature are subordinated to politics, and freedom of thought becomes impossible, as the protagonist's doomed struggle for self-expression and human contact shows. The totalitarian government of the novel is general enough that it can be read as a representation of both fascist and socialist dictatorships.

Decades after Orwell's vision of the future, international news and war reportage are as one-sided as ever. Orwell's unnerving legacy leaves us questioning to what degree our own freedom is mired in doublethink. **ER**

EVELYN WAUGH

Born: Arthur Evelyn St. John Waugh, October 28, 1903 (London, England); died April 10, 1966 (Combe Florey, Somerset, England).

Style and genre: Waugh was a novelist and travel writer whose work is wittily satirical with a darkly humorous edge.

Evelyn Waugh's comic genius has probably not been equaled in British literature. Born the upper-middle class son of a publisher, Waugh was educated at Lancing College and Oxford University. Between the two World Wars he socialized with the fast set on a merry-go-round of cocktail parties, mixing with families such as the Guinnesses, Asquiths, and Churchills. He enjoyed the hedonistic frenzy of the avant-garde populated by Robert Byron, Anthony Powell, and John Betjeman at a time when the Edwardian rules of the old order had disappeared and the bleakness of the 1930s was snapping at their heels.

Influenced by the camp Catholicism and wit of author Ronald Firbank, Waugh's first two novels, *Decline and Fall* and *Vile Bodies*, lampoon the decadence of high society and the private education system of which he was a part. A creator of absurdist plots and bungling characters, he captures the zeitgeist of the age with wry humor, exposing its hypocrisies and tempering his satire with a sense of decency informed by his own conversion to Roman Catholicism in 1930.

Waugh continued to examine the fading aristocracy's foibles masterfully in *A Handful of Dust* and *Brideshead Revisited*. He was not averse to turning his attention elsewhere, tackling the blunders of British colonialism in *Black Mischief* and parodying sensational journalism as never before in *Scoop*. Despite approaching middle age, Waugh took up the call to arms in World War II and saw active service. He later drew on his experiences in his *Sword of Honour* trilogy in which he turns his mordant humor to the rise of communism, the end of English gentlemanliness, and the horrors of war. Waugh died of a heart attack at his countryside home, still the master of farce. **CK**

Signature titles

Novels

Decline and Fall, 1928
Vile Bodies, 1930
Black Mischief, 1932
A Handful of Dust, 1934
Scoop, 1938
Put Out More Flags, 1942
Brideshead Revisited, 1945
The Loved One, 1948
Men at Arms, 1952
Officers and Gentlemen, 1955
Unconditional Surrender, 1961

"News is what a chap who doesn't care much about anything wants to read."—*Scoop*

ABOVE: The satirical novelist Evelyn Waugh photographed in 1943.

RAYMOND QUENEAU

Born: February 21, 1903 (Le Havre, France); died October 25, 1976 (Paris, France).

Style and genre: Raymond Queneau, the French poet and novelist, was a forerunner of postmodernism who played with language and used mathematics as an inspiration.

French novelist and poet Raymond Queneau was fascinated by language and by challenging the conventions of traditional spelling, style, and vocabulary. He often argued that the real subject of his work was not the stories he told, but the language itself.

His first novel, *The Bark Tree* (later renamed *Witch Grass*) was published in 1933 and was the story of a series of comic characters in Paris. It was notable for its use of slang and French as it was spoken by ordinary people.

Among his most important works is *Exercises in Style* in which the same story is retold in ninety-nine different ways—from an official letter, to a sonnet, to a publisher's blurb simply by altering the tone and style.

His most popular novel, *Zazie in the Metro*, was published in 1959 and also makes playful use of language. It tells the story of a young girl on a visit to see her uncle in Paris. She crosses the city and is involved in a complicated series of farcical events. It uses slang, swearwords, and phonetics. It was well received by the public who liked its playfulness and it was adapted for the stage, turned into a comic book, and was filmed by the French director Louis Malle.

In 1960, Queneau, who had always been interested in mathematics and the relation between mathematics and literature, collaborated with a number of writers and mathematicians to form the *Ouvroir de littérature potentielle* (OuLiPo) to experiment with writing under various constraints. Queneau used this technique to write *Hundred Thousand Billion Poems*—a book of ten sonnets in which each page is split into fourteen strips. He estimated it would take 200 million years to read all the possible combinations. **HJ**

"Religions tend to disappear with man's good fortune."

ABOVE: One of the leaders of the OuLiPo, Queneau was a constant innovator.

Signature titles

Novels

The Bark Tree (later renamed *Witch Grass) (Le Chiendent)*, 1933

We Always Treat Women Too Well (as Sally Mara) *(On est toujours trop bon avec les femmes)*, 1947

Exercises in Style (Exercises de style), 1947

Zazie in the Metro (Zazie dans le metro), 1959

The Blue Flowers (Les Fleurs bleues), 1965

The Flight of Icarus (Le Vol d'Icare), 1968

Poetry

Hundred Thousand Billion Poems (Cent mille milliards de poèmes), 1961

ANAÏS NIN

Born: February 21, 1903 (Neuilly, France); died January 14, 1977 (Los Angeles, California, U.S).

Style and genre: Nin was a French diarist and eroticist whose lifestyle was every bit as risqué as her novels and short stories.

Signature titles

Novels

House of Incest, 1936
Cities of the Interior
Children of the Albatross, 1947
The Four-Chambered Heart, 1950
A Spy in the House of Love, 1954
Ladders to Fire, 1959
Seduction of the Minotaur, 1961

Short stories

Under a Glass Bell, 1944
The Delta of Venus, 1978 (published posthumously)

Nonfiction

The Diary of Anaïs Nin Volumes 1–7 (published from 1966 to 1978)

Born to a Cuban father and a Danish mother, Anaïs Nin lived in different European locations before moving to New York with her mother and two brothers at the age of eleven. Her father, Joaquin, who she later alleged had fondled her as a child, abandoned the family at the same time. Her diaries, which were started at around this time, were to become her defining work: journals that, although extremely personal, speak in universal themes of womanhood and artistic ambition.

Nin married in 1923 and moved back to Paris with her husband, the banker Hugh Guiler. She began writing fiction and embarked on an affair with the writer Henry Miller, a passionate and long-lasting involvement that heavily influenced her own writing, particularly the astonishing *House of Incest*. A regular contributor of short stories to magazines, two anthologies were produced in Nin's lifetime, although the straightforwardly erotic pieces for which she is now better known were not anthologized until after her death. These erotic stories were originally written for a private collector in the 1940s, allegedly for a dollar per page.

The works published in her lifetime, including a series of novels in the 1940s and 1950s, are notable for their sensuality and strong female lead characters. Her writing no doubt drew on her own experience of extramarital affairs, to which her husband turned an indulgent blind eye, including a relationship with Rupert Pole that lasted twenty-five years. Nin eventually became a popular lecturer across the United States, tirelessly commuting between her husband in New York and her lover in California—until the end, the epitome and antithesis of the willful, independent woman that she so wanted to be. **PS**

"Love never dies a natural death. It dies because we don't know how to replenish its source."

ABOVE: Anaïs Nin photographed in Chicago, Illinois, c. 1972.

RIGHT: Nin's erotic stories, written during the 1940s, were not published until 1978.

DELTA OF VENUS

EROTICA BY ANAÏS NIN

ALAN PATON

Born: January 11, 1903 (Pietermaritzburg, KwaZulu-Natal, South Africa); died April 12, 1988 (Durban KwaZulu-Natal, South Africa).

Style and genre: Stylistically, Paton's writing is lyrical. Thematically, much of his work engages with issues of the racially charged relationships of apartheid South Africa.

Alan Paton spent his childhood watching the rights of South Africa's black majority dwindle while those of the white majority expanded—a situation that would inform his literature and politics. He was the founder and president of the Liberal Party that opposed South African apartheid, which, during his lifetime, was considered provocative by the racist government and inadequate by anti-apartheid activists.

Paton's most famous book, *Cry, the Beloved Country*, was influenced by another novel, Laurens van der Posts's *In a Province* (1934). It tells the story of a Zulu man who travels to Johannesburg in search of his only son, who, he discovers, has murdered the son of a white man. The two fathers connect because of the murder and strike up a kind of friendship. This interracial friendship headed a variety of responses to the novel, which changed with the tide of South African politics. A few months after its publication, the National Party came to power in South Africa, ushering in the apartheid era with it. In the year of Paton's death, *Cry, the Beloved Country* had sold over fifteen million copies and apartheid had been abolished.

Paton's Christian upbringing influenced his writing and much of his work has biblical resonance. He has also written biographies and autobiographies, perhaps fittingly, given that his canon amounts to a biography of South Africa during a crucial time in its history. Perhaps what is less well known is that Paton provided evidence to mitigate the sentencing of Nelson Mandela during his 1964 trial. Mandela later said of Paton that "*Cry, the Beloved Country* . . . is also a monument to the future. One of South Africa's leading humanists, Alan Paton vividly captured his eloquent faith in the essential goodness of people in his epic work." **JSD**

"To give up the task of reforming society is to give up one's responsibility as a free man."

Signature titles

Novels

Cry, the Beloved Country, 1948
Too Late the Phalarope, 1953
Instrument of Thy Peace, 1968
Case History of a Pinky, 1972
Ah, But Your Land is Beautiful, 1981
Save the Beloved Country, 1989

Short stories

Tales from a Troubled Land, 1961

Autobiography

Towards the Mountain, 1980
Journey Continued: An Autobiography, 1988

ABOVE: A press shot of South African writer Alan Paton taken in 1950.

GEORGES SIMENON

Born: February 13, 1903 (Liège, Belgium); died September 4, 1989 (Lausanne, Switzerland).

Style and genre: A prolific Belgian novelist and author of the Maigret detective series, Simenon's psychological novels are written in a direct, pared-down prose.

Georges Simenon learned his trade as a journalist on a local newspaper and as a writer of pseudonymous pulp fiction. His most famous creation, introspective Parisian police detective Commissaire Maigret, made his debut in 1930. Maigret was, in some ways, the opposite of his creator—a domesticated husband whereas Simenon was an epic womanizer—but shared the author's fascination with the psychology of murder. Simenon wrote large numbers of short, realist novels, typically describing emotional crises in the lives of outwardly dull "ordinary people." He published around 450 volumes of fiction. No single work stands superior to the rest, but most possess a disturbing insight into character and a sharp sense of atmosphere. **RG**

Signature titles

Novels

The Man Who Watched Trains Go By (*L'homme qui regardait passer les trains*), 1938

Three Beds in Manhattan (*Trois chambres à Manhattan*), 1946

The Stain on the Snow (*La neige était sale*), 1948

My Friend Maigret (*Mon ami Maigret*), 1949

The Clockmaker of Everton (*L'Horloger d'Everton*), 1954

The Little Man from Archangel (*Le Petit homme d'Arkhangelsk*), 1957

Maigret Has Scruples (*Les scrupules de Maigret*), 1958

Maigret in Court (*Maigret aux Assises*), 1960

The Train (*Le Train*), 1961

Maigret and the Ghost (*Maigret et le fantôme*), 1964

NANCY MITFORD

Born: Nancy Freeman-Mitford, November 28, 1904 (London, England); died June 30, 1973 (Versailles, Paris, France).

Style and genre: The prominent themes in Mitford's brilliantly witty writing include social mores and classes, and barely concealed autobiographical details.

Nancy Mitford was born into one of the most eccentric families in Britain. The daughter of Lord and Lady Redesdale, Nancy was one of six vastly different sisters: the others became a Nazi, a Moseleyite, a socialist, the Duchess of Devonshire, and a contented housewife. The sisters have been the subject of numerous dramas and their unusual aristocratic existence informed all of Nancy's works. She escaped the mayhem by moving to Paris and concentrating on her writing. Her books are still in print and remain literary favorites. They are keenly observed, witty, and clever, and have inspired generations of writers. Nancy's large circle of friends included Evelyn Waugh, and their correspondence has been published. **LH**

Signature titles

Novels

Highland Fling, 1931

Christmas Pudding, 1932

The Pursuit of Love, 1945

Love in a Cold Climate, 1949

Biographies

Madame de Pompadour, 1954

Voltaire in Love, 1957

The Sun King, 1966

Frederick the Great, 1970

PABLO NERUDA

Born: Neftalí Ricardo Reyes Basoalto, July 12, 1904 (Parral, Chile); died September 23, 1973 (Santiago, Chile).

Style and genre: Neruda's works are characterized by a voracious appetite for love, life, and language, and an unending capacity for invention and reinvention.

Signature titles

Poetry

Twenty Love Poems and a Song of Despair, 1924
Residence on Earth, 1947
The Heights of Macchu Picchu, 1947
Canto General, 1950
The Captain's Verses, 1952
Elemental Odes, 1957
100 Love Sonnets, 1960

Nonfiction

Memoirs, 1973

Neruda's output is staggering: more than fifty books, comprising some 3,500 pages of verse, selling perhaps more than a million copies, and translated into several dozen languages.

In the 1920s, Neruda quickly established a reputation as a lyricist of intensity and prodigious invention, publishing five volumes of verse by the age of twenty-two. His second book, *Twenty Love Poems and a Song of Despair*, was a popular success and became an instant "classic" for its elemental elegance, impossible tendernesses, and deep melancholy.

Lacking a steady income, in 1927 Neruda took a series of unpaid consulships in Asia. Over the next five years, he increasingly identified with the oppressed masses whose ancient cultures and contemporary ways of life he saw as being crushed by capitalism, corruption, and the colonial order. During these years he wrote *Residence on Earth*, at times an astounding and surrealistic expression of personal and collective anguish.

Further consulships in Spain and France put Neruda in contact with the Spanish avant-garde and the antifascist cause. With the outbreak of the Spanish Civil War in 1936, he worked

ABOVE: A portrait of the Chilean writer in London in 1965.

RIGHT: Neruda campaigning for president in Santiago, Chile, in 1969.

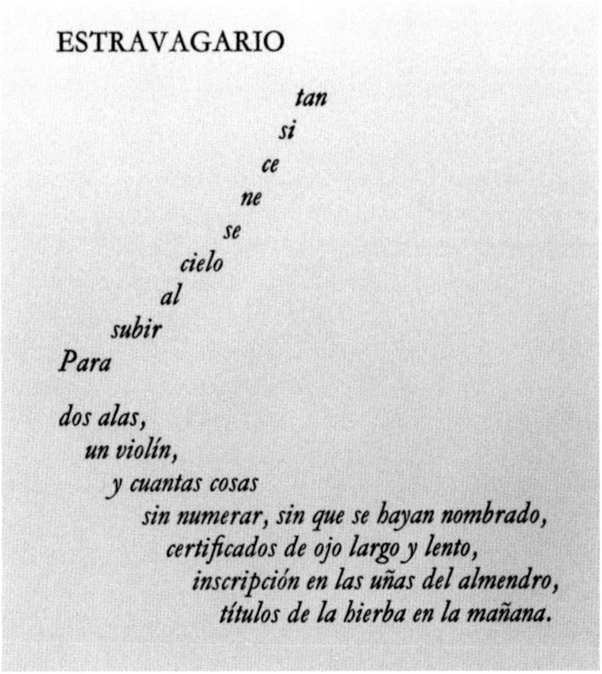

ESTRAVAGARIO

tan
si
ce
ne
se
cielo
al
subir
Para

dos alas,
un violín,
y cuantas cosas
sin numerar, sin que se hayan nombrado,
certificados de ojo largo y lento,
inscripción en las uñas del almendro,
títulos de la hierba en la mañana.

LEFT: The poem "Estravagario" (published in 1958) written in the form of a calligramme.

to mobilize support for the Republicans. In 1940, he began work on an epic poem detailing the flora and fauna, history, mythology, and political struggles of the Latin-American people. Inspired by the grandeur of pre-Columbian civilizations, in 1947 Neruda wrote the *Heights of Macchu Picchu*, later making the poem the centerpiece of his epic, *Canto General*.

In 1945, Neruda was elected a senator and joined the Communist Party. After criticizing the right-wing regime of President Videla, he went into hiding, later exile, to avoid arrest. By 1952, the climate had changed and Neruda returned to Chile, both wealthy and famous. His final decades were marked by conjugal happiness (with Matilde Urrutia), many voyages, and a prodigious output and reinvention. The works of this period are among Neruda's simplest and finest, and include *The Captain's Verses*, *Elemental Odes*, and *100 Love Sonnets*. He was awarded the Nobel Prize in 1971. **CH**

Hot Off the Press

Pablo Neruda's collection of militant verse, *Spain in My Heart* (1937), has one of the most unusual publishing histories of the century. Anonymous publication in Spain did not go unnoticed by the Chilean authorities and Neruda was promptly dismissed from his consulship. In October 1937, Neruda published the volume in Santiago to great success, selling out four editions by 1938. Later that year, an edition was published by Republican troops on the eastern front of the Spanish Civil War, using a mobile press and paper manufactured from old flags and uniforms.

ALEJO CARPENTIER

Born: December 26, 1904 (Lausanne, Switzerland); died April 24, 1980 (Paris, France).

Style and genre: Cuban novelist, musicologist, and inspiration to Latin American literature, Carpentier is believed to be the father of magical realism.

Alejo Carpentier grew up in a French-speaking household of comfort and cosmopolitanism. When his father disappeared in 1922, Carpentier left university for journalism, publishing in avant-garde journals, agitating against the dictator Machado, and promoting the nascent Afro-Cuban movement. Throughout his career, Carpentier would attempt to fuse these three strands—timeless cosmopolitanism, utopian politics, and deep knowledge of Latin America's black, indigenous, and colonial heritages—into a syncretic vision of Cuban identity.

In a round-up of dissidents in 1927, Carpentier was thrown in jail. Upon release he escaped to Paris, where he remained until 1939, apprenticing in surrealism and researching Latin American ethnology. His first major work was *Music in Cuba*, a pioneering cultural history and comprehensive account of Cuban identity, tracing five centuries of Euro-African musicology. This was followed by *The Kingdom of this World*, a kaleidoscopic narrative of the Haitian Revolution (1791–1804) and its aftermath, both recounting and enacting the interpenetration of political events and religious beliefs—what Carpentier called "the marvelous real." Resident in Caracas between 1945 and 1959, during the years of Venezuela's oil-financed "progress," Carpentier worked in advertising and radio, and made trips to the Amazon. These polarities animate his 1953 masterpiece, *The Lost Steps*, concerning a disaffected New York musicologist who discovers the true roots of postindustrial man in a magical transformative process. Perhaps his finest work is the sumptuous *Explosion in a Cathedral*, a Goya-inspired account of the arrival of Enlightenment, and the guillotine, in the Caribbean, and a veiled history of the twentieth century. **CH**

"New worlds had to be lived before they could be analyzed."—*The Lost Steps*

Signature titles

Novels

The Kingdom of this World, 1949

The Lost Steps, 1953

The Chase, 1956

The War of Time, 1958

Explosion in a Cathedral, 1962

Concierto Barroco, 1974

Reasons of State, 1974

The Harp and the Shadow, 1979

Nonfiction

Music in Cuba, 1946

ABOVE: The Cuban writer, essayist, and musicologist photographed in 1976.

RIGHT: Carpentier at a book signing on March 19, 1976.

GRAHAM GREENE

Born: Henry Graham Greene, October 2, 1904 (Berkhamsted, England); died April 3, 1991 (Vevey, Switzerland).

Style and genre: Greene was an English novelist concerned with ambivalent moral and political issues and the overriding influence of Roman Catholic teachings.

Greene managed that rarest of feats of combining huge popularity with critical acclaim. His novels are thrillers heavily laden with politics, crime, and intrigue, exploring questions of twentieth-century morality. The masterful control of tension, realistic dialogue, and gripping storytelling captivates audiences and lends a cinematic quality to his work, resulting in many of his novels making a successful translation to film.

The modest success of his first novel, *The Man Within* (1929), encouraged Greene to quit his job at *The Times*. His next two books sank without a trace, but he found success with *Stamboul Train* (1932). This compelling mix of thriller and murder-mystery, interlaced with a sharp moral and philosophical subtext, has been attributed to Greene's conversion to Catholicism. Questions of faith play a central role in *Brighton Rock*. The main character, the violent gang leader Pinkie Brown, is a Roman Catholic defeated by a combination of his own dedication to evil and eternal damnation and persistent hounding by the cheerful, kindhearted Ida Turner, who, though not religious, has a strong moral sensibility. There is little

Signature titles

Novels

Brighton Rock, 1938
The Power and the Glory, 1940
The Ministry of Fear, 1943
The Heart of the Matter, 1948
The End of the Affair, 1951
The Quiet American, 1956
Our Man in Havana, 1958
A Burnt-Out Case, 1961
The Comedians, 1966
The Honorary Consul, 1973
The Human Factor, 1978

ABOVE: A late photo of thriller and murder-mystery writer Graham Greene.

RIGHT: Greene pictured drinking with the film director Carol Reed in 1951.

LEFT: The 1961 cover of *A Burnt-Out Case*, published by William Heinemann, London.

ambiguity in the Catholic theme pervading *The Power and the Glory*, seen by many as Greene's finest literary achievement. The story of a nameless "whiskey priest" in rural Mexico, where the Catholic Church has been outlawed, it is a brutal exposure of man's weakness and the redemptive powers of religion.

Travel inspired much of Greene's later work. While working for the Foreign Office in Sierra Leone during World War II, he wrote *The Heart of the Matter*. In *The Quiet American* (set in Vietnam), *Our Man in Havana* (Cuba), and *A Burnt-Out Case* (Belgian Congo), the omnipresent battle between good and evil for the individual resides against a backdrop of squalid locations, laced with danger and political espionage. **SG**

Shirley Is Innocent

In 1937, Graham Greene caused uproar when his critical review of *Wee Willie Winkie* claimed that the young Shirley Temple displayed in her performance "a certain adroit coquetry which appealed to middle-aged men." The subsequent libel lawsuit brought by Twentieth Century Fox against the *Night and Day* publication resulted in its closure, yet it has remained a secret for seventy years that Greene was forced to flee Britain to avoid potential imprisonment. As a country without extradition, Mexico was the chosen destination. The rest, as they say, is history.

JEAN-PAUL SARTRE

Born: Jean-Paul Charles Aymard Sartre, June 21, 1905 (Paris, France); died April 15, 1980 (Paris, France).

Style and genre: Sartre expounded his ideas in various literary forms and centered on the notion that the individual has absolute freedom of choice.

One of the giants of twentieth-century philosophy, Sartre's influence on modern thought has been immense. As he describes in his short but stunning autobiography *Words*, he was the son of a naval officer, whose early death landed him in the care of his young mother and grandparents. His grandfather doted on the young Sartre and as an educationalist was proud to see him develop into a precocious, if rather affected, reader. Even at an early age, Sartre had resolved to be a writer.

Sartre specialized in philosophy at the École Normale Supérieure, where he met the feminist writer Simone de Beauvoir, with whom he developed a lifelong romantic and intellectually fruitful attachment. He served a period of military service, but was later taken prisoner when the Germans overran France. His experience of World War II helped to form some of the moral thinking from which his later more influential writing developed.

Sartre's philosophical doctrines are explored across a large and varied oeuvre that includes novels, short stories, plays, articles, and pamphlets, as well as his more esoteric academic

Signature titles

Philosophical works

Being and Nothingness (*L'Être et le néant*), 1943

Critique of Dialectical Reason (*Critique de la raison dialectique*), 1960

Novels

Nausea (*La Nausée*), 1938

The Age of Reason (*L'Âge de raison*), 1945

The Reprieve (*Le Sursis*), 1947

Iron in the Soul (*La Mort dans l'âme*), 1949

Autobiography

Words (*Les Mots*), 1964

Plays

The Flies (*Les Mouches*), 1943

No Exit (*Huis Clos*), 1945

Literary criticism

What is Literature? (*Qu'est-ce que la littérature?*), 1948

ABOVE: Jean-Paul Sartre photographed in Paris in 1971.

RIGHT: Sartre and André Gide relaxing in Cuverville, France, in 1945.

LEFT: Gerard Fromanger's 1976 portrait of Sartre from the series "Splendours II."

publications. His existential and phenomenological sympathies are explored in his novel *Nausea*, in which he traces his hero's responses to the absurdity and contingency of life. He further explores these ideas in his semi-autobiographical trilogy of novels known together as *The Roads to Freedom* (1945–1949). Set in postwar Paris, the trilogy revolves around the life of Mathieu, a philosophy teacher, and his group of friends. His best known philosophical work is *Being and Nothingness*, in which he explores the relationship of the individual's consciousness to the world around him. Sartre was offered the Nobel Prize for Literature in 1964 but turned it down, in a typical display of political resistance. **GM**

Set Yourself Free

Sartre was committed to communicating to as large an audience as possible, his message being that individuals should take action to further both personal and human freedoms. Like other existentialists, he placed the individual at the forefront of his philosophy, emphasizing the phenomenological notion that all experience is subjective and capable of being altered by an effort of will. He sought to warn of the *mauvaise foi* (bad faith) by which we delude ourselves into believing that our choices are restricted by circumstances and that we are therefore not to blame for our actions.

ELIAS CANETTI

Born: July 25, 1905 (Rustchuk [present-day Ruse], Bulgaria); died August 13, 1994 (Zurich, Switzerland).

Style and genre: A novelist and playwright, Canetti was fascinated by the psychology of crowds and the twin human longing for (and need to obey) power.

The son of a businessman descended from Spanish Jews, Elias Canetti grew up speaking Ladino, the Jewish variety of Spanish, and Bulgarian. He learned English as a boy when the family moved to Manchester, England, and German when he and his mother settled in Vienna in 1913, after his father's death. Educated in Zurich and Frankfurt, Canetti was awarded a doctorate in chemistry at Vienna University and it was in German that he wrote his novels and plays. Getting caught up in angry mobs rioting through the streets in Vienna in the 1920s made a horrifying impression on him and inspired his 1935 novel, *The Deception*, which dealt with "the human comedy of madness." Banned by the Nazis, the story focused on the plight of the individual in a world that had fallen to pieces around him and with which it no longer seemed possible to get to grips in conventional fiction.

In 1938, Canetti left Vienna and journeyed to Paris. He then moved to England and settled in London where he remained for most of the rest of his life. He had intended to write more novels, but he abandoned fiction and instead devoted himself to researching the behavior of crowds. He also studied the psychology and tempting allure of fascism, which he believed could only be understood through scientific approaches. His study *Crowds and Power*, in which he maintained that society's fundamental need was "the humanization of power," was the first product of these labors and, although criticized as not adequately rigorous in scientific terms, the work was credited with a compelling force. Later in the 1960s, Canetti published selections from his notes in *The Human Province* and subsequently wrote three volumes of autobiography. **RC**

"All the things one has forgotten scream for help in dreams."—*The Human Province*

Signature titles

Novel

The Deception (*Die Blendung*), 1935

Nonfiction

Crowds and Power (*Masse und Macht*),1960

The Human Province (*Die Provinz des Menschen*), 1973

Play

Dramen, 1964

Memoirs

The Tongue Set Free (*Die gerettete Zunge*), 1977

The Torch in the Ear (*Die Fackel im Ohr*), 1980

The Play of the Eyes (*Das Augenspiel*), 1985

ABOVE: A December 1983 photograph of Elias Canetti in Zurich.

VASSILY GROSSMAN

Born: December 12, 1905 (Berdichev, Ukraine); died September 14, 1964 (Moscow, Russia).

Style and genre: Grossman's masterpiece *Life and Fate*, a searing epic of life in Soviet Russia, was deemed by the Kremlin as too dangerous to be read.

Vassily Grossman trained as an engineer but turned to full-time writing in 1930. At the outbreak of World War II he became a correspondent in Stalingrad for the Red Army newspaper. His eyewitness accounts of the horrors of battle made him a national icon and he followed the Red Army to the death camp in Treblinka and then on to Hitler's bunker.

After the war, Grossman took part in the *Black Book*, a project organized by the Jewish Anti-Fascist Committee to document the Holocaust. It was suppressed by the Soviet government and led Grossman to question his loyalty to the state. This, together with his wartime experiences and his growing bitterness about life in Soviet Russia, culminated in his novel *Life and Fate* written in the 1950s. It has been described as the *War and Peace* of the twentieth century and is a sweeping epic with a huge cast of characters. Its central tenet is that even under a totalitarian regime, the human spirit cannot be crushed.

It is a theme that Grossman returned to in his next novel *Forever Flowing*. However, he did not see either of them published in his lifetime. Grossman submitted *Life and Fate* for publication in 1960 and was told by the Kremlin it could not be published for two hundred years because it was deemed too dangerous. The KGB destroyed his manuscripts, copies, and notebooks, but one copy survived and was smuggled to Switzerland. Grossman died in 1964, never knowing whether his work would be read. *Life and Fate* was published in Switzerland in 1980, in English in 1985, and finally became available in Russia in 1988, with *Forever Flowing* published there the following year. *Life and Fate* is now considered a masterpiece of twentieth-century fiction. **HJ**

"'Soviet Realism' was just as imaginary as the romances of the 18th century."—*Forever Flowing*

Signature titles

Nonfiction

A Writer at War: A Soviet Journalist with the Red Army, 1941–1945

Novels

Life and Fate, 1980

Forever Flowing, 1989

ABOVE: A sepia image of Vassily Grossman taken in 1945.

ANTHONY POWELL

Born: December 21, 1905 (London, England); died March 28, 2000 (Frome, England).

Style and genre: Powell is best known for his twelve-volume sequence *A Dance to the Music of Time*, distinguished by its dry wit, rich cast of characters, and subtly oblique and allusive web of narrative.

Anthony Powell made a small but distinct impression on the British literary scene in the 1930s as the author of five sardonic, modernist novels that pointedly ignore the earnest social and political concerns of the era. Although often deliriously funny, these works are savage and sad in their depiction of wearying parties, mechanical sexual encounters, and the friction of human egotism in the absence of either pleasure or feeling.

After a decade's break from fiction, Powell embarked on the monumental *A Dance to the Music of Time* sequence of novels, on which his reputation inevitably depends. The narrator of *Dance* follows a path through life identical to that of its author: the son of an undistinguished army officer, he was educated at Eton and Oxford and spent the interwar years in London, drifting between seedy nightclubs and stuffy drawing rooms. He married into an eccentric aristocratic family, served in the army during World War II, and enjoyed a growing literary reputation after the war. The function of the narrator is not so much to experience as to observe. Through his ironic, detached consciousness, we watch a swarming cast of characters meet and diverge, converse and copulate, prosper and decline.

Powell's autobiography and the diaries he published late in life project an image of the author as a crusty upper-middle-class conservative, which has tended to obscure the aesthetic radicalism of his work as a novelist. *Dance* is sometimes characterized as "social comedy," but although often low key and consistently funny, the series is overall far darker and more artistically ambitious than that term suggests.

The authors Powell himself most admired were not Austen or Trollope, but Dostoevsky, Proust, and Balzac. Formally innovative and unflinchingly committed to an ideal of literary excellence, Powell should be recognized as the most interesting native English novelist of the twentieth century. **RG**

Signature titles

Novels

Afternoon Men, 1931
Venusberg, 1932
From a View to a Death, 1934
Agents and Patients, 1936
What's Become of Waring, 1939
A Dance to the Music of Time
A Question of Upbringing, 1951
A Buyer's Market, 1952
The Acceptance World, 1955
At Lady Molly's, 1957
Casanova's Chinese Restaurant, 1960
The Kindly Ones, 1962
The Valley of Bones, 1964
The Soldier's Art, 1966
The Military Philosophers, 1968
Books Do Furnish a Room, 1971
Temporary Kings, 1973
Hearing Secret Harmonies, 1975

ABOVE: Powell at home in Frome, near Somerset, England, December 28, 1983.

RIGHT: The twelfth book in the *Dance* series, published by Heinemann, London, 1975.

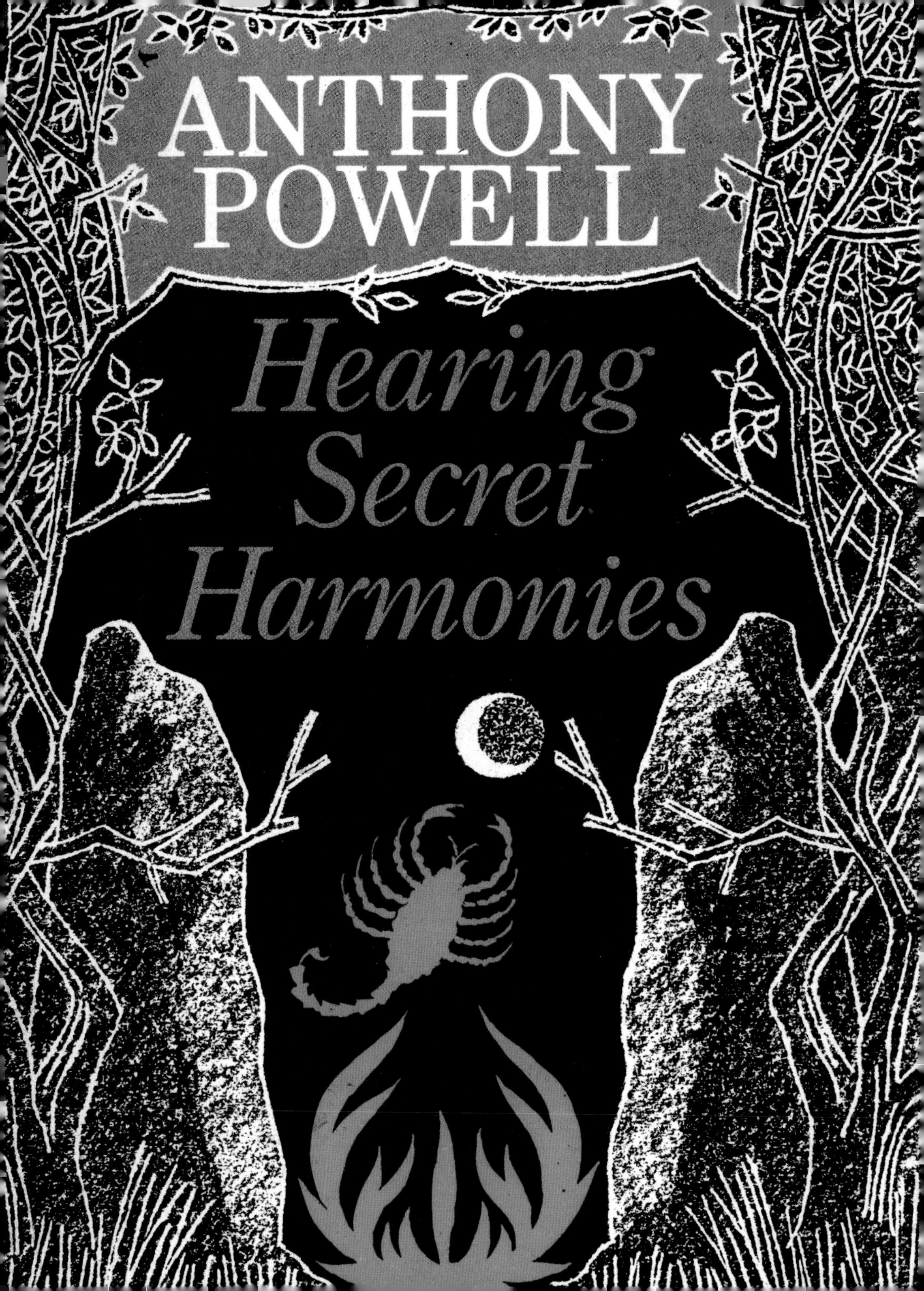
ANTHONY
POWELL
Hearing
Secret
Harmonies

DINO BUZZATI

Born: October 16, 1906 (Belluno, Italy); died January 28, 1972 (Milan, Italy).

Style and genre: Buzzati was an Italian fantasy writer who explored the uncanny nature of human existence using a broad range of experimental forms and techniques, including fairy tales, comic books, and science fiction.

Signature titles

Novels

Barnabò of the Mountains (*Barnabò delle montagne*), 1933

The Tartar Steppe (*Il deserto dei Tartari*), 1940

Larger Than Life (*Il grande ritratto*), 1960

A Love Affair (*Un amore*), 1963

Short stories

Sixty Stories (*Sessanta racconti*), 1958

Earthly Chronicles (*Cronache Terrestre*), 1972

Illustrated works

The Famous Invasion of the Bears in Sicily (*La famosa invasione degli orsi in Sicilia*), 1945

Comic Strip Poem (*Poema a fumetti*), 1969

Dino Buzzati worked for most of his life as a journalist in Milan, yet his imagination repeatedly returned to the strange mountainous landscapes of his childhood. His novels take their characters on psychological expeditions through those bleak, beautiful surroundings, a motif that has led to comparisons with Kafka. Although Buzzati lived through political turmoil in Italy, he never asserted his political allegiances. His literature has an escapist bent and takes place on the social margins; in *The Tartar Steppe*, Giovanni Drogo waits a lifetime at a lonely border fort for an invading army that never arrives. Buzzati was never afraid to query and disrupt literary borders, experimenting widely with different styles and genres. **TM**

WILLIAM EMPSON

Born: September 27, 1906 (Yorkshire, England); died April 15, 1984 (London, England).

Style and genre: Empson was a sagelike English poet and critic whose witty and intricate exploration of ambiguities reflected his passion for argument.

Signature titles

Poetry

Poems, 1934

The Gathering Storm, 1940

Literary criticism

Seven Types of Ambiguity, 1930

Some Versions of Pastoral, 1935

The Structure of Complex Words, 1951

Milton's God, 1961

To friends, Empson was as notorious for the disorderliness of his personal life as for his well-ordered poems. He was an undergraduate prodigy—he began *Seven Types of Ambiguity* aged twenty-two—but was expelled from Cambridge University when a cleaner found contraceptives in his room (a shocking find in 1929). Empson lived a peripatetic life, much of it in China, while he composed the pioneering works of criticism and poetry that made him a leading figure in the Auden generation. (Winston Churchill borrowed one of Empson's titles, *The Gathering Storm*, for a volume of his Nobel Prize–winning history of World War II.) In later life, Empson wrote impassioned attacks on Christian belief and morality. **MS**

MARIO SOLDATI

Born: November 11, 1906 (Turin, Italy); died June 19, 1999 (Tellaro, La Spezia, Italy).

Style and genre: Writer, director, scriptwriter, and essayist, Soldati was at home in many mediums, but his work often touched on the theme of the "other"—a general sense of dislocation and detachment from life.

Among the Italian intellectuals of the twentieth century, Mario Soldati is one of the most complex and difficult to define. His multifaceted work ranged from playwriting to directing films; from writing narratives to conducting inquests on television; and from essayist discourses to reports on trifling current events. His language became drier the graver the subject matter, making any kind of incident sound as though it demanded a joke. A minimalist, you could say.

The risk of having such an extensive range of artistic outlets is for his work to seem fragmentary and dispersed, yet his numerous contributions in various artistic fields always boiled down to one very contemporary topic: the "other." For Soldati the "other" meant many things: the impossibility of definitively planting roots and settling down; the inability to surrender to the routines of work and emotional life; and on a deeper psychological level it gives expression to the urges of the unconscious, the forgotten, to those areas deep in the brain where reason cannot penetrate. This is why, in Soldati's writings, there are no protagonists who are able to escape the anguish of dealing with the ghosts of their past or of trying to understand the urges of their unconscious minds. None of his characters are able to escape making a "confession." His protagonists are made to reassess their own existence through nationalizations that approach the "nausea" of Sartre and the "indifference" of Moravia. And even when the escape (a recurrent word in Soldati's works) materializes into a trip to the United States (one of the author's favorite countries), Soldati is drawn to the unforeseen and the unpredictable—by an "other" that finds its ideal expression in the theme of wandering. **FF**

"The feverish desire to leave at all costs, for no reason, burned him like a fire."—*The Two Cities*

Signature titles

Nonfiction

America First Love (America primo amore), 1935

Novels

Dinner with the Commendatore (A cena col commendatore), 1950

The Capri Letters (Le lettere da Capri), 1955

The Confession (La confessione), 1956

The Emerald: A Novel (Lo smeraldo), 1974

The Fire (L'incendio), 1981

1900–19

ABOVE: A portrait of Soldati in the 1980s wearing his trademark bow tie.

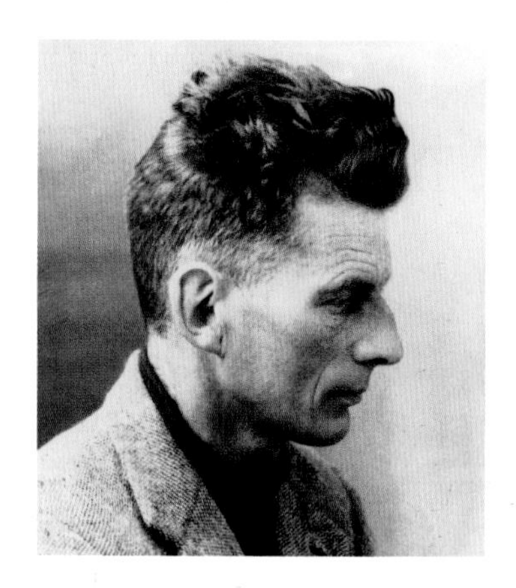

SAMUEL BECKETT

Born: Samuel Barclay Beckett, April or May 13, 1906 (Foxrock, Ireland); died December 22, 1989 (Paris, France).

Style and genre: Beckett's work expresses the loneliness and anguish of the human condition. His minimalist style is full of black humor about life's bleakness.

Samuel Beckett's writing is more often thought to articulate the perils of the "human condition" than to reflect his life specifically. Yet the mystery surrounding his experience as a courier in Nazi-occupied France and his friendship with Irish writer James Joyce have deeply contributed to the bleakness and confusion that are signatories of his writing style, particularly in the later and best known works.

Beckett was born in the Dublin district of Stillorgan. Although his birth certificate records his birth on May 13, 1906, Beckett claimed that he was actually born on Good Friday, April 13, 1906. Whether he intentionally changed the date of his birth inspires much speculation. He once said that he "likes all these lies and legends—the more there are, the more interesting I become." His early life was sheltered from the events of World War I. He passed his time reading in the countryside, swimming, riding motorcycles, and attending several distinguished private schools. After obtaining a degree from Trinity College, Beckett moved to Paris to lecture in English at the distinguished École normale supérieure. Although he was dissatisfied with his post as a lecturer, Beckett found his writing electrified by an encounter and subsequent friendship with self-exiled Irish writer James Joyce. Joyce exerted a huge influence on Beckett's early writing and became the locus of a major stylistic retraction in his postwar writing.

Beckett's writing career began well before World War II, yet the turmoil and aftermath of the conflict left a profound mark on his later and most influential writing. Prior to the war, he had scant success with poems, novels, and reviews. In 1937, a pimp stabbed Beckett in Paris and the writer almost died. The randomness of this event—the pimp, ironically named Prudent, claimed in court he had no reason for the attack—resonated with Beckett for the rest of his life. In 1940, Beckett

Signature titles

Plays
Waiting for Godot, 1952
Endgame, 1957
Krapp's Last Tape, 1958
Happy Days, 1961
Footfalls, 1975
Rockaby, 1981

Novels
Murphy, 1938
Malone Dies, 1951
Watt, 1953
The Unnamable, 1953
Dream of Fair to Middling Women, 1992

Novellas/short stories
More Pricks Than Kicks, 1934
Stories and Texts for Nothing, 1954
First Love, 1973
Stirrings Still, 1988

Poetry
Whoroscope, 1930
What is the Word, 1989

Nonfiction
Proust, 1931

ABOVE: A photograph of Beckett in profile taken c. 1950.

ABOVE: Beckett at Le Petit Café on Boulevard St. Jacques, Paris (1985).

became involved with a French resistance cell that resulted in a long stretch of hiding. He doled the time away by writing *Watt* (completed in 1945), a novel with a dramatically pared-down style that signaled his break from Joyce's weighty influence.

Beckett emerged from the war melancholic and defeated, but with an intense desire to continue to write. He soon became interested in the dramatic form as a relief from the unwieldiness of his novels. Working against Joyce's principle that writing should be exuberant and concerned with outward manifestations, Beckett wrote plays and novels that dealt with impoverishment and loss. In 1949, he completed *Waiting for Godot*, a play about two clowns who endlessly await the arrival of a mysterious figure named Godot. The play was an international sensation and, along with

"Nothing is funnier than unhappiness, I grant you that."—*Endgame*

Waiting for Godot

It is difficult to know what has intrigued audiences more: the curious dialogue in *Waiting for Godot* or the identity of Godot. The play concerns two tramps, Vladimir and Estragon, who idle away their time bantering while they await the arrival of a mysterious person named Godot. A young boy often appears to insist that Godot will keep his appointment, but at the end of the play, Godot has yet to arrive.

Immediately striking to the play's first audiences was the dialogue between the tramps. Beckett brought the tedium of ordinary conversation (insults, bawdy words, and digressions) to a stage ill accustomed to performing them—it is a play, to quote a famous review, "where nothing happens twice." The script was expurgated in some early productions in England, but when the play received overwhelmingly favorable reviews from two British critics in 1955, it became an overnight sensation.

The identity of the absent character Godot has also been a puzzle for Beckett's audiences. Beckett claimed to have borrowed the word from the French slang for boot, "*godillot, godasse*," in order to emphasize the prominent role of feet in the play. However, Godot has more often been taken to symbolize an absent "God," a figure of rebirth and redemption for a postwar world. This is an interpretation that Beckett denounced, claiming that the play was written in French and the name "Godot" has no resemblance to the French word for God, "*Dieu*." "If Godot were God," said Beckett, "I would have called him that." Beckett's denial of Godot as God does not mark him as a nihilist. While Godot (whatever he stands for) does not arrive, the play emphasizes, in a sympathetic but humiliating manner, how humans pass the time in the meanwhile.

plays such as *Endgame, Happy Days, and Krapp's Last Tape*, confirmed his stature as an important experimental dramatist.

After the success of *Waiting for Godot*, Beckett was able to support himself as a writer in Paris. In 1969, he was awarded the Nobel Prize in Literature: "For his writing which—in new forms for the novel and drama—in the destitution of modern man acquires its elevation." In the ensuing decades, Beckett wrote many radio plays and began to stage his own productions in Berlin, Paris, and London. Approaching the 1980s, his plays and prose pieces took on an even more concentrated examination of the human condition: soliloquies expressing loneliness, survival, and loss became completely unhinged from elements of plot and staging.

Although Beckett's body of work does not offer clear hope for a despairing world, it is not simply pessimist or nihilist. His last pieces of writing, *Stirrings Still* and *What is the Word,* are testimony to his stoical claim that humans must tread resolutely on, even when near the end. **SD**

RIGHT: Beckett examining stills from his movie *Film*, 1964.

LOUIS MacNEICE

Born: Frederick Louis MacNeice, September 12, 1907 (Belfast, Northern Ireland); died September 3, 1963 (London, England).

Style and genre: MacNeice was an Irish poet, playwright, and critic who is most often associated with the Auden generation of 1930s poetry.

The pull of both Ireland and England is strongly felt in Louis MacNeice's work. Educated at Oxford, he was a lecturer in classics in Birmingham and London. His love of the classics pervades his poetry, but he is best remembered for the dazzling linguistic innovation of such poems as "Snow" and "Bagpipe Music." His rapprochement with the politically committed writing of the 1930s is evident in his *Poems* and especially in his *Autumn Journal*, prompted by the Munich crisis, the Spanish Civil War, and events in prewar London. Later, he experienced a fresh burst of creative energy with *Visitations*, *Solstices*, and *The Burning Perch*. He wrote a number of radio plays, a book on Yeats, and an unfinished autobiography. **SR**

Signature titles

Poetry

Poems, 1935

The Earth Compels, 1938

Autumn Journal, 1939

Visitations, 1957

Solstices, 1961

The Burning Perch, 1963

Anthologies

Collected Poems, 2007

DAPHNE DU MAURIER

Born: May 13, 1907 (London, England); died April 19, 1989 (Par, Cornwall, England).

Style and genre: Her writing is characterized by superb historic research, exciting themes tense with emotion and passion, and exceptionally well-thought-out plots. Alfred Hitchcock turned her short story "The Birds" into one of his greatest movies.

Daphne grew up in a privileged home among a creative family. She began writing at a young age and had her first novel published while in her twenties. She fell in love with the county of Cornwall, and its beaches, rugged landscape, and richly mythic history inspired most of her stories. Confused by her sexuality, she married a distinguished soldier, Sir Frederick Browning (known as "Boy"), with whom she had three children, but she also fell in love with women, including Gertrude Lawrence. These deep, emotional mood swings influenced her melodramatic plots and helped her evoke high-strung moments of tension. She was an international success, but after the death of Boy, Daphne became reclusive. **LH**

Signature titles

Novels

Jamaica Inn, 1936

Rebecca, 1938

Frenchman's Creek, 1941

The King's General, 1946

My Cousin Rachel, 1951

The Flight of the Falcon, 1965

The House on the Strand, 1969

Short stories

The Birds and Other Stories, 1952

Don't Look Now, 1971

Biographies

The du Mauriers, 1937

The Infernal World of Branwell Brontë, 1960

Nonfiction

Vanishing Cornwall, 1967

Enchanted Cornwall, 1989

W. H. AUDEN

Born: Wystan Hugh Auden, February 21, 1907 (York, England); died September 29, 1973 (Vienna, Austria).

Style and genre: Auden was an English poet and essayist whose mastery of form and moral authority show throughout his long writing career and many styles.

In 1922, the fifteen-year-old Auden was asked by a schoolmate whether he had ever tried to write poetry. The answer was no, but the moment awoke within him a sense of vocation. With characteristic smartness and within five years, Auden had written some of the most distinctive poems of the decade. He garnered the attention of T. S. Eliot and became the figurehead of what would become known as the "Auden generation." Throughout his life, Auden's poetry would maintain a sense of absorbed playfulness, effortless precocity, and anarchic, schoolboyish mischief.

Auden worked through a number of stylistic phases. His early poems of modernist obliquity and menacing, impersonal diction led into a mid-period (at an age when most poets are still finding their feet) of political commitment and authority in the fight against fascism. After his emigration to the United States in 1939, he entered a late phase that combined a more relaxed, diffuse style with Christian humility and wisdom.

His best-known poems come from the mid-period: "Spain," "Musée des Beaux Arts," "In Memory of W. B. Yeats," and "September 1, 1939" resound with a sense of moral pronouncement that is still powerful today (the latter was widely cited in the aftermath of the 9/11 attacks on New York). After he left England, Auden came to regret some of the political boldness and moral assurance of these poems and revised or excluded them from future editions. The poet became a much-loved celebrity, writing librettos for Benjamin Britten and Stravinsky and enjoying the liberality of gay life in Greenwich Village, New York. In old age, he was known for his wrinkled, creased face ("My face looks like an egg upon a plate," he wrote when still young) and eccentric mannerisms. **MS**

"A poet is, before anything else, a person who is passionately in love with language."

Signature titles

Poetry

Poems, 1930

Poems

"Out on the Lawn I Lie in Bed," 1936
"Letter to Lord Byron," 1937
"Spain," 1937
"Miss Gee," 1938
"Musée des Beaux Arts," 1940
"In Memory of W. B. Yeats," 1940
"September 1, 1939," 1940
"The Sea and the Mirror," 1944
"In Praise of Limestone," 1948
"Horae Canonicae," 1954

Literary criticism

The Dyer's Hand, 1962

ABOVE: Auden in London, June 1972, a year before his death.

ALBERTO MORAVIA

Born: Alberto Pincherle, November 28, 1907 (Rome, Italy); died September 26, 1990 (Rome, Italy).

Style and genre: Moravia was a prolific novelist whose works explored the moral sterility behind the glittering surfaces of the Italian bourgeoisie.

Alberto Moravia recorded the alienating force of money on the Italian upper-middle classes. His explorations of their thwarted and occasionally piquant desires have led critics to make comparisons between him and the French existentialists.

Moravia was a psychologically rigorous novelist; in works such as *Agostino* and *The Empty Canvas*, the individual consciousness of the protagonist becomes a kaleidoscope in which social shams are revealed. Although his characters spend their time navel-gazing and his novels look inward at a country crippled by social claustrophobia, Moravia himself was an accomplished travel writer and an open-minded intellectual; he would not suffer conformists and was never one himself. **TM**

Signature titles

Novels

The Time of Indifference (*Gli indifferenti*), 1929

Two Adolescents (*Agostino*), 1944

The Woman of Rome (*La Romana*), 1947

The Conformist (*Il conformista*), 1951

Two Women (*La ciociara*), 1957

The Empty Canvas (*La noia*), 1960

Short stories

Roman Tales (*Racconti romani*), 1954

Travel writing

Which Tribe Do You Belong To? (*A quale tribù appartieni?*), 1972

PAULINE RÉAGE

Born: Anne Desclos (also known as Dominique Aury), September 23, 1907 (Rochefort-sur-Mer, France); died April 26, 1998 (Corbeil-Essonnes, France).

Style and genre: Réage was the controversial author of erotic fiction featuring the total submission of women to men.

Since its publication in 1954, *Story of O* caused a scandal for its explicit sexuality and its depiction of women as subservient to men. Many feminist critics attacked the book as a misogynist fantasy and speculated that the novel was actually written by a man (the most likely suspect was Jean Paulhan, who wrote the introduction). However, in 1994 it was confirmed that the novel was written by Pauline Réage (one of the pen names of Anne Desclos). In an interview, she claimed the novel was a fantasy that she wanted to share with her lover, Paulhan, and he encouraged her to publish it. For some, *Story of O* is emblematic of women's internalized oppression; for others, it is an erotic tale of a woman who gives herself entirely for love. **IJ**

Signature titles

Novels

Story of O, 1954

Return to the Château, 1969

1900–19

MAURICE BLANCHOT

Born: September 22, 1907 (Quain, France); died February 20, 2003 (Yvelines, France).

Style and genre: A philosopher and literary critic who examined the "question of literature," Blanchot played a key role in shaping post-structuralist literary theory.

A philosopher, novelist, and literary critic, Maurice Blanchot has been credited as an enormously important influence on the thinking of post-structuralist writers such as Derrida and Barthes. Concerned with the philosophy of language, in his essays Blanchot questions whether it is possible to describe reality in abstract literary terms, which are distinct from everyday experience. A conscious engagement with the act of writing—and of reading—is a recurring theme in his work, which forces a re-evaluation of what our understanding of literature is and how we should respond to it.

Blanchot studied philosophy at the University of Strasbourg and during the 1930s worked as a political journalist in Paris. While serving as the editor of both a stridently anti-German nationalist magazine and a mainstream conservative daily, he was also an outspoken critic of the ruling government and anti-Semitic legislation. During World War II, he was active in the Resistance, and in 1944, he came close to being executed by a Nazi firing squad. After the war, his sympathies shifted markedly to the left, and he retreated to the rural south of France. This self-imposed isolation was connected to his poor health, but also to his need for a secluded space in which to formulate ideas. Between 1953 and 1968, Blanchot made his name with a monthly article for the *Nouvelle Revue Française* and continued to write novels and critical essays. Deliberately blurring the traditional divide between genres, he wove narratives with literary theory and philosophical investigation with plots. He re-entered the public eye only to speak out against the French occupation of Algeria during the 1950s and to lend his intellectual support to the left-wing student uprising of May 1968. **MK**

"A writer never reads his work . . . he cannot remain face to face with it."

Signature titles

Essays

Faux Pas, 1943
The Work of Fire, 1949
The Space of Literature, 1955
The Book to Come, 1959
The Infinite Conversation, 1969
The Writing of the Disaster, 1980
A Voice from Elsewhere, 2002

Novels

Thomas the Obscure, 1941
Death Sentence, 1948

ABOVE: Blanchot, a notable recluse who refused to be photographed, in a rare picture.

RICHARD WRIGHT

Born: September 4, 1908 (Roxie, Mississippi, U.S.); died November 28, 1960 (Paris, France).

Style and genre: Wright was concerned with the "race question." He is known for his documentary detail, philosophical determinism, and communist polemics.

Richard Wright's controversial writings reflect the historic trauma of segregation and racial oppression in the United States, but they also work to produce a sort of trauma in the reader. In the autobiographical *Black Boy*, Wright reflected on his artistic awakening and on his lonely youth in the Mississippi Delta. His father abandoned the young family, which was then presided over by Richard's zealous grandmother—for whom fiction was "the devil's lies." In 1927, Wright left for Chicago, where he worked as a dishwasher before moving up to the post office, joining the Communist Party, and eventually publishing his first book of short stories, *Uncle Tom's Children*.

In 1940, now based in New York City, Wright published the work that would solidify his reputation as the United States's leading black novelist. *Native Son* is the story of Bigger Thomas, an inarticulate black thug who ruthlessly murders the daughter of his rich employer. Bigger's multiple atrocities were intended to shock white readers into the realization that the United States itself had created this monster—that Bigger's poisonous attitudes were the logical outcome of the United States's institutionalized racism. The work was (and remains) deeply controversial, and critics vociferously attacked the novel, charging that Wright had essentially confirmed racist white fears toward violent and sexually threatening black males.

Wright, however, continued to publish on the issue of race and in 1946 moved to Paris. There he found himself in the circle of Jean-Paul Sartre, Albert Camus, and other French existentialists, and in 1953, he published his own existential fiction, *The Outsider*. Wright was increasingly charmed by the Japanese haiku form and had written more than 4,000 such poems by the time he died. **IW**

"Don't leave inferences to be drawn when evidence can be presented."

Signature titles

Novels

Native Son, 1940

The Outsider, 1953

Savage Holiday, 1954

The Long Dream, 1958

Short stories

Uncle Tom's Children, 1938

Eight Men, 1961

Nonfiction

Black Power, 1954

The Color Curtain, 1956

Pagan Spain, 1957

White Man, Listen!, 1957

Autobiographies

Black Boy, 1945

American Hunger, 1977

ABOVE: Wright photographed in a library in 1943.

SIMONE DE BEAUVOIR

Born: January 9, 1908 (Paris, France); died April 14, 1986 (Paris, France).

Style and genre: French writer and existentialist philosopher, Simone de Beauvoir was an inspiration to postwar feminists with her book *The Second Sex*, a study of the history of the oppression of women.

The daughter of a Montparnasse lawyer who told her she was ugly—at fifty-one she wrote that she loathed her own appearance—de Beauvoir was educated at private schools and went on to study philosophy at the Sorbonne in Paris. It was there, in 1929, that she first met Jean-Paul Sartre, with whom she would have a lifelong relationship, though they lived separately and both would have affairs with others. As a feminist, she rejected marriage on principle and disapproved of the conventional family, and she would have no children. She worked as a teacher, lived in Paris during the German occupation, and in 1943 published her first novel, *L'Invitee*, which dealt with existentialist themes and preoccupations.

Spirited and brave, and fond of a drink, she went on to produce philosophical books and essays, more novels and a play. In the late 1940s she had a long love affair with the American writer Nelson Algren and in 1949 published *The Second Sex*, a two-volume study of the history of the oppression of women, which denounced the whole notion of "the eternal feminine" as a myth calculated to promote male dominance. It created shock and outrage at the time. The Roman Catholic

Signature titles

Novels

She Came to Stay (L'Invitee), 1943

The Blood of Others (Le Sang des autres), 1945

All Men are Mortal (Tous les hommes sont mortels), 1945

The Mandarins (Les Mandarins), 1954

Nonfiction

The Second Sex (Le Deuxième sexe), 1949

The Long March (La longue marche), 1957

Autobiographies

Memoirs of a Dutiful Daughter (Mèmoires d'une jeune fille rangée), 1958

The Prime of Life (La Force de l'age), 1960

Force of Circumstance (La Force des choses), 1963

All Said and Done (Tout compte fait), 1972

Adieux: A Farewell to Sartre (La Cérémonie des adieux suivi es Entretiens avec Jean-Paul Sartre), 1981

1900–19

ABOVE: The stoic Simone de Beauvoir in a February 1968 image.

RIGHT: De Beauvoir at a school in Marseille where she taught from 1931 to 1943.

ABOVE: Grinning existentialists Jean-Paul Sartre and Simone de Beauvoir in 1959.

Church banned it and it helped to power the feminist movement: though some feminists would later criticize her for playing second fiddle to Sartre. Her later novel, *The Mandarins,* about politically committed intellectuals in France in the postwar years, won the Prix Goncourt.

In 1956, she and Sartre visited the U.S.S.R. and Communist China, with which she sympathized, and in the 1960s she traveled widely in Cuba, Russia, Egypt, Israel, and Japan. She published her autobiography in four volumes, demonstrated in support of rioting students, and campaigned for abortion, contraception, and women's rights. She also wrote about the horrors of aging and society's neglect of the elderly. Sartre died in 1980 and she aroused fresh controversy with a book the following year that, in saying adieu to him, gave brutal accounts of his physical and mental decay in his last years. When she died, she was buried with him in Montparnasse. **RC**

Adam and Eve

"God did not spontaneously choose to create Eve as an end in herself. . . . She was destined by Him for man; it was to rescue Adam from loneliness that He gave her to him, in her mate was her origin and her purpose. She was a conscious being, but naturally submissive. And therein lies the wondrous hope that man has often put in woman; he hopes to fufill himself as a being by carnally possessing a being, but at the same time confirming his sense of freedom through the docility of a free person. No man would consent to be a woman, but every man wants women to exist."—*The Second Sex*

CESARE PAVESE

Born: September 9, 1908 (the Langhe, Italy); died August 26, 1950 (Turin, Italy).

Style and genre: Pavese was an Italian poet, novelist, translator, and journalist who agonized over his personal failings in the troubled context of fascist Italy and reflected these insecurities in his writing.

Cesare Pavese was born in the hills but brought up in the city; his writing was never sure where it was most at home. His early poems (in *Hard Labor*) set the tone for his later works as they questioned whether traditional, rural ways of living had become defunct in an age of technological upheaval. Although he was committed to his craft, Pavese eschewed personal and political commitments. He drew much inspiration from U.S. and English classics and their stylistic variety galvanized his own literary experiments. Pavese has been criticized for not joining the resistance movement and the protagonists of novels such as *The House on the Hill* and *The Moon and the Bonfires* are fragile barometers of his own political guilt. **TM**

Signature titles

Poetry

Hard Labor (*Lavorare stanca*), 1936

Death Will Come and It Will Have Your Eyes (*Verrà la morte e avrà i tuoi occhi*), 1951

Novels

The Harvesters (*Paesi Tuoi*), 1941

Dialogues with Leucò (*Dialoghi con Leucò*), 1947

The Prison (*Il carcere*), 1948

The House on the Hill (*La casa in collina*), 1948

The Beautiful Summer (*La bella estate*), 1949

The Moon and the Bonfires (*La luna e i falò*), 1950

Diary

The Business of Living (*Il mestiere di vivere*), 1952

MALCOLM LOWRY

Born: Clarence Malcolm Lowry, July 28, 1909 (New Brighton, England); died June 27, 1957 (Ripe, England).

Style and genre: Novelist, short-story writer, and poet, Lowry spent much of his short life submerged in alcoholism and mental difficulties.

Lowry's masterpiece was his novel *Under the Volcano*, set in Mexico. He started it in the 1930s at a time when Europe itself seemed in danger of destruction by a political volcano and it made his name in America, though ignored in England. The youngest of four sons of a rich businessman, Lowry went to Cambridge University before restless years spent living in London, Paris, Hollywood, Mexico—with his American first wife; it was not a happy marriage—Canada, and Italy before returning to England in the 1950s. His life was punctuated by drinking bouts and mental troubles, and he died of alcohol and possibly an overdose of pills. His short stories, poems, and letters were published posthumously in the 1960s. **RC**

Signature titles

Novel

Under the Volcano, 1947 (republished 1962)

Short stories

Hear Us O Lord from Heaven Thy Dwelling Place, 1961

Anthologies

Selected Poems, 1962

Selected Letters, 1965

EUGÈNE IONESCO

Born: Eugen Ionescu, November 26, 1909 or 1912 (Slatina, Romania); died March 28, 1994 (Paris, France).

Style and genre: Prolific in the theater of the absurd, Ionesco's unorthodox plays of the 1950s and 1960s explored the absurd meaninglessness of life.

Eugène Ionesco's surrealist, one-act "anti-plays," such as *The Lesson*, caught the existentialist tide of 1950s Paris and helped to establish an absurdist theater whose exponents have included major figures of twentieth-century drama—from Samuel Beckett and Edward Albee to Harold Pinter and Tom Stoppard. Ionesco's plays are characterized by a lack of traditional plotting, narrative thread, and characterization, and themes include death, man's inability to shape events, and the nature of inanimate objects. They feature bizarre, often grotesquely comic, and apparently arbitrary episodes—such as a chatting couple discovering they are married to each other (*The Bald Soprano*) or the stage filling up with empty chairs (*The Chairs*). Their spare, fragmented language points up the failure of words to foster meaningful communication in an alienated bourgeois world filled with empty relationships.

Ionesco's broken and stilted use of words was in part inspired by his own study of English during the late 1940s, when he was struck by the strangeness of the phrases in his English textbook. Linguistic issues were very much a part of his background. Brought up in Romania and Paris, with a Romanian father and French mother, Ionesco studied French at Bucharest University and finally settled in Paris in the 1940s. A career as a playwright did not come until Ionesco was entering middle age but his first one-act piece, *The Bald Soprano*, was hailed as the point of departure for a new revolution in drama.

After the success of his one-act plays, Ionesco tackled longer formats. These often seemed to lose the force and focus of his shorter dramas, although *Rhinoceros* proved enduringly popular. Later works explored dreams and the world of the subconscious. **AK**

"Ideologies separate us. Dreams and anguish bring us together."

Signature titles

Plays

The Bald Soprano/The Bald Prima Donna (*La Cantatrice chauve*), 1950

The Lesson (*La Leçon*), 1951

The Chairs (*Les Chaises*), 1952

The New Tenant (*Le Nouveau locataire*), 1955

Rhinoceros (*Le Rhinocéros*), 1960

Exit the King (*Le Roi se meurt*), 1962

A Hell of a Mess (*Ce formidable bordel*), 1973

Journeys among the Dead (*Voyages chez les Morts*), 1981

ABOVE: Ionesco pictured at his home office on July 1, 1973.

JEAN GENET

Born: December 19, 1910 (Paris, France); died April 15, 1986 (Paris, France).

Style and genre: A thief, homosexual, and male prostitute who hymned the delights of anal eroticism, Jean Genet was a leading figure in French avant-garde theater.

Signature titles

Novels

Our Lady of the Flowers (Notre-Dame des fleurs), 1943

Miracle of the Rose (Miracle de la rose), 1946

Autobiography

The Thief's Journal (Journal du voleur), 1949

Plays

The Maids (Les Bonnes), 1947

The Balcony (Le Balcon), 1956

The Blacks (Les Nègres), 1958

The Screens (Les Paravents), 1961

Jean Genet's life began badly and got worse. Illegitimate, he was abandoned by his mother to be brought up in orphanages, a foster home, and a reformatory. A professional thief, and proud of it, he spent much time in prisons. In the 1930s, he lived by his wits, wandering Europe as a beggar, thief, pickpocket, drug dealer, and male prostitute, of which he would later write a self-glorified account in *A Thief's Journal*. It was while serving a prison sentence in France for theft that he began writing. His first novel, *Our Lady of the Flowers*, celebrated the criminal underworld, whereas *Miracle of the Rose* described the reform school at Mettray where he had spent part of his adolescence before escaping to serve briefly in the Foreign Legion, which he then deserted.

Genet later turned his hand to plays, in which he explored the problems of identity and the human appetite for role-playing that would also fascinate Samuel Beckett and Eugène Ionesco. His reputation grew among intellectuals, including Jean Cocteau and Jean-Paul Sartre, and when he was convicted of theft yet again in 1948 and faced an automatic life sentence, well-known writers interceded and he was granted a pardon.

ABOVE: A black and white photograph of the young Genet during his troubled youth.

RIGHT: Genet (far right) in Paris in 1968 at a political demonstration and sit-in.

Genet's work was often difficult; he managed to combine foregrounding his criminality and homosexuality—and a preoccupation with murder and violent death—with religiosity, including his own quest for "saintliness" through degradation and self-abasement. Repudiating the bourgeois world that had rejected him, he wrote of criminals as victims of society. Described as the "theater of hatred," his plays were intended to shock, and succeeded. *The Balcony* was set in a brothel whose clients became their fantasy selves and *The Blacks* was written for a black cast in white masks and led up to a white woman's ritual rape and murder. Sartre wrote an approving book about him, *Saint Genet, Actor and Martyr*, but François Mauriac described him as "like a squirrel in a cage, imprisoned in the dungeon of a vice from which he cannot escape." Genet wrote little after the mid-1960s, though in his later years he spent time with the Black Panthers in America and the Palestine liberationists. **RC**

ABOVE: Genet on stage at a Black Panther rally with Elbert Howard, May 1, 1970.

The Would-Be Saint

"Though saintliness is my goal, I cannot tell what it is. My point of departure is the world itself, which indicates the state closest to moral perfection. Of which I have known nothing, except that without it my life would be in vain. Unable to arrive at a definition of saintliness—no more than of beauty—I want at every moment to create it, that is, to act so that everything I do may lead me to what is unknown to me, so that at every moment I may be guided by a will to saintliness until the time when I am so luminous that people will say, 'He is a saint,' or more likely, 'He was a saint.'"—*A Thief's Journal*

GONZALO TORRENTE BALLESTER

Born: June 13, 1910 (Serantes, Spain); died January 27, 1999 (Salamanca, Spain).

Style and genre: Ballester's work is steeped in the influence of his Galician roots and moves between the two extremes of a combination of myth and reality to an emphasis on intellect and rationalism.

Gonzalo Torrente Ballester wrote primarily novels, but also literary criticism, plays, essays, and even history books. He combined his love of teaching with writing, holding university professorships or teaching high school for most of his life. Despite writing for an anarchist newspaper during his student days, in 1937 he joined Franco's Falange party. He seemed to keep to his leftist ideals, however, and his first novel, *Javier Mariño,* was censored by Franco's regime when published in 1943. Throughout the 1960s he had increasing problems with government censors, perhaps because in 1962 his name was linked with a strike of Asturian miners, and he lost his teaching post at the university. Critics mostly ignored his 1963 novel, *Don Juan*, Torrente's personal favorite, because of his public stance against political policies. In 1966, he left Spain to take up a teaching post at the State University of New York at Albany.

Torrente returned to Spain in 1970 and became increasingly popular, gaining important literary renown. He was accepted as a member of the Real Academia Española in 1977, won Spain's National Prize for Literature in 1981, and in 1985 was honored with the Cervantes Prize. Torrente's fiction owed much to the superstitions of the family who raised him in rural Galicia; this background gave his work an irony and elements of the supernatural, set against the picturesque yet rough Galician landscape. Although he wrote some plays, none of them were ever staged, and Torrente himself acknowledged that they were more for reading than viewing. One of the most important Spanish contemporary novels is *La saga/fuga de J.B.*, a metaliterary work of postmodern fantasy that is rich in imagination and intellect, which brought the author great popular fame. **REM**

"Neither the past nor the future exists. All is present."

Signature titles

Novels

Javier Mariño, 1943

Iphigenia (Ifigenia), 1950

Don Juan, 1963

Off-side, 1969

The Sleeping Princess Goes to School (La princesa durmiente va a la escuela), 1985

King Amaz'd: A Chronicle (Crónica del rey pasmado), 1989

ABOVE: A portrait of Gonzalo Torrente Ballester taken in 1981.

FLANN O'BRIEN

Born: Brian O'Nolan, October 5, 1911 (Strabane, Ireland); died April 1, 1966 (Dublin, Ireland).

Style and genre: O'Brien is considered by many to be the most dazzlingly clever and entertainingly obtuse Irish novelist since James Joyce.

Flann O'Brien was one of the many pseudonyms of Brian O'Nolan, an Irish civil servant who was best known to his contemporaries as a talented newspaper satirist and best known since for his strong claim to being the first postmodern novelist. His comic masterpieces *At Swim-Two-Birds* and *The Third Policeman* raise pastiche and satire to the level of philosophical inquiry and are still among the most psychologically astute and consistently hilarious metafictions ever written.

The fifth of twelve children, O'Brien was raised in an Irish-speaking household and wrote his master's thesis on Irish language poetry. *At Swim-Two-Birds* is, most basically, the story of a student of Irish language poetry, not unlike O'Brien himself, writing a novel about a novelist and the novel he is writing. It includes characters from Irish mythology such as Finn MacCool and a pookah. These layers of fiction refuse to remain discrete, and O'Brien leaves no conundrum unexploited, from the man who is born at the age of twenty-five to the novelist held captive by his own characters.

These mindbenders, however, are nothing compared with the "pancakes" presented to the reader in O'Brien's next novel, *The Third Policeman*. In a story told like Lewis Carroll by way of Hieronymous Bosch, O'Brien drops a murderous protagonist into a bizarre country, where even the physical act of riding a bicycle creates an insoluble metaphysical dilemma. Although arguably a more accomplished piece of writing than *At Swim-Two-Birds*, *The Third Policeman* was a commercial failure, and O'Brien did not write another English language novel until *The Dalkey Archive* in 1964. **SY**

"I declare to God if I hear that name Joyce one more time I will surely froth at the gob."

ABOVE: A photographic portrait of O'Brien taken in Dublin *c.* 1940.

Signature titles

Novels

At Swim-Two-Birds, 1939
The Third Policeman, 1939–1940
The Poor Mouth, 1941
The Dalkey Archive, 1964

MERVYN PEAKE

Born: Mervyn Laurence Peake, July 9, 1911 (Kuling, China); died November 17, 1968 (Burcot, England).

Style and genre: Peake was a writer who produced eccentric imagery and drama in cool, restrained prose, creating an enclosed, engrossing universe all its own.

Mervyn Peake spent the first twelve years of his life in China, the son of a British missionary doctor. It was an unusual upbringing that would be reflected in his vivid, caricaturelike illustrations and imaginative fiction.

The drawings came first. Peake exhibited his artwork at the Royal Academy in the 1930s and illustrated a book of nursery rhymes. Just before World War II, he published a children's book, *Captain Slaughterboard Drops Anchor*. It has a simple story but marvelously detailed drawings of creatures such as the Dignipomp, which bears a marked resemblance to Cicero.

It was not until after the war that Peake produced the first of the books that would form his legacy. *Titus Groan* is a monumental achievement, a huge, dripping, Gothic cathedral of a novel. It covers the birth and infancy of the titular hero, but the focus is on the strange, insular, distorted world of Titus's castle, Gormenghast, and its inhabitants. Peake had intended to tell Titus's entire life story in a cycle of books, but he managed only three, and by the time he wrote the last, *Titus Alone*, he was already suffering from Parkinson's disease.

Between the Gormenghast novels, however, Peake brought out some lighter fare: *Mr. Pye*, from 1953, is a cheerful allegory about a do-gooder who sets out to save the people of Sark, but God has other ideas. Thanks to fables such as these and the fantasy elements of the Gormenghast novels, Peake is sometimes thought to be a children's author. Nothing could be further from the truth. The Gormenghast books throb with a fierce, repressed sexuality and their depiction of evil is horrifyingly informed by Peake's experiences in World War II. Peake may have a cultish appeal, like Tolkien, but his fiction belongs to no earth other than our own. **CO**

"There is a kind of laughter that sickens the soul. Laughter when it is out of control . . ."

Signature titles

Novels

Titus Groan, 1946

Gormenghast, 1950

Mr. Pye, 1953

Titus Alone, 1959

ABOVE: Mervyn Peake photographed around the time *Titus Groan* was published.

ELIZABETH BISHOP

Born: February 8, 1911 (Worcester, Massachusetts, U.S.); died October 6, 1979 (Boston, Massachusetts, U.S.).

Style and genre: Bishop was one of the most important American poets of the twentieth century; her poetry addresses our relationship with the natural world.

Elizabeth Bishop was neither a very well-known poet during her lifetime, nor very prolific, but since her death, she has become recognized as a major force in American poetry.

Her early life was a difficult one. Her father died before she was a year old, and her mother was confined to a mental institution when Bishop was five; she never saw her again. Her grandparents sent her to Vassar College in Poughkeepsie, New York, where, under the influence of the poet Marianne Moore, Bishop began writing.

She disliked personal, confessional poetry and instead focused on observation and precise imagery. She wrote with great clarity and lyricism about her travels in France, Ireland, Spain, Italy, and North Africa. Bishop was not a prolific writer but she was a perfectionist and spent a long time polishing each poem. As a result, she is regarded as a "poet's poet."

In 1951, Bishop was awarded a traveling fellowship from Bryn Mawr College and set off for South America where she stayed for fifteen years. In 1956, while living in Brazil, Bishop was given the Pulitzer Prize for her collection of poetry *North & South—A Cold Spring*. In 1970, she began teaching at Harvard and that year was awarded the National Book Award for Poetry for *The Complete Poems*. Her reputation was further enhanced with the publication of her last collection *Geography 111* in 1976. It won the National Book Critics Circle Award and consists of ten poems including major works: "In the Waiting Room," "Crusoe in England," and "One Art."

"I'm not interested in big-scale work as such. Something needn't be large to be good."

Bishop died in Boston in 1979 at the age of sixty-eight. Since her death, her reputation has grown and her highly accessible poetry has become popular with a wider audience than during her lifetime. **HJ**

Signature titles

Poetry

North & South—A Cold Spring, 1946

Questions of Travel, 1965

The Complete Poems, 1969

Geography 111, 1976

Edgar Allan Poe & The Juke Box: Uncollected Poems, Drafts, and Fragments, 2006

ABOVE: A photograph of Elizabeth Bishop taken on May 10, 1956.

TENNESSEE WILLIAMS

Born: Thomas Lanier Williams III, March 26, 1911 (Columbus, Mississippi, U.S.); died February 25, 1983 (New York, New York, U.S.).

Style and genre: Williams was a major American dramatist whose plays, mostly set in the South, examined the pained lives of isolated individuals.

Signature titles

Novella

The Roman Spring of Mrs. Stone, 1950

Short stories

The Field of Blue Children, 1939

The Yellow Bird, 1947

The Poet, 1948

Plays

The Glass Menagerie, 1945

A Streetcar Named Desire, 1947

The Rose Tattoo, 1951

Cat on a Hot Tin Roof, 1955

Orpheus Descending, 1958

Night of the Iguana, 1961

Small Craft Warnings, 1973

Something Cloudy Something Clear, 1983

Depressive, hypochondriac, painfully shy, and homosexual, Tennessee Williams's life was as theatrical as his plays. Born to an abusive, alcoholic father and a heroically long-suffering mother, Tennessee—a nickname he adopted at the age of twenty-eight—wrote into his plays all the neuroses and isolation he had experienced in his life, from his first-produced composition in 1931 until his death in 1983.

Williams's travels would take him from Missouri to California to British Columbia, writing all the while, but most of his life was spent living between Key West, New Orleans, and New York. He began studying for a degree at the University of Missouri, but was removed by his father; he later graduated from the University of Iowa in 1938. *The Glass Menagerie*, Williams's first major success, deals, like most of his plays, with the pained lives of isolated individuals. The next thirty years were ones of considerable public success. He received his first Pulitzer Prize for *A Streetcar Named Desire*, a gritty, steamy exposé of the faded romance of the South, and a second for *Cat on a Hot Tin Roof*, a quasi-autobiographical play—Williams was often desired by women, for whom he felt no attraction. The 1960s were his self-dubbed "Stoned Age," a period of all-consuming drug dependency. After receiving an award for *Night of the Iguana* in 1961, Williams saw no further real success until *Small Craft Warnings* in 1973.

"All your Western theologies . . . are based on the concept of God as a senile delinquent."

Williams's reputation in his final decade became compromised after years of addictions. He died alone in a hotel room in New York; the police report suggested that his use of drugs and alcohol may have contributed to his death. Williams's life work, however, resulted in his name being synonymous with the twentieth-century American canon. **JS**

ABOVE: Williams sits for a portrait in an undated photograph.

MAX FRISCH

Born: May 15, 1911 (Zurich, Switzerland); died April 4, 1991 (Zurich, Switzerland).

Style and genre: Frisch was a prolific Swiss novelist, playwright, and diarist whose work has been acclaimed internationally; his themes include moral dilemmas, the search for identity, and personal freedom.

Max Frisch began his career as a journalist and published his first novel, *Jurg Reinhart,* in 1934. He then trained as an architect and, following the outbreak of World War II, served in the Swiss army. After the war, he started to write plays, including *The Chinese Wall*, a grim farce set in a fictionalized China, and *When the War Was Over*, which takes as its theme guilt and responsibility and the defeatist mentality that consumed individuals in Russian-occupied Berlin.

In the early 1950s, Frisch returned to writing novels. He published his masterpiece *I'm Not Stiller* in 1954. Written as a journal in seven sections, it is the story of a man in prison who claims not to be himself. The themes of personal identity and self-acceptance recur throughout Frisch's work. In *Homo Faber*, published in 1957, Frisch again examines the search for personal identity. The work explores the strange events that undermine the life and sense of security of a UNESCO engineer, whose plane crashes in a Mexican desert; he subsequently falls in love with a woman who, it eventually becomes clear, is his daughter from a love affair in the past.

In the early 1960s, Frisch wrote his most famous plays: *Andorra*, which deals with anti-Semitism; and *Firebugs*, a dark comedy about a town that is being attacked by arsonists. In the latter work, Frisch explores how victims become accomplices in their own misfortunes.

Frisch is considered one of Switzerland's most distinguished writers and his work has been acclaimed internationally. Throughout his life he won numerous literary awards including the Georg Büchner Prize and the Neustadt International Prize. Frisch gave up writing toward the end of his life because of ill health; he died in Zurich in 1991. **HJ**

"Technology is the knack of so arranging the world that we don't have to experience it."

Signature titles

Novels

I'm Not Stiller (Ich bin nicht Stiller), 1954

Homo Faber, 1957

A Wilderness of Mirrors (Mein Name sei Gantenbein), 1964

Bluebeard, 1982

Plays

The Chinese Wall (Die Chinesische Mauer), 1946

When the War Was Over (Als der Kreig zu Ende war), 1949

Andorra, 1961

Firebugs (Bierdermann and die Brandstifter), 1963

Biografie, 1967

Jonas und sein Veteran, 1989

ABOVE: The writer Max Frisch photographed in 1970.

WILLIAM GOLDING

Born: September 19, 1911 (Newquay, Cornwall, England); died June 19, 1993 (Perranarworthal, Cornwall, England).

Style and genre: Nobel Prize–winning English novelist whose often allegorical fiction presents humans stripped of the trappings of conventional existence.

One of literature's great pessimists, William Golding was born in Cornwall to a schoolteacher father and a suffragette mother. It was a household of radical politics and unstinting faith in scientific rigor. Golding began writing at a young age, but studied science at his parent's instigation before switching to English in the final year of his Oxford degree. He published *Poems* while still at university, but did not write his first novel until after World War II, when he served in the Royal Navy.

Golding became a teacher after the war and became a full-time writer only in 1961, after the considerable success of *Lord of the Flies*. To this day, this is the novel that most clearly defines most people's view of Golding. It presents a dystopian vision of children stranded on a deserted island, whose initial good intentions and fledgling democratic instincts give way to primitive tribalism—a postwar comment on the fragility of civilization. The theme of base instincts overriding good intentions returns throughout Golding's work, notably in *The Spire*, Golding's underrated 1964 allegory of worldly ambition and egoism. After retiring from teaching in 1961, Golding spent a year as writer-in-residence at Hollins University, Virginia, before returning to Salisbury, England, where he lived with his wife for the next twenty years.

In 1983, Golding received the Nobel Prize in Literature, and in 1984 he published *The Paper Men*, a powerful indictment of celebrity and moral vacuity that may have reflected his own dissatisfaction with the literary industry from which he made his living. In 1985, he returned to Cornwall, and in 1988 he was knighted by the queen. He died of heart failure in 1993, leaving behind a draft of the novel *The Double Tongue*, which was published three years later. **PS**

Signature titles

Novels

Lord of the Flies, 1954
The Inheritors, 1955
Pincher Martin, 1956
Free Fall, 1959
The Spire, 1964
The Pyramid, 1967
The Scorpion God, 1971
Darkness Visible, 1979
The Paper Men, 1984
To the Ends of the Earth
Rites of Passage, 1980
Close Quarters, 1987
Fire Down Below, 1989

"Fancy thinking the Beast was something you could hunt and kill!"—*Lord of the Flies*

ABOVE: Golding poses for a photo in front of his home in Wiltshire, England, in 1983.

RIGHT: Hugh Edwards as Piggy and James Aubrey as Ralph in *Lord of the Flies* (1963).

CZESŁAW MIŁOSZ

Born: June 30, 1911 (Šeteniai, Lithuania); died August 14, 2004 (Krakow, Poland).

Style and genre: Winner of the 1980 Nobel Prize in Literature, Miłosz has been called a visionary poet for his unmetered, philosophical, multivocal poetry, which is at once intimate yet impersonal.

Miłosz's work as a poet and political writer is inseparable from the history of European wars and occupations in the twentieth century. Miłosz lived and wrote in Warsaw during World War II, witnessing the Warsaw Uprising; however, unlike younger Polish poets who came of age during that war, Miłosz does not abjure representation of the Holocaust. His descriptions are mediated by a poetic imagination, and come about through speaking about responsibility, about the failure to intervene, and about the scandal of surviving when many friends have fallen. In "Dedication," the very thing that kills "you" strengthens the poet himself, by becoming content for his art. Art itself is culpable, a fact made manifest in the act of representing.

Miłosz emigrated to the United States in 1960 and taught Polish literature at Berkeley. When he received the Nobel Prize in Literature in 1980, he cut short his attendance at the ceremony so he could teach his undergraduates. The award largely introduced Poland to Miłosz's work, which had been censored for his opposition to communist rule.

His poetry draws heavily on animal imagery and the inhumanity of nature, figures that are often used to show a disorienting disproportion between inner states of mind and external exigencies. "Song of a Citizen" portrays a material existence from selling goods on the black market at the same time as it describes the states of consciousness of unreality that war gives rise to. In these mournful and catastrophic poems, doubt and hope coexist.

Miłosz's poetry proliferates with polarities and antitheses, and thus exceeds attempts to define it. Minute and immense reaches of time and space are juxtaposed in verse that reaches out to a range of mythologies and cultures for its subject matter. Miłosz was influenced by thinkers from Swedenborg and Dostoevsky to Bakhtin and Simon Weil—whom he dubbed

Signature titles

Novel

The Issa Valley, 1981

Memoir

Native Realm, 1951

Nonfiction

The Captive Mind, 1953

Poetry

Bells in Winter, 1978

Visions from San Francisco Bay, 1982

The Rising of the Sun, 1985

Facing the River, 1995

Second Space, 2004

ABOVE: The poet photographed while attending Mass in Lublin, Poland, in 1981.

LEFT: Miłosz at a reading of his work at the Jagiellonian University, Krakow, in 1981.

"Ariel" in relation to his "Caliban." A philosophical and moral inquiry plays out in his work in the relation between the self and other people. In "What Does It Mean," the speaker envisions "a town where the postmaster gets drunk every day / Out of grief at remaining identical only to himself." If there is any unifying sentiment, it might be in the injunction to do what one can with each day, spoken by an unearthly voice in "On Angels" and echoed in "Bobo's Metamorphoses," in which "ecstasy at sunrise" is repeated "from childhood to old age." **ER**

Failure of the Intellect

Miłosz's nonfiction work *The Captive Mind* is a harrowing account of the psychological suicide that afflicts intellectuals and artists living under the communist regime. The work follows four professionals—Alpha, the Moralist; Beta, the Disappointed Lover; Gamma, the Slave of History; and Delta, the Troubadour—who compromise their identity in order to conform to the ideas of the State. Miłosz deftly outlines the conflicting instincts of man toward the "necessity" of government and religion, and that of intellectual freedom.

NAGUIB MAHFOUZ

Born: December 11, 1911 (Cairo, Egypt); died August 30, 2006 (Cairo, Egypt).

Style and genre: Mahfouz's historical work, in the tradition of Arab storytelling, demonstrates substantial psychological understanding, rich characterization, and a focus on the political and cultural modernization of his native Egypt.

Mahfouz began writing when he was seventeen, but his novels draw on memories crystallized from earlier childhood. The museums he visited with his mother provided the riches of Egyptian history that have since evolved into the themes of many of his works. *Abath Al-Aqdar*, *Radubis*, and *Kifah Tibah* were supposed to be part of a much larger thirty-volume work spanning the history of Egypt. Two Cairo districts—al-Abbasiya and al-Jamaliyyah—have been reincarnated as settings in most of Mahfouz's early novels. His most famous work, *The Cairo Trilogy*, is set against the backdrop of the streets where Mahfouz grew up, and the work is prized throughout the Arab world for its depiction of traditional Egyptian urban life. Equally formative was the 1919 revolution in Egypt, which seven-year-old Mahfouz watched from his window as English soldiers fired into crowds of demonstrators.

The Egyptian Revolution of 1952 made Naguib Mahfouz put down his pen for years. When he started to write again, his literature had changed—metaphors veiled political opinions in his novels as the psychological effects of Egyptian social change played itself out around him. As a reader of Western detective novels and Russian classics, an admirer of James Joyce, and a connoisseur of the Arab literary canon, Mahfouz's work often comments on modernization and the effects of Western influence in Egypt.

Despite being the first Egyptian to be awarded the Nobel Prize for Literature, Mahfouz's name was added to the death list drawn up by Islamic fundamentalists for defending the fatwa issued against Salman Rushdie. He survived twelve years following a knife attack near his home, on the very streets that he helped immortalize. **JSD**

"The writer interweaves a story with his own doubts, questions, and values. That is art."

Signature titles

Novels

Mockery of the Fates (Abath Al-Aqdar), 1939
Radubis, 1943
Kifah Tibah, 1944
Khan Al-Khalili, 1944
Midaq Alley, 1947
The Cairo Trilogy
Palace Walk, 1956
Palace of Desire, 1957
Sugar Street, 1957
Children of Gebelaawi, 1959
The Thief and the Dogs, 1961
Adrift on the Nile, 1966
Miramar, 1967
Arabian Nights and Days, 1981

ABOVE: An undated photograph of the Egyptian novelist and Nobel laureate.

LAWRENCE DURRELL

Born: February 27, 1912 (Jullundur, India); died November 7, 1990 (Sommières, France).

Style and genre: Novelist, poet, travel writer, humorist, translator, and dramatist, Durrell wrote brilliant characterizations and exotic descriptions of Alexandria.

The success of Lawrence Durrell's series *The Alexandria Quartet* has largely overshadowed his other work, which includes novels, plays, poetry, humorous pieces, and a series of translations. *The Alexandria Quartet*, however, brought him international recognition and placed him at the forefront of his profession. The four books cover, in a particularly innovative and expressive way, events that took place in Alexandria prior to and during World War II.

Durrell was born in India and educated in England from the age of eleven. He was unhappy in England and failed his university exams. Around this time, he decided to become a writer, although he also worked in various diplomatic services and taught. He moved to Corfu with his first wife in 1935, the year in which his first novel, *Pied Piper of Lovers*, was published. In 1937, he met the American writer Henry Miller in Paris, and the two became lifelong friends, collaborating on several projects with the hopes of instigating a literary movement.

Durrell fled Greece before the advancing Nazis in 1941 and settled in Cairo. The following year, he moved to Alexandria, where he met his second wife, Eve Cohen, on whom he based the character Justine in the first book of *The Alexandria Quartet*. In 1945, Durrell relocated to Rhodes and then, in 1947, to Argentina. From 1949 to 1952, he worked in Belgrade as a press attaché, during which time his writing was curtailed. In 1952 he moved to Cypress, hoping to resurrect his literary career. He began work on *The Alexandria Quartet* before being caught up in the conflict between the Cypriots, Turkish Cypriots, and British, an experience he later recorded in *Bitter Lemons*. Leaving Cypress, Durrell moved to Sommières, France, where he lived for the rest of his life. **TamP**

"Everyone loathes his own country and countrymen if he is any sort of artist."

ABOVE: Lawrence Durrell pictured on a French television program in 1982.

Signature titles

Novels

Pied Piper of Lovers, 1935
The Alexandria Quartet
- *Justine*, 1957
- *Balthazar*, 1958
- *Mountolive*, 1958
- *Clea*, 1960

The Revolt of Aphrodite
- *Tunc*, 1968
- *Nunquam*, 1970

The Avignon Quintet, 1974–1985

Travel writing

Bitter Lemons, 1957
Sicilian Carousel, 1977
Caesar's Vast Ghost, 1990

PATRICK WHITE

Born: May 28, 1912 (London, England); died September 30, 1990 (Sydney, New South Wales, Australia).

Style and genre: Novelist and playwright of epic, psychological works dissecting the Australian narrative and exploring the personal and national search for identity.

Patrick White spent his formative years moving between England and Australia, feeling an outsider in both countries. He came from a tradition of landowners that subscribed to the Australian national stereotype of manly men, one that could not easily understand his literary aspirations, let alone his homosexuality. A delicate, asthmatic child, he was sent away to school for his health, and later studied in Cambridge—separations that further emphasized his difference from his family. As a young man, he worked on his uncle's sheep station, but the inheritance he received on his father's death meant he could support himself as a writer.

White continued to feel a deep attachment to the Australian bush, however, and after World War II he settled on a small working farm outside Sydney with his Greek partner, Manoly Lascaris. A recurring theme in his work is the issue of what it means to be Australian, confronted on all sides by a vast emptiness. His early novels were well received in America and England, but panned by critics at home for being "un-Australian." Not until the publication of *Voss* in 1957 did he gain popular recognition at home in Australia; but by 1973, when he became the first (and, to date, the only) Australian to be awarded the Nobel Prize in Literature, Patrick White had become firmly established as one of the great writers of the twentieth century. Belligerent, contradictory, and prone to fits of rage, White regarded his unharnessed personal demons as a requisite of creative inspiration. He refused interviews and invitations to awards ceremonies, but thrived on gossip and entertaining. Despite his hatred of public speaking, during the 1980s he campaigned vociferously for nuclear disarmament. **MK**

"I think it is impossible to explain faith. It is like trying to explain air . . ."

Signature titles

Novels

The Tree of Man, 1955

Voss, 1957

Riders in the Chariot, 1961

The Eye of the Storm, 1973

The Twyborn Affair, 1979

Short stories

The Burnt Ones, 1964

The Cockatoos, 1974

Plays

The Ham Funeral, 1947

Signal Driver: A Morality Play for the Times, 1982

Memoir

Flaws in the Glass, 1981

ABOVE: Patrick White at an antinuclear/peace demonstration in 1981.

JORGE AMADO

Born: Jorge Amado de Faria, August 10, 1912 (Ilheus, Brazil); died August 6, 2001 (Salvador, Brazil).

Style and genre: Amado's early work deals with class struggle whereas his later work emphasizes the sensual and humorist side of Brazilian psychology.

The most translated author in Brazil, Jorge Amado grew up in Bahia, northern Brazil, on his grandfather's cocoa plantation. There he quickly became familiar with a double standard that would surface in much of his work—that is, the way wealthy plantation-owning men asserted their masculinity by being loyal to their promiscuity, and women their femininity through loyalty to their men. This double standard is played out in what is arguably Amado's most popular novel, *Gabriela, Clove and Cinnamon*, in the relationship between the beautiful migrant worker, Garbriela, and Nacib, who hires her to cook in his bar.

Amado's career was punctuated by several turbulent events: the public burning of six of his novels by then-president Getulio Vargas; exile due to his communist views; and the eventual realization that he was "of better use to the people as a writer than by spending my time on party activity." His work falls into two discrete writing phases: Class struggle dominates the first phase, as in *The Violent Land*, in which many of his provincial characters struggle to survive. With *Gabriela*, he beckoned in a new era. His post-exile work emphasizes the sensual and humorist side of the Brazilian psychology. It was Amado's portrayal of this psychology that would come to be his biggest export to the rest of the world.

Several of Amado's books have been adapted for television and film, including *Gabriela*, even if the novel was criticized at the time of its publication for reinforcing third-world depictions of women. *Dona Flor and Her Two Husbands* and *The Violent Land* both saw Amado nominated for the Nobel Prize for Literature. But it has been the outside view of his homeland, which he has done so much to mold, that will be his lasting legacy to readers everywhere. **JSD**

"I . . . believe in changing the world and I believe literature has a huge importance."

Signature titles

Novels

O País do Carnaval, 1931

Cacau, 1933

Sea of Death (Mar Morto), 1936

The Violent Land (Terras do Sem Fim), 1943

Gabriela, Clove and Cinnamon (Gabriela, Cravo e Canela), 1958

Shepherds of the Night (Os Pastores da Noite), 1964

Dona Flor and Her Two Husbands (Dona Flor e Seus Dois Maridos), 1966

Tent of Miracles (Tenda dos Milagres), 1969

Tieta, the Goat Girl (Tieta do Agreste), 1977

Farda Fardão Camisola de Dormir, 1979

*Showdown (Tocaia Grande),*1984

O Compadre de Ogum, 1995

ABOVE: Amado pictured in 1990 when he won the Cino del Duca literary award.

ALBERT CAMUS

Born: November 7, 1913 (Mondovi, Algeria); died January 4, 1960 (near Sens, France).

Style and genre: Camus's themes include isolation of man in an alien environment, absurdist notions of life and universe, and exploration of morality and the human condition.

Albert Camus was a novelist, playwright, essayist, and philosopher, whose work addressed the alienation and disillusionment facing man in the postwar age. His father was killed in combat during World War I, less than a year after Camus was born, and his mother moved the family to an impoverished working-class area of Algiers. A keen student, he won a scholarship to the Algiers lycée, progressing to the

Signature titles

Novels

The Stranger (L'étranger), 1942

The Plague (La Peste), 1947

The Fall (La Chute), 1956

Short story

Exile and the Kingdom (L'exil et le royaume), 1957

Play

Caligula, 1938

Nonfiction

The Myth of Sisyphus (Le Mythe de Sisyphe), 1942

The Rebel (L'homme révolté), 1951

ABOVE: A studio portrait of Albert Camus dating from c. 1950.

RIGHT: Illustration by Édouard Legrand from the French NRF edition of *The Plague*.

ABOVE: Camus smoking a cigarette on a balcony outside his publishers in 1955.

University of Algiers to study philosophy. Camus was a committed sportsman, excelling at soccer, but severe attacks of tuberculosis thwarted any ambitions as an athlete.

Camus turned his attention to literature, digesting the French classics and left-wing politics, and briefly joined the Algerian Communist Party in 1935, before serving as a journalist for the socialist paper *Alger-Republicain*. He also had a deep love of the theater, writing, producing, and acting for the Théâtre du Travail. His play *Caligula* was written shortly before his more admired literary work, although it was not produced until 1945.

"But what is happiness except the simple harmony between a man and the life he leads?"

The author moved to France at age twenty-five and, at the outbreak of World War II, joined the resistance movement during the German occupation, working as an editor for the underground Parisian daily *Combat*. It was during these tumultuous times that he finished his first and

Camus and Sartre

Despite a critical clash of opinions that severed a once-healthy friendship, Camus and Sartre are today often spoken of in the same sentence. Although Camus rejected the label "existentialist" and Sartre eagerly took on the mantle, the two helped shape the postwar world through their philosophy and literature.

Camus's *The Stranger* mirrored many of the views expressed in Sartre's earlier novel, *Nausea*, and the two finally met in Paris in 1943 at the opening of Sartre's play *The Flies*. Together with Simone de Beauvoir, they would meet at Café de Flore on the Left Bank and share their views. The friendship was fascinating to the outside world, the pair even appearing together in a photo for the American magazine *Vogue*, as the champions of the French intelligentsia. Politics soon drove a wedge between them, as Camus refused to accept communism and Sartre actively embraced it; they also clashed over the situation in Algeria, where Camus favored a continued French role and Sartre espoused independence at a time when the idea was unthinkable to most of his countrymen. Their differences even generated into open letters of criticism of each other's work in the printed press.

The two never spoke to each other again after 1952, yet after Camus's untimely death in 1960 Sartre's generous eulogy of his former friend hinted at the deep respect that such huge men of words held for each other.

most celebrated novel, *The Stranger*. The novel follows the young Algerian Meursault, who is put on trial for shooting an Arab. It is not the nature of the crime that offends the court, but his refusal to feign remorse. Meursault is considered subhuman and a danger to society for his lack of conformity, and this emotional detachment and alienation ultimately leads to his death. The sense of the absurd and portrayal of the world as meaningless is a recurring theme of Camus's, for which he would be labeled an existentialist novelist alongside his one-time friend Jean-Paul Sartre.

The philosophical essay *The Myth of Sisyphus* continued his exploration of the absurd and man's futile search for meaning in an unintelligible world. Camus presents a series of paradoxical dualisms, such as the assertion that the value of life is great but cheapened by the fact that death renders it meaningless, concluding that, to survive, it is best to abandon ambition and focus on the everyday.

Camus's persistent faith in man's inherent goodness, however, is best conveyed in *The Plague*, an allegorical account of the Nazi occupation of France, in which the citizens of the Algerian town Oran are ravaged by a plague of rats and are quarantined from the outside world. The resulting triumph of the human spirit is a result of a unilateral decision to work together rather than to seek a personal solution.

Camus tackled the concept of rebellion in his book-length essay *The Rebel*. In the 1950s, he also devoted much of his time to human rights issues, campaigning for the worldwide abolishment of capital punishment and speaking out against the Soviet repression of the 1956 Hungarian Revolution. His final complete work of fiction, *The Fall*, is an elegantly crafted series of monologues by the successful Parisian defense lawyer Jean-Baptiste Clamence. Clamence's story amounts to a confession, as he describes the good he has done in life for the weak and unfortunate, only to reveal the complacent hypocrisy of his actions that are performed for his own satisfaction. In 1957, at the age of forty-four, Camus received the Nobel Prize in Literature. He died three years later in a car accident. **SG**

RIGHT: Cover of the paperback of *L'étranger* published by Editions Gallimard in 1957.

ALBERT CAMUS

L'ÉTRANGER

Texte intégral

BARBARA PYM

Born: June 2, 1913 (Oswestry, England); died January 11, 1980 (Oxford, England).

Style and genre: Recognized as one of the most underrated writers of the twentieth century, Pym wrote satirical tragic-comic novels about quiet English middle-class lives.

Barbara Pym's novels are full of what she described as "excellent women"—intelligent, sensible spinsters living quiet lives often revolving around the church and village activities. Pym drew on her own experience of growing up in rural Shropshire, where her mother was assistant organist at the local church. The vicars and curates who were regular visitors at her home formed the basis of some of her most memorable characters.

After studying English at Oxford, Pym wrote her first novel in 1935, when she was only twenty-two. She submitted *Some Tame Gazelle*, a story of two spinsters in their fifties, to numerous publishers although it was not accepted until 1950. Following its success, she produced five more novels, including *Excellent Women* and *Less than Angels*, which were all well received and established her reputation for elegantly written comic prose. However, in 1963, when she submitted her seventh novel, *An Unsuitable Attachment*, to her publisher, it was rejected for being out of step with the times—in all it was rejected by a further nineteen publishers.

Pym continued writing but could no longer get published. In 1977, however, her career was revived when Philip Larkin described her as the most underrated writer of the twentieth century. As a result, her books were reprinted and her novel, *Quartet in Autumn*, a poignant tale about four characters on the verge of retirement, was short listed for the Booker Prize. It was followed in 1978 by *The Sweet Dove Died*, which was about an older woman's relationship with a younger man. Pym did not only enjoy renewed fame in England, her work was also published internationally to great acclaim. Sadly she died just two years later, from breast cancer, at the age of sixty-six. **HJ**

"How absurd and delicious it is to be in love with somebody younger."—*The Sweet Dove Died*

Signature titles

Novels

Some Tame Gazelle, 1950
Excellent Women, 1952
Jane and Prudence, 1953
Less than Angels, 1955
A Glass of Blessings, 1958
No Fond Return of Love, 1961
Quartet in Autumn, 1977
The Sweet Dove Died, 1978
A Few Green Leaves, 1980

ABOVE: Barbara Pym photographed in 1979, the year before she died.

ANGUS WILSON

Born: August 11, 1913 (Bexhill, England); died May 31, 1991 (Bury St. Edmunds, England).

Style and genre: Biting wit, social observations of English class, and a love of the macabre constitute Wilson's oeuvre, as well as open reference to homosexuality.

Angus Wilson was one of England's first openly gay writers. He was possessed of a brilliant brain and during World War II he worked as a code breaker, but he suffered some kind of breakdown thought to have been brought on not only by the stress of the job but also by gossip about his homosexuality (which was then illegal). He had recovered by the end of the war and on the advice of his psychiatrist began writing. His first two published works, *The Wrong Set* and *Such Darling Dodos*, were collections of short stories. These were followed by his first novel *Hemlock and After,* which tells the story of a middle-aged novelist attempting to set up a writers' center in a country house and draws upon Wilson's own homosexual experiences.

During the 1950s and 1960s Wilson produced a series of novels that garnered a significant amount of critical acclaim. They included *Anglo-Saxon Attitudes,* which tells of an archeologist who knows he has been involved in a hoax, and *The Middle Age of Mrs. Eliot*, a novel about a widow who finds herself in financial difficulties. *The Old Men at the Zoo* explores the near future and *No Laughing Matter*, perhaps his most ambitious novel, is a family saga that spans some fifty years.

Wilson also wrote essays on Émile Zola, Charles Dickens, and Rudyard Kipling and from 1966 he was a lecturer in English literature at the University of East Anglia. In 1970, he jointly founded the university's now widely acclaimed creative writing course with the novelist Malcolm Bradbury. Illustrious alumni include the novelists Angela Carter, Ian McEwan, and Kazuo Ishiguro as well as the British poet laureate Andrew Motion. In 1980, Wilson was honored with a knighthood for his services to literature. After a long illness, he died in 1991. **HJ**

"I have no concern for the common man except that he should not be so common."

Signature titles

Short stories

The Wrong Set, 1949

Such Darling Dodos, 1950

Novels

Hemlock and After, 1952

Anglo-Saxon Attitudes, 1956

The Middle Age of Mrs. Eliot, 1958

The Old Men at the Zoo, 1961

Late Call, 1964

No Laughing Matter, 1967

As If by Magic, 1973

Setting the World on Fire, 1980

ABOVE: A portrait of Angus Wilson later in life, taken in 1981.

RALPH ELLISON

Born: March 1, 1914, (Oklahoma City, Oklahoma, U.S.); died April 16, 1994 (New York, New York, U.S.).

Style and genre: Ellison wrote naturalistic fiction leavened with philosophical speculation and essays focusing on the relationship between race and aesthetics.

Although he published only one novel in his lifetime, *Invisible Man*, Ralph Ellison ranks as one of the most important American writers of the twentieth century. Born into a poor black family in Oklahoma, he won a scholarship to study music at Tuskegee Institute, the Alabama school made famous by its first principal, Booker T. Washington. While Tuskegee's library granted him access to the inspirational world of modernist literature, his time in Alabama would also introduce him to the Southern legacy of slavery and segregation that still cast a shadow over African-Americans.

The protagonist of *Invisible Man* follows a trajectory similar to his creator's. He leaves his family to study and, like Ellison, heads to New York City without completing his studies. Before he can take up his scholarship he must box, blindfolded, against other black youths for the entertainment of local white dignitaries. Later, working as a left-wing activist in Harlem, he finds himself caught up in a storm of racial violence. Finally, he retires to a basement, resolving to live as an invisible man, before returning to confront white society with the discrimination that has driven him underground. If the greater part of the novel is written in a straightforward naturalistic style, the surreal, nightmarish aspects of African-American life threaten to overwhelm the narrative at any moment.

"Who knows but that, on the lower frequencies, I speak for you?"—*Invisible Man*

While Ellison was critical of the racism of American society, he eschewed the militant attitudes adopted by Richard Wright and James Baldwin. His brilliant essays spoke out against racial and cultural segregation: He demonstrated how white American identity had always been constructed in relation to black Americans and celebrated the power of jazz to bring both races together. **CT**

Signature titles

Novels

Invisible Man, 1952

Juneteenth, 1999 (incomplete)

Essays

Shadow and Act, 1964

Going to the Territory, 1986

Short stories

Flying Home and Other Stories, 1996

ABOVE: The provocative essayist Ralph Ellison pictured in 1964.

ROBERTSON DAVIES

Born: August 28, 1913 (Thamesville, Ontario, Canada); died December 2, 1995 (Orangeville, Ontario, Canada).

Style and genre: One of Canada's most popular and influential novelists, Davies's work is steeped in myth, magic, and satire.

Robertson Davies's first love was drama and he produced his first commercially successful play, *Fortune, My Foe*, in 1948. In the 1960s he turned to academic life and joined Trinity College at the University of Toronto where he taught literature.

Davies's masterpiece is the Deptford Trilogy—comprising *Fifth Business*, *The Manticore*, and *World of Wonders*—which follows the lives of three characters intertwined by the simple act of throwing a snowball. It is a world of myth and magic and its cast includes saints and devils. His next works, *The Rebel Angels*, *What's Bred in the Bone*, and *The Lyre of Orpheus*, known as the Cornish Trilogy, satirize academic life and center around Francis Cornish, a mysterious spy, art collector, and forger. **HJ**

Signature titles

Novels

The Deptford Trilogy
- *Fifth Business*, 1970
- *The Manticore*, 1972
- *World of Wonders*, 1975

The Cornish Trilogy
- *The Rebel Angels*, 1981
- *What's Bred in the Bone*, 1985
- *The Lyre of Orpheus*, 1988

Murther and Walking Spirits, 1991

The Cunning Man, 1994

CLAUDE SIMON

Born: October 10, 1913 (Tananarive, Madagascar); died July 6, 2005 (Paris, France).

Style and genre: Simon was a representative of the 1950s avant-garde *nouveau roman* movement. His long-sentenced, stream-of-consciousness writing often examined war and the experiences of time.

Claude Simon was born in Madagascar, but after his father was killed during World War I he was raised by his mother and her family in Perpignan, close to the Spanish border. He lived a colorful life: gunrunning for the Republicans during the Spanish Civil War; being captured by the Germans; escaping on his transfer to a prison camp in France to join the Resistance movement; and then living after the war by producing wine and selling his writing. Simon's first four novels follow mostly traditional forms, but his 1957 title, *The Wind*, won him international recognition for its innovative, *nouveau roman* style, in which the plot is simply one element of the novel. Simon won the Nobel Prize in Literature in 1985. **REM**

Signature titles

Novels

The Cheat (Le Tricheur), 1945

The Tightrope (La Corde raide), 1947

Gulliver, 1952

The Anointment of Spring (Le Sacre du printemps), 1954

The Wind. Attempted Restoration of a Baroque Altarpiece (Le Vent. Tentative de restitution d'un retable baroque), 1957

The Flanders Road (La Route de Flandres), 1960

The Palace (La Palace), 1962

Story (Histoire), 1967

Conducting Bodies (Les Corps conducteurs), 1971

The Georgics (Le Géorgiques), 1981

The Invitation (L'invitation), 1987

The Acacia (L'acacia), 1989

The Botanical Garden (Le Jardin des plantes), 1997

DYLAN THOMAS

Born: Dylan Marlais Thomas, October 27, 1914 (Swansea, Wales); died November 9, 1953 (New York, New York, U.S.).

Style and genre: Welsh poet and playwright with lyrical musical quality to his writings, Dylan Thomas is famous for his play *Under Milk Wood*.

Dylan Thomas was one of the twentieth century's most influential lyrical poets. He was brought up in Swansea, Wales, but his father refused to have Welsh spoken in the house. Instead, Thomas was immersed in Shakespeare, local folklore, and the Bible, all of which, it is thought, helped to provide inspiration for the intense imagery and vivid metaphors he was to become famous for in his own writings.

Thomas moved to London in 1934 and his first poetry collection, *Eighteen Poems*, was published in the same year. Although many found its surreal imagery hard to understand, it earned him praise from the likes of poet Edith Sitwell. A second book, *Twenty-Five Poems*, published two years later, cemented his reputation. Throughout his life Thomas's poems dealt with morbid themes. One of his latest and greatest works, "Do not go gentle into that good night," details his feelings on seeing his father on his deathbed and contains the famous line: "Rage, rage against the dying of the light." Although his rich rhetorical poetry seemed to be an almost free-flowing

Signature titles

Poetry

Eighteen Poems, 1934
Twenty-Five Poems, 1935
The Map of Love, 1939
The World I Breathe, 1939
New Poems, 1943
Deaths and Entrances, 1946
Selected Writings, 1946
Twenty-Six Poems, 1950
Collected Poems, 1952
In Country Sleep, 1952

Short stories

Portrait of the Artist as a Young Dog, 1940
Adventures in the Skin Trade, 1955
A Child's Christmas in Wales, 1955

Play

Under Milk Wood, 1954

Film script

The Doctor and the Devils, 1953

Letters

Letters to Vernon Watkins, 1957

ABOVE: Dylan Thomas photographed for *Picture Post* on August 10, 1946.

RIGHT: Thomas working at home in South Leigh, Oxfordshire, on January 1, 1948.

stream of consciousness, his notes show that his visionary style was created by an almost obsessive amount of labor.

In 1937, Thomas married Caitlin Macnamara and for a short time lived in Laugharne, in west Wales, saying he could write only in Wales. He completed what was to be his most famous work, *Under Milk Wood*, in 1954. Set in the fictionalized seaside town of Llareggub ("Bugger all" backward), his "play for voices" was in turn lyrical, tender, and comedic. He also wrote many short stories of note, later collected in *Portrait of the Artist as a Young Dog* and *Adventures in the Skin Trade*.

As well as being an accomplished poet and playwright, Thomas was an entertaining radio broadcaster, working for the BBC between 1937 and 1953. These broadcasts and his poetry tours of the United States and Britain—not to mention his reputation for wild living and hard drinking—provided him with a strange mix of fame and notoriety. **JM**

ABOVE: The Welsh poet with his wife Caitlin at the pub in an undated photograph.

"Cold Beer Is Bottled God"

No account of Dylan Thomas would be complete without mention of alcohol. Both in London and in the United States, Thomas became infamous as an objectionable drunkard, albeit one who was often entertaining. Sadly, the years of drinking caught up with him in the Chelsea Hotel in New York on his fourth tour of the United States, when he was only thirty-nine. Suffering from alcohol poisoning, it was there that he uttered the words that many people quote as his last: "I've had eighteen straight whiskeys. I think that's the record." Nevertheless, he did not actually die until a few days later.

JULIO CORTÁZAR

Signature titles

Poetry

Presencia, 1938

Los reyes, 1949

Short stories

The End of the Game and Other Stories (Final del juego), 1956

Blow Up and Other Stories, 1967

Around the Day in Eighty Worlds, 1967

All Fires the Fire (Todos los fuegas el fuego), 1973

Unreasonable Hours (Deshoras), 1994

Novels

Hopscotch (Rayuela), 1963

Final Exam (Ultimo Round), 1969

A Manual for Manual (Libro de Manuel), 1973

Born: August 26, 1914 (Brussels, Belgium); died February 12, 1984 (Paris, France).

Style and genre: Cortázar was an Argentine fabulist whose ludic, fantastic stories and nonlinear, genre-defying longer works produce a fusion of Poe, Borges, surrealism, and jazz.

The son of a diplomat, with a talent for languages, Cortázar taught school for more than fifteen years before moving to Paris in 1951. Many of his short stories portray a secret, fantastic, and terrifying world fusing dreams and awakenings. His seminal 1963 novel, *Hopscotch*, opens with the proposition that it may be read either from beginning to "the end" (there are 155 chapters) or in an aleatory manner, beginning with chapter 73 and following footnoted prompts to compose a seemingly random sequence. The resulting kaleidoscopic journey—moving, irreverent, and profound—captured the anarchic energy of the 1960s and ensured Cortázar's stature as one of the fathers of magical realism. **CH**

MARGUERITE DURAS

Signature titles

Novels

Les impudents, 1942

The Sea Wall (Un barrage contre le Pacifique), 1942

The Square (Le Square), 1955

The Ravishing of Lol Stein (Le Ravissement de Lol V. Stein), 1964

India Song, 1973

The Lover (L'amant), 1984

Practicalities (La Vie materielle), 1987

Screenplay

Hiroshima Mon Amour, 1959

Born: Marguerite Donnadieu, April 4, 1914 (Gia Dinh, Indochina—now Vietnam); died March 3, 1996 (Paris, France).

Style and genre: Representative of *nouveau roman* who as a poetic memoirist of French Indochina deftly examined female consciousness, madness, and cinema.

Born in Indochina, Marguerite Duras's life and works were intertwined with the dramatic events of twentieth-century Europe, including the dissolution of colonialism, the Nazi genocide, the sexual revolution, and the dominance of cinema. Her novels and screenplays examine the inability of language to bear witness to cultural events. The fallibility of personal and political histories, informed and deformed by desire, is at the core of her best known works—the poetic screenplay for *Hiroshima Mon Amour*, the play for voices *India Song*, and the semiautobiographical novel *L'amant*. Having taken herself as subject, her writing grew increasingly abstract and influenced by her alcoholism. **SM**

WILLIAM BURROUGHS

Born: William Seward Burroughs II, February 5, 1914 (St. Louis, Missouri, U.S.); died August 2, 1997 (Lawrence, Kansas, U.S.).

Style and genre: Leading literary figure of Beat Generation known for his fragmented nonlinear narrative style, spoken-word performances, and as an artist.

William S. Burroughs is regarded as one of the most influential writers of twentieth-century literature, whose influence extended across the arts and shaped an entire generation of young creative talents. He is also one of the most controversial literary figures, whose work has sparked both ardent admiration and scathing attack. His debilitating drug addiction, homosexuality, and repeated clashes with the law formed the foundation for much of his work, which was profoundly influenced by his opiate use.

In *Naked Lunch*, Burroughs's most famous book, he used a new literary style, referred to as "cut up" technique, bringing together fragmented and seemingly random passages and characters in a literary collage. His friend, the artist and writer Brion Gysin, employed the same technique in his works, and influenced him in this respect. *Naked Lunch* was published in 1959 and was immediately branded obscene. Its notoriety spread across Europe and America, and it became iconic of the Beat Generation. At the time of its publication, Burroughs had moved into "the Beat Hotel," a dilapidated hostel in Paris that was also home to the photographer Harold Chapman and the poets Peter Orlovsky, Allen Ginsberg, and Gregory Corso.

Burroughs wrote throughout his life, including *Cities of the Red Night*, *The Place of Dead Roads*, and *The Western Lands*, and taught briefly at the City College of New York. He spent his last years in Lawrence, Kansas, where he became involved with spoken-word performance and developed a painting technique called "action art." Burroughs died at age eighty-two, following a heart attack. He remains an influential figure whose work is referenced repeatedly in contemporary literature, film, and television. **TamP**

"Every man has inside himself a parasitic being who is acting not at all to his advantage."

Signature titles

Novels

Junkie, 1853

Queer, 1951–1953 (published 1985)

Naked Lunch, 1959

The Soft Machine, 1961

Dead Fingers Talk, 1963

Cities of the Red Night, 1981

The Place of Dead Roads, 1983

The Western Lands, 1987

Nonfiction

The Job: Interviews with William S. Burroughs, 1969

Jack Kerouac, 1970 (with Claude Pelieu)

Letters to Allen Ginsberg, 1953–1957

ABOVE: Burroughs poses for photographer William Coupon in the 1990s.

BOHUMIL HRABAL

Born: March 28, 1914 (Brno, Czechoslovakia); died on February 3, 1997 (Prague, Czech Republic).

Style and genre: Influenced by the surrealists, Hrabal's lyrical, exuberant prose contains touches of irony, symbolism, humor, and magical realism.

Signature titles

Novels

Dancing Lessons for the Advanced Age, 1964
Closely Watched Trains, 1965
I Served the King of England, 1971
Cutting It Short, 1974
Lovely Wistfulness, 1977
Too Loud a Solitude, 1977
The Little Town where Time Stood Still, 1978
Vacant Lots, 1986
In-House Weddings, 1986

Short stories

The Little Town where the Time Stood Still, 1978
Bambino di Praga, 1990
Total Fears: Letters to Dubenka, 1990
Sunny Days, 1998

Bohumil Hrabal belongs to the new wave of twentieth-century Czech experimentalists. His stream-of-consciousness prose abounds in comic relief, Czech folklore, and vernacular witticisms. Pervading his work is his compassionate treatment of ordinary people whose lives are punctuated by the kind of lyrical naivety or freakishness that implicates them in events much larger than themselves. And yet, in their desperate attempt to give meaning to their otherwise meaningless existence, they often realize that heroism lies in the comic relief brought on by the most ordinary life events.

Among the most acclaimed of Hrabal's novels is *Closely Watched Trains*, a lyrical depiction of the virginal railroad apprentice Milo Hrma, who survives his suicide attempt only to die a heroic, albeit accidental death when blowing up a German transport full of ammunition. Like most of Hrabal's characters, Dittie, the waiter protagonist from *I Served the King of England*, is propelled uncannily by his comic ambitions into external events that are beyond his control. From a humble servant of the emperor of Ethiopia, a father to a mentally ill offspring of the new German race, to a millionaire who sabotages his own fortune by drawing the attention of the communist authorities, Dittie loses his life's purpose in the name of a Švejk-like honesty. One of the most accomplished of Hrabal's novels is *Too Loud a Solitude*, a political satire on communist censorship and "cultural cleansing," in which the protagonist attempts to salvage books renounced by Husák's regime from being exterminated by the hydraulic press. After the fall of communism, Hrabal's work was no less critical of the budding Czech democracy, which he treated with a dose of infectious parody and skepticism. **PR**

"If I knew how to write, I'd write a book about the greatest of man's joys and sorrows."

ABOVE: Bohumil Hrabal pictured on a visit to Paris, France, in 1995.

ADOLFO BIOY CASARES

Born: September 15, 1914 (Buenos Aires, Argentina); died March 8, 1999 (Buenos Aires, Argentina).

Style and genre: Bioy Casares was a South American novelist who created classic works in the genre of magical realism and collaborated with Jorge Luis Borges.

Bioy Casares, or Bioy, as he was often affectionately known, wrote his first work of fiction at the age of eleven. He was a great friend of Jorge Luis Borges, with whom he collaborated to write detective novels and other works under the pseudonyms H. Bustos Domecq and B. Suárez Lynch. Although he seems to always have been in the literary shadow of Borges, the older writer himself acknowledged Bioy Casares's help in leading him from baroque fussy prose into a more streamlined classical style. Borges, in turn, encouraged Bioy Casares to move away from surrealism and stream of consciousness. The two were introduced in 1932 by Victoria Ocampo, a writer and intellectual of great esteem in Argentina, described by Borges as *la mujer más Argentina* ("the most Argentine woman").

In 1940, Bioy Casares married Victoria's younger sister, Silvina, and in that same year published what is arguably his most important work, *The Invention of Morel*. An established classic of Latin American fiction, it combines magical realism, science fiction, fantasy, and terror. It is perhaps his most famous work, one that both Luis Borges and Octavio Paz called "perfect" for its quality of a faultless tale formed with no superfluity of language or plot. In 1954, Bioy Casares and his wife Silvina adopted a baby girl the novelist had fathered with another woman. After Bioy Casares died, his estate was awarded to another illegitimate child, Fabián Bioy. Bioy Casares was an active member of Argentinian cultural life, producing many novels and works of short fiction, as well as the collaborations with Borges and a detective novel written with his wife Silvina. In 1990, he was awarded the Cervantes Prize, the most prestigious award given in the Spanish-speaking world. **REM**

"There are no hallucinations here: I know these people are real . . ."—*The Invention of Morel*

Signature titles

Novels

The Invention of Morel (La Invención de Morel), 1940

A Plan for Escape (Plan de evasión), 1945

Dream of Heroes (El Sueño de los héroes), 1954

Diary of the War of the Pig (Diario de la guerra del cerdo), 1969

Asleep in the Sun (Dormir al sol), 1973

The Adventures of a Photographer (La Aventura de la fotógrafo en La Plata), 1985

An Uneven Champion (Un campeón desparejo), 1993

ABOVE: The author of classic magical realism poses for a picture in 1994.

OCTAVIO PAZ

Born: Octavio Paz Lozano, March 31, 1914 (Mexico City, Mexico); died April 19, 1998 (Mexico City, Mexico).

Style and genre: Poet and essayist whose poems explore themes of love, eroticism, and the nature of time; and whose essays deal with politics, history, and economics.

Octavio Paz's poetry is lyrical and political, erotic and existential, above all beautiful and profound. From an early age he wanted to be a poet and, encouraged by Pablo Neruda, he began to write, publishing his first poems in 1931. Paz's grandfather, Ireneo Paz—a novelist, publisher, liberal intellectual, and former soldier for President Porfirio Díaz—introduced the young Octavio to authors such as Juan Ramón Jiménez, Gerardo Diego, and Antonio Machado. Paz's father was often away from home in his role as secretary to Emiliano Zapata. Because of this connection, the family went into exile in the United States after Zapata's assassination in 1919.

Paz also spent time in Spain during the Spanish Civil War, where he fought on the Republican side. His time in the United States and Europe influenced his writing in ways both formalistic and political. He experimented with the techniques of modernism and surrealism, and communist ideologies entered his poetry. When the Spanish Republicans murdered

Signature titles

Play

The Daughter of Rappaccini (*La hija de Rappaccini*), 1956

Poetry

Wild Moon (*Luna silvestre*), 1933

Between the Stone and the Flower (*Entra la piedra y la flor*), 1941

Liberty under Oath (*Libertad bajo palabra*), 1949)

Eagle or Sun? (*Águila o sol?*), 1951

Sunstone (*Piedra del sol*), 1957

Eastern Slope (*Ladera este*), 1969

Poemas (*1935–1975*), 1979

Essays

The Labyrinth of Solitude (*El laberinto de la soledad*), 1950

The Bow and the Lyre (*El arco y la lira*), 1956

Alternating current (*Corriente alterna*), 1967

Children of the Mire (*Los hijos del limo*), 1974

SVENSKA AKADEMIEN
har vid sin sammankomst
den 11 oktober 1990
i överensstämmelse med
föreskrifterna i det av
ALFRED NOBEL
den 27 november 1895 upprättade
testamentet beslutat att
1990 års Nobelpris i litteratur
skall tilldelas
OCTAVIO PAZ
"för en lidelsefull diktning med vida
horisonter, präglad av sinnlig intelligens
och humanistisk integritet".
STOCKHOLM DEN 10 DECEMBER 1990

ABOVE: Octavio Paz pictured in a library in 1982.

RIGHT: Paz's diploma for receiving the Nobel Prize in Literature in 1990.

ABOVE: Paz interacts with students from Cornell University, New York, in 1966.

one of his friends, he became extremely disillusioned, although he never abandoned his advocacy for freedom of speech.

Paz traveled extensively, working as a journalist and founding several literary journals and magazines. In 1945 he took a post in the Mexican diplomatic service, working in New York, Paris, India, Japan, and Geneva. During this period, he wrote his brilliant study of Mexican life, identity, and thought, *The Labyrinth of Solitude*, as well as his most famous poem "Sunstone." In 1962, Mexico named him its ambassador to India, but in 1968 he resigned his diplomatic position in protest at the government's massacre of students in Plaza Tlatelolco, just before the Olympic Games were to be held in Mexico City. Paz won the prestigious Cervantes Prize in 1981, the Neustadt Prize in 1982, and was awarded the Nobel Prize in Literature in 1990. He died of cancer at the age of eighty-four in Mexico City. **REM**

Sunstone

"Sunstone," arguably Octavio Paz's greatest and most well-known poem, takes its name from the planet Venus: goddess of love in Roman mythology—and the symbol of the sun and water in Aztec legend. Written in 1957, it is a circular poem, modeled on the Aztec calendar stone, which begins where it ends:
"a crystal willow, a poplar of water,
a tall fountain the wind arches over,
a tree deep-rooted yet dancing still,
a course of a river that turns, moves on,
doubles back, and comes full circle,
forever arriving."

ROLAND BARTHES

Born: Roland Gérard Barthes, November 12, 1915 (Cherbourg, France); died March 25, 1980 (Paris, France).

Style and genre: French essayist and literary critic whose writings on semiotics were instrumental for movements such as structuralism and New Criticism.

Before writing literary manifestos such as *Writing Degree Zero* and *Mythologies*, Roland Barthes received several degrees in classics, grammar, and philology from the University of Paris. In 1976, after spending several years teaching at Centre National de la Recherche Scientifique, he was appointed to the chair of literary semiology at the Collège de France. The appointment both recognized Barthes as a leading literary theorist and acknowledged the intellectual importance of semiotics, the study of signs and symbols as communicative behavior.

Barthes is largely responsible for advancing structuralism—the application of concepts from structural linguistics to social and cultural phenomena—within cultural and literary studies. With a rollicking, sensual, and wildly personal writing style, he revealed the conventions and social functions that exist in advertising, fashion, photography, and literature. His best known work is the essay "The Death of the Author," which argues against using the biographical context of an author to understand the meaning of a text. Although psychoanalyst Jacques Lacan and philosophers Michael Foucault and Jacques Derrida received Barthes warmly in the 1970s, his early work, specifically *On Racine*, sparked fiery debate among more traditional French critics. Some academics accused Barthes of denigrating classical literature by viewing it as a "system" of signs rather than as a body of art with cultural roots. His late works, particularly *Camera Lucida*, which he wrote after the death of his mother, probe communication theory through more personal and biographical writings. In 1975, five years before his death, Barthes turned his critical apparatus on himself, producing an autobiography that radically rewrites the conventions of the genre. **SD**

"What the public wants is the image of passion, not passion itself."

Signature titles

Essays

Writing Degree Zero, 1953
On Racine, 1963
The Fashion System, 1967
Elements of Semiology, 1968
Mythologies, 1957
The Pleasure of the Text, 1973
A Lover's Discourse: Fragments, 1977
Camera Lucida: Reflections on Photography, 1980

Autobiography

Roland Barthes by Roland Barthes, 1975

ABOVE: Roland Barthes in a photograph from 1975.

SAUL BELLOW

Born: Solomon Bellows, June 10, 1915 (Lachine, Quebec, Canada); died April 5, 2005 (Brookline, Massachusetts, U.S.).

Style and genre: Nobel Prize–winning Jewish-American novelist who vividly explored male identity and spirituality amid postwar alienation.

Although he was born in Canada, the son of Russian Jews, Bellow grew up and lived in Chicago, and it was his depiction of urban life in that city that made his name. His breakthrough novel was *The Adventures of Augie March*, which inaugurated a new era of postwar confidence and exuberance in American fiction. In it, Bellow discovers a voice fluent and capacious enough to capture the manic expansion and variety of 1950s America, through a combination of fast-talking banter, wise-guy coinages, Yiddish slang, and poetic accuracy.

Martin Amis, among others, has described *Augie March* as the end of the quest for the Great American Novel. But Bellow followed it with works of equal ambition, from the exuberant picaresque of *Henderson the Rain King* to the desperate and hilarious intellectualism of *Herzog*, about a "suffering joker" who writes unsent letters to past lovers, dead philosophers, and the U.S. president. The book begins, "'If I am out of my mind, it's all right with me,' thought Moses Herzog," and shows Herzog coming to terms with the wreckage of his personal life (his wife has left him for his best friend) and the uselessness of his nonstop verbal flow. Difficulties with women are a persistent theme in Bellow. He described himself as a "serial husband," the last of his five wives being less than half his age, and he fathered a child in 1999 at the age of eighty-four, a year before he published his last novel.

When Bellow was awarded the Nobel Prize in Literature in 1976, the committee commended his "human understanding and subtle analysis of contemporary culture." What makes Bellow great, however, is the transmission of these qualities through an irresistibly memorable and quotable prose style, as felicitous as it is funny, and as accurate as it is expansive. **MS**

"A fool can throw a stone in a pond that 100 wise men cannot get out."

Signature titles

Novels

Dangling Man, 1944
The Victim, 1947
The Adventures of Augie March, 1953
Seize the Day, 1956
Henderson the Rain King, 1959
Herzog, 1964
Mr. Sammler's Planet, 1970
Humboldt's Gift, 1975
More Die of Heartbreak, 1987
Ravelstein, 2000

Essays

To Jerusalem and Back, 1976
It All Adds Up, 1994
Graven Imges, 1997

ABOVE: Saul Bellow poses for the camera in 1982.

ARTHUR MILLER

Born: October 17, 1915 (New York, New York, U.S.); died February 10, 2005 (Roxbury, Connecticut, U.S.).

Style and genre: Miller is best known for his dramatic social criticism, interest in Jewish identity, obsession with time and history, and psychological realism.

Like Tennessee Williams, the U.S. playwright with whom he is most often compared, Arthur Miller peaked young. His greatest artistic and commercial achievements—*All My Sons*, *Death of a Salesman*, and *The Crucible*—came in a six-year surge of writing (1947–1953) that also included *Focus*, a novel exploring anti-Semitism, and *An Enemy of the People*, an adaptation of Ibsen. Miller continued to write for more than fifty years, without matching the successes of his youth.

Miller's enduring works engaged with the pressing social concerns of postwar American life. He believed that drama has a social function and saw the theater as an arena for confronting coercive national myths. *Death of a Salesman*, his masterpiece, portrays the dehumanizing effects of consumer culture through the immolation of salesman Willy Loman. *The Crucible*, a story of witch-hunts in seventeenth-century Salem, analogizes the McCarthyite witch-hunts of the 1950s.

In 1956, Miller was summoned before the House Un-American Activities Committee (HUAC), where he was found in contempt of Congress for refusing to "name names." His bravery in the face of HUAC bought him the moral capital that he would spend for the rest of his life. Later that year, Miller left his wife and family for Marilyn Monroe. Miller's plays are haunted by history, particularly the Depression and the Holocaust, and are frequently obsessed with the relationships between fathers and sons. But while Miller dedicated much of his career to exploring father–son relationships on the stage, he never publicly recognized the existence of one of his own sons, Daniel, who was born with Down's syndrome. Even in death, it seems as though Arthur Miller is haunted by the past. **IW**

"The theater is so endlessly fascinating because it's so accidental. It's so much like life."

Signature titles

Novel

Focus, 1945

Plays

The Man Who Had All the Luck, 1944

All My Sons, 1947

Death of a Salesman, 1949

An Enemy of the People, 1950

The Crucible, 1953

A View from the Bridge, 1955

After the Fall, 1964

The Price, 1968

The American Clock, 1980

Broken Glass, 1994

Autobiography

Timebends: A Life, 1987

ABOVE: The American playwright Arthur Miller sits for a photograph c. 1960.

GIORGIO BASSANI

Born: March 4, 1916 (Bologna, Italy); died April 13, 2000 (Rome, Italy).

Style and genre: Bassani was a poet and writer who was among the major representatives of Italian literature in the 1950s and 1960s and best known as the "writer of memories."

In the fifteenth and sixteenth centuries, Ferrara—the splendid town in the Emilia-Romagna region of Italy—was one of the centers of the Renaissance movement. The town also had some notable sons in the twentieth century: one was the painter Giorgio de Chirico, the father of metaphysical art, and another was the poet and writer Giorgio Bassani, who dedicated a series called *Ferrara Novel* (*Romanzo di Ferrara*) to the city.

Bassani was always known as the "writer of memories," someone who evoked the past to render it immortal. His vision was closer to art than to conventional storytelling, at times seeming like the literary equivalent of the visions that Giorgio de Chirico expressed in his paintings. Maybe it was for that reason that Bassani initially devoted his time almost uniquely to writing poetry, depicting a stylized, barren reality stifled by dry yet fundamental words.

But poetry was not the best vehicle for Bassani to deliver the historical descriptions he wanted to convey, and so he decided to absorb the Ferrara setting into the more solid branch of his narrative. The novel *The Garden of the Finzi-Continis* was immediately recognized as Bassani's magnum opus. It relates the incidents that occurred among the provincial bourgeoisie during the years of the fascist regime, of which the author (who was of Jewish ancestry) became victim after the introduction of the Race Laws in 1938. The book gives a deep insight into these events. Through a young, unnamed narrator, it depicts the awkwardness of an adolescence full of torment and a pure and simple desire to live. It is no coincidence that in 1972 Vittorio de Sica turned the book into a film that won the Academy Award. **FF**

"This was our vice: to walk ahead with our heads perennially turned backward."

ABOVE: Bassani pictured in 1964 on the publication of *Behind the Door*.

Signature titles

Novels

A Town in the Plains (Una città di pianura), 1940

The Last Years of Clelia Trotti (Gli ultimi anni di Clelia Trotti), 1955

A Night in '43 (Una notte del '43), 1955

Five Stories of Ferrara (Cinque storie Ferraresi), 1956

Glasses Made of Gold (Gli occhiali d'oro), 1958

The Garden of the Finzi-Continis (Il giardino dei Finzi-Contini), 1962

Behind the Door (Dietro la porta), 1964

The Heron (L'airone), 1968

The Smell of Hay (L'odore del fieno), 1972

ROALD DAHL

Born: September 13, 1916 (Llandaff, Cardiff, Wales); died November 23, 1990 (Great Missenden, Buckinghamshire, England).

Style and genre: Dahl's ingenious, often grisly imagination was best expressed by his made-up words, fantastic plots, and larger-than-life characters.

The possessor of an incredible imagination, Roald Dahl wrote for both adults and children. His works were inspired by his life—people he knew or events he had experienced—and the stories told to him by his mother. The fourth of six children, he was born in Wales to Norwegian parents, who named him after the explorer Roald Amundsen. His sister Astrid died of appendicitis when he was three years old; their father died of pneumonia just a few months later.

Dahl's works emphasize his bipartite nature—part Norwegian, part British, but never fully either. As a child he was often unhappy at school—according to his autobiography, *Boy,* bullies inspired many of the characters in his stories. *Charlie and the Chocolate Factory* was inspired by his school being chosen to taste chocolates for Cadbury. His second autobiography, *Going Solo*, tells of his adventures as a pilot for Shell Oil Company in what is now Tanzania. During World War II, Dahl served with the RAF and in 1940 survived a plane crash in the Libyan desert, despite the aircraft bursting into flames.

After leaving the Royal Air Force, Dahl began working for the British government's war effort in the United States, where he had more articles published. In 1952 he married the actress Patricia Neal and they had five children; tragically their eldest daughter died at the age of seven and their son was permanently disabled in an accident. The couple divorced in 1983, after Dahl had begun an affair with Felicity Crossland, who became his second wife. Dahl was a great campaigner and fundraiser for children's charities, both in the United Kingdom and overseas. The author died at his home in Buckinghamshire and there are now two museums in the county dedicated to his works. **LH**

"A little nonsense now and then is relished by the wisest men."

Signature titles

Children's fiction

James and the Giant Peach, 1961

Charlie and the Chocolate Factory, 1964

The BFG, 1982

Children's poetry

Revolting Rhymes, 1982

Dirty Beasts, 1983

Novel

My Uncle Oswald, 1979

Short stories

Kiss Kiss, 1959

Tales of the Unexpected, 1979

Autobiographies

Boy: Tales of Childhood, 1984

Going Solo, 1986

ABOVE: Roald Dahl photographed during the 1970s.

RIGHT: The cover of the first U.S. edition of Dahl's short story collection *Kiss Kiss* (1960).

ROALD DAHL
Kiss
Kiss
Eleven fine new stories by the author of SOMEONE LIKE YOU
ROALD
DAHL
Kiss
Kiss
Michael
Joseph

CAMILO JOSÉ CELA

Born: May 11, 1916 (Iria Flavia, Spain); died January 17, 2002 (Madrid, Spain).

Style and genre: Camilo José Cela was an iconoclastic Spanish writer of darkly comic and often brutally grotesque vision; his novels resound with social realism and formal experimentation.

Cela's youth was largely uneventful, save for a couple of bouts of tuberculosis. In 1934, he entered university with the aim of studying medicine and law, but abandoned his studies after wandering into a lecture on literature by the poet Pedro Salinas. During the bombing of Madrid in 1936, he wrote his first book of poetry, and fought briefly on the side of Franco before being made invalid by a shrapnel wound.

Cela's first novel, *The Family of Pascual Duarte*, was both a popular and a critical success, sending shockwaves through an exhausted and impoverished Spanish society still recovering from the Civil War that had claimed more than half a million lives and at least as many exiles. Written in the first person, the novel presents Pascual's death-row confession to matricide and a life of loathing, debasement, and violence. Cela's next novel, *Rest Home*, continued his necrological explorations in a more formally stylistic mode, portraying the final months of seven terminally ill, tubercular patients. Perpetually unsatisfied, Cela again experimented, and in 1946 completed his

Signature titles

Novels

The Family of Pascual Duarte (La Familia de Pascual Duarte), 1942

Rest Home (Pabellón de Reposa), 1944

The Hive (La Colmena), 1951

Mrs. Caldwell Speaks to Her Son (Mrs. Caldwell habla con su hijo), 1953

San Camilo, 1969

Mazurka for Two Dead Men (Mazurca para dos muertos), 1983

Christ Versus Arizona (Christo versus Arizona), 1988

Travel writing

Journey to the Alcarria (Viaje a la Alcarria), 1948

ABOVE: The Nobel Prize winner pictured in 2001, the year before he died.

RIGHT: In 1956 with Ernest Hemingway (left), one of Cela's great influences.

ABOVE: Cela poses while smoking a cigar in a photograph from 1972.

masterpiece, *The Hive*. Rejection by the censors, however, meant it was not published until 1951, in Argentina, where it was subject to cuts. Employing more than 300 characters, the novel recounts three days in the life of Madrid, whose denizens are paralyzed by despair, poverty, boredom, and fear. *Mrs. Caldwell Speaks to Her Son* followed in 1953, a poetic exploration of the lucid but surreal reminiscences of an elderly English woman, whose only son drowned many years ago.

With increasing mastery of the novel form, Cela began to branch out into other genres: eight books of travel writing, notably *Journey to the Alcarria*; lexicographic researches (*Secret Dictionary*, a thesaurus of forbidden words and phrases); more than a dozen collections of short stories; and a series of anti-novels of great complexity. In each of these explorations, Cela remained faithful to his vision of excavating the instinctive drives of a beloved, horrible but human Spain. In 1989, a Nobel Prize in Literature recognized Cela's preeminent position at the crossroads of postwar Spanish fiction. **CH**

Sacrificial Lamb

The confession of Camilo José Cela's Pascual Duarte holds up a dark mirror to Franco's Spain. His abusive parents; his brother's death in a vat of oil; his sister's flight into prostitution; his rape of his wife; his murder of his sister's and wife's lovers; his matricide—this simple but rancid report on reality is rendered ambiguous by Pascual's references to determinism. The jury is still out on whether Pascual Duarte is the sacrificial lamb his name implies, or an unrepentant sociopath—and what those judgments might mean for the survivors of Francoism.

CARSON McCULLERS

Born: Lula Carson Smith, February 19, 1917 (Columbus, Georgia, U.S.); died September 29, 1967 (Nyack, New York, U.S.).

Style and genre: McCullers was a Southern Gothic in both life and work; her haunting oeuvre centered on loneliness.

Recognized as a Woman of Achievement by the state of Georgia, Lula Carson Smith left her Southern birthplace at the age of seventeen, when she moved to New York to study piano at the Juilliard School of Music—but her work is proof of the adage that though you can take the girl out of the South, you cannot take the South out of the girl. McCullers's fiction's obsessive circling around failure, loss, and rejection can be seen as echoing the South's (poor) relation to the North.

This obsession is echoed as much by McCullers's biography as by American history. Her first story, "Wunderkind," came out of creative writing classes that she took at Columbia in lieu of studying at Juilliard (she apparently lost the tuition money), and narrated an adolescent piano prodigy's sense of failure. *The Heart Is a Lonely Hunter*, her first novel, was published in 1940, three years after she married failed writer Reeves McCullers, whom she was to divorce the year the novel was published, and then remarry in 1945.

McCullers spent World War II in a commune in Paris, associating with modernist writers such as W. H. Auden. However, it was only after she remarried Reeves that McCullers's major fiction was written, including *The Member of the Wedding*, which she successfully adapted as an award-winning Broadway play, and the passionate love story *The Ballad of the Sad Café*. Reeves's suicide in 1953, and a series of strokes, meant that McCullers finished only one further novel, *Clock Without Hands*, before her death in 1967. Her reputation, however, received a posthumous burnish from critically acclaimed film adaptations by John Huston (*Reflections in a Golden Eye*, 1967) and Robert Ellis Miller (*The Heart Is a Lonely Hunter*, 1968). **SM**

"I live with the people I create and it has always made my essential loneliness less keen."

Signature titles

Novels

The Heart Is a Lonely Hunter, 1940
Reflections in a Golden Eye, 1941
The Member of the Wedding, 1946
Clock Without Hands, 1961

Short stories

The Jockey, 1941
The Ballad of the Sad Café, 1951
The Mortgaged Heart, 1971

Play

The Square Root of Wonderful, 1958

Poetry

Sweet as a Pickle and Clean as a Pig, 1964

Autobiography

Illumination and Night Glare, 1999 (published posthumously)

ABOVE: McCullers photographed at her home in September 1961.

ROBERT LOWELL

Born: Robert Traill Spence Lowell IV, March 1, 1917 (Boston, Massachusetts, U.S.); died September 12, 1977 (New York, New York, U.S.).

Style and genre: An American poet, Lowell wrote of history and personal suffering, often based on his own manic depression and troubled relationships.

Robert Lowell was perhaps the best bred of all twentieth-century writers. The Lowells were one of the most distinguished families in America—"the Lowells talk only to Cabots, and the Cabots talk only to God," as the saying went. Lowell's forebears included two notable poets, James Russell Lowell and Amy Lowell, as well as colonial pioneers, Revolutionary War generals, and Harvard presidents. But much of the burden of Lowell's early work was to free himself from his ancestors, and to come to terms with the guilt he felt at their role in oppressing Native Americans. His famous name concealed a sense of family life as something acrimonious and painful, which would do much to influence his own later relationships (he married three times) and his mental well-being. Lowell spent his life at the mercy of a violently unstable psyche, and throughout his life he suffered from manic depression. "He goes into the mental hospital now and again and occasionally gets dangerous," Ted Hughes wrote in a letter; during his "dangerous" phases, Lowell was the victim of delusions, believing himself to be Caligula or Napoleon.

Lowell's poetry, however, survived and was perhaps indebted to his mental turmoil. The poems of his early years, such as the Pulitzer Prize–winning collection *Lord Weary's Castle*, are intensely wrought and highly rhetorical, while the breakthrough volume *Life Studies* contained freer forms and a direct treatment of often painful autobiographical material. Lowell also collected and many times revised seemingly endless sequences of unrhymed sonnets, in volumes such as *Notebook*, *History*, and *The Dolphin*. In all of these works, Lowell's gifts of phrase-making, vivid images, and rhythmical vigor place him among the most important poets of the century. **MS**

"The light at the end of the tunnel is just the light of an oncoming train."

Signature titles

Poetry

Land of Unlikeness, 1944
Lord Weary's Castle, 1946
The Mills of the Kavanaughs, 1951
Life Studies, 1959
Imitations, 1960
For the Union Dead, 1964
The Old Glory, 1965
Near the Ocean, 1967
Prometheus Bound, 1969
Notebook, 1970
For Lizzie and Harriet, 1973
History, 1973
The Dolphin, 1973
Day by Day, 1977

ABOVE: An undated portrait photograph of Robert Lowell.

HEINRICH BÖLL

Born: December 21, 1917 (Cologne, Germany); died July 16, 1985 (Bornheim-Merten, West Germany).

Style and genre: Böll was seen as one of his country's leading literary explorers of the problems of Germany during and after World War II.

Born into an artistic home (his father was a sculptor), Böll trained briefly as a bookseller after leaving school. In 1938, he embarked on several years as a soldier, first doing German national service and then joining the World War II effort. The war took him to several parts of Europe and saw him wounded, a victim of serious typhus, and interned by the Americans and British. For a free-thinking pacifist, such wartime experiences were especially unbearable, flying in the face of Böll's highly moral core as he fought a war he wished "might be lost."

Böll had begun writing in 1938, and now his painful army term provided ample fodder for the postwar writing career he began to carve out steadily. He settled with his wife and sons in a war-damaged house in Cologne, surrounded by the city's bomb-torn rubble. Slowly he rebuilt the house while producing early stories that detailed the grim realities of a soldiering life: *The Train Was on Time* and *Adam, Where Art Thou?*

Realism was the keynote of these works, but later books showed increasing experimentation and symbolism, as in *Billiards at Half Past Nine*. His tone was often severe and satirical and his thinking fiercely independent—he believed strongly in accepting individual responsibility. Böll probed a range of subject matter, from German postwar guilt and social problems to organized Catholicism (though a Catholic himself), corporate greed, amoral journalism, and terrorism. *Group Portrait with Lady* is a particularly impressive novel. Its map of the changing scenery of German life from World War I to the 1970s is unpicked via the story of a war-widow who is fighting to save her Cologne apartment block from demolition. Böll's books were highly successful during his life and he received a Nobel Prize in Literature in 1972. **AK**

"Soon is nothing and Soon is a lot. Soon is everything. Soon is death..."—*The Train Was on Time*

Signature titles

Novels

The Train Was on Time (Der Zug war Pünktlich), 1949
Adam, Where Art Thou? (Wo warst du, Adam?), 1951
Billiards at Half Past Nine (Billard um halb zehn), 1959
The Clown (Ansichten eines Clowns), 1963
Group Portrait with Lady (Gruppenbild mit Dame), 1971

ABOVE: Heinrich Böll pictured at home in 1982.

ANTHONY BURGESS

Born: John Burgess Wilson, February 25, 1917 (Manchester, England); died November 22, 1993 (London, England).

Style and genre: Prolific and multitalented English writer and composer who is best known for his linguistic invention and his historical and cultural range.

Although he disliked its fame, Anthony Burgess's most important book is *A Clockwork Orange*, his dystopian morality tale of youth violence told in *nadsat*, a slangy combination of English and Russian. The book became infamous when director Stanley Kubrick placed an embargo on his own movie adaptation of it, fearing copycat attacks. But Burgess published more than fifty other books with the same irrepressible creative energy. He boasted of producing 2,000 words every day while maintaining a ferocious intake of alcohol and tobacco, living in exile in Rome and Monaco. *Earthly Powers* is an epic overview of the twentieth century, while *The Long Day Wanes* portrays the declining British Empire in Malaya. **MS**

Signature titles

Novels

The Long Day Wanes

Time for a Tiger, 1956

The Enemy in the Blanket, 1957

Beds in the East, 1959

A Clockwork Orange, 1962

Enderby

Enderby, 1968

Enderby Outside, 1968

The Clockwork Testament, 1974

Napoleon Symphony, 1974

Earthly Powers, 1981

Autobiographies

Little Wilson and Big God, 1987

You've Had Your Time, 1990

JUAN RULFO

Born: May 16, 1917 (Sayula, Mexico); died January 7, 1968 (Mexico City, Mexico).

Style and genre: Mexican novelist, short-story writer, and photographer whose seminal stature in Latin American literature rests on, as stated by Gabriel García Márquez (an avowed fan), "no more than 300 pages."

Orphaned at the age of ten, Rulfo began publishing short stories in the 1940s. Grants from the Centro Mexicano de Escritores allowed him to complete his two sole publications. Rulfo's characters eke out an existence in the arid, impoverished Jalisco plain of the revolutionary years, obsessed by memories of an atavistically violent past. In *Pedro Páramo*, Juan Preciado's voyage in search of his dead father, the deserted, specter-populated village he encounters, and his own death and afterlife are intertwined with an account of the life of his father, a local strongman who, through avarice and lust, brings ruin upon the village. The novel's multiple voices design a space of historical, existential, and mythic proportions. **CH**

Signature titles

Short stories

The Burning Plain (El Llano en llamas), 1953

Novel

Pedro Páramo, 1955

MURIEL SPARK

Born: February 1, 1918 (Edinburgh, Scotland); died April 13, 2006 (Tuscany, Italy).

Style and genre: Internationally respected Scottish postmodern novelist, poet, biographer, and writer of short stories, who writes wry commentaries on modern life.

Scottish author Muriel Spark revealed her talent for writing at a young age, when she won the Walter Scott prize for poetry at the age of twelve. She married at nineteen and moved to Africa, but she became unhappy with her husband and returned to London in 1944. There she got a job producing anti-Nazi propaganda for the British Foreign Office.

Spark began her literary career three years later as biographer and editor for the *Poetry Review*. In 1954, she converted to Roman Catholicism, a central event that was to shape her life and works; she said it gave her something "original to say." Her study of the Book of Job was to inspire her first novel, *The Comforters*, published three years later. This tale of a Catholic convert who finds she is the only one who can hear the sound of a typewriter recording her thoughts, as if she were a character in a story, earned her many plaudits from literary critics and was described by Evelyn Waugh as "brilliantly original and fascinating." However, the novel that was to bring her the widest acclaim and recognition of her great observational talents was *The Prime of Miss Jean Brodie*, published in 1961. Jean Brodie, an unconventional and charismatic schoolteacher with her own ideas on how to teach her favorite pupils, is acclaimed as one of the greatest characters of modern fiction.

Spark wrote more than twenty books, producing many wry commentaries on modern life that dealt with serious issues with a feather-light touch. She could make surreal happenings seem like everyday occurrences. In 1967, she moved to Italy, where she lived for the rest of her life. She was made a dame in 1993 and won many literary awards, including the British Literature Prize and the David Cohen British Literature Prize for Lifetime Achievement. **JM**

"I don't like a lot of laughter but I like a certain amount of wit in almost everything."

Signature titles

Novels

The Comforters, 1957
Memento Mori, 1959
The Ballad of Peckham Rye, 1960
The Prime of Miss Jean Brodie, 1961
The Girls of Slender Means, 1963
The Mandelbaum Gate, 1965
Loitering with Intent, 1981
A Far Cry from Kensington, 1988
Symposium, 1990
Reality and Dreams, 1996
The Finishing School, 2004

Short stories

The Go-Away Bird, 1958
Bang-bang You're Dead, 1982

ABOVE: The Scottish novelist in a photograph taken in Paris in 1991.

ALEXANDER SOLZHENITSYN

Born: December 11, 1918 (Kislovodsk, U.S.S.R.).

Style and genre: Solzhenitsyn is a renowned novelist, playwright, essay writer, and historian who wrote realistic stories of Russia under communist rule and about the dissident experience.

"During all the years until 1961, not only was I convinced that I should never see a single line of mine in print in my lifetime, but, also, I scarcely dared allow any of my close acquaintances to read anything I had written because I feared that this would become known," said Alexander Solzhenitsyn, talking about the days before his groundbreaking novel *One Day in the Life of Ivan Denisovich* was published in 1962.

It was groundbreaking because to have a novel published in the Soviet Union that exposed the deprivations of the gulag labor camp was unheard of, and perhaps more so because in the novel the dissident Solzhenitsyn was drawing on his own experience as a camp inmate. It was an event that would set the writer on course as a literary giant and future Nobel Laureate. It also heralded his style of writing that tackled the horrors of the communist totalitarian state, which led to his twenty-year period in exile abroad from 1974.

Solzhenitsyn grew up wanting to be a writer but was unable to receive a literary education in Rostov where he lived with his widowed mother, and was unsuccessful in his attempts to get

Signature titles

Novels

One Day in the Life of Ivan Denisovich, 1962

The First Circle, 1968

Cancer Ward, 1968

August 1914, 1971

The Gulag Archipelago, 1973–1978

October 1916, 1983

Essays

Live Not By Lies, 1974

The Russian Question at the End of the Twentieth Century, 1995

Play

The Love-Girl and the Innocent (or The Tenderfoot and the Tart), 1969

ABOVE: Solzhenitsyn standing outside his U.S. home in exile in May 1989.

LEFT: An animated Solzhenitsyn the day after his return from exile on May 27, 1994.

Return of a Dissident

In 1990, Mikhail Gorbachev, the last leader of the former Soviet Union, restored Solzhenitsyn's citizenship, and in 1991 the treason charges against the writer were dropped. Solzhenitsyn returned to Russia in 1994 after twenty years in exile, and 2,000 people went to eastern Russia's Magadan airport to meet him. The former dissident then embarked on a two-month-long train journey across Russia to Moscow with the intention of meeting ordinary people.

He met with a mixed reaction: some saw him as an irrelevance to contemporary Russia, and others as a hero for his stand against communist totalitarianism and his advocacy of human rights.

The homecoming was a shock for Solzhenitsyn, who was astonished by what he saw en route—a country suffering economic hardship and in the grip of corruption and organized crime. He attacked President Boris Yeltsin for allowing the country to become tainted by the materialism and secularism of the West, and in 1998 refused to accept the highly respected Order of St. Andrew from the president—presented to mark the writer's eightieth birthday—because he felt that Yeltsin had led Russia into a state of ruin.

Since then Solzhenitsyn has met President Vladimir Putin—ironically a former head of the KGB—when Putin visited the author at his home outside Moscow in 2000. The meeting took place after Solzhenitsyn criticized Putin's failure to pull Russia "out of the ruins into which it had fallen." It seems that despite his aging years the author known as "the conscience of Russia" has a voice that still has an audience at the highest level.

his writings published in the 1930s. Instead he studied mathematics at the local university. During World War II Solzhenitsyn served on the front line, in the artillery, but was arrested in 1945 because censors discovered disrespectful references to Communist Party leader Joseph Stalin in a letter written to a friend that the authorities deemed "libelous speech"; Solzhenitsyn was sentenced to eight years in Siberia's correctional camps.

After serving time in various work camps, Solzhenitsyn—because of his flair for mathematics—was sent to work in a scientific research facility, known as a *sharashia*. His experiences there formed the basis for *The First Circle*, which was first published in the West in 1968. After he had served his eight-year sentence, Solzhenitsyn was sentenced again, this time to internal exile for life, in southern Kazakhstan. In 1953 he was diagnosed with cancer; he was eventually allowed to be treated in a clinic in Tashkent, where his cancer was cured. He drew on this experience for his novel *Cancer Ward*.

At the age of forty-two, tired of writing in secret, Solzhenitsyn succeeded, with the aid of editor Alexander Tvardovsky, in getting *One Day in the Life of Ivan Denisovich* published in 1962. However, the Soviet authority's liberal thaw was temporary; in 1964 permission to publish *Cancer Ward* was refused and in 1965 the KGB seized Solzhenitsyn's writings, including the manuscript for *The First Circle*. Undeterred, Solzhenitsyn continued to write, working on his epic literary history of the Soviet system and the formation of the gulags, *The Gulag Archipelago*. His works were then illicitly circulated as *samizdat*, or "self-published" literature.

His books were also published in the West, winning him the Nobel Prize in Literature in 1971, although he did not travel to Sweden to receive the prize because he was afraid he would be refused entry back into the Soviet Union. When the first part of *The Gulag Archipelago* was published in Paris, the Soviet authorities could take no more of Solzhenitsyn's frank and realistic exposés of the system and, in 1974, he was stripped of his citizenship and deported to West Germany. On the day that

ABOVE: Solzhenitsyn talks to the world's press after being deprived of his Soviet citizenship in February 1974.

the KGB broke into his home to arrest him for deportation, Solzhenitsyn wrote an essay "Live Not By Lies," calling on citizens to take a moral stand against the communist system.

Solzhenitsyn settled in the United States where he received a warm welcome. However, as a patriot and follower of the Russian Orthodox Church, he often ruffled feathers because of his critiques of what he saw as the West's spiritual vacuum and love of materialism. After the fall of the Berlin Wall and the arrival of glasnost, he returned to Russia in 1994. He has continued to write and speak out unreservedly against totalitarianism of any kind. The bravery of this champion of human rights means that the suffering experienced by ordinary people under communist rule has been brought to life on the pages of his work and can never be forgotten. **CK**

"Own only what you can carry with you. . . . Let your memory be your travel bag."

DORIS LESSING

Born: Doris May Taylor, October 22, 1919 (Kermanshah, Persia [now Iran]).

Style and genre: Writer of both realist and science fiction novels, Lessing is known for her irreverence and her rigorous scrutiny of inequality and hyprocrisy in both male–female and race relations.

Born in Persia, Doris Lessing and her family moved to a farm in Rhodesia (Zimbabwe) when she was a toddler. She grew up in what she describes as "a mud hut, but full of books." She left school at thirteen, home at fifteen, and was married by nineteen. She left her first husband after a few years and became involved in a local communist book club, where she met her second husband. Before long, having become disillusioned both with that marriage and the Communist Party, she moved to London with her youngest son and began work on her first novel, *The Grass Is Singing*, which explored race relations in Africa.

Lessing's lack of formal education did not hinder her—self-educated and a fierce proponent of free-thinking, she went on to a truly prolific writing career. Her early books closely reflect her life experience, and *The Children of Violence* series follows protagonist Martha Quest as she traces a path similar to Lessing's own. Her most famous work, *The Golden Notebook*, is experimental in form, comprising a number of colored notebooks belonging to protagonist Anna Wulf, each one dedicated to a segment of her divided self, until she has a breakdown, and finds a kind of wholeness in her final notebook.

For her next project, influenced by Sufi mysticism, Lessing turned to science fiction: In the *Canopus in Argos* series, aliens document their dealings with a planet much like Earth over a period of about a million years.

"Man, who is he? Too bad to be the work of God: Too good for the work of chance!"

When made a Companion of Honour by the British queen in 1999, Lessing revealed that she had earlier turned down the offer of becoming a Dame of the British Empire because "there is no British Empire." She won the Nobel Prize in 2007—the oldest person ever to receive the award. **CQ**

Signature titles

Novels

The Children of Violence

Martha Quest, 1952

A Proper Marriage, 1954

A Ripple from the Storm, 1958

Landlocked, 1965

The Four-Gated City, 1969

The Golden Notebook, 1962

Science fiction

Canopus in Argos: Archives vol. 1–5, 1979–1984

Short stories

To Room Nineteen, 1978

The Temptation of Jack Orkney, 1978

Autobiographies

Under My Skin, 1994

Walking in the Shade, 1997

ABOVE: The prolific Doris Lessing in a photograph taken in 1991.

J. D. SALINGER

Born: Jerome David Salinger, January 1, 1919 (New York, New York, U.S.).

Style and genre: American author of one novel and several short stories whose prevailing themes are adolescent alienation and the loss of innocence. Salinger is known for his reclusive nature.

The world's most famous recluse and author of the seminal teenage adolescent novel, Salinger has produced a small but exceptional body of work. He grew up in Manhattan and spent a short period studying at New York and Columbia universities, only leaving to dedicate his time to writing. It was not until returning from service in the U.S. Army during World War II that Salinger's work reached a wider audience with regular published stories appearing in the *New Yorker*.

Salinger's one and only novel, *The Catcher in the Rye*, gained instant acclaim when released in 1951. The book is narrated by the sensitive and rebellious teenager Holden Caulfield as he spends a few days drifting in New York City. In his colloquial voice Holden exposes his sense of unease at the passing of childhood and the rage he feels for the "phoney" adult world that awaits him. Holden has become an icon for teenage angst and alienation, contributing to the book's reputation as one of the twentieth century's most important texts, studied in schools and colleges throughout the English-speaking world.

Salinger's next release, *Nine Stories*, was a collection of short stories featuring the Glass family and the effect the suicide of the eldest son, Seymour, has on various family members. "A Perfect Day for Bananafish" and "For Esme—with Love and Squalor" are the outstanding stories, adding to the author's burgeoning reputation, yet the intrusion that success brought on Salinger's personal life made him withdraw into himself. Two further books followed—*Franny and Zooey,* published in 1961, and *Raise High the Roof Beam, Carpenters,* and *Seymour: An Introduction*, published together in 1963—before the storytelling ground to a halt leaving a deafening silence from a truly creative voice. **SG**

"I am a kind of paranoiac in reverse. I suspect people of plotting to make me happy."

Signature titles

Novel

The Catcher in the Rye, 1951

Short stories

Nine Stories, 1953

Franny and Zooey, 1961

Raise High the Roof Beam, Carpenters, and *Seymour: An Introduction,* 1963

ABOVE: A rare image of Salinger, from 1951, the year *The Catcher in the Rye* came out.

PRIMO LEVI

Born: July 31, 1919 (Turin, Italy); died April 11, 1987 (Turin, Italy).

Style and genre: Holocaust survivor and author of novels, memoirs, poems, and short stories, Levi's reputation rests principally on his reflections on his time as a prisoner in Auschwitz.

Born to a comfortably off Jewish-Italian family, Levi was a scientist by training, graduating in chemistry at Turin University in 1941, the year after Italy had entered World War II. Levi's professional training would later help him to survive when, in 1943, he was captured by Germans after escaping to northern Italy with a group of antifascist friends, hoping to join up with the resistance movement. He was sent to Auschwitz in Poland and employed as a slave laborer in a synthetic rubber factory, thereby escaping death. Auschwitz was liberated by the Russians in 1945 and, after months of waiting for repatriation, Levi returned to Turin, where he went to work as a chemical technician in a factory making paint and resins; he became the factory's general manager in 1961.

Levi's Auschwitz experiences inspired his first book, *If This Is a Man*. He said he had been left with an overwhelming need to write, not just as a moral duty, but as a psychological need. He described himself as a normal man who "fell into a maelstrom and got out of it more by luck than by virtue," since when he had felt curious about "maelstroms large and small, metaphorical and actual." His insights into the psychology of both those who ran the camp and the prisoners made a tremendous impression and he wrote two further books in the 1950s and 1980s based on his wartime experiences. He wrote about the horrors he had seen and endured with remarkable detachment and humanity, somehow managing to convey an optimistic sense of hope. Levi's short stories, novels, poems, and essays were also admired. Ultimately, though, he could not escape his overwhelming pessimism, committing suicide in April 1987; his concentration camp number was inscribed on his gravestone. **RC**

"Our language lacks words to express this offense . . ."

—*If This Is a Man*

Signature titles

Novels

If This Is a Man/Survival at Auschwitz (Se questo è un uomo), 1947

The Truce/The Reawakening (La Tregua), 1958

The Drowned and the Saved (I Sommersi e i salvati), 1986

Short stories

Technical Error (Vizio de forma), 1971

Meditations

The Periodic Table (Il sistemo periodico), 1975

Poems

The Collected Poems of Primo Levi (Shema), 1976

ABOVE: Portrait of Primo Levi taken in January 1986.

IRIS MURDOCH

Born: Jean Iris Murdoch, July 15, 1919 (Dublin, Ireland); died February 8, 1999 (Oxford, England).

Style and genre: Murdoch's tangled plotlines are filled with dark humor, obsession, and coincidence, reflecting the power of myth and magic to both clarify and distort.

Moral philosopher and prolific novelist, Iris Murdoch is almost as famous for the way she lived as for the books she wrote. As a young woman, studying then teaching at Oxford, she lived promiscuously, both personally and intellectually. She elicited a number of proposals from various writers and philosophers before finally settling into marriage with literary critic John Bayley. Although Murdoch continued to have affairs, she and Bayley lived in happy squalor for forty years, writing, reading, and playing poker. In 2001, Bayley's biography of her life and eventual deterioration from Alzheimer's disease was made into a film called *Iris*, starring Kate Winslet and Judi Dench.

In her 1961 essay, "Against Dryness," Murdoch argues that "philosophy is not in fact at present able to offer us [a] complete and powerful picture of the soul"—but that literature can give us a sense of the dense complexity of life and of people. Although her characters are often wrapped up in high-minded philosophies like Platonism or Freudian psychoanalysis, they are never simply mouthpieces for these points of view. Instead, Murdoch puts these discourses to the test by embodying them in characters whose moral urges clash with sexual ones, and by failing to distinguish between true mystics and manipulative enchanters. For example, Charles Arrowby, narrator of the Booker Prize–winning *The Sea, the Sea*, is a retired playwright and theater director who has decided, like Prospero in Shakespeare's *The Tempest*, to abjure magic and learn to be good—a task that proves decidedly difficult as past relationships refuse to loosen their grip on this jealous and rapacious old man. This wryly absurd yet tender novel is Murdoch in top form, examining the impossibility of seeing things clearly and the difficulty of letting go. **CQ**

"Love is the supremely difficult realization that something other than oneself is real."

Signature titles

Novels

Under the Net, 1954

The Sandcastle, 1957

The Bell, 1958

A Severed Head, 1961

The Italian Girl, 1964

The Nice and the Good, 1968

The Sea, the Sea, 1978

Philosophic works

Sartre: Romantic Rationalist, 1953

The Fire and the Sun, 1977

Existentialists and Mystics, 1997

Poetry

A Year of Birds, 1978

Poems by Iris Murdoch, 1997

ABOVE: Murdoch poses for the camera in an undated photograph.

RAY BRADBURY

Born: August 22, 1920 (Waukegan, Illinois, U.S.).

Style and genre: An iconic author from the 1950s golden age of science fiction, Ray Bradbury's atmospheric tales bridge the gap between American Gothic and Kurt Vonnegut's satiric irreverence.

There are few writers of American genre fiction who have a stronger claim to lasting relevance than Ray Bradbury. Or, at least, there are not many who can claim to have won an O. Henry Award, a World Fantasy Award, a National Book Foundation Medal for a Distinguished Contribution to American Letters, and an Emmy. Like his contemporary Isaac Asimov, Bradbury's influence on science fiction has been so profound that his writing has both established and transcended the genre, to make him one of the major pop-cultural icons of the twentieth century.

Bradbury's prolific output has included close to 600 short stories and eleven novels, not to mention his poetry, plays, essays, screenplays, and an exhibit for the giant geosphere Spaceship Earth at the Epcot Center in Florida. His first novel, *The Martian Chronicles*, is a series of chronological short stories that are set in a future history of Martian colonization, with a timeline loosely analogous to U.S. history from the conquistadors to World War I. This episodic structure, which he also uses in *The Illustrated Man* and *The Halloween Tree*, plays to Bradbury's talents. Although he is most famous for his dystopian novel *Fahrenheit 451*—a meditation on the dangers of censorship that, for decades, has appeared on U.S. high-school reading lists—most of his best work has been in the form of short stories. Like his fellow golden age sci-fi writers, the short story was where Bradbury cut his teeth, selling his work to periodicals such as *Planet Stories* and *Fantastic Adventures*. At their best, his parables of postwar America evoke the era's peculiar mood of combined optimism and paranoia more successfully than the work of any other writer, then or since. **SY**

Signature titles

Short stories

Dark Carnival, 1947
The Illustrated Man, 1951
The October Country, 1955
I Sing the Body Electric, 1969
Bradbury Stories: 100 of His Most Celebrated Tales, 2003

Novels

The Martian Chronicles, 1950
Fahrenheit 451, 1953
Dandelion Wine, 1957
Something Wicked This Way Comes, 1962
The Halloween Tree, 1972
Farewell Summer, 2006

"What could he say in a single word, a few words, that would sear all their faces?"—*Fahrenheit 451*

ABOVE: Photograph of the writer Ray Bradbury taken in 1984.

RIGHT: Cover of a magazine featuring one of Bradbury's early sci-fi stories in 1949.

A.N.C.
PLANET
stories
SPRING
20c
FICTION HOUSE MAGAZINES
ROBERT ABERNATHY
RAY BRADBURY
ALFRED COPPEL
Anderson
ETERNAL ZEMMD MUST DIE! . . . .
"Oh Zemmd-beware the Outcast's daughter. Beware the Convict from cold Mercury. These two speak death!"
Novel by HENRY HASSE

PAUL CELAN

Born: Paul Antschel, November 23, 1920 (Bukovia, Romania [now Ukraine]); died April 20, 1970 (Paris, France).

Style and genre: Paul Celan is one of the most important poets to have emerged in the postwar period. He wrote intensely haunting poems about the Holocaust.

Paul Celan grew up in a Jewish, German-speaking family in Romania. He briefly studied medicine in France, but returned to Romania in 1939 to study literature and languages. With the Nazi occupation, Celan was forced into a ghetto where he began writing his own poetry and translated Shakespeare's sonnets. Later he was sent to a labor camp and became separated from his parents who were both killed.

It is these experiences, his guilt, and loss that form the basis of Celan's poems. His collection *Poppy and Memories* established him as an exceptional poet of the Holocaust. This volume contains his best known and most anthologized poem, "Death Fugue" ("Todesfugue"), which is an evocation of life in the Nazi death camps.

During the 1950s Celan's poems became increasingly minimalist and fractured, reflecting the broken world through which he had lived. Celan wrote in German, "the language of his mother's murderers," but he believed that the German language must be set free from history. When he won the Bremen Prize for German Literature in 1958, he said: "Only one thing remained reachable, close, and secure amid all losses: language. Yes, language. In spite of everything, it remained secure against loss."

"Nothing can prevent a poet from writing, not even the fact that he's Jewish and German."

In the 1960s, Celan wrote more volumes of poetry that were internationally acclaimed. He also translated the works of other writers including Osip Mandelstam, Paul Valéry, and Henri Michaux. However, Celan's mental state became increasingly fragile. He was wrongly accused of plagiarizing the work of fellow poet Yvan Goll and suffered a breakdown followed by periodic bouts of depression. He killed himself by throwing himself into the River Seine in Paris in 1970. **HJ**

Signature titles

Poetry

Sand from the Urns (Der Sand aus den umen), 1948

Poppy and Memories (Mohn und Gedachtnis), 1952

From Threshold to Threshold (Von Schwelle zu Schwelle), 1955

Speech-grille (Sprachgitter), 1959

The No-One's Rose (Die Niemandsrose), 1959

Breath-turn (Atemwende), 1967

Threadsuns (Fadensonnen), 1968

Lightforce (Lichtzwang), 1970

Snow-part (Schneepart), 1971

ABOVE: Celan photographed in 1967, three years before he killed himself.

ISAAC ASIMOV

Born: Isaak Judah Ozimov, January 2, 1920 (Petrovichi, Soviet Union); died April 6, 1992 (New York, New York, U.S.).

Style and genre: A writer from the American golden age of science fiction, Asimov had such a staggering influence on the genre that he almost personifies it.

Although virtually every writer in this book can claim to have left an indelible impact on world literature, few have invented their own words. Asimov is one of the writers on this shorter list, having coined the term "robotics" and arguably inventing the discipline it names. Asimov's short stories are among the first to talk about robots in the modern sense (humanlike machines with computers for brains); and his "three laws" governing robot behavior are still discussed, as the technology of artificial intelligence catches up with the ethical situations described in his fiction more than fifty years ago.

Asimov's other most famous contribution to the genre is his *Foundation* series of novels. It is based on the premise that, in the future, we will be able to apply Gibbon's thesis from *The Decline and Fall of the Roman Empire* (basically that the growth and decline of civilizations follow certain consistent patterns) in a scientific discipline called "pyschohistory." The series details the millennia following a psychohistorian's application of this discipline, to create a Foundation that will shorten the duration of the chaos that inevitably exists between the peaks of intergalactic civilizations.

Asimov published prodigiously, from the time he started writing in 1939 until 1958, when he abandoned fiction and turned to popular science instead. When Asimov returned to fiction again in the 1980s, it was to write several novels that tied his robot short stories and novels to the *Foundation* series, as a continuous mythology. In a certain sense, this was unnecessary, as these two universes were already united in their articulation of Asimov's basic thesis: If we could make full use of our rational capacity, we might be able to save ourselves. **SY**

"I write for the same reason I breathe—because if I didn't, I would die."

Signature titles

Short stories

I, Robot, 1950

Nightfall and Other Stories, 1969

The Bicentennial Man and Other Stories, 1976

Novels

Foundation, 1951

Foundation and Empire, 1952

Second Foundation, 1953

Caves of Steel, 1954

The End of Eternity, 1955

Naked Sun, 1957

Foundation's Edge, 1982

Robots of Dawn, 1983

Robots and Empire, 1985

Foundation and Earth, 1986

ABOVE: Asimov, the master of science fiction, pictured during the 1980s.

CHARLES BUKOWSKI

Born: Henry Charles Bukowski, August 16, 1920 (Andernach, Germany); died March 9, 1994 (San Pedro, California, U.S.).

Style and genre: Bukowski was a hell-raising novelist and poet, whose notorious drinking habits and individual style earned him cult status.

Signature titles

Poetry

Burning in Water Drowning in Flame: Selected Poems 1955–1973, 1974

War All the Time: Poems 1981–1984, 1984

Roominghouse Madrigals: Early Selected Poems 1946–1966, 1988

Last Night of the Earth Poems, 1992

Betting on the Muse, 1996

Novels

Flower, Fist, and Bestial Wall, 1960

Confessions of a Man Insane Enough to Live with Beasts, 1965

All the Assholes in the World and Mine, 1966

Notes of a Dirty Old Man, 1969

Fire Station, 1970

Factotum, 1975

Women, 1978

For one so closely identified with the United States, it comes as something of a surprise to learn that Charles Bukowski was born in Germany, to a German mother and a U.S. serviceman father. The family moved to the United States in 1922, when Bukowski's father's service ended, and after a bright start were stung by the effects of the Great Depression. Often unemployed, Bukowski's father would allegedly get drunk and beat him. This, coupled with an extreme and long-lasting case of acne, made the young Bukowski feel unwanted, a theme that flickers throughout his novels and poems, most notably in his autobiographical 1982 novel *Ham on Rye*. Indeed, much of his work seems to be nakedly about himself; his 1971 novel *Post Office* recounts a version of his own experiences working for the institution during the 1950s and 1960s, and features the first appearance of his literary alter ego, Henry Chinaski.

As well as working for the post office, Bukowski spent these two decades contributing poetry and journalism to various Los Angeles magazines, drinking extremely heavily, and living in poverty. Identified by many with the Beat writers, it was a label Bukowski resisted, preferring to remain isolated: the poet of Skid Row. His entire adult life was lived in Los Angeles, and his ambivalent relationship with the city looms large in his work. While its racetrack and bars were constant companions into his later years, there is a sense pervading his work that Los Angeles can also be a deeply impersonal, unforgiving city. Bukowski died of leukemia, aged seventy-three, leaving behind a wife, Linda, and a body of work that amounts to an outsider's library, stylistically unique, possessing thematic solidarity with those people whom he never truly left: anyone at the margins, anyone who did not belong. **PS**

"Some people never go crazy. What truly horrible lives they must lead."—*Betting on the Muse*

ABOVE: Bukowski photographed at his Los Angeles home in 1978.

FRIEDRICH DURRENMATT

Born: January 5, 1921 (Konolfingen, Switzerland); died December 14, 1990 (Neuchâtel, Swtizerland).

Style and genre: The "Swiss Aristophanes," Durrenmatt wrote brilliantly amusing, if puzzling, dramas for both the theater and radio.

Durrenhant studied theology at Berne University, but started writing cabaret songs and plays, the first of which was produced in 1947. Many of his plays were set in the past, but were meant to illuminate the present. His refusal to take sides or, as he said, "lay the egg of explanation" intrigued and baffled audiences. His savage humor ruled out tragedy as having no place in the contemporary world because there were no moral standards. He saw the world as "something monstrous" that must be accepted, but not surrendered to. In *The Visit*, often considered his masterpiece, a rich old woman returns to her hometown and bribes the townspeople to kill the now eminently respectable citizen who raped her as a girl. **RC**

Signature titles

Plays/radio dramas

It is Written (Es steht geschrieben), 1947

Romulus the Great (Romulus der grosse), 1949

An Angel Comes to Babylon (Ein Engel kommt nach Babylon), 1953

The Visit (originally titled *Der Besuch der Alten Dame)*, 1956

Gesammelte Hörspiele, 1961

STANISŁAW LEM

Born: September 12, 1921 (Lwów, Poland); died March 27, 2006 (Krakow, Poland).

Style and genre: A writer of science fiction, satire, and philosophy, Lem's work is characterized by the exploration (often in comic language) of themes such as rise of technology, the nature of intelligence, and the human failure to communicate.

Lem was born to secular Jewish parents, raised as a Catholic, but considered himself an atheist. During the Nazi occupation of Poland in World War II, he had false papers so avoided the concentration camps, and joined the resistance against the Germans. In 1946, Soviet Ukraine annexed eastern Poland, and Lem published works of poetry, several dime novels, and had his first science fiction work serialized in a magazine—*Nowy S'wiat Przygód* (*New World of Adventures*). Lem could not speak plainly in Soviet-controlled Poland, so he used science fiction to express his ideas. He is the best known, non-English-writing science fiction author of the twentieth century, and recognized as equal to H. G. Wells and Olaf Stapledon. **REM**

Signature titles

Novels

Eden, 1959

Return from the Stars, 1961

Solaris, 1961

Memoirs Found in a Bathtub, 1961

His Master's Voice, 1968

Fiasco, 1986

Short stories

The Cyberiad, 1967

A Perfect Vacuum, 1971

JOSÉ SARAMAGO

Born: José de Sousa Saramago, November 16, 1922 (Azinhaga, Portugal).

Style and genre: Saramago's writing is characterized by a distinctive narrative voice; he uses fantasy and allegory as a mask for commentary on subjects such as politics, historical events, and the human condition.

José Saramago was born to a family of landless peasants in 1922, a background that he considers to have made him the man and writer he is today. In 1924 Saramago's father moved the family to Lisbon in search of a better life. Here his father found work as a policeman and young Saramago entered grammar school. When the family could no longer afford his education, Saramago was sent to a technical school to become a car mechanic. However, he spent long periods in his native village with his maternal grandparents—visits that fueled his imagination, while also forging a pessimistic pragmatism that would characterize his life and works.

When Saramago was three years old, Portugal underwent a military coup and for the next forty-eight years was ruled by a fascist regime headed by António Salazar. The adult Saramago held and lost a number of jobs, sometimes because of his political stance (in 1969 he joined the Portuguese Communist Party). He published his first novel in 1947, but would not publish again until 1966, when he began to produce regularly. It was not until 1982, with the publication of the satirical novel *Baltasar and Blimunda (Memorial do Convento)*, that Saramago began to gain international recognition.

Saramago's works are allegorical and fantastical, and many have much in common with South American writers of magical realism. In *Baltasar and Blimunda*, the protagonists dream of escape by building a flying machine powered by human will, whereas in *The Stone Raft*, the Iberian peninsula breaks off and floats around the Atlantic Ocean. Saramago's novels are not merely flights of fantasy, however, but a commentary on life under political dictatorship. They deal with questions of the human condition, our need to

Signature titles

Novels

Baltasar and Blimunda, 1982
The Year of the Death of Ricardo Reis, 1984
The Stone Raft, 1986
The History of the Siege of Lisbon, 1989
The Gospel According to Jesus Christ, 1991
Blindness, 1995
The Tale of the Unknown Island, 1997
The Cave, 2000
The Double, 2002
Seeing, 2004
Death with Interruptions/Death at Intervals, 2005

Travel writing

Journey to Portugal (Viagem a Portugal), 1981

"Man stopped respecting himself when he lost the respect due to his fellow creatures."

ABOVE: Saramago at an exhibition in 2007 to commemorate his eighty-fifth birthday.

LEFT: The cover of the Harvill Press edition of *The Double* (2004), illustrated by Tom Gauld.

connect as humans, to live in community with each other, and yet keep our individuality. His 1991 novel, *The Gospel According to Jesus Christ,* was met with outrage, censorship by the Portuguese government, and exclusion from the European Union literary contest. Saramago and his second wife, Pilar del Río, a Spanish journalist and translator of his works, took up symbolic exile on Lanzarote in the Canary Islands. He was awarded the Nobel Prize in Literature in 1998 and has continued to write into his eighties. **REM**

What's in a Name?

When the young José was just seven years old and ready to enter grammar school, he had to take his birth documents to the school. On this occasion, the family learned that the village clerk, either because he was drunk or as a prank, had registered José's family name at birth as "Saramago," a demeaning nickname meaning "wild radish," which the villagers gave to José's father. Although dismayed, his father had to take that official name as well—the first time in history a son has named his father, Saramago said in an interview for the *New York Times*.

ALAIN ROBBE-GRILLET

Born: August 18, 1922 (near Brest, France); died February 18, 2008 (Caen, France).

Style and genre: A controversial experimental novelist, Alain Robbe-Grillet was also author of several screenplays, including Alain Resnais's *Last Year in Marienbad,* as well as a film director.

Born in Brittany, Alain Robbe-Grillet began a career as an agricultural scientist, but later worked as an editor for Éditions de Minuit, a celebrated avant-garde publishing house in Paris whose authors included Samuel Beckett. He was a leading exponent and theoretician of the *nouveau roman*, the "new novel," or *anti-roman*, "anti-novel," which developed in the 1950s and whose practitioners were sometimes known as "the Minuit school." It was based on a determination to free the novel from the patterns and precedents of the nineteenth century because they were felt to reflect a social order that had ceased to exist and values that were no longer believed in.

Robbe-Grillet maintained that the traditional novel was out of place in the postwar world. He rejected the political commitment of writers like Jean-Paul Sartre. In his book *Towards the New Novel,* 1963, he said that his fiction was "attentive to the ties that exist between objects, gestures, and situations, avoiding all psychological and ideological 'commentary' on the actions of the characters. . . . The true writer has nothing to say. What counts is the way he says it."

The results were highly controversial and he was criticized for abandoning plot and character for mysterious ambiguities and inconsistencies. Unintelligibility, it seemed, was meant to reflect the incomprehensible real world. The reader of *In the Labyrinth* is transported to and from various different labyrinths, physical and mental, whereas in *The House of Assignation* the "same" characters appear and reappear as different people. Robbe-Grillet also wrote film scripts, from 1963 directed baffling and increasingly sado-masochistic films, and later wrote an "imaginary autobiography" in three volumes. **RC**

Signature titles

Novels

The Erasers (Les Gommes), 1953

The Voyeur (Le Voyeur), 1955

In the Labyrinth (Dans le labyrinthe), 1959

The House of Assignation (La Maison de Rendez-vous), 1965

Films

Last Year in Marienbad (L'Année dernière à Marienbad), 1961

L'Immortelle, 1963

Trans-Europ-Express, 1966

Autobiographies

Ghosts in the Mirror (Le Miroir qui revient), 1985

Angèlique ou l'enchantement, 1988

The Last Days of Corinth (Les Derniers jours de Corinthe), 1993

"The reader does not view the work from the outside. He too is in the labyrinth."

ABOVE: Photograph of Robbe-Grillet taken in February 1994.

RIGHT: The writer pictured in 1978 in the United States, where he spent some time.

JACK KEROUAC

Born: Jean-Louis Lebris de Kerouac, March 12, 1922 (Lowell, Massachusetts, U.S.); died October 21, 1969 (St. Petersburg, Florida, U.S.).

Style and genre: Jack Kerouac's work is an amalgamation of fiction and autobiography. He wrote without coherent structure or traditional frameworks.

Signature titles

Novels

The Town and the City, 1950
On the Road, 1957
The Subterraneans, 1958
The Dharma Bums, 1958
Maggie Cassidy, 1959
Doctor Sax, 1959
Lonesome Traveler, 1960
Big Sur, 1962
Visions of Gerard, 1963
Desolation Angels, 1965

ABOVE: The author in the 1985 television documentary "What Happened to Kerouac?"

The prominent figure of the Beat movement, Jack Kerouac was born in the United States to French-Canadian immigrants, only learning to speak English at the age of six. A complex, rebellious character, Kerouac dropped out of Columbia University to work as a merchant seaman before enlisting in the U.S. Navy during World War II, only to be discharged for possessing a schizoid personality. He also spent a brief time in prison for assisting his friend Lucien Carr in disposing of evidence in a murder case. With his life seemingly in danger of spiraling disastrously out of control, he returned to Columbia in 1944 and befriended the likes of Allen Ginsberg and William Burroughs, who in later years would become the arch protagonists of the Kerouac-coined Beat Generation. This group of writers and poets experimented with drugs, listened to progressive jazz, and flirted with Zen Buddhism as they sought a way of looking at and understanding the world in a new and visionary way through literature.

Finally able to realize his desires to write, Kerouac completed his first published novel, *The Town and the City*, in between undertaking a number of road trips back and forth across the

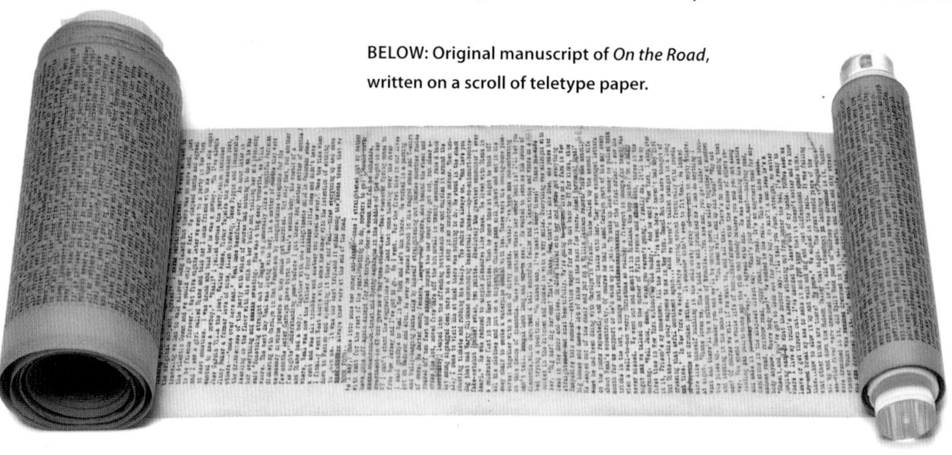

BELOW: Original manuscript of *On the Road*, written on a scroll of teletype paper.

United States. These trips became the subject of his most recognized work, *On the Road*, which was reputedly written in a three-week period in April 1951. Kerouac displayed a revolutionary style of writing, eschewing traditional fictional styles in favor of a spontaneous, stream-of-consciousness approach. The book is semiautobiographical and relies upon the use of real-life characters interjected into the frenzied transcoastal trips of Sal Paradise (Kerouac) and the penniless idealists he meets along the way, fueled by drugs, alcohol, and love, in search of kicks among the postwar sterility of the United States. This is best exemplified by the character Dean Moriarty, who is based on a friend Neal Cassady. William Burroughs noted how Kerouac had tapped into a new national consciousness with a truly groundbreaking piece of work, highlighting "the alienation, the restlessness, and the dissatisfaction."

Further novels, including *The Dharma Bums* and *Desolation Angels*, continued the autobiographical theme featuring other prominent Beat writers. The self-mythology and style of prose has kept Kerouac culturally influential for more than fifty years. **SG**

ABOVE: Kerouac leans in closer to the radio to hear himself on a broadcast in 1959.

Songs of Kerouac

Jack Kerouac and his oeuvre have provided a constant source of inspiration to musicians worldwide:

- "Before you could say Jack Kerouac you'd turn your back and I'd be gone." —"The Other Kind," Steve Earle
- "Curiosity killed the cat / Kerouac's *Dharma Bums* and *On the Road*." —"Cleaning Windows," Van Morrison
- "While I'm reading *On the Road* by my man Jack Kerouac." —"3-minute Rule," Beastie Boys
- "There are nights when I think Sal Paradise was right . . ."—"Boys and Girls of America," The Hold Steady

PIER PAOLO PASOLINI

Born: March 5, 1922 (Bologna, Italy); died November 2, 1975 (Ostia, Italy).

Style and genre: Pier Paolo Pasolini was a poet, novelist, and later essayist and polemicist. He wrote many screenplays and directed films on many aspects of Italian life, religion, and mythology.

During World War II, Pier Paolo Pasolini took shelter at Casarsa, in the region of Friuli, northern Italy. Here he formed a circle of young Friulian-speaking poets and wrote his Friulian-language collection of poems, *The Poems at Casarsa*, later complemented by *The Best Youth*. In the early 1950s, Pasolini moved to Rome. Struggling initially to make ends meet, he spent time with the underprivileged, whose lives became the theme of his novels *The Ragazzi* and *A Violent Life* (1959).

In the 1960s, after writing various screenplays, Pasolini began to dabble in filmmaking. The hard life of the destitute suburbs was the focus of films such as *Acattone* (1961). Religion as a tragic calling was the theme of *The Gospel According to St. Matthew* and *Teorema*. *The Decameron* dealt with the novelistic genre. *Salò, or the 120 Days of Sodom* (*Salò o le 120 giornate di Sodoma*, 1975) is a highly original re-reading of the Italian Social Republic. *Oedipus Rex* (*Edipo re*, 1967) and *Medea* (1969) confront Greek myths with contemporary society.

After his critical literary writings, Pasolini arrived at the final stage of social protest, with a passionate and polemical participation in national life through the publication of his writings in newspapers and periodicals. By rigorously analyzing the degrading and degraded aspects of the chaotic Italian society that emerged from World War II, Pasolini linked Italians' loss of identity to their striving for general economic well-being at all costs. He predicted the environmental and moral disasters caused by the exodus to the cities, with their promise of jobs. In his lucid despair about the fate of the world, Pasolini identified the prevalent economic model, based on industrial-scale profits, as the major cause for the evils of contemporary society. **CC**

"Death determines life. Life acquires meaning only when it is finished."

Signature titles

Poetry

The Poems at Casarsa (Le Poesie a Casarsa), 1950

The Best Youth (La meglio gioventù), 1954

The Ashes of Gramsci (Le ceneri di Gramsci), 1957

The Religion of My Times (La religione del tempo), 1961

Poetry in the Shape of Roses (Poesia in forma di Rosa), 1964

Novels

The Ragazzi (Ragazzi di Vita), 1954

Screenplays

MammaRosa, 1962

The Gospel According to St. Matthew (Vangelo secondo Matteo), 1964

Teorema, 1968

The Decameron (Il Decamerone), 1971

ABOVE: The Italian poet, novelist, and filmmaker photographed in 1970.

1920–39

PHILIP LARKIN

Born: August 9, 1922 (Coventry, England); died December 2, 1985 (Hull, East Yorkshire, England).

Style and genre: Philip Larkin is one of the great twentieth-century poets, also a novelist and jazz critic. He was the leading voice of a group of young English writers.

Philip Larkin famously remarked that his biography could begin with his life at the age of twenty-one and omit nothing of importance, and he seemed to pride himself on the absence of conventional sources of poetic inspiration: "Deprivation is for me what daffodils were for Wordsworth." He was educated at St. John's College, Oxford, and the city in wartime provides the setting for his first novel, *Jill*. His second novel, *A Girl in Winter*, was an ambitious study of loneliness in the symbolist manner of Virginia Woolf, but further efforts at fiction failed. In 1945, Larkin discovered Thomas Hardy's poetry and became a great admirer of his work. Larkin's first major collection of poems, *The North Ship*, is often criticized for its high-flown Yeatsian rhetoric, but its significance lies in its wartime mood of elegiac lyricism and its tenacious sense of survival.

During the 1950s, Larkin was linked with "The Movement," an anti-Romantic group of young English writers. In 1955, he became the Librarian at the University of Hull, in East Yorkshire, where he spent the rest of life. The city and its surrounding landscape provided striking images of postwar English society, which were to feature prominently in his poems. *The Less Deceived* is skeptical about the promise of freedom, carefully reassessing traditional values and attitudes to work, love, and religion. *The Whitsun Weddings* takes us from the austerity of the 1950s to the affluence of the 1960s, whereas *High Windows* registers the break-up of the postwar social consensus.

Larkin's poetry found unsentimental meaning in the mundane details of daily life and he became one of the best loved English poets of the late twentieth century. In 1984 he was offered, but declined, the position of poet laureate after the death of Sir John Betjeman. **SR**

"I think writing about unhappiness is probably the source of my popularity."

Signature titles

Poetry

The North Ship, 1945
The Less Deceived, 1955
The Whitsun Weddings, 1964
High Windows, 1974
Philip Larkin: Collected Poems, 1988

Novels

Jill, 1946
A Girl in Winter, 1947

Nonfiction

All What Jazz: A Record Diary, 1961–1971

ABOVE: At John Betjeman's memorial service at Westminster Abbey, London, in 1984.

KINGSLEY AMIS

Born: April 16, 1922 (London, England); died October 22, 1995 (London, England).

Style and genre: Sir Kingsley Amis was a famous English novelist, poet, critic, and satirist, known for his comic wit. He was made a Commander of the British Empire (CBE) in 1990.

ABOVE: Portrait of Kingsley Amis taken in the 1970s.

Signature titles

Novels

Lucky Jim, 1954

That Uncertain Feeling, 1955

The James Bond Dossier, 1965

The Anti-Death League, 1966

Colonel Sun, 1968 (written under the pseudonym Robert Markham)

The Green Man, 1969

The Alteration, 1976

Jake's Thing, 1978

The Old Devils, 1986

Father of the novelist Martin Amis, Sir Kingsley Amis is regarded as one of the great British literary figures of the twentieth century. He is remembered for his piercingly sharp, satirical comic wit that threads through his novels.

Amis based his novels on contemporary British life, often referencing experiences from his own life. He was associated with a group of young British writers referred to as "The Angry Young Men," because of the sardonic and, at times, radical nature of their work, which was critical of the contemporary social conventions and political climate, although Amis himself—and a number of other writers—rejected this label. Drawing from his own experiences as a lecturer and teacher, Amis developed the "campus" novel. Set in and around universities, works such as *Lucky Jim* portrayed student and teacher life with exacting clarity and dry humor and formed a model for authors like Howard Jacobson and Tom Sharpe.

By the 1960s, Amis was beginning to move away from the precise realism of his early novels, embracing a more alternative and controversial reality that, in part, reflected his interest in reading works of science fiction. This can be seen, for example, in *The Anti-Death League* and *The Alteration*, which question conventional religious beliefs, mirroring Amis's own atheistic views. It was during the 1960s that he became involved with Ian Fleming's James Bond, writing critical pieces and *The James Bond Dossier* and penning the Bond book *Colonel Sun*, under a pseudonym. Amis wrote prolifically, producing novels as well as many critical essays and volumes of poetry. In 1986, he won the Booker Prize with *The Old Devils*, which is widely considered, along with *Lucky Jim*, to be one of his best works. **TamP**

"If you can't annoy someone there is little point in writing."

WILLIAM GADDIS

Born: December 29, 1922 (New York, New York, U.S.); died December 16, 1998 (East Hampton, New York, U.S.).

Style and genre: Gaddis is a novelist with a dry satirical voice. His novels address the United States's modern cultural and social situation, and are often complex.

William Gaddis was one of the postwar literary giants, whose work has influenced the development of postmodern literature and writers such as Thomas Pynchon, Don DeLillo, and Christopher Wunderlee. His first novel, *The Recognitions*, was published after he had spent some years traveling. It is a monumental, complex work that creates a series of tightly wrought and intertwined plots with fifty characters, their stories evolving over a thirty-year period. At the center of the book is the theme of art forgery, which becomes an allusion to fraud and forgery on a greater, more metaphysical level. *The Recognitions* did not receive the reception Gaddis was hoping for, although it is considered one of his best works.

Gaddis's next work, *JR*, is another immense and complicated narrative that satirically addresses corporate America and its obsession with money. The novel, in which the main character is an eleven-year-old boy, is penned almost entirely in continuous dialogue, written as spoken, with interrupted sentences and lacking in grammar. This book won Gaddis a National Book Award, and he began to get a small but dedicated following. *Carpenter's Gothic* was a smaller undertaking and was more successful commercially. Again written in near continuous dialogue, it presents Gaddis's sardonic and pessimistic world view. *A Frolic of his Own* continues his ironic voice, this time using litigation as its vehicle. It is cleverly conceived and the complicated story artfully exposes the difference between the ideal of justice and the reality of the law. Gaddis's final work, the novella *Agape Agape*, was planned to be a nonfiction piece before Gaddis decided to turn it into a dramatic monologue that reiterates his themes from earlier works. **TamP**

"Writing is all about what happens between the reader and the page."

Signature titles

Novels

The Recognitions, 1955

JR, 1975

Carpenter's Gothic, 1985

A Frolic of His Own, 1994

Novella

Agape Agape, 2002 (published posthumously)

ABOVE: The American writer William Gaddis photographed in Paris, France, 1993.

KURT VONNEGUT, JR.

Born: November 11, 1922 (Indianapolis, Indiana, U.S.); died April 11, 2007 (New York, New York, U.S.).

Style and genre: Satirical novelist, playwright, and essay writer whose wittily dark, surreal comedies often have semiautobiographical themes.

Being a student in the 1970s meant that Kurt Vonnegut, Jr. was almost required reading in order to be considered hip. His satirical novels appealed to a generation that smoked dope, listened to Pink Floyd, and were against the Vietnam War. Vonnegut's darkly comic works feature recurring characters and inventions, and surreal worlds that are part science fiction, part absurd, and part real. They play with form, structure, and typography in the manner of satirical novelist Laurence Sterne, frequently featuring Vonnegut's own doodles.

Yet the author's fast, choppy pace of writing and flippant, almost throwaway, style belie the seriousness of his subject matter. Vonnegut served as an infantryman in World War II, and was captured and taken prisoner in 1944. He survived the 1945 Allied bombing raid on Dresden, as he, along with six other prisoners of war, were held in an underground meat locker in Schlachthof-Fünf—Slaughterhouse-Five. After the bombing, he and his colleagues were put to work burying the city's dead. This horrific experience inspired Vonnegut's best-seller *Slaughterhouse-Five, or The Children's Crusade*. The human race's capacity for self-destruction was a frequent theme in his work, and he drew heavily on his own experiencs in his writing.

"I am a pacifist, I am an anarchist, I am a planetary citizen, and so on."

Vonnegut was an antiauthoritarian Luddite, humanist, environmentalist, and supporter of civil liberties, but his novels are never overtly political nor cynical, having a metaphysical tone tempered by hope that human kindness may prevail. He wrote his last novel in 1997, and turned to writing essays that on occasion struck a more political tone, particularly on the futility of the Iraq War. After his death, a generation of readers, such as film director Michael Moore, continue to use humor in fighting the establishment. **CK**

Signature titles

Short stories

Welcome to the Monkey House, 1968

Novels

Player Piano, 1952

Mother Night, 1961

Cat's Cradle, 1963

God Bless You, Mr. Rosewater, or Pearls Before Swine, 1965

Slaughterhouse-Five, or The Children's Crusade, 1969

Breakfast of Champions, or Goodbye Blue Monday, 1973

Slapstick, 1976

Deadeye Dick, 1985

Bluebeard, 1987

Play

Happy Birthday, Wanda June, 1970

ABOVE: Portrait of Kurt Vonnegut, Jr., photographed in 1984.

NADINE GORDIMER

Born: November 20, 1923 (Transvaal, South Africa).

Style and genre: Nadine Gordimer's novels relay the tensions between black and white people in apartheid and post-apartheid South Africa. She is known for her concise writing style, with an emphasis on detail and restrained voice.

As a child Nadine Gordimer was kept at home with a seemingly weak heart, and in so doing her mother inadvertently facilitated her daughter's early writing career. Gordimer's first short story, "Come Again Tomorrow," was published when she was only fourteen in the Johannesburg magazine *Forum*. By her twenties, she was published regularly—an auspicious start for an author who would come to be awarded fifteen honorary degrees and win multiple awards, including the Booker and Nobel Prize in Literature. Gordimer spent one year at university in South Africa, and has since dedicated her life to writing. She has written thirteen novels and ten short-story collections.

Gordimer has dedicated most of her work to criticism of the apartheid system. She deals mostly with the psychological tensions that are embedded within a racially contentious South Africa. The racial law in South Africa is showcased in *Occasion for Loving* through the relationship between white (and married) Ann Davis, her black (and married) lover, the painter Gideon Shibalo, and Jessie Stilwell, a liberal woman who facilitates their relationship. Another aspect of apartheid that Gordimer chronicles closely is the theme of the master–servant relationship, as in *July's People* and *The Late Bourgeois World* (1966). *Burger's Daughter* was written following the brutal Soweto Uprising and *The House Gun* looks at the violence of the postapartheid South African society.

"Writing is some kind of affliction as the most solitary of occupations."

Despite growing up in a society that accepted Gordimer as "normal," three of her works have been banned. She has refused to go into exile, and holds iconic status in South Africa and abroad. The many facets of apartheid unfold within Gordimer's canon, providing an alternative narrative of those events that her writing career has now outlived. **JSD**

Signature titles

Short stories

Face to Face, 1949

Six Feet of the Country, 1956

Livingstone's Companions, 1971

Town And Country Lovers, 1980

Writing and Being, 1995

Beethoven Was One-Sixteenth Black and Other Stories, 2007

Novels

Occasion for Loving, 1963

A Guest of Honor, 1971

The Conservationist, 1974

Burger's Daughter, 1979

July's People, 1981

The House Gun, 1988

The Pickup, 2001

ABOVE: Nadine Gordimer photographed in May 2006.

YAŞAR KEMAL

Born: Kemal Sadık Gökçeli, 1923 (Hemite, now Gokçedam, Osmaniye, Turkey).

Style and genre: One of Turkey's most influential writers, Yaşar Kemal is renowned for his lyrical stories of village life and for his stark realism. A highly successful novelist, he also writes poetry and short stories.

Signature titles

Novels

Memed, My Hawk, 1955
The Wind from the Plain, 1960
Iron Earth, Copper Sky, 1963
The Undying Grass, 1968
They Burn the Thistles, 1968
The Saga of a Seagull, 1976
The Sea-Crossed Fisherman, 1978

Yaşar Kemal was born in the shadow of the Taurus mountains in Turkey in 1923 and it is this landscape that provides the backdrop for some of his novels. He was the son of a wealthy landlord and, while still a young child, he saw his father murdered, which resulted in his developing a speech impediment that lasted for many years. He went to secondary school for only two years, leaving at the age of fourteen to look after his mother after his sisters died.

Kemal grew up listening to folk tales and began writing poetry and short stories. He worked as a journalist but it was his first novel *Memed, My Hawk,* published in 1955, that established his reputation both in Turkey and internationally. It is the story of a young village boy who becomes an outlaw, fights injustice, and becomes a legend. His exploits on behalf of the poor continued in a number of sequels. *Memed, My Hawk* has now been published in forty different languages.

Kemal also wrote about the poor and dispossessed in an epic trilogy: *The Wind from the Plain*; *Iron Earth, Copper Sky;* and *The Undying Grass*. These novels focus on the harsh lives of a group of villagers who work as cotton pickers. Later novels, such as *The Saga of the Seagull*, set in a Black Sea fishing town, and *The Sea-Crossed Fisherman*, move away from the landscape of his earlier work and focus on the chaos of city life.

"People have always created their own worlds of myths and dreams . . ."

Kemal's concern about the oppressed has continued throughout his life. In 1995 he was arrested and given a twenty-month suspended sentence for a piece he wrote for the German magazine *Der Spiegel* about the position of Turkish Kurds. Kemal has won numerous Turkish and international literary awards that are testament to the universal appeal of his work. **HJ**

ABOVE: Kemal pictured at the Académie universelle des cultures in Paris in 2003.

NORMAN MAILER

Born: January 31, 1923 (Long Branch, New Jersey, U.S.); died November 10, 2007 (New York, New York, U.S.).

Style and genre: Mailer is known for narrating through a stylized version of his own ego, for an often baroque prose style, and for the sheer bulk of his novels.

If you wanted to compress Norman Mailer's life into a single adjective, you could do worse than the word "fertile"—here is a man who left no shortage of offspring, literary or otherwise. "Fertile" is certainly the right word for an imaginative consciousness that gave us a novel about ancient Egypt (*Ancient Evenings*), a first-person account of the life of Jesus (*The Gospel According to the Son*), a 1,300-page chronicle of the CIA (*Harlot's Ghost*), and a meditation on the genesis of Adolf Hitler (*The Castle in the Forest*).

All this from an author who is remembered not primarily as an imaginative writer, but as a journalist. A cofounder of the New Journalism of the 1960s, Mailer penned essays on race ("The White Negro") and books on politics (*Miami and the Siege of Chicago*). He reached the apotheosis of the genre with *The Executioner's Song*, an account of Gary Gilmore, the killer who campaigned for his own execution.

Mailer's life encapsulated a staggering breadth of experience: he served in World War II (and wrote about it in *The Naked and the Dead*), cofounded the *Village Voice* newspaper, and ran for the mayor of New York City (his slogan was: "The Other Guys are the Joke"). His essays expounded on everything from space travel to birth control.

Mailer was a theoretician (and an occasional practitioner) of violence, and was fascinated by boxing, a topic that excited some of his best writing. In *The Fight*, he documented the Ali–Foreman "Rumble in the Jungle." He caused a stir at a press conference for the Paterson–Liston fight in 1962 by sitting in Sonny Liston's chair and refusing to vacate it. The chair might as well be Norman Mailer's place in the literary canon: Ask him to leave, but he is not going anywhere. **IW**

"Machismo is not the easiest cloak to wear or the easiest role to assume in life."

Signature titles

Novels

The Naked and the Dead, 1948
The Deer Park, 1955
An American Dream, 1965
Ancient Evenings, 1983
Tough Guys Don't Dance, 1984
Harlot's Ghost, 1991
The Gospel According to the Son, 1997
The Castle in the Forest, 2007

Nonfiction

Advertisements for Myself, 1959
The Armies of the Night, 1968
Miami and the Siege of Chicago, 1968
The Fight, 1975
The Executioner's Song, 1979

ABOVE: The pugnacious Mailer poses for a portrait taken in New York in 1987.

ITALO CALVINO

Born: October 15, 1923 (Santiago de Las Vegas, Cuba); died September 19, 1985 (Siena, Tuscany, Italy).

Style and genre: Italian novelist and critic who made bold experiments with narrative technique that redefined the boundaries of what was possible in a novel.

Signature titles

Novels

The Path to the Nest of Spiders (Il sentiero dei nidi di ragno), 1947

Our Forefathers (I nostri antenati), 1960

Marcovaldo, or the Seasons in the City (Marcovaldo ovvero le stagioni in città), 1963

Cosmicomics (Le cosmicomiche), 1965

Invisible Cities (Le città invisibili), 1972

The Castle of Crossed Destinies (Il castello dei destini incrociati), 1973

If On a Winter's Night a Traveler (Se una notte d'inverno un viaggiatore), 1979

Mr. Palomar (Palomar), 1983

Essays

The Uses of Literature (Una pietra sopra), 1980

Italo Calvino was born in Cuba of Italian parents. He was never afraid to express his antipathy for convention or the expectations of others. As a schoolboy in Italy, he ruffled his Roman Catholic teachers by declaring himself exempt from religious instruction. Although his parents were scientists, he was adamant that he wanted pursue a literary career. He refused to be conscripted into Italian dictator Benito Mussolini's fascist forces, instead he joined a communist partisan group in 1944 to combat them. His first novel, *The Path to the Nest of Spiders*, drew on these experiences and was welcomed as a classic neo-realist text.

Calvino married in 1964 and three years later moved to Paris, the center of literary innovation in the 1960s. His work in the 1950s had already demonstrated an interest in a variety of modes of storytelling, and in the recurrent motifs of fables and fairy tales, but now his experiments with narrative became as ingenious as they were audacious. In *Cosmicomics*, a cell formula called Qfwfq relates the evolution of the universe in twelve tales, while *The Castle of Crossed Destinies* is a strange commentary on a pack of Tarot cards that offers a meditation on fate and human destiny. *Invisible Cities* is an extraordinary

ABOVE: Photograph of Italo Calvino taken during the 1980s.

RIGHT: Unposed portrait of the Italian writer, date unknown.

collection of imaginary conversations between Marco Polo and Khublai Khan, in which the explorer describes and categorizes fifty-five fantastic utopias. These novels—if that is what they are—disrupt the idea that narrative should be linear, as they employ unusual framing devices and advertise their proximity to other kinds of prose writing.

Calvino was an important member of the experimental OuLiPo organization, whose members included Raymond Queneau and Georges Perec. He also knew Roland Barthes, whose playful post-structuralist theory percolated into Calvino's work. This is most evident in the explorations that form the basis of *If On a Winter's Night a Traveler*. The serious thought that informed Calvino's fiction and criticism meant that he was never far from academic circles; it seemed appropriate that his sudden death interrupted a series of lectures that he was invited to give at Harvard University. **TM**

ABOVE: Calvino photographed by Sophie Bassouls in a Paris cafe in February 1981.

The Great Experiment

If On a Winter's Night a Traveler is probably the most important novel ever to have been inspired by writer's block. It is a baffling but compelling game of metatextual experiments. The novel compiles a series of first chapters of different novels that are connected by a loose narrative about the act of reading. "You are about to begin reading Italo Calvino's new novel," it begins, but the first chapter of that novel is interrupted by the revelation that the book is misprinted and "you" must go in search of another copy—which turns out to be an entirely different novel.

JOSEPH HELLER

Born: May 1, 1923 (Brooklyn, New York, U.S.); died December 12, 1999 (Long Island, New York, U.S.).

Style and genre: A twentieth-century unrelenting satirist, known for his opening lines, Joseph Heller challenged bureaucracy and the illogical nature of warfare.

Signature titles

Novels

Catch-22, 1961, reworked as a play in 1971
Something Happened, 1974
Good as Gold, 1979
God Knows, 1984
Picture This, 1988
Closing Time, 1994
Portrait of an Artist, as an Old Man, 2000

Plays

We Bombed in New Haven, 1967
Clevinger's Trial, 1973

Screenplays

Sex and the Single Girl, 1964

Autobiographies

No Laughing Matter, 1988
Now and Then, 1998

Joseph Heller was a Jewish New Yorker who loved writing from an early age. After leaving high school, he had several jobs, including working as an apprentice to a blacksmith, before signing up to the U.S. Army Air Corps in 1942, aged nineteen. He became a B-25 bombardier, a position that informed the scathing war consciousness that built the character of Yossarian in *Catch-22*, Heller's first and most famous work.

After obtaining a master's degree in English from Columbia University and having spent a year as a Fulbright Scholar at St. Catherine's College, Oxford, Heller's first published work was a short story in 1948, written while working as a copywriter for an advertising agency. He continued to write at home, and the seeds of *Catch-22* were first sown in the early 1950s. The novel was finally published in 1961, and met first muted, then overall acclaim. The fast-paced, meandering plot and grotesque comedy of the novel served to question combat-related acts of honor as demonstrative of insanity, with the terrifed Yossarian portrayed as the most lucid "crazy" man in the forces. The resolutely contradictory machinations of war administration and its organized deaths also come under caustic scrutiny. The no-win "Catch-22" predicament has since been assumed into common parlance. In 1970, the film version of *Catch-22* was released, with Alan Arkin playing Yossarian.

"His only mission each time he went up was to come down alive."—*Catch-22*

Before completing any further novels, Heller wrote various TV and film scripts, plus a Broadway play, which again propagated Heller's prevailing thoughts on the ridiculous nature of war. His second novel *Something Happened* was released in 1974. This was followed by several other works, but none reached the widespread acclaim afforded his first novel. **LK**

ABOVE: The author of *Catch-22* poses for a portrait in February 1998.

OUSMANE SEMBÈNE

Born: January 1, 1923 (Ziguinchor, Senegal); died June 9, 2007 (Dakar, Senegal).

Style and genre: Called "the father of African film," Ousmane Sembène brought French Marxism thrillingly to life in fiction, film, and practice in Senegal through his novels and films.

Ousmane Sembène was the son of a fisherman. Called up to fight for the colonial masters at the end of the World War II, Sembène became a dock worker and postwar radical agitator in France. Returning to Senegal post-liberation in 1960, with an education in Marxism and world literature, Sembène turned from political to creative agitation. He published four novels and made seven films, including *La Noire de. . .*, before writing his satire *Xala*, which he adapted for the screen.

Translated into English in the 1980s, his novels appeared in the Heinemann African writers' series, while his films won many prizes, culminating in Cannes' prestigious "Un Certain Regard" ("A Certain Glance") for his final film *Moolaadé*. **SM**

Signature titles

Novels

The Black Docker (Le docker noir), 1956

God's Bits of Wood (Les Bouts de bois de Dieu), 1960

Xala, 1973

Niiwam, 1987

Screenplays

La noire de . . ., 1966

Ceddo, 1976

Gelwaar, 1992

Moolaadé, 2004

SHUSAKU ENDO

Born: March 23, 1923 (Tokyo, Japan); died September 29, 1996 (Tokyo, Japan).

Style and genre: Endo is one of Japan's best-loved twentieth-century novelists. He explored complex moral issues, in particular and the relationship between East and West and Christianity.

Shusaku Endo converted to Catholicism as a child and his faith is often at the heart of his novels. He is frequently compared to the English Catholic writer, Graham Greene, who described him as one of the finest writers of the twentieth century.

In the early 1950s Endo studied French Literature at the University of Lyon. His first short story, *To Aden*, is about his travels to Europe. In 1955 he was awarded the prestigious Akutagawa Prize for his short novel, *White Men*. However, it was *Silence* that established his international reputation. The book focuses on the martyrdom of Japan's Christian converts in the sixteenth and seventeenth centuries and describes how a Portuguese priest has his faith severely tested. **HJ**

Signature titles

Short stories

To Aden, 1954

Wonderful Fool, 1959

Novels

White Men, 1955

Yellow Man, 1956

The Sea and Poison, 1958

Volcano, 1960

Silence, 1966

Upon The Dead Sea, 1973

A Life of Jesus, 1973

Song of Sadness, 1977

The Samurai, 1980

Play

The Golden Country, 1970

MICHEL TOURNIER

Born: December 19, 1924 (Paris, France).

Style and genre: Michel Tournier tells old stories from a new point of view. He writes mythic, sometimes fantastical novels, which are highly readable, but also notable for their depth.

Michel Tournier is one of the most important French writers of the last fifty years. His work is often inspired by German culture (as a child, he spent his summers in Germany), by Roman Catholicism, and by the work of the French philosopher Gaston Bachelard. He studied philosophy at the Sorbonne and at Tübingen University in Germany.

He began his writing career in radio and television and wrote three novels, which he did not consider worth publishing. His breakthrough came with *Friday*, which won him the Grand Prix du Roman of the Académie Française. It is a retelling of Daniel Defoe's Robinson Crusoe story, in which Robinson Crusoe chooses to stay on his island rather than return to civilization. The French public were becoming tired of difficult *nouveau roman* novels and so Tournier soon found a large and loyal readership.

Tournier followed *Friday* with *The Ogre* (formerly called *The Elf King)*, which is considered to be his masterpiece. A story of innocence and obsession, the story follows the fortunes of Abel Tiffauges—the ogre of the title—a French prisoner who helps run a Nazi military training camp, but who dies rescuing a Jewish child. The book became an international best-seller and he won the most prestigious literary award in France, the Prix Goncourt.

"I can't live except in obscurity and . . . I only live at all through misunderstanding."—*The Ogre*

Tournier has also written novels that rework the myth of Castor and Pollux in *Gemini* and the story of the Magi—*The Four Wise Men*. This recounts the tale of the fourth wise man who did not reach Bethlehem for Christ's birth, but traveled from India and rescued a group of children from the Massacre of the Innocents. Tournier's autobiography was translated and published as *The Wind Spirit* in English in 1988. **HJ**

Signature titles

Novels

Friday (Vendredi ou les limbes du Pacifique), 1967

The Ogre (Le Roi des aulnes), 1970

Gemini (Les Météores), 1975

Friday and Robinson (Vendredi ou la vie sauvage), 1977

The Four Wise Men (Gaspard, Melchior, et Balthazar), 1980

The Midnight Love Feast (Le Medianoche amoureux), 1989

The Mirror of Ideas (Le Miroir des idées), 1994

Autobiography

The Wind Spirit (Le vent paraclet), 1977

ABOVE: Tournier pictured in a French garden in 2006.

JAMES BALDWIN

Born: August 2, 1924 (Harlem, New York, U.S.); died November 30, 1987 (St.-Paul-de-Vence, France).

Style and genre: Baldwin was a groundbreaking, controversial African-American novelist, playwright, poet, essayist, and civil rights activist.

"One writes out of one thing only—one's own experience," said James Baldwin in *Autobiographical Notes*. A gay African-American, he was writing at a time when a wind of change was sweeping across America with the Civil Rights Movement—Malcolm X and Martin Luther King were his friends. Baldwin tackled the hardships of being poor and African-American, and, more controversially, explored themes of homosexuality and interracial relationships that were taboo at the time.

Born into a poor family in New York's Harlem, Baldwin's stepfather, a preacher, was not too fond of his stepson's bookish ways and enthusiasm for Charles Dickens. Yet Baldwin followed his stepfather into the pulpit before leaving to work on the New Jersey railroads. He eventually moved to Greenwich Village, New York, and worked as a freelance writer. In 1948, he headed for Paris and mixed with the American expatriate circle that included Ernest Hemingway, Richard Wright, and F. Scott Fitzgerald. Although he did return to the United States, Baldwin found it easier to write about his home country from a distance.

Yet Baldwin's early years informed his writing, and his prose owes much to the Pentecostal church and the King James Bible. His first novel, *Go Tell It on the Mountain,* examines racism and religion. His novel, *Giovanni's Room,* tells of a young, white American in France. Left alone by his fiancée, and haunted by his teenage love for a boy, he begins a relationship with an Italian man, Giovanni.

Baldwin's novels depict people of all colors, nations, and sexual orientations with unsparing honesty regarding their faults. His anger at society's injustice is revealed in his work, but he is more concerned to portray human fallibility as the common factor that links people the world over. **CK**

"I began plotting novels at about the time I learned to read."—*Notes of a Native Son*

Signature titles

Poetry

Jimmy's Poems, 1983

Novels

Go Tell It on the Mountain, 1953

Giovanni's Room, 1956

Another Country, 1962

Play

The Amen Corner, 1954

Essays

Autobiographical Notes, 1952

Notes of a Native Son, 1955

ABOVE: Baldwin poses at his home in the south of France in September 1985.

TRUMAN CAPOTE

Born: Truman Streckfus Persons, September 30, 1924 (New Orleans, Louisiana, U.S.); died August 25, 1984 (Los Angeles, California, U.S.).

Style and genre: Capote's writing has a unique journalistic approach, with reminiscences of childhood and the American South, and intrigue with high society.

A colorful and flamboyant character, Truman Capote was an author of outstandingly polished prose, both in fiction and nonfiction. His early writing belonged to the Southern Gothic tradition, but he would later become more widely known for his journalistic novel *In Cold Blood*.

Much of Capote's youth was occupied with writing. He left school at the age of seventeen, and worked at the *New Yorker*. Capote achieved early literary recognition in 1945, winning the

Signature titles

Short stories

A Tree of Night and Other Stories, 1949

Novella

Breakfast at Tiffany's, 1958

Novels

Other Voices, Other Rooms, 1948

In Cold Blood, 1966

Answered Prayers: The Unfinished Novel, 1987 (published posthumously)

Play

The Grass Harp, 1951

ABOVE: Capote photographed in 1970 in his Palm Springs garden, California.

RIGHT: Capote in 1980, posing with a copy of *Interview* magazine featuring his likeness.

O. Henry Memorial with his debut novel, *Other Voices, Other Rooms*. The book was a sensitive account of adolescence in the Deep South, discussing homosexual issues in a frank manner that courted nearly as much controversy as the suggestive back-cover photograph of the author.

Literary success saw Capote immerse himself among the celebrities of the day, attending endless parties and frequently appearing in gossip columns. Moving in such circles provided the inspiration for one of his most popular works, the novella *Breakfast at Tiffany's*. The book's accessibility lies in the linear plot, sparkling dialogue, and creation of one of the most engaging characters in American fiction, Holly Golightly, a lady with a mysterious past who floats through life searching for a place where she belongs. The subsequent Hollywood adaptation starring Audrey Hepburn cemented Capote's reputation as a gifted storyteller, an art he would use to great effect in his next project.

In Cold Blood signaled a radical departure from Capote's previous output as he strove to revolutionize the fields of journalism and literature with his pioneering "nonfiction novel." The book is a chilling account of the vicious murder of a Kansas farming family by two young psychopaths. The novel incorporates Capote's personal involvement with the story as he became enmeshed in the lives of the murderers and townspeople, by undertaking numerous interviews over a six-year period leading up to the execution of the two men. He masterfully avoids emotional attachment, simply telling the harrowing facts in a powerfully evocative narrative.

A seminal piece of work, *In Cold Blood* attained instant classic status and brought the author unparalleled wealth and fame in the literary world. It proved to be the pinnacle of his career as later works failed to match his earlier success. Capote would later be ostracized by the glamorous elite he so admired after selected extracts of a late novel, *Answered Prayers*, describing the intimate details of his social circle, appeared in *Esquire* magazine. However, the novel remained incomplete up to his death. **SG**

ABOVE: Capote dancing with Marilyn Monroe in New York, 1955.

How the Camera Shot Capote to Fame

Harold Halma's provocative back-cover author photo for *Other Voices, Other Rooms* created a huge surge of interest in Capote, instigating his overnight fame. The image, innocuous by today's standards, captures the young Capote lounging seductively on a chaise longue. His sultry yet childlike pose appeared in bookstore display windows across America, provoking intrigue in some and outrage in others. Ever the self-publicist, Capote was delighted with the publicity it generated; it vindicated his faith in the power of the image and ensured further memorable photo shoots of the author.

JANET FRAME

Born: August 28, 1924 (Dunedin, Otago, New Zealand); died January 29, 2004 (Dunedin, Otago, New Zealand).

Style and genre: Saved from lobotomy by a literary prize, Frame put New Zealand on the map with her vivid evocations of madness.

Signature titles

Short stories

The Lagoon and Other Stories, 1951

You Are Now Entering the Human Heart, 1983

Novels

Owls Do Cry, 1957

Faces in the Water, 1961

Scented Gardens for the Blind, 1963

Living in the Maniototo, 1979

Autobiographies

To the Is-Land, 1982

An Angel at My Table, 1984

The Envoy from Mirror City, 1985

When *An Angel at My Table* scooped prizes at film festivals in 1990, it brought to global attention two New Zealand women artists. Jane Campion went on to make *The Piano*, while Janet Frame, whose three-volume autobiography Campion had adapted, found her work celebrated around the world.

Frame's collection of stories, *The Lagoon*, was published when she was ricocheting between institutions for a (false) diagnosis of schizophrenia. A hospital worker, who read that Frame had won the Hubert Church Memorial Award, postponed her lobotomy. *Owls Do Cry*, was the first novel in a career that brilliantly investigated mental states on the edge. **SM**

LUIS MARTÍN SANTOS

Born: November 11, 1924 (Larache, Morocco); died January 21, 1964 (San Sebastian, Spain).

Style and genre: Luis Martín-Santos's interest in psychiatry infused his writing. He used modernist techniques, second-person point of view, and interior monologue.

Signature titles

Poetry

Grana Grey (Grana gris), 1945

Novels

Time of Silence (Tiempo de silencio), 1962

Time of Destruction (Tiempo de destrucción), 1975 (posthumous, unfinished)

Nonfiction

Dilthey, Jaspers, and the Understanding of Mental Illness (Dilthey, Jaspers y la comprensión del enfermo mental), 1955

Freedom, Temporality, and Transference in Existential Psychoanalysis (Libertad, temporalidad y transferencia en el psicoanálisis existencial), 1964

Apólogos y otras prosas inéditas, 1970

Luis Martín-Santos studied medicine at the University of Salamanca, then psychiatry at Madrid University and acted as director of the Psychiatric Sanatorium in San Sebastian for thirteen years. He wrote many essays in his quest to develop a psychology of the whole person, publishing a collection of ideas—*Dilthey, Jaspers, and the Understanding of Mental Illness*.

In 1962, Martín-Santos produced a novel that translated the narrative structures, modernist techniques, and linguistic complexity of James Joyce's Ulysses into Spanish. This novel, *Time of Silence*, provided a subjective and innovative approach at odds with the social realism prevalent in Spain. *Time of Destruction*, the second novel in this projected trilogy, was left unfinished by his death in an automobile accident. **REM**

GORE VIDAL

Born: Eugene Luther Gore Vidal, October 3, 1925 (West Point, New York, U.S.).

Style and genre: American novelist, playwright, scriptwriter, and essayist, famous for his wit and scathing (often controversial) opinion of American politics, and for his frank treatment of sexual themes, particularly in his essays.

When Gore Vidal's third novel, *The City and the Pillar*, was published, it caused an instant rage of publicity because of its open treatment of homosexuality. This was the first book in America to address the subject with such frankness, and was considered scandalous by the public and critics. However, it firmly established Gore Vidal's reputation as one of the most talented and controversial writers.

Vidal's work is notorious for its sharp wit and unashamed frankness, and through his continuing career he has addressed topics such as sexuality and politics with a disarming bluntness that has earned him both appreciation and loathing. For a period during the 1950s, and following *The City and the Pillar*, sales of his books decreased and he turned to scriptwriting, most famously reworking the script for *Ben Hur* and suggesting a gay subtext. However, this was not acknowledged by lead Charlton Heston. During the 1960s, Vidal's career as a novelist once again took off with the publication of *Julian*, *Washington D.C.*, and the satirically humorous *Myra Breckinridge*, which addressed transsexuality and feminism. From this period on, Vidal's novels fall roughly into two categories: the historical and/or political work such as *Lincoln* and sardonic comedies similar to *Myra Breckinridge* and *The Smithsonian Institution*.

Vidal's fame rests also on his work as an essayist, a medium through which he airs his controversial political, sexual, and social views with a dynamism and turn of phrase that is rarely matched. His political views, which are ardent, have been well documented, and have at times brought him trouble, in particular with the political analyst William F. Buckley Jr., with whom Vidal has had an on-going war of words and litigation. **TamP**

"In writing and politicking, it's best not to think about it, just do it."—Gore Vidal

Signature titles

Novels

The City and the Pillar, 1948
Julian, 1964
Washington D.C., 1967
Myra Breckinridge, 1968
Lincoln, 1984
The Smithsonian Institution, 1998

Screenplay

Ben Hur, 1959

ABOVE: Photograph of Gore Vidal taken in October 2006.

1920–39

FLANNERY O'CONNOR

Born: March 25, 1925 (Savannah, Georgia, U.S.); died August 3, 1964 (Milledgeville, Georgia, U.S.).

Style and genre: Flannery O'Connor's fiction takes place in rural, Southern settings, featuring crude characters and a focus on the quest for God in an irreverent world.

When Flannery O'Connor was twenty-five, she was struck down by lupus, the wasting sickness that had killed her father ten years earlier. This first encounter with the disease seemed set to kill her—instead she was forced to live out the rest of her short adult life as an invalid in the rural isolation of her mother's Georgia farmhouse. Life with the debilitating effects of lupus gave her a keen sense of her own mortality: her work proclaims her preoccupation with death.

The South of O'Connor's stories is peopled with the small-minded, the selfish, the crippled, and the insane. A devout Roman Catholic, she chose to write about sinners rather than saints: her two novels portray the difficulties that religious believers face in a profane world. In *Wise Blood*, Hazel Motes attempts to establish a "Church Without Christ," a faith unblemished by sin, only to be frustrated by the interference of a pimply adolescent eager to provide him with a "new Jesus." *The Violent Bear It Away* sees Francis Tarwater struggle with the mission with which his zealous grandfather has entrusted him: baptizing his mentally disabled young cousin to spite his irreligious uncle. In each book a series of violent events leads the protagonist toward redemption.

While her themes—suffering and salvation—may be serious, O'Connor's style is resolutely comic. Much of her fiction revolves around some grotesque incident: a pervert's theft of a woman's wooden leg, or a young man running wild in a gorilla suit. No aspect of life is too mean to be worthy of her attention, or too macabre to carry a spiritual meaning. In her stories, God's grace is made manifest in the most unlikely situations, often in moments of defeat, reversal, and embarrassment than in victory or celebration. **CT**

"Death has always been brother to my imagination."

—Flannery O'Connor

Signature titles

Short stories

A Good Man is Hard to Find, 1955

Everything That Rises Must Converge, 1965

Novels

Wise Blood, 1952

The Violent Bear It Away, 1960

ABOVE: O'Connor poses for a portrait during the 1950s.

YUKIO MISHIMA

Born: Kimitake Hiraoka, January 14, 1925 (Shinjuku, Tokyo, Japan); died November 25, 1970 (Tokyo, Japan).

Style and genre: Japanese writer of novels, short stories, essays, poetry, and plays on themes of decaying physical beauty, suicide, masochism, and homoeroticism.

Yukio Mishima is probably the best known Japanese writer to Western readers. He was nominated three times for the Nobel Prize in Literature. He also had a very public suicide, dying by *seppuku*—a ritual involving self-disembowelment.

The manner of Mishima's death reflected the preoccupations of his work. In his forty novels, twenty short-story compilations, and eighteen plays, Mishima explores Japanese society grappling with Western values as those of Imperial Japan fall away. His first novel, *Confessions of a Mask,* propelled him to success. It tells the story of a man discovering his homosexuality. It is said to be semiautobiographical and although a husband and father, Mishima's own sexuality has never been made clear. **CK**

Signature titles

Novels

Confessions of a Mask, 1948

Forbidden Colors, 1953

The Sound of Waves, 1954

The Temple of the Golden Pavilion, 1956

The Sailor Who Fell from Grace with the Sea, 1963

The Sea of Fertility Tetralogy, 1966–1971

Way of the Samurai, 1967

Plays

Five Modern Noh Plays, 1956

Tenth Day Chrysanthemum, 1961

Madame de Sade, 1965

CARMEN MARTÍN GAITE

Born: December 8, 1925 (Salamanca, Spain); died July 22, 2000 (Madrid, Spain).

Style and genre: Martín Gaite's early work focused on a realistic criticism of social injustice, convention and monotony of society, especially as it affected women. Later, she concentrated on preoccupations such as the passage of time and chance.

One of only two women in the Spanish Royal Academy at the time of her death, Carmen Martín Gaite's work has highlighted the constraints on women in patriarchal societies. It deals with issues Spanish women have faced throughout history. Her later works are infused with elements of myth, folklore, fairy tales, and fables.

As a post–Spanish Civil War writer, Martín Gaite wrote about social consequences of Franco's regime. She was awarded the Nadal Prize for *Behind the Curtains*, the Prince of Asturias Prize for Literature in 1988, and the National Prize for Literature in 1978 and 1994. Her work links the realism of mid-century Spanish literature and the more intimate modern novel. **REM**

Signature titles

Short stories

El balneario, 1954

Las ataduras, 1960

Complete Stories (Cuentos completos), 1978

Novels

Behind the Curtains (Entre visillos), 1957

Ritmo lento, 1963

Retahílas, 1974

Fragmentos de interior, 1976

The Back Room (El cuarto de atrás), 1978

Variable Cloud (Nubosidad variable), 1992

The Farewell Angel (La Reina de las Nieves), 1994

Living's the Strange Thing (Lo raro es vivir), 1996

Irse de casa, 1998

Los parentescos, 2001 (posthumous, unfinished)

JOHN BERGER

Born: November 5, 1926 (London, England).

Style and genre: John Berger is a visionary whose revolutionary meditations on "ways of seeing" continue to redefine readers' responses—and responsibilities—to art, culture, and politics.

It is almost impossible to discuss the scope of John Berger's six-decade career as humanist Marxist essayist, artist and art critic, screenwriter, and public intellectual without defining him as and through his collaborations. Profoundly gifted as a writer, Berger's greatest gift is perhaps the generosity with which he has worked alongside creators such as director Simon McBurney, artist Juan Muñoz, and composer Gavin Bryars. In addition, his essay collections have introduced readers to the work of Middle Eastern and Latin American writers, artists, and activists, including a wonderful exchange with the enigmatic revolutionary Subcomandante Marcos (*The Shape of a Pocket*).

Berger, author of more than a dozen books of nonfiction, is almost as elusive as the Chiapas guerrilla. Renowned for his study of Western high art, *Ways of Seeing* (1972), which he developed while working as art critic for socialist magazine *The New Statesman*, he is a widely exhibited artist, and a dazzling novelist who focuses on lives and places marginalized by industrial capitalism. Like Marcos, Berger lives outside of cosmopolitan centers, in a village in the Alps, and observes international politics and culture vividly and mordantly.

Prescient and politicized, Berger's *Hold Everything Dear: Despatches on Survival* blends erotic poetry, reportage from Palestine, and economic theory, into a multifaceted meditation on the relationship between freedom and desire that is opposed to all walls: between countries and people, between genres and media. Whether he is looking at the lives of working folk, his memories (*Here Is Where We Meet*), a friend's painted wall (*I Send You This Cadmium Red*, with John Christie, 2000), Titian, or photographs of mountains, Berger's nomadic eye is profoundly local and brilliantly global. **SM**

Signature titles

Novels

G, 1972

Into their Labours—a Trilogy

Pig Earth, 1979

Once in Europa, 1987

Lilac and Flag, 1990

Nonfiction

Ways of Seeing, 1972

About Looking, 1980

Essays

The Shape of a Pocket, 2001

Hold Everything Dear: Despatches on Survival and Resistance, 2007

Memoirs

Here Is Where We Meet, 2005

"[Art] . . . makes sense of what life's brutalities cannot . . ."

—*Let Seven Men Write Your Poem*

ABOVE: Berger pictured during the making of the video "Vanishing Points" in 2005.

DARIO FO

Born: March 24, 1926 (San Giano, Varese Province, Italy).

Style and genre: An extrovert Italian actor, writer, comedian, storyteller, Fo is a performer. He employs comedic methods of the ancient Italian *commedia dell'arte* in his work, and runs a theater company.

Dario Fo was the son of a railroad worker and the family moved frequently when he was young. In 1940, Fo moved to Milan to study architecture. His family was opposed to Mussolini's facist regime and although Fo was conscripted into the army in World War II, he escaped and went into hiding.

When Fo was awarded the Nobel Prize in Literature in 1997, the reactions of the Italian intellectuals were closer to bewilderment than joy. Fo is not a writer in the strict sense of the word. But it would be wrong to define him as an actor, as few people see in him the qualities of a pure "performer." His writings overturn legends and genres, and make use of a vocabulary filled with meaning and regional expressions threatened by media's influence on the Italian language.

One of the most significant episodes of his career was his participation in the Italian television program *Canzonissima* in 1962. Together with his wife, Franca Rame, Fo showed himself to be both humorous and sarcastic, but below the surface there were veiled attacks against the political classes, the economic miracle's "false" promise of freedom, and the exploitation of the workers. Despite the cloak of sarcasm and derision, Fo was effectively banned from television after this appearance, but it only served to multiply the number of his admirers. In the aftermath, theaters showing his works were all sold out. So much so that, during the years leading up to the student protests of 1968, Fo moved his plays into communal institutions such as town halls, and even gyms, thus underlining that his art was part of everyday life. Just like in the visual arts, the performer Fo broke with the established rules, refuting the traditions of the theater in order to lower himself to the level of modern life. **FF**

"A thousand children butchered for one of yours, a river of blood for a cupful."—*Comic Mystery*

Signature titles

Plays

Poor Little Thing (Poer nano), 1952

The Worker Knows 300 Words, the Boss 1000: That's Why He's the Boss (L'operaio conosce 300 parole, il padrone 1000: per questo è lui il padrone), 1969

Comic Mystery (Mistero buffo), 1969

Accidental Death of an Anarchist, 1970

Can't Pay? Won't Pay! (Non si paga, non si paga!), 1974

The Pope and the Witch (Il papa e la strega), 1989

Johan Padan and the Discovery of the Americas (Johan Padan a la descoverta de le Americhe), 1991

The Dysfunctional Bicefalo (L'anomalo Bicefalo), 2003

ABOVE: The Nobel Prize–winner pictured at an awards ceremony in 1998.

ALLEN GINSBERG

Born: Irwen Allen Ginsberg, June 3, 1926 (Newark, New Jersey, U.S.); died April 6, 1997 (New York, New York, U.S.).

Style and genre: Beat Generation poet and counter-cultural activist whose visionary poetry captures the spirit of bohemian life in the fifties and sixties.

Allen Ginsberg's father, Louis, was a high-school English teacher and minor poet. His mother, Naomi, whose unstable mental health caused her epileptic seizures and bouts of paranoia, spent much of her life in mental hospitals and was an active member of the Communist Party in the post-Depression years. These influences would show through in Ginsberg's work. He wrote a great deal about his mother's mental illness, most memorably in his poem *Kaddish*, an elegy for Naomi modeled on traditional Jewish ritual and considered by many to be his masterpiece. He was also committed to radical political causes both in his writing and in his personal activism. Ginsberg lent a strong presence to many anti-Vietnam rallies, leading the crowd in Buddhist chants of "Om."

Ginsberg's breakthrough poem was *Howl*, which he described as "an emotional time bomb that would continue exploding in U.S. consciousness in case our military-industrial-nationalist complex solidified into a repressive police bureaucracy." The poem is written in long lines influenced by Whitman, William Blake's prophetic books, and the cadences of the Old Testament. Its content includes celebrations of gay sex, outlaw living, and cultural change, and it was the subject of an obscenity trial. It became the best-known work of the Beat Generation, along with Kerouac's *On the Road*, and it cemented Ginsberg's place among the leading countercultural icons of his age.

"I saw the best minds of my generation destroyed by madness . . ."—*Howl*

Ginsberg spent his life traveling, including two-years in India learning to meditate. He was dedicated to pharmaceutical experimentation in the interests of expanding his consciousness. Although he became a much-garlanded establishment figure, he never forsook his radical principles. **MS**

Signature titles

Poetry

Howl, 1955

Kaddish, 1958

Planet News, 1968

The Fall of America, 1973

Plutonian Ode, 1982

ABOVE: Ginsberg photographed in New York in 1988 by William Coupon.

JOHN FOWLES

Born: March 31, 1926 (Leigh-on-Sea, Essex, England); died November 5, 2005 (Lyme Regis, Dorset, England).

Style and genre: A postmodernist novelist, poet, and essayist who explored existentialist themes. His playfulness called traditional narrative form into question.

John Fowles's first three novels—*The Collector*, *The Magus*, and *The French Lieutenant's Woman*—all met with considerable success and made him a rising star on the British literary scene in the 1960s. Yet, for most, they represent the peak of his powers, and perhaps his later lack of critical acclaim for works such as *Daniel Martin* contributed to the slowing down of his production of work. In 1988, Fowles suffered a stroke that saw him spend the rest of his life as somewhat of a recluse in his beloved West Country home in Lyme Regis, with his frankly honest journals being published to reveal a rather intolerant man, given to strong dislikes and prejudices, who was only too happy to avoid the literary limelight.

Nevertheless, his early works have continued to be hugely popular, achieving almost cult status. In subject matter they are incredibly diverse: *The Collector* tells the disturbing story of a misfit who abducts a woman, and even falls into the thriller category; *The Magus* is a sprawling Shakespearean chronicle of a young man's coming of age while teaching English on a Greek island; and *The French Lieutenant's Woman* is part-romance, part-pastiche of the Victorian novel, telling the tale of a fallen woman. What unites them all, apart from Fowles's talent for storytelling, is his postmodern playfulness with the traditional narrative form, with alternative endings, the shifting of the narrator's voice, and suggestion that the characters have a life of their own outside his works. An atheist, Fowles was drawn to the writings of French existentialists such as Jean-Paul Sartre. Fowles's work not only gives existentialism its very own British twist, it also asks the reader to make his or her own conclusions about the characters he creates and their fate. **CK**

Signature titles

Novels

The Collector, 1963

The Magus 1965, revised 1977

The French Lieutenant's Woman, 1969

The Ebony Tower, 1974

Daniel Martin, 1977

Mantissa, 1982

A Maggot, 1985

"Your characters become much more real to you than anyone can imagine."—John Fowles

ABOVE: Photograph of John Fowles taken in December 1999.

GÜNTER GRASS

Born: October 16, 1927 (Danzig [now Gdansk], Poland).

Style and genre: Grass's writing uses strong, thought-provoking political and historical themes, unravels plots through fantastical situations, and addresses issues of guilt and acceptance in postwar Germany.

The leading spokesman of contemporary German literature, Günter Grass is equally adept as a poet, playwright, and sculptor. His works incur a strong socialist element and his groundbreaking debut novel, *The Tin Drum*, remains the work that is best known to English-speaking readers. The controversial revelation, in 2006, that Grass served in Hitler's Waffen SS during World War II has damaged the reputation of a man who received the Nobel Prize in Literature in 1999.

Grass passed through the Hitler Youth movement in his native Danzig before a call-up to the Waffen SS at the age of seventeen. Wounded in battle, he spent the remainder of the war in an American POW camp. Afterward, he studied art in Düsseldorf and Berlin, flitting between jobs including farm

Signature titles

Novels

The Tin Drum (Die Blechtrommel), 1959

Cat and Mouse (Katz und maus), 1961

Dog Years (Hundejahre), 1963

Local Anesthetic (Örtlich betäub), 1969

From the Diary of a Snail (Aus dem tagebuch eine schnecke), 1972

The Flounder (Der butt), 1977

The Rats (Die Rätten), 1987

The Call of the Toad (Unkenrufe), 1992

Crabwalk (Mein krebsgang), 2002

Autobiography

Peeling the Onion (Beim haüten der zweibel), 2007

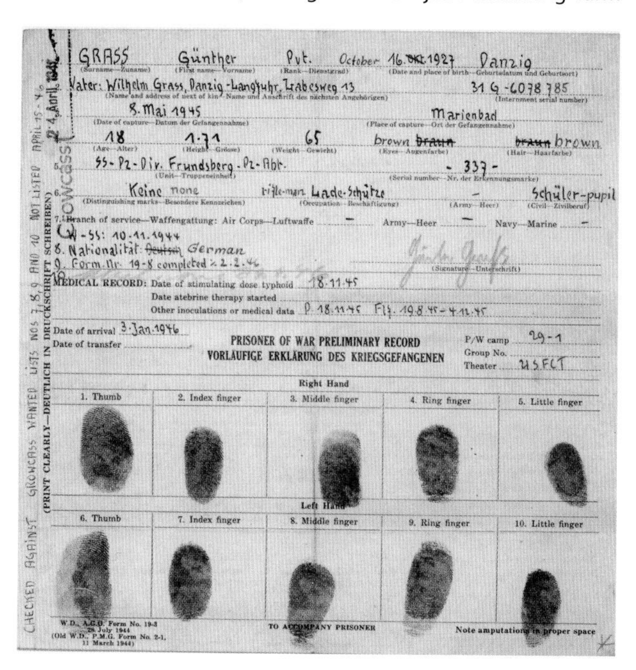

CHECKED AGAINST GROWCASS WANTED LISTS NOS 7, 8, 9 AND 10 NOT LISTED APRIL 15-46

(PRINT CLEARLY—DEUTLICH IN DRUCKSCHRIFT SCHREIBEN)

GRASS (Surname—Zuname) Günther (First name—Vorname) Pvt. (Rank—Dienstgrad) October 16. Okt. 1927 Danzig (Date and place of birth—Geburtsdatum und Geburtsort)

Vater: Wilhelm Grass, Danzig-Langfuhr, Labesweg 13 (Name and address of next of kin—Name und Anschrift des nächsten Angehörigen) 31 G-6078785 (Interment serial number)

8. Mai 1945 (Date of capture—Datum der Gefangennahme) Marienbad (Place of capture—Ort der Gefangennahme)

18 (Age—Alter) 1.71 (Height—Grösse) 65 (Weight—Gewicht) brown braun (Eyes—Augenfarbe) braun brown (Hair—Haarfarbe)

5. SS-Pz-Div. Frundsberg-Pz-Abt. (Unit—Truppeneinheit) -337- (Serial number—Nr. der Erkennungsmarke)

6. Keine none (Distinguishing marks—Besondere Kennzeichen) rifle-man Lade-Schütze (Occupation—Beschäftigung) – (Army—Heer) Schüler-pupil (Civil—Zivilberuf)

7. Branch of service—Waffengattung: Air Corps—Luftwaffe – Army—Heer – Navy—Marine –

W-SS: 10.11.1944

8. Nationalität: Deutsch German

9. Form Nr. 19-8 completed 2.2.46 (Signature—Unterschrift)

10. MEDICAL RECORD: Date of stimulating dose typhoid 18.11.45

Date atebrine therapy started

Other inoculations or medical data P. 18.11.45 Flf. 19.8.45-4.12.45

Date of arrival 3. Jan. 1946

Date of transfer

PRISONER OF WAR PRELIMINARY RECORD
VORLÄUFIGE ERKLÄRUNG DES KRIEGSGEFANGENEN

P/W camp 29-1
Group No.
Theater USFCT

Right Hand

1. Thumb	2. Index finger	3. Middle finger	4. Ring finger	5. Little finger

Left Hand

6. Thumb	7. Index finger	8. Middle finger	9. Ring finger	10. Little finger

W.D., A.G.O. Form No. 19-3, 28 July 1944 (Old W.D., P.M.G. Form No. 2-1, 11 March 1944)

TO ACCOMPANY PRISONER

Note amputations in proper space

ABOVE: Grass's work deals with issues of acceptance and guilt in postwar Germany.

RIGHT: Grass's prisoner-of-war record from 1945.

ABOVE: Grass (left) on the set of the film version of *The Tin Drum*, 1979.

laborer, miner, graphic artist, sculptor, and jazz musician. In 1955, Grass joined the socially critical writer's association Gruppe 47 and published his first poems and plays, although to little acclaim. It was while he was working in Paris that he completed his allegorical and picaresque novel, *The Tin Drum*, which upon release instantly made Grass a household name within Germany. The story, which tells of Oscar Matzerath, who at the age of three receives a tin drum and refuses to grow physically after recoiling from what he pertains to be a duplicitous adult world, is a response to the guilt of Grass's homeland after the war.

"Today I know that everything watches, that nothing goes unseen . . ."—*The Tin Drum*

Although dark and disturbing, Grass imaginatively exaggerates his own experiences of living in Danzig through the rise of Nazism, the Soviet invasion, and postwar German

Peeling the Onion

When Grass publicly acknowledged for the first time his membership to the Waffen SS at the age of seventeen, after years of condemnation of the Nazis, it caused more than a mild commotion in the literary world. Far from having opposed the Nazis, he had walked among them as a soldier in one of their most notorious organizations. For a man of such visible socialist credentials, a committed and outspoken critic of Germany's treatment of its Nazi past, and someone who had made a career from satirizing the views of those at odds with his own strong beliefs, the accusations of hypocrisy were predictably numerous.

The full extent of his involvement in the Waffen SS is described in *Peeling the Onion* and despite the author asking us to suspend belief when insisting he never actually fired a shot, he is fiercely critical of his younger self. The book does not aim to admonish guilt or seek redemption, but it has thrown up important issues of authorial ethics, as well as the expectations the audience places on an author's behavior.

For some, the revelation has discredited him as a moral authority, while others argue that Grass's own feelings of guilt at his complicit stand have been integral to the unforgiving moral questions asked in so many of his works. Like many of his novels, it is an issue that looks likely to continually divide opinion.

reconstruction. Oscar remains out of step with the marching rallies of the Nazi hordes by steadily beating his drum, exerting a piercing scream, and mocking the absurdity of the events unfolding around him.

Two further works followed on to form the *Danzig Trilogy*, still set in wartime against the constant backdrop of the Polish-German dualism of Danzig. *Cat and Mouse* is the tale of Joachim Mahlke, a high school student with a protruding Adam's apple (the mouse of the title), told through the eyes of the unreliable narrator, Pilenz. He reminisces about their youth in Hitler's Germany and explores what it means to be human in an age of war. *Dog Years* is even more challenging stylistically, with its use of invented words and dense, twisted imagery. The tale is told from three distinct viewpoints across an apocalyptic period in Germany's history and serves as a harrowing journey into the German psyche of the twentieth century.

During the 1960s, Grass participated in election campaigns for his friend the Social Democrat leader Willy Brandt; an experience incorporated into the book *From the Diary of a Snail*. While serious in intent, Grass appears as a comic character, willfully attempting to do the right thing despite many obstacles. It signaled a more playful and satirical approach to tackling the political and historical issues that, at times, threaten to bewilder the reader in their magnitude. *The Flounder* details the battle of the sexes from the Stone Age to the present in a fantasy tale that is enlivened with wit, puns, food, and sex, finding a receptive audience outside Germany.

Grass's books are intellectual and experimental in form, theme, and language, challenging our reading of the past—something he continued into the new century with *Crabwalk*. This account of the sinking of the *Wilhelm Gustloff*, a German cruise ship loaded with refugees, by a Soviet submarine in 1945, is told through the eyes of a journalist born to one of the few survivors. The story embraces the issue of guilt by looking to the past—an issue Grass would have himself after the publication of his memoirs, *Peeling the Onion*, in 2007. **SG**

GABRIEL GARCÍA MÁRQUEZ

Born: March 6, 1927 (Aracataca, Colombia).

Style and genre: Colombian Nobel Prize winner whose fictions are deeply rooted in traditions of Caribbean folklore and magic, Colombian history, international politics, and the vicissitudes of the heart.

Raised by his grandparents, whose folk stories and superstitions would figure prominently in his fiction, Márquez began his career as a journalist. In 1955 his serialized account of a shipwrecked sailor doubled the circulation of opposition newspaper *El Espectador*. His left-wing politics were confirmed after witnessing a massacre of students by government troops. In 1959, Castro made Márquez bureau chief of Prensa Latinaó Bogota, a post he resigned in 1961. After four years in Mexico City working as a journalist and writing screenplays, Márquez began *One Hundred Years of Solitude*, which was published in 1967 to immediate and enormous acclaim.

Márquez's previous novels may be seen as discrete pieces of an as yet undefined fictional totality. *One Hundred Years*, with its wheel-of-time narrative, gives magisterial, exhilarating shape to the middle kingdom of Macondo. In prose of Biblical cadence and poetic imagination, the novel recounts a century in the lives and loves of the village: the plague of insomnia, the return of the dead, the disappearance of an entire train of workers, the woman who eats dirt, time itself paralyzed, the destruction of the village, and of how it was all foretold.

Subsequent novels weave similar concerns around differing focal points. *The Autumn of the Patriarch* explores the pathology of the dictator, while *The General in His Labyrinth* dissects the solitude of the statesman; both works question the supposed correspondence of facts and personalities. *Chronicle of a Death Foretold* recounts a surreal transformation, under the aegis of an implacable resignation to fate, of victims into executioners, and vice versa. *Love in the Time of Cholera* and *Of Love and Other Demons* return to and plumb deeper the various nymphomanias of the heart. **CH**

"The only advantage to fame is that I have been able to give it a political use."

Signature titles

Novels

One Hundred Years of Solitude (Cien años de soledad), 1967

The Autumn of the Patriarch (El otoño del patriarca), 1975

Chronicle of a Death Foretold (Crónica de una muerte anunciada), 1982

Love in the Time of Cholera (El amor en los tiempos del cólera), 1981

The General in His Labyrinth (El general en su laberinto), 1989

Of Love and Other Demons (Del amor y otros demonios), 1994

Novellas

No One Writes to the Colonel (El coronel no tiene quien le escriba), 1961

In Evil Hour (La mala hora), 1962

ABOVE: García Márquez in an undated photograph.

JOHN ASHBERY

Born: July 28, 1927 (Rochester, New York, U.S.).

Style and genre: John Ashbery is a much-heralded American poet of the New York School, who unites the mainstream writers and the avant-garde with his canny, elusive, playful poems.

John Ashbery is that rarest of birds: an experimental poet who has managed to garner wide acclaim, and a writer of challenging texts that are also enticingly lyrical, surprising, and beautiful. Studying at Harvard, Ashbery made friendships with writers such as Robert Creeley, Robert Bly, Kenneth Koch, and Frank O'Hara that would come to define the landscape of postwar American poetry. With the latter two, Ashbery would become known as a key player in the "New York School" of poets distinguished by a stylish, colloquial, *flâneur*-like poetry strongly influenced by the visual arts, and especially by the painters of abstract expressionism. But Ashbery's work also shows the strong imprint of surrealism, perhaps because of the time he spent in Paris working as an art critic.

Ashbery's first collection, *Some Trees*, was selected for the Yale Younger Poets Prize in 1956 by the writer W. H. Auden, on whom he had written a thesis at Harvard. *The Tennis-Court Oath*, his second book, surprised readers with its sharply disjunctive, nonlinear, surrealistic style. In 1975, Ashbery found wide acclaim for *Self-Portrait in a Convex Mirror*, making a clean sweep of the Pulitzer Prize, the National Book Award, and the National Book Critics Circle Award. The title poem in this collection takes off from Parmigianino's work of the same name to investigate the convexities and complications of subjectivity, and the ways that language moves in pursuit of a self that it can never quite fix down. Since then, Ashbery has produced his unique, unparaphrasable poetry at a steady rate. Some of his best work is to be found in collections such as *Houseboat Days*, *As We Know*, *Wakefulness,* and *Girls on the Run*, the latter a book-length narrative poem based on the work of outsider artist Henry Darger. **MS**

"We are afloat / On our dreams as on a barge made of ice . . ."

—"My Erotic Double"

Signature titles

Poetry

Some Trees, 1956
The Tennis-Court Oath, 1962
The Double-Dream of Spring, 1970
Three Poems, 1973
Self-Portrait in a Convex Mirror, 1975
Houseboat Days, 1977
As We Know, 1979
A Wave, 1984
Flow Chart, 1991
And the Stars Were Shining, 1994
Wakefulness, 1998
Girls on the Run, 1999
Chinese Whispers, 2002
A Worldly Country, 2007

ABOVE: Ashbery poses outdoors in a wicker chair in New York, August 1964.

JUAN BENET

Born: Juan Benet Goita, October 7, 1927 (Madrid, Spain); died January 5, 1993 (Madrid, Spain).

Style and genre: Juan Benet's style broke with traditional Spanish narratives. However, contemporaries saw the quality, uniqueness, and importance of his work.

When the Spanish Civil War broke out in 1936, Juan Benet's father died and the family fled the capital for San Sebastian in the Basque region of northern Spain, returning to Madrid when it was safe again in 1939. After completing high school, Benet entered the School of Civil Engineering in Madrid, earning an advanced degree in 1954. He worked as a highway engineer at first in Finland, then in Spain, until 1961, when he published his first work, a collection of short stories called *You'll Never Amount to Anything*.

His first novel, *Return to Región*, triggered a critical reaction, and much interest, for its break from traditional narratives. Written in an experimental and complex style, it focuses on characters living in a fictional area of Spain called Región, which is perhaps loosely based on León in mountainous northern Spain. The area of Región is difficult to get to, very isolated, and provincial, and some critics see in this description a metaphor for Spain itself. The novel is full of myth and allegory, is written in a style that demands much of the reader, and is deeply sarcastic. It is the first in a trilogy based in Región, and was followed by *A Meditation* in 1969 and *A Winter Journey* in 1972.

In addition to his fiction, Benet wrote critical essays and plays. One of his best known is his essay *Inspiration and Style (La inspiración y el estilo)*, which expounded on his ideas about literature. He insisted that literature should be more about style than about telling stories or persuasive arguments. Benet has been grouped with an international jet set of literary voices, including Marcel Proust, James Joyce, and William Faulkner, with Faulkner's influence especially prevalent in Benet's work. **REM**

"Philosophy is the science that complicates things that everybody knows."

Signature titles

Novels

Return to Región (Volverás a Región), 1967
A Meditation (Una meditación), 1969
A Winter Trip (Un viaje de invierno), 1972
Rusty Spikes (Herrumbrosas lanzas), 1983
The Knight of Saxony (El caballero de Sajonia), 1991

ABOVE: A photograph of Benet taken in Spain in 1980.

EDWARD ALBEE

Born: Edward Harvey, March 12, 1928 (Washington, D.C., U.S.).

Style and genre: A Pulitzer Prize–winning acclaimed American playwright, best known for *Who's Afraid of Virginia Woolf?*. His mix of theatricality and biting dialogue helped reinvent postwar American theater in the early 1960s.

Signature titles

Plays

The Zoo Story, 1958
The Sandbox, 1960
The Death of Bessie Smith, 1960
Who's Afraid of Virginia Woolf?, 1962
The Ballad of the Sad Cafe, 1964
A Delicate Balance, 1966
Box and Quotations from Chairman Mao Tse-Tung, 1969
Seascape, 1975
Finding the Sun, 1982
The Man Who Had Three Arms, 1983
Three Tall Women, 1991
Fragments, 1993
The Goat or Who Is Sylvia?, 2001
Peter and Jerry, 2004

There are few writers who have won the Pulitzer Prize more than once, but acclaimed American playwright Edward Albee has managed to win it three times. Always a great experimenter, Albee's twists on dramatic subjects and styles tend to garner equal amounts of praise and derision from theater critics, but no one could deny their innovation. As Albee himself says, "From the very beginning I must have been wired differently." Albee was adopted as a baby into a rich family, but said he never fit in at home—he and his parents were too different in outlook. He was thrown out of numerous private schools, and later dropped out of college. At the age of twenty he chose to live a more bohemian life in Greenwich Village, New York, as he had been told that was where all the interesting people were.

It was here, two days before his thirtieth birthday, that he wrote the startling one-act play *The Zoo Story* about a drifter who, after meeting a stranger in a park, provokes him to violence. This was the start of a series of realistic yet absurdist short plays that were to provide him with his first real public acclaim. However, it was his first work to last longer than fifty-five minutes, a controversial Broadway hit depicting marital strife, called *Who's Afraid of Virginia Woolf?* that brought him the fame his writing deserved. He followed this with his first two Pulitzer Prize–winning plays, *A Delicate Balance* and *Seascape*.

"A playwright is someone who lets his guts hang out on the stage."—Edward Albee

By the 1980s, the popularity of Albee's work suffered a decline and it seemed that he may disappear from public view. But in 1991, *Three Tall Women*, a play about a dying woman who has spurned her gay son, brought renewed interest in Albee (and earned him his third Pulitzer) and he was soon back in demand, where he has remained to this day. **JM**

ABOVE: Edward Albee photographed in London in 2006.

CARLOS FUENTES

Born: Carlos Fuentes Macias, November 11, 1928 (Panama City, Panama).

Style and genre: Although born in Panama, Carlos Fuentes is a Mexican novelist and critic, known especially for his narrative experimentalism and deep excavations in Mexican and Latin American history.

Much like the murals of Diego Rivera, Carlos Fuentes's novels explore Mexican identity in its political, historical, social, psychological, and mythic dimensions. In addition to being a novelist, Fuentes has also held diplomatic posts and been an unofficial ambassador of Latin American culture.

Fuentes's early novels portray an urban, contemporary Mexico ruled by economic (and mythic) determinism, historical amnesia, and an ossified image of its revolutionary past. The protagonists suffer the stagnation of the society they have helped to build as a kind of death-in-life. In *Where the Air Is Clear*, this takes a panoramic and kaleidoscopic form, with multiple characters and points of view representing all the strata of society. *The Death of Artemio Cruz* focuses on the title character's deathbed hallucination, recounted in three alternating voices—"I," "you," and "he"—a conglomeration of warring selves that achieves fusion only in death. *The Old Gringo* offers a slightly less pessimistic vision. American spinster Harriet Winslow also endlessly reviews her past in revolutionary Mexico, but shows evidence of having changed her puritan attitudes and grown as a woman. Equally dark, but also more ludic, are *Christopher Unborn*, in which a narrator-fetus awaits his birth on October 12, 1992, and *Terra Nostra*, a vast circular epic of 1492–1999, best described as the New World's re-conquest of the Old. In both novels, apocalypse wars with utopia and both end with the potential for a new Genesis.

"The novel indicates that we are becoming. There is no final solution. There is no last word."

A supporter of Cuba's Fidel Castro and the Sandinistas of Nicaragua, and a sometimes harsh critic of the United States, Fuentes has been refused entry there many times, although in 1987 he became Harvard's first professor of Latin American Studies. **CH**

Signature titles

Novels

Where the Air Is Clear (La región más transparente), 1958

The Death of Artemio Cruz (La muerte de Artemio Cruz), 1962

A Change of Skin (Cambio de piel), 1967

Terra Nostra, 1975

The Hydra's Head (La cabeza de la hydra), 1978

The Old Gringo (Gringo viejo), 1985

Christopher Unborn (Cristóbal Nonato), 1987

Essays

Contra Bush, 2004 (untranslated)

ABOVE: Portrait of Carlos Fuentes taken in October 2006.

ELIE WIESEL

Born: September 30, 1928 (Sighet, Romania).

Style and genre: Accepted as one of the greatest Holocaust writers, Wiesel is known for his spare, straightforward prose, the simplicity of which lends enormous power to his message of peace and tolerance.

Signature titles

Novels

Dawn, 1961

Day/The Accident, 1962

Memoirs

Night, 1960

Legends of our Time, 1968

All Rivers Run to the Sea, 1995

And the Sea Is Never Full, 1999

Nonfiction

One Generation After, 1971

A Jew Today, 1978

After the Darkness, 2002

Essayist, novelist, memoirist, and short-story writer, Elie Wiesel is the author of more than forty fiction and nonfiction books and the recipient of the 1986 Nobel Peace Prize. More than a writer, he is a survivor and a messenger. He was appointed Chairman of the U.S. Holocaust Memorial Council in 1978 by President Jimmy Carter, and won the Congressional Medal of Freedom in 1985. Now an American citizen, Wiesel lives in New York and teaches at Boston University. He and his wife founded the Elie Wiesel Foundation for Humanity, an organization fighting for human rights worldwide.

Wiesel was born and spent his early years in the northern Romanian town of Sighet, where a Jewish community had been established in 1640. In 1944, at the age of fifteen, he was deported by the Nazis, along with his parents and three sisters, to the concentration camp of Auschwitz. Separated from his mother and sisters on arrival, Wiesel never saw his mother or his younger sister again; his two older sisters survived. Weisel and his father stayed together during their time at Auschwitz and were transported together to Buchenwald, but his father died just before the camp's liberation in April 1945.

ABOVE: A portrait of Wiesel by William Coupon, taken in New York,1984.

RIGHT: Wiesel with the press after receiving the U.S. Congressional Gold Medal in 1985.

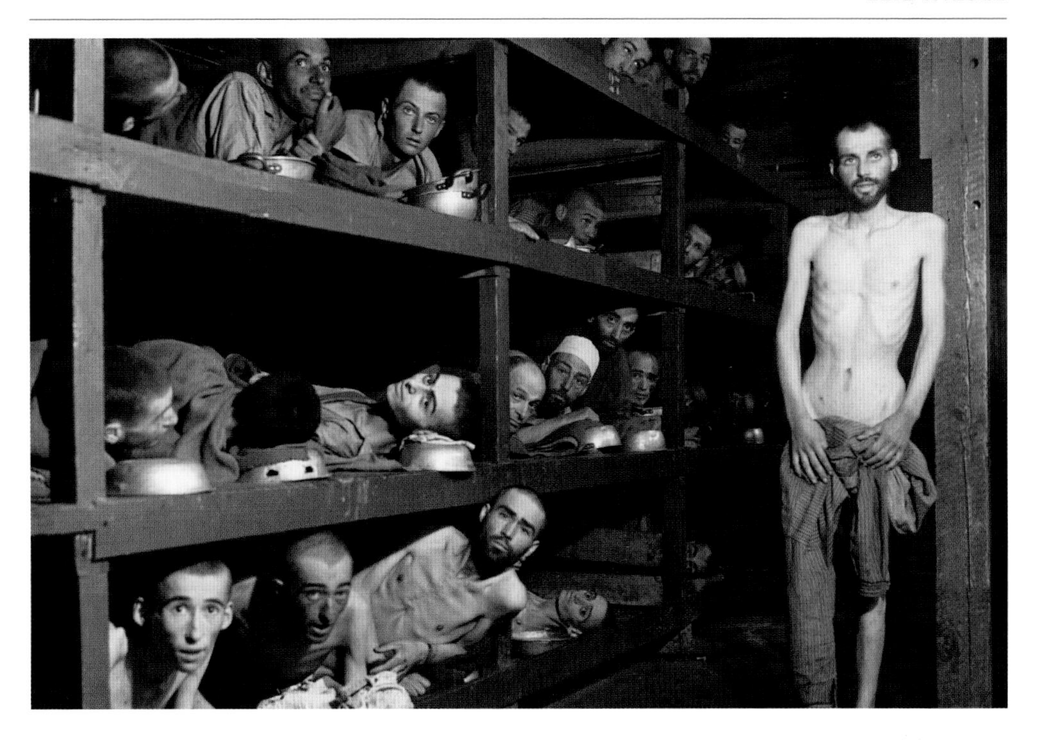

ABOVE: Elie Wiesel (middle row, seventh from left) at Buchenwald, April 16, 1945.

Wiesel studied philosophy and psychology at the Sorbonne in Paris after his liberation, and became a journalist. His postwar silence was broken in 1958 when his first and most famous book, *Night*, was published. A concise, bleak memoir detailing his horrific wartime experiences, *Night* eventually won international acclaim and sold over five milion copies.

After being granted American citizenship in 1963, Wiesel settled in New York and worked as a feature writer for *The Jewish Daily Forward* newspaper. He continued to write and publish novels, plays, and essays in French, and developed a strong international reputation. The majority of Wiesel's books focus on the events of the Holocaust, and the lectures he delivers center around his opposition to racial and religious persecution. His life's work has been to ensure that the death of six million Jews during the Holocaust will not be forgotten, in the hope that memory will prevent repetition. **LP**

The Publication of *Night*

Despite having been translated into more than thirty languages, *Night* narrowly escaped being lost to the world entirely. Francois Mauriac, a French novelist and Nobel Prize winner, persuaded Wiesel to break his ten-year silence and write about his Holocaust experiences. When Wiesel produced *Night*, Mauriac personally delivered it to countless publishers, but he failed to secure publishing success. Rejected by many publishers on the grounds that it was too morbid, *Night* was taken on by a small publishing house, but sold fewer than 1,500 copies between 1960 and 1963.

WILLIAM TREVOR

Born: William Trevor Cox, May 24, 1928 (Mitchelstown, County Cork, Ireland).

Style and genre: William Trevor is an Irish novelist, short-story writer, and playwright. His upbringing as a Protestant in Roman Catholic Ireland gave him a strong sense of the present caught in the toils of the past.

Born to a middle-class Protestant family, William Trevor grew up in a succession of Irish provincial towns. He was awarded a degree in history at Trinity College, Dublin, and then worked as a teacher while trying to establish himself as a sculptor. Marrying and moving to England in the 1950s, he begrudgingly worked as a copywriter in a London advertising agency.

Trevor's first novel, A *Standard of Behavior*, published in 1958, attracted little attention, but in the 1960s he began to build up a reputation with further novels and with much-admired short stories. *The Old Boys*, in which a group of former school boys plot and connive against each other, while still in the grip of the mutual hatreds and rivalries of their school days, won the British literary Hawthornden Prize.

Trevor thinks that writing "suffers from too much introspective attention," and has set some of his tales in his native Ireland, some in England. He has won praise for his skillful characterization, wry humor, a sense of the macabre, and spare, subtly effective prose.

Strongly influenced by Irish history and politics, Trevor's work often centers on the inescapable influence of the past on human lives, and he wrote with what has been called "a bleak objectivity" about the Northern Ireland Troubles and the long, tragic conflict between the Irish and the English. Some of his novels deal with the tensions between the Protestant landowners in Ireland and their Roman Catholic tenantry. *Fools of Fortune* is the story of a doomed love affair between an Irish woman and an Englishman. He has also adapted some of his work for the theater (including *The Old Boys*), radio, and television, and has won numerous prizes and awards. **RC**

Signature titles

Short stories

The Day We Got Drunk on Cake and Other Stories, 1967

The Ballroom of Romance and Other Stories, 1972

Angels at the Ritz and Other Stories 1975

The Stories of William Trevor, 1983

Novels

The Old Boys, 1964

The Children of Dynmouth, 1976

Fools of Fortune, 1983

Felicia's Journey, 1994

"Uncommonly well written, gruesome, funny, and original."

—*Evelyn Waugh on* The Old Boys

ABOVE: Portrait of Irish author William Trevor taken in 1993.

MAYA ANGELOU

Born: Marguerite Johnson, April 4, 1928 (St. Louis, Missouri, U.S.).

Style and genre: Maya Angelou is best known for her frank autobiographies, but she is a poet, playwright, historian, and essayist as well. She is also a performer with a career that has seen her in films and theater.

Maya Angelou's start in life at a public school in Arkansas, a victim of rape, and a teenage mother, may not have seemed propitious first steps to Washington's Capitol Hill, yet it was partly by telling that story in the first volume of her six-part autobiography *I Know Why the Caged Bird Sings* that led to her reciting one of her poems—*On the Pulse of the Morning*—at Bill Clinton's first inauguration as president in 1993. She is only the second poet in U.S. history to have done this.

Angelou's frank account of growing up bright, female, and black in the American South before World War II reveals her suffering at the hands of racism and sexism, her bewilderment at her treatment, and her saving escape into literature. Tireless, inspirational, and multitalented, her easy lilting prose, canny powers of description, wry humor, and ultimately optimistic tale shot her into the best-seller lists and to fame. Ironically, Angelou started writing the book to help her recover from her grief after the assassination of her friend, Martin Luther King.

Yet Angelou is much more than an autobiographer. Her early years saw her work as a singer and actress, and she has continued to perform and produce, winning an Emmy Award nomination for Best Supporting Actress for her role in the television series *Roots* (1977). As a writer she has produced plays, screenplays, and most notably poetry: *Just Give Me a Cool Drink of Water 'Fore I Diiie* was nominated for the Pulitzer Prize. Her talent has inspired a generation of African-American women, Oprah Winfrey being one famous example. She is Reynolds Professor of American Studies at Wake Forest University. Her ability to find hope in the face of despair has, unsnobbishly, led her to supply words for Hallmark greeting cards. Nothing stops this bird from singing. **CK**

"There is no greater agony than bearing an untold story inside you."

Signature titles

Poetry

Just Give Me A Cool Drink of Water 'Fore I Diiie, 1971

The Complete Collected Poems of Maya Angelou, 1994

Autobiographies

I Know Why the Caged Bird Sings, 1969

Gather Together in My Name, 1974

A Song Flew up to Heaven, 2002

Essay

Even the Stars Look Lonesome, 1977

ABOVE: The multitalented Maya Angelou photographed in 2005.

PHILIP K. DICK

Born: Philip Kindred Dick, December 16, 1928 (Chicago, Illinois, U.S.); died March 2, 1982 (Santa Ana, California, U.S.).

Style and genre: An American science-fiction writer and countercultural icon, whose brilliant tales of phantasmagoric paranoia are among the most original.

The astonishingly prolific Philip K. Dick lived almost his entire life in Northern California. He attended Berkeley for a year, where he briefly operated a record store and ran a classical music program on the radio. He was married five times and had three children. Between 1950 and 1970, he wrote more than sixty novels and hundreds of short stories, the highlights of which are among the most breathtakingly inventive flights of fancy ever taken by an American author.

Dick rarely strayed far from the familiar conventions of science fiction, but his work is always recognizable. His major themes are ultimately epistemological: how do we know what we know? Dick ties his narratives around the problem, usually with motifs of schizophrenia and drug use, both of which he writes about from personal experience. What keeps these novels from flying off the rails is that his often wryly humorous accounts of future technology are resolutely grounded in the everyday reality of mid-century America. In *The Three Stigmata of Palmer Eldritch*, the colonization of Mars is reduced to a flight to the suburbs; maybe you can afford more property on the Red Planet and there is less worry about pollution, but there is

Signature titles

Short stories

Selected Stories, 2002

Novels

Solar Lottery, 1955

Time Out of Joint, 1959

The Man in the High Castle, 1962

Martian Time-Slip, 1964

The Three Stigmata of Palmer Eldritch, 1965

Dr. Bloodmoney, 1965

Do Androids Dream of Electric Sheep?, 1968

Flow My Tears, the Policeman Said, 1974

Confessions of a Crap Artist, 1975

A Scanner Darkly, 1977

Radio-Free Albemuth, 1985

ABOVE: Philip K. Dick photographed during the 1970s.

RIGHT: An android of Dick is interviewed for the NextFest in Chicago in 2005.

ABOVE: Darryl Hannah as Pris in the film *Blade Runner*, based on one of Dick's novels.

also nothing to do except pop pills and have affairs with your neighbors. The most charming aspect of Dick's fiction is that his characters are just as preoccupied with these workaday problems as they are with more genre-appropriate concerns—aliens and evil, dystopian conspiracies.

Although Dick's work would enjoy a second life on the silver screen, he was best known in his lifetime for his novel *The Man in the High Castle*. Despite being more speculative fiction than science—the novel is set in an alternate history, where the Axis won World War II. It is classic Dick in its resistance of its own premise: The titular character is a science-fiction writer, who has written a book about an alternate history where the Allies won World War II. This kind of gesture is what makes Dick so interesting; he invites us to wonder whether the reality in his novels might be the real one, and the world in which we read them the fiction. **SY**

Dick and the Movies

Dick died of a stroke before he could enjoy the success of Ridley Scott's film *Blade Runner* (1982), which is based on his novel *Do Androids Dream of Electric Sheep?*. Scott's film was a smash, and helped to create the aesthetic later called cyberpunk. Other films based on Dick's work include *Total Recall* (1990), Stephen Spielberg's *Minority Report* (2002), and Richard Linklater's *A Scanner Darkly* (2006). *The Economist* reported in 2004 that movies based on Dick's fiction had grossed nearly US $700 million.

MILAN KUNDERA

Born: April 1, 1929 (Brno, Czechoslovakia).

Style and genre: Milan Kundera writes philosophical prose with themes of melancholy, exile, and transformation. There are musical influences, and he uses metaphysical symbolism, dialectics of memory, and erotic transcendentalism.

Milan Kundera is a Franco-Czech writer of worldwide acclaim whose work is famous for its philosophical agility, lyrical eloquence, and musical quality. Inspired by his father, a professor of music and a close friend of the Moravian composer, Leos Janâjek, Kundera refined the melodic yet disciplined tenor of his prose during his studies of musical composition and literature at Charles University in Prague, and later as a lecturer at the Film Academy. When his burgeoning literary and academic career was interrupted by the Prague Spring in 1968, Kundera was forced to go into exile in France.

His early novels examine the many ideological perversions of the communist regime through characters who are victimized by history, but also by their personal choices. A Nietzschean reflection on good and evil, Kundera's first novel, *The Joke*, is a philosophical tour de force in which the protagonist earns himself an expulsion from the university, merely for ridiculing the regime in a postcard addressed to his girlfriend. Tragicomic undertones also pervade *The Book of Laughter and Forgetting*, a series of melancholy vignettes depicting the personal struggle of characters whose lives were variously compromised by the Husak government. Forced out of their professions or exiled from their country, Kundera's protagonists rely on memories to construct a sense of belonging out of feeling deracinated, if not weightless in the face of life's many burdens, a notion developed further in *The Unbearable Lightness of Being*. Kundera's recent novels written in French (*Immortality, Slowness, Identity*, and *Ignorance*), ponder the complexities of human desire, identity, and individual history, exposing the ephemeral, destructive ethos of contemporary society. **PR**

Signature titles

Poetry

Man: A Broad Garden, 1953

Novels

The Joke, 1967

The Book of Laughter and Forgetting, 1978

The Unbearable Lightness of Being, 1982

Immortality, 1988

Slowness, 1994 (as a play, 1968)

Identity, 1996

Ignorance, 2000

Plays

The Owner of the Keys, 1962

Jacques and His Master, 1971

Essays

The Art of the Novel, 1960

The Curtain, 2005

"A novel that does not uncover a hitherto unknown segment of existence is immoral."

ABOVE: The Czech writer Kundera in a photograph taken in 1980.

CHRISTA WOLF

Born: Christa Ihlenfeld, March 18, 1929 (Landsberg an der Warthe, Poland).

Style and genre: Christa Wolf, novelist, essayist and literary critic, is one of the most distinguished writers to emerge from former East Germany. German fascism, humanity, feminism, and self-discovery are prevalent themes in her work.

Christa Wolf is closely associated with East Germany where she wrote critically about the regime. Her first novel *Divided Heaven* was published in 1963, but it was *The Quest for Christa T*, a story concerning the pressure for women to conform, that established her. *Cassandra*, is perhaps her most important novel and her biggest international success. It is a reworking of Aeschylus's portrayal of Cassandra in *Agamemnon*. *What Remains* is a more autobiographical work based on her life under surveillance by the Ministry of State Security—the Stasi—and although written in 1979, it was published much later. Wolf won the Heinrich Mann Prize in 1963, the National Prize in 1978, and the Georg Büchner Prize in 1980. **HJ**

Signature titles

Novels

Divided Heaven (Der geteilte Himmel), 1963

The Quest for Christa T, 1969

Cassandra, 1983

Medea's Voices, 1996

Autobiography

What Remains, 1979, published 1990

MILORAD PAVIĆ

Born: October 15, 1929 (Belgrade, Serbia).

Style and genre: Poet, writer, and literary historian Milorad Pavić, pushes the limits of narrative structure, using crosswords, tarot cards and dual beginnings as an integral part of his novels.

Milorad Pavić has produced some of the most innovative and intriguing works in post modernist fiction. He believes that the reader has nearly the same rights as the author so can choose how his work should be read. His first novel, *Dictionary of the Khazars* is a mock history told in three versions—Christian, Islamic, and Jewish and in male and female versions that differ by one paragraph. *Landscape with Tea* is partly written in the form of a crossword puzzle and *Inner Side of the Wind*, based on the story of Hero and Leander, can be read back to front. *Last Love in Constantinople* comes complete with a set of Tarot cards, which the reader can use to choose the order in which to read the chapters. **HJ**

Signature titles

Novels

Dictionary of the Khazars, 1984

Landscape with Tea, 1988

The Inner Side of the Wind or The Novel of Hero and Leander, 1991

Last Love in Constantinople, 1994

JOHN OSBORNE

Born: December 12, 1929 (London, England); died December 24, 1994 (Shropshire, England).

Style and genre: A British playwright famed for sparking a revolution in 1950s theater. He gave the first voice to the "angry young man" of postwar Britain.

Signature titles

Plays

Look Back in Anger, 1956

The Entertainer, 1957

Luther, 1961

Inadmissable Evidence, 1964

A Patriot for Me, 1965

West of Suez, 1971

Watch It Come Down, 1976

Déjàvu, 1992

Autobiographies

A Better Class of Person, 1981

Almost a Gentleman, 1991

John Osborne was the angry young (and older) man incarnate, famed for his raging against, among other things: a postwar society that failed to deliver, suburban values, his mother, his wives, and critics. This rage burst on to the stage with a landmark play that brought international acclaim: *Look Back in Anger*.

Osborne is admired for creating passionate, tour-de-force speeches for his leads. The 1950s and 1960s was the golden age for a dandyish, witty, and outspoken Osborne, who was fêted in London and New York. He wrote great plays such as *The Entertainer*, *Luther*, and *Inadmissable Evidence*. Subsequent decades were peppered with plays like *Watch it Come Down* and *Déjàvu*, which revisits the cast of *Look Back in Anger*. **AK**

HANS MAGNUS ENZENSBERGER

Born: November 11, 1929 (Kaufbeuren, Germany).

Style and genre: Enzensberger is one of Germany's most important postwar poets. His work is characterized by his radical views and themes of civil unrest over economic and class-based issues.

Signature titles

Poetry

Blindenschrift, 1964

Mausoleum: 37 Ballads from the History of Progress (Mausoleum: 37 Balladen aus der Geschichte des Fortschritts), 1975

The Sinking of the Titanic (Der Untergang der Titanic: Eine Komödie), 1978

The Number Devil (Der Zahlenteufel: Ein Kopfkissenbuch für alle, die Angst vor der Mathematik haben), 1997

Where Were You Robert? (Wo warst du, Robert?), 1998

Lighter than Air: Moral Poems (Leichter als Luft: Moralische Gedichte), 1999

Critical prose

The Consciousness Industry: On Literature, Politics, and the Media, 1974

Hans Magnus Enzensberger's first poetry collection was published in 1957 and he was soon established as Germany's "angry young man." His political poetry, written in a clear, concise style was well received. His reputation as a poet who spoke for the oppressed with compassion, grew rapidly. In the 1960s, Enzensberger began moving beyond poetry and wrote for the theater, radio, and opera. He was awarded the Georg Büchner prize for his third collection of poetry *Blindenschrift* in 1964, and became a member of the literary movement Gruppe 47, a group of political writers that included Heinrich Boll. In *The Sinking of the Titanic,* the liner becomes a metaphor for modern society and the gap between rich and poor is explored. **HJ**

JOHN BARTH

Born: May 27, 1930 (Cambridge, Maryland, U.S.).

Style and genre: Resolute, postmodernist, short-story writer, and novelist, Barth produces unconventional narratives that play with truth, authorial power, and epistemology.

John Barth was a key player in forming the genre of metafiction, a playful and self-referential style of writing that invites the reader into the creative process that has built the text. Postmodernism had thrown forward-thinking authors into a ferment of authorial and ontological doubt. This fueled writers such as Barth to revise conventional modes of storytelling into hyperactive, insecure, yet daring alternatives, bristling in the face of narrative's newly recognized constraints.

Barth initially studied music theory and orchestration at the Juilliard School in New York. Abandoning music, he gained an undergraduate degree, majoring in journalism, then a Master's degree from Johns Hopkins University in Maryland. He went on to pursue various academic posts, teaching English at Penn State, Buffalo, Boston, and Johns Hopkins Universities.

In 1957, *The Floating Opera*, an unconventional novel about a suicidal lawyer's life, was published. Its peculiarity split the critics, with some accusing Barth of too frenzied a style, designed to confuse the reader. Elsewhere, the work was received as refreshing, bold, and in keeping with burgeoning postmodern writing movements. Further novels were well received, most notably *The Sot-Weed Factor* and *Giles Goat-Boy*.

In 1968, the energetic, prankish stories of *Lost in the Funhouse* showed more fully Barth's wish to experiment with the status quo. Here, textual play served to underline the exhausted nature of written language, but nonetheless demonstrated the scope for dynamic, innovative, textual forms to permeate the canon. Barth has won several awards, including the National Book Award, the F. Scott Fitzgerald Award for Outstanding Achievement in American Fiction, and the PEN/Malamud Award for Excellence in the Short Story. **LK**

"I am not a philosopher, except after the fact; but I am a mean rationalizer."—*The Floating Opera*

Signature titles

Novels

The Floating Opera, 1957

The End of the Road, 1958

The Sot-Weed Factor, 1960

Giles Goat-Boy, 1966

The Tidewater Tales, 1987

Coming Soon!!!: A Narrative, 2001

Short stories

Lost in the Funhouse, 1968

Novellas

Chimera, 1972

Where Three Roads Meet, 2005

ABOVE: Portrait of Barth taken May 18, 1997, the year he won the F. Scott Fitzgerald Award.

DEREK WALCOTT

Born: January 23, 1930 (Castries, St. Lucia).

Style and genre: Caribbean poet, painter, and dramatist, Walcott's writing lays bare the complexities thrown up by multicultural roots. His themes of journeying and exile draw on the poetry of Homer.

The Caribbean landscape has had a powerful shaping effect on Derek Walcott's work, but so too has the painful colonial legacy of the place. Much of Walcott's poetry has been inspired by his profound sense of being "divided to the vein" by his African and European ancestry. The English-speaking son of a Methodist family in a French-speaking Catholic community, Walcott quickly acquired an awareness of both the potential artistic fruitfulness and the personal and social conflicts that came with a complex multicultural inheritance.

In his life and in his work, Walcott has often been drawn by the compelling image of the castaway, caught between different places, cultures, and languages. *In A Green Night* brought him recognition worldwide. The title, echoing a line from Andrew Marvell's great poem of religious exile, "Bermudas," is one of many rueful reminders that the Renaissance was a green age of learning, but also a time of colonial darkness and oppression. Displacement and dislocation are evident in later titles such as *The Castaway* and *The Gulf*. Walcott comes to

Signature titles

Poetry

In A Green Night, 1962
The Castaway and Other Poems, 1965
The Gulf and Other Poems, 1969
Another Life, 1973
The Star Apple Kingdom, 1979
Collected Poems, 1948–1984, 1986
Omeros, 1990
The Bounty, 1997
Tiepolo's Hound, 2000
The Prodigal, 2004

Plays

Ione, 1957
Ti-Jean and His Brothers, 1958
Dream on Monkey Mountain, 1967

ABOVE: A studio portrait of Derek Walcott taken in 2000 by Horst Tappe.

RIGHT: Walcott at home in St. Lucia in January 2005.

terms with the psychological effects of the African diaspora by finding parallels in the epic poetry of Homer. However, he once observed that "The classics can console, but never enough."

Even so, the idea of the epic journey persists in his work, especially in *Omeros*, with its punning emphasis on the Greek name for Homer and the circular quest for home. *Another Life* sets out to rediscover and repossess a distinctively Caribbean cultural inheritance. "My generation," he said, "had looked at life with black skins and blue eyes." In *Sea Grapes*, he returns to the sights and sounds of his native St. Lucia, and in *The Star Apple Kingdom*, he adopts the Trinidadian creole of a sailor-poet named Shabine. Walcott has consistently argued against a literature of either revenge or remorse and that "truly tough aesthetic" continues to be worked out in his most recent work, including *The Bounty*, *Tiepolo's Hound*, and *The Prodigal*. Walcott was awarded the Nobel Prize in Literature in 1992. **SR**

ABOVE: *Street in Gros Îlet*, a watercolor by Walcott painted in 2002.

A Dramatic Side

Derek Walcott has played a major role in developing a distinctive Caribbean theatrical tradition. His play *Ione* blends Caribbean folk elements with the legacy of classical drama. His ambition of creating a theater where "someone could do Shakespeare or sing calypso with equal conviction" was to be realized in his work with the Trinidad Theater Workshop and in the production of powerful plays like *Ti-Jean and His Brothers* and *Dream on Monkey Mountain*. Walcott has also collaborated on musicals such as *The Joker of Seville* (1974) with Galt MacDermot and *The Capeman* (1998) with Paul Simon.

TED HUGHES

Born: Edward James Hughes, August 16, 1930 (Mytholmroyd, West Yorkshire, England); died October 28, 1998 (Devon, England).

Style and genre: An English poet with a prolific output, Hughes's vivid use of language characterized his work. He was English poet laureate from 1984 to 1998.

The poems of Ted Hughes remained firmly rooted, throughout his career, in the local vernacular of the Calder Valley where he grew up, and closely attached to a landscape that he came increasingly to elegize in its state of postindustrial ruination. His father was a survivor of World War I, and several early poems, including "Six Young Men" and "Wilfred Owen's Photographs," reflect on the colossal tragedy of 1914 to 1918. Hughes's education in archeology and anthropology at Cambridge University was to shape and sustain a lifelong interest in the natural environment, as well as in cultures and languages other than his own. It was in Cambridge that he met Sylvia Plath, and after their marriage in June 1956 he spent two years (1957–1959) in the United States.

The Hawk in the Rain immediately established Hughes's reputation as a bold and energetic poet, working against the predominant "movement" ethos of the time, with its preference for traditional forms and accessible subject matter. Linguistic vitality was Hughes's distinguishing characteristic, although frequently this was confused with violence. *Lupercal* and *Wodwo* further consolidated his appeal as a writer alive to the energies of nature and "the elemental power-circuit of the universe." *Crow*, with its striking illustrations by Leonard Baskin, showed Hughes to be a poet with a powerful myth-making imagination and a dark sense of humor. In later volumes, such as *Moortown Diary* and *Remains of Elmet*, Hughes brought a new ecological urgency and sensitivity to his writings on the English landscape. He also helped to bring Russian, East European, and other non-English poets to prominence in Britain through the influential magazine *Modern Poetry in Translation*. **SR**

"Maybe, if you don't have that secret confession, you don't have a poem."

Signature titles

Poetry

The Hawk in the Rain, 1957
Lupercal, 1960
Wodwo, 1967
Crow, 1970
Moortown Diary, 1979
Remains of Elmet, 1979
River, 1983
Flowers and Insects, 1986
Birthday Letters, 1988
Wolfwatching, 1989
Tales from Ovid, 1997
Collected Poems of Ted Hughes, 2003

ABOVE: Hughes in 1986 at a twenty-four-hour outdoor reading.

J. G. BALLARD

Born: James Gordon Ballard, November 15, 1930 (Shanghai, China).

Style and genre: English novelist and short-story writer whose themes of natural disaster, the erotic and psychic potential of technology, and the violence underlying late capitalism make him an essential contemporary commentator.

Ballard has been a unique figure in English writing for more than fifty years, and the category of the Ballardian has become central to an understanding of the postmodern world. Ballard began as a writer of science fiction, but immediately twisted its conventions to his own elegant purpose for his disaster novels, *The Crystal World*, *The Drowned World,* and *The Drought.* Here the end of the world seems not so much a disaster as the occasion for a strangely beautiful reconsideration of our inner lives.

Ballard's breakthrough came with *The Atrocity Exhibition*—the beginning of what Martin Amis calls Ballard's "concrete-and-steel period." This book is a scintillating, experimental catalog of the pathological atrocities of late capitalism, with sections such as "The Facelift of Princess Margaret" and "Why I Want to Fuck Ronald Reagan." Ballard followed this work with *Crash*, his even less compromising elaboration on the erotic possibilities of road accidents. When Ballard presented *Crash* to his publisher, its first reader commented, "The author of this book is beyond psychiatric help," which Ballard welcomed as a mark of his literary success. In 1996, *Crash* found its ideal director in David Cronenberg's memorable film adaptation.

Some of the roots of Ballard's compulsive images and anxieties were revealed in *Empire of the Sun*, his autobiographical account of growing up in a Japanese prisoner-of-war camp. The book was an unaccustomed commercial success and was filmed by Steven Spielberg. Ballard soon returned to the darker territory of his habitual preoccupations, however. From the nineties onward, he produced a series of novels that stylishly subvert our notions of community and literary form, such as *Cocaine Nights*, *Super-Cannes,* and *Kingdom Come.* **MS**

"I see my books as warnings. I'm the man at the side of the road who yells 'Slow down!'"

Signature titles

Novels

The Crystal World, 1962
The Burning World, 1965
The Drowned World, 1966
The Atrocity Exhibition, 1970
Crash, 1973
Concrete Island, 1974
High Rise, 1975
Cocaine Nights, 1996
Super-Cannes, 2000
Kingdom Come, 2006

Autobiography

Empire of the Sun, 1984

ABOVE: Detail from a photograph of Ballard on a railway platform taken October 9, 1992.

HAROLD PINTER

Born: October 10, 1930 (London, England).

Style and genre: Pinter is known for his distinctive use of language, pauses, and sense of menace—the "Pinteresque"—as well as for his interest in memory. More recently, he has gained notoriety for his polemical poetry and speeches.

The effect of Harold Pinter's drama is difficult to describe. While critics often invoke the phrase "comedy of menace," it is surely the latter of those terms that Pinter's audiences have felt most acutely. Consider the plot of what is frequently called Pinter's masterpiece, *The Homecoming*. The reunion in question finds Teddy and his American wife returning to his family home in London. She is initially unsettled by the strange house and its all-male occupants; her trepidation seems well founded when Teddy's father and brothers approach her sexually. However, when they brazenly ask her to remain as their prostitute and au pair girl, her sole concern is for a good salary.

On the face of it, such a plot would seem to present few opportunities for knee-slapping laughter. Yet many of Pinter's early works are often deliberately humorous. Plays such as *The Dumb Waiter* and *The Birthday Party* are crowded with jokes, verbal repartee, and physical comedy. As his plays enact the sudden reversals for which Pinter is famous and veer toward hostility, brutality, or violence, it is too easy to forget their

Signature titles

Plays

The Room, 1957
The Birthday Party, 1958
The Caretaker, 1960
The Homecoming, 1965
Landscape, 1968
Silence, 1969
Old Times, 1971
No Man's Land, 1975
Betrayal, 1978
A Kind of Alaska, 1981
One for the Road, 1984
Mountain Language, 1988
Party Time, 1991
Moonlight, 1993
Ashes to Ashes, 1996
Celebration, 1999

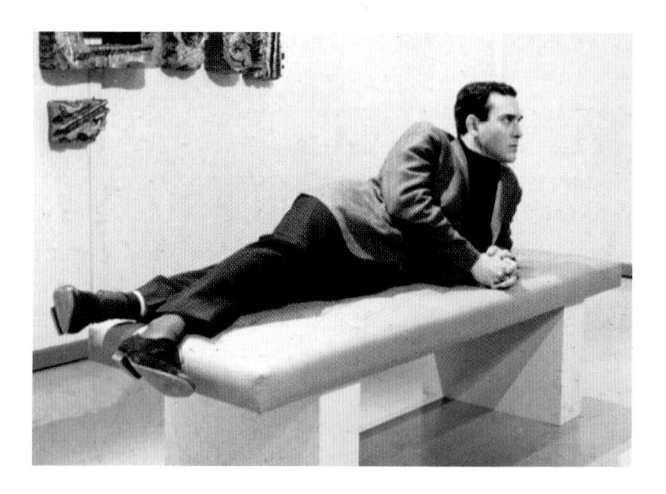

ABOVE: A photograph taken in May 2005 in Paris, the year Pinter won the Nobel Prize.

RIGHT: Harold Pinter poses for a photo shoot with George Konig in 1964.

ABOVE: Pinter in September 2007 at his writing desk in his London home.

comedic aspects. Pinter forces us to recognize the ways that laughter and language can sanitize the ugliness and perversity endemic to human power relationships—a recognition whose stylistic expression is sometimes called "Pinteresque."

Pinter's body of work resists easy categorization, although one may indulge in a few generalizations. His work almost uniformly rejects sentimentality, which is suggested in the contrapuntal relationship between the titles of his plays and their subject matter—between the warmth implied by "The Homecoming" and its chilling contents. His works categorically eschew exposition and denouement and are thus formally opposed to the structure of the well-made play. Finally, his characters are often deeply ambiguous and their motivations are as obscure to other characters as they are to the audience.

Pinter retired from writing plays in 2003, but still writes poetry and screenplays. He won the Nobel Prize in 2005. **IW**

Pinter at the Movies

Although Harold Pinter is best known as a playwright and poet, he is also a prolific screenwriter, with more than twenty-five film scripts to his credit. In his cinematic efforts, Pinter is interested mainly in adapting other writers' work. He has produced screenplays for John Fowles's *The French Lieutenant's Woman*, Margaret Atwood's *The Handmaid's Tale*, Ian McEwan's *The Comfort of Strangers*, Franz Kafka's *The Trial*, and most recently Anthony Shaffer's *Sleuth*. He has also adapted Proust's *In Search of Lost TIme* and Shakespeare's *King Lear*, although they have never been produced.

CHINUA ACHEBE

Born: Albert Chinualumogu Achebe, November 16, 1930 (Ogidi, Nigeria).

Style and genre: Describing the effects of Western culture on traditional Igbo society, Achebe's style tends toward spoken language, Igbo parables, and pidgin. His essays challenge critics to recognize African literature on its own terms.

Chinua Achebe spent his childhood watching two worlds unfold and has since done much to reconcile those worlds through writing. In the process, he has earned twenty-two honorary doctorate degrees and many literary awards, including the Man Booker International Prize (2007) and the Nigerian National Merit Award (1979). Achebe's devout Christian parents christened him Albert, after Prince Albert, but also instilled in him the practices of the traditional Igbo society. He adopted his Igbo name, which translates as "may God fight on my behalf," after graduating from the University College of Ibadan. Accordingly, he laid the framework in his own life for the social change in Nigeria that so much of his literature explores.

Achebe's first novel, and arguably his most well known, is *Things Fall Apart*. It tells the story of strongman Okonkwo and the downfall that comes about when he is not able to adapt to the new authority of the British district commissioner and the missionary church. *No Longer at Ease* and *Arrow of God* trace similar colonial trajectories, revealing for the first time the conflicts facing traditional Nigerian ways of life as the colonial powers began establishing their influence. Later works, such as *A Man of the People,* examine the internal conflicts that have occurred within Nigeria as a result of colonial presence. This second phase of Achebe's writing career aligns with the civil war in Nigeria, in which Achebe served as a Biafran diplomat. Using pidgin language and Igbo parables throughout much of his canon, Achebe developed a new paradigm for writing African novels. Defending the use of English and rejecting European notions of art, he transposed the oral tradition of storytelling into the format of the novel, and in so doing founded a new type of African literature. **JSD**

Signature titles

Novels

Things Fall Apart, 1958

No Longer at Ease, 1960

Arrow of God, 1964

A Man of the People, 1966

Anthills of the Savanna, 1987

Poetry

Christmas in Biafra and Other Poems/ Beware, Soul Brother and Other Poems, 1971

Children's fiction

How the Leopard Got His Claws, 1972

The Flute, 1977

Nonfiction

The Trouble with Nigeria, 1983

Hopes and Impediments, 1988

Home and Exile, 2000

"Our ancestors created their myths and told their stories for a human purpose."

ABOVE: Chinua Achebe at an award ceremony in Germany on October 13, 2002.

RIGHT: The revised edition of *Arrow of God* was published by Day in 1967.

Arrow of God

CHINUA ACHEBE

EDNA O'BRIEN

Born: December 15, 1930 (Tuamgraney, County Clare, Ireland).

Style and genre: O'Brien draws affecting portraits of contemporary women as isolated, unfulfilled, and repressed. Her writing is noted for its frank sexuality and lyrical description, and has powerful echoes of James Joyce.

Edna O'Brien's own life provided rich material for her work. Born in a small village in the west of Ireland, she had a withdrawn childhood spent writing stories. She later spent some years in a Catholic convent, preparing to be a nun, before heading for the worldly lights of Dublin. There she qualified as a pharmacist, had some pieces published in the *Irish Press*, and eloped with novelist Ernest Gebler. The two married in 1951, settling first in County Wicklow and then in London.

Divorce came in the 1960s, a few years after the great success of O'Brien's first novel, *The Country Girls*. Following on from this book, *The Lonely Girl* and *Girls in Their Married Bliss* formed a trilogy that drew on painful experience and also garnered praise. The trilogy charts the fortunes of girls brought up in a repressively Catholic rural Ireland, who escape to Dublin and London and become trapped in unhappy marriages. The books were banned in Ireland for their frankness.

Themes of dramatically doomed love continued to thread their way through O'Brien's work, from the moving *August Is a Wicked Month*, in which the love-starved heroine's son and husband are killed, to *I Hardly Knew You*, in which the female protagonist visits the sins of former partners on her lover by killing him. In *House of Splendid Isolation*, O'Brien entered a political dimension and began a trilogy that addresses a range of Irish issues: the IRA, abortion, and national identity. O'Brien is considered especially talented at short stories. Themes are similar to those in her novels, and much-admired works include "The Love Object" and "The House of My Dreams." She has also written screenplays for filmed versions of her stories and novels, as well as plays, nonfiction pieces about Ireland, and a very personal biography of James Joyce. **AK**

"... mental disturbance by literature is a healthy and invigorating thing."

Signature titles

Novels

The Country Girls, 1960
The Lonely Girl/Girl with Green Eyes, 1962
Girls in Their Married Bliss, 1964
August Is a Wicked Month, 1965
I Hardly Knew You, 1977
House of Splendid Isolation, 1994
Wild Decembers, 1999
The Light of Evening, 2006

Short stories

The Love Object, 1968
A Scandalous Woman, 1974
Lantern Slides, 1990

Biography

James Joyce, 1999

ABOVE: O'Brien at the Edinburgh Book Festival, Scotland, August 19, 2002.

JUAN GOYTISOLO

Born: January 5, 1931 (Barcelona, Spain).

Style and genre: Goytisolo criticizes Spain for its repressive Roman Catholic values and betrayal of its multicultural past. His style is avant-garde, modernist, and provocative, with a reproachful undercurrent of political and social issues.

Born just before the Spanish Civil War, Goytisolo grew up hating the Francoist regime, blaming it for the death of his mother (killed in an air raid in Barcelona) and the breakdown of his family (his father, a Francoist, was imprisoned by the Republicans). Indeed, his works indicate conflicted feelings for Spain as a country as well. He said in an interview in the *Guardian* in August 2000, "It would have been impossible to have a third life in Spain. I love Spanish culture but hate Spanish society; I can't live there." This is a reference to his self-imposed exile, begun in 1956, in Paris and Morocco.

Goytisolo's bisexuality, despite a lifelong relationship with a Frenchwoman named Monique Lange, contributes to his work and also to his feelings about traditionalist, repressionistic Spanish culture. His first novel, *The Young Assassins,* was published in 1954 to critical acclaim. Under Franco's regime the book was banned, as was all his work until the dictator's death in 1975. After the publication of a collection of short stories called *The Party's Over*, Goytisolo broke with the realism of his earlier work and began writing more experimentally. He considers his first adult novel to be *Marks of Identity*, disowning his earlier novels. Considered by some to be his masterwork, *Count Julian* deals with a reinvention of the Spanish language, seen as a political power tool. Goytisolo also wrote a two-volume autobiographical work in the mid-1980s, which is considered masterful and groundbreaking in its honesty. He settled in Marrakech because of his love of Islamic culture and its attitude toward his sexuality, which is accepted but not to be named. His lifelong battle against Catholic, nationalist Spain is bound up with his quest for moral, sexual, and political freedom. **REM**

"His works . . . are like pages torn out of the book of experience."—*New York Times*

Signature titles

Novels

The Young Assassins (*Juegos de manos*), 1954

Fiestas, 1958

Marks of Identity (*Señas de identidad*), 1966

Count Julian (*Reivindicación del conde don Julián*), 1970

Juan the Landless (*Juan sin tierra*), 1975

The Marx Family Saga (*La saga de los Marx*), 1993

State of Siege (*El sitio de los sitios*), 1995

The Garden of Secrets (*Las semanas del jardín*), 1997

A Cock-Eyed Comedy (*Carajicomedia*), 2000

The Blind Rider (*Telón de boca*), 2003

Short stories

The Party's Over (*Fin de fiesta*), 1962

ABOVE: Goytisolo pictured at a book fair in Sarajevo, Bosnia, September 28, 2000.

E. L. DOCTOROW

Born: Edgar Lawrence Doctorow, January 6, 1931 (New York, New York, U.S.).

Style and genre: A critically acclaimed contemporary American author of novels with historic themes, Doctorow's often controversial, insightful, and probing style stretches the boundaries of his literary genres.

ABOVE: Doctorow at the PEN Montblanc Literary Gala, New York, April 20, 2005.

Signature titles

Novels

Welcome to Hard Times, 1960
The Book of Daniel, 1971
Ragtime, 1975
Loon Lake, 1980
World's Fair, 1985
Billy Bathgate, 1989
The March, 2005

E. L. Doctorow is a celebrated contemporary author whose compelling works bring American history to life, finely balancing recorded fact with literary fiction to create insightful, questioning, and gripping stories such as *Billy Bathgate* and *The March*. Doctorow vividly paints passages from history, evoking scene and atmosphere through his beautiful prose, while the sharpness of his narrative style lends his work immediacy and a striking, realistic edge.

The Book of Daniel, Doctorow's third novel, was his first commercially successful book. A fictional account based on the Rosenberg spy case, it reveals the complexities of Cold War America. Fast-paced and thrilling, it established Doctorow's reputation as a leading American author. Four years later, Doctorow published *Ragtime*. A breathtaking and multilayered novel set in the decade prior to World War I, it brings together factual and fictional characters and plays out their role in historic and imaginary events. Doctorow creates such a compelling version of the period that the boundaries between fact and fiction are totally obliterated. The book won the first National Book Critics' Circle Award for Fiction in 1976 and was also voted one of the top one hundred best English language novels of the twentieth century by the editorial board of the Modern Library. In 2005, *The March* yet again confirmed Doctorow's position among the higher echelons of modern writers. Set during the American Civil War, it paints a fictitious account of General William Tecumseh Sherman's infamous military rampage across the country. The novel was a finalist for the National Book Award in 2005 and won the National Book Critics' Circle Award the same year. In 2006, it won the PEN/Faulkner Award. **TamP**

"The reason we need writers is because we need witnesses to this terrifying century."

THOMAS BERNHARD

Born: Nicolaas Thomas Bernhard, February 9, 1931 (Heerlen, the Netherlands); died February 12, 1989 (Gmunden, Austria).

Style and genre: In Bernhard's novels and plays, existential disgust reaches the critical mass where it becomes indistinguishable from love . . . or just a joke.

Enfant terrible of postwar Austria and self-proclaimed "exaggeration artist," Thomas Bernhard was the son of a domestic servant. She died when he was nineteen, and he never met his father. His maternal grandfather, who was also a writer, was an important figure for him, even if he was not, by Bernhard's reckoning, a role model. By Bernhard's reckoning, of course, he had *no* role models.

His earliest years were spent in Vienna, then in Seekirchen, near Salzburg, as well as in Bavaria. The years of World War II had a profound influence on his adolescence, which was traumatically spent in national socialist boarding schools, first in Thuringia and later in Salzburg. The Salzburg Johanneum reverted to being a Catholic school after 1945, providing Bernhard with the schema for his notorious designation of the Austrian state as "National-Socialist-Catholic."

Bernhard's work was formally influenced by studies in music, acting, and philosophy. His first novel, *Frost*, is filled largely by the misanthropic monologues of the aging artist Strauch, delivered on long walks through dismal alpine surroundings. Death, insincerity, brutality, stupidity—questions that recur with an insane determination throughout Bernhard's work—are studied with patient attention to the individual capable of asking them. A young doctor serves both as Strauch's audience and as our narrator, creating a space between reader and artist in which seduction can only occur consciously. Bernhard spent most of his life in and around Salzburg, plagued by defective lungs. In *Old Masters: A Comedy*, he honors the death of his soul mate and "life person" Hedwig Stavianicek, who was thirty-five years his senior. He outlived her by a mere five years. **JK**

"We only really face up to ourselves when we are afraid."

Signature titles

Novels

Frost, 1963

The Lime Works, 1970

Correction, 1975

Wittgenstein's Nephew, 1982

Extinction, 1986

Plays

A Party for Boris, 1968

Ritter, Dene, Voss, 1984

Histrionics, 1984

Poetry

In Hora Mortis, 1958

Under the Iron of the Moon, 1958

Autobiography

Gathering Evidence, 1975–1982

ABOVE: Bernhard pictured in March 1981 discussing his courtyard farm in Ohlsdorf.

TONI MORRISON

Born: Chloe Anthony Wofford, February 18, 1931 (Lorain, Ohio, U.S.).

Style and genre: African-American author, whose sinuously poetic novels combine the innovative narrative techniques of the Harlem Renaissance with the allusive symbolism of the magical realists.

In 2006, *The New York Times Book Review* chose Toni Morrison's novel *Beloved* as the best American novel of the previous twenty-five years. The choice caused a surprising controversy—surprising because the book had won the Pulitzer Prize and its author had received the Nobel Prize in Literature in 1993.

The reason for the grumbling seemed to be that although Morrison's mastery of the form is unquestioned, her novels are so unique within the context of American letters that they can hardly be considered representative. Morrison's fiction shares its thematic concerns and literary techniques with the international movement loosely called "post-colonialism," but her work differs from that of writers such as Salman Rushdie and Gabriel García Márquez in its resolute domesticity, the politics of her novels emerging from their sexual ethics rather than the other way around. Her writing has a depth of feeling and character development in stories that, in less competent hands, could become top-heavy with historical revisionism.

Morrison wrote her first novel, *The Bluest Eye*, fifteen years into her career as a university lecturer in English literature, supporting two children on a single income. Her second novel, *Sula*, was nominated for a National Book Award and her third, *Song of Solomon*, won the National Book Critics Circle Award. These early works exemplified Morrison's skill at interweaving texts with networks of allusion and applying themes inspired by postmodern literary theory without drifting into abstraction.

Beloved was inspired by the story of a runaway slave who killed her children rather than have them taken back to the plantation. This work, like *Jazz* and *Paradise*, is correspondingly built around singular traumatic experiences, employing them with a narrative spareness that grounds Morrison's rich, evocative prose. Her latest novel, *Love*, adds complexity to the interpersonal dynamics of these previous works, but many of

Signature titles

Novels

The Bluest Eye, 1970
Sula, 1973
Song of Solomon, 1977
Beloved, 1987
Jazz, 1992
Paradise, 1999
Love, 2003

ABOVE: This portrait by Dana Lixenberg appeared in *Book Magazine*, January 2003.

ABOVE: Oprah Winfrey recommends *Song of Solomon* nineteen years after it was written.

their themes—the difficulty of sharing space, the relationship between traumatic history and the present, and the meaning of the dead to the living—continue to be explored.

That a novelist as uncompromisingly literary as Toni Morrison should enjoy such a wide, popular readership in the United States owes much to her appearances on the American talk show *Oprah*. The host of the show, Oprah Winfrey, produced and starred in the 1998 movie of *Beloved*, and made *Song of Solomon* one of the first recommendations of her famous book club. Winfrey brings Morrison on the show for everything from leading discussion groups of her novels to talking about what it means to have true self-esteem. **SY**

"Freeing yourself was one thing; claiming ownership of that freed self was another."

TOM WOLFE

Born: Thomas Kennerly Wolfe, March 2, 1931 (Richmond, Virginia, U.S.).

Style and genre: Tom Wolfe is a high-profile, erudite journalist, novelist, and surveyor of culture, documenting American society throughout its changing economic and social seasons.

Tom Wolfe was an all-around high achiever throughout his school years, choosing Washington and Lee University over Princeton to study English. In the mid-1950s, he began a long-running career as a newspaper journalist, providing him with the scope to report on a myriad of social changes that came about in 1960s America; race was one of his principal preoccupations. Wolfe worked for the *Washington Post* and the *New York Herald-Tribune*, often providing his own illustrations, and was a leading force in the New Journalism movement.

Wolfe's first book, *The Kandy-Kolored Tangerine-Flake Streamline Baby* was a volume of selected articles about the 1960s. More nonfiction successes came in the form of such works as *The Pump House Gang*, *The Electric Kool-Aid Acid Test*, *Radical Chic & Mau-Mauing the Flak Catchers*, and *The Painted Word*. In much of his work, Wolfe's theories on writing have been ill-received by contemporary writers, who fail to share his dedication to realist, journalistic approaches to fiction.

Wolfe's first and most famous novel, *The Bonfire of the Vanities*, was written in two-week installments initially published in *Rolling Stone* magazine. It was later released as a complete novel to far-reaching success. Critics applauded its astute encapsulation of 1980s money-mad America. *A Man in Full* is another of Wolfe's most striking works, with principal character Charlie Croker no longer able to loom over the United States's shifting multicultural demographics with the same authority as in the days of a younger, more compliant society. Tom Wolfe has won several prestigious literary awards, including the American Book Award for nonfiction, the Columbia Journalism Award, and the Dos Passos Prize for Literature from Longwood University. **LK**

Signature titles

Novels

The Bonfire of the Vanities, 1987
Ambush at Fort Bragg, 1997
A Man in Full, 1998
I Am Charlotte Simmons, 2004

Nonfiction

The Kandy-Kolored Tangerine-Flake Streamline Baby, 1965
The Electric Kool-Aid Acid Test, 1968
The Pump House Gang, 1968
Radical Chic & Mau-Mauing the Flak Catchers, 1970
The Painted Word, 1975
The Right Stuff, 1979
The Purple Decades, 1982
Hooking Up, 2000

"The attitude is we live and let live . . . it's an example of freedom from religion."

ABOVE: Tom Wolfe photographed at his New York home in October 2004.

DONALD BARTHELME

Born: April 7, 1931 (Philadelphia, Pennsylvania, U.S.); died July 23, 1989 (Houston, Texas, U.S.).

Style and genre: Short-story writer and novelist whose surrealistic, postmodernist works are formally experimental, linguistically innovative, and vertiginously comic.

Donald Barthelme is one of only a few major artists whose greatest work has come in short forms. "Fragments are the only forms I trust," Barthelme said; yet his broken-off short stories have a startlingly coherent and precise impact on the reader.

Born in Philadelphia, Barthelme moved at an early age to Houston, Texas, where he worked as a reporter, speechwriter, and director of the Houston Contemporary Arts Museum. His artistic career began in 1962, when he moved to New York to found the magazine *Location*. Soon afterward, his first story was published in the *New Yorker*, and in 1964, his first collection of stories, *Come Back, Dr. Caligari*, appeared. These tales, like many of Barthleme's narratives, use striking juxtapositions and collagelike techniques and seem strongly influenced by surrealists such as Max Ernst, Marcel Duchamp, and René Magritte.

Although Barthelme had significant scruples about the term, he might fairly be described as the United States's greatest exponent of the postmodern short story. His work turns us back toward awareness of the medium in which we receive it; as avant-garde writer Robert Coover said, Barthelme's work is "bleakly comic, paradoxical, and grounded in the beautiful absurdities of language." Barthelme has also published several novels. *Snow White* is a helter-skelter retelling of the fairytale; *The Dead Father* is a freewheeling attack on all forms of authority—personal, cultural, and textual—wherein a monolithic father of voracious and mournful libido traverses a mythical landscape, only to find himself heading toward the site of his burial. Barthelme has been a major influence on the generation of fiction writers who followed him, and his imprint can be seen in the work of writers David Foster Wallace, Dave Eggers, and Péter Esterházy. **MS**

"I opened the door and the new gerbil walked in. The children cheered wildly."—"The School"

Signature titles

Novels

Snow White, 1967

The Dead Father, 1975

Paradise, 1986

The King, 1990

Short stories

Come Back, Dr. Caligari, 1964

Unspeakable Practices, Unnatural Acts, 1968

City Life, 1970

Guilty Pleasures, 1974

Sixty Stories, 1980

Forty Stories, 1987

ABOVE: A photograph of Barthelme taken by Jerry Bauer in the 1980s.

ALICE MUNRO

Born: Alice Laidlaw, July 10, 1931 (Wingham, Ontario, Canada).

Style and genre: Canadian short-story writer who explores, from a mostly female perspective, the full range of human relationships with sadness and stoicism, an astounding capaciousness, and a quick, flinty wit.

To compare Alice Munro with Anton Chekhov, that other master of the short story, is an understandable commonplace. Both write with a simplicity and muted naturalism that is deceptively transparent; both are innovators of the form without being overtly "experimental"; and both allow the intricate intimacies of character to guide the plot, instead of the other way around. We may also resort to the comparison simply because both authors are otherwise so difficult to describe. We might ask of either of them, how is it that so much can happen when so little actually seems to happen?

Many of Munro's stories are, as she once said of *Lives of Girls and Women*, "autobiographical in form but not in fact." Like many of her protagonists, Munro grew up on the wrong side of the tracks in a household that did not value learning and creativity, especially in girls. She learned to dissemble at an early age, and many of her characters carry a secret life around inside themselves. Intensely observant, these characters are astonished and even archly amused when their personas are mistaken for their true selves.

Most of Munro's stories are resolutely Canadian. They are grounded in the distinctions of class and custom that make up life in small-town Ontario, or in the Vancouver suburbs of the 1960s. However, the narratives are never simply of a place, and loop back and forth in time to capture the emotion of a moment. Munro's brilliance is in her ability to pinpoint those often unexamined elements that can determine the arc of a whole life: the submerged memory of betrayal, the compromised ambition, the private shame and the private pretension, the love you wish you had never admitted to yourself. **CQ**

"That's something I think is growing on me as I get older: happy endings."

Signature titles

Short stories

Dance of the Happy Shades, 1968
Lives of Girls and Women, 1971
Something I've Been Meaning to Tell You, 1974
Who Do You Think You Are?, 1978
The Moons of Jupiter, 1982
The Progress of Love, 1986
Friend of My Youth, 1990
Open Secrets, 1994
The Love of a Good Woman, 1998
Hateship, Friendship, Courtship, Loveship, Marriage, 2001
Runaway, 2004
The View from Castle Rock, 2006

ABOVE: Alice Munro photographed in New York, February 1, 2005.

IVAN KLÍMA

Born: September 14, 1931 (Prague, Czechoslovakia).

Style and genre: With a Kafkaesque vision, Klíma's narratives are distinguished by themes of religion, social justice, and political struggle, and liberally laced with erotic vulnerability.

A winner of many literary prizes including the 2002 Franz Kafka literary award, Ivan Klíma is a master of political yet deeply personal prose. Underscored by his traumatic childhood in the Terezin concentration camp, his work exposes the cruelties of human struggle for survival that are often underpinned by ironic, if not endearing, innuendoes. Persecuted during the communist regime, Klíma was banned as a writer and forced to undertake menial jobs. Nonetheless, his artistic devotion to the study of human nature remained unshaken.

From *Judge on Trial*, *Love and Garbage*, *Waiting for the Dark, Waiting for the Light*, *Ultimate Intimacy*, or to his more recent *No Saints or Angels*, Klíma's narratives are interlaced with protagonists whose sentimental yet honest attempts at reconciling various moral, ethical, and political conundrums leave them suspended between right and wrong, fidelity and betrayal, political beliefs and propaganda. In a Kafkaesque manner, Klíma explores his characters' psyche through their everyday trials, as they vacillate between a solipsistic search for freedom and a moral commitment to honor. *Judge on Trial*, Klíma's most political work, examines the plight of Adam Kindl, a high court judge, who complies with the totalitarian system only to avoid his own conflicting loyalties.

In his most recent novels, *No Saints or Angels* and *The Premier and the Angel*, Klíma provides a skeptical view of Czech life after communism as he points to the pervading Western consumerism and the increasing homogenization of European culture under the yoke of yet another political golem, the ever-expanding European Union. Critical of human injustice, Klíma is undeniably a political realist whose fiction comments on the struggle between the fallible self and the world. **PR**

"Humanity needs more tolerance, solidarity, and humility."

Signature titles

Novels

Judge on Trial, 1986
Love and Garbage, 1988
Waiting for the Dark, Waiting for the Light, 1993
Ultimate Intimacy, 1996
No Saints or Angels, 1999
The Premier and the Angel, 2003

Plays

The Castle, 1964
The Master, 1967

Nonfiction

The Spirit of Prague and Other Essays, 1994
Between Security and Insecurity, 2000
Karel Čapek: Life and Work, 2001

ABOVE: Ivan Klíma photographed in Paris, October 10, 2002.

UMBERTO ECO

Born: January 5, 1932 (Alessandria, Italy).

Style and genre: Italian semiotician, philosopher, and novelist whose densely allusive, scholarly works are among postmodern metafiction's most popular successes. Eco has also written children's books and academic works.

No one would have guessed that *The Name of the Rose*—a detective novel set in a medieval Italian monastery against the backdrop of the Franciscan poverty debate—would have been such a popular success, least of all its author. Eco was already an established semiotician at the University of Bologna when he wrote the novel; he has famously said that his inspiration was simply that he felt like poisoning a monk.

However, there is a good deal more that happens in this book than its author might lead you to believe. For one thing, there is Eco's intimate knowledge of his subject matter; his monks think the way monks would, in the densely intertextual networks of scripture, commentary, and Neoplatonic philosophy that characterized the educated medieval mind. It is an extremely dense novel for a historical murder mystery, but though its casual readers can sometimes find it hard to follow the philosophical discussions, they have typically found it even harder to put the book down.

Less of a commercial success than its predecessor, Eco's next novel, *Foucault's Pendulum*, was nonetheless at the beginning of a genre that, in the wake of *The Da Vinci Code*, could be to the twenty-first century what the detective novel was to the nineteenth: the art-historical thriller. It tells the story of three publishers of occult books who concoct a single conspiracy theory that encompasses all of history, from the pyramids to the Nazis. In the process, Eco writes with rare enthusiasm for ideas in and of themselves; there are few writers anywhere who have more clearly decided to share them with their readers simply for the pleasure of it. Eco has received numereous honorary doctorates from academic institutions worldwide. **SY**

"A dream is a scripture, and many scriptures are nothing but dreams."

Signature titles

Novels

The Name of the Rose (Il nome della rosa), 1980

Foucault's Pendulum (Il pendolo di Foucault), 1988

The Island of the Day Before (L'isola del giorno prima), 1994

Baudolino, 2000

The Mysterious Flame of Queen Loana (La misteriosa fiamma della regina Loana), 2004

Children's fiction

The Bomb and the General (La bomba e il generale), 1966

The Three Astronauts (I tre cosmonauti), 1966

ABOVE: Writer and journalist Umberto Eco in Paris, October 17, 2007.

RIGHT: Umberto Eco takes time out from writing to practice the recorder, 1983.

JOHN UPDIKE

Born: John Hoyer Updike, March 18, 1932 (Reading, Pennsylvania, U.S.).

Style and genre: Updike is a prolific producer of fiction, nonfiction, and poetry; he writes rich, densely layered physical descriptions (with explicit portrayals of sex) that focus on marriage, adultery, parenthood, and religious faith.

If the modern American male author—since Hemingway and Mailer—is expected to be an adventurer, a political creature, a man of the world, John Updike is something of a curiosity. His fiction is resolutely domestic in its scope. Most of his novels take place in the middle-class Pennsylvania of his youth or the privileged New England of his middle and mature years. His characters lead apparently comfortable lives, yet Updike masterfully lays open their sexual, ethical, and religious discomforts. Unusually for a male novelist, marriage and its discontents are his overriding obsessions: many of his novels and short stories turn upon adultery, divorce, and remarriage.

Updike's literary career began in August 1954, when, following many rejected submissions, *The New Yorker* finally published one of his poems. Between 1955 and 1957, he worked as a staff writer for the magazine, producing sketches of New York life for its "Talk of the Town" section. Updike's great versatility as a writer may be traced to his time as a journalist—his continued association with the magazine has produced hundreds of stories, reviews, poems, and sketches.

It is as a novelist, however, that Updike has produced his finest work. In Harry "Rabbit" Angstrom—his vision of the American Everyman—Updike found his ticket to critical and commercial success. Through the course of four novels, we follow Rabbit's journey from troubled youth to complacent middle age. While each book reflects the social tensions of a slice of postwar American history, Updike's eye is always focused on Rabbit's personal epiphanies and crises. Like many of Updike's characters, Rabbit shares the author's questioning religious faith: he struggles to live as a Christian in a secular, divided world. **CT**

"Being naked approaches being revolutionary; going barefoot is mere populism."

Signature titles

Novels

Rabbit, Run 1960

Couples, 1968

Rabbit Redux, 1971

Rabbit Is Rich, 1981

The Witches of Eastwick, 1984

In the Beauty of the Lilies, 1996

Short stories

The Music School ,1966

Too Far to Go: The Maples Stories, 1979

The Early Stories 1953–1975, 2003

Poetry

The Carpentered Hen and Other Tame Creatures, 1958

Telephone Poles and Other Poems, 1963

ABOVE: Smiling as usual, Updike is pictured in Boston, Massachusetts, October 15, 2002.

V. S. NAIPAUL

Born: Vidiadhar Surajprasad Naipaul, August 17, 1932 (Chaguanas, Trinidad and Tobago).

Style and genre: Naipul writes with irony and concision; his ability to analyze the pessimistic side of human nature has earned him comparisons to Joseph Conrad.

Born in Trinidad into a family of Indian Brahmin origin, Naipaul's father was a short-story writer who encouraged his son's writing from a young age. "If it were not for the short stories my father wrote," Naipaul has said, "I would have known almost nothing about the general life of our Indian community." The figure of his father appears in some of Naipaul's novels, most notably in *A House for Mr. Biswas*, one of Naipaul's better known novels, which recounts the story of an unlucky Brahmin Indian living in Trinidad, and his search for a house of his own.

Naipaul has often portrayed the figure of the lonely wanderer, or outsider, in his work—a theme drawn from his own experience as both an Indian in West India and a West Indian in England. Much of his work fittingly traces such effects of colonialism on its former subjects. When V. S. Naipaul was awarded the Nobel Prize in Literature in 2001, he was praised "for having united perceptive narrative and incorruptible scrutiny in works that compel us to see the presence of suppressed histories."

As with much of Naipaul's thinly veiled travel fiction, such as the vision of Africa unraveled in *A Bend in the River*, he has attracted much negative attention. Criticism for his racist judgment of "half-made societies" has been forthcoming to say the least. Fellow West Indian and poet Derek Walcott said: "If Naipaul's attitude toward Negroes, with its nasty little sneers . . . was turned on Jews, how many people would praise him for his frankness?" Despite being West India's best known English writer, Naipaul, who was knighted in 1990, has declared that he "had no faith in the survival of the novel"—a controversial view from the 2001 Nobel laureate from whom we have come to expect nothing less. **JSD**

"I am the kind of writer that people think other people are reading."

Signature titles

Novels

The Mystic Masseur, 1957
The Suffrage of Elvira, 1958
Miguel Street, 1959
A House for Mr. Biswas, 1961
Mr. Stone and the Knights Companion, 1963
The Mimic Men, 1967
In a Free State, 1971
Guerrillas, 1975
A Bend in the River, 1979
Finding the Centre, 1984
The Enigma of Arrival, 1987
A Way in the World, 1994
Half a Life, 2001

ABOVE: Naipaul photographed in his apartment in London, April 7, 1994.

SYLVIA PLATH

Born: October 27, 1932 (Boston, Massachusetts, U.S.); died February 11, 1963 (London, England).

Style and genre: The American confessional "New Poet," Plath lived in 1960s England, searingly documenting her interior life as daughter, wife, and mother.

The protest of feminist critics about Ted Hughes's betrayal of Plath, his first wife, and her related suicide, is where most people's knowledge of Plath begins. As the title of his final collection suggests, his poetic reputation was overshadowed by being "Her Husband." Likewise, her death threatens to obfuscate the verbal music of her three slim volumes of poetry, and its heady Yeatsian brew of biography and mythography.

Plath had biography in spades to mythologize: a suicide attempt led to electroshock therapy; on first meeting Hughes, she bit him. Due to these biopic-perfect spikes, there was blanket Plath coverage long before John Madden's film *Sylvia*, to the point that Jacqueline Rose was moved to write a critique of the Plath biog-industry, *The Haunting of Sylvia Plath*. But Plath herself started it with *The Bell Jar*, a pseudonymously published and thinly veiled autobiographical novel that follows Esther Greenwood from an internship at a New York magazine to internment in a mental institution.

The stifling "bell jar" Plath places over her 1950s protagonist resonated with women readers in the 1960s (and 1970s, when it was eventually published in the United States). Born in 1932, Plath was a harbinger of revolution: she studied at Smith College as *The Feminine Mystique* was being written; her suicide in 1963, and the publication of her final, furious poems in *Ariel*, connected electrically with the nascent feminist movement.

Influenced by fellow New England poet Robert Lowell, she mined her lived and imagined life for poetic material. Sex, fever, motherhood, and writing itself are seen through a fractured microscope lens, hysterical symptoms of a life-consuming disease. Posthumously, she was a propulsive influence on feminist poets and readers, and a Pulitzer winner. Few (Gwyneth Paltrow included) have come close to the scintillating, scalpel-sharp dissection of her lines. **SM**

Signature titles

Novel

The Bell Jar, 1963 (published under the pseudonym "Victoria Lucas")

Short stories

Johnny Panic and the Bible of Dreams, 1977

Poetry

The Collected Poems, 1981

Ariel: The Restored Edition, 2004

Children's fiction

The It-Doesn't-Matter-Suit, 1996

ABOVE: A copy made in 2003 of an undated black and white portrait of Plath.

RIGHT: A relaxed Sylvia Plath pictured on the beach c. 1954.

JOE ORTON

Born: John Orton, January 1, 1933 (Leicester, England); died August 9, 1967 (London, England).

Style and genre: Orton was a playwright whose black comedies use epigrammatic dialogue and farcical plots to subvert conventional morality and satirize authority.

Brought up on a working-class housing estate in the English Midlands, Joe Orton was failed by the school system and consigned to humdrum clerical work by the age of fifteen. He found an escape through acting, winning a scholarship to the Royal Academy of Dramatic Art, where he met his lifelong partner, Kenneth Halliwell. Both Orton and Halliwell failed as actors and by the start of the 1960s were living on government support in a cheap apartment in then-unfashionable Islington in London. They collaborated in writing unpublishable camp novels and perpetrating subversive pranks, including the humorously creative defacing of library books—a crime that earned them six months in jail in 1962.

Orton's breakthrough came when he began writing without Halliwell. The BBC accepted his radio play *The Ruffian on the Stair* in 1963, and the following year his sinister Pinteresque comedy *Entertaining Mr. Sloane* was staged in London to critical acclaim. After initial bad reviews and much rewriting, the spoof detective drama *Loot* carried Orton's reputation to new heights.

In 1967, Orton's status as a trendy figure in swinging London was confirmed by an invitation to write a screenplay for the Beatles. The diary he kept during this period portrays a life that was split between celebrity, homosexual promiscuity, and a collapsing relationship with Halliwell. In August 1967, Halliwell beat Orton to death with a hammer, before taking his own life.

"The Ten Commandments. She was a great believer in some of them."—*Loot*

Joe Orton's plays are remarkable for their unstaunchable flow of paradoxical wit and the extremism of their offense to conventional sensibilities—from the unceremonious treatment of a mother's corpse in *Loot* to the display of Winston Churchill's penis in the posthumously performed *What the Butler Saw*. **RG**

Signature titles

Plays

The Ruffian on the Stair, 1964
Entertaining Mr. Sloane, 1964
Loot, 1965
The Eringham Camp, 1966
The Good and Faithful Servant, 1967
Funeral Games, 1968
What the Butler Saw, 1969

Autobiography

The Orton Diaries, 1986 (published posthumously)

ABOVE: Orton photographed at his Islington home, October 1, 1966.

SUSAN SONTAG

Born: January 16, 1933 (New York, New York, U.S.); died December 28, 2004 (New York, New York, U.S.).

Style and genre: Sontag was an American Renaissance woman of letters who used her position as a public intellectual to address issues from Vietnam to AIDS.

Voracious, various, and vociferous, Susan Sontag was so dominant an intellectual figure that TV-show *Saturday Night Live* had a stock wig (black with a dramatic white streak) for parodying her. Whether making Brahmin-toned pronouncements on television, or cutting through media hyperbole with clear-sighted prose, Sontag was—but was in fact too idiosyncratic to be called—the voice of a generation.

Born in the liberal Jewish community in New York City in 1933, Sontag studied philosophy, literature, and theology at Harvard and Oxford Universities. She famously told the *Paris Review* that she left academia because she "really wanted every kind of life, and the writer's life seemed the most inclusive." Her academic training gave her photographic recall: her essays are whirlwind tours of the Western canon and beyond—particularly into visual media.

Mid-century American cinematic taste was shaped by the critical "rivalry" between modernist Europhile Sontag—who wrote seriously about film before it was the done thing—and the more populist Pauline Kael, but Sontag's interest in film extended beyond reviewing: she wrote and directed her own screenplays, including *Brother Carl*, shot in Israel during the 1973 war. Sontag's humanist fierceness and fearlessness, combined with the delicately savage irony that infuses her prose, also saw her directing *Waiting for Godot* in besieged Sarajevo in 1993. In her final book, *Regarding the Pain of Others*, written as she underwent chemotherapy treatment, Sontag asked unsparingly how and why people look at images of others in pain. With a gift for saying the unsayable in inimitable prose, Sontag could be called the conscience of the mid-century. **SM**

"The only interesting answers are those that destroy the questions."

Signature titles

Novels

The Benefactor, 1963

Death Kit, 1967

The Volcano Lover, 1992

Plays

A Parsifal, 1991

Alice in Bed, 1993

Lady from the Sea, 1999

Nonfiction

Against Interpretation, 1966

Illness as Metaphor, 1978

AIDS and its Metaphors, 1988

Regarding the Pain of Others, 2003

Short stories

I, etcetera, 1977

The Way We Live Now, 1986

ABOVE: Sontag photographed at a book signing in 1992.

JERZY KOSINSKI

Born: Josek Lewinkopf, June 14, 1933 (Łodz, Poland); died May 3, 1991 (New York, New York, U.S.).

Style and genre: Kosinski was a Polish-American novelist accused of fraudulently marketing his life story; he wrote sadistic existentialist vignettes.

Jerzy Kosinski was at various points in his life a penniless paint-chipper, a professor at Yale and Princeton, and a darling of the glitterati. As a writer, he turned his life into myth. His first novel, *The Painted Bird*, was presented as being based on his experiences as a lost child wandering through the villages of Eastern Europe during World War II. The book leaves a haunting impression of a countryside full of cruel and superstitious peasants. However, Kosinski lived through the war at home with his family, who changed their name from Lewinkopf to conceal their Jewish identity. An exposé in the *Village Voice* in 1982 revealed that Kosinski could never have had many of the experiences he describes in *The Painted Bird*; it also claimed that his books were heavily edited without due credit to the editors, and in one case, plagiarized from a Polish source.

Kosinski would never entirely recover from these accusations of fraud. However, given his recurrent depiction of the self as a shifting series of momentary fictions, it is not surprising that he would approach his public image as a chameleonic object.

Kosinski found the oppression of intellectual life under communist rule to be intolerable and emigrated to the United States to pursue doctoral studies at Columbia. The signature disinhibition of Kosinski's writing contrasts markedly with the climate of suppression of his youth. Using the English language helped him to examine his experiences from the outside—an act that he identifies as the crucial movement of art.

Kosinski's novels present a world of moral depravity without so much as a word about how disturbing these descriptions are. In his second book, *Steps*, which won the 1969 National Book Award, sexuality is the key to a wider understanding of human nature. Here, as in *The Devil Tree*, beauty arouses the desire to destroy, and self-possession is sought through violent sexual control of others. **ER**

Signature titles

Novels

The Painted Bird, 1965
Steps, 1969
Being There, 1971
The Devil Tree, 1973
Cockpit, 1975
Blind Date, 1977
Passion Play, 1979
Pinball, 1982
The Hermit of 69th Street, 1988

Essays

The Art of the Self: Essays à propos Steps, 1968
Passing By: Selected Essays, 1962–1991, 1992

ABOVE: A detail of a portrait photograph of author Jerzy Kosinski.

RIGHT: A poster for the film adaptation of Kosinski's novel *Being There*, 1979.

BEING THERE

PHILIP ROTH

Born: March 19, 1933 (Newark, New Jersey, U.S.).

Style and genre: Roth's intricate plotlines feature doppelgängers, alter egos, and alternative life histories, and an interest in identity, both Jewish and American; in 1998 he won the Pulitzer Prize for *American Pastoral.*

Signature titles

Novels

Portnoy's Complaint, 1969
My Life as a Man, 1974
The Professor of Desire, 1977
The Ghost Writer, 1979
Zuckerman Unbound, 1981
The Counterlife, 1986
Sabbath's Theater, 1995
American Pastoral, 1997
The Human Stain, 2000

Short stories

Goodbye, Columbus, 1959

Nonfiction

Reading Myself and Others, 1975
Shop Talk, 2001

Throughout his literary career, Philip Roth has reworked the fabric of his own life into material for his fiction. His work is peopled with alternative versions of himself, men who go by the names of Nathan Zuckerman, David Kapesh, and even Philip Roth. These alter egos allow him to experiment with the different facets of his own identity: writer, son, husband, American, Jew. Zuckerman, his most enduring creation, has led a life broadly similar to Roth's own. Both men were born into Jewish families in suburban New Jersey, achieved success with a controversial novel, and struggled with complex sex lives and a disapproving Jewish-American establishment. Yet there are also key differences: where Zuckerman's parents are mortified by his frank, explicit book *Carnovsky*, Roth's own parents were fiercely proud of their son's achievements.

The book that launched Roth's career was the provocative *Portnoy's Complaint*. Breathlessly, theatrically, the protagonist unfolds his history of sexual dysfunction to his psychoanalyst. The novel established the themes that would dominate Roth's work from then on: fascination with sex in all its comic, obscene glory; tortured affairs between Jewish men and Gentile women; and tense, difficult family relations. In the 1990s, Roth produced a trilogy of extraordinary novels that expanded his artistic vision. Each draws on a particular period of modern American history, examining how one man's life can express the hopes, fears, and prejudices of a nation. The finest of them, *American Pastoral*, won the Pulitzer Prize for fiction in 1998. In *The Plot Against America*, Roth turned from "counterlives" to counterhistory, imagining the election of a fascist government in 1940s America and charting its impact on a fictionalized version of his own family. **CT**

"The Jewish man with parents alive . . . will remain a fifteen-year-old until they die."

ABOVE: Detail from a photograph of Roth in New York City, May 23, 2007.

CORMAC McCARTHY

Born: Charles McCarthy, July 20, 1933 (Providence, Rhode Island, U.S.).

Style and genre: Winner of numerous awards, McCarthy uses historical Western American themes and often controversial, harrowing, or violent subject matter, threading a gritty realism with "greater or universal" truths into his stories.

Cormac McCarthy is one of the more enigmatic modern writers. He has consistently shunned publicity and interviews, yet despite his reticence, his name is one of the most recognized of contemporary American authors.

McCarthy's writing career can be roughly divided into two halves, one incorporating his first four works, *The Orchard Keeper*, *Outer Dark*, the controversial and disturbing *Child of God*, and *Suttree*. These established him as a literary figure of some note. *Child of God*, in particular, caused a publicity storm, hailed as brilliant by some critics and sharply rejected by others. In characteristic McCarthy style, the story addressed complex and dark themes written in a direct, nonjudgmental way. The subject matter was highly controversial, but more so was McCarthy's treatment of it and the equanimity with which he depicted the main character and perpetrator, reflecting the notion of all humanity united through being children of God. His next work, *Suttree*, was more favorably received and is considered one of his finest pieces.

The publication of *Blood Meridian* in 1985 marked the start of McCarthy's second branch of writing, addressing Western American themes. It is these books for which he is most famous today, in particular the best-selling *All the Pretty Horses*, which is the first book of his Border Trilogy. McCarthy's ability to transfer the reader straight into the landscape of his novels is legendary and is achieved through his striking realism and evocative language, which, combined with his piercing insight and meditations on life and humanity, makes him one of the United States's leading contemporary writers. The Coen Brothers' 2007 film of *No Country for Old Men* won four Oscars as well as numerous other awards. **TamP**

"Everything you do closes a door somewhere ahead of you."

Signature titles

Novels

The Orchard Keeper, 1965
Outer Dark, 1968
Child of God, 1974
Suttree, 1979
Blood Meridian, 1985
All the Pretty Horses, 1992
The Crossing, 1994
Cities of the Plain, 1998
No Country for Old Men, 2005
The Road, 2006

ABOVE: A photograph of McCarthy soon after the 2008 Academy Awards ceremony.

CEES NOOTEBOOM

Born: Cornelius Johannes Jacobus Maria Nooteboom, July 31, 1933 (The Hague, the Netherlands).

Style and genre: One of the most important contemporary writers from the Netherlands and frequently mentioned as a potential Nobel Prize candidate.

Cees Nooteboom is best known outside his native Holland for his novels, but he considers himself first and foremost a poet. His work is inspired by his extensive travels and much of what he writes has a sense of restlessness. He wrote his first novel, *Philip and the Others*, in 1956, following a hitchhiking trip across Europe; in several of his books his characters explore not only the world around them but also their inner selves.

Nooteboom's work is experimental, cerebral, and has a playful quality and lightness of touch. It is also full of literary allusions. In *The Knight Has Died*, published in 1963, one of Nooteboom's characters is writing a book about a dead friend who was writing a book about a writer who has died. After its publication, Nooteboom concentrated on poetry and travel writing and did not write another novel for seventeen years. Perhaps Nooteboom's most highly regarded travel book is *Roads to Santiago*, about his journeys in Spain, which mixes lyrical description with poetry and philosophy.

Nooteboom's later novels include *The Following Story*, an intricate story of love and death in fewer than a hundred pages. It tells of a Dutch teacher, Herman Mussert, who goes to bed in Amsterdam and wakes up in Lisbon. He has no idea how he got there but recognizes the room as one in which he had slept with another man's wife some three years earlier. In Mussert's last moments, as he lies dying on the bed, he recalls past moments of his life. At the end he journeys up the Amazon toward the unknown. Nooteboom has won a number of literary prizes including the 1982 Pegasus Prize for Literature. *The Following Story* won the European Literary Prize for Best Novel in 1993. He is also frequently cited as a likely candidate for the Nobel Prize in Literature. **HJ**

"He remains a writer's writer, whose books seem metaphors for art itself."—Ed Park, *Village Voice*

Signature titles

Novels

Philip and the Others, 1956
The Knight Has Died, 1963
Rituals, 1980
A Song of Truth and Semblance, 1981
In the Dutch Mountains, 1984
All Souls Day, 1999
Lost Paradise, 2004

Novella

The Following Story, 1991

Poetry

The Captain of the Butterflies, 1997

Travel writing

Roads to Santiago, 1992

ABOVE: Cees Nooteboom photographed in Paris, November 29, 1990.

ALAN BENNETT

Born: May 9, 1934 (Leeds, Yorkshire, England).

Style and genre: English playwright known for his use of irony, wry humor, and pathos, who blends serious issues seamlessly with the mundane and the everyday. Bennett writes novels and plays for radio, television, and the stage.

The absolute epitome of the phrase "national treasure," Alan Bennett has been delighting readers and audiences with his unique, stylish work since the 1960s. After spending his formative years in Yorkshire, Bennett won a scholarship to study at Exeter College, Oxford, and graduated in 1957. It was at Oxford that he met Dudley Moore who recommended Bennett for the satirical review *Beyond the Fringe* with ex-Cambridge Footlights players Peter Cook and Jonathan Miller. First performed at the Edinburgh Festival in 1960, the show later enjoyed success in London's West End and in New York.

Bennett's best known work is the *Talking Heads* monologues, written for the BBC. The two series, each comprising six monologues, were aired ten years apart, the first in 1988 and the second in 1998. The speeches cover such issues as incest, alcoholism, murder, mental illness, and dementia. On the surface, however, Bennett's achingly real characters are simply detailing for the viewer the mundane events of their ordinary lives. Bennett writes sensitively, moving between the everyday and the horrific or the painfully sorrowful with such grace and ease that the viewer simply cannot spot the seams.

In 1994, Bennett was nominated for an Oscar for his screenplay of the film *The Madness of King George,* an adaptation of his 1992 play *The Madness of George III*. His most recent play, *The History Boys*, was nominated for seven Tony Awards in 2006 and won six. He wrote the screenplay for the successful 2006 film of the same name. Bennett's critically acclaimed books, which showcase his dry humor and deft use of language to perfection, include a set of three novellas entitled *Three Stories* and two collections of essays and memoirs, *Writing Home* and its sequel, *Untold Stories*. **LP**

"I write plays about things that I can't resolve in my mind. I try to root things out."

Signature titles

Plays and screenplays

Afternoon Off, 1979
One Fine Day, 1979
Talking Heads, 1988
The Madness of George III, 1992
Talking Heads, 1998
Telling Tales, 2000
The History Boys, 2004

Novellas

Three Stories, 2003
The Uncommon Reader, 2007

Nonfiction

The Lady in the Van, 1989
Writing Home, 1994
Untold Stories, 2005

ABOVE: Bennett at the International Book Festival Edinburgh, Scotland, August 11, 2007.

1920–39

WOLE SOYINKA

Born: Akinwande Oluwole Soyinka, July 13, 1934 (Abeokuta, Nigeria).

Style and genre: Soyinka uses both traditional Western African and Western avant-garde stylistic devices in his mystical writing, sometimes drawing on Yoruba parables; one of his primary themes is the repetition of history.

On being awarded the Nobel Prize in Literature in 1986, the first black African ever to have been granted the accolade, Wole Soyinka commented: "Some people think the Nobel Prize makes you bulletproof. I never had that illusion." His statement reflects a lifetime of political activism that has led to jail sentences and exile. This includes being arrested for criticizing elections as fraudulent; being accused of conspiring in support of the Biafran civil war; speaking out against the corrupt exploitation of Nigeria's oil supply by Shell; supporting the release of human rights activist Ken Saro-Wiwa, who was held and hanged by General Sani Abacha; and addressing the payment of reparations to Africa from the West.

Soyinka is the son of a well-respected teacher and community leader in the Yoruba tribe. In his Nobel speech he paid tribute to his countryman Chinua Achebe. Despite his connection with universities and activism worldwide, Soyinka has never relented from taking Nigeria and its politics as the single most important theme of his writing. His primary preoccupation has been writing about the "oppressive boot and the irrelevance of the color of the foot that wears it."

A Dance of the Forests, a celebration of Nigeria's independence, tied Nigerian politics to Soyinka's work from that point on. His best-known play, *Death and the King's Horseman*, tells of the death of a chief and the tribe who are prevented by a British colonial subject from performing the ritual Yoruba killing of his horse, thereby throwing the tribe into catastrophic confusion. Soyinka chronicled his time in prison (1967–1969) in *The Man Died*, a prose account first written on toilet paper, and has recorded the story of late-twentieth-century Nigeria ever since. In April 2007, Soyinka called for the cancellation of Nigeria's presidential elections because of the fraud and violence that he claims tainted the process. **JSD**

Signature titles

Plays

A Dance of the Forests, 1963

The Strong Breed, 1963

The Lion and the Jewel, 1963

Death and the King's Horsemen, 1975

King Baabu, 2001

Poetry

A Shuttle in the Crypt (Poems from Prison), 1969

Essay

Myth, Literature, and the African World, 1976

Memoir

You Must Set Forth At Dawn: A Memoir, 2006

The Man Died, 1972

ABOVE: Soyinka is the first black African to be awarded the Nobel Prize in Literature.

RIGHT: A young Wole Soyinka photographed in 1966.

PER OLOV ENQUIST

Born: September 23, 1934 (Hjoggböle, Västerbotten, Sweden).

Style and genre: Enquist writes novels and plays characterized by an investigative style, often exploring real events or people that are ambiguous or complex and dealing with them in a narrative, fictional form, but with a journalistic flair.

Per Olov Enquist began his literary career in the 1960s, when writers were influenced by the French *nouveau roman* writers such as Claude Simon, Nathalie Sarraute, and Michel Butor. These writers were looking for new ways of expression and style, and Enquist chose to develop an investigative-reporter style, based on his experience as a newspaper columnist and television reporter. Most of Enquist's writing is the result of a tremendous amount of research, giving a journalistic flair to the facts, which are then combined with the richness and flexibility of the novel form. Life in Västerbotten, where Enquist was born and raised, was heavily influenced by Laestadianism, a conservative Lutheran revival movement of the mid-nineteenth century. Many of Enquist's works reflect life in this isolated and pious community.

Enquist gained international fame with his 1999 novel, *The Visit of the Royal Physician*, based on Johan Friedrich Struensee, the personal physician to the mentally ill Danish king Christian VII. In this work, the doctor begins to issue reformist statutes without the king's permission, aided and abetted by the headstrong queen, Caroline Mathilde. Struensee was executed by a faction that regained power, using many of the reforms that he himself had instigated. The novel raises interesting questions about the clash between pure idealism and political power. In 2004, *The Story of Blanche and Marie* was published. The novel explores the relationship between Blanche Wittman, Professor J. M. Charcot's famous hysteria patient, and Marie Curie, Polish physicist and Nobel Prize winner. Enquist uses their friendship to speak of science and love, once again using historical fact to create a brilliant and insightful novel. **REM**

Signature titles

Novels

The Magnetist's Fifth Winter, 1964
The Legionnaires, 1968
The March of the Musicians, 1978
Downfall, 1985
Captain Nemo's Library, 1991
The Visit of the Royal Physician, 1999
The Story of Blanche and Marie, 2004

"By the way, it is doubtful if one can ever become divorced."
—Narrator, *Downfall*

ABOVE: A portrait of Swedish writer Per Olov Enquist.

ALASDAIR GRAY

Born: December 28, 1934 (Glasgow, Scotland).

Style and genre: Gray is a Scottish novelist whose works combine science fiction, fantasy, and realism. He often illustrates his works himself and gives them a distinctive flair through an original use of typography.

Alasdair Gray was born in Glasgow to working-class parents. During World War II, he was evacuated with his mother and sister to a farm in Perthshire, and from there to the town of Stonehouse in Lanarkshire. These childhood experiences would eventually find their way into Gray's first great work, *Lanark*, and also into some of his later novels.

When the war was over, the family reunited in Glasgow and Gray attended school, doing well in English and art. During this period, he also began taking classes in art appreciation at the Kelvingrove Art Gallery and Museum. In 1952, the year Gray's mother died, he entered the Glasgow School of Art, and two years later began work on *Lanark*, which would not be published until 1981. While an art student, Gray worked on the first of many murals, called "Horrors of War" for the Scottish-U.S.S.R. Friendship Society—an organization that is still in existence today in Glasgow. In the decades after leaving art school, Gray made his living by teaching, painting scenery and murals, and writing radio plays and television documentaries. During this time he also pursued his own writing, and after the publication of *Lanark* he was finally able to fully devote himself to writing, designing, and illustrating books, mostly his own.

A traditional Scotsman, Gray's work is sharply humorous and precise, at times dark with a realism that he insists must be heard; the truth is never romanticized. His novels often have no happy endings, but his craft is to present the cleansing and the relief elsewhere. An entertaining read, Gray is also a social and political writer, and is particularly good at creating strong female characters. His novel *Poor Things*, which was published in 1992, won both the Whitbread Prize and the Guardian Fiction Prize. **REM**

"Work as if you live in the early days of a better nation."

Signature titles

Novels

Lanark, 1981
1982, Janine, 1984
The Fall of Kelvin Walker, 1985
McGrotty and Ludmilla, 1990
Poor Things, 1992
A History Maker, 1994
Old Men in Love, 2007

Short stories

Unlikely Stories, Mostly, 1983
Ten Tales Tall & True, 1993
The Ends of Our Tethers, 2003

Poetry

Old Negatives, 1989
Sixteen Occasional Poems, 2000

ABOVE: A portrait photograph of Gray taken by Marius Alexander in 1996.

KENZABURO ŌE

Born: January 31, 1935 (Ōse, Japan).

Style and genre: One of Japan's leading contemporary writers, Ōe was awarded the Nobel Prize in Literature in 1994. His novels deal with philosophical, social, and political themes.

One of seven children (and whose father died when he was just nine years old), Kenzaburo Ōe is one of the most influential contemporary writers from Japan. His work covers a wide range of subjects but a central theme is isolation and outcasts.

Ōe studied French literature at Tokyo University where he was strongly influenced by French writing; he wrote his dissertation on the work of Jean-Paul Sartre. He wrote his first novel, *Nip the Bud, Shoot the Kids*, in 1958. It tells the story of how war tears apart the lives of young people living in the forests of idyllic rural Japan, and has been compared to William Golding's masterpiece, *Lord of the Flies*. Between 1958 and 1961, he published a series of novels about the occupation of Japan, notable for their explicit sexuality and violence.

But it was the birth of Ōe's son, Hikari, in 1963 that was to change the direction of his writing. Hikari was born with brain damage and the theme of the "idiot-son"—Ōe's own description—recurs throughout his work. Much of it is starkly autobiographical: *Teach Us to Outgrow Our Madness* and *The Day He Himself Shall Wipe My Tears Away* both focus on the father of a disabled son. The father does not understand his own father and, in turn, the disabled child does not understand his father. Hikari's story is further explored in *The Silent Cry*, about a family with a disabled child who move back to the village from which they originally came, and the difficult relationship between the husband and wife. Ōe's later work tackles a number of themes. *Somersault*, for example, explores the nerve gas attack on the Tokyo metro in 1995 by a doomsday cult, in which twelve died and fifty were severely injured. Ōe, who lives in Tokyo, was awarded the Nobel Prize in Literature in 1994. **HJ**

"I have survived by representing these sufferings of mine in the form of the novel."

Signature titles

Novels

Nip the Buds, Shoot the Kids, 1958
A Personal Matter, 1964
The Silent Cry, 1967
Teach Us to Outgrow Our Madness, 1977
The Day He Himself Shall Wipe Away My Tears
Prize Stock
Teach Us to Outgrow Our Madness
Aghwee the Sky Monster
A Quiet Life, 1990
Somersault, 2003

Nonfiction

A Healing Family, 1995

ABOVE: Kenzaburo Ōe photographed in Tokyo, Japan, December 13, 2004.

RIGHT: A Japanese collection of Ōe's talks on writing, reading, language, and politics.

骨太でいながら、こまやかで、
深味のある情報も、
ユーモアにもみちている、
大江さんの話を、活字で読みたい。

講演会の感想から

集英社　定価1470円 本体1400円

CAROL SHIELDS

Born: Carol Ann Warner, May 16, 1935 (Oak Park, Illinois, U.S.); died July 16, 2003 (Victoria, Canada).

Style and genre: Canadian poet and novelist who wrote about ordinary lives with uncommon depth, clarity, poignant sympathy, and a surprisingly wicked wit.

Carol Shields did not start writing fiction and poetry until she was in her thirties. Born just outside Chicago, she studied at the University of Exeter in England. For over twenty years, she taught at universities: first the University of Ottawa, where she wrote a master's thesis on Susanna Moodie, and then at the Universities of British Columbia and Winnipeg. She and her husband had five children, and at first she wrote because she found little literature that spoke of this experience.

Though Shields also wrote poetry and short stories, she is celebrated for her novels, which explore everyday moments of bewilderment and happiness with a profound humanity. In *The Stone Diaries*, the unassuming Daisy Goodwill tells us the story of her life as she drifts from childhood to old age over the course of the twentieth century. The *New York Times* said of the novel that it "reminds us again why literature matters." *Larry's Party* met with equal critical and commercial success, and has since been adapted as a musical. In the novel, Larry Weller has a revelation, at the center of the Hampton Court maze in London, that he can do something important with his life—build mazes. Shields's last novel, *Unless*, is her most frankly feminist work, about a writer who struggles to understand how her daughter ended up mute and living on the street with a sign reading "Goodness" hanging from her neck. *Unless* made the top ten list of Britain's best-loved books written by women, and was adapted for the theater by Shields's daughter.

The recipient of numerous honorary degrees and prizes, Shields is the only writer to have won both the American Pulitzer Prize and the Canadian Governor General's Award, made possible because of her dual citizenship. She also won the prestigious Charles Taylor Award for her biography of Jane Austen. Shields was diagnosed with breast cancer in 1998 and died in 2003. **CQ**

Signature titles

Novels

Small Ceremonies, 1976
The Box Garden, 1977
A Fairly Conventional Woman, 1982
Various Miracles, 1985
Swann, 1987
Republic of Love, 1992
The Stone Diaries, 1993
Larry's Party, 1997
Dressing Up for the Carnival, 2000
Unless, 2002

Short stories

The Orange Fish, 1989

Plays

Departures and Arrivals, 1990
Thirteen Hands and Other Plays, 2001

Poetry

Others, 1972
Intersect, 1974
Coming to Canada, 1992

Biography

Jane Austen, 2001

ABOVE: Carol Shields pictured at home in Victoria, Canada, November 27, 2001.

RIGHT: *Unless* was shortlisted for the Man Booker Prize for Fiction in 2002.

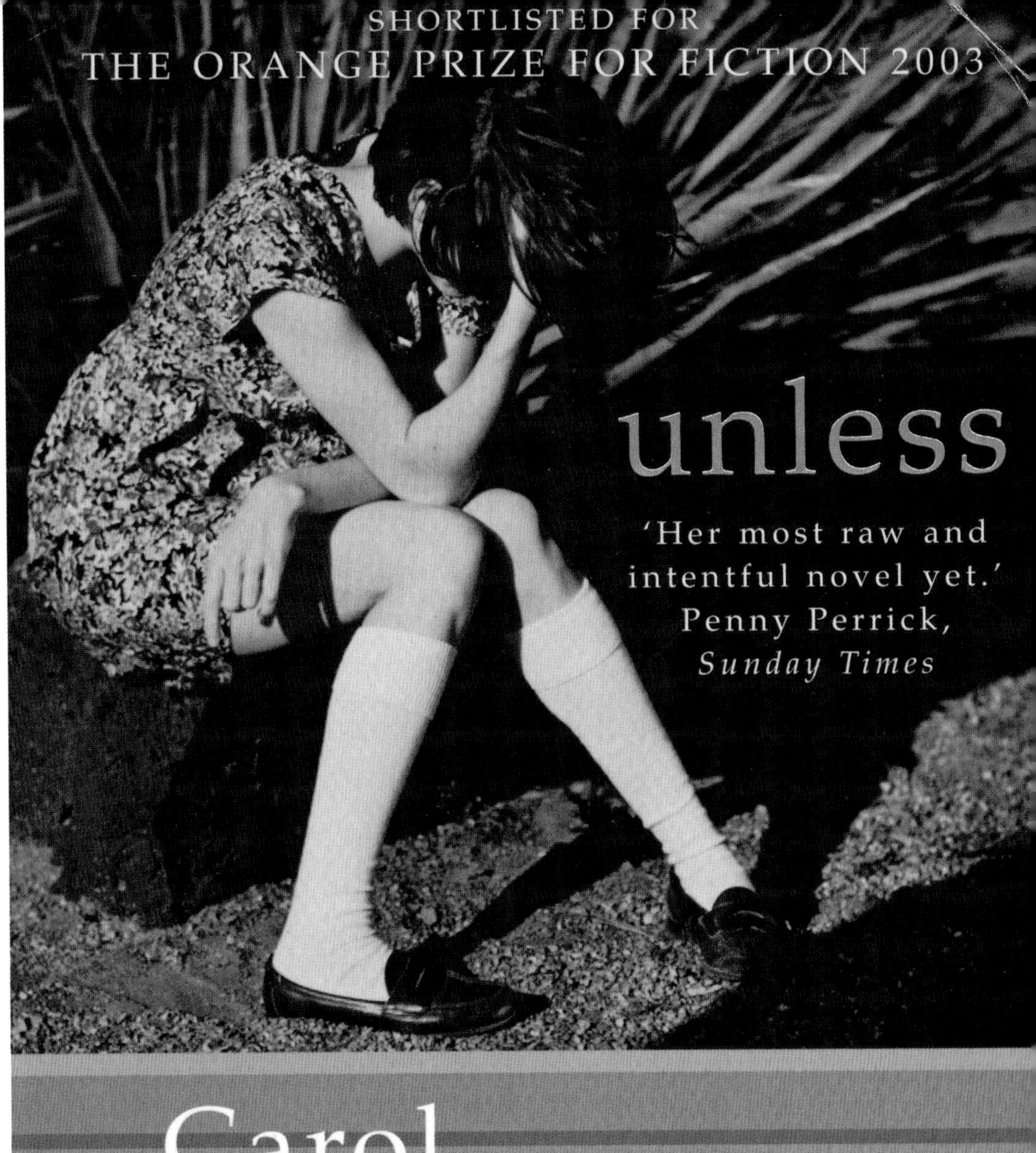

Carol Shields

SHORTLISTED FOR THE MAN BOOKER PRIZE

ANDRÉ BRINK

Born: May 29, 1935 (Vrede, South Africa).

Style and genre: A leading South African writer, Brink's novels challenge the apartheid regime yet champion the Afrikaans language. He has twice been shortlisted for the Booker Prize and won the 2003 Commonwealth Writers regional award.

André Brink established his reputation as one of the leading literary opponents of South Africa's apartheid regime with a series of deeply political novels. He grew up in a conservative Afrikaans family but in the 1960s he spent time as a student in Paris, where he met black students and gained another perspective on the country of his birth. He then decided that he had to return to South Africa so that he could play a part in fighting the political system.

Brink—along with Breyten Breytenbach—was a leading figure in a literary movement called *Die Sestigers* (The Sixty-ers), a group of writers who wanted to bring the techniques used in European experimental writing to literature written in Afrikaans. They also wanted to use their own language to speak out about the political situation. Brink's novel *Looking on Darkness*, about the relationship between a black South African man and a white woman, questioned the laws on racial segregation and was banned under tough censorship laws in 1973—the first time the laws had been applied to a work in Afrikaans. In response, Brink translated it into English to bring his work to a wider audience. All his subsequent works have been written simultaneously in both Afrikaans and English.

Brink soon developed an international following, and his novels have been translated into more than twenty languages. *An Instant in the Wind*, the story of a relationship between a white woman and a black man, and *Rumors of Rain*, about unrest in Soweto, were both shortlisted for the Booker Prize for Fiction. A later novel, *The Other Side of Silence*, set in colonial Africa in the early twentieth century, won a Commonwealth Writers regional award for Best Book in 2003. **HJ**

"Don't you think people are like landscapes to be explored?"

—Elisabeth, *An Instant in the Wind*

Signature titles

Novels

Looking on Darkness, 1974
An Instant in the Wind, 1976
Rumors of Rain, 1978
A Dry White Season, 1979
The Wall of the Plague, 1984
States of Emergency, 1988
An Act of Terror, 1991
On the Contrary, 1993
Imaginings of Sand, 1996
Devil's Valley, 1998
The Other Side of Silence, 2002
Before I Forget, 2004
Praying Mantis, 2005

ABOVE: Brink at his home in Rosebank, Capetown, South Africa, October 13, 2006.

E. ANNIE PROULX

Born: Edna Annie Proulx, August 22, 1935 (Norwich, Connecticut, U.S.).

Style and genre: Proulx writes about rural America, characterizing the countryside and people with dry precision and economy peppered with wry humor. She has won numerous book awards, including the Pulitzer Prize and National Book Award.

E. Annie Proulx only took up writing in earnest in her fifties, yet she has swiftly ascended to the highest ranks of contemporary American authors with her gritty realism and dry, precise writing style. Her books and stories evoke rural America with striking clarity and vision, but it is perhaps the characters who people her work that are most compelling.

Proulx wrote short stories intermittently for several decades and, in 1988, she published them as a volume, *Heart Songs*, which was released to favorable reviews. Her first novel, *Postcards*, was not published until 1992 but it was an immediate success. It won her the PEN/Faulkner Award for Fiction, making her the first female writer to receive the accolade. This was followed by *Shipping News*, which gained a Pulitzer. Before writing *Shipping News*, Proulx visited Newfoundland, where the story is set, and immersed herself in the life of a rural and slightly decaying fishing village. This provides the backdrop for the story of a man struggling to cope with life and his move to the hometown of his ancestors, subtly tracing his emotional growth and his gradual reestablishment of self. It is a poignant book that expertly combines perceptive character development with unexpected plot twists and droll humor.

More recently, Proulx was at the center of a public storm generated by the release of the film *Brokeback Mountain*, based on her short story. The story revolves around two rural ranch hands who have a romantic and sexual relationship—blowing apart the all-American macho cowboy figure. Proulx later stated that her literary exploration of homosexuality among American ranch hands was based on years of observation and her own conclusions on homophobia in the Midwestern states. **TamP**

"I'm desperate to write. I'm crazy to write. I want to write."

Signature titles

Novels

Postcards, 1992

Shipping News, 1993

Accordion Crimes, 1996

That Old Ace in the Hole, 2002

Short stories

Heart Songs and Other Stories, 1988

Close Range: Wyoming Stories, 2000

Bad Dirt: Wyoming Stories 2, 2004

Nonfiction

Sweet and Hard Cider: Making It, Using It and Enjoying It, 1980

ABOVE: Prizewinning author Annie Proulx pictured in September 2001.

THOMAS KENEALLY

Born: October 7, 1935 (Homebush, New South Wales, Australia).

Style and genre: Keneally is a prolific novelist and playwright whose historical works are often heavily researched and express a particular interest in Australia's political and social history.

Signature titles

Novels

The Place at Whitton, 1964
Bring Larks and Heroes, 1967
A Dutiful Daughter,1971
The Chant of Jimmie Blacksmith, 1972
Ned Kelly and the City of the Bees, 1978
Schindler's Ark, 1982
Flying Hero Class, 1991
Bettany's Book, 2001

Plays

Halloran's Little Boat, 1968
Childermas, 1968
Bullie's House, 1981

Nonfiction

Homebush Boy: A Memoir, 1995

Thomas Keneally is one of Australia's most prominent writers, and indeed public figures. A staunch supporter of Australia's independence from Britain, his novels often focus on historical events in Australian history (penal colonies, the sidelining of the indigenous Aboriginals), the push and pull between Australia's vulnerabilities and strengths, religious faith, and the day-to-day struggles and joys of ordinary people.

Having abandoned his training to be a Catholic priest prior to becoming ordained, he worked as a teacher until the publication of *The Place at Whitton*, a Gothic horror set in a seminary. Keneally continued to publish his novels regularly to appreciative Australian and worldwide audiences, notably *Bring Larks and Heroes*, *The Chant of Jimmie Blacksmith* (a story featuring a main character of both Aboriginal and white Australian parentage, made into a film in 1978), and *Confederates*. Keneally is best known for *Schindler's Ark*, a meticulous and powerful delving into Oskar Schindler's part in Holocaust history. Keneally's chance meeting with a "Schindler survivor" spurred him to write the novel. He took an interest in what he called the "ethnic hysteria" of the Holocaust and in the challenge of delivering the problematic and paradoxical character of Schindler to the public. Having done this, *Schindler's Ark* was awarded the 1982 Booker Prize, and the novel then inspired the 1993 Steven Spielberg film adaptation *Schindler's List*.

"I found both literature and the church very dramatic presences in the . . . 1950s."

Thomas Keneally has received many awards, including the Royal Society for Literature Award and the C. Weichhardt Award for Australian Literature, and has won the Miles Franklin Literary Award no less than three times. He is also on the list of Australian Living Treasures, as appointed by the National Trust of Australia. **LK**

ABOVE: Champion of Australian culture and independence, Keneally in 1994.

RIGHT: Photograph of Schindler with a list of Jews whom he saved from the Holocaust.

te of Honou
68911
68920
Panzer
Oppenheim
Schneider Israel
Nussbaum Wilhelm
Nussbaum Richard
Pemper Stefan
68 930
Perl Salomon
Posner Baruch
Mühlrad Aleksander
Pemper Jakob
Leser Jakob
68940
Müller Moses
Pechner Simon
Lewkowicz Natan
Melzer Josef
Mützenmacher Rubin
Lewkowicz Hermann
Rosenzweig Maks
Horowitz Bronislawa

ISMAIL KADARE

Born: January 28, 1936 (Gjirokaster, Albania).

Style and genre: Albania's best known poet and novelist, Kadare's work focuses on Albanian culture, history, and folklore and the impact of the past upon the present. Kadare won the Man Booker International Prize in 2005.

Signature titles

Novels

The General of the Dead Army, 1963
Why These Mountains Brood, 1964
The Wedding, 1968
The Castle, 1970
The Three-Arched Bridge, 1978
Broken April, 1980
The Palace of Dreams, 1981
The Concert at the End of the Winter, 1988
The Successor, 2005

Memoir

Albanian Spring: The Anatomy of Tyranny, 1995

Ismail Kadare has been a leading figure in Albanian literature for more than forty years. His first novel, *The General of the Dead Army*, an epic story of postwar Albania, was published in 1963. Although Albania was cut off from the outside world, Kadare's work was smuggled out of the country in the 1980s and translated into French. A number of his novels, including *The Palace of Dreams*—a Kafkaesque tale of the absurdity of totalitarianism—were banned by Enver Hoxha's repressive regime. Kadare finally sought political asylum in France in 1990 but now splits his time between France and Albania. In 2005, Kadare achieved world recognition when he won the inaugural Man Booker International Prize. **HJ**

A. S. BYATT

Born: Antonia Susan Drabble, August 24, 1936 (Sheffield, Yorkshire, England).

Style and genre: British fiction writer of social realism, historical pastiche, and fairy tale, her work is erudite, richly allusive, and unapologetically literary. She is the recipient of numerous awards, including the Booker Prize for *Possession*.

Signature titles

Novels

The Virgin in the Garden, 1978
Still Life, 1985
Babel Tower, 1996
A Whistling Woman, 2002
Possession: A Romance, 1990
The Biographer's Tale, 2000

Short stories

Sugar and Other Stories, 1987
The Matisse Stories, 1993
The Djinn in the Nightingale's Eye, 1994
Elementals: Stories of Fire and Ice, 1998
Little Black Book of Stories, 2003

Essays

Passions of the Mind: Selected Writing, 1991
On Histories and Stories: Selected Essays, 2000
Portraits in Fiction, 2001

A. S. Byatt decided early on that the only way to avoid being overly influenced by any one author was to read them all, and it seems from her fiction that she has. Passionate about narrative of all kinds, her characters are often writers, or at least great readers, themselves. She is also an insatiable polymath, and her stories teem with images and metaphors taken from the fields of art history and language theory, entomology, genetics, and abstract mathematics. Her *Frederica Quartet* is a history of intellectual trends as much as it is the coming-of-age story of its titular protagonist; the best-selling *Possession* follows two sleuthing academics on the trail of a secret love affair between Victorian poets. **CQ**

MARIO VARGAS LLOSA

Born: Jorge Mario Pedro Vargas Llosa, March 28, 1936 (Arequipa, Peru).

Style and genre: Multifaceted Peruvian journalist, essayist, and novelist whose fiction manifests a keen social conscience through a variety of different techniques. Llosa is considered one of Latin America's leading authors.

Mario Vargas Llosa is one of the preeminent witnesses to the condition of twentieth-century Latin America. Born in southwestern Peru to a comfortable middle-class family, at age one Mario was taken to Cochabamba, Bolivia, after his parents separated. There he lived with his mother and grandparents until he was ten, when his parents were reconciled and he returned to Peru. Following a stint at a military academy, Llosa studied literature in Peru before traveling to Madrid where he obtained his doctorate.

It was with his move to Paris and the publication of a collection of short stories in 1959 that Llosa's writing career began to take off. His early novels from this period are ambitious conflations of autobiography and left-leaning social commentary, with *The Time of the Hero*—set in the military academy that Llosa had attended—perhaps the best of them. He moved to Barcelona in 1970 and then back to Peru five years later. It was around this time that his political views began to change. Initially an enthusiastic supporter of Castro's Cuba, Llosa seemed to investigate the validity of such projects in novels such as *The Real Life of Alejandro Mayta*, and find them wanting. Indeed, by 1993, Llosa was standing as a conservative candidate in the Peruvian presidential election—which he lost.

"There is an incompatibility between literary creation and political activity."

Because his novels are by turns funny and surreal, tragic and optimistic, and because his own political views are so murky, Llosa is best read without any preconceptions at all. His masterpiece, *The Feast of the Goat*, perhaps best encapsulates the author's greatness: it is investigative and probing of Latin America, but while it judges people, it refuses to condemn them. Llosa now lives in Madrid and London. **PS**

Signature titles

Novels

The Time of the Hero (La ciudad y los perros), 1963

The Green House (La casa verde), 1966

Captain Pantoja and the Special Service (Panteleón y las visitadoras), 1973

The War of the End of the World (La guerra del fin del mundo), 1981

The Real Life of Alejandro Mayta (Historia de Mayta), 1984

Who Killed Palomino Molero? (¿Quién mato a Palomino Molero?), 1986

The Feast of the Goat (La fiesta del chivo), 2000

The Way to Paradise (El paraíso en la otra esquina), 2003

Nonfiction

A Fish in the Water (El pez en el agua), 1993

ABOVE: Llosa at the 2003 International Book Festival in Edinburgh, Scotland.

GEORGES PEREC

Born: March 7, 1936 (Paris, France); died March 3, 1982 (Paris, France).

Style and genre: Experimental French novelist and member of OuLiPo, Perec is celebrated for his mastery of wordplay and the elaborate mathematical construction of his books.

The playfulness and delight in language expressed in Perec's work stand in stark contrast to the tragic circumstances of his childhood. The son of Jewish immigrants, Perec felt alienated in French society: "I am French, I have a French first name, Georges, and a French surname, or almost, Perec." The crucial word is "almost." Perec's sense of the difference a single letter can make (since a true Frenchman would be Perrec or Pérec) is reflected in his novels' focus on minute linguistic detail. But the sense of something missing also relates to the terrible loss Perec suffered early in life: his father was killed in 1940 fighting for the French Foreign Legion; his mother died in Auschwitz.

Perec's first novel, *Things*, won the Prix Renaudot for its critique of middle-class commodity fetishism and the consumer society. But in 1967, Perec became a member of OuLiPo, the "Ouvroir de Littérature Potentielle" (Workshop for Potential Literature), a loose band of writers and mathematicians who sought to apply formal constraints and mathematical principles in the composition of literary texts. This was the critical influence on his greatest books. Along with minor forms, like palindromes, multilingual word puzzles,

Signature titles

Things: A Story of the Sixties (Les choses: Une histoire des années soixante), 1965

Which Moped with Chrome-plated Handlebars at the Back of the Yard?, (Quel petit vélo à guidon chromé au fond de la cour?), 1966

A Man Asleep (Un homme qui dort), 1967

A Void (La disparition), 1969

The Exeter Text: Jewels, Secrets, Sex (Les revenentes), 1972

Species of Spaces (Espèces d'espaces), 1974

W, or The Memory of Childhood (W, ou le souvenir d'enfance), 1975

Life: A User's Manual (La vie mode d'emploi), 1978

ABOVE: Perec in 1982 in Paris at the literary show "Apostrophes."

RIGHT: With Alain Corneau on the set of *Serie Noire*; Perec contributed dialogue.

and crosswords, Perec composed works of large-scale ambition using externally imposed constraints. Most notorious is his novel *A Void*. The French title is *La Disparition*, which might be expected to translate as *The Disappearance*, except that the word "disappearance" contains the letter "e" and the novel is a lipogram (a text that excludes a letter of the alphabet). The fact that Perec chose to exclude "e," the most common letter in French, demonstrates his amazing skill and inventiveness; but there is nothing cold about *A Void*, which carries a sense of unspoken tragedy in the way that people or things can be made to disappear. This ability to make highly experimental writing entertaining and moving may be Perec's greatest legacy, and it shows in his masterpiece, *Life: A User's Manual*. It is through the elaborate formal gamesmanship of the book that its myriad stories, and the central tale of the eccentric puzzle-maker, realize their sweeping emotional force. **MS**

ABOVE: Perec on location for the filming of *Un Homme Qui Dort* in the 1960s.

Writing with Constraints

Life: A User's Manual has an unusual structure: "I imagine a Parisian apartment building whose façade has been removed, so that all the rooms in the front, from the ground floor up to the attics, are instantly and simultaneously visible." As well as "describing the rooms thus unveiled and the activities unfolding in them," the novel also uses "formal procedures" to determine its narrative—such as "a polygraph of the moves made by a chess knight" and "an orthogonal Latin bi-square of order 10" (that is, a ten-by-ten grid with a letter and a number in each square).

Signature titles

Plays

The Garden Party, 1963
Memorandum, 1965
The Increased Difficulty of Concentration, 1968
Audience, 1970
Private View, 1970
Protest, 1970
Largo desolatio, 1985
Temptation, 1986
Leaving, 2008

Memoir

To the Castle and Back, 2007

VÁCLAV HAVEL

Born: October 5, 1936 (Prague, Czechoslovakia).

Style and genre: Václav Havel's role as the first president of the Czech Republic has overshadowed his writing career, but his plays, poems, and essays remain hugely influential. Following the 1968 Prague Spring his work was banned from the theater.

Václav Havel grew up in a wealthy family in Prague. He was regarded as a member of the bourgeoisie and so was not allowed to attend university. Instead, he became a stagehand in Prague, studied drama by correspondence course, and began writing fiction. His first play was *The Garden Party*, a satire on bureaucracy that was performed as part of a season of absurdist theater. It was followed by *Memorandum*, which is set in a bureaucratic organization where an artificial language is introduced; it is intended to improve communication between people but has absurd results. Although the play is a satire of the communist system, it has universal appeal due to the way in which it explores office politics, and has subsequently been performed around the world.

Following the Prague Spring in 1968, Havel's work was banned from the theater and he became increasingly politically active. During the 1970s and 1980s, he was repeatedly arrested and imprisoned, and in 1978 he wrote about this experience in a series of one-act plays—*Audience*, *Private View*, and *Protest*—that describe a dissident playwright's run-ins with the authorities. During the 1980s, Havel became a leader of the Czech human rights movement, though he continued to write plays. These include *Largo desolatio*, which was written after a long period in prison and focused on a writer who finds it hard to face his difficulties, and *Temptation*, a reworking of the legend of Faust. Havel was a leading figure in the Velvet Revolution that saw the overthrow of communism in Czechoslovakia, and he was elected president in 1989. He then became the first president of the Czech Republic in 1993. Havel continues to write and produced his memoirs, *To the Castle and Back*, in 2007. **HJ**

"There's always something suspect about an intellectual on the winning side."

ABOVE: Havel in 1990 during his presidency of Czechoslovakia.

DON DELILLO

Born: November 20, 1936 (New York, New York, U.S.).

Style and genre: Postmodern master of the American novel, DeLillo dissects national paranoia and ideological formation in the postwar world with a poetic, precise prose style, acute awareness of rhythm, and colloquial speech.

When *Underworld* was published in 1997, it was immediately hailed as an epic masterpiece of cold war consciousness—"an aria and a wolf-whistle of our half-century," as Sri Lankan-born Canadian novelist Michael Ondaatje wrote. It certainly was a book conceived and executed on a grand scale, covering 800 pages and fifty years of civic history.

It begins with the astounding set piece of a panoramic sixty-page description of a baseball match, as the Dodgers play off against the Giants in 1951. Along the way, the book includes memorable cameos for public figures such as Frank Sinatra, J. Edgar Hoover, and comedian Lenny Bruce. With a cover boldly branded with the negative-print image of the Twin Towers, *Underworld* seemed remarkably proleptic of the terror that would hit New York in 2001, and to which DeLillo would address himself in *Falling Man*.

But in a sense, all of DeLillo's books had been looking forward to an age in which paranoia seemed to be the only legitimate response to the sway of events. In novels such as *Americana*, *White Noise*, *Libra*, and *Mao II*, the collision of power and terrorism with the ordinary, extraordinary lives of people was brought to memorable life. *Libra*, in particular, with its insight into the minds of Lee Harvey Oswald and the FBI investigator charged with cataloguing the assassination of John F. Kennedy, brought to new light the workings of personal destiny and political machination. The other characteristic that distinguishes DeLillo is the virtuosity of his prose. He writes sentences and paragraphs full of throwaway felicities, daring word choices, and fast-paced hipster talk, all with an unwavering rhythmic sense and an ear for colloquial speech that is close to a gift of perfect pitch. **MS**

"I've come to think of Europe as a hardcover book, America as the paperback version."

Signature titles

Novels

Americana, 1971
End Zone, 1972
Great Jones Street, 1973
White Noise, 1985
Libra, 1988
Mao II, 1991
Underworld, 1997
The Body Artist, 2001
Falling Man, 2007

Plays

The Day Room, 1986
Valparaiso, 1999
Love-Lies-Bleeding, 2005
The Word for Snow, 2007

ABOVE: Don DeLillo at the Hay Festival in Britain in 2003.

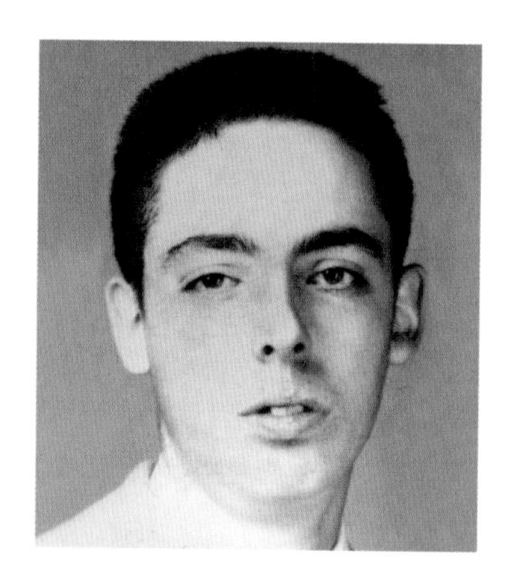

Signature titles

Novels
V., 1963
The Crying of Lot 49, 1966
Gravity's Rainbow, 1973
Vineland, 1990
Mason & Dixon, 1997
Against the Day, 2006
Short stories
Slow Learner, 1984

THOMAS PYNCHON

Born: May 8, 1937 (Glen Cove, Long Island, U.S.).

Style and genre: Pynchon is a reclusive American postmodern novelist, whose epics of endless deferral are known for their ebullient prose, gonzo historicism, and mastery of playful pastiche.

Pynchon's fabulously inventive novels proceed from what is basically a simple theme: The best things are either irrecoverably lost, or we never had them in the first place. The pleasure of his work thus resides less in the destination than in the journey, as he oscillates crazily between unsatisfactory extremes along every axis imaginable; utopianism and fascism, culture and counterculture, Eros and Thanatos, and anything in between. Like his contemporary Salinger, Pynchon is famously reclusive and has been so rarely photographed that when he appeared in the prime-time cartoon *The Simpsons*, in 2004, he was drawn with a bag over his head.

Pynchon's extravagant prose is certainly in full force in his early works *V.* and *The Crying of Lot 49*, and finds perhaps its most emotionally grounded expression in his later novel *Mason & Dixon*. But he pulls off his most impressive symbolic gymnastics in the novel widely considered his masterpiece, *Gravity's Rainbow*. It is ostensibly the story of U.S. serviceman Tyrone Slothrop, stationed in London during World War II, who discovers that a map of his sexual conquests corresponds exactly to a map of Nazi bombing patterns. (And, as always, there is a lot more to it than that.)

"If they can get you asking the wrong questions, they don't have to worry about the answers."

Gravity's Rainbow displays all of the hallmarks of Pynchon's fiction—in particular, his talent for the comical resistance of narrative progression, in which he is equaled only by eighteenth-century masters like Laurence Sterne and Henry Fielding. By constantly interrupting Slothrop's quest with everything from song-and-dance numbers to the story of an undying light bulb on the run from General Electric, Pynchon not only amuses us, but asks more generally: What are we in such a hurry to find out anyway? **SY**

ABOVE: Portrait photograph of Thomas Pynchon in his youth, taken in 1955.

ANITA DESAI

Born: June 24, 1937 (Mussoorie, Delhi, India).

Style and genre: Desai is a contemporary Indian author exploring female psychology and the notion of the family unit as both stifling and supportive. Her common themes are the demise of traditional values and Western portrayals of India.

Anita Desai spent her childhood speaking German at home to a German mother (her father was Indian), negotiating the city that she grew up in, Delhi, in Hindi, and writing in English. By the time her first short story was published in a children's magazine, the importance of language had asserted itself in her life—an auspicious literary beginning for a nine-year-old.

Shortly after she married, Desai's 1963 debut *The Peacock* was published in the United Kingdom by an imprint specializing in British Commonwealth writing. At a time when Indian writers composing narratives about India in English was rare, Desai can be considered a literary pioneer.

Many of Desai's leading female characters are anglicized middle-class women. They are independent women, such as Bim Das in *Clear Light of Day*, beautiful married women such as Aruna in *Fasting, Feasting*, or struggling women, such as Aruna's sister, Uma. Whatever their outer selves, it is the inner life of these characters—their alienation, family tension, and suppression by the traditional Indian culture that has shaped them—that is reiterated throughout most of Desai's canon. Understanding these women has sparked much debate among Desai's critics: are they more accessible or alienated from Western audiences? Are they more Indian or European? Unstitching Western views about India is another current driving Desai's short stories and novels. Her very exploration of East and West, tradition and modernity, reflects her view of a country that blends them all. With *The ZigZag Way*, set in Mexico and Cornwall via Vienna and New England, Desai's male protagonist undergoes a search for identity that draws him into the company of pioneering women, as his author heads out in yet another direction. **JSD**

"I aim to tell the truth about any subject, not a romance or fantasy, not avoid the truth."

Signature titles

Novels

Voices in the City, 1965
Bye-Bye, Blackbird, 1971
Where Shall We Go This Summer?, 1975
Fire on the Mountain, 1977
In Custody, 1984
Journey to Ithaca, 1996
Fasting, Feasting, 1999
The Zigzag Way: A Novel, 2004

Children's fiction

The Peacock Garden, 1974
Cat on a Houseboat, 1976
Village by the Sea, 1982

Short stories

Diamond Dust, 2000

ABOVE: Desai at the 2004 International Book Festival, Edinburgh, Scotland.

TOM STOPPARD

Born: Tomáš Straussler, July 3, 1937 (Zlin, Czechoslovakia).

Style and genre: An eminent English dramatist, Stoppard is famous for his metaphysical wit and challenging ethical conundrums. He established the Tom Stoppard Prize in 1983 to assist authors of Czech origin.

Signature titles

Plays

Rosencrantz and Guildenstern Are Dead, 1966
The Real Inspector Hound, 1968
Jumpers, 1972
Travesties, 1974
Every Good Boy Deserves Favor, 1977
The Real Thing, 1982
Arcadia, 1993
The Invention of Love, 1997
Rock 'n' Roll, 2006

Screenplays

Brazil, 1985 (co-author)
Empire of the Sun, 1987
Shakespeare in Love, 1998 (co-author)

Born in Czechoslovakia, Stoppard moved with his family to Singapore in 1939 to escape the Nazi invasion. His father was killed in a Japanese prison camp after fighting for the British during World War II. Stoppard was educated in England from 1946, and took his stepfather's name.

Stoppard's early troubles profoundly influence his work, much of which deals with conflicts between different ethical and political philosophies. He worked as a journalist after leaving school and had his first television play broadcast in 1963. However, it was in 1966 that he made his commercial and critical breakthrough with *Rosencrantz and Guildenstern Are Dead*—an exploration of two peripheral characters from Shakespeare's *Hamlet*. With characteristic comic sympathy, Stoppard imagines the characters as unwilling and unknowing victims of Hamlet's fury. Although not overtly political, the play explores the themes of marginalization and lack of representation that would increasingly dominate Stoppard's later work. A trip to the Soviet Union in 1977 provided the catalyst for a sustained period of human rights activism, and a renewed interest in the fate of Czechoslovakia.

The Tom Stoppard Prize was inaugurated in 1983, to provide support to Czech dramatists, while plays such as *Every Good Boy Deserves Favor* and *Rock 'n' Roll*, both of which explore the limits of left-wing political philosophy in the context of the cold war, further demonstrate his sympathies. Stoppard has also written extensively for television and film, including the Oscar-winning script for *Shakespeare in Love* (1998), directed by John Madden. Stoppard was awarded a knighthood by the queen in 1997 and has won countless awards for theater, both in London and New York. **PS**

"Eternity's a terrible thought. I mean, where's it all going to end?"

ABOVE: Photograph of Tom Stoppard taken by Francesco Guidicini in 2002.

HUNTER S. THOMPSON

Born: Hunter Stockton Thompson, July 18, 1937 (Louisville, Kentucky, U.S.); died February 20, 2005 (Woody Creek, Colorado, U.S.).

Style and genre: Thompson's subjective style of reporting laced with fiction and forthright political commentary gave exposure to 1960s counterculture.

Hunter S. Thompson was the creator of the pioneering "gonzo" journalism—a style of reporting that eschews objectivity and places the writer at the heart of the story. Known for his hedonistic lifestyle and rebellious personality, Thompson drove a gaping hole through conventional writing, becoming a counterculture icon in the process.

Thompson's books evolved from newspaper and magazine articles and it was an assignment to infiltrate the Hell's Angels motorcycle gang that resulted in Thompson's being offered the chance to expand his experiences in a book, *Hell's Angels: The Strange and Terrible Saga of the Outlaw Motorcycle Gangs.* This graphic account of life at the heart of a gang that most Americans feared, and about which they knew very little, launched his writing career and he was commissioned to write for the likes of *Esquire, Harper's,* and *Rolling Stone.*

An assignment from *Sports Illustrated* to cover the Mint 400 motorcycle race in Nevada was the catalyst for Thompson's most memorable work, *Fear and Loathing in Las Vegas: A Savage Journey to the Heart of the American Dream.* The chief protagonists Raoul Duke (Thompson's alter ego) and his attorney Dr. Gonzo go in search of the American Dream, only to discover that the idealism of the 1960s has suddenly turned to cynicism with the advent of the new decade. Some of his most humorous and controversial writing appeared in *Fear and Loathing: On the Campaign Trail '72* as he chronicled the 1972 U.S. presidential race and openly criticized Richard Nixon in a series of amusing diatribes. Thompson's literary output diminished in later years as he continued to report on politics and compiled his magazine articles in the four volume *Gonzo Papers.* **SG**

"The person who doesn't scatter the morning dew will not comb gray hairs."

Signature titles

Novels

Hell's Angels: The Strange and Terrible Saga of the Outlaw Motorcycle Gangs, 1966

Fear and Loathing in Las Vegas: A Savage Journey to the Heart of the American Dream, 1972

Memoir

Kingdom of Fear: Loathsome Secrets of a Star-Crossed Child in the Final Days of the American Century, 2003

Nonfiction

Fear and Loathing: On the Campaign Trail '72, 1973

Gonzo Papers Vol. 1: The Great Shark Hunt: Strange Tales from a Strange Time, 1979

Better Than Sex: Confessions of a Political Junkie, 1994

ABOVE: Thompson photographed at home in Woody Creek, Colorado, February 11, 2003.

RAYMOND CARVER

Born: May 25, 1938 (Clatskanie, Oregon, U.S.); died August 2, 1988 (Port Angeles, Washington, U.S.).

Style and genre: Short-story writer dubbed "the American Chekhov" for his spare and sensitive depiction of working-class life and the difficulties of domesticity.

Raymond Carver lived in straitened circumstances for much of his sadly short life. The son of a sawmill worker and a waitress, he found himself working dead-end jobs, as a delivery man, mill hand, or hospital janitor, to support the family he started young (in the typical postwar pattern, he was a father of two before he had turned twenty-one). Unable to find time to write, he became increasingly, ruinously dependent on alcohol. But out of this he managed to craft stories of a rare beauty, as striking for the restraint with which they leave things unsaid as for their portrayals of the regularly down-at-heel and drunken.

It was not until the publication of *Will You Please Be Quiet, Please?* in 1976 that Carver found any recognition. Soon after this, estranged from his first wife and children, he began what he called his second life; he gave up drinking and met the writer Tess Gallagher, who would be his companion for the rest of his life. There followed the flowering of his major achievements, in the collections *What We Talk About When We Talk About Love* and *Cathedral*, with stories written in a style cut back—as Carver said—"to the marrow, not just to the bone."

Since Carver's death, as the original drafts came to light, it has emerged that this spare style was as much the result of editor Gordon Lish's labors as the author's; but either way, it represents a distinct achievement. Successful film adaptations of literary works are perhaps rare, but Carver's stories have been the basis for not one, but two. First, Robert Altman made a patchwork of Carver stories into the panorama of *Short Cuts*, then, in 2006, "So Much Water So Close to Home" was transplanted into small-town Australia for *Jindabyne*, adding a level of class and racial tension to Carver's sensitive domestic tale. **MS**

"I never wrote so much as a line worth a nickel when I was under the influence of alcohol."

Signature titles

Short stories

Will You Please Be Quiet, Please?, 1976

What We Talk About When We Talk About Love, 1981

Cathedral, 1983

Where I'm Calling From, 1988

Poetry

All of Us: The Collected Poems, 1996

Anthology

Fires: Essays, Poems, Stories 1983

ABOVE: Raymond Carver poses for a photographic portrait in the 1980s.

JOYCE CAROL OATES

Born: June 16, 1938 (Lockport, New York, U.S.).

Style and genre: Oates has a compelling, page-turning writing style and uses vivid descriptions with a strong sense of the visual, in-depth characterization, and historic accuracy.

Joyce Carol Oates is a master of thought-provoking fiction that draws the reader into its characters' lives as she takes the American Dream and turns it inside out. Seemingly happy situations secretly underlined with tension characterize many of her works, as do autobiographical and biographical experiences woven into fiction.

Born during the Great Depression in a working-class suburb of New York, Oates was always more interested in books than in her parents' farm. She began writing in earnest at the age of fourteen, and when she was twenty-six, her first novel, *With Shuddering Fall,* was published; five years later, *them* won the National Book Award. The novel centers on issues at the heart of contemporary U.S. society: divisions between black and white; male and female; rich and poor. Oates later described the novel, and in essence her writing style thus: "This is a work of history in fictional form—that is, in personal perspective, which is the only kind of history that exists."

Throughout Oates's oeuvre, real lives are placed into fictional settings, inspired by stories related or people she has met. Her plots differ widely. The lyrical and mesmerizing *The Falls* is seemingly a love story of a new bride widowed at Niagara Falls—but a love story with a twist. The controversial *Rape: A Love Story* is a hard-hitting but beautifully told novel about a brutalized woman and child, and the men who attacked them. *Blonde* is a biographical novel about Norma Jean Baker (aka Marilyn Monroe), which tells the story through the imagined voice of the character. An astonishingly prolific writer, Oates also writes short stories, essays, plays, poetry, and—under the pseudonyms Lauren Kelly and Rosamond Smith—suspense thrillers. **LH**

"Love commingled with hate is more powerful than love. Or hate."

Signature titles

Novels

them, 1969
Childwold, 1976
Bellefleur, 1980
You Must Remember This, 1987
Because It Is Bitter, and Because It Is My Heart, 1990
We Were the Mulvaneys, 1996
Man Crazy, 1997
Blonde, 2000
Middle Age: A Romance, 2001
Rape: A Love Story, 2003
The Falls, 2004
Missing Mom, 2005
The Gravedigger's Daughter, 2007

ABOVE: Joyce Carol Oates photographed in London, England, in August 2006.

CARYL CHURCHILL

Born: September 3, 1938 (London, England).

Style and genre: Churchill is an important twentieth-century playwright whose radical and often experimental work explores issues of female oppression, social inequality, and thwarted political desire.

Caryl Churchill spent much of her childhood in Montreal, Canada, but returned to England to study English at Oxford, where she began writing her first plays. Since then, her output has been prolific and wide-ranging, in both style and content.

Churchill's bold and innovative approach has earned her a reputation as the leading woman writer in the "new wave" of British playwrights. Her writing emerges from a staunch but not necessarily didactic left-wing perspective and adopts a range of inventive angles to explore feminist themes. Many of her plays reject strict linear plotting, are episodic in nature, juxtapose two hugely disparate theatrical worlds, and thus assume overall a distinctly Brechtian quality.

Much of this work has grown out of collaborative workshops with theater groups such as Joint Stock or with English theater director Max Stafford-Clark. Two such examples are *Cloud Nine* and *Top Girls*, plays that make liberal use of anachronism to investigate their social and political themes. In *Cloud Nine*, the sexual mores of two epochs are examined by placing the same characters in the years 1879 and 1979 respectively, though the characters age only twenty-five years. By this ingenious method, Churchill is able to compare the responses of a patriarchal Victorian society to sexual unconformity with that of the supposedly more enlightened, unprejudiced era of the 1970s. In the first act of *Top Girls*, a dinner party is held in honor of Marlene, a successful businesswoman. Her guests are eminent women from a range of historical periods and together they cause drunken mayhem. This is contrasted with the far more sober second act, in which Marlene struggles with the practical and social realities of life as a businesswoman in Thatcherite Britain. **GM**

"We need to find new questions, which may help us to answer the old ones . . ."

Signature titles

Plays

Owners, 1972
Light Shining in Buckinghamshire, 1976
Cloud Nine, 1979
Top Girls, 1982
Softcops, 1984
A Mouthful of Birds, 1986
Serious Money, 1987
Ice Cream/Hot Fudge, 1989
Mad Forest, 1990
The Skriker ,1994
Thyestes, 2001
A Dream Play, 2005

ABOVE: Portrait photograph of Churchill taken by Gemma Levine *c.* 1985.

MANUEL VÁZQUEZ MONTALBÁN

Born: July 27, 1939 (Barcelona, Spain); died October 18, 2003 (Bangkok, Thailand).

Style and genre: Novelist, poet, short-story writer, essayist, biographer, journalist, food writer, social critic, political commentator, and gastronome, Montalbán is also known for his detective novels.

Manuel Vázquez Montalbán was a prolific writer whose oeuvre spanned a host of genres, and a vast range of topics. Yet he is perhaps best known as the creator of a series of detective novels featuring his alter-ego character, private detective José "Pepe" Carvalho—a Barcelona sleuth whose passion for food reflects Montalbán's own gastronomic interests. The Carvalho series has been translated into twenty-four languages and adapted for television. In his youth Montalbán was a leading member of Catalonia's Communist Party, when it was dangerous to oppose Franco's regime, and his outspokenness earned him a spell in prison. Montalbán's novels, essays, and journalism frequently tackle thorny social issues. **CK**

Signature titles

Novels

I Killed Kennedy (Yo maté a Kennedy), 1972

Angst-ridden Executive (La soledad del manager), 1977

Southern Seas (Los mares del sur), 1979

Galíndez, 1991

Olympic Sabotage (Sabotaje olímpico), 1993

The Strangler (El estrangulador), 1994

Buenos Aires Quintet (Quinteto de Buenos Aires), 1997

Erec and Enide (Erec y Enide), 2002

Poetry

Memory and Desire (Memoria y deseo), 1986

Essays

*Report about Information (Informe sobre la Información),*1963

MARIE-CLAIRE BLAIS

Born: October 5, 1939 (Quebec City, Quebec, Canada).

Style and genre: Novelist, poet, and playwright, Blais writes insightful social commentary, often combining elements of reality and fantasy. In 1972 she was awarded Canada's highest civilian honor, the Order of Canada.

Marie-Claire Blais's work offers a poignant, perspicuous account of humanity and society. She addresses morality, spirituality, and the mundane with similar insight, often breaking literary conventions and creating compelling characters and scenes, occasionally placed within a fantasy framework. Her first novel, *Mad Shadows*, published in 1959 when she was just twenty years old, was critically acclaimed; it was quickly followed by *Tête Blanche* in 1960. Perhaps her best known and most acclaimed novel is *A Season in the Life of Emmanuel*, which won the Prix France-Canada and the Prix Médicis. She was also awarded the Order of Canada in 1972 and made a Chevalier of the French Ordre des Lettres. **TamP**

Signature titles

Novels

Mad Shadows (La Belle bête), 1959

Tête Blanche, 1960

A Season in the Life of Emmanuel (Une Saison dans la vie d'Emmanuel), 1965

The Wolf (Le Loup), 1970

Thunder and Light (Dans la foudre et la lumière), 2001

Play

Wintersleep (Sommeil d'hiver), 1984

SEAMUS HEANEY

Born: April 13, 1939 (Mossbawn, County Derry, Northern Ireland).

Style and genre: Irish poet, writer, and winner of the Nobel Prize in Literature, Heaney believes poetry to be a redemptive act. His themes include religious and political oppression, and the inspirational qualities of nature.

Signature titles

Poetry

Death of a Naturalist, 1966
Door into the Dark, 1969
Wintering Out, 1972
North, 1975
Field Work, 1979
Station Island, 1984
The Haw Lantern, 1987
Seeing Things, 1991
The Spirit Level, 1996
Electric Light, 2001
District and Circle, 2006

Plays

The Cure at Troy, 1990
The Burial at Thebes, 2004

Nonfiction

Preoccupations: Selected Prose 1968–1978, 1980
The Government of the Tongue, 1988
The Redress of Poetry: Oxford Lectures, 1995
Finders Keepers: Selected Prose 1971–2001, 2002

ABOVE: Heaney at the International Book Festival, Edinburgh, Scotland, August 2006.

RIGHT: At home in Ireland with his wife and children in 1977.

Seamus Heaney's first major book of poems, *Death of a Naturalist*, is rooted in the rural life and labour of County Derry, where he grew up on a farm. The opening poem, "Digging," has come to be regarded as the signature piece of Heaney's poetic vocation, neatly balancing his fidelity to the land and physical labor on the one hand, and a commitment to the life of the imagination and the intellect on the other. *Door into the Dark* was published as sectarian violence became more widespread and intense in the aftermath of the Catholic civil rights marches, and the book was to mark a political, as well as a psychological, threshold in Heaney's career. Several poems in *Wintering Out* declare their solidarity with those who have suffered oppression in Ireland's long political and religious struggles, but Heaney's confrontation with the political tumult of the 1970s is much more explicit in *North*.

Field Work is a reassessment of the poet's responsibilities after ten years of political antagonism in the north. It shows a strong and continuing interest in the land itself as a source of

inspiration and sustenance. In *Station Island*, Heaney follows the penitential rites of pilgrims visiting an island closely associated with St. Patrick and the coming of Christianity to Ireland, where he meditates on his own vocation as a poet. His continuing belief in the possibilities of lyric form is given ample expression in *The Haw Lantern* and in *Seeing Things*, which initiates a more reflective and visionary mode in Heaney's poetry. A tentative optimism prevails in *The Spirit Level*—the first collection of poems to appear after the ceasefire in 1994—in *Electric Light* and *District and Circle*, all of which revisit places and themes associated with Heaney's earlier work.

Heaney was appointed Professor of Poetry at Oxford University, England, in 1988, and awarded the Nobel Prize in Literature in 1995. Like Yeats before him, Heaney has held fast to the idea of poetry as a potentially redemptive act, daring to believe that "the end of art is peace." **SR**

ABOVE: Pictured here in 1996, Heaney was often inspired by his surroundings.

Heaney's "Bog Poems"

In 1969, as political violence intensified, Heaney began to reconsider his vocation and to search for what W. B. Yeats had termed "befitting emblems of adversity." Heaney was to find appropriate images in the work of the Danish archeologist P. V. Glob, whose studies of Iron Age sacrificial victims preserved in peat bogs suggested a terrifying parallel with the victims of ritualistic killings in Northern Ireland. Glob's vivid account of the discovery of the Tollund man and the Grauballe man in *The Bog People* (1969) inspired Heaney's compelling series of "bog poems" in *Wintering Out* (1972) and *North* (1975).

AMOS OZ

Born: Amos Klausner, May 4, 1939 (Jerusalem, Israel).

Style and genre: The works of novelist, short-story writer, political essayist, and peace activist Amos Oz are rooted in his Israeli homeland; his themes include the frailty of human nature.

Signature titles

Novels

Where the Jackals Howl, 1965

Elsewhere, Perhaps, 1966

My Michael, 1968

To Know a Woman, 1989

Memoir

A Tale of Love and Darkness, 2005

Nonfiction

Help Us to Divorce, 2004

Amos Oz, the renowned Israeli writer of fiction and nonfiction says that if he had to sum up his entire literary work in one word it is "families" and in two words, "unhappy families." His characters suffer loneliness, inner conflict, and rootlessness and reflect the realities of modern-day Israeli life. One of the most prominent contemporary Hebrew writers, as well as one of the most influential and respected intellectuals in Israel, Oz was brought up by his Eastern European parents in Jerusalem. His mother, who suffered from depression, committed suicide when he was thirteen and Oz says that the profound trauma he suffered influenced his decision to become a writer.

Oz's first collection of short stories, *Where the Jackals Howl*, was published in 1965 and is an allegory of the problems that the State of Israel faces. A year later, it was followed by *Elsewhere, Perhaps*, a novel about life on an Israeli kibbutz. Oz gained recognition, however, with his next novel, *My Michael*, the tale of a woman's retreat from an unhappy marriage into a world of fantasy, set against the backdrop of Israel's turbulent history. Among his later work, Oz's memoir *A Tale of Love and Darkness* stands out. It tells his own story of living as a child in war-torn Jerusalem, the effect of his mother's suicide, and looks back at 120 years of family history.

"I find the family the most mysterious and fascinating institution in the world."

As a prolific political essayist, Amos Oz focuses on the complexities of the relationship between the Jews and the Arabs and is a vigorous advocate of a two-state solution to the Israeli-Palestinian conflict and a Palestinian homeland. Oz's work is now translated in over thirty languages and he has won a number of international literary prizes including the Chevalier de la Légion d'Honneur (France) in 1997, the Israel Prize for Literature in 1998, and the Goethe Prize in 2005. **HJ**

ABOVE: Oz at the International Festival of Literature in Rome, Italy, June 23, 2005.

RIGHT: Oz's memoir *A Tale of Love and Darkness* is a touching family saga.

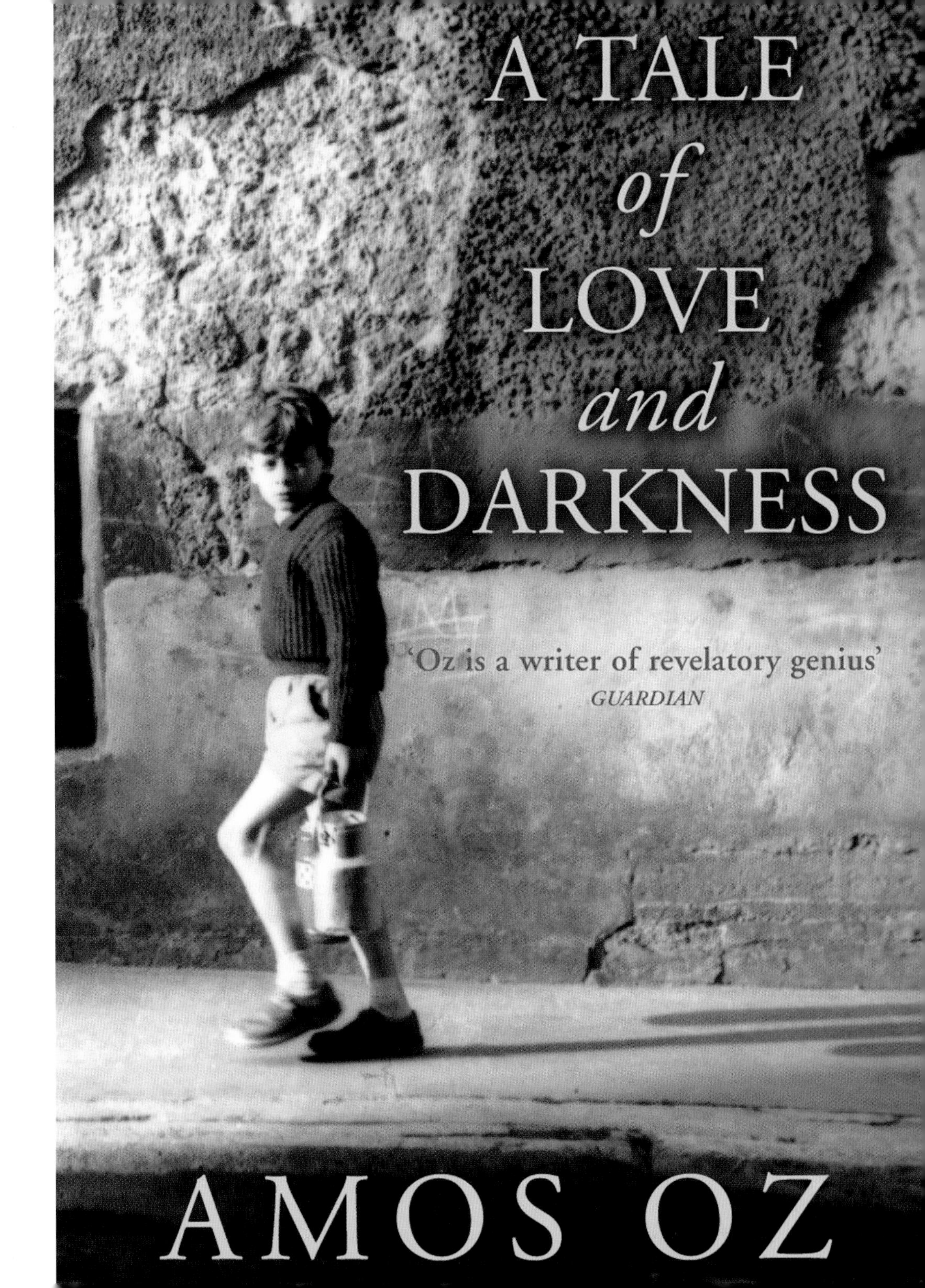
A TALE
of
LOVE
and
DARKNESS
'Oz is a writer of revelatory genius'
GUARDIAN
AMOS OZ

MARGARET ATWOOD

Born: November 18, 1939 (Ottawa, Canada).

Style and genre: Canadian poet and novelist, Atwood combines a well-developed sense of irony and verbal playfulness with a penetrating insight into contemporary issues, from gender relations to the environment.

In an interview, Margaret Atwood once rejected the term "literary icon," saying that the true celebrities were the "rock stars, Elizabeth Taylor." One wonders if she was not being a little disingenuous. After all, her latest novels have been best sellers as well as critical successes, her fiction and poetry have been translated into over thirty languages, and Atwood herself has received sixteen honorary degrees and has won awards at a rate of more than one per year since the late 1970s.

Although Atwood is often described as a feminist author, her work is never polemical or mere political allegory. "I didn't invent feminism and it certainly didn't invent me," she has said. "But I'm naturally sympathetic to it." Gender issues are central to her work, and she has explored cultural ideals of femininity, the representation of women's bodies in art, and male–female relationships, as well as what she calls "bad female behavior." Perhaps it would be more accurate to call her a student of the female psyche, which she chronicles with unsparing insight and a double-edged wit. And, of course, there are bigger themes at play in her work as well: the

Signature titles

Novels

The Edible Woman, 1969

The Handmaid's Tale, 1985

Cat's Eye, 1988

The Robber Bride, 1993

Alias Grace, 1996

The Blind Assassin, 2000

Oryx and Crake, 2003

The Penelopiad, 2005

Short stories

Dancing Girls, 1979

Bluebeard's Egg, 1985

Wilderness Tips, 1991

The Tent, 2006

Poetry

Eating Fire: Selected Poetry 1965–1995, 1998

Children's fiction

Princess Prunella and the Purple Peanut, 1995

Rude Ramsay and the Roaring Radishes, 2003

Nonfiction

Survival, 1972

Negotiating with the Dead, 2002

ABOVE: Atwood poses for a dramatic portrait in Toronto, Canada, May 2, 2006.

RIGHT: Photograph of Atwood taken November 10, 1994 by Sophie Bassouls.

conflict between nature and technology, the limits of rationality and historical knowledge, and the inevitability of death.

ABOVE: At home with her cat, Fluffy, in January 1989; the title of her book *Cat's Eye* refers to a type of marble.

Atwood's father was a forest entomologist, and Margaret spent much of her youth in remote Northern Quebec, where he was a researcher; she did not complete a full year of school until grade eight, but she read a lot, and was totally at home in the wilderness. She was first encouraged as a writer by a high school English teacher, who read one of her poems and said, "I can't understand this at all, dear, so it must be good!" She took her bachelor's degree at the University of Toronto, where she studied under Northrop Frye and self-published her first collection of poetry, which won a college prize. After graduating, she wrote another book of poetry, *A Circle Game*, and this time took home Canada's top literary

"A divorce is like an amputation: you survive it but there's less of you."

The Queen of CanLit

When Margaret Atwood's *Survival* was first published in 1972, it addressed the question: why should we bother with Canadian literature? The answer might now seem obvious, when international literary superstars like Michael Ondaatje, Alice Munro, Carol Shields, and Rohinton Mistry (and of course Atwood herself) all hail from the Great White North, but the number of recognized authors before them was extremely limited. There *were* Canadian writers, of course, but Canadian readers were mostly indifferent to homegrown talent. Atwood argued that Canadians preferred foreign writers because of a deep-rooted inferiority complex—the lasting legacy of the colonial mindset.

Survival, described simply as a "short, easy-to-use guide to Canadian Literature," sold extremely well for a book of essays. It argued not only that there *was* a canon of "CanLit," with its own distinct preoccupations, but that it should be read, studied, and talked about. Part criticism, part manifesto, this witty and impassioned critique traced the motif of Canadian characters as survivors with victim mentalities, from the hardships of the colonists to the survival of both French and English cultures against their neighbors to the south. Frankly nationalistic, *Survival* was the clarion call for a major surge in Canadian cultural production, and the 1970s saw the growth of publishing houses (including the House of Anansi, which Atwood helped to establish), theater and film production, and Canadian authors being taught in Canadian schools.

RIGHT: Dust jacket of *Alias Grace*, published by Doubleday, New York, 1996.

accolade, the Governor General's Award. A few years later, she published her first novel, *The Edible Woman*, and she has alternated between the two genres ever since, explaining that while poetry is at the heart of her relationship with language, fiction encapsulates her moral vision of the world.

It was with *A Handmaid's Tale*, about a fictional U.S. theocracy, that Atwood came to prominence on the international scene. In this dystopian novel a plague (or biological weapon—it is never made clear) has rendered much of the population infertile; our narrator Offred, officially stripped of her rights and property, is an unwilling handmaid, forced to bear her master a child. Atwood insists that her work is not science fiction, which connotes aliens and space ships, but rather "speculative fiction," because she writes of things that could happen (and indeed, Offred's flashbacks reveal a world very much like our own). The novel has been adapted as a feature film and, more recently, an opera. *Oryx and Crake*, Atwood's other experiment within the speculative fiction genre, is a cautionary tale about genetic engineering and the environment. Although books of ideas, these novels are grounded in richly evoked settings and well-drawn characters, and work as both social commentary and literary fiction.

Atwood's other novels show her restlessly toying with literary conventions, both high and low brow, from epic (*The Penelopiad*) and bildungsroman (*Cat's Eye*) to crime (*Alias Grace*) and historical fiction (*The Blind Assassin*). And those are just the novels; besides her poetry, Atwood is also a prolific writer of criticism and reviews, screenplays and radio scripts, and children's books. Her work has also inspired a number of adaptations—*Edible Woman* as a successful play, *The Robber Bride* as a TV movie, and *Alias Grace* as a mini-series.

Notorious for her quick tongue and acerbic wit, Atwood has frightened more than a few interviewers, but as she put it in her book, *Negotiating with the Dead*, "It took me a long time to figure out that the youngest in a family of dragons is still a dragon from the point of view of those who find dragons alarming." **CQ**

ALIAS GRACE

A NOVEL

MARGARET ATWOOD

GAO XINGJIAN

Born: January 4, 1940 (Ganzhou, China).

Style and genre: Gao Xingjian was the first Chinese to be awarded the Nobel Prize in Literature, yet his criticism of the regime has made him *persona non grata* in China; his fragmented narrative is a critical account of the Cultural Revolution.

Gao Xingjian's career as a dramatist began with his appointment as screenwriter to the Beijing People's Art Theater. His first play, *Warning Signal*, was well received but he soon fell out of favor with the regime. *Bus Stop*, a Beckett-inspired satire of a cross-section of Beijing society waiting for a bus that never comes, was decried as "the most pernicious piece of writing since the foundation of the People's Republic of China," and he became a target in the "Anti-Spiritual Pollution Campaign" of 1983.

After graduating in 1962 from the prestigious Beijing Foreign Languages Institute, where he studied French language and literature, Gao worked as a translator. The violence and absurdity of the Cultural Revolution (1966–1976) left a tremendous imprint on his oeuvre, and he developed a strong aversion toward mass ideology, turning instead to an introspective individualism.

Gao's lyrical novel *Soul Mountain* is a philosophical odyssey that takes the narrator on a journey to the mystical Chinese Southwest, in search of the true meaning of life. Even more personal is his novel *One Man's Bible,* published in 1990. Employing a fragmented narrative as in *Soul Mountain*, the narrator speaks as political activist, victim, and outside observer to give an account of his experiences during the Cultural Revolution.

"I began writing my novel *Soul Mountain* to dispel my inner loneliness. . . ."

Following an invitation to visit Europe in 1987, Gao decided not to return to China. He settled in Paris and became a French citizen in 1998. His plays remain banned in China. After settling in France, and prior to receiving the 2000 Nobel Prize in Literature, Gao continued to write, but also gained recognition as a painter. His ink drawings are reproduced in a book entitled *Return to Paintings*, which was published in 2002. **FHG**

Signature titles

Novels

Buying a Fishing Rod for My Grandfather, 1986

Soul Mountain, 1989

One Man's Bible, 1999

Plays

Warning Signal, 1982

Bus Stop, 1983

Wild Man, 1985

The Other Shore, 1986

Escape, 1990

Between Life and Death, 1991

Essays

Cold Literature, 1990

Parisian Notes, 1990

The Case for Literature, 2000

ABOVE: Gao Xingjian, the Nobel laureate, pictured in November 2006.

EDMUND WHITE

Born: January 13, 1940 (Cincinnati, Ohio, U.S.)

Style and genre: One of the most highly regarded American writers, with a body of work that spans novels, literary criticism, and biography, White chronicles gay life and the impact of AIDS in America and France.

Born in Cincinnati, Ohio, Edmund White grew up in Chicago. After studying Chinese at the University of Michigan he worked as a journalist in New York. His first novel, *Forgetting Elena,* is a witty exploration of life on an island community. It was followed by a work of nonfiction, *The Joy of Gay Sex*, a guide to the erotic, emotional, and social fulfilment of a gay lifestyle.

But it is *A Boy's Own Story*, a deeply touching work of autobiographical fiction, for which White is best known. It tells of a boy growing up in 1950s America and escaping his difficult childhood by immersing himself in art, literature, and his imagination. The work is the first of a trilogy that also includes *The Beautiful Room is Empty*, which charts the narrator's move into adulthood and the birth of gay liberation; and *The Farewell Symphony* (named after the Hadyn work in which instrumentalists leave the stage one by one until just one violin is left), which tells of the rise of AIDS and of the narrator who has outlived most of his friends. The trilogy is a moving chronicle of American gay life spanning forty years.

In 2000, White published *The Married Man*, a haunting account of a middle-aged American in Paris. It is considered by many to be his finest work to date. White returned to autobiography in 2005 with *My Lives*, but instead of taking a conventional chronological approach in the work, each chapter takes a theme such as My Europe, My Friends, and My Shrinks. As well as fiction, White has produced a critically acclaimed biography of French writer Jean Genet, a study of Marcel Proust, and a reflection about Paris—*The Flâneur: A Stroll Through the Paradoxes of Paris*, which takes the reader on an amble through the streets of Paris, introducing us to the places where guidebooks never venture. **HJ**

"I think sincerity was my sole aesthetic and realism my experimental technique."

Signature titles

Novels

Forgetting Elena, 1973

Nocturnes for the King of Naples, 1978

A Boy's Own Story, 1982

The Beautiful Room is Empty, 1988

The Farewell Symphony, 1997

The Married Man, 2000

Fanny: A Fiction, 2003

Hotel de Dream, 2007

Autobiography

My Lives: An Autobiography, 2005

Nonfiction

The Joy of Gay Sex, 1977

Genet: A Biography, 1993

The Flâneur: A Stroll Through the Paradoxes of Paris, 2001

ABOVE: A studio portrait of Edmund White taken in 2005.

J. M. COETZEE

Born: John Maxwell Coetzee, February 9, 1940 (Cape Town, South Africa).

Style and genre: Coetzee is a South African Nobel Prize–winning novelist known for his spare yet complex prose, frank depictions of violence, and unflinching portrayal of the legacies of colonialism.

Signature titles

Novels

Dusklands, 1974
In the Heart of the Country, 1977
Waiting for the Barbarians, 1980
Life & Times of Michael K, 1983
Foe, 1986
Age of Iron, 1990
The Master of Petersburg, 1994
Disgrace, 1999
Elizabeth Costello: Eight Lessons, 2003
Slow Man, 2005
Diary of a Bad Year, 2007

Memoirs

Boyhood: Scenes from Provincial Life, 1997
Youth: Scenes from Provincial Life II, 2002

ABOVE: A photograph of Coetzee at the International Parliament of Writers in 2005.

It is not surprising that, having lived most of his life under the apartheid regime in South Africa, J. M. Coetzee has spent his writing career analyzing the relationship between the personal and the political uses and abuses of power. What is notable is the intellectual honesty with which he treats the realities of torture, brutality, and injustice, and the difficulty of remaining an innocent bystander to colonialism of all kinds.

Coetzee studied at the University of Cape Town and the University of Texas, Austin, where he earned a doctorate on the work of Samuel Beckett who, along with Kafka and Dostoevsky, remains an important influence. In fact, two of his novels—*The Life and Times of Michael K* and *The Master of Petersburg*—owe especial debts to those two authors.

In 2003, when Coetzee was awarded the Nobel Prize, the Swedish Academy called him "a writer of solitude." The description is apt: His novels are constantly reconfiguring the problems of communication, whether between individuals or cultures. In *Foe*, his fictional response to Daniel Defoe's genre-defining novel *Robinson Crusoe*, Coetzee adds a point of view to the original narrative: that of a woman shipwrecked on the same island. Friday travels with her back to London after Crusoe dies, but is unable to tell his own story, as his tongue has been cut out. In Coetzee's most celebrated novel, *Disgrace*, a professor's daughter is the victim of a violent crime, but she decides not to pursue her attackers. Her father must be stripped of dignity before he is able to fully acknowledge the difficulty of his ethical position, as a white man in South Africa. This allegory of the post-apartheid nation offers no consoling vision at its close, which is indicative of the uncompromising clarity with which the author addresses his themes.

The Academy's portrayal of Coetzee is also appropriate because the novelist values solitude himself. He did not even

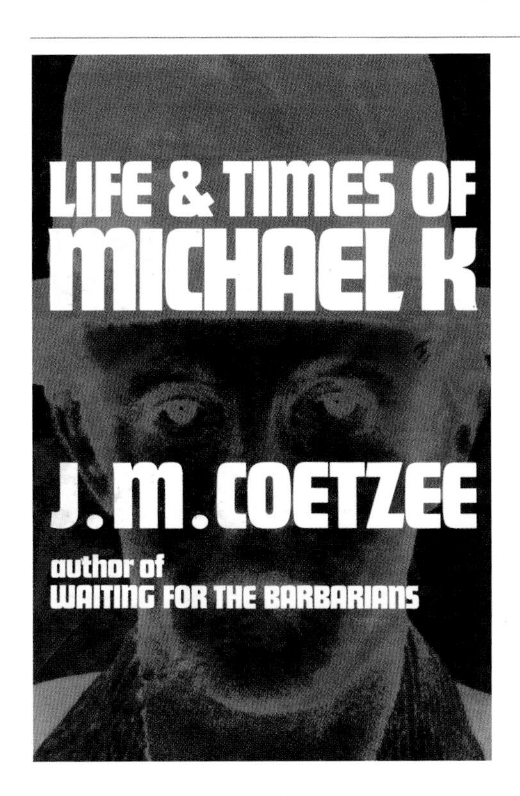

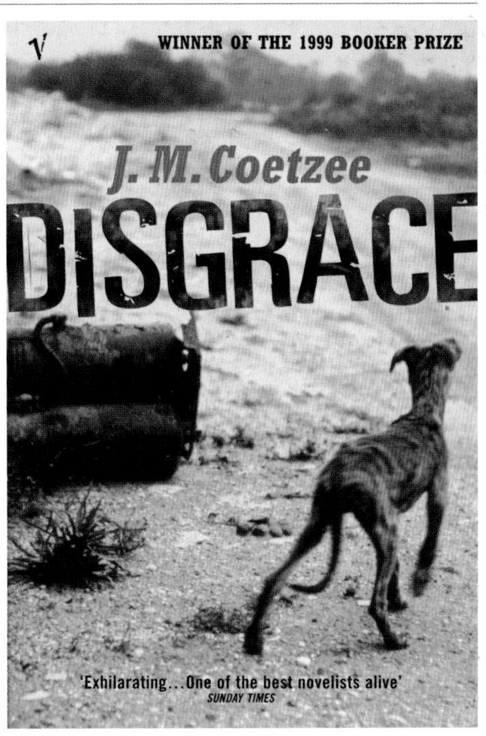

show up to receive his two Booker Prizes in person. He did attend the ceremony for the Nobel Prize, however, saying that he would certainly have made his mother proud.

Controversy has always dogged J. M. Coetzee. In a report commissioned by the African National Congress (ANC), Coetzee's novel *Disgrace* was held up as an example of the kind of white racism still prevalent in post-apartheid South Africa—though many readers and critics rose to his defense. His being awarded the Nobel Prize sparked a parliamentary debate when the opposition party called on the ANC to apologize for its close-minded critique of the novel. In a startling turnaround, President Thabo Mbeki summoned the nation to celebrate their compatriot's success. **CQ**

"Sometimes one has the intuition that the intellect by itself will lead one nowhere."

ABOVE LEFT: *Life & Times of Michael K*, a tale of hardship in apartheid South Africa.

ABOVE: *Disgrace* has a white man coming to terms with his post-apartheid country.

1940–59

ANGELA CARTER

Born: Angela Olive Stalker, May 7, 1940 (Eastbourne, East Sussex, England); died February 16, 1992 (London, England).

Style and genre: Carter was a prolific novelist, journalist, and editor, seen as a postmodern Mother Goose spinning folk tales of transgression and desire.

Signature titles

Novels

The Magic Toyshop, 1967

Heroes and Villains, 1969

The Infernal Desire Machines of Dr. Hoffman, 1972

Nights at the Circus, 1984

Wise Children, 1991

Short stories

The Bloody Chamber and Other Stories, 1979

Black Venus, 1985

American Ghosts and Old World Wonders, 1993

Nonfiction

The Sadeian Woman and the Ideology of Pornography, 1978

Expletives Deleted: Selected Writings, 1992

The Infernal Desire Machines of Dr. Hoffman—the title of one of Angela Carter's best-known novels—could equally belong to the author herself. Carter's stories, whether created for page, stage, screen, or radio, are wonders of invention. Part of an anti-realist strain of British fiction stretching back to *A Midsummer Night's Dream*, Angela Carter brought out the grotesque and sexual energies of fantasy, creating twentieth-century fairy tales for adults.

London, Carter's lifelong home, is an atmospheric presence in her books, particularly in her late novels, *Nights at the Circus* and *Wise Children,* which look at the capital through the saucy gazes of working girls. Carter imbibed socialist politics from her family, and her characters often both see, and see through, the glitter of consumerism. Feminism became part of her life after divorce from her first husband and three years in Japan, from 1969 to 1972. Returning to London, she became associated with the newly founded Virago Press, which, as well as rescuing many modernist women's novels, enjoyed its most notorious success with her study *The Sadeian Woman*.

Although Carter's pre-1969 novels brim with her trademark Gothic and fevered narrative and vocabulary, her post-Japan writing has a refined sense of purpose and a mordant wit. Having edited a collection of fairy tales from around the world (with its controversial inclusion of the overtly sexual Inuit story of Sedna), she riffed productively on Perrault's morality tales in her short stories. "The Company of Wolves," filmed by Neil Jordan from Carter's screenplay, is the best-known of these. With Carter's usual voracity, the film is a tricksy series of mirror image tales-within-a-tale-within-a-tale. The film is a fitting memory to a surrealist Scheherazade. **SM**

"It is, perhaps, better to be valued as an object of passion than never to be valued at all."

ABOVE: Angela Carter pictured in her office during the 1980s.

BRUCE CHATWIN

Born: May 13, 1940 (Sheffield, South Yorkshire, England); died January 18, 1989 (Nice, France).

Style and genre: Chatwin's travel writing interweaves fact and fiction with a strong sense of history, a clear narrative voice, and personal experience.

Art historian turned journalist, Bruce Chatwin became a celebrated travel novelist, rather than a travel writer, filling his books on travel with as much imagination as reality. In his celebrated *Songlines*, he explored the world of Aboriginal mythology and culture, while weaving his own thoughts and stories into those of the Aborigines' traditions—a style criticized by purists but received enthusiastically by readers. His travel writing was seldom written from the expected angle, rushing on in a style that entices the reader into Chatwin's mind as much as into the country he is writing about, darting from history, through fictional musings, into travel journalism.

Chatwin's style changed from book to book. The lyrical, evocative prose of *In Patagonia* encouraged a new generation to explore Argentina and Chile, wanting to experience the elusive journey the nomadic Chatwin claimed as nonfiction; *On the Black Hill* saw Chatwin turning from a transient, expansive subject to the claustrophobically closed-in subject of identical twins who remain resolutely in one place. Another departure, *The Viceroy of Ouidah* was a difficult, uncomfortable novel about slavery, as Chatwin attempted to get into the mind of the slave traders. His vast subject matter and the author's exploration of differing writing styles emphasize the contradictions of Chatwin's own life, veering wildly between styles and genres. He was a controversial, chameleon-like man who lived his life as he traveled—taking daring risks and refusing to follow convention. He became a celebrity for his scandalous lifestyle instead of his writing, living among New York socialites and gay icons, journeying with nomads and living an openly homosexual lifestyle, while yet remaining married to his much-loved wife, Elizabeth. **LH**

"Losing my passport was the least of my worries, losing a notebook was a catastrophe."

Signature titles

Novels

The Viceroy of Ouidah, 1980

On the Black Hill, 1982

Utz, 1988

Anthologies

What Am I Doing Here?, 1989

Anatomy of Restlessness, 1997

Nonfiction

In Patagonia, 1977

The Songlines, 1987

Winding Paths, 1998

ABOVE: Chatwin photographed in Paris during a book promotion tour in 1984.

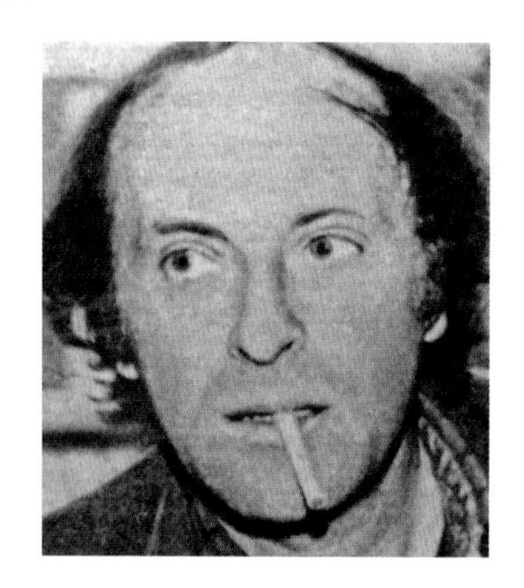

JOSEPH BRODSKY

Born: Iosif Alexandrovich Brodsky, May 24, 1940 (Leningrad [now St. Petersburg], Russia); died January 28, 1996 (New York, New York, U.S.).

Style and genre: Brodsky was a Russian-American poet and essayist who survived the Soviet gulag to become a Nobel Prize winner and U.S. poet laureate.

After his death from heart failure in 1996, Joseph Brodsky became one of the most elegized of twentieth-century poets, his life celebrated with poems by fellow Nobel Laureates Derek Walcott and Seamus Heaney, leading Irish poet Paul Muldoon, and a host of others. He also received the honor of translation by some of his most accomplished contemporaries, including Walcott, Richard Wilbur, and Anthony Hecht. If this suggests that Brodsky was merely a "poet's poet," nothing could be further from the truth. Brodsky had a genius for sociability and friendship: Robert Lowell called him a "spendthrift talker," and it is his appetite for "pepper vodka" that Heaney remembers in his elegy. These qualities are reflected in the energy, generosity, and love of worldly detail in Brodsky's poems.

It is almost miraculous that all this survived the ordeals that Brodsky faced. Socially disadvantaged as a Russian Jew, he left school at fifteen and worked in a series of menial jobs until he came into the orbit of Russian poet Anna Akhmatova, who admired the combination of modernity with traditional forms

Signature titles

Plays

Marbles, 1989

Democracy!, 1991

Poetry

Elegy to John Donne, 1967

A Part of Speech, 1977

Verses on the Winter Campaign, 1980

To Urania: Selected Poems, 1965–1985

Lullaby of Cape Cod, 1975

So Forth: Poems, 1996

Discovery, 1999 (published posthumously)

Essays

Less Than One, 1986

Watermark, 1992

On Grief and Reason, 1996

ABOVE: Brodsky photographed posing with a cigarette in 1970.

RIGHT: Brodsky embraces his publisher on hearing of his Nobel Prize win in 1987.

LEFT: An undated photo of Brodsky; his work earned world acclaim and Soviet scorn.

in his poems. Within a few years, he had become well known, but this brought with it suspicion from the authorities. In 1964, having been denounced as a "social parasite" (the court deemed Brodsky insufficiently educated: "a pseudo-poet in velveteen trousers"), he was sentenced to five years' hard labor on a state farm in the far north of the U.S.S.R. Following international protests by writers and intellectuals, he was released after eighteen months of breaking rocks, carting manure, and chopping logs, but he continued to be harassed by the authorities. In 1971, having been ordered to leave the country, he arranged a new life in the United States, becoming, with the help of W. H. Auden, poet-in-residence at the University of Michigan. Publication in English translations soon followed, and eventually Brodsky was composing original poems in English. He won the Nobel Prize in 1987 and served as the first Clinton-era American Poet Laureate in 1992. **MS**

On Trial as a "Parasite"

A transcript of Brodsky's trial in 1964 was smuggled out and published in the West. Asked by the judge, "Who recognized you as a poet?" Brodsky replied, "No one. Who placed me among the human race?" Asked why he did not earn a regular wage for the Motherland, Brodsky said, "I have one suit, an old one, but still a suit. I don't need a second one. I have worked. I have written poems," and described his work as "spiritual labor." The judge told him, "Forget the big words," and sentenced him to five years' hard labor; but the crude philistinism of the proceedings brought the U.S.S.R. embarrassment and discredit.

ANNE TYLER

Born: October 25, 1941 (Minneapolis, Minnesota, U.S.).

Style and genre: Tyler is a Pulitzer Prize–winning novelist famous for documenting American twentieth-century middle-class family life using subtle, gentle humor peppered with sharp irony. Tyler is known for her endearing characters.

American writer Anne Tyler is known for her insightful descriptions of the often-bizarre everyday life of American middle-class families. Although often eccentric, her characters encapsulate infuriating yet endearing personality types who really could be living next door. Her most acclaimed books are *The Accidental Tourist*, about an unhappy travel writer on a bittersweet journey of loss and recovery, and the Pulitzer Prize–winning *Breathing Lessons*, the story of a couple who have been married for twenty-eight years examining their life as they travel to a funeral. A famously private person, Tyler declined interviews even after winning the Pulitzer. She lives in Baltimore, Maryland, where many of her novels are set. **JM**

Signature titles

Novels

If Morning Ever Comes, 1964
The Tin Can Tree, 1965
A Slipping-Down Life, 1970
The Clock Winder, 1972
Celestial Navigation, 1974
Searching for Caleb, 1975
Earthly Possessions, 1977
Morgan's Passing, 1980
Dinner at Homesick Restaurant, 1982
The Accidental Tourist, 1985
Breathing Lessons, 1988
Saint Maybe, 1991
Ladder of Years, 1995
A Patchwork Planet, 1998
Back When We Were Grownups, 2001
The Amateur Marriage, 2004
Digging to America, 2006

PETER HANDKE

Born: December 6, 1942 (Griffen, Austria).

Style and genre: Austria's leading avant-garde writer, Handke is a prolific author who works across genres; his works are often controversial and are characterized by experimentation with language.

Peter Handke is a prolific writer. He writes plays, novels, and short stories, and collaborated with the German filmmaker Wim Wenders on the screenplay of his 1987 film *Wings of Desire*. Handke first came to public attention in 1966 with his exhilarating drama *Offending the Audience*, which attacked conventional notions of the theater. In the play, the audience is told by actors that they are in fact the actors around which the drama unfolds. Other plays that challenge our ideas of drama include *The Hour We Knew Nothing of Each Other*, which has 450 characters and no dialogue at all. Handke was nominated for the Heinrich Heine literary prize in 2006, but the prize was withdrawn following his controversial support of Serbia. **HJ**

Signature titles

Novels

The Hornets (Die Hornissen), 1966
The Goalie's Anxiety at the Penalty Kick (Die Angst des Tormanns beim Elfmeter), 1970
My Year in the No-Man's-Bay (Mein Jahr in der Niemandsbucht),1998

Plays

Offending the Audience (Publikumsbeschimpfung) 1966
The Hour We Knew Nothing of Each Other (Die Stunde, da wir nichts voneinander wußten), 1992

Short stories

The Left-Handed Woman (Die linkshändige Frau), 1976

RIGHT: A undated photo of Handke in Kragujevac, Serbia.

ISABEL ALLENDE

Born: Isabel Allende Llona, August 2, 1942 (Lima, Peru).

Style and genre: Allende is a Chilean–American novelist and short-story writer whose work is characterized by magical realism, dreamlike, lyrical prose, and autobiographical themes.

Signature titles

Novels

The House of the Spirits (La casa de los espíritus), 1982

Of Love and Shadows (De amor y de sombra), 1984

Eva Luna, 1985

The Infinite Plan (El plan infinito), 1991

Daughter of Fortune (Hija de la fortuna), 1999

Portrait in Sepia (Retrato en sepia), 2000

My Invented Country (Mi país inventado), 2003

Zorro, 2005

Inés of My Soul (Inés de mi alma), 2006

Nonfiction

Paula, 1994

Aphrodite: A Memoir of the Senses (Afrodita: cuentos, recetas y otros afrodisiacos), 1998

In drawing on her life as subject matter, Isabel Allende weaves stories that are a mix of memory, dream, and fantasy in the magical realist tradition, leading to comparisons with author and literary giant Gabriel García Márquez. Like Márquez, Allende's stories are largely set in Latin America and have a fairy-tale quality, portraying a romantic but turbulent world that is inhabited by spirits, superstition, poverty, close-knit communities and families, and the stamp of the heel of the dictator's boot. However, her work differs from that of Márquez in that her protagonists are largely female and the content of her works is more transparently autobiographical.

Although Chilean, Allende was born in Peru, where her father was the Chilean ambassador; he was also a cousin of Salvador Allende, the president of Chile from 1970 to 1973. After her father's "disappearance" in 1945, the family lived in Bolivia, Lebanon, and then Chile. Following the 1973 coup, led by General Augusto Pinochet, that saw Salvador Allende killed, Isabel Allende helped various political dissidents flee the country. Her actions put her in danger and she was forced to flee to Venezuela, and eventually to the United States.

ABOVE: Allende poses for the camera in 1984, in the early days of her literary career.

RIGHT: Allende attended this 1973 Paris protest against the Chilean dictatorship.

Allende's first novel, *The House of the Spirits*, started life as a letter to her dying grandfather. Part romance and part a thinly veiled account of Salvador Allende's rise to power, the author charts the growth of revolutionary socialism in Chile, and the fallout after the coup d'état as the country becomes riddled with secret police, and inhabitants disappear, escape into exile, or simply live in fear. It is Allende's deftness as a storyteller and the novel's magical realism that makes the violence of the events tolerable. Her next novel, *Of Love and Shadows*, follows the fortunes of two journalists investigating the fate of a young woman who has "disappeared" under Chilean military rule.

Allende has continued to draw on her own experiences—for example, being the mother of a dying child. She excels at portraying subjects such as the injustice of life under a junta and the obscenity of poverty, but all the while offers a glimmer of hope in the form of her resilient female characters. **CK**

ABOVE: Winona Ryder stars in *The House of the Spirits* (1993), based on Allende's novel.

Honoring a Daughter

Allende's memoir *Paula* developed from a letter to her daughter, Paula, as she lay in a coma. The book relates the story of Allende's life and Paula's illness. Paula died in 1992, and Allende went on to establish a charity in her daughter's honor that offers education and healthcare to women and children. Allende's first work after a long period of mourning was a collection of recipes for dishes with aphrodisiac properties—*Aphrodite: A Memoir of the Senses*. Allende said, "I knew that I was reaching the end of a long tunnel of mourning . . . with a tremendous desire to eat and cuddle once again."

PETER CAREY

Born: May 7, 1943 (Bacchus Marsh, Victoria, Australia).

Style and genre: Carey is a post-colonial Australian novelist, whose satirical and fantastical works are noted for their playfulness with the truth, time, narrative, and history; he has won the Booker Prize twice.

Signature titles

Novels

Bliss, 1981
Illywhacker, 1985
Oscar and Lucinda, 1988
The Tax Inspector, 1991
The Unusual Life of Tristan Smith, 1994
Jack Maggs, 1997
True History of the Kelly Gang, 2000
My Life as a Fake, 2003
Theft: A Love Story, 2006

Short stories

The Fat Man in History, 1974
War Crimes, 1979
Exotic Pleasures, 1990

Children's fiction

The Big Bazoohley, 1995

Peter Carey spent one lackluster year studying zoology before starting work at an advertising agency in 1962. It was then that he embarked on his literary education, discovering and being inspired by the works of authors such as William Faulkner, James Joyce, Franz Kafka, and Samuel Beckett. He continued to work in advertising in Melbourne and London, but began writing during evenings and weekends. After twelve years of rejections, Carey's first manuscript to be accepted for publication was *The Fat Man in History*, a short-story collection that brought him overnight success. In 1980, he set up his own advertising agency in Sydney and worked part time, before leaving the industry for good and relocating to America, where he teaches a creative writing course at New York University, and devotes the rest of his week to writing.

Carey is one of only two authors (with J. M. Coetzee) to have won the Booker Prize twice: for *Oscar and Lucinda* and *True History of the Kelly Gang*. The tale of the outlaw Ned Kelly, which is proffered as the "real" diaries of the fugitive bushman, is typical Carey, freely mixing historical and fictional characters while playing games with the truth, chronology, and narrative voice. A tangled web of improbable reality and exotic imagined events is integral to *My Life as a Fake*, a story of hoax and counter hoax constructed around a genuine literary fraud of the 1940s; and in *Illywhacker*—Australian slang for conman—the allegedly 139-year-old narrator cheerfully introduces himself as "a terrible liar." Some domestic critics take umbrage with Carey for writing from an Australian perspective while living outside the country, but his darkly humorous fables can be seen as both a fantastical reflection of society and satirical critiques of capitalism. **MK**

"I have a greater sense of community in New York than almost anywhere I've ever lived."

ABOVE: Peter Carey photographed in January 2001.

REINALDO ARENAS

Born: July 16, 1943 (Province of Oriente, Cuba); died December 7, 1990 (New York, New York, U.S.).

Style and genre: Arenas was a poet of revolutionary freedom—not only in Castro's Cuba, but also in his own sexual and literary revolution within and against it.

Reinaldo Arenas is perhaps best known through Julian Schnabel's cinematic adaptation of his posthumously published autobiography, *Before Night Falls (Antes que anochezca)*. That a Cuban writer, who fought with Castro's guerrillas as a teenager, should enter popular consciousness through an American film embodies the contradictions that galvanized Arenas's literary career. Although he died tragically young, Arenas produced a wealth of novels, poetry, autobiography, and journalism—all the more astonishing considering that much of it was produced under state censorship, in prison, or when the author was suffering from AIDS-related illnesses.

Arenas's journey from impoverished farm boy to New York literary underground is characterized by his prodigious self-fashioning. Plying his pen in self-defense as much as self-definition, Arenas demonstrated a courage that was as tensile and as fragile as a torch song. His writing resists all stable truth, mythologizing not as escapism but to escape dogmatism.

Resonating with postmodernism and magical realism, Arenas's works gained a following outside Cuba—having been smuggled off the island to be published abroad. In 1980, thanks to a bureaucratic error, he left the island for New York, long disillusioned with a regime that branded him a non-person. In the United States, his writing flourished, representing gay experience more explicitly and more polemically (often in contexts such as forced labor camps), and shaping narrative from the tension between political dogma and individual freedom. Arenas's 1990 suicide, following the completion of his *Pentagony* series of novels, *Before Night Falls*, and a volume of poetry about living with AIDS, embodied his message of individual freedom. **SM**

"My message is not a message of failure, but rather one of struggle and hope."

Signature titles

Novels

Hallucinations (El mundo alucinante), 1966

Pentagony (Pentagonia)

- *Singing from the Well (Celestino antes de alba)*, 1967
- *The Palace of the White Skunks (Palacio de las blanquísimas mofetas)*, 1980
- *Farewell to the Sea (Otra vez el mar)*, 1982
- *The Color of Summer (El color de verano)*, 1982
- *The Assault (El asalto)*, 1990

Old Rosa (La vieja Rosa), 1980

Graveyard of the Angels (La loma del angel), 1987

Doorman (Portero), 1990

Autobiography

Before Night Falls (Antes que anochezca), 1992

ABOVE: The Cuban poet and novelist pictured in Paris, France, in 1986.

MICHAEL ONDAATJE

Born: Philip Michael Ondaatje, September 12, 1943 (Colombo, Sri Lanka).

Style and genre: Ondaatje is a Sri Lankan–Canadian, Booker Prize–winning novelist and poet; he is a magician of the local and the intimate, shifting between identities and between rhapsodic fiction and observant poetry.

Signature titles

Novels

Coming Through Slaughter, 1976

Running in the Family, 1982

In the Skin of a Lion, 1987

The English Patient, 1992

Anil's Ghost, 2000

Divisadero, 2007

Poetry

The Collected Works of Billy the Kid, 1970

There's a Trick with a Knife I'm Learning to Do, 1979

The Cinnamon Peeler, 1991

"There's a trick with a knife I'm learning to do." So Michael Ondaatje entitled his 1979 Governor General's Award–winning (GGA) collection of poetry. At thirty-six, Ondaatje had already published three volumes of poetry (collected in *Trick*) and garnered a previous GGA—the most prestigious Canadian literary award, for his verse novel, *The Collected Works of Billy the Kid*, published in 1970.

The finessed knife trick, which runs through Ondaatje's work, is that of the disappearing man, from the unseizable Billy, through Ondaatje senior (recorded in *Running in the Family*), to vanished jazz musician Buddy Bolden in *Coming Through Slaughter*, the faceless, eponymous *English Patient*, the unidentified corpse who is *Anil's Ghost*, and Coop who makes cards and himself disappear in *Divisadero*.

In the Skin of a Lion, the prequel to *The English Patient* and Ondaatje's emblematic work, traces the impression left by what vanishes: here, it is in the weft of connections created by the disappearance of millionaire Ambrose Small. Like both Billy the Kid and Bunny Bolden, Ambrose Small is an historical figure whom Ondaatje makes the absent center of an erotic map of a formational—and formative—Toronto.

"It doubles your perception, to write from the point of view of someone you're not."

Ondaatje's language is delicately intrusive, as much sensing as sensual. Often, it draws on a specific register or practice to reveal a character: bomb defusal is Kip's trick in *The English Patient* as poker is Coop's. Revealing the working of the tricks that isolate these characters positions Ondaatje's work as he plays with the dual etymology of *Divisadero*: both a division, and a place from which things are visible. Ondaatje's knife trick is to take the violent absence or abcess, and show us magic. **SM**

ABOVE: Ondaatje photographed in October 2007.

ALICE WALKER

Born: February 9, 1944 (Eatonton, Georgia, U.S.).

Style and genre: Walker's work is infused with strong themes of feminism, and civil and human rights. She has a hypnotically lyrical writing style and often interweaves ancient African mythology into modern stories.

Known as much for her political activism as her poetry and novels, Alice Walker has become one of the best-loved contemporary American writers. Her work encompasses themes integral to the lives of anyone who has suffered prejudice. Her most famous book, *The Color Purple,* won the Pulitzer Prize and was made into a film; her groundbreaking novel, *Possessing the Secret of Joy,* controversially explored the theme of female genital mutilation in tribal Africa. Walker's poetry delves into both personal and worldwide themes, from her own traumatic experiences of an unwanted pregnancy and suicidal depression to global issues of political corruption.

Walker grew up in a poor family in an America where strict segregation of blacks and whites was still in force. Blind in one eye and facially scarred after a childhood accident, the young Walker was a reclusive, nervous child and adolescent who found her identity through schoolwork. She won a scholarship to Spelman College—a university specifically for black women—in her native Georgia. Later, she transferred to a college in New York and spent a year as an exchange student in Africa, where she fell in love with the continent, particularly its traditions, myths, and folklore—a fascination that has influenced much of her work.

In her early twenties, Walker married a civil rights lawyer (whom she later divorced) and had a daughter (born in 1969). A member of the civil rights movement in the United States during the 1960s—she met Martin Luther King in 1962—and a spokesperson for the anti-apartheid movement, the women's movement, and the anti-nuclear movement, Alice Walker remains a political activist. She lives in California, where she runs her own publishing company, Wild Trees Press. **LH**

"The quietly pacifist peaceful always die to make room for men who shout."

ABOVE: A picture of the writer and political activist Alice Walker taken in 1989.

Signature titles

Novels

The Color Purple, 1983

The Temple of My Familiar, 1989

Possessing the Secret of Joy, 1992

By the Light of My Father's Smile, 1998

Now Is the Time to Open Your Heart, 2004

Short stories

You Can't Keep a Good Woman Down, 1982

The Way Forward Is With a Broken Heart, 2000

Poetry

Goodnight Willie Smith, I'll See You in the Morning, 1979

Horses Make a Landscape Look More Beautiful, 1984

A Poem Traveled Down My Arm, 2005

ARMISTEAD MAUPIN

Born: May 13, 1944 (Washington, D.C., U.S.).

Style and genre: A journalist turned writer, Maupin documents the gay scene and other alternative lifestyles in San Francisco and is best known for his series *Tales of the City,* which started off as a newspaper serial.

Signature titles

Novels

Tales of the City, 1978
More Tales of the City, 1980
Further Tales of the City, 1982
Babycakes, 1984
Significant Others, 1987
Sure of You, 1989
Maybe the Moon, 1992
The Night Listener, 2000
Michael Tolliver Lives, 2007

Like the works of a queer Dickens of San Francisco, Maupin's *Tales of the City* is both invaluable social document and irrepressible celebration. It is not just the breathlessly observant descriptions—and the grueling schedule of a weekly newspaper serial—that mark the series as the work of a former journalist. Vietnam veteran Armistead Maupin may have sharpened his pen in the conservative press in North Carolina during the turbulent late 1960s, but it was a move to San Francisco in 1971 that liberated both pen and man.

Like his best-loved *Tales* character, Michael "Mouse" Tolliver, Maupin came from a staunchly conservative family, discovering his sexuality in his mid twenties. Within three years of his move to San Francisco, Maupin was turning his ear for reportage to the celebrities, post-hippies, protoyuppies, queers, and roller-skating nuns of his adopted city. In pot-smoking landlady Anna Madrigal, Maupin created a transgender heroine who was "mother of us all." She oversaw an alternative family of boarders that readers worldwide have adopted (or been adopted into) for over thirty years, with 2007 seeing the belated publication of a seventh novel, *Michael Tolliver Lives*. The title's significance

ABOVE: Maupin snapped in 2006 at the after party for the movie *The Night Listener*.

RIGHT: Maupin laughs with Terry Anderson, co-screenwriter of *The Night Listener* (2006).

ABOVE: Maupin and Terry Anderson, with whom he had a twelve-year relationship.

is perhaps in its unsaid—"With AIDS." From the fourth book of the series (*Babycakes*) on, Maupin was among the first to chronicle the so-called "gay plague" as it struck the bathhouses, clubs, and characters who were his central subjects. Never afraid of controversy, Maupin adapted the first *Tales* novel for American public television network PBS in 1993. The miniseries achieved both the network's highest rating for a dramatic program and enough complaints about onscreen nudity, gay sex, and drug use for it to drop plans to adapt the sequels.

America's pay cable network Showtime screened *More* and *Further Tales* in 1998 and 2001 respectively, and Maupin's novel *The Night Listener* was made into a 2006 feature film starring Toni Collette and Robin Williams. *The Night Listener*'s protagonist, gay radio serialist Gabriel Noone, offers a profound insight into the world of a much-loved writer whose passion lies in telling the truth—even when the truth is fiction. **SM**

Truth and Fiction

Maupin is famous for eliding the gap between truth and fiction in his work, not least in the case of his name, which (although real) is an anagram of "Is a Man I Dreamt Up." Mouse's brief affair with a movie star in *Further Tales* is based on Maupin's own relationship with Rock Hudson. *Maybe the Moon* is an imagined autobiography of Tamara de Treaux, the dwarf actor who played E.T., while *The Night Listener* concerns the Antony Godby Johnson hoax, a traumatized HIV-positive adolescent with whom Maupin corresponded, and who turned out to be his adoptive mother's literary invention.

W. G. SEBALD

Born: Winfried Georg Maximilian Sebald, May 18, 1944 (Wertach im Allgäu, Germany); died December 14, 2001 (Norfolk, England).

Genre and style: Sebald's elegiac novels focus on personal and collective memory using a mixture of fiction, history, and half-remembered images.

W. G. Sebald, known as Max, was born in a village high up in the mountains in the Bavarian Alps during World War II. His father returned home a stranger following his release from a prisoner-of-war camp in France in 1947 and never spoke of his wartime experiences. Silence, memory, and Germany's past were to become central themes of Sebald's writing.

Sebald studied German literature at Freiburg University and graduated in 1965. He then moved to the United Kingdom to become a "lektor" at the University of Manchester and in 1970 was awarded a lectureship in German at the newly created University of East Anglia (U.E.A.). In 1987, he was appointed as chair of German literature at U.E.A. and in 1989 became the founding director of the British Center for Literary Translation.

It was not until Sebald was in his forties that he began to write the highly idiosyncratic novels that brought him international recognition. He created a new literary form—part novel, part travelog, part memoir, and part documentary. There is little dialogue, no paragraphs, and no chapters, and these melancholic works are scattered with black-and-white images—old photographs, newspaper cuttings, and postcards—that add to their dream-like quality. Despite spending more than half his life in England, Sebald wrote his novels only in German and claimed not to trust himself to translate them. Three of his four novels—*Vertigo*, *The Emigrants,* and *Austerlitz*—explore the collective past of Europe, while *The Rings of Saturn* is a meditation, told in fragments, of one man's walk through the East Anglian landscape. Sebald was acclaimed by literary critics and was beginning to find a wider readership when he was killed in a car crash in Norfolk in 2001. **HJ**

"... those who have no memory have the ... greater chance to lead happy lives."

Signature titles

Novels

Vertigo (Schwindel Gefühle), 1990

The Emigrants (Die Ausgewanderten: Vier Lange Erzahlungen), 1992

The Rings of Saturn (Die Ringe Der Saturn: Eine Englische Walfahrt), 1995

Austerlitz, 2001

Poetry

For Years Now, 2001

After Nature (Nach der Natur), 2002

The Unrecounted (Unerzählt), 2003 (published posthumously)

ABOVE: Sebald pictured in 1999; he did not begin to write until in his forties.

JOHN BANVILLE

Born: December 8, 1945 (Wexford, Ireland).

Style and genre: Banville is an Irish author of intricate allusive prose filled with word play and black humor; he is known for tightly constructed novels echoing larger philosophical questions and is also the author of mysteries by "Benjamin Black."

In some ways, Banville's novels tell the same story over and over again, about the vagaries of perception and representation, and the slippery nature of selfhood. He spends his early novels digesting metaphysical ideas; four novels examining scientists (Copernicus, Kepler, Newton, and a mathematician named Swan in *Mefisto*); and a loose trilogy following an artist-murderer trying to come to terms with his crime (*The Book of Evidence*, *Ghosts*, *Athena*). All these works are densely allusive, not only of each other, but of literary classics, from *The Tempest* to Banville's idols Nabokov and Proust. What connects all his work is a desire to give his prose "the kind of denseness and thickness that poetry has."

Banville never went to college, and left home at a young age to work at Aer Lingus, the national airline of the Irish Republic. This gave him the opportunity to become extremely well traveled, and, like his hero Beckett, he writes as comfortably about continental settings as he does about Ireland. *Shroud*, for example, the story of a literary theorist with a secret past, lucidly evokes the city of Turin. The privileged landscape of his novels, however, is the psyche of artists and people who think about art, and in his Booker Prize–winner *The Sea*, an elderly art historian returns to the seaside cottage where he spent his childhood summers to mourn the death of his wife. In his Booker speech, Banville said: "When I started writing I was a great rationalist and believed I was absolutely in control. But the older one gets, the more confused, and for an artist I think that is quite a good thing: you allow in more of your instinctual self; your dreams, fantasies, and memories. It's richer, in a way." Banville has also published mysteries under the pseudonym Benjamin Black. **CQ**

"Writers are just like other people, except slightly more obsessed."

Signature titles

Novels

Long Lowkin, 1970
Doctor Copernicus, 1976
Kepler, 1981
The Newton Letter, 1982
Mefisto, 1986
The Book of Evidence, 1989
Ghosts, 1993
Athena, 1995
Shroud, 2004
The Sea, 2005

As Benjamin Black

Christine Falls, 2006
The Silver Swan, 2007
The Lemur, 2008

ABOVE: The Irish writer John Banville pictured in May 2007.

JULIAN BARNES

Born: January 19, 1946 (Leicester, England).

Style and genre: Barnes is a British novelist, essayist, and journalist known for his cool irony, playfulness with form and convention, and what Joyce Carol Oates called his "pre-postmodern humanism."

Julian Barnes has said of his creative process that "in order to write, you have to convince yourself that it's a new departure not only for you but for the entire history of the novel." This tenet has served him well, as each book he produces makes him more difficult to categorize as a writer. As Martin Amis put it: "What he's really good at is creating a suspense through themes and ideas, which is very rare."

Barnes's parents were both French teachers, and he himself is a conspicuous Francophile. In his first (and only semiautobiographical) novel, *Metroland*, a furiously bored and striving teenager makes his way to Paris during the upheavals of 1968; *Cross Channel* is a collection of stories about England's relationship with France; and *Something to Declare* gathers essays on the same topic. But it is in *Flaubert's Parrot*, Barnes's third and breakthrough novel, that English restraint and French flamboyance collide in the most inventive way. A crazy hybrid of forms, from bestiary to examination paper, the novel catalogues a retired doctor's obsession with the biographical trivia surrounding the author of *Madame Bovary*, only gradually exposing the grief that drives his literary ecstasies.

Julian Barnes's command of voice and form is obvious in the convention-challenging range of some of his other novels: *A History of the World in 10½ Chapters* is a collage of fantasy, revisionist history, and art criticism (the half chapter is a lengthy "parenthesis" on the writer's love for his wife); *England, England* is a satire of British amusement-park sensibility, set in the near future; *Arthur and George* is the imaginative exploration of a forgotten moment in British history, when the creator of Sherlock Holmes is called upon to defend a wrongly accused solicitor. All his work is an eloquent combination of languid irony and emotional perspicuity, and the themes of love, betrayal, and the nature of truth and authenticity. **CQ**

Signature titles

Novels

Metroland, 1980
Before She Met Me, 1982
Flaubert's Parrot, 1984
Staring at the Sun, 1986
A History of the World in 10½ Chapters, 1989
Talking it Over, 1991
The Porcupine, 1992
England, England, 1998
Love, etc, 2000
Arthur and George, 2005
Nothing To Be Frightened Of, 2008

Short stories

Cross Channel, 1996
The Lemon Table, 2004

Essay

Something to Declare, 2002

As Dan Kavanagh

Duffy, 1980
Fiddle City, 1981
Putting the Boot In, 1985
Going to the Dogs, 1987

ABOVE: A portrait photograph of author Julian Barnes in his home.

RIGHT: *Metroland's* cover artwork, recalling London Underground posters of the 1920s.

METROLAND

Julian Barnes

JAMES KELMAN

Born: June 9, 1946 (Glasgow, Scotland).

Style and genre: A novelist, short-story writer, and playwright, Kelman's depictions of working-class Scottish life, themes of alienation, and social commentary on bourgeois society uses Glaswegian dialect, monologue, and rhythmic prose.

The angry voice, sense of alienation, use of internal monologue by his characters, and almost impenetrable language of James Kelman's novels and short stories have drawn comparisons to Samuel Beckett, James Joyce, and Franz Kafka.

Raised in Glasgow, in his teens Kelman emigrated to the United States with his family, but he later returned to Scotland. He read the usual stories for a young boy of that era before coming to realize that scenes of working-class Scottish life and the language of the Glasgow tenement were absent in fiction. A left-wing campaigner for social justice, Kelman seems to regard this as an almost political act on the part of a capitalist, bourgeois society. He gives life to that voice, and has become almost a contemporary Robert Burns in bringing the lilt of the Scottish language to the page, peppered frequently with the vernacular. His work reveals the life of the downtrodden, embittered man in the pub with a pint in his hand, the trials of urban life on the dole, and having to be an opportunist to make a living.

Kelman studied philosophy at Strathclyde University, but left before completing the course. In 1971, he joined a writing group at the University of Glasgow, and went on to write his first collection of short stories, *An Old Pub Near the Angel*. He came to public acclaim in 1994 with his novel *How Late it Was, How Late*, which somewhat contentiously won the Booker Prize. It tells the story of an unemployed Glaswegian and petty criminal who wakes up in a police cell. Kelman moved out of familiar territory with *Translated Accounts*, where his characters live under martial law in an unnamed state, but once again, he portrays the dispossessed and explores the politicization of language. **CK**

"He is the Cooler King of Scottish prose."
—Tim Adams, *The Observer*

Signature titles

Novels

The Busconductor Hines, 1984
A Chancer, 1985
A Disaffection, 1989
How Late it Was, How Late, 1994
Translated Accounts, 2001
You Have to Be Careful in the Land of the Free, 2004
Kieron Smith, Boy, 2008

Short stories

An Old Pub Near the Angel, 1973
Not Not While the Giro, 1983
Greyhound for Breakfast, 1987

Plays

Hardie and Baird and Other Plays, 1991

ABOVE: James Kelman in a photograph taken in 1994.

PHILIP PULLMAN

Born: October 19, 1946 (Norwich, Norfolk, England).

Style and genre: Pullman is a pedagogue with a flair for otherworldly histories and historical otherworlds; his Milton-for-children *His Dark Materials* series stirred hearts, minds, and Catholic controversy.

There are few characters in contemporary literature more appealing and resonant than Lyra Belacqua, the courageous, inventive, effervescent heroine of Philip Pullman's *His Dark Materials* series. The trilogy takes as its raw material Satan's journey in Milton's *Paradise Lost* and begins in a world like ours; yet it deviates when John Calvin becomes Pope of a theological Enlightenment, and when his Satanic figure, Lord Asriel, astonishes a group of academics with the claim that Dust (evidence of original sin) is also the heretical evidence that other universes exist—and can be reached. Lyra, Asriel's sheltered niece, follows her uncle to the end of the Earth and achieves what he could only dream of—entering another universe to bring Death to an end.

Called Silvertongue by the armored bear who elects himself her protector, Lyra embodies what Pullman clearly conceives as the highest calling, that of the storyteller—by which he does not mean "fantasist." Indeed, the narrator remarks that Lyra, like all good liars, lacks imagination. At her most triumphant moment, Lyra harrows Hell by telling the harpies who guard the dead piquantly true stories of her experiences in the material world. It is this sensory and sensual world that Pullman's novels bring vividly to life, with young characters who are not only brave and loyal, but also pragmatic, wounded, and staunchly real. In Sally Lockhart, the protagonist of an earlier series set in a mock-Dickensian London, Pullman presents a sharp-shooting, book-balancing orphan of the Indian mutiny, a proto-New Woman with a talent for detective work and forming an alternative family. Like Lyra, she learns to unlock her heart through the stories she tells and is told, inviting the reader to do the same. **SM**

"Men pass in front of our eyes like butterflies, creatures of a brief season."

Signature titles

Children's fiction

Sally Lockhart
- *The Ruby in the Smoke*, 1985
- *The Shadow in the North*, 1986
- *The Tiger in the Well*, 1991
- *The Tin Princess*, 1994

The White Mercedes, 1992 (republished as *The Butterfly Tattoo*, 2001)

The Firework-Maker's Daughter, 1995

His Dark Materials
- *Northern Lights (The Golden Compass)*, 1995
- *The Subtle Knife*, 1997
- *The Amber Spyglass*, 2000

Lyra's Oxford, 2003

ABOVE: Philip Pullman, expert creator of other worlds, pictured in November 2003.

ELFRIEDE JELINEK

Born: October 20, 1946 (Mürzzuschlag, Austria)

Style and genre: Jelinek is a highly controversial playwright and novelist who uses controlled, biting satire and often-shocking content to critique the sexual and societal oppressions of contemporary life.

An extremely politicized left-wing feminist, Jelinek has long been a thorn in the side of conventional Austrian society. Some passionately opposed her 2004 Nobel Prize in Literature, and her novel *Lust* has been described as pornographic. She has even been accused of treason, for her criticism of right-wing government ministers. One contradiction of Jelinek as a person is her sensitive, anxious, phobia-prone introversion on one hand, and her combative spirit on the other.

In Jelinek's view, the great fight is against the patriarchal repression of women, the overly restrictive Austrian mind-set (especially within Austrian Catholicism), empty political rhetoric, and crass commercialism. Other targets are violence, control, and discrimination—especially classism, nationalism, and racism, which she often links with Austria's Nazi past.

Jelinek, who published her first novel in 1970, comes from a part-Jewish background and attended a convent school and university in Vienna. She also undertook musical training as a child at the Vienna Conservatory and is often praised for the musicality of her prose. Other literary qualities include acidic irony and an experimental layering of language. Her characters seem like empty husks in a brutally deconstructed world where she suggests no clear solutions. She says her language aims to offer up possibilities for an escape from oppression without dictating which path should be taken. Jelinek's typical creation is the woman enslaved within a domestic setting, such as the sado-masochistic Erika in *The Piano Teacher* (made into a controversial film in 2001), a mature woman still living with her controlling mother. *Bambiland* blends CNN news reports of the Iraq war with Greek tragedy to comment on contemporary politics and the media. **AK**

"I don't do what I do willingly, but I have to do it."

Signature titles

Novels

We're Decoys, Baby! (Wir sind Lockvögel Baby!), 1970

Women as Lovers (Die Liebhaberinnen), 1975

Wonderful, Wonderful Times (Die Ausgesperrten), 1980

The Piano Teacher (Die Klavierspielerin), 1983

Lust, 1989

Plays

What Happened After Nora Left Her Husband; or Pillars of Society (Was geschah, nachdem Nora ihren Mann verlassen hatte oder Stützen der Gesellschaften), 1980

Bambiland, 2003

ABOVE: A photograph of Elfriede Jelinek taken in October 1997.

PAUL AUSTER

Born: February 3,1947 (Newark, New Jersey).

Style and genre: Auster is known for labyrinthine theoretical novels with deceptively simple surfaces and existential detective fiction all with an overarching concern for coincidence, chance, and the unexpected in everyday experience.

Brooklyn-based writer Paul Auster reacquaints readers with the essential strangeness of writing. In his novels, characters impersonate one another, represent aspects of an absent individual, are named "Paul Auster," represent what they are not, or write fictions whose plots reveal more about their author than the author's own narration, or that refer back to the reader's own reality. He uses fiction to investigate the implications of post-modernism for the relation between writing and the writer. The realization that we have no direct access to reality means that the writer is cut off from truly knowing himself. Because the writer is inherently "other" to himself, in *City of Glass* and *The Invention of Solitude* the consideration of the self from the outside makes possible a more intimate form of autobiography.

Auster's notion of writing as rooted in struggle has both biographical and philosophical origins. In "White Spaces," the thing that eludes us is what "propels us into speech"—writing is the record of the struggle to bridge the gap between words and the objects they represent. However, Auster's career began with years of poverty, in which writing meant voluntary misery on a practical level. After leaving graduate school at Columbia, Auster took on an array of odd jobs in order to pay the bills while leaving time to write. He lived for a time in Paris, earning his living as a translator. Creative attempts at bringing in cash included a detective novel, an attempt at a pornographic novel (thankfully abandoned), the invention of a card game, and numerous translating, editing, and ghostwriting projects. Auster's novels attempt to break down the boundary between living and writing, but in doing so they reveal a reciprocal incompatibility between the two spheres. **ER**

"Who are you? And if you think you know, why do you keep lying about it?"—*City of Glass*

Signature titles

Novels

The New York Trilogy

City of Glass, 1985

Ghosts, 1986

The Locked Room, 1986

In the Country of Last Things, 1987

Oracle Night, 2003

The Brooklyn Follies, 2005

Man in the Dark, 2008

Essays

The invention of Solitude, 1982

The Art of Hunger, 1982

Screenplays

The Music of Chance, 1993

Smoke, 1995

ABOVE: Auster photographed at a literary gala in New York in April 2005.

SALMAN RUSHDIE

Born: Ahmed Salman Rushdie, June 19, 1947 (Bombay [now Mumbai], India).

Style and genre: Rushdie is an Indian-born author most famous for his patchwork use of Hindu legend, Islamic theology, and the classics of Western literature to "write back" to both the British Empire and the political chaos left in its wake.

Salman Rushdie grew up in the Kashmir region of the Indian subcontinent. Though today the region is polarized by an ongoing feud for possession between India and Pakistan, Rushdie has said in an interview that he remembers it in his childhood mostly as a place of religious tolerance.

All of Rushdie's writing can be characterized by a desire to bring this trait of his native country to the world at large. His experimental combinations of disparate symbols, modes, dialects, and allusions are grounded in an attempt to find a new shared experience, in a world that no longer helps us distinguish between ourselves and everyone else. Rushdie is a spokesperson for the transnational experience, whose

Signature titles

Novels

Grimus, 1975

Midnight's Children, 1981

Shame, 1983

The Satanic Verses, 1988

The Moor's Last Sigh, 1995

The Ground Beneath Her Feet, 1999

Shalimar the Clown, 2005

Children's fiction

Haroun and the Sea of Stories, 1990

Nonfiction

The Jaguar Smile, 1987

Imaginary Homelands: Essays and Criticism 1981–1991, 1991

Step Across This Line: Collected Nonfiction 1992–2002, 2002

ABOVE: Rushdie photographed in 2005 at the Edinburgh International Book Festival.

RIGHT: Rushdie poses in 1988 beneath a framed Indian textile in his London home.

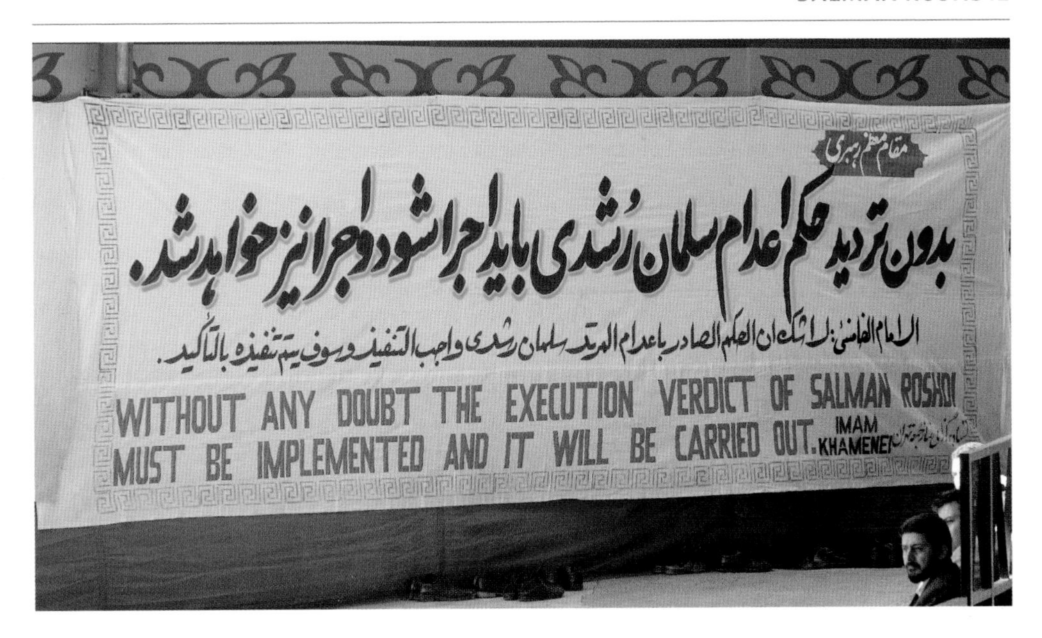

ABOVE: A 2004 banner in Tehran, Iran, confirms Ayatollah Khomeini's 1989 fatwa.

restlessly experimental fiction constantly looks for new ways to undermine the old dichotomies between East and West, progressive and fundamentalist, colonized and colonizer, by showing how he himself, in spite of his self-contradictions, can nonetheless stand as a model for a new kind of coherence.

It was with his second novel, *Midnight's Children*, that Rushdie made his first indelible imprint on the literary world. The novel is a fabulistic allegory of India's independence that cleverly reworks the narrative of Laurence Sterne's *Tristram Shandy*: the "Midnight's Children" of the title are the 1,001 people born at midnight on the first official night of India's independence, in 1947, and whose fortunes are intimately intertwined with the then-fledgling democracy. Rushdie himself was also born in 1947, and there are several autobiographical elements to the story. This combination of disparate sources contributes a good deal to the feeling that Rushdie's readers are witnessing the birth of a new world of

"To be Kashmiri was to value what was shared far more highly than what was divided."

The Fatwa

When the Ayatollah Khomeini of Iran called on faithful Muslims to assassinate Salman Rushdie for what was interpreted as the blasphemous nature of *The Satanic Verses*, the threat was not idle. Bookstores were firebombed, effigies of the author were burned, and the novel's Japanese translator was stabbed to death. A 1989 Hezbollah bombing in Britain seems to have been an attempt on Rushdie's life, and Britain broke diplomatic ties with Iran over the issue in the same year. For almost a decade, Rushdie stopped making public appearances and he still travels with a large security retinue.

In 1998, as a precondition for renewing diplomatic relations with Britain, Iran backed down from its stance. Though the fatwa is still valid and Rushdie's life is still in danger, the author's assassination is no longer an official goal of the Iranian government. Even before this breakthrough, Rushdie had relaxed his security measures, even participating in a gag on the *David Letterman Show* in 1995 (the idea being that Letterman's ratings were so low, that Rushdie thought it would be a good place to hide). Rushdie has called the experience "a degree course in worthlessness, my own personal and specific worthlessness."

fiction. The novel won the Booker Prize, and in 1993 was honored with the "Booker of Bookers," as the best novel to have won the Booker in the twenty-five years of the prize's existence. Rushdie's subsequent fiction has similarly used surreal and phantasmagoric means to explore his key issues. *Shame*, set in a fictional, fun-house Pakistan, fictionalizes that country's history as a family drama; *The Satanic Verses* is an apocalyptic allegory of the battle between good and evil, faith and fanaticism; *Haroun and the Sea of Stories* began as a bathtime story for Rushdie's son, but ultimately became a meditation on the role of the artist; and *The Ground Beneath Her Feet* is the Orpheus myth, reimagined as the lives of Indian-born rock stars. In *Shalimar the Clown*, Rushdie returns to his key political issues with new urgency, as extremism threatens to overwhelm the polyvocal pluralism that underwrites both his narrative method and his politics. Though these summaries convey something of the comic inventiveness that gives these novels their appeal, underlying them all is the same ethical imperative to respect difference without resorting to brutality, and the same sadness that this imperative is rarely heeded.

Rushdie's novel *The Satanic Verses* was to have major political consequences. The novel contains a fictional reworking of an apocryphal event from Muslim history, involving the prophet Muhammad. Interpreted by hard-line Islamicists as sacrilegious, this depiction of the prophet led to an explosion of controversy, culminating in a fatwa issued by the Ayatollah Khomeini of Iran calling for Rushdie's assassination.

Bolstered in part by the clash of civilizations that erupted over *The Satanic Verses*, Rushdie has become a genuine literary superstar, to such a degree that it could reasonably be asked whether any other living author deserves the name. Rushdie has used this status as an outspoken critic of both militant Islam and U.S. involvement in the Middle East, a combination of stances that has left him alienated from almost everyone. But then again, Rushdie has always stood with one foot on either side of a fault line, and tried to convince his readers that they should do the same. **SY**

PAULO COELHO

Born: August 24, 1947 (Rio de Janeiro, Brazil).

Style and genre: A Brazilian author concerned with spiritual enlightenment and personal fulfillment, Paulo Coelho advocates having the courage to recognize and realize your dreams.

Paulo Coelho's books should be seen in the context of his personal journey toward spiritual understanding and self-acceptance. While he does not advocate any one faith as "correct," his broad religious themes draw on elements of Catholicism, Eastern mysticism, and indigenous Latin American Earth worship. As a young man, he rebelled against his rigid Jesuit schooling and family's wish that he study engineering, and was committed to a psychiatric hospital. Later, Coelho followed the hippie trail around Peru, Bolivia, and Mexico, before finding success writing lyrics for Brazilian rock stars. His plans to found a radical Alternative Society in Minas Gerais were viewed as subversive by the military dictatorship, and he was imprisoned and tortured.

In 1986, Coelho traveled the ancient Spanish pilgrims' path to Santiago de Compostela; this incredible experience formed the basis of *The Pilgrimage*, which suggests that meaning and truth are to be found in simplicity, and celebrates the extraordinary in the everyday. The existential questions raised in *The Alchemist*, conversations with "the inner child of [his] soul," resonated with millions, and the novel became an international best-seller during the 1990s. Coelho's election to the Brazilian Academy of Letters in July 2002 was controversial; despite mass market popularity, his works have been criticized by some as poorly written, overly reliant on external sources, and more akin to self-help books than literature. Others praise his profoundly moving humanist and universal message. In fluid prose he offers guidance and meditations for a happier, more fulfilling life, inviting readers to become "warriors of light" and embark on their own spiritual journey, analyzing less and feeling more. **MK**

"When we are high up, everything looks very small."

—*The Fifth Mountain*

ABOVE: Coelho pictured during a photo shoot in August 2003.

Signature titles

Novels

The Pilgrimage, 1987
The Alchemist, 1988
The Greatest Gift, 1991
The Valkyries, 1992
By the River Piedra I Sat Down and Wept, 1994
The Fifth Mountain, 1996
Veronika Decides to Die, 1998
The Devil and Miss Prym, 2000
Eleven Minutes, 2003
The Zahir, 2005
The Witch of Portobello, 2006

Anthologies

The Manual of the Warrior of Light, 1997
Like the Flowing River, 2006

STEPHEN KING

Born: September 21, 1947 (Portland, Maine, U.S.).

Style and genre: King's works typically focus on supernatural events occurring within inauspicious locations, with the main characters cast as outsiders who achieve revenge. His blistering pace of plot is tempered with chilling suspense.

The best-selling author of more than fifty novels, and synonymous with the horror fiction genre, Stephen King is the master of exploiting everyday fears in the reader by creating extraordinary events within realistic settings.

While working as an English teacher, King published his first novel, *Carrie*, the story of a high-school outsider who is bullied and tormented but who gradually discovers that she has telekinetic powers, which she uses against her tormentors. The work became a huge overnight success, allowing King to concentrate on his writing full-time. *Carrie* exhibited the recurring motif for much of his subsequent novels—the idyllic small town that suffers inexplicable supernatural forces. In *Salem's Lot*, two boys in a small New England town are terrorized by vampires, and in the mammoth *It*, a monstrous child-killer strikes fear throughout a fictional Maine town.

Another popular prop in King's novels is the writer as main character. The violent, alcoholic would-be writer Jack Torrance in *The Shining* is interrupted in his work by evil spirits in a haunted hotel, gradually losing his sanity and life. *Misery* tells the sinister tale of the novelist Paul Sheldon rescued from a car crash by his number-one fan, Annie Wilkes, who kidnaps him and forces him through torturous methods to write another book. King has frequently delved into fantasy and science fiction genres, most notably with *The Green Mile*, a six-volume collection set on the death row of a 1930s penitentiary, and the seven books of *The Dark Tower* series, which chronicle the adventures of the Gunslinger, who exists in a desolate world parallel to our own. King was the 2003 recipient of The National Book Foundation Medal for Distinguished Contribution to American Letters. **SG**

"Only enemies speak the truth; friends and lovers lie endlessly, caught in the web of duty."

Signature titles

Novels

Carrie, 1974
Salem's Lot, 1975
The Shining, 1977
The Stand, 1978
The Dead Zone, 1979
Cujo, 1981
Christine, 1983
It, 1986
Misery, 1987
The Green Mile, 1996
The Dark Tower (series), 1982–2004

Short stories

Skeleton Crew, 1985

ABOVE: Stephen King pictured at the Sundance Film Festival in 2006.

DAVID MAMET

Born: November 30, 1947 (Chicago, Illinois, U.S.).

Style and genre: Best known for his often aphoristic dialogue that swings from the blunt to the baroque, from the ornate to the plain ornery. Mamet's drama contains lines of irresistible linguistic vitality and highly stylized expressions of character.

David Mamet is one of America's most celebrated and prolific playwrights, as well as one of its harshest critics. His plays frequently portray, in startling, cringe-inducing detail, the intimate consequences of sweeping societal debasement. His most memorable creations—Ricky Roma from *Glengarry Glen Ross*, Don Dubrow, Bobby, and Teach from *American Buffalo*, Bernie from *Sexual Perversity in Chicago*—live in a facile and tawdry America whose founding principle of personal opportunity has become a license for selfishness. From this corruption of national identity flow all the sexual, economic, and political perversions that surface in his plays.

While it is sometimes argued that Mamet's works do not sufficiently observe the requirements of conventional plotting, much of his best work is underwritten by a recognizable pattern of collective degeneration, in which some flashpoint of social alienation (for example, the raucously amoral capitalism of *Glengarry Glen Ross*) leads to a more local, personal vision of tragedy. He populates his stage with hucksters, creeps, and small-time crooks, united by their passion for salesmanship, which always amounts to the selling of a particular self.

Mamet fashions characters who are difficult to identify with or even tolerate, morally speaking, but who are nevertheless overflowing with an irresistible linguistic vitality. Audiences frequently praise the "realism" of his urban rhythms, although his lines are actually tightly controlled and highly stylized expressions of character. His language also has intoxicating beauty. Mamet is by turns disgusted and depressed with the moral, intellectual, and even physical corruption of his society—yet never has the decline of an empire been so much fun. **IW**

Signature titles

Plays

The Duck Variations, 1972
Sexual Perversity in Chicago, 1974
American Buffalo, 1977
The Woods, 1977
Edmond, 1982
Glengarry Glen Ross, 1983
The Shawl, 1985
Speed-the-Plow, 1988
Oleanna, 1992
The Cryptogram, 1994

Nonfiction

Writing in Restaurants, 1986
A Whore's Profession: Notes and Essays, 1994
On Acting, 1999

"Every reiteration of the idea that nothing matters debases the human spirit."

ABOVE: A photograph of David Mamet taken in Venice *c.* 2001.

JAMES ELLROY

Born: Lee Earle Ellroy, March 4, 1948 (Los Angeles, California, U.S.).

Style and genre: Ellroy is a revisionist writer of hard-boiled crime fiction whose novels have plots so Byzantine, characters so desperate, and syntax so clipped that they make Raymond Chandler look like Henry James.

You could argue that James Ellroy's autobiography, *My Dark Places*, is the most hard-boiled book he ever wrote. It describes, in heartbreaking detail, the sensational murder of Ellroy's mother when he was ten; his uneasy adolescence, growing up with his irreponsible father; and the toll that these experiences took on him as an adult, including addictions that were typical (drugs, alcohol), untypical (breaking and entering) and, fortunately for his readers, formative (crime novels).

Ellroy was already an established writer when he turned to a subject near to his heart: the murder of the so-called "Black Dahlia," an unknown Hollywood actress whose body was discovered around the same time as Ellroy's mother. Ellroy's fictionalized account of this murder kicked off the series of novels for which he is still best known, *The L.A. Quartet*. These four novels all take place in the same Los Angeles of the 1950s, and characters and plotlines overlap from book to book. The gritty underbelly of the City of Angels emerges from briefly sketched, unobtrusive details, without ever retreading the territory already mapped out by Raymond Chandler and Nathaniel West. Ellroy not only has a native's knowledge of the city, but evokes without overplaying the brutal power politics and racism that characterized law enforcement in the decades after the Iron Curtain and before internal affairs.

Ellroy's subsequent novels have applied this mentality of brutal expediency to the national stage, fictionalizing the Kennedy assassination and its aftermath. Although something is lost when Ellroy gives up the immediacy of his Los Angeles setting for the national stage, he reveals himself to be at the height of his narrative powers, setting up dozens of plot lines and characters that almost miraculously resolve. **SY**

Signature titles

Novels

L.A. Quartet
- *The Black Dahlia*, 1987
- *The Big Nowhere*, 1988
- *L.A. Confidential*, 1990
- *White Jazz*, 1992

American Underworld Trilogy
- *American Tabloid*, 1995
- *The Cold Six Thousand*, 2001
- *Blood's a Rover*, 2008

Short stories

Hollywood Nocturnes, 1994
Crime Wave, 1999

Autobiography

My Dark Places, 1996

"I am a master of fiction. I am also the greatest crime writer who ever lived."

ABOVE: A portrait of gritty crime writer Ellroy taken in September 2006.

IAN McEWAN

Born: June 21, 1948 (Aldershot, Hampshire, England).

Style and genre: McEwan is a British author of pitiless psychological realism whose work features exacting detail and threatening atmospheres against a backdrop of historical events. He is particularly interested in the relation between the sexes.

Ian McEwan's novels and short stories are known for their intense psychological portraits of protagonists thrust into extraordinary circumstances—be they violent, romantic, or both—that disrupt their sense of themselves and sometimes of reality itself. McEwan's stories often focus on a moment of ethical choice, exploring not just the difficult decision itself, but the question that follows: How does one live with it? The answer is often wrapped up in what one critic aptly described as "the art of unease."

McEwan's work can be divided into two periods: he earned the moniker "Ian Macabre" for his dark and claustrophobic early work, which is filled with incest, murder, and sadomasochism. *The Cement Garden*, for example, follows three children who decide to bury their dead mother in the basement, to avoid being taken into care. In *The Comfort of Strangers*, an English couple vacationing in Venice come under the spell of a charismatic local, who puts not just their comfort but also their lives at risk.

With his subsequent novels, McEwan seemed to have experienced a change of heart, perhaps because, as he put it, after having children, "you find that whether you like it or not, you have a huge investment in the human project somehow succeeding." McEwan's later work is frequently set against the backdrop of historical eras and events: the aftermath of World War II in *The Innocent* and *Black Dogs*; an only slightly exaggerated Thatcherite England in *The Child in Time*; the shadow of terrorism in *Saturday*. *Atonement*, his most challenging and ambitious novel, ranges from a prewar upper-class household to the disastrous retreat at Dunkirk in 1940, to London in 1999. **CQ**

"One has to have the courage of one's pessimism."
—Ian McEwan, *Guardian*, 1983

Signature titles

Novels
The Cement Garden, 1978
The Comfort of Strangers, 1981
The Child in Time, 1987
The Innocent, 1990
Black Dogs, 1992
Enduring Love, 1997
Amsterdam, 1998
Atonement, 2001
Saturday, 2005

Short stories
First Love, Last Rites, 1975
In Between the Sheets, 1978

Novella
On Chesil Beach, 2007

ABOVE: Ian McEwan photographed in 2007, the year *On Chesil Beach* was published.

PASCAL QUIGNARD

Born: April 23, 1948 (Verneuil-sur-Arve, France).

Style and genre: Quignard is an award-winning French writer known for his erudite and iconoclastic approach to fiction, his experimentation with writing styles, and his melding of other disciplines with his writing.

Pascal Quignard is well regarded in France for ambitious and distinctive work that follows, loosely, in the tradition of other writer-thinkers such as Bataille and Blanchot. He aims for what he calls a "genre-free" literature—not, however, in order to create a new or hybrid genre, but to instigate a dialogue, involving both collaboration and contest, between fictional invention and critical modes of thought (from anthropology to psychoanalysis, and beyond). Quignard has won a number of prestigious awards, including the Prix Goncourt (2002) for *In Front of My Hermitage*. Nevertheless, he is probably best known for *All the World's Mornings*, a novel about the seventeenth-century viol player and composer Marin Marais, which was turned into a feature film in the early 1990s.

Quignard has had a distinguished and varied career: philosopher, professor, musician and musicologist, translator (from Latin, Greek, and Chinese), and editor. These diverse interests inform the scope and shape of his work, with its characteristic mixture of elements of fiction, theory, journal, dream, poetry, essay, citation, and aphorism. His novels are unconventional in their narrative structures and polyvocality. *In Front of My Hermitage* is, like much of Quignard's work, built upon the principle of fragmentation, with its series of narrative sketches or extracts that neither begin nor conclude. Quignard described it as "a sequence of beginnings of novels, stories, landscapes, autobiographical fragments." Though some readers have found this approach alienating, Quignard puts it at the center of his project: "To write, I seek the succession of scenes without connection so as not to interpret for the reader. . . . Fragments of life are always more moving." **ST**

"To experience as thought something that is trying to find expression."—*Les Ombres errantes*

Signature titles

Novels

Carus, 1979

The Salon in Wurttemberg: A Novel (Le Salon du Wurtemberg), 1986

A Technical Difficulty Concerning Fragments (Une gêne technique à l'égard des fragments), 1986

The Stairways of Chambord (Les Escaliers de Chambord), 1989

All the World's Mornings (Tous les matins du monde), 1991

Sex and Terror (Le Sexe et l'effroi), 1994

Hatred of Music (La Haine de la musique), 1996

In Front of My Hermitage (Les Ombres errantes), 2002

ABOVE: Quignard, pictured here in 1989, is also a musicologist and a philosopher.

PATRICK SÜSKIND

Born: March 26, 1949 (Ambach am Starnberger See, Bavaria, Germany).

Style and genre: Writer of novels, plays, essays, and screenplays, Süskind is known for his quirky, existential tales of obsession and the absurdity of life; his work often features bizarre scenarios inhabited by solitary, obsessive characters.

Little is known about the private life of reclusive writer Patrick Süskind, given that he refuses to give interviews or make public appearances. It is known, however, that his father was a journalist and Süskind followed in the tradition of writing by producing screenplays and a play, *The Double Bass*, that proved highly popular on the German stage.

The work that catapulted Süskind to fame was his short novel *Perfume: The Story of a Murderer* that was adapted into a film in 2006. Set in eighteenth-century France, it tells the story of Jean-Baptiste Grenouille, a misfit and misanthropic character who lacks any body odor, but whose powerful sense of smell leads him to create best-selling perfumes. Yet his obsession to create the ultimate scent leads him into dark territory. Part thriller, partly a tale of the emperor's new clothes, Süskind's powerful descriptions of the smell of people, objects, and locations, from the stench of a market to the dizzying scents of flower blossom, and the seductive odor of a beautiful young girl, leave readers sniffing the world around them for days afterward with a heightened olfactory awareness.

Süskind's most successful work since has been his novella *The Pigeon*, which takes the reader into a Kafkaesque world tinged with modern-day Gothic horror. This time the protagonist is bank security guard Jonathan Noel, whose lonely but ordered existence is shattered when a pigeon comes home to roost. Süskind's capacity to create bizarre scenarios inhabited by solitary, obsessive characters makes compelling reading. His narratives have been called magical realism, perhaps because of their sense of the absurd, but they also follow an existential tradition as their protagonists attempt to find meaning, purpose, and significance. **CK**

"He doesn't smell at all. He's possessed by the devil."

—*Perfume: The Story of a Murderer*

Signature Titles

Novels

Perfume: The Story of a Murderer (Das Parfum), 1985

The Story of Mr. Sommer (Der Geschichte von Herrn Sommer), 1991

Three Stories and a Reflection (Drei Geschichten), 1995

Play

The Double Bass (Der Kontrabass), 1981

Novella

The Pigeon (Die Taube), 1987

ABOVE: A thoughtful looking Süskind in an undated photograph.

Signature titles

Novels

A Wild Sheep Chase, 1982

Hard-Boiled Wonderland and the End of the World, 1985

Norwegian Wood, 1988

South of the Border, East of the Sun, 1992

The Wind-up Bird Chronicle, 1995

Sputnik Sweetheart, 1999

Kafka on the Shore, 2002

Short story

The Elephant Vanishes, 1985

Nonfiction

Underground, 2000

1940–59

ABOVE: Murakami pictured on a Tokyo rooftop in April 2004.

RIGHT: The U.S. dust jacket of Murakami's 1999 novel *Sputnik Sweetheart*.

HARUKI MURAKAMI

Born: January 12, 1949 (Kyoto, Japan).

Style and genre: Murakami is a former jazz-club owner whose novels and short stories blend conversational prose, meandering narratives, and a penchant for the bizarre, and have been compared to everything from magical realism to cyberpunk.

It is not surprising that Haruki Murakami became a writer on impulse when he was on the cusp of thirty. He was at a Yakult Swallows game in 1978 when the U.S. player Dave Hilton hit a double. Something clicked, and Murakami realized that he could write a novel. He went home and started writing that very night; a year later, his first book was published.

This story is exactly the kind of offbeat turn of events that draws readers into Murakami's world. Seemingly mundane objects and events show themselves to have extraordinary significance, like the titular sheep of *Wild Sheep Chase* with a birthmark shaped like a star, or the bottle of Cutty Sark in *The Wind-Up Bird Chronicle* that has something to do with astral projection. Murakami's novels include meditations on Western pop culture and the clash between tradition and postmodernity in Japan, but typically they are not "about" Japan in any particular way; his characters are recognizable to anyone living in the developed world. From his realistic novels (*Norwegian Wood*) to his most speculative (*Hard-Boiled Wonderland and The End Of The World*), the dominant theme of his work is absence; and whether it is the absence of a woman, a memory, or a sheep, there is always an underlying suspicion that what is missing is not lost, but was never there in the first place.

Murakami's nonfiction book *Underground: The Tokyo Gas Attack and the Japanese Psyche* is his most explicit meditation on Japanese culture, as evidenced by the title. But the book's form in describing the sarin gas attacks on Tokyo's subways by the Aum Shinrikyo cult in 1995 is telling as well: Murakami lets his interviews with both the cult members and the survivors of the attacks speak for themselves. The complex plurality of the voices that emerges from this minimal approach is emblematic of what works in Murakami's best fiction: instead of seizing control, he sits back to see where the story will take him. **SY**

SPUTNIK SWEETHEART • A NOVEL BY HARUKI MURAKAMI

MARTIN AMIS

Born: August 25, 1949 (Oxford, England).

Style and genre: Martin Amis is a controversial and much imitated English novelist and critic whose dizzying, extravagant style reflects on masculinity and violence, both personal and political.

Signature titles

Novels

The Rachel Papers, 1973

Dead Babies, 1975

Money, 1984

London Fields, 1989

Time's Arrow: Or the Nature of the Offense, 1991

The Information, 1995

Night Train, 1997

Yellow Dog, 2003

House of Meetings, 2006

Nonfiction

Visiting Mrs. Nabokov: And Other Excursions, 1993

Experience, 2000

The War Against Cliché, 2001

Martin Amis has grown up in the public eye. The son of English novelist Kingsley Amis, he published *The Rachel Papers*, a novel of precocious quick-wittedness and loose-cannon sexual appetite, at age twenty-four. Since then, his every move has been scrutinized by the media and his works have brought him an unprecedentedly high profile for an English novelist.

Amis's masterpiece trilogy of low life and conspicuous consumption in modern London (*Money*, *London Fields,* and *The Information*) was followed by a record of midlife crisis in the memoir *Experience*, reflecting on the death of his father and his own loss of innocence. After that came his turn as a post-9/11 political commentator, for which he has garnered unprecedented column inches with his views on "Islamism."

Yet despite the glare of flashbulbs that follows him, Amis has always been a writer committed to the craft, concerned, above all, to turn a good sentence. His style is unmistakable. He is the most spectacular crafter of character names since Dickens: *Money* alone features John Self (an appropriate Everyman for the "Me Decade" of the 1980s), Butch Beausoleil, Lorne Guyland (an Englishman's joke, perhaps, on how Americans pronounce "Long Island"), Spunk Davis, and Caduta Massi. He riffs out new verbs and unexpected adjectival couplings, while his paragraphs brim with baroque, wise-guy repetitions and absurdly self-multiplying lists. Even when tackling the gravest subject matter, as in his Holocaust novel *Time's Arrow* or in *House of Meetings*, set in the Soviet Gulag, Amis has an irrepressible urge toward verbal innovation; in *Time's Arrow*, events and even sentences are run backward, as a reverse chronology invites the reader to reconsider the causes of historical atrocity. **MS**

"Only in art will the lion lie down with the lamb, and the rose grow without thorn."

ABOVE: A portrait of Martin Amis from October 2007.

PEDRO JUAN GUTIÉRREZ

Born: January 27, 1950 (Matanzas, Cuba).

Style and genre: Cuban writer, artist, and journalist, Pedro Juan Gutiérrez, is a master of dirty realism and focuses on contemporary life in Havana; his semiautobiographical novels feature his alter ego Pedro Juan.

Pedro Juan Gutiérrez writes stories soaked with sex, rum, poverty, and hedonism with the crumbling city of Havana as a backdrop. His work has been compared with that of Charles Bukowski, the American writer whose work, too, is characterized by violence and sexual imagery.

Gutiérrez began selling ice cream and newspapers when he was eleven years old and then he was employed variously as a a soldier, swimming instructor, technical designer, and then a journalist and artist specializing in painting and sculpture. In 1994, Gutiérrez suffered a personal and ideological crisis when his marriage ended badly and Cuba's economic difficulties reached a peak. It was then that he decided to write and he produced the *Dirty Havana Trilogy*. It is semiautobiographical and features the author's alter ego, Pedro Juan, in a series of encounters around the city, each of which ends in sex or violence. Although it is not overtly political, the novel reflects on life and its problems in Fidel Castro's Cuba.

Gutiérrez was allowed to promote the novel in Italy and Spain but on his return to Cuba he lost his job as a journalist so now concentrates on fiction and his art. Banned in Cuba, the *Dirty Havana Trilogy* has been published in twenty countries. His next novel, *Tropical Animal* returns once again to the adventures of Pedro Juan. In this work he visits Sweden where he finds himself haunted by memories of sexual encounters with his lover, Gloria. In *The Insatiable Spider Man*, drunken anti-hero, Pedro Juan is now fifty and his relationship with his wife Julia is falling apart. In a series of vignettes he seeks solace in rum and steamy sexual encounters. Despite his grim depictions of everyday life in Cuba, Gutiérrez's love of the island and its culture is evident in his work. **HJ**

"My books are not journalism, sociology, or anthropology in any way, shape, or form."

Signature titles

Novels

Dirty Havana Trilogy: A Novel in Stories (Trilogia sucia de La Habana), 2001

Tropical Animal (Animal Tropical), 2002

The Insatiable Spider Man (El insaciable hombre araña), 2005

ABOVE: A 2007 portrait of Gutiérrez by Ulf Andersen.

1940–59

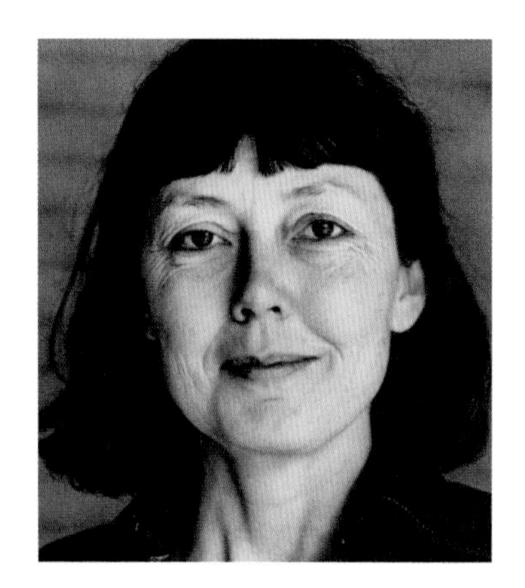

ANNE CARSON

Born: June 21, 1950 (Toronto, Ontario, Canada).

Style and genre: An elusive yet volcanic modernist poet, Carson blurs the borders between ancient and contemporary, modernist and postmodernist, Canadian and American in her fiction, scholarship, and poetry.

Signature titles

Poetry

Glass, Irony and God, 1995

Autobiography of Red, 1998

Men in the Off Hours, 2000

Nonfiction

Eros the Bittersweet, 1986

Anthology

Decreation, 2005

Translation

Grief Lessons, 2007

In lieu of an author photograph on the jacket of *Glass, Irony and God,* the 1995 poetry collection that asserted Anne Carson's claim to the major league, there is a painting of a volcano by the author. The volcano recurs at the climax of *Autobiography of Red,* a verse novel adaptation of some Greek fragments, which was a surprise international success.

The volcano, over which flies Geryon, a red-winged monster from Greek myth, who in *Autobiography of Red* is also a contemporary gay man, is at once geographical and literary. This commingling of components begins with the epigraph, taken from the Emily Dickinson poem "The Only Secret People Keep." Carson's open secret lies in her idiosyncratic and playfully enigmatic appropriation of the works of other literary giants. Samuel Beckett, Gertrude Stein, Emily Brontë, Virginia Woolf, Sappho, and Catullus all appear in this guise in her work: as latches, as she describes adjectivily in *Autobiography.*

A classicist whose scholarly essays (often focused on gender) are as oblique and formally inventive as her poetry, Carson is seen as an iconoclast by academics, and an interloper by the poetic mainstream. Winning the first Griffin Poetry Prize, as well as the T. S. Eliot Award (the first woman to do so), piqued literary reviewers, but her popularity transcends them, not least with a citation on the television show *The L Word.*

"Each morning a vision came to me. . . .[I realized] these were naked glimpses of my soul."

Carson's own sexuality—along with much of her biography—is deliberately obscured, even as she excavates the lives of other writers. Secrets, in all their disguises and revelations, lie at the heart of her work. It is more than fitting that she has translated four plays by Euripides, himself a master of the inner workings of human character, as well as revelation as an instigator of volcanic events. **SM**

ABOVE: A portrait of the poet Anne Carson by Allen McInnis.

PÉTER ESTERHÁZY

Born: April 14, 1950 (Budapest, Hungary).

Style and genres: One of Hungary's leading contemporary authors, Esterházy writes experimental novels set against the turbulent history of Central and Eastern Europe and uses postmodern techniques to play with time and character.

Péter Esterházy is a member of one of Hungary's most prominent families, which can trace its roots back to the twelfth century. His ancestry is central to his most well-known work, *Celestial Harmonies*, published in 2000. The novel traces the rise of his family during the Austro-Hungarian Empire and its decline under communism. Like Esterházy's other works, *Celestial Harmonies* abandons the conventions of narrative prose and instead uses postmodern techniques—time ebbs and flows, characters turn into one another, and the author plays with the reader. Esterházy has won Hungary's leading literary prize and numerous European literary awards. His work has been translated into more than twenty languages. **HJ**

Signature titles

Novels

The Transporters, 1983

A Little Hungarian Pornography, 1984

The Book of Hrabal, 1990

The Glance of Countess Hahn-Hahn/Down the Danube, 1991

She Loves Me, 1993

Celestial Harmonies, 2000

JAVIER MARÍAS

Born: September 20, 1951 (Madrid, Spain).

Style and genre: Marías writes stories of intrigue, love, family, espionage, violence, mystery, and imagination. His complex novels attract popular as well as literary recognition in Spain, and increasingly in the English-speaking world.

Javier Marías's father accepted a position at Wellesley College in the United States, just a few months after Javier's birth in Madrid. This early exposure to American culture resulted in Marías's fascination with English literature, and he has become a highly regarded literary translator. This interest is manifested in his own work—all his protagonists/narrators are translators or interpreters, who never fully identify themselves or reveal their identities. As a translator, Marías recognizes the act of choosing one word or phrase over another, to most authentically and honestly capture the meaning of the original text. This act of choosing, and the space between two choices, is often the centerpiece of some of his best work. **REM**

Signature titles

Novels

The Man of Feeling (El hombre sentimental), 1986

All Souls (Todas las almas),1989

A Heart So White (Corazón tan blanco), 1992

Written Lives (Vidas escritas), 1992

Tomorrow in the Battle Think on Me (Mañana en la batalla piensa en mí), 1994

When I Was Mortal (Cuando fui mortal), 1996

Dark Back of Time (Negra espalda del tiempo), 1998

Your Face Tomorrrow (Tu rostro mañana)

Fever and Spear (Fiebre y lanza), 2002

Dance and Dream (Baile y sueño), 2004

Veneno y sombra y adiós, 2007

ORHAN PAMUK

Born: Ferit Orhan Pamuk, June 7, 1952 (Istanbul, Turkey).

Style and genre: Pamuk is an avant-garde writer whose earlier works were more naturalistic, while later ones use postmodern techniques to examine the tension between Western-style living in a non-Western country.

"A new star is born in the East," wrote the *New York Times* when Orhan Pamuk's third novel, *The White Castle*, was published in translation. The publication launched him onto an international platform, one that has remained intricately connected to and exactly defined by Pamuk's "Turkishness."

Pamuk was educated at a prestigious prep school in Istanbul, and went on to study architecture. After three years, however, he abandoned architecture and went on to study at the Institute of Journalism. After graduating, he lived with his mother while he wrote his first novel. The flat in Istanbul where Pamuk now writes overlooks the Golden Horn, with views of the Topkapi Palace on one side and the bridge linking Europe and Asia on the other. The rapidity of social change in Turkey takes center stage in Pamuk's books; he claims that most of the country's struggles pivot around the two views from where he sits and witnesses the westernization of Turkey.

Although he does not want to be seen as a distinctly political writer, Pamuk has become known for being openly critical of the state, specifically of its violations of human rights, women's rights, its failure to move toward a real democracy, its banning of books, and its version of the Kurdish problem. Being one of the first writers from a Muslim country to speak out against the fatwa issued against Salman Rushdie has invited death threats issued to him by Turkish ultra-nationalists. As if to counteract the political context that has been so remarkable in Pamuk's emergence as Turkey's most notable author (he was awarded the Nobel Prize in 2006), his actual novels blend mystery, fantasy, philosophical debates, and games. He is a compelling storyteller and manages to build complex narratives with almost ironic detachment. **JSD**

"I want to describe the psychological state of the people in a certain city."

Signature titles

Novels

Cevdet Bey and His Sons, 1982
The Silent House, 1983
The White Castle, 1985
The Black Book, 1990
The New Life, 1995
My Name Is Red, 1998
Snow, 2002

Screenplay

Secret Face, 1992

Essay

Other Colors, 1999

Memoir

Istanbul: Memories and the City, 2003

ABOVE: Pamuk, pictured here in 2006, is the first Turkish person to receive a Nobel Prize.

VIKRAM SETH

Born: June 20, 1952 (Calcutta, West Bengal, India).

Style and genre: Seth is a poet, novelist, librettist, children's writer, travel writer, and memoirist famed for his realism, satirical edge, and detail; he has won numerous awards, including the 1994 Commonwealth Writers Prize for *A Suitable Boy*.

Vikram Seth has produced the longest novel published in a single volume in the English language, *A Suitable Boy*, and yet despite its 1,471 pages it made best-seller lists, garnered awards, and shot the author to fame.

Born into a middle-class family in Delhi, Seth was educated in India, and later studied economics at Oxford University and Stanford University in California. Yet Seth was more interested in writing, and produced the first of his five volumes of poetry, *Mappings,* in 1980, following it up with *From Heaven Lake: Travels Through Sinkiang and Tibet*, which won him the Thomas Cook award for travel writing. His first novel, *The Golden Gate,* tells the lives of young professionals in San Francisco, written as a series of sonnets.

But the book that put him on the map was *A Suitable Boy*. Set in post-Independence India, it charts the fortunes of a mother's search for a suitable husband for her rebellious daughter. Focusing on four families and three possible candidates, Seth's epic novel is inhabited by a Dickensian cast of characters grappling with old traditions and a new post-colonial political landscape beset by tensions between Muslim and Hindu communities. Packed with romance, history, and humor, what sustains the novel is Seth's ability to create plausible characters and give an insight into Indian family life, and he has admitted to drawing on characters within his own circle in order to do so. Since the publication of *A Suitable Boy*, the polymath Seth—he writes in English rather than his native Hindi—has gone on to write poetry, a children's book, a libretto, a family memoir, and another novel, *An Equal Music*, that examines the life of a violinist and what happens when he meets his long-lost love. **CK**

> "Easy writing makes damn hard reading, and I think the opposite is true as well."

ABOVE: Seth photographed on World Book Day in 2005.

Signature titles

Novels

The Golden Gate, 1986

A Suitable Boy, 1993

An Equal Music, 1999

Poetry

Mappings, 1980

The Humble Administrator's Garden, 1985

All You Who Sleep Tonight, 1990

Three Chinese Poets, 1992

Children's fiction

Beastly Tales, 1991

Nonfiction

From Heaven Lake: Travels Through Sinkiang and Tibet, 1983

Two Lives, 2005

ROBERTO BOLAÑO

Born: April 28, 1953 (Santiago, Chile); died July 15, 2003 (Barcelona, Spain).

Style and genre: Bolaño was a Chilean writer whose novels of the disappeared or forgotten fuse Jim Morrison's wanton lyrics with James Joyce's modernist lingo, written with a savage irony.

Signature titles

Novels

Nazi Literature in the Americas (Literatura nazi en América), 1996

The Savage Detectives (Los detectives salvajes), 1998

2666, 2004

Novellas

Distant Star (Estrella distante), 1996

By Night in Chile (Nocturno de Chile), 2000

In 1974 Bolaño cofounded the infrarealists, a group of surrealist-punk provocateurs best known for infiltrating "bourgeois" poetry readings to scream out their own verses. From 1993 until his death, he published a series of innovative and intense works about what he called "astronauts on lost planets with no possible escape." These include *Nazi Literature in the Americas*, an encyclopedia of fictitious authors; *Distant Star*, a biography of a fascist poetaster and assassin; and *By Night in Chile*, the confessions of a priest-poet and Pinochet collaborator. Perhaps his most remarkable book is *The Savage Detectives*, an anti-lyrical epic about two poets who, while searching for a lost poet, themselves become lost. **CH**

ALAN HOLLINGHURST

Born: May 26, 1954 (Gloucestershire, England).

Style and genre: Celebrated for the high style of his sonorous prose, Hollinghurst depicts sexuality, obsession, art, and English society since the 1980s; he won the Booker Prize in 2004 for *The Line of Beauty*.

Signature titles

Novels

The Swimming-Pool Library, 1988

The Folding Star, 1994

The Spell, 1998

The Line of Beauty, 2004

When Alan Hollinghurst won the Booker Prize in 2004, one tabloid ran with the headline, "Booker Won By Gay Sex." The irony is not just that the book contains less sex than most of his previous works, but that Hollinghurst writes with equal nuance, dry humor, and insight about class, music, architecture, politics, and family life. He also writes about books: *The Line of Beauty* frequently invokes Henry James; *The Swimming-Pool Library* recasts the "deflected sexuality" of novels by E. M. Forster, Ronald Firbank, and L. P. Hartley in a spirit of sexual openness; and *The Folding Star* triangulates Nabokov's *Lolita*, Mann's *Death in Venice,* and doomed fin-de-siècle symbolism. Hollinghurst's comments on English life offer unique, rarefied pleasures. **MS**

DAVID GROSSMAN

Born: January 25, 1954 (Jerusalem, Israel).

Style and genre: One of Israel's most perceptive writers, Grossman uses stream-of-consciousness and other modernist narrative techniques to examine the complex issues of life for today's Israelis and Palestinians in his fiction and nonfiction.

David Grossman was born in Jerusalem to Yizchak Grossman, originally from Austria, and Michaela, a Jerusalemite. From a very early age, Grossman had a flair for journalism and storytelling, beginning work as a radio youth correspondent at the age of ten. He served his mandatory time in the Israeli military service before attending Hebrew University, where he studied philosophy and theater. He continued his radio work (his book *Duel* first aired as a radio drama in 1982) and was a presenter of a children's radio broadcast and a slapstick radio program until 1988, when he resigned as a protest against restrictions on journalistic work, especially regarding Palestinian issues. An ardent advocate for peace, in 2006 Grossman joined with two fellow authors—Amos Oz and A. B. Yehoshua—in pleading with the Israeli prime minister to reach a cease-fire agreement between Israel and Hezbollah forces in Lebanon. Two days later, and shortly before the cease-fire, Grossman's twenty-year-old son, Uri, was killed when a Hezbollah missile destroyed his tank.

Grossman found fame as a writer in 1983 with his first novel *The Smile of the Lamb*—a wrenching work that explores the intricacies of a soldier's experience in the West Bank. His nonfiction work *The Yellow Wind*, published in 1987, recounts his own observations of the Palestinians living in the West Bank under Israeli occupation. The *New York Times* compared Grossman's second novel, *See Under: Love*, published in 1986, to such iconic literary works as William Faulkner's *The Sound and the Fury*, Günter Grass's *The Tin Drum*, and Gabriel García Márquez's *One Hundred Years of Solitude*. Grossman himself acknowledges Franz Kafka and Heinrich Böll as his literary influences. **REM**

"The rocks will be white from the heat, and the mountains will crumble . . ."—*The Yellow Wind*

Signature titles

Novels

The Smile of the Lamb, 1983
See Under: Love, 1986
The Book of Intimate Grammar, 1991
The Zigzag Kid, 1997
Be My Knife, 1998
Someone to Run With, 2000
Her Body Knows, 2003

Children's fiction

Duel, 1982

Nonfiction

The Yellow Wind, 1987
Sleeping on a Wire: Conversations with Palestinians in Israel, 1992

1940–59

ABOVE: The Israeli writer David Grossman in a photograph taken in 2003.

KAZUO ISHIGURO

Born: November 8, 1954 (Nagasaki, Japan).

Style and genre: Ishiguro is a Japanese-British novelist who explores the power of the unconscious in elliptical, intricately structured plotlines and scrupulously unfussy prose, tackling questions of personal ethics in a context of historical trauma.

Kazuo Ishiguro's narrators tend to have one thing in common: They are in thrall to their memories. They are driven by a desire for origin and identity, and a deep and often unconscious need to make the stories of their lives palatable to themselves. That said, they are also typically unreliable: their narratives are structured around silences and omissions, and the reader must patch together what really happened from all the details the storytellers are at pains to leave out.

Ishiguro, who came to England in 1960 as a five-year-old boy, claims that he never felt like an immigrant, because until he was an adult his parents believed they would return to Japan. It was only in 1982 that he became a British citizen and finally relinquished the suppositions of his youth. Ishiguro says that, expecting to return to Japan, he had always written "with translation in mind," which may account for the deceptively calm surface of his prose. His first two novels are set in the shadows of the bombs at Nagasaki and Hiroshima, respectively. In *A Pale View of Hills*, Etsuko grieves the suicide of her oldest daughter while she relives but refuses to untangle her memories of life just after the war; in *An Artist of the Floating World*, painter Masuji Ono struggles to reconcile his prewar enchantment with imperialist ideals, with the shame he feels in the aftermath of defeat.

Perhaps because his early work pegged him as a Japanese novelist, in his next novel—the Booker Prize–winning *The Remains of the Day*—Ishiguro manages to out-British the British. This quietly heartbreaking story follows Stevens, the elderly head butler at Darlington Hall, as he winds his way across the English countryside, taking in the view and only haltingly revealing the depth of his personal regrets.

Ishiguro's commitment to narrative innovation shines through in his next novels, which follow a certain dream logic

Signature titles

Novels

A Pale View of Hills, 1982
An Artist of the Floating World, 1986
The Remains of the Day, 1989
The Unconsoled, 1995
When We Were Orphans, 2000
Never Let Me Go, 2005

Screenplays

The Saddest Music in the World, 2003
The White Countess, 2005

ABOVE: Ishiguro in 2005, photographed on the publication of his novel *Never Let Me Go*.

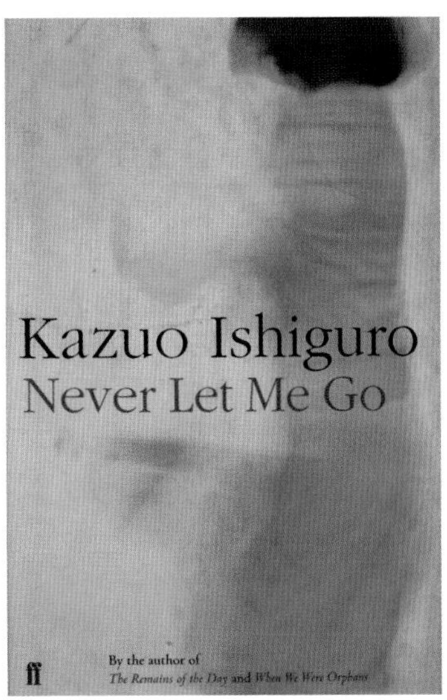

ABOVE: Ishiguro's recent novel addresses the rights of potential human clones.

LEFT: The author, posing in his London home, has played guitar since he was fifteen.

that belies the power of the irrational in our lives. *The Unconsoled* is about a pianist trying to give a very important concert in an unnamed European city; in *When We Were Orphans*, a celebrated detective returns to 1930s Shanghai to recover his parents, missing since he was a child. *Never Let Me Go* is a chilling parable that defies genre expectations. Whatever the form, all of Ishiguro's work reconfigures questions of personal ethics in the face of historical trauma. Both *When We Were Orphans* and *Never Let Me Go* were shortlisted for the Booker Prize—the latter was nominated as runner-up. **CQ**

Writing for Film

Ishiguro asserts "I'm a kind of enthusiastic amateur when it comes to screenplays." Besides a handful of scripts for BBC television, he also wrote the script for the Canadian film *The Saddest Music in the World* (2004). Director Guy Maddin put his stamp on it (as Ishiguro notes, the prosthetic legs filled with beer were not in the original script) but the premise, that all the suffering in the world has to literally compete for our sympathy and attention, is pure Ishiguro. Other credits include the Merchant Ivory production *The White Countess* (2006), about a love affair set in Shanghai on the eve of war.

HANIF KUREISHI

Born: December 5, 1954 (Bromley, Kent, England).

Style and genre: Kureishi is an English playwright, screenwriter, filmmaker, novelist, and short-story writer; he writes about a global London, father-son relationships, and cultural inbetweenness, all while using autobiographical material.

Hanif Kureishi's London has been assimilated by its citizens into a culturally hybrid though still largely segregated space. By emphasizing multiplicity of experience, Kureishi gracefully sweeps aside expectations that he represents the voice of a particular ethnic group in his writing.

The concerns of Kureishi's characters range over a wide spectrum of issues: the relationship between imagination and culture, the constructed nature of desire, the experience of cultural in-betweenness, and the father-son relationship. Coming from a family on his father's side that competed for book-learning and knowledge, Kureishi grew up reading and writing. His first success came as a playwright and screenwriter. In *My Beautiful Laundrette*, two young men, one Asian and one English, revive a failing laundrette and fall in love into the bargain—a partnership that friends and family are keen to wipe out. In *Sammy and Rosie Get Laid*, their open relationship is upset when Sammy's father comes to London amid rising racial tensions to bury his shady political past.

Writer-characters in Kureishi's work call attention to their use of autobiographical material in their fiction: for example, Jay in *Intimacy* describes "writing as I read myself within." Kureishi has courted controversy for portraying friends and lovers in unflattering ways in his writing, most notably after the publication of *Intimacy*. In response, he maintains that his work is essentially imaginative. In *My Ear at His Heart*, Kureishi compares recollections of a shared past by his uncle and father to show the radical rendering involved in giving one's version of events. The way in which each version fills in the suppressed content of the other forecloses any possibility of a singular truth. **ER**

Signature titles

Novels

The Buddha of Suburbia, 1990
The Black Album, 1995
Intimacy, 1998
Gabriel's Gift, 2001
The Body, 2003
Something to Tell You, 2008

Plays and screenplays

Sammy and Rosie Get Laid, 1987
London Kills Me, 1991
My Beautiful Laundrette, 1996
My Son the Fanatic, 1997
Sleep With Me, 1999
The Mother, 2003
Venus, 2007

"Religions may be illusions, but they are important and profound illusions."

ABOVE: Hanif Kureishi pictured in London in April 2007.

COLM TÓIBÍN

Born May 30, 1955 (Enniscorthy, County Wexford, Ireland).

Style and genre: Tóibín is an Irish journalist and novelist whose work explores creativity and personal identity with a keen eye for detail and cadence, especially in the context of complicated Irish heritages and homosexual identities.

With a family steeped in Irish history, both political and domestic, it should come as no surprise that Colm Tóibín's early novels deal with these very subjects. His first, *The South*, focuses on a young Protestant woman from County Wexford and her experiences in Barcelona. Although geographically distant, the parallels between Franco-era Catalonia and Ireland's own struggles are clear, and Tóibín re-evaluates assumptions about his homeland through the prism of another. His own experiences in Barcelona in the years immediately post-Franco inform the novel, which was followed by *The Heather Blazing*, a more directly Irish work.

A journalist throughout the 1980s, working both in Dublin and during travels in South America, Tóibín's fiction manifests a keen eye for detail and cadence, most notably in *The Master*, his 2004 imagining of the personal life and thoughts of the American writer, Henry James. Tóibín's understanding of James seems almost uncanny, and his meditative, balanced prose is at times indistinguishable from that of the master's itself. The novel conflates Tóibín's homosexuality with James's repressed longings, and explores the nature of the personal sacrifices required to produce great art.

Tóibín still works as a journalist, both in Ireland and for publications such as the *London Review of Books* and its New York counterpart. Increasingly involved in America, he has been visiting professor at Stanford University, California, and has lectured at the American University in Washington, D.C. He travels extensively, and is an accomplished travel writer, although his 2006 collection of short stories, *Mothers and Sons*, proves that his heart remains, for the time being at least, firmly in Ireland, and especially in Dublin. **PS**

"Tóibín's genius is that he makes it impossible for us to walk away."—The *New Yorker*

Signature titles

Novels

The South, 1990

The Heather Blazing, 1992

The Story of the Night, 1996

The Blackwater Nightship, 1999

The Master, 2004

Short stories

Mothers and Sons, 2006

Nonfiction

Homage to Barcelona, 1990

Bad Blood: A Walk Along the Irish Border, 1994

Love in a Dark Time: Gay Lives from Wilde to Almodóvar, 2002

ABOVE: A portrait of the Irish writer from August 2002.

ARTHUR JAPIN

Born: July 26, 1956 (Haarlem, the Netherlands).

Style and genre: One of the Netherlands' best-loved and best-selling contemporary novelists, Japin has also written award-winning stage and screenplays; most of his novels focus on historical subjects.

Arthur Japin studied language and literature at the University of Amsterdam and then went to drama school in London. He has acted on stage, screen, and on television, and sung with Dutch National Opera; but it is his novels—the majority of which focus on historical subjects—that have brought him international acclaim.

The Two Hearts of Kwasi Boachi was published in 1997 and became an instant best seller. It has subsequently been adapted for the stage and turned into a film and an opera. Based on a true story, it is the deeply humane tale of two African princes who are taken to Holland in the nineteenth century as guests of the royal family. Caught between two cultures they are neither African nor Dutch. It is a novel that has been compared with the works of Joseph Conrad and the great South African writer Nadine Gordimer.

Japin's second novel, *The Lion Dreaming* is a highly entertaining novelized version of his relationship in Rome with Rosita Steenbeek, who became the last lover of the Italian film director Frederico Fellini. His third novel, *In Lucia's Eyes*, also has a historical subject at its center: It is based on a small reference in Casanova's memoirs to a woman with whom he fell in love at the age of seventeen and then met later in an Amsterdam brothel, where he finds her horribly disfigured. Japin expands the anecdote into an intricately plotted story of love and sacrifice.

Japin's novels are now translated and published in twenty countries and they have won a number of literary prizes, including the 2005 Libris Award for *In Lucia's Eyes*. He has been a writer in residence at a number of universities, including Cambridge University and New York University. **HJ**

"The first ten years of my life I was not black."

—*The Two Hearts of Kwasi Boachi*

Signature titles

Novels

The Two Hearts of Kwasi Boachi, 1997

The Lion Dreaming, 2002

In Lucia's Eyes, 2003

Short stories

Dooi & Zeep, 2004

Plays and screenplays

Heijermans!, 1991

Magonia, 2001

ABOVE: An undated photograph of Japin, who is also an actor and singer.

RICHARD POWERS

Born: June 18, 1957 (Evanston, Illinois, U.S.).

Style and genre: Powers's novels deal with contradictory impulses and with huge themes of technology and science in the modern world, often juxtaposed with more intimate, microcosmic personal stories.

An old photograph of three farmers inspired Richard Powers to quit his job as a computer programmer and devote himself to his first novel, *Three Farmers on Their Way to a Dance*.

Powers uses his knowledge of science and technology to formulate questions that resonate with our postmodern uncertainties, such as *The Gold Bug Variations*, which deals with genetics, computer science, and music. His 2006 novel, *The Echo Maker*, explores the effects of a rare neurological disorder that causes the sufferer not to recognize those closest to them, while still knowing acquaintances perfectly well. Powers has received many awards and is recognized as one of America's most praised as well as most productive writers. **REM**

Signature titles

Novels

Three Farmers on Their Way to a Dance, 1985
Prisoner's Dilemma, 1988
The Gold Bug Variations, 1991
Operation Wandering Soul, 1993
Galatea 2.2, 1995
Gain, 1998
Plowing the Dark, 2000
The Time of Our Singing, 2003
The Echo Maker, 2006

IRVINE WELSH

Born: September 27, 1958 (Leith, Edinburgh, Scotland).

Style and genre: Welsh's work features a wealth of local vernacular; black comedy; unremitting tragedy; extreme, violent behavior; and alcohol and narcotic abuse—all set against a working-class Edinburgh backdrop.

Contemporary Scottish writer Irvine Welsh blew a hole through the British literary scene with his debut novel *Trainspotting* in 1993. A controversial author, the amalgamation of twisted storylines, flawed characters, authentic local dialect, and extreme subject matter has produced consistent success. In Welsh's follow-up novel, *Marabou Stork Nightmares*, the chief protagonist, lying in a coma, delves into a fantasy safari world to avoid facing his terrible past as both a victim and perpetrator of sexual violence. Firmly ensconced as one of Britain's most bankable authors, Welsh produced a sequel to *Trainspotting* with *Porno*, catching up with Renton and Sick Boy as they attempt to break into the pornographic industry. **SG**

Signature titles

Novels

Trainspotting, 1993
Marabou Stork Nightmares, 1995
Ecstasy: Three Tales of Chemical Romance, 1996
Filth, 1998
Glue, 2001
Porno, 2002
The Bedroom Secrets of the Master Chefs, 2006

Short stories

The Acid House, 1994
If You Liked School You'll Love Work, 2007

MICHEL HOUELLEBECQ

Born: Michel Thomas, February 26, 1958 (Réunion Island, Indian Ocean).

Style and genre: Controversial French novelist Houellebecq advocates nihilism, writes brutally about sex, and has been taken to court for his opinions on Islam; his novels register the disintegration of European culture in a cash-based era.

Michel Houellebecq has always been an ambiguous character; his critics can never agree as to whether he is a naive doomsayer or a wily performer who has merely taken on his misanthropic role to launch critiques of European society. He has frequently rewritten his own life story through the various protagonists named "Michel," who appear in his bitter but darkly comic fiction. He seems to have worked as a French civil servant during the 1980s, for example, but our knowledge of that period of his life is largely inferred from the descriptions of "Michel's" office-bound drudgery in his first novel, *Whatever.*

In the 1990s, Houellebecq began to live a solitary life in Ireland. Although he claimed that he had been motivated by tax purposes, it was a symbolic relocation; he had moved to the western edge of Europe, where he could be simultaneously apart from and a part of the continent. His novels register the disintegration of European culture in an era where the cash nexus offers a framework not only for business transactions but also for sexual relationships. They are dense with sex scenes that some critics have accused of being pornographic but that challenge the reader to consider his or her own complicity in a society governed by mass consumption.

Houellebecq's most notorious novel to date is probably *Platform*. Published in 2001, it apparently condoned sex tourism, and its protagonist made generalizing statements that condemned the Islamic world. Outrage was not confined to France; the Moroccan newspaper *Libération* printed a photograph of Houellebecq with the headline "This Man Hates You." In 2002, Houellebecq was taken to court by Muslim groups in France, although he was acquitted of inciting racial hatred after a controversial ruling. **TM**

Signature titles

Novels

Whatever (L'extension du domain de la lutte), 1994

The Elementary Particles/Atomised (Les Particules élementaires), 1998

Platform (Plateforme), 2001

The Possibility of an Island (La Possibilité d'une île), 2005

Poetry

The Pursuit of Happiness (La Poursuite du bonheur), 1992

"I am a child who no longer has the right to tears."

—*The Pursuit of Happiness*

ABOVE: Houellebecq in a photograph taken in September 2005.

BENJAMIN ZEPHANIAH

Born: April 15, 1958 (Birmingham, England).

Style and genre: Zephaniah is a Rasta revolutionary who "dubbed-up" Britain, turned down an honor from the Queen, and charged a nation's hearts with fire; he brought black art forms to the front of the stage.

Dr. Benjamin Obadiah Iqbal Zephaniah, to give the poet and novelist his full name, is a local poet as Wordsworth was. Zephaniah's home turf is the Handsworth district of Birmingham, England, a largely Caribbean area made famous by John Akomfrah's documentary, *Handsworth Songs*.

Like Akomfrah, Zephaniah was part of a wave of radical Caribbean artists and intellectuals who challenged, and changed, British culture in the early 1980s, standing up to the National Front not by assimilating but by defiantly bringing black art forms to the front of the stage. Zephaniah, who had been performing his poetry since he was thirteen, was an initiator—or, better, instigator—of the dub poetry scene that brought liveness, performance, vernaculars, music, and charisma into a dull, elitist, literary world.

As well as recording with Bob Marley's band, The Wailers, Zephaniah used his street-sharp verbal skills to fillet politicians and received histories. In BBC TV's *Dread Poets' Society*, Zephaniah recreated his train journey from Birmingham to Cambridge—from the margins to the center of privilege—when he was shortlisted for a Creative Fellowship at Trinity College. He did not get the job, but rebutted with the film, in which he meets John Keats and Percy and Mary Shelley, and measures himself against them. Summoned to Buckingham Palace to receive an Order of the British Empire in 2003, Zephaniah spoke out against Orders, Britishness, and Empire, turning the so-called honor down. In full voice against Tony Blair, Zephaniah secured his status as hero of the outspoken and those without a voice. His recent award-winning novels and poetry for children are inspiring a new generation to stand and speak with him. **SM**

"Smart big awards and prize money is killing off black poetry . . ."—*Bought and Sold*

Signature titles

Novel

Face, 1999

Poetry

Pen Rhythm, 1980

Talking Turkeys, 1994

Propa Propaganda, 1996

Too Black, Too Strong, 2001

Children's fiction

Refugee Boy, 2001

Teacher's Dead, 2007

Music

Naked, 2004

ABOVE: The Rastafarian poet and writer pictured in December 2002.

JEANETTE WINTERSON

Born: August 27, 1959 (Manchester, England).

Style and genre: A gender-bending novelist whose work is playfully inventive and in which the carnal is suffused with myth, the cosmic, and the evangelical; Winterson's first novel won the Whitbread Prize in 1985.

Signature titles

Novels

Oranges Are Not the Only Fruit, 1985
Boating for Beginners, 1985
The Passion, 1987
Sexing the Cherry, 1989
Written on the Body, 1992
Gut Symmetries, 1997
The World and Other Places, 1998
The Power Book, 2000
Lighthousekeeping, 2004
Weight, 2005
The Stone Gods, 2007

Children's fiction

The King of Capri, 2003
Tanglewreck, 2006

Adopted into a Pentecostal family in a Northern English industrial town, Jeanette Winterson was brought up to be a missionary, writing sermons at age eight, and preaching them at twelve. There were only six books in the house, including the Bible and Mallory's *Le Morte d'Arthur*, but as a teenager Winterson scoured the rummage shops for more, reading in secret. Her first novel, *Oranges Are Not the Only Fruit*, is a semiautobiographical account of what came next: falling in love with a recent convert to the church—another girl—and leaving home at sixteen. In quirky, aphoristic, nonlinear prose, Winterson's tale of sexuality and creativity brought her enormous critical success as a fresh new voice on the London literary scene. Her next few novels lived up to this promise, garnering both acclaim and a devoted following.

Winterson's stories combine love triangles and androgyny with fantastical versions of historical moments (*The Passion* follows Napoleon's chicken chef and a Venetian gondolier with webbed feet as they become romantically intertwined), with an interest in science and philosophy (the Grand Unified Theory of quantum physics provides the punning acronym in *Gut Symmetries*). When the press developed a more prurient appetite for the details of Winterson's private life, she responded rather cheekily, nominating her own novel as the best of the year, and spreading outrageous rumors about having exchanged sexual favors with suburban housewives for their Le Creuset cookware. This only created more furor and notoriety, however, and Winterson withdrew to the country to write, and to champion organic farming and sustainable hunting; she also runs her own organic delicatessen in London. **CQ**

"Everything in writing begins with language. Language begins with listening."

ABOVE: A portrait of Jeanette Winterson taken in August 2004.

WILL SELF

Born: September 26, 1961 (London, England).

Style and genre: Self is an English novelist, short-story writer, blogger, and journalist whose grotesque, raucous, modern satires are hilarious and penetrating in equal measure; he writes manic prose marked by its intellectual vibrancy.

In England, Will Self is ubiquitous. He claims to have published 350,000 words per year for eight years in succession, and with his endless supply of newspaper articles, novels, critical introductions, and psychogeography manuals, this is believable. A far cry, then, from the boy who grew up in a Jewish family in North London, was drinking in his early teens, and was taking heroin before he even got to university (Oxford University, no less). Although Self has not taken drugs since 1998, they overshadowed the early part of his career, which really took flight with *The Quantity Theory of Insanity* in 1991, a collection of short stories whose manic prose and intellectual vibrancy attracted plaudits from reviewers and readers alike. Novels and short stories followed throughout the 1990s, and as Self's first marriage broke down, his career blossomed, with the 1997 *Great Apes* providing its high point to date. The novel describes a society in which apes have all the trappings and intelligence of civilization while humans are exhibited in zoos; it is a rabid satire on human arrogance and stupidity. Ironically, it was at about this time that Self experienced his own arrogant, stupid moment, causing controversy by smoking heroin on Prime Minister John Major's jet while reporting on a general-election campaign.

Since giving up drugs, Self has been nothing short of prodigious in his output, publishing several novels and nonfiction works, as well as carving out a lucrative and high-profile media career. Perhaps more than anything else, Self has become a chronicler of London, where he lives with his second wife, walking, investigating, and seemingly breathing its sidewalks, buildings, and waterways. As he says of why he writes: ". . . it's my way of mediating the world as I see it around me." **PS**

"What excites me is to disturb the reader's fundamental assumptions."

Signature titles

Novels

Cock and Bull, 1992
My Idea of Fun, 1993
Great Apes, 1997
How the Dead Live, 2000
Dorian, an Imitation, 2002
The Book of Dave, 2006

Short stories

The Quantity Theory of Insanity, 1991
Grey Area, 1994
Tough, Tough Toys for Tough, Tough Boys, 1998
Dr. Mukti and Other Tales of Woe, 2004

Nonfiction

Feeding Frenzy, 2001
Psychogeography, 2007

ABOVE: A photograph of Self taken in London on September 5, 2006.

ARUNDHATI ROY

Born: Suzanna Arundhati Roy, November 24, 1961 (Shillong, Meghalaya, India).

Style and genre: Roy is a Booker Prize–winning Indian writer known for her rhythmic prose and lyrical descriptions of Kerala; she is also the author of several collections of political essays espousing humanitarian themes.

Born to a Christian mother and a Bengali Hindu father, Indian writer Arundhati Roy grew up in the small village of Aymanam, Kerala, the setting of her first and only novel, *The God of Small Things*. At age sixteen she moved to Delhi and lived in a squatter's colony selling bottles. She currently resides in Delhi with her second husband, filmmaker Pradip Krishen. Despite training as an architect at the New Delhi School of Planning and Architecture, Roy has dedicated her life to writing.

Prior to writing her novel, she produced two screenplays for films directed by her husband: *In Which Annie Gives It Those Ones*, a television film about architecture students, in which Roy stars, and *Electric Moon*. She also played a role in Krishen's award-winning *Massey Sahib* (1985).

It was shortly after working on these films that Roy began work on her novel, dedicating 1992 to 1996 to writing *The God of Small Things*. Intricate and tragic, with lyrical descriptions of Kerala's lush green landscape, this semiautobiographical tale of forbidden love and a troubled family in 1960s India is shown through the eyes of young twins Rahel and Esthappen. The novel was published to great international acclaim, and with it Roy became the first Indian woman to win the prestigious Booker Prize in 1997.

Since her novel, Roy has turned her attention to politics, and is a social activist like her mother, Mary, who fought against Christian inheritance law in India to give women an equal part of their fathers' estates. She works as a political writer and has become involved in humanitarian causes, protesting against nuclear warfare and the Narmada Dam Project, among other things. In 2004, Roy was awarded the Sydney Peace Prize for her advocacy of peace and human rights. **LP**

"The Great Stories are the ones you have heard and want to hear again."—*The God of Small Things*

Signature titles

Novel

The God of Small Things, 1997

Nonfiction

The Cost of Living ,1999

The Algebra of Infinite Justice, 2002

Power Politics, 2002

War Talk, 2003

An Ordinary Person's Guide to Empire, 2004

Public Power in the Age of Empire, 2004

The Checkbook and the Cruise Missile: Conversations with Arundhati Roy, 2004

Screenplays

In Which Annie Gives It Those Ones, 1989

Electric Moon, 1992

ABOVE: A photograph of Roy in 1999, two years after she won the Booker Prize.

BRET EASTON ELLIS

Born: March 7, 1964 (Los Angeles, California, U.S.).

Style and genre: Ellis is a controversial cult novelist and short-story writer famed for his young, vacuous, depraved characters and depiction of extreme situations; he often uses a stream-of-consciousness technique to write of recurring characters.

Despised and adored in equal measure, Bret Easton Ellis is very difficult to ignore. His novels enact and satirize vacuity, both moral and intellectual, while his protagonists are unified by their lust for depravity. Ellis populates his novels with a cast of characters who reappear across the different titles, linked for the most part by a connection with Camden College, New Hampshire, a place apparently based on Ellis's own experiences at Bennington College, Vermont. Raised in the San Fernando Valley, he studied music at college and spent the early 1980s as a part-time musician in various bands. His first novel, *Less Than Zero*, was published while he was still a student. Its success saw him move to New York, where he became a member of the literary Brat Pack that also included Tama Janowitz and Jay McInerney and raised establishment hackles in the late 1980s and early 1990s.

With *American Psycho*, Ellis's satire on the excesses of the 1980s, he reached his apotheosis. Dropped by one publisher for its extreme violence and perceived misogyny, it was eventually published in 1991 to a mixture of outrage and admiration. Death threats and hate mail followed, although the book sold extremely well. The aftermath of its publication triggered something of a collapse, and Ellis had problems with drinking, drugs, and relationships in the ensuing years.

His father (on whom he based his most controversial character, Patrick Bateman) died in 1992, and then, in 2004, so did his lover and friend, Michael Wade Kaplan, aged thirty. Both deaths inform—and to an extent haunt—his novel *Lunar Park*, in which a character called Bret Easton Ellis is a parody of the author, and is tormented by ghosts from his past, both fictional and real. **PS**

"I didn't think anyone outside of [Los Angeles] would read *Less Than Zero*."

Signature titles

Novels

Less Than Zero, 1985
The Rules of Attraction, 1987
American Psycho, 1991
Glamorama, 1998
Lunar Park, 2005

Short stories

The Informers, 1994

ABOVE: A photograph of Ellis in March 2006 on a tour promoting *Lunar Park*.

J. K. ROWLING

Born: Joanne Rowling, July 31, 1965 (Yate, South Gloucestershire, England).

Style and genre: Rowling is the creator of the most successful fiction serial ever; her novels are rich with humor, adventure, and classical allusion and explore themes of friendship, family, identity, and the nature of good and evil.

One thing stands out when reading the frank and funny autobiographical note on the web site of J. K. Rowling, and that is how many of the critical points in her life involve trains. Not only did her parents meet on a train, but the idea that became her seven-novel serial about the boy wizard Harry Potter occurred to her on a crowded and delayed Manchester to London train, only to be metaphorically derailed by her mother's death and becoming a single parent. The image of Rowling scribbling her first novel in an Edinburgh café, baby stroller at her side, has entered modern mythology in much the same way as King's Cross 9¾, the railway-station departure platform for the Hogwarts Express. This fictional train transported Potter and a generation of readers into a decade-long adventure through seven epic books, garlanded and disparaged in equal measure.

It is too early to determine whether Potter—along with his friends Hermione Granger, Ron Weasley, and Neville Longbottom; the guardian adults of the Order of the Phoenix; and his nemeses Severus Snape and the terrifying Lord Voldemort—will persist in the same way as Lewis Carroll's Alice and Frank Baum's Dorothy. However, it is unquestionable that Rowling's series not only revolutionized the fortune of independent publisher Bloomsbury Publishing, but also ushered in a revitalized era of children's fiction. Considerable commercial concerns notwithstanding, the *Harry Potter* series has popularized literacy. Rowling's humanist vision of young people engaged in learning to save the world is reflected in her support for the Children's Voice, a campaign to rescue children from much the same maltreatment and neglect that make Potter's escape into the world of wizardry so poignant and effective. **SM**

"I just write what I wanted to write. I write what amuses me. It's totally for myself."

Signature titles

Novels

Harry Potter and the Sorcerer's Stone, 1997
Harry Potter and the Chamber of Secrets, 1998
Harry Potter and the Prisoner of Azkaban, 1999
Harry Potter and the Goblet of Fire, 2000
Harry Potter and the Order of the Phoenix, 2003
Harry Potter and the Half-Blood Prince, 2005
Harry Potter and the Deathly Hallows, 2007

Short stories

Fantastic Beasts and Where to Find Them, 2001
Quidditch Through the Ages, 2001
The Tales of Beedle the Bard, 2007

ABOVE: Rowling at the 2007 film premiere of *Harry Potter and the Order of the Phoenix*.

DAVID MITCHELL

Born: January 12, 1969 (Southport, Lancashire, England).

Style and genre: Mitchell is an inventive British novelist of fantastical, wide-ranging, and epic works that string together a series of contrasting narratives, which are linked tangentially yet add up to a greater whole.

David Mitchell hit the ground running: his first novel, *Ghostwritten*, won the John Llewellyn Rhys Prize in 1999, and in 2003 he was named one of the twenty best young British novelists by *Granta* magazine. It was a case of the right book at the right time. *Ghostwritten* is the quintessential fin-de-siècle novel: it leaps lightly from a homicidal Japanese cultist to a body-hopping ghost, crisscrossing the globe and the centuries. Each chapter is a separate story with its own voice, but tiny shared details create subtle parallels between them, cultivating a spooky sense that everything ultimately connects in a manner reminiscent of the pleasurable paranoia of Thomas Pynchon's universe.

Mitchell's next book, *number9dream*, is more conventionally novelistic than *Ghostwritten*, and critics welcomed its story line about a geeky nineteen-year-old trying to find out the identity of his father. Yet Mitchell had plenty of tricks up his sleeve. The narrative takes wild digressions into cyber worlds, cinematic daydreams and—in an extraordinary act of ventriloquism—the mind of a World War II kamikaze submarine pilot.

Cloud Atlas reverts back to the style of *Ghostwritten*, making dazzling leaps across genres and venturing into science fiction. Even here, Mitchell takes liberties: he serves up an Isaac-Asimov-style techno-dystopia, full of clones and holograms, and follows it up with a Riddley-Walker-style neo-primitive dystopia, all animal skins and superstition. Some found the juxtapositions indigestible; others giddily went along for the ride.

"Probably, in a parallel universe not far from here, I'm working for Nintendo."

Black Swan Green is semiautobiographical and much calmer. Its narrator is a boy grappling with the pains of growing up, but behind the coming-of-age tale are deeper themes. **CO**

Signature titles

Novels

Ghostwritten, 1999
number9dream, 2001
Cloud Atlas, 2004
Black Swan Green, 2006

ABOVE: Mitchell at the Edinburgh International Book Festival in August 2004.

SARAH KANE

Born: February 3, 1971 (Brentwood, Essex, England); died February 20, 1999 (London, England).

Style and genre: A playwright of enormous raw power, Kane's work caused outraged controversy; she is now seen as a beacon of edgy, outspoken theater.

"This Disgusting Feast of Filth" ran the *Daily Mail* headline. The target was Sarah Kane's first full-length play, *Blasted*, which had premiered at London's Royal Court theater, a bastion of controversial new writing. Kane had studied drama at Bristol and Birmingham universities and was a recent Master's graduate at the age of twenty-three when *Blasted* struck. The play is now seen as a milestone of 1990s theater.

Kane was part of a group of young British "Nihilists," chafing against the complacency and materialism of their times. Sharply intelligent and great fun, with short blonde hair and an all-black wardrobe, Kane blended powerful emotions with an uncompromisingly provocative outlook. In her teens, her parents' Christianity had helped push her toward evangelism, and something of this zeal stayed with her. Graphic violence, extreme sex, and bodily functions hallmarked her visceral plays, shot through with political and ethical issues. *Blasted* starts in a hotel room and explodes into a bloody war-zone, inviting reflection on the contemporary political situation in Bosnia. Kane ran workshops across Europe and was better appreciated abroad than at home. As the 1990s progressed, some British critics began to see why leading dramatists including Harold Pinter had defended her earlier plays. Influenced by writers as diverse as Shakespeare and Edward Bond, Kane tore theatrical naturalism apart. She stressed imagery rather than dialogue in plays such as *Cleansed*, which was set in a concentration camp. In *Crave*, an essay in obsessional love, Kane counters structural norms by creating a kind of theatrical poem, and poetic strands weave through *4:48 Psychosis*—completed in 1999 and premiered in 2000, the year after her depression-induced suicide at twenty-eight. **AK**

"My responsibility is to the truth, however difficult that truth happens to be."

Signature titles

Plays (dates when performed)

Blasted, 1995
Phaedra's Love, 1996
Cleansed, 1998
Crave, 1998
4:48 Psychosis, 2000

ABOVE: A headshot of the playwright Sarah Kane *c.* 1998.

CHIMAMANDA ADICHIE

Born: September 15, 1977 (Enugu, Nigeria).

Style and genre: Adichie is a Nigerian novelist whose work explores issues of common human understanding, ethnical allegiances, class, and race; she uses Igbo phrases whose meaning she evokes without providing a translation.

It is said that Chimamanda Adichie is doing for the contemporary generation of Nigerian writers what Chinua Achebe did for his generation. That she cites the grandfather of African writing as having emboldened her to be a writer is not unique; that she is tracing his footsteps (literally, having spent her childhood in the very house Achebe inhabited thirty years earlier) to become one of the writers shaping the very different landscape of writing coming out of Nigeria is more so. Where Achebe explored the clash between British colonial culture and traditional Nigerian Igbo life, Adichie reaches into the legacy that such a history has left behind.

Adichie grew up in the university town of Nsukka. She published her first poetry collection before completing high school and went on to study medicine before deciding to move to the United States to join her sister. After completing a degree in communications and political science, she later gained a master's degree in creative writing.

Adichie's first novel, *Purple Hibiscus*, is narrated by fifteen-year-old Kambili Achike, and traces the story of a Nigerian family struggling under its evangelical father through the political turmoil of 1990s Nigeria. The novel won the Commonwealth Writers' Best First Book Prize and the Hurston/Wright Legacy award for debut fiction. While the youth of *Purple Hibiscus*'s narrator ensures that politics do not dominate the story, Adichie's second novel, *Half of a Yellow Sun*, weaves the lives of three characters through the political tumult of Nigeria's civil war. Adichie says: "I do think that I, as a person who writes realist fiction set in Africa, almost automatically have a political role." She certainly has a role in shaping contemporary Nigerian literature. **JD**

"A new writer endowed with the gift of ancient storytellers."—Chinua Achebe

Signature titles

Novels

Purple Hibiscus, 2003

Half of a Yellow Sun, 2006

Short stories

You in America, 2001

The Grief of Strangers, 2004

Ghosts, 2004

Tomorrow is Too Far, 2006

The Time Story, 2006

Play

For Love of Biafra, 1998

ABOVE: Adichie photographed in London in June 2007 after winning the Orange Prize.

CONTRIBUTORS

Richard Cavendish (RC) is a historian who regularly covers anniversaries of past events in *History Today* magazine.

Claudio Cazzola (CC) teaches literature, Latin, and Greek at the Ludovico Ariosto state high school in Ferrara and is also an adjunct professor of Latin language at the School of the Humanities at the University of Ferrara. He has published essays and papers on classical (Homer, Lucretius, Horace), humanistic (culture at the court of the House of Este), and contemporary literature (Giorgio Bassani).

Stephanie DeGooyer (SD) is a PhD candidate in English at Cornell University. She studies eighteenth-century philosophy and literature.

Jenny Doubt (JSD) completed her MA from the University of Sussex and has since worked as a senior editor in illustrated book publishing in London, England. Originally from Canada, Jenny also works as a freelance writer, focusing particularly on postcolonial literature.

Fabriano Fabbri (FF) is a professor of the History of Contemporary Art at the University of Bologna. His books deal with the relationship between high and low culture, from literature to art to music videos; including *Sesso arte rock'n'roll,* (Atlante, Bologna, 2006).

Simon Gray (SG) studied Media at Sheffield Hallam and has been a freelance writer for over ten years specializing in the fields of travel, music, and the arts. His first book is due for publication in 2009.

Reg Grant (RG) is a freelance writer. He has extensive knowledge of modern European literature, especially post–World War II French fiction.

Frederik H. Green (FHG) was educated at St. John's College, Cambridge, and Yale University, where he is currently completing his PhD dissertation in Chinese Literature. His research interests include the reception of European Modernism in East Asia.

Paul Gareth Gwynne (PG) has a BA in English with Latin (Reading); MA in English Renaissance Literature (York); and PhD in Combined Historical Studies: the Renaissance (Warburg Institute, London). He lives and works in Italy, where he is Director of Interdisciplinary Studies at the American University of Rome.

Lucinda Hawksley (LH) is an art historian, biographer, and freelance writer, with a specialism in the nineteenth and early twentieth centuries. Her books include *Essential Pre-Raphaelites* and *Katey: The Life and Loves of Dickens's Artist Daughter.*

Colman Hogan (CH) teaches literature and film at Ryerson University, Toronto, and has recently become a father. He is the co-editor of *The Camp: Narratives of Internment and Exclusion* (2007).

Ian Johnston (IJ) is a PhD student at Queen's University. He teaches Shakespeare's Drama, and is working on a dissertation on sadomasochistic literature. He currently resides in Kingston, Ontario.

Helen Jones (HJ) is a freelance journalist and writes for national newspapers and magazines in the UK and the US.

Lara Kavanagh (LK) has a BA in English and French from the University of Leeds, and a Masters in twentieth century literature from King's College London. She has written literary, entertainment, and travel articles for both print and online publications.

Ann Kay (AK) studied English and American Literature and Art History at Kent University. She has a strong interest in drama, swapping early plans to become an actress for a long career as a writer and editor in nonfiction publishing.

Carol King (CK) is a freelance journalist. She has a degree in English Literature from the University of Sussex.

Melanie Kramers (MK) is an English and French graduate from the University of Leeds. She has worked in book and magazine publishing for a number of years, and is currently living in Argentina.

John Koster (JK) is from Loveland, Ohio. A graduate of Hampshire College in Amherst, Massachusetts, he is currently a doctoral student in German Literature and Theory at the University of Toronto.

Thomas Marks (TM) is writing a DPhil on nineteenth-century poetry and architecture at Magdalen College, Oxford, where he also teaches nineteenth-and twentieth-century English Literature. He is a regular contributor to *The Times Literary Supplement* and other literary journals.

Sophie Mayer (SM) is a writer whose works have appeared in academic journals, literary magazines, and newspapers in the U.K., U.S., Canada, and Australia. She is the author of *The Cinema of Sally Potter* (Wallflower, 2008) and the forthcoming poetry collection *The Private Parts of Girls* (Salt, 2009).

Jamie Middleton (JM) is a freelance writer and editor for various lifestyle magazines and books. Based in Bath, he has worked on a range of diverse subjects from the Milau Bridge and Jaguar cars to laptops and fine wines.

Geoff Mills (GM) studied English at Reading and London Universities and is currently enrolled at the "National Academy of Writing." He teaches English in a small private college in Worcestershire.

Robin Elam Musumeci (REM) works as a property law paralegal and holds a Masters degree in English Literature from Trinity College, Hartford, Connecticut. She has lived in the United States and England, and loves to read, write, and travel.

Carrie O'Grady (CO) grew up in Toronto, and now works for the *Guardian* newspaper in London, England.

Julian Patrick (JP) is a professor of English and Comparative Literature at the University of Toronto. He has directed the Literary Studies program at Victoria College and has edited books on Ben Jonson and literary theory.

Laura Pearson (LP) lives in London, where she works as an editor. She previously worked as a copywriter for a television shopping channel, answered directory enquiries calls, and fitted the plastic seals onto the lids of jars of pickled onions.

Timothy Perry (TP) is a specialist in ancient Greek literature, which he teaches at the University of Toronto.

Tamsin Pickeral (TamP) is a freelance writer and researcher specializing in art, architecture, literature and horses.

Mariapia Pietropaolo (MP) specializes in Roman elegy at the University of Toronto.

Cynthia Quarrie (CQ) is writing her doctoral dissertation on the contemporary British novel at the University of Toronto, where she lives with her husband and infant son.

Pavlina Radia (PR) is a lecturer at University of Toronto Scaborough. Her main interests include literature, gender studies, and writing composition.

Erin Rozanski (ER) is a PhD student at the University of Toronto, studying Contemporary Literature.

Stephen Regan (SR) is Professor of English at the University of Durham, where he is also Director of the Basil Bunting Centre for Modern Poetry. His books include *Irish Writing: An Anthology of Irish Writing 1789–1939* (Oxford University Press, 2004) and *Irelands of the Mind: Memory and Identity in Modern Irish Culture* (Cambridge Scholars Press, 2008).

Peter Scott (PS) is a journalist who lives and works in northwest London.

Donald Sells (DS) is a PhD candidate in Classical Philology at the University of Toronto whose interests include fifth century Greek drama (specifically Old Comedy), as well as Hellenistic poetry and papyrology.

Andrew Smith (AS) is a New Zealander, and, like most of his compatriots, he currently lives in Australia. He is undertaking a PhD in English Literature at the University of Melbourne, researching the role played by ruins in descriptions of landscape in eighteenth- and early nineteenth-century British literature.

Matthew Sperling (MS) is Lecturer in English at Hertford College, Oxford, and is writing a doctoral thesis on Geoffrey Hill and Philology.

Julie Sutherland (JS) completed her PhD at Durham University and now teaches at Kwantlen University College in Canada. She also manages a professional theater company (Pacific Theatre) in Vancouver, British Columbia.

Sophie Thomas (ST) is a lecturer in English at the University of Sussex, where she teaches eighteenth and nineteenth-century literature, visual culture, and critical theory. She is the author of *Romanticism and Visuality: Fragments, History, Spectacle*.

Christopher Trigg (CT) studied medieval literature at Trinity Hall, Cambridge. He is currently writing his doctoral dissertation on American Literature at the University of Toronto.

Claire Watts (CW) has a degree in French from King's College London. She has been a freelance writer and editor for the last twenty years and spends far too much time reading when she ought to be working.

Ira Wells (IW) is a doctoral candidate in American literature at the University of Toronto. He is currently completing a dissertation on gender in American literary naturalism.

Stephen Yeager (SY) has a PhD in English Literature. He lives in Toronto.

GLOSSARY

Académie Française
The official authority on the French language, made up of elected members. It is responsible for regulating French, for instance, agreeing when new words, grammatical structures or forms of punctuation should be accepted into the language.

Beat Poets
Writers associated with the Beat movement, a rebellious cultural movement in the 1950s and 1960s. The Beat Generation were young people who refused to be bound by accepted conventions and whose music and writing focused on self-expression.

Calligramme
A poem, or piece of prose, in which the words are written in a shape, usually one that reflects the subject matter of the writing. Calligrammes were created by the poet Guillaume Appollinaire.

Canon
The definitive list of an author's works; this must be works that are known without doubt to be by the named author, it cannot refer to disputed works.

Canto
The name for a section or division of a long poem.

Eclogue
A short pastoral poem. Often a poem that contains dialogue.

Epic
A long poem or work of prose that focuses on a narrative, one that usually involves heroic actions or legendary figures. A good example of an epic is Homer's *Iliad*.

Extant
Works that are still in existence; as opposed to works that are known to have been written by a particular author but have been destroyed or lost.

Extemporaneous poetry
Poetry created without any preparation.

Formalism
A style of writing that is more concerned with form than creative content.

Humanist movement
In the Renaissance period, this was a movement that saw a return to ancient Greek and Roman belief systems, as opposed to the accepted medieval ways of thinking. Today, the Humanist movement follows a belief system attaching supreme importance to human beings and their concerns, as opposed to religious or supernatural beliefs.

Idiom
A colloquial expression where the words have a different meaning from their usual interpretation. An idiom loses meaning if translated into a foreign language, for example "it is raining cats and dogs" or "it cost an arm and a leg."

Lost Generation
Those writing after World War I, whose values and experiences had been formed in the prewar world they grew up in, a world that no longer existed.

Metaphysical
Something that transcends the body, the physical and the accepted laws of nature. Often used to describe a group of English poets who were active in the seventeenth century.

Metatext
A piece of writing that explains or describes another text.

Ode
A lyrical poem usually complimentary and written to, or about, a particular person or thing. Originally, odes were written to be sung.

OuLiPo
A French writers' group whose name is an acronym for Ouvroir de Litterature Potentielle.

Polemical
An attack, often in the form of an essay or poem; a verbal debate; usually controversial subject matter.

Poststructuralism
A movement that came after Structuralism, often critical of its forerunner. Poststructuralism looks at the duality of the language and ideas behind Structuralism and strives to move language forward.

Protagonist
The main character or "hero" in what is usually a work of fiction although it is occasionally used to describe a real person.

Rhetoric
Language that is persuasive, effective in getting its message across, and often overly grand.

Saga
An elongated story that usually tells of heroic progress and/or a family's progress over several generations. Often associated with Icelandic and ancient Norse writing.

Sonnet
A poem that contains fourteen lines; in English literature it is often associated with William Shakespeare.

Structuralism
Writing that is characterized by analysis of the linguistic process.

Sturm und Drang
Literally "Storm and stress." Originally a German term, now refers to literature in which passion and emotion are unconfined and given free reign.

Tercet
Three lines of poetry that are linked together by rhyming or connected in some other way, for example by their subject matter.

Vernacular
A language that is native to a particular area, or country, such as a local dialect.

INDEX